BEFORE LEWIS AND CLARK
VOLUME II

BEFORE LEWIS AND CLARK

DOCUMENTS ILLUSTRATING THE
HISTORY OF THE MISSOURI
1785-1804

Edited

with an introductory narrative

by

A. P. NASATIR

VOLUME II

Introduction to the Bison Book Edition by
James P. Ronda

University of Nebraska Press
Lincoln and London

Introduction to the Bison Book Edition copyright © 1990 by
the University of Nebraska Press
Manufactured in the United States of America

First Bison Book printing: 1990
Most recent printing indicated by the last digit below:
10   9   8   7   6   5   4   3   2   1

Volume II: ISBN 0-8032-8362-8 (paper)
ISBN 0-8032-3321-3 (cloth)
Set of Volumes I and II: ISBN 0-8032-3322-1

Library of Congress Cataloging-in-Publication Data
Before Lewis and Clark: documents illustrating the history of the Missouri, 1785–
1804 / edited, with an introductory narrative, by A. P. Nasatir.
p.   cm.
Reprint, with a new introd. Originally published: St. Louis: St. Louis Historical
Documents Foundation, 1952.
"Bison book edition."
Includes bibliographical references.
ISBN 0-8032-3322-1 (set).—ISBN 0-8032-3320-5 (v. 1.—ISBN 0-8032-8361-X (v.
1: pbk.).—ISBN 0-8032-3321-3 (v. 2).—ISBN 0-8032-8362-8 (v. 2: pbk.)
1. Missouri River Valley—History—Sources. 2. Fur trade—Missouri River Valley—History—Sources. I. Nasatir, Abraham Phineas, 1904–   .
F598.B44   1990
978—dc20
89-25080   CIP

Originally published as the second of two volumes by the
St. Louis Historical Documents Foundation in 1952

Introduction to the Bison Book Edition
By James P. Ronda

On a hot August day in 1805 Captain Meriwether Lewis and a small party of explorers became the first Europeans to reach the headwaters of the Missouri River. Lewis and his men looked at the trickle of water and could only wonder that they had reached "the most distant fountain of the waters of the mighty Missouri." A decade earlier François Luis Hector Carondelet, governor general of Louisiana, spoke with equal enthusiasm about "the mighty Missouri."[1] That rhetoric was matched by the efforts of Jacques Clamorgan and the Missouri Company to forge a Spanish empire up the great river, across the mountains, and on to the Pacific coast. This struggle, its ultimate failure, and the resulting shifts in the political fortunes of the Missouri provide the focus for the second volume of Abraham P. Nasatir's monumental collection, *Before Lewis and Clark*. The second volume presents documents for the decade 1796–1806. For Spain, those years were filled with great hope, mounting danger, and, finally, shattered dreams.

The compelling diaries and letters found in this volume have value and interest in themselves. They tell the reader a story of great adventure and high drama. But they are also part of a larger and more complex sequence of events. For that reason they call for understanding in a wider context. Some of that context can be found in a July 1795 report drafted by Jacques Clamorgan and Antonio Reilhe (it is printed in full in Volume I of *Before Lewis and Clark*). Directed to Governor General Carondelet, the report begins by recounting the struggles of the Missouri Company to explore and trade on the great river. Those efforts had been dogged by bad luck and Indian hostility. But more important, there was the undeniable presence of rival Canadian traders. The men from Quebec and Montreal were not only an economic threat but a political one as well. "The commerce of the English," wrote Clamorgan and Reilhe, "daily encroaching on our possessions requies a check in this far and distant region" (p. 336). That "check," as the enterprising promoters put it, was an ambitious scheme to link the Spanish Missouri with territories on the Pacific coast. What Clamorgan and his associates proposed was a chain of fortified trad-

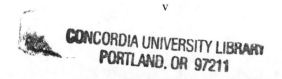

ing posts marching up the Missouri, over the Rockies, and on to the Columbia. These forts would bind Indian allies to the Spanish interest and might prove "a barrier which the foreigners will dare not to cross" (p. 337). This powerful vision of transcontinental empire was much like that fashioned by the Canadian traders Peter Pond and Alexander Henry. Later, Sir Alexander Mackenzie and John Astor would urge their governments to build similar commercial empires.

Clamorgan and his fellow entrepreneurs were not idle dreamers. The documents printed in Volume I of *Before Lewis and Clark* illustrate the ways Missouri Company officials sought to bring their western vision to life. The journey of Jean Baptiste Truteau and the Lecuyer expedition were initial steps in an imperial march across the continent. It was with the arrival of James Mackay that Spain's Missouri River fortunes took a dramatic turn. An experienced Canadian trader, Mackay had already been involved in efforts to find routes and passes to the Pacific. By the time he reached St. Louis in 1793 and took on Spanish citizenship, he was a frontiersman and explorer of considerable skill.

That skill did not go long unnoticed and by late summer 1795 Mackay was appointed leader of a major Missouri Company expedition. Trade and exploration beyond the Rockies were Mackay's twin goals. By November 1795 Mackay's party was at the Omaha village of Chief Black Bird. Trade relations with the Oto and Omaha Indians now seemed established and Mackay was ready to continue toward the Arikara and Mandan villages. A preliminary reconnaissance made by Mackay's lieutenant, John Evans, revealed the impressive power of the Sioux as a blockading force on the river. January 1796 found Evans, Mackay, and their party holed up at Fort Charles on the Missouri. Thinking to check the English, they had nearly been checkmated by weather and Indian hostility.

It was during January that Mackay drafted new and comprehensive exploration instructions for Evans. Both the document and its intended recipient are worth some attention. John Evans, dreamer and explorer, had come to the Missouri country in search of the mythical Welsh Indians. The belief that a Welsh prince named Madoc had guided refugees across the Atlantic to create a race of pale-skinned Indians was one of the most durable tales in North America. Thomas Jefferson believed it, and the legend continues to charm the naïve and unsuspecting. In 1792 a group of London Welsh intellectuals hired young Evans to cross the Atlantic and find Madoc's children. A year later Evans showed up in St. Louis and somehow ingratiated himself with Mackay and the Missouri Company. Now in the winter of 1795–96 Evans was about to be sent up the Missouri to find unicorns, lost Welsh folk, and a way through the Stony Mountains to the Western Sea.[2]

If Evans was a character straight out of fantasy and Central Casting, the instructions that Mackay carefully framed for him had their origins firmly in geography and geopolitics of the day. Printed in full in this volume, they amount to a remarkably well thought-out plan for scientific and geographic discovery. The goal set for Evans was plain—"a passage from the sources of the Missouri to the Pacific Ocean." Along the way Evans was to make careful notes on plants and animals new to the world of science. And in that wonderful blend of fantasy and imagination the West often produced, Mackay urged Evans to keep a sharp eye out for unicorns. Because native people were essential as both allies and trading partners, the Evans expedition was to pay special attention to "the nations, their size, their dwellings, their land, and their productions" (p. 411, below). Although there is no evidence that Jefferson ever saw Mackay's exploration plan, the instructions drafted for Lewis and Clark bear a striking resemblance to the Scot's remarkable design for a way West.

As the documents in Volume II of *Before Lewis and Clark* plainly reveal, the Evans expedition never got past the Mandan villages. In fact, what happened to Evans among the Mandans is itself a commentary on the international, multicultural complexities of the upper Missouri and the northern plains. By the 1790s the Mandan and Hidatsa villages had become a grand plains marketplace. Indians of many bands and tribes came to exchange everything from horses and fancy beadwork to corn and squash. Traders from the Hudson's Bay Company and the North West Company joined resident Europeans to make the villages a vast country store. When John Evans reached the Mandans in late September 1796, he found a British post and several traders. With more daring than good sense, he seized the trading house and planted a Spanish flag firmly over it. Nasatir documents the flurry of correspondence as North West Company officers struggled to deal with this sudden shift in the balance of Missouri River power. French Canadian traders like René Jusseaume and Baptiste La France did more than write heated letters. At one point Jusseaume attempted to persuade several Indians to kill Evans. The plot miscarried, but it was just one more reason to abandon the quest for the Pacific. In early May 1797 Evans quite the Mandans and headed back downriver. His northern plains sojourn was perhaps the high-water mark for Spanish exploration on the Missouri.

As the records in *Before Lewis and Clark* make clear, Spanish interest in the Missouri and a path to the Pacific did not suddenly cease after the Mackay-Evans failure. The irrepressible Jacques Clamorgan kept the dream alive in dozens of letters and petitions. The Missouri Company was reorganized as Clarmorgan, Loisel, and Company. The real effort after 1797 was trade with those tribes along the river. Clamorgan continued to call for expansion west beyond the mountains, but his calls fell on deaf ears. Increased British competition on the northern plains, the fear of

American invasion, and uncertainties in European politics meant that the vision of a Spanish empire stretching across the West was nearly dead. Men like Régis Loisel and Pierre-Antoine Tabeau—French by nationality but carrying Spanish trade permits—now worked the river and dreamed only of profit, not of reaching the Pacific. Any glimmer of a Spanish hope died in 1800 with the secret treaty of San Ildefonso. That piece of European diplomacy returned the Missouri to France. It also laid some of the groundwork for the Louisiana Purchase. Charles Dehault de Lassus, Lieutenant Governor of Louisiana, wrote a terse epitaph for Spanish dreams on the Missouri. In his list of trade licenses for the period 1799–1804, he put the phrase "the Devil may take it all" next to the date 1804 (p. 592). The Americans had come. The age of Lewis and Clark was dawning on the Missouri.

NOTES

1. Gary E. Moulton, ed., *The Journals of the Lewis and Clark Expedition*, 6 vols. to date (Lincoln, 1983–   ), 5:74; Nasatir, ed., *Before Lewis and Clark*, I:254.

2. Bernard DeVoto, *The Course of Empire* (Boston: Houghton Mifflin, 1952), 373–79; James D. McLaird, "The Welsh, the Vikings, and the Lost Tribes of Israel on the Northern Plains: The Legend of the White Mandan," *South Dakota History* 18 (Winter 1988): 250–52.

CONTENTS
VOLUME TWO

Chapter VII 1799

Chapter VIII 1800

ILLUSTRATIONS
VOLUME II

DOCUMENTS
Chapters IV-XII

CHAPTER IV

1796

I

TRUDEAU'S [TRUTEAU'S] DESCRIPTION OF THE UPPER MISSOURI[1]

Containing an exact account of the most remarkable rivers that empty there from above the great river Platte to above the Mandan and Gros Ventres nations, of their name and their distance with a general idea of the savage people recently visited by the subjects of his Catholic Majesty, of their customs, religions, maxims, usages, commerce and other remarks—as well of those who dwell upon the banks of this great river, as of those who wander over the neighboring countries to the westward.

By Jean Baptiste Trudeau [Truteau], *voyageur.*

---

[1]This is a document that Ara Timouian ("Catholic Exploration of the Far West" in *Records* of the American Catholic Historical Society of Philadelphia, XLVIII, 345) says is among the Nicollet papers in the Library of Congress. It was formerly in the State Department. It is printed in French and in English in the *Mississippi Valley Historical Review*, VIII (1921), 157-179, where the late Annie Heloise Abel has scholarly edited it and preceded it (*Ibid.,* VIII, 149-157) with a closely reasoned argument that Truteau was the *ancien traiteur* and supplier of information to Perrin du Lac. Parts of this document have been printed also in *Medical Repository,* Second Hexade, III, 314-315. This was one of the manuscripts given to Dr. Mitchell by Nicolas Boilvin in the winter of 1805-1806. Dr. Mitchell says that he did not print more since the physical geography and trading intelligence resembled Mr. McKay's narrative which he printed in Volume IV, 27-36.

The material contained in this "Description" was also used by, and perhaps it was expressly written for, Victor Collot (*cp.* J. C. Bay's [ed.] edition of Victor Collot's *A Journey in North America* (Firenze, 1924). See A. H. Abel [ed.], *Tabeau's Narrative of Loisel's Expedition to the Upper Missouri* (Norman, 1939), 15. In connection with this document use Truteau's "Journal" (Chapter II, Document XXII) ; Collot, *op. cit*; and F. M. Perrin du Lac, *Voyages dans les Deux Louisianes et Chez les Nations Sauvages du Missouri* (Paris et Lyon, 1805) ; German edition (M. Mueller ed., Leipzig, 1807) ; English edition (London, 1807, in Sir Richard Phillip, *Collection of Modern and Contemporary Voyages,* volume VI). Perrin du Lac's map

The Missouri river comes from the west northwest and, in some places from the northwest. It empties into the Mississippi river five leagues above St. Louis of the Illinois.

No one has been able to learn exactly where this river has its source. It is common belief, according to the report of some savages, that it comes from the great mountains of rock which they say cross, from the north to the south, this vast country yet unknown to civilized nations. Up to the mouth of the river Platte, the waters of the Missouri flow between two chains of steep hills which wind as it winds. In some places, they are situated rather far from the great river.

On the banks, which are between the hills and the river, there are large low prairies on which one generally sees herds of the wild cattle that pasture there. Beyond these hills are vast prairies which extend without interruption up to the foot of the mountains of rock which rise up in the west, being cut only by the several rivers which cross them, on the edge of which one sees only little woods, thin and of trees low. These large prairies, or great waste lands are completely sterile; scarcely grass grows there. Upon the banks of the Missouri, one finds, here and there, some wooded point, narrow and short, supplied only with small cottonwoods, willows, and also thin woods. This river is diversified by a number of islands covered with trees that are so interlaced with vines that one can hardly pass. It is almost everywhere half a league in width. Its bed is less deep than is the case lower down and it is frequently found covered with sandbars, or banks of sand, very extensive, which form several channels that make the way, in certain places, difficult; but there is always enough water at all times to carry the largest pirogues. The little flatboats, or barges, would be, (however) the most suitable conveyances for traveling there.

In no place does one meet with those masses of driftwood that are named *enbaras* such as are commonly found upon the lower part of the river and overcome only with difficulty and danger. Neither does one find any dangerous shoal, broken up or in otherwise bad conditions. The farther one ascends toward its beginning, the less rapid one finds its course;

is published in *Missouri Historical Society Collections*, IV, opposite p. 18; in *South Dakota Historical Collections*, volume II, back cover; in the French edition and in the German edition, of Perrin du Lac, I, opposite page 206. See also A. H. Abel, "A New Lewis and Clark Map" in *Geographical Review*, I, (1916). 329-345, and the Evans map printed between pages 344-345. See also the first three maps in Thwaites, *Original Journals of the Lewis and Clark Expeditions*, VIII; and F. J. Teggart, "Notes Supplementary to any Edition of Lewis and Clark" in *American Historical Association, Annual Report, 1908*, I, 185-195.

Truteau's "Description" shows where he was in the summer of 1795 and that he made a journey to the Chaguennes. In his "Journal," Truteau says he had made trips to the interior for over twenty-six years.

Strikingly similar to Truteau's "Description" is Collot, *A Journey in North America*, I, chapter XVIII, pp. 271-300.

the only inconvenience suffered there is in not finding, in the time of low water, any place suitable for mooring the pirogues so that they may be sheltered from the winds which are very frequent and very high in this country and one is often compelled to unload the pirogues every time the wind blows which happens almost every day.

The great river Platte empties into the Missouri, on the left in ascending, two hundred leagues above the mouth of the latter. At fifty leagues higher, on the right, one finds the little river of the Sioux which is navigable with hunting canoes only. Its source is not far from its outlet. Thirty leagues higher, on the left, dwells the Omaha nation. Their huts are built two leagues distant from the banks of the Missouri. These savages go out to hunt in summer and return to their villages only in August. Six leagues above the Omaha, one finds, on the north bank, the great river of the Sioux which comes from the north east north. It is navigable only with little pirogues. The Sioux nations that frequent the St. Pierre and Des Moines rivers come at different times of the year to hunt the buffalo and other wild animals. Forty-five leagues from there on the same side, goes out the river St. James, a beautiful river, very abundant in beaver and other wild animals. It has, according to the report of the savages, a course of more than a hundred leagues and comes also from the north. It disembogues into several other little rivers, one of which is named the river of the red stone. It takes its name from a quarry of this stone that is found upon its banks. At twenty-five leagues above the James river, on the left, one finds the river Qui Court. It has its source in the west southwest and very far from its mouth. According to the report of the savages, it is the most abundant in beaver and otter of all the known rivers; but it flows with such swiftness and is so full of water falls that it is impossible to navigate it, either in ascending or in descending.

The Ponca nation has its habitations placed at two leagues higher than its mouth. Their huts are built upon a hill on the edge of a great plain about a league from the Missouri. The buffalo, the deer, and beaver are common in this place. At thirty-five leagues higher, on the same side, there goes out a river named the White river. Its waters are white. Its source is a little way from its mouth. Fifteen leagues above this river, the Missouri makes a detour of ten leagues. It turns in this place to the southwest and resumes its usual course after ten leagues of detour.

Fifteen leagues higher, on the left in ascending, one finds a river, named by the savages Tranquil Water, and by the French, the Little Missouri. This river is small. The water runs only in the springtime at the melting of the snow or after some heavy rain. At other times one sees only some ponds of water without flow. One branch of the Sioux, called the *Oconona*, formerly friends and allies of the Arikara, wandered habitually along the banks of this stream.

The Arikara, called for short the Ree, had their dwellings ten leagues higher upon the left bank. These they abandoned during my stay among them, in order to withdraw nearer to the Mandan. One can count five hundred warriors of this nation.

Two leagues above the dwelling of the Ree issues forth the river of the Cheyenne which some hunters have named the Fork. This river is rather wide but shallow so that one can navigate it only with much difficulty. It has its source very far from its mouth, in the hills of precipitous rocks, in the direction of the setting sun. In its upper part, it divides into many branches, well supplied with wood and very abundant in beaver.

About thirty leagues from its mouth, upon one of its tributaries, called the river of the Bunch of Cherries, the Cheyenne built there some permanent huts, around which they cultivated little fields of maize and tobacco; but, furthermore, this nation, which is divided into three bands, or hordes, of which the largest bears the name of Cheyenne, the second is called Ouisy, the third Chouta, wanders without cessation the length of this river and crosses, in search of wild cows, even many chains of hills that separate, by several ranges, these vast prairies. On the other side of these various hills, on this side of the great river Platte, several little lakes, or bogs, are found, which seem, they say, by the quantity and the great size of the huts which these animals have built there and which they inhabit, to be the place whence have come all the beavers and the otters that are scattered in all the other rivers.

Several savage wandering peoples scour this country, such as are the Kiowa, the *Tocaninanbiche*, the *Tokiouako*, the *Pitapahato*, all allies of the Cheyenne but speaking different languages. The Cheyenne know very well how to hunt the beaver, the skins of which they barter with the Sioux for merchandise; and the others would not fail likewise to kill many of them if they were led to it by traders who would take the skins in exchange for merchandise.

The great nation of the Comanche [Pados] which roams along the banks of the river Platte is, at the place of the territory of the Arikara, only ten days' march by warriors from the Missouri river which distance can be estimated as sixty or eighty common leagues. The *Hahitannes*, or wandering bald-headed people, occupy all the country beyond the great river Platte as far as along the banks of the Arkansas river and extend themselves the length of the great mountains which separate New Mexico from this part of southern Mexico.

When I had dealings with the Cheyenne people, in the course of the summer of 1795, where I saw and spoke to many chiefs and leading men

379

of the *Tocaninanbiche* and Kiowa nations, I inquired of all if, in their long war marches beyond the mountains, they had not discovered some river the waters of which might possibly flow toward the setting sun. They told me that two years before the Cheyenne and Kiowa, their allies, had formed a considerable war party in which the great chief of the Cheyenne took part, who himself reported to me this fact for certain :—that, having crossed the mountains, they had come, after many days' journey, to the banks of a wide and deep river, well timbered, the waters of which appeared to go in the direction of the winter sunset; that, along this river which they had followed in descending, they had discovered seven huts of unknown savages; having attacked them and defeated them, they found in their booty none of the small effects coming from white men, all of their utensils being of their own invention. Their huts were made of rush matting and of long straw. The large animals of the skins of which the savages are accustomed to make their tents are absolutely wanting in this country. Their garments, their shoes, and even the saddlecloths were of skins of beaver, of otter, of kid, of deer, of wolf, of fox, of hare, and so forth. They have, as all the others, the use of the bow and arrow, the armor of which is of stone or bone. A little bag full of Indian corn, which they found among their baggage, gave them occasion to inquire of some women prisoners if their nation cultivated that plant. They answered no; but that in the lower part of this river there was a large village of savages who sowed and reaped a great quantity of it. These women had hung around their neck and ears some shells of various kinds and shapes, pierced and threaded on little strings of leather. They asked them where they obtained this kind of glass bead. They answered that at the mouth of this river appeared a large body of water, the other bank of which was not visible; that the water rose and fell considerably at certain times of the day and night; that the savages that had their homes about there attached to the end of a long line large pieces of meat which they threw into the water when deep and drew out when it ebbed; that a quantity of these shells were found adhering to these pieces of meat; and that, having detached them, they pierced them and hung them thus around the neck and ears for ornament.

The Missouri, above the river of the Cheyenne, turns to the northeast the distance of four or five leagues and, afterwards, it turns again to the west as far as the Mandan. On the north side from there up to the Gros Ventres, it receives only a single river, which issues forth about sixty leagues above the mouth of this river of the Cheyenne. On the west side of the Missouri there are five rivers all of inconsiderable size. It is estimated that the Mandan village is distant one hundred leagues from the entrance of this river of the Cheyenne.

The Mandan count only three hundred warriors. This nation is divided into three villages, the largest of which is situated on the western side of the Missouri and the two smaller ones upon the other bank opposite, quite near this river.

The Gros Ventres are more numerous. They can put upon foot eight hundred warriors. They are divided into two villages situated upon the bank of the Missouri on the left in ascending, about two leagues above the Mandan. They are all settled in their dwellings, which they leave only by the brigades either for war or to hunt the buffalo.

Near the villages of the Mandan and Gross Ventres, the woods of the Missouri are thicker and of larger full-grown trees than upon the lower part of this river; that is to say, from the mouth of the great river Platte in ascending to this place.

The Assiniboin, a wandering nation to the north of the Missouri, with whom the English traders of Canada and of Hudson bay traffic in peltries, visit the Mandan and the Gros Ventres, from whom they obtain horses, corn, and tobacco in exchange for guns and other merchandise that they bring there.

At fifty leagues above the Gros Ventres, to the west of the Missouri there discharges a large river, called the river of the Yellowstone, which is almost as broad and deep as the Missouri. This great river has its source in the mountains of rocks in the western part. Its banks are well supplied with wood. There are found firs, pines, North American firs, birches, cedars, and every other tree. The buffalo and other wild animals rove in herds along its banks. Many little rivers that flow into it abound in beaver beyond all belief. The nation of the Crow, a numerous people, dwells along its banks, and, higher up, in ascending toward its source, are situated several other savage nations that are still unknown to us. The savages assured me that it was very deep along distance from its mouth. A Canadian, named Menard, who, for sixteen years has made his home with the Mandan, whither he came from the north, and who has been several times among the nation of the Crows in company with the Gros Ventres, their allies, has assured me that this river was navigable with pirogues more than a hundred and fifty leagues above its mouth, without meeting any falls or rapids. They take usually fifteen or twenty days of a slow march on land to go from the Mandan to the Crow nation. A fort built at the entrance of this river would be very profitable for the opening up of a large trade in peltries, not only with the nations situated upon the banks of this beautiful river, but likewise with those that roam the banks of the Missouri above its outlet. Such are the *Chiouitounes* and the Snake nation of which we have only slight knowledge. A large part of the Assiniboin nation, which roams over the land north of the Missouri, would have a much shorter distance to come to trade its peltries at this fort than to carry them to the English fort on the Red river.

The western and northern part of the Missouri, from the White river thirty-five leagues above the Ponca up to this river that I have said flows into the Missouri sixty leagues above the Cheyenne river, is visited only by the Sioux nations, called Teton, who are divided into four wandering tribes; they roam also over the west side of this river in order to hunt the buffalo and the beaver which are found there in greater numbers than upon the other side. The Sioux tribes are those who hunt most for the beaver and other good peltries of the Upper Missouri. They scour all the rivers and the streams without fearing any one. They carry away every springtime, from out of our territory, a great number of them, which they exchange for merchandise with the other Sioux, situated on the St. Peter's and Des Moines rivers, frequented by the traders of Canada. It would be easy to establish upon the Missouri storehouses of merchandise to provide for their needs and to secure the trade of their peltries.

At the beginning of the month of April, the Sioux wander far from the banks of the Missouri and usually return in the course of the months of July and August and scour its two banks until springtime; for this is the only time when one can pass the places which they are accustomed to visit with any safety in order to come among the nations situated on the upper Missouri.

All the savage peoples which I have mentioned in this description, that is to say, those which dwell on the west of the Missouri, are the mildest and the most humane toward us of all the people of the universe. They have a great respect and a great veneration for all white men in general, whom they put in the rank of divinity, and all that which comes from them is regarded by these same people as miraculous. They do not know how to distinguish among civilized nations, English, French, Spanish, et cetera, whom they call indifferently white men or spirits.

Trade is carried on with them very peaceably. He who does not think what is given him in exchange for his peltries is enough carries it away, nevertheless, without murmur or threat. I would say, finally, that, having myself visited all the savage nations situated on the east and west of the Mississippi and all those who dwell on the lower Missouri, I have never found any who approach these in kindness and good will toward us. There is as great difference between them as between day and night.

II

STATE OF THE INDIAN NATIONS
Who dwell to the West and North-west
of the Mississippi,
lately discovered.

NATIONS.	NUMBERS.	RIVERS NEAR WHICH THEY RESIDE, WITH THEIR LATITUDES.
Castor	600	The sources of the Sahaskawan, and at the foot of the Yellow Mountains, in the 54th degree of latitude.
Black-foot	1500	The same; near lat. 52.
Sacue	400	Sources of the Daim, and at the foot of the Yellow Mountains; lat. 50.
Wandering part of the Asseniboine.	500	Southern branch of the Sahaskawan; lat. 47, long. 115.
Great Nation		Between the Daim River and the lake Placote.
Great-foot	1000	North-western branch of the Missouri at the foot of the Yellow Mountains, lat. 50.
Asseniboine, settled	1000	Upper part of the Asseniboine River; lat. 52, long. 115.
The Christin-aux.	500	South of the Asseniboine, near the Red River; lat. 47, long. 110.
Sauteux Nation	1000	The whole course of the Red River; between the 46th and the 47th degrees of north latitude, and the 100th and 106th of west longitude.

[1]V. Collot, *A Journey in North America* (Firenze, 1924), I, 303-310. Compare with Perrin du Lac, *Voyage Dans les Deux Louisianes*, and other accounts including Collot's account of his travels in his *Journey*; with Truteau's "Description" (Document I, Chapter IV) and *Tabeau's Narrative of the Loisel Expedition to the Upper Missouri* etc. I have collected many hundreds of documents relating to Collot in the Mississippi Valley which abundantly document every move he made while in the Upper Mississippi Valley.

In a statement of the materials collected by General Collot during his journey for the French Republic under Adet's instructions, through the West, Northwest, Upper and Lower Louisiana, lasting nine months and covering 7600 miles (Archives du Ministère des Affaires Étrangères, Paris, Séries, Correspondance Politique: États Unis, Supplément, volume XXVIII, folios 44-46 *verso*) are listed a topographical description of the timber work of the country from the sources of the Ohio, the Lakes, the Upper part of the Mississippi, and the Missouri as far as the Montagnes Jeaunnes, Mississippi, and Gulf of Mexico; a particular description of the Missouri as far as the Mandannes, etc, etc., and a map of that area.

NATIONS.	NUMBERS.	RIVERS NEAR WHICH THEY RESIDE, WITH THEIR LATITUDES.
Grand division of the Sioux	1000	The whole of the river St. Peter, and upon the river St. Lewis.
Lesser division of the Sioux		On the Crow or Yellow Rock River.
Crow-Quill		Crow River, and the bottom of the Yellow Mountains.
Red-Bead		The same.
Orignal		At the fork of the Missouri.
Bigbellied	500	Fifty leagues above Titon River; lat. 53; long. 115.
Mandane	1000	On the banks of the Missouri, ten leagues above the Bigbellied nation.
Pitapahata		Northern bank of the Cherry-branch River.
Tokiwako		Southern bank of the Cherry-branch River.
Kayoha		The same.
Chaguiennes		Confluence of the above river.
Tokaninambich		South-western branch of the Chaguinne River.
Arricaras	500	Western bank of the Missouri, and the mouth of the Chaguienne River.
Richaare		Sources of the Little Missouri.
Blue-Bead nation		Southern bank of the Little Missouri.
Poncas		Western bank of the Missouri, and the mouth of the river Qui-court.
Mahas	1100	Western bank of the Missouri, opposite the Great Sioux River.
Panimaha	600	Platte river to the confluence of Wolf River.
Panis	800	Southern bank of Platte River, and opposite the mouth of Wolf River.
Otoktata	800	Mouth of Plate River, and upon the western bank of the Missouri.
Padou		Banks of the south-western branch of Plate River.
Cans		On the river Cans, where it divides, 60 leagues from its mouth.
Republican nation		South-western branch of the river Cans, near its source.
Great Osages	9000	Near the sources of the Great Osages, and of the Lead-mine River.

NATIONS.	NUMBERS.	RESIDE, WITH THEIR LATITUDES. RIVERS NEAR WHICH THEY
The Serpent and Chiouitanon nations	2000	Westward of the Yellow Mountains.
Maskego		Eastward of Lake Winipeg; lat. 63, long. 104, W.
Bungi		Northward of York River; lat. 53, long. 97, W.
Chipiwian	800	Latitude 57; longitude 110.
Total	24600	

III

CARONDELET TO ALCUDIA, NEW ORLEANS, JANUARY 8, 1796[1]

El Baron de Carondelet, brigadier of the Royal Armies, political and military governor of Louisiana, has learned that during the last year the English constructed a fort in the Mandanas nation, situated on the Missouri 440 leagues from the city of St. Louis, Illinois, some 200 [leagues] according to conjecture, from New Santa Fé, and consequently in the midst of Spain's possessions. Drawing a line from the Mississippi via the Missouri, then reascending toward Nootka Sound he proposes some sure and inexpensive means for restraining the usurpations of the English on the Spanish territory situated to the north of Louisiana and of New Mexico to repress the clandestine commerce which they [the English] are carrying on in the Spanish establishments of Illinois, taking the richest peltries out of Spanish territory; [and] lastly to conciliate the friendship of the warlike Indian nations which are located north of the Ohio, Mississippi and Missouri rivers, forming, a barrier against the English and Americans.

No. 65 *Reservada*

Most Excellent Sir:

The matter to which this confidential report treats directly concerns the boundaries of the possessions of Spain towards the North and Northeast of Louisiana and the New Kingdom of Mexico, extending to the

---

[1]A.H.N., Est., leg. 3900. Written in Spanish. The important annexes to this letter (with some exceptions) are omitted. They are given from their originals in their proper chronological places and are referred to by document number in the notes to this document. An incomplete copy of Carondelet's letter in Carondelet's handwriting is in the Bancroft Library. (I have given the Bancroft Library a complete copy). A draft of this letter without its annexes is in A.G.I., P. de C., leg. 2364.

South Sea by Nootka Sound, within which [boundaries] the English are making their way secretly and forming settlements which in a short time will secure them possession of that same territory which they do not at present dare to claim by the least right of ownership.[2] I hope that Your Excellency will deign to take the matter into consideration with all the attention that it deserves and perhaps consider it of sufficient importance to discuss in the Council of State[3] the means that I propose to use and which I have already begun to put into practice, to drive the English from those frontiers.[4]

An annual expenditure of ten thousand *pesos*,[5] establishment of two forts on the San Pedro and Mongoina rivers,[6] with a troop of fifty men-at-arms in each; approval of the decree placed at the bottom of the recommendation included in the confidential official letter no. 66,[7] the results of which from this very year will result in an increase in the income of the royal custom-house of not less than twenty thousand *pesos,* to be duplicated progressively in the years to come; [and] confirmation of the privileges of the Company of Discoverers of the Missouri—these in brief are the four means that I propose, and upon which the whole plan depends. Its outcome is infallible and it will save Spain[8] from very serious disagreement with England in the future.

---

[2]Referring to the activities of the Northwest and Hudson's Bay Companies.

[3]This is discussed in the Council of State on May 27, 1796 (Document XVII). See *Minuta del Acta del Consejo de Estado* for that date, A.H.N., Est., printed in full in Nasatir and Liljegren, "Materials for the History of the Mississippi Valley", in *Louisiana Historical Quarterly*, XXI, (1938), reprint, pp. 62-72, see esp. pp. 62 and 65-71.

[4]For the matters discussed here see the various articles by A.P. Nasatir referred to in the notes to the documents in this volume including especially the following:

"Anglo-Spanish Rivalry in the Upper Missouri", *Mississippi Valley Historical Review*, XVI (1929-1930), 359-382; 507-530.

"Jacques D'Eglise on the Upper Missouri", *Ibid.*, XIV (1927), 47-56.

"Spanish Exploration of the Upper Missouri", *Ibid.*, XIV (1927), 57-71.

"John Evans: Explorer and Surveyor," *Missouri Historical Review*, XXV (1931), 219-239; 432-460; 585-608.

"Anglo-Spanish Frontier on the Upper Mississippi 1786-1796," *Iowa Journal of History and Politics*, XXIX (1931), 155-232.

"Anglo-Spanish Rivalry in the Iowa Country, 1797-1798", *Ibid.*, XXVIII (1930), 337-389, etc.

See also Carondelet's military report of November 24, 1794, in Robertson, *Louisiana under Spain, France and the United States*, I, 294-345, etc.

[5]See Clamorgan to Carondelet, New Orleans, September 20, 1796, A.G.I., P. de C., leg. 2364 and also leg. 188-3; Clamorgan to Trudeau, St. Louis, March 1, 1797; Trudeau to Delassus, November 24, 1800, A.G.I., P. de C., leg. 2366; Trudeau to Clamorgan, March 3, 1797, Missouri Historical Society, Clamorgan Collection, and others translated in *American State Papers, Public Lands*, VIII, 233-236. See also Louis Houck, *History of Missouri* (Chicago, 1908), I, 333.

[6]The construction of these posts had been proposed many years before by Perez, Miró, and more recently by Trudeau and Carondelet.

[7]Number 66 is of the same date and place as number 65, January 8, 1796, and is in A.H.N., Est., leg. 3900. It was written by Carondelet as a plea to the Prince of Peace that the royal assent be granted to the concession for which Todd had petitioned him and which petition forms annex number 6 to this document and is given *below*.

I was informed at the beginning of my government in these provinces, that the Spanish settlements of the [Illinois] were going from bad to worse from day to day because of the thronging of the English into the fur trade of the Missouri River, as well as through the smuggling [contraband trade] which they carried on from Canada with those same settlements of ours providing them with everything that they need at a price much lower than that current in New Orleans, five hundred leagues distant from St. Louis, Illinois.[9] I therefore concerned myself seriously with means to stop these abuses and sent orders to my lieutenant-governor to seize by force the smaller English boats[10] that are found with goods in the country on the west bank of the Mississippi.

As a matter of fact, when the Lieutenant-Governor, Don Zenon Trudeau, captain of the fixed regiment of Louisiana, sent an expedition from St. Louis, Illinois, at the end of October of the year 1793, it succeeded in confiscating, at a distance of forty-one leagues, some goods and merchandise belonging to Don Andrés Todd, Don Nicholas Marchesseau, and Josiah Bleaklay, citizens of Michelimakinak in Canada, as is shown in the accompanying memorial, no. 1.[11]

At the same time I managed to arouse the citizens of the settlements of the Illinois to organize their forces to save the Missouri trade. As a result of these provisions, and seconded by the zeal, energy, and disinterestedness of Don Zenon Trudeau, the most desirable citizens of St. Louis formed a company under the name of the Discoverers of the Missouri, and under the leadership of a citizen named Don Santiago Clamorgan,[12] a well-trained [informed] active man, of good reputation. He suggested to me on the fifth of May, 1794, the regulation which follows under no. 2,[13] and the following instructions, no. 3.[14] In view of the utility, ad-

---

[9]These were given royal assent. See *below*. The decision is found in many other places as well, some of which will be cited in its proper place.
[9]Cf. Todd to Carondelet, New Orleans, December 18, 1795, annex no. 6 given *below*. It is also in A.G.I., Sto. Dom., 87-1-24 (old numbering), transcript in Bancroft Library. A draft in English is in A.G.I., P. de C., leg. 2364.
[10]*las embarcaciones menores Ingleses.*
[11]This annex is given here. It is Todd to Carondelet, New Orleans, December 18, 1795, cited in note 9. *Idem to Idem*, New Orleans, December 21, 1795, annex no. 1, given *below*, draft in A.G.I., P. de C., leg. 129. The seizure is discussed in greater detail in the petition of Todd, McGill and Company, Josiah Bleakely, Charles Bellerive and Nicolas Marchesseau to Carondelet by J. Jones, their attorney in fact, A.G.I., P.de C., leg. 201. This affair entered into the correspondence between the governors-general of Spanish Louisiana and Canada, see Dorchester to Carondelet, August 21, 1794, A.G.I., P. de C., leg. 2371, calendared in *Report* of the Canadian Archives, 1891, State Papers, Lower Canada, 113; and enclosed in Dorchester to Duke of Portland, no. 68, October 26, 1795, calendared in *Ibid.*, 114, enclosed in Dorchester to Portland, no. 70. This is fully discussed in A.P. Nasatir, "Anglo-Spanish Frontier on the Upper Mississippi, 1786-1796," *Iowa Journal of History and Politics,* XXIX (1931), 198-231.
[12]See A.P. Nasatir, "Formation of the Missouri Company", *Missouri Historical Review,* XXV (1931), 3-15.
[13]Chapter II, document IX.
[14]Chapter II, document XVIII.

387

vantages, and lack of injury to the royal treasury of these instructions (and regulation), I approved them on the eighteenth of July of the same year, with ten others, with the restrictions that appear at the foot, offering in addition in the name of the king three thousand *pesos*[15] to the one who should succeed in first reaching the South Sea, [this I did] partly to arouse those people to a dangerous undertaking by greed and the reward, and partly in consideration of the fact that such a discovery was important to the state; for it would determine its boundaries in a permanent fashion by founding a settlement with all the necessary arrangements to prevent the English or the Russians from establishing themselves or extending themselves on those coasts, remote from the other Spanish possessions and near Nootka Sound.

The greatest obstacles that the Missouri Company has met in its first two expeditions amount merely to the two following:[16] One consists in securing passage through the nations established on the Lower Missouri; and the other in avoiding encounters with bands from those nations that live to the north of the Missouri. These, being at war with the ones who live on its banks, do not want our traders to supply them with arms or ammunition. Therefore, by trading with the English from Hudson Bay, Michelimakinac, Montreal, etc., they attempt through the instigation of the latter, who wish to secure all that trade, to destroy and plunder all our people whenever they find them on the shores of that Missouri River. However, in general all those tribes try to prevent us from supplying those of the Upper Missouri with firearms. They are continually at war with them and if they lack arms, they are exposed to stealing, to frequent depredations, and even to having their members sold as slaves.

The first of the tribes which it is difficult to pass is that of the Mahas, two hundred eighty leagues distant from St. Louis, Illinois. Beyond these are the Poncas, three hundred and fifty leagues from the same city, where the first expedition had to spend the winter.[17] After passing these, the others are: the nation of the Ricaras, four hundred leagues from St. Louis,

---

[15]Carondelet's letter to Trudeau, New Orleans, July 12, 1794 (Chapter II, document XIV) in which he approves the Company's articles of incorporation is the only letter in which the prize is mentioned as being only 2000 *pesos*. All other letters and documents give the prize as 3000 *pesos*, e.g. letters of Carondelet to Clamorgan, New Orleans, September 16 and October 26, 1796, Missouri Historical Society, Clamorgan Collection, translated in *American State Papers, Public Lands*, VIII, 235-236.
Carondelet's prize offer was confirmed by the Council of State, May 27, 1796— See *below*, and Nasatir and Liljegren, "Materials for the History of the Mississippi Valley," *op. cit.*, reprint, p. 70.

[16]Under Truteau and Lecuyer. See Nasatir, "Anglo-Spanish Rivalry on the Upper Missouri", in *Mississippi Valley Historical Review*, XVI (1929), reprint pp. 14-20.

[17]Truteau spent his first winter at a place in what is now Charles Mix County, South Dakota, a little above and opposite the site of the later Fort Randall. They began the construction of the fort on November 11, 1794 and departed from there on March 25, 1795. This was located below the Sioux habitat but above those of the Ponca and Omaha. See Truteau's *"Journal"*, Chapter II, document XXII.

in which we learned that the first expedition, which arrived there on the fifteenth of May, 1794,[18] was raising a fort; that of the Mandanas, forty leagues lower down, where the expedition was to arrive sometime during the summer,[19] the nations of the Gros Ventres, the Panis Hocá, Cheyenne. [etc]. These are the natives which are more civilized than those below and receive our traders with much friendship and good faith. The other nations established further up wish to attract our traders to their villages according to the report which the Mandans gave us.

Of the two obstacles which I have just mentioned, the first will be overcome without difficulty by means of the decision reached by the Company to erect three forts [factories—store houses] protected by a palisade and some swivel guns among the Oto, Maha, and Ponca nations. These garrisons will cause the Spanish flag to be respected, will protect the passage of the Company's smaller boats and will drive the English traders from the river. If His Majesty consents to a patrol of the Missouri with one or two galliots of small tonnage, flat-bottomed and armed with six two-pound cannons, some swivel guns and twenty sailors, it will protect its commerce and the Company's expeditions in the most difficult places. If its banners float over the banks, it is certain that all those nations will form the highest opinion of the Spanish nation and will cease to trade with the English whose advance towards the Missouri already deserves serious attention as is shown by the map which accompanies no. 4. In it [map] is marked out the path that the English follow and the line of forts built by them from Lake Superior to the Mountains of the Black Rock, not far distant from the South Sea according to the opinion of travelers.[20]

But, as the statement of two English deserters from the very place shows—a copy of which accompanies, no. 5,[21] the company called the *North Company* has just taken a bold step in building a fort this year on the Missouri itself[22] about a half league distant from the village of the Mandans

---

[18]Obviously an error, for Truteau left St. Louis on June 7, 1794. If the error is one for 1795 then perhaps it helps to fix the arrival of Truteau among the Arikara for Carondelet had received the missing (middle) portion of Truteau's diary which has not been found as yet.

[19]These problems are discussed in Nasatir, "Anglo-Spanish Rivalry on the Upper Missouri", *op cit.*

[20]In A.H.N., Est., leg. 3900 there is a folder which states that there is a map which is under separate cover. I was unable to locate this map in the A.H.N. However, there is a plat which was enclosed in Truteau's instructions which is in A.G.I., P. de C., leg. 2363 which I am convinced is the map referred to. Miguel Gómez del Campillo, *Relaciones Diplomáticas entre España y los Estados Unidos*, vol. I (Madrid, 1944) 293, says "No. 4 *era un mapa que no ha a parecido.*"

[21]Chapter III, document XII.

[22]Fort built by Jusseaume. See "Extracts from Journals of McKay and Evans in *Medical Repository*, second hexade, IV, 27-36 and in *Wisconsin Historical Society Proceedings*, 1915 LXIII, 190-195. Carondelet's information coming as it does from letters written and documents sent to him by Trudeau, a number of them are included in this volume of documents. The information about the fort is taken from Chapter III, document XII.

and consequently in the midst of Spanish possessions. Such action indicates that if our government does not use the most prompt and active measures to restrain the trespassing of the English companies of Montreal, Michelimakinac, and Hudson Bay, they will shortly get possession of the immense territory drained by the Missouri River. They will establish themselves on it, pass beyond the mountains of the *Roca Negra* [Black Rock] and turn their hand to settlements so that that of Nootka Sound will extend to the shore of the South Sea. Then Spain will find herself quite unable to prevent the commerce that their trading houses will carry on with the *Provincias Internas* and California, whose inhabitants, in addition, will find themselves plundered by the savage tribes which will then be dependent on the English and will be provided with firearms by them.[23]

If the government itself intends to dislodge the English from their settlement near the Mandans, four hundred leagues away from St. Louis, Illinois, from where the expedition must start, its expense would probably be more than fifty thousand *pesos* and even though it should win a most complete momentary success, nothing would be gained, because the same company would return and again raise the English flag, further up or further down the river, and it would be necessary to keep constantly on the move to restrain it.[24]

In order to maintain a hundred armed men in the line of forts which it is building among the Oto, Maha, Ponca, Ricara, Mandan, and other tribes and which it plans to continue gradually until it reaches the South Sea, our Company has requested the annual sum of ten thousand *pesos*.[25] Through the granting of this request it is evident that the above-mentioned Company will succeed not only in driving the English from the Missouri,

---

[23]This fear had been urged before and was continually being urged afterward. See Nasatir, "Anglo-Spanish Rivalry on the Upper Missouri", *op. cit.;* Nasatir, "Jacques Clamorgan: Colonial Promoter of the Northern Border of New Spain" in *New Mexico Historical Review,* XVII (1942), 101-112. The idea that Louisiana was a barrier for the protection of Spain's *Provincias Internas* constitutes a theme which is worthy of a writer. The English had been trading constantly in the area since the 1780's—witness the activities of Jusseaume, Menard, Thompson, and later Henry, Larocque, etc.

[24]Patrolling the Missouri and Mississippi rivers as a measure, which, together with forts strategically located, would effectively stop these incursions, was suggested much earlier than this time by lesser Spanish officials than Carondelet and by traders. Some of the suggestions made were ordered by Carondelet in his secret instructions to Carlos Howard. See Nasatir, "Anglo-Spanish Rivalry in the Iowa Country 1797-1798," *Iowa Journal of History and Politics,* XXVIII, (1930) 337-389; Liljegren. "Jacobinism in Spanish Louisiana 1792-1797," *Louisiana Historical Quarterly,* XXII (1939), reprint pp. 47-51.

[25]There was a great deal of haggling over the payment of the money which indeed was never paid by the government. Clamorgan attributed to the refusal of the government to pay the company 10.000 *pesos* annually as promised the failure of the company's project. Carondelet steadfastly urged the payment of the 10,000 *pesos* but the Intendant quibbling over wordage persistently refused to allow the payment.

but also in keeping them away from it and from that frontier without any communication at all with the savage nations which are near [or approach] the *Provincias Internas* and California. Finally, at the end of the ten years of exclusive privilege, our Company will be strong enough to do without [this] apparent aid and support of the State. I say "apparent" because in reality in payment of the ten thousand *pesos* advanced annually to the Company, the royal treasury will collect more than thirty thousand *pesos* annually from the value of the customs duties which will be paid both for the exportation of peltries from the province and for the importation of goods necessary for trade.

When this first obstacle is overcome with such advantage to the state, it remains to oppose the Sioux, Sauteux, Osniboine [Assiniboine] and other nations that live to the North of the Missouri. These nations, trading with the English, make frequent raids on that river and rob and kill our traders when they meet them. Although it is true that the Company's forts and posts [factories-trading houses] will contribute in great part to keep those savages at a distance, one must consider that a single robbery committed in the course of a year will be sufficient to intimidate the traders and consequently to retard the Company's progress. The only means of overcoming this difficulty will be found in the admission and acceptation which, with the greatest appreciation and desire, we have given to the proposals of the English merchant, Don Andrés Todd, established at Michelimakinak. Through the delivery of the forts on the Strait [Detroit] and elsewhere agreed upon between the English and Americans for the coming month of June, he was afraid of losing the profitable branch of the fur trade which he is carrying on with the nations situated to the north of the Ohio, Mississippi and Missouri rivers. Therefore, he offered to transfer his house to Louisiana and to carry on his business from there under the conditions mentioned in the document that accompanies, no. 6.[26] From its contents Your Excellency will be informed of the powerful motives that urged the Intendant Don Francisco Rendón and myself to assent to this proposal.[27] However, besides those reasons that are evident in the document, I will add some considerations to prove that that was the only way to win the savage nations located north of the Missouri to allegiance to Spain and to free the shores of that river from their depredations.

As a matter of fact, since Don Andrés Todd is one of the principal shareholders in our Missouri Company; and since the greater part of the merchandise and goods used on its three expeditions[28] were supplied by his house which will receive in payment part of the skins on its return,

---

[26]See *below*. Also found in A.G.I., Sto.Dom., 87-1-24 (old numbering), transcript in Bancroft Library. Draft in English in A.G.I., P. de C., leg. 2364.

[27]A.G.I., Sto. Dom., 87-1-24 (old numbering), transcript in Bancroft Library.

[28]See Chapter III, document XIII which is annex no. 7 to this letter. This is discussed in Nasatir, "Anglo-Spanish Frontier on the Upper Mississippi 1786-1796."

it follows that he will assist its undertakings in every possible way. It also [logically ensues] that he will influence to cease their hostility and attacks against the traders of our [Company],[29] those nations of the Upper Mississippi and north of the Missouri who hold him in great respect and have traded with his house for years.

The statement [representation] of Todd, mentioned above, and the reply of the director of the Company of the Discoverers of the Missouri, Don Santiago Clamorgan, a copy of which accompanies, no. 7,[30] are other truths strengthened and proved by experience. The English from Hudson Bay, Montreal, Michelimakinak, etc., have succeeded not only in securing and usurping the profitable fur trade of the North and of all our own settlements of Illinois, but they also supply and furnish [the latter] at prices much lower than those current at New Orleans. This they do in spite of the great expense and the difficulties which they experience in transporting their merchandise a distance as great by water as by land, since from Montreal they are subjected to more than twenty portages before reaching the Mississippi.[31] For this reason they use on the trip only bark canoes which they carry overland on their heads. Nevertheless, on account of the exemption from export and import duties on the goods intended for this trade, it was [is] enough to counterbalance all those difficulties. Stopping smuggling which is carried on more than five hundred leagues from the capital would cost the royal treasury more than it was worth; would expose the king's vassals to reprisals on the part of the savages, and the court to complaints from England that would be incapable of adjustment as is evidenced by those sent to me by Lord Dorchester resulting from the confiscation mentioned in the aforesaid memorial of Don Andrés Todd.[32]

By accepting the proposals in this memorial, the motives for disagreement between the two courts will cease to exist; the smuggling which the English carry on with Illinois will be stopped; [and] the royal revenue will be increased not only by the whole value of the duties paid for goods taken up the Mississippi to the Illinois settlements for the consumption of its inhabitants and for its trade with the savages, but also by all the duties paid for the many furs of the Missouri Company and Don

[29]The word "company" is omitted in the copy in the Bancroft Library.
[30]Chapter III, document XIII.
[31]See Todd's petition to Carondelet, annex no. 6, *below;* Perrault's "Narrative" in *Michigan Pioneer and Historical Collections,* XXXVII; W. E. Stevens, *Northwest Fur Trade* (Urbana, 1926); H. A. Innis, *Fur Trade in Canada* (New Haven, 1930); G. C. Davidson, *Northwest Company* (Berkeley, 1918), etc. etc.
[32]Dorchester to Carondelet, August 21, 1794, A.G.I., P. de C., leg. 2371, calendared in *Report* of the Canadian Archives, 1891, State Papers, Lower Canada, 113, and enclosed in Dorchester to Portland, no. 68, October 26, 1794, calendared in *Ibid.,* 117; Carondelet to Dorchester, June 12, 1795, calendared in *Ibid.* 114, enclosed in Dorchester to Portland, no. 70. See Nasatir, "Anglo-Spanish Frontier on the Upper Mississippi 1786-1796."

Andrés Todd when they are shipped out from Valiza. Up to the present time all of these articles have been sent to Canada, and have produced nothing for the royal treasury. By accepting these terms, the population will also be increased. Likewise, there will be an increase in the business of our establishments of Illinois with all the traders, clerks, employees, and sailors that the Company and Todd will maintain in their pay and will attract from Canada. The navigation and the commerce of Louisiana will be increased. A line of forts will be established on the Missouri which will be extended to the South Sea. These in time will become so many more settlements, many in number, which will mark the boundary and protect the *Provincias Internas* on the North against the encroachment of the Americans and the English, [in the same manner that] the Mississippi marks the boundary on their West. Finally, we will deprive the Americans of the friendship and alliance with the savage nations that live near the Strait [Detroit] whom they propose to bring to our side. If we were assured of our influence over them as we are over those who live to the South of the Ohio, we would add this new obstacle to the advance which the English and the Americans are making towards us.[33]

It is true that Intendent Don Francisco Rendón and I have lowered the import and export duties on the goods necessary for Todd's trade with the Indians from fifteen per cent to six for one year and until His Majesty decides what may seem best to him for the future.[34] Your Excellency will bear in mind not only that there was no opportunity [time] to consult the court, but also that a report could not even be received before the month of July, while the transfer of the Strait [Detroit] to the United States by England was to take place in June,[35] leaving no other means to Don Andrés Todd to avoid the ruin of his business except to come to terms with the United States. The latter would have received him with open arms, and probably would have exempted his goods from all import [duties], since those that are paid in America are returned to the merchants as rewards which they receive for expending their effects among the Indians. In the second place we had in mind the privileges and sacrifices the state makes in favor of the English company of Don Guillermo Panton[36] whose trade with our nations to the South is free of all duties,

---

[33]Carondelet and Trudeau were in continual fear of American and British aggression and of their attacking Spanish Louisiana. Anglo-American ingenuity and fearlessness stood face to face with Latin temperament and lack of action. It was a plain case of action versus words, and although the officials in and of Spanish Louisiana spoke and wrote a good deal and oftimes acted, the higher officials paid little heed.

[34]See above. This was confirmed by Spain, May 27, 1796.

[35]This refers to the fulfillment of the terms of Jay's treaty.

[36]Panton, Leslie and Company. See Whitaker, *Spanish American Frontier*, 38 ff., esp. 40, and A. P. Whitaker [ed.], *Documents Relating to the Commercial Policy of Spain in the Floridas* (Deland, 1931), etc.

for the sole purpose of keeping those tribes friendly [attached] to Spain. Since it is of no less importance to attract to our allegiance [devotion] the warlike natives who live between the Strait [Detroit] and the Ohio, and who have been abandoned by the English for political reasons that have not yet come to the notice of the public, we thought that we were doing the state an essential service by taking advantage of an opportunity, as unexpected as it was fortunate. [By our action we sought] to acquire for Spain a preponderance of forces against the United States; to expel the English from our frontiers in the North; to protect the Spanish settlements of Illinois from the the raids and plunderings of the savage nations, which is the principal cause of their backwardness in agriculture; to put an end to the smuggling between the English and these very settlements; to increase our trade by water at the expense of theirs; and finally, to add from this year on [*desde este Año*]—*more than thirty thousand pesos to the custom-house receipts.*

If, in addition to motives so strong as those to which I have just referred, one considers that the reduction of royal revenue in favor of Don Andrés Todd applies only to the goods necessary for trading with the Indians and the furs obtained from it, one draws the natural conclusion that if it had been denied, the royal treasury would have collected nothing at all from them; for, in that case, the aforesaid Todd would not have decided to transfer his trading house from Michilimakinac to this province, and his goods and furs which will begin this year to go by way of the Mississippi, would have been sent by way of Canada or by way of the Ohio to the Atlantic Ocean. Neither should objection be made that a reduction of taxes in favor of a foreigner is harmful to the rest of the[37] [trade] of Louisiana or the Missouri Company, since his privilege extends no further than the particular commerce of the savage nations to the north of the Ohio and the Missouri; but even though this were true, it would be easy to do away with this disparity, by hearkening to the many petitions that the Intendant Don Francisco Rendón and I have made in an endeavor to have all export and import duties reduced to the same six percent which was paid before the war in this colony. That action, instead of lessening the income of the royal customs, would unquestionably contribute to its rapid increase. It would also promote [increase] its population, agriculture, commerce, navigation, etc.; and it would completely gain the loyalty and good will of these colonists in favor of Spain,—advantages that can never be attained by coercion or force. A moderate export and import duty to foreign countries and freedom to trade with all, would rapidly transform Louisiana into a useful, rich, and well-populated Spanish possession. An opposite course, on the other hand, would

---

[37] Here ends the copy in the Bancroft Library.
[38] A.H.N., Est., leg. 3899; draft in A.G.I., P. de C., leg. 178.

cause it to be for many years, as it now is, a French colony, burdensome, barren and deserted, which the great pecuniary sacrifices made by Spain for thirty years have not yet completely conquered for the monarchy.

In view of all that I have set forth in this official letter as well as in my confidential letter, no. 36, under date of June 3, 1794,[38] I hope that Your Excellency will see fit to pass it all on to His Majesty to obtain his approval [first] for the four points that I urge for the success of the proposed plan of establishing a frontier line of [posts] between Spain's northern possessions from the Mississippi to the South Sea, extending towards Nootka Sound, strong enough to restrain the encroachments of the English. And lastly, to insure once for all the peace and prosperity of Louisiana by securing from the king reduction to the pre-war six percent rate of Import and export duties to foreign countries.

May God, Our Lord, preserve Your Excellency for many years. New Orleans, January 8, 1796. Most Excellent *Señor,*

Le Baron de Carondelet [rubric]

Most Excellent *Señor* Príncipe de la Paz.

[Annex without number]
New Orleans, January 8, 1796[39]

The Baron de Carondelet makes it known that he is sending on this date to this ministry an *expediente* of supreme interest to the State; for it shows, with proof, the recent usurpations of the English to the north of the *Provincias Internas* and New Mexico.

Most Excellent Sir:

My dear and most respected Sir: On this date I am sending to the ministry in charge of Your Excellency an *expediente* of supreme interest to the State, for it demonstrates with proof the recent usurpations by the English to the north of the internal provinces and New Mexico. These usurpations are aimed at nothing less than opening a path to those provinces. Simply by a glance at the topographical map which forms a part, under no. 4,[40] of the confidential *expediente* no. 65, Your Excellency will perceive the designs of the British and the dangers which menace the kingdom on that frontier.

The remedy which I propose is certain, and will not cost the royal treasury 20,000 *pesos;* if, on the contrary, the favorable moment which

---

[39]On the same date Carondelet sent no. 66 *res.* urging Spain to grant to Todd the exclusive commerce with the Indian nations of the Upper Missouri [*sic*], paying six per cent duty, etc. A.H.N., Est., leg. 3900.

There is a note in the margin, probably by the Príncipe de Paz saying: "May 2, 1796. I will look it over carefully and with pleasure. I know about the views [plans] of the English. I know their ambitious plans and I am going to reproach them."

[40]See note 20.

now offers itself is lost, it is inevitable that the usurpations of England, consecrated by time, will some day be the cause of war, or of great sacrafice on the part of Spain.

With this motive I again place myself at the orders of Your Excellency, whose life I pray God to keep many and happy years.
New Orleans, January 8, 1796.

I kiss the hands of Your Excellency.   Your most humble and devoted servant,

Baron de Carondelet [rubric]

His Excellency el Príncipe de la Paz

[Annex without number]
Article 3.[41]

It has been established that at all times it will be permitted to the subjects of His Majesty and to the inhabitants of the United States, as well as to the Indians resident in the two parts of the territory bounded as has just been pointed out, to pass and repass, by land or by means of interior navigation, from one country to the other belonging to the two contracting parties in the continent of America (excepting solely the part within the limits of the Company of Hudson Bay); and to navigate or make use of all the lakes, rivers, or any communication by water, in order that the two may pursue their respective traffic and commerce.   But it must be understood that this article does not extend to the admission of vessels from the United States either in the ports, roadsteads, bays, or other anchorages in the aforesaid territories of His Majesty, or in that part of the rivers within the territory belonging to His Majesty lying between the mouth and the highest port of entry, unless it be in small boats carrying on a "bona fide" trade between Montreal and Quebec under those regulations which will be formed to prevent all possibility of fraud or illicit traffic.   And on the same terms, neither will English vessels be admitted proceeding from the sea within the rivers belonging to the United States beyond the highest or most elevated ports of entry, coming from the sea.   Nevertheless, in accordance with the Treaty of Peace, *the Mississippi River will be entirely open to both contracting parties, and it has been agreed, besides, that they can reciprocally go and use all the ports and places on the east bank of the said river, whether belonging to Great Britain or the United States, as freely as is practiced in any place or port on the Atlantic which belongs to them respectively.*[42]

---

[41]Annex without number. Articles three and four of Jay's Treaty. Compare with the treaty as published in S. F. Bemis, *Jay's Treaty* (New York 1923), 322-325. The definitive edition of Jay's Treaty is in D. Hunter Miller (ed.) *Treaties and other International Acts of the United States of America* vol. II. (Washington, 1921).
[42]The underlining is in the original.

396

All goods and merchandise whose introduction is not entirely prohibited in the dominion of His British Majesty in America will be admitted in the aforesaid territories referred to in the articles; and trade in them [will be] permitted to the inhabitants of the United States, who will not be subject to new or greater duties than those which would be paid there by Brittanic subjects who bring the goods from Europe. On equal terms, goods and merchandise whose introduction is not prohibited in the jurisdiction of the United States may be traded in by Brittanic subjects in those places without paying new or greater duties than the Americans themselves pay in their own vessels. At the same time, each may respectively take from the ports and places of the other, with perfect equality, those goods and products whose exportation is not prohibited.

Neither of the two contracting parties will pay any import duty on the peltries which may be brought, by land or interior navigation, respectively, into the territory of the other; nor will the Indians pay, in pass- and repassing with their own effects, any duty or impost of any kind whatsoever. But goods and merchandise conducted in bales or bulky boxes not generally used by the Indians will not be considered as goods belonging to them in good faith.

In going from one part to the other, no demand will be made for higher duties than those paid by the natives of the country in crossing rivers, boundaries, etc.; nor will any charge be made for goods which are solely conducted with the object of again embarking them in another place. But since the only purpose if this stipulation is to establish for both parties facility and convenience in their respective traffic, it is established that it will not be permitted to make sales or exchanges during their transit, in regard to which suitable regulations will be made.

Since it is desired by this article to establish that the local advantages enjoyed by each party in its territory may be extended to both districts, in order to cement friendship and neighborliness, both governments will promote the greatest justice and necessary protection in all cases that may occur.

Art. 4.

As it is still uncertain whether the Mississippi River extends so far to the north that it may be cut by a line drawn exactly to the west from the Lake of the Woods, in the way that is expressed in the Treaty of Peace between His Majesty and the United States, it has now been agreed that necessary measures shall be taken in common accord by the government of His Majesty in America and that of the United States to have an exact examination made by persons named by both sides, to [who will] go together and explore the said river from a degree of latitude lower down than the Falls of San Antonio to the origin or principal origin, of the same river and adjacent parts; and if from this examination it results that it is not possible to draw the line referred to above, then the two contracting parties, by means of friendly and cordial negotiations, will discuss the best means of regulating the boundaries in that part with regard for justice and mutual advantage, which was the object of the preceding Treaty.

[Annex without number]

May, 1796[43]

Most Excellent Sir: The governor of Louisiana and Western Florida, Baron de Carondelet, represents to Your Excellency in his letter no. 65 of the 8th of last January the measures which he has taken and the means by which he has availed himself to restrain the contraband trade carried on by the English in the Spanish establishments of Illinois, and he proposes at the same time the measures which seem to him most feasible to prevent the English and Americans from carrying forward their usurpations.

Carondelet, having learned in the beginning of his government that the Spanish establishments of St. Louis Illinois were declining from day to day through the entrance of the English into the fur trade on the Missouri River, and [through] the contraband trade which they were carrying on from Canada, providing our establishments with all the utensils they needed at lower prices than those of New Orleans, distant 500 leagues from Illinois,—ordered his lieutenant-governor to confiscate by force any small English ships found with goods in territory on the western side of the Mississipi.

In fulfillment of this order, Lieutenant-Governor Don Zenon Trudeau armed an expedition in the latter part of October, 1793, and with it, at a point forty-one leagues above St. Louis, Illinois, took possession, of various goods belonging to Don Andrés Todd and other inhabitants of Michelimakinak. At the same time Carondelet persuaded some well-to-do inhabitants of St. Louis, Illinois, to form a company under the title of "Discoverers of the Missouri," under the direction of Don Santiago Clamorgan, an active and well-informed man. Carondelet also approved the regulation and instructions which they presented to him in May, 1794, and which he now sends indicated with the [enclosures] numbers 2 and 3, granting to the company the exclusive privilege of trade with all the Indian nations of the Missouri who live beyond that of the Poncas. He promised, besides, a reward of three thousand *pesos* to the one who should arrive first at the South Sea, a very important discovery, for besides fixing its

---

[43]Annex without number. This seems to be the summary which Montarco prepared for the Council of State. Compare it with the *minuta* of the session of the Council of State for May 27, 1796, in Nasatir and Liljegren, "Materials for the History of the Mississippi Valley," reprint pp. 65-71.

limits it would undoubtedly lead to an establishment capable of preventing the English and Russians from establishing themselves on those remote coasts.

The greatest obstacles encountered by the Company of the Missouri in its first two expeditions were the dangers offered by the passage through the nations of the Lower Missouri and those north of the same river, who do not wish to permit our traders to carry arms or munitions to their enemies living on the banks of that river, partly on account of the interest which they have in it and partly through the instigations of the English of Hudson Bay, who aspire to embrace all that commerce.

The passage through the nations of the Lower Missouri may be assured without difficulty by means of the three forts which the Company has erected among the Otto, Maha, and Ponca nations. Still greater advantage, [will be obtained] if His Majesty will consent that one or two flat-bottomed galleys, armed with six cannon, swivel-guns, and twenty sailors, shall patrol the river and protect the expeditions in the most dangerous passes.

These precautions (says Carondelet) are all the more indispensable since the English now leave no doubt of their intentions toward the Missouri, as is evidenced both by the line of forts marked on the map [enclosure] no. 4, which they have established from Lake Superior to the mountains of *Roca Negra,* not far distant (it is believed) from the South Sea, and also particularly by the attempt of the English company called "Of the North", which in this present year has built a fort on the Missouri, half a league from the *pueblo* of the Mandanas, in the midst of the Spanish possessions, according to the declaration of the English deserters, a copy of which is enclosed under no. 5.

In view of this, the governor of Louisiana believes that it is necessary to hasten to take all the most feasible means to restrain the usurpations of the English Companies of Montreal, Michelimakinak, and Hudson Bay; to prevent them from possessing themselves of the immense territory bathed by the Missouri; and, after passing the mountains of *Roca Negra,* to restrain them from uniting their establishments with that of Nootka Sound, and carrying on all the commerce with the *provincias internas* and the Californias. But in view of the fact that if the government attempts by itself to dislodge the English from their establishments next to the Mandanas, distant more than 400 leagues from St. Louis, Illinois, from which the expedition would have to start, it would have to spend more than 50,000 *pesos* (and perhaps with little result, because the English Company could establish itself further up or further down), Carondelet proposes that 10,000 *pesos* shall be granted annually to the Company mentioned for the maintenance of 100 armed men in the forts which it has built and intends to build until it comes to the South

Sea; he adds that when the ten years of exclusive privilege which have been granted to that Company are past, the government will no longer need it, and that in the meantime the royal treasury will gain more than 30,000 *pesos* annually from the export duties on the peltries and the import duties on the goods necessary for the trade.

Although the forts of the Company may help to restrain the forays of the Sioux, Sauteux, Osniboine [Assiniboine] nations and the rest of the nations who live north of the Missouri, forming the second obstacle to the establishment of that Company the governor of Louisiana proposes, as the only means of overcoming this difficulty, that His Majesty should consent to the petition (enclosure no. 6) of the English merchant Don Andrés Todd, citizen of Michelimakinak, and permit him to introduce all the goods necessary for trade with the Indians and to take out the peltries and other products of the country, under the pre-war six percent duty. On these terms Todd promises to assure the friendship of the Indians, with whom he has very close relations, because of the many years during which he has managed the greater part of the commerce of Canada. He also says that he is obliged to send down by way of the Mississippi in the course of the present year, four thousand bales of peltries, which, at the rate of forty-five *pesos,* would bring into the royal treasury 10,800 *pesos,* not taking into consideration the product from the exchanges, or the advantages of the increase in population, industry, consumption, and navigation, or most important, the exclusion of the American traders, who, if these steps are not taken would possess themselves of the said commerce, to the great injury of Louisiana and the *Provincias Internas* of New Spain.

At the same time Carondelet states that in accord with the Intendant Don Francisco Rendón, he has granted to Todd the favor of reducing the import and export duties from fifteen percent to six percent, for the term of one year and until His Majesty comes to a decision in view of the whole business, being influenced in this determination not only by the reasons stated above but by many others of greater importance.

Don Andrés Todd, afraid of losing the rich fur trade which he had with the nations situated north of the Ohio, Mississippi, and Missouri Rivers through the conveyance of the forts of the Strait and the rest agreed upon between the English and the Americans for the month of next June, offered to transfer his trade to Louisiana and continue it under the conditions mentioned. In this state of things, in case his petition should be denied, or the decision of His Majesty, which could not arrive until July, should have to be waited for, Todd would be compelled, in order to avoid ruin, to take sides with the United States. The latter would not have failed to accept him with his eagerness, and to admit his goods free of all duty; for, duties paid in the aforesaid States, are returned to the merchants when they expend their goods among the Indians. Consequently are lost in an irreparable manner the advantages offered by a merchant as intelligent as Todd, with sufficient powers [means], and one of the principal persons interested in the Company of the Missouri, to which he has furnished all the goods necessary for the three expeditions which it has made, and who is, above all, a friend of the Indians with whom the Company has to trade.

The exemption from import and export duties enjoyed by the English of Hudson Bay, Michelimakinak, etc., has been the principal reason why they have usurped not only all of the fur trade of the North and of our own establishments in Illinois, but is also the reason why they have furnished the latter with all the goods they have needed at lower prices than those current in New Orleans, in spite of the great expense and difficulties caused them by the long distance they had to come by land or water. And His Majesty has followed these principles in granting various privileges to the English house of Don Guillermo Panton, excusing him from all duties in the trade which he has with our Indian nations of the South, with the object of preserving their friendship.

Besides, says Carondelet, the reduction of duties in favor of Todd does not damage in any way the rest of the commerce of Louisiana or that of the Company of Missouri, since its [Todd's] privilege does not extend to any more than the particular trade with the savage nations north of the Ohio and of the Missouri; and for this reason he calls to mind his previous representations and those of the Intendent Rendón for the general reduction of all import and export duties to the same six percent, as a certain means of increasing the royal exchequer, of promoting agriculture and commerce, of conciliating the good will of the colonists and of transforming Louisiana, which is to-day as backward as it is uncultivated and uninhabited, into a well-populated, useful, and abundant province.

Lastly, Carondelet believes that by accepting the proposals of Todd, the contraband trade with the English will cease, and with it a motive for quarrels between our court and that of England, as has just been proved in the complaints directed by Lord Dorchester in regard to the attachment that was placed upon Todd. This memorial, which he encloses, recommends to the generosity of His Majesty that he shall deign to order the return to Todd of the 7,860 *pesos,* the value of the effects and goods seized by Don Zenon Trudeau.

To sum up, the Baron de Carondelet proposes four methods to restrain encroachments of the English on the Spanish territory north of Louisiana, and to repress the contraband trade which they [the English] are carrying on in the Spanish establishments of Illinois, in order to win the friendship of the nations living north of the Ohio, Mississippi, and Missouri Rivers, [thus] forming of the barrier against the English and Americans.

1. The confirmation and royal approbation of the Company of Discoverers of the Missouri.

2. An annual grant of 10,000 *pesos* for a period of ten years to the said Company.

3. The establishment of two forts on the San Pedro and Mongoina Rivers with a garrison of fifty men.

4. The approbation and concession to Don Andrés Todd of the reduction of import and export duties in his commerce with the nations north of the Ohio and the Missouri.[44]

[Annex without number]

Aránjuez, May 25, 1796[45]
To the Governor of New Orleans

Since on this same day the resolutions of the King in his Council of State relative to the project and means explained in Your Excellency's

---

[44]Todd was granted the exclusive trade of the Indian nations of the Mississippi north of the Missouri. Delays in engaging in it caused Todd to propose a number of changes in his contract in February, 1796, including an extension of his exclusive trade from five to ten years; he declared it would be necessary to construct forts to prevent the Americans from intruding into Spanish territory (which forts Carondelet said, must be confined to the entrances of the San Pedro and Des Moines rivers and be built at Todd's expense); a militia of 100 men to defend the forts which Todd would feed, maintain and pay including a sergeant, two corporals and four soldiers of the regular troops (Carondelet remarked that Todd must petition for this); a flag for the forts, medals and flags for the Indians, guns for the forts, goods and *engagés* to be imported and exported free of duty, and to protect Todd's investment in case Spain gives up or cedes Louisiana. A.G.I., P. de C., leg. 2371. This savors a great deal of Clamorgan's work or/and influence.

[45]Annex without number. This is evidently a marginal note. The date is most likely an error in copying, for the decision was not taken until May 27. On May 29 Montarco returned the documents (here presented) and the topographical plan which the Prince of Peace had sent to him a few days before, together with the royal order sanctioning the Missouri Company, etc. At the same time Montarco dispatched a copy of the decision of the Council of State to the *Ministerio de Hacienda*. Copies were also directed to Diego de Gardoqui who in turn forwarded the news and the royal order to the Governor of Louisiana and the Intendant of Louisiana. Montarco to Gardoqui, Aránjuez, May 29, 1796, A.G.I., Sto. Dom., 87-3-22 (old numbering), copy in the Missouri Historical Society, Spanish Archives, no. 97; Gardoqui to Intendant of Louisiana, June 11, 1796, A.G.I., P. de C., leg. 129; and Gardoqui to Governor of Louisiana, Aránjuez, June 11, 1796, *Ibid.*, leg. 176/2; translated in Houck, *Spanish Régime in Missouri*, II, 179-180, and in many other documents.

letter, number 65 of the tenth of February [January?] for restraining the plans of the English in the Northwest of America, by favoring the trading Companies [The Missouri Company] and the Merchant Don Andrés Todd, have been communicated to Your Excellency by the Ministery of the Exchequer, I will omit repeating to Your Excellency the decision of His Majesty.

[Annex no. 1][46]

Sir: Don Andrés Todd, in his name and that of Nicolas Marchessau and Jonas Bleaklay, places himself at the royal feet of Your Majesty and with the proper respect declares:

That in the latter part of October, 1793, at a point [forty] one league further up than the establishments of St. Louis, Illinois, there were confiscated at the order of Captain Don Zenon Trudeau,[47] Lieutenant-Governor of the establishments on the west bank, on land as well as on the river, various effects and merchandise suitable for trade with the Indians, whose principal cost, without including that of the crew, and equipment and salaries of the oarsmen,[48] amounts to the sum of 7,860 *pesos.*[49]

---

[46]There is a draft of this letter in A.G.I., P.de C., leg. 129.

[47]Carondelet had ordered Trudeau to confiscate all English boats, together with their goods, that were found to be in the territory west of the Mississippi. *Minuta del Acta del Consejo de Estado*, May 27, 1796, in Nasatir and Liljegren, "Materials for the History of the Mississippi Valley", *op. cit.* For a full account of the seizure see Nasatir, "Anglo-Spanish Frontier on the Upper Mississippi 1786-1796."

[48]There is a more extended account of the seizure in the petition of Todd, McGill and Company, Josiah Bleakley, Charles Bellivos and Nicholas Marchesseau to Carondelet presented by J. Jones their attorney-in-fact. A.G.I., P.deC., leg. 201.

[49]The accounts as to the amounts of the value of the goods confiscated seem to vary:

Todd says 7860 *pesos.* See text.

Jones says $8814 dollars, 1 *livre*, 11 *sols*, 6 *deniers* original cost at Michilimackinac. Bleakley's cargo was returned except for $162 worth of goods. Petition of Todd, McGill and Co., etc. *op. cit.*

One itemized account is as follows:

Amount of goods seized from Basil Proulx as per invoice	3736.4
Amount of goods seized from Charles Bellivos as per invoice	15,538.1
Livres........	19,274.14

Nineteen thousand two hundred and seventy four *livres* fourteen sols. Amount belonging to Andrew Todd at the Michilimackinac prices exclusive of men's wages, etc.

Amount of goods seized from Amable Duroche the property of Nicholas Marchesseau—agreeable to his invoice, exclusive of men's wages, etc.	6,325.9
Amount of goods seized from Jacob Franks as per invoice as sworn to by him	14,808.15
Deduct amount of Indian credits received on account	1,227.
	13,581.15
Deduct amount received back from Capn Trudeau on said account	690.4
	12,891.11

Señor, the supplicant cannot contest the territorial rights of His Majesty, nor can he contest the propriety of the reasons and motives which actuated the Governor in stopping without previous warning a commerce which has always been provided with goods by the merchants of Michelimakinak,[50] since the means of the inhabitants of your establishments of Illinois are not sufficient to support the immense expense of expeditions made from New Orleans, (on account of the poverty of their fortunes). Without this relief they would be ruined to-day by the innumerable Indian nations of the west and frontiers of the New Kingdom of Mexico.

The good faith with which they have pursued this commerce in the presence of the knowledge and patience of those commandments— for really, in any other way, they would have fallen victims to the fury of the Indians,—leads them to appeal to the noble heart and generosity of His Majesty, supplicating that you will deign, in view of the reasons stated, to order that the aforesaid capital of 7,860 *pesos* be returned to them, under the promise of their not taking part again in this trade except by legitimate means and through the province of Louisiana. With this object, the supplicant had taken his measures in the petition[51] which

---

Amount of sundries taken out of Josiah Bleakley's boat on the Mississippi	721.7
Amount of sundries taken from Josiah Bleakley's men in said boat	88.10

Libres	13,701.8

Thirteen thousand seven hundred and one *livres eight sols*
Amount belonging to Josiah Bleakley at the Michilimackinac prices exclusive of men's wages, etc.

Amount of goods the property of Andrew Todd	19,274.14
Amount of goods the property of Nicholas Marchesseau	6,325.9
Amount of goods the property of Josiah Bleakley	13,701.8

Total amount in *livres*	39,301.11

New Orleans, 19 December, 1795.
Andrew Todd for self and the others interested.

Attached to Todd's petition, A.G.I., P.de C., leg. 129.
Trudeau sold some of the goods seized for something like $2860.
Houck, *History of Missouri*, I, 330.

[50]John Rice Jones did protest, however. Petition of Andrew Todd, McGill and Company and others by Jones, their attorney in fact, A.G.I., P. de C., leg. 201. Jones also protested the methods of handling the men seized and the bringing of some of them to St. Louis where they and their papers were examined and some of their goods confiscated.

[51]The petition is dated New Orleans, December 18, 1795, see annex no. 6, *below.* It is also in A.G.I., Sto.Dom., 87-1-24 (old numbering), transcript in Bancroft Library. A draft in English is in A.G.I., P. de C., leg. 2364.

he has just presented to your governor and intendant, with the intention of placing Spain in quiet and peaceful possession of the rich fur trade of the nations of the west, which will remain entirely attached to Spain. This favor will attract to the establishments named, a considerable increase in commerce and population, and their inhabitants will ceaselessly bless the mild government of His Majesty.[52]

New Orleans, December 21, 1795.

Sire,

At the royal feet of His Majesty
Andrés Todd [rubric]

[Report of *Señor* Baron de Carondelet] :

[On the margin of the previous writing appears the following report] :[53]

Sire: The just motives which impelled my Lieutenant Governor of the establishments of Illinois to send an expedition to restrain the clandestine commerce of the English on the Mississippi, appear in the *expediente* which was sent on the 2nd of July, 1794, to the Ministry of State; but, because it is true that this same commerce has been carried on for years, and cannot be cut off except by reduction of the import and export duties on goods by way of the Mississippi to the six percent (added to the freedom of trade granted to the colony since the beginning of the war) : and because of the great advantages which the royal treasury will draw from the establishment of the supplicant in Louisiana, I consider him worthy of the favor which he solicits of the liberal piety of Your Majesty, which you will determine as best pleases you.

New Orleans, January 8, 1796.
Baron de Carondelet [rubric].[54]

---

[52]Carondelet, the governor-general, and Rendón, the Intendant of Louisiana, granted Todd his petition on December 21, 1795. This may have impelled Todd to petition for the recovery of the value of the goods which the Spaniards had seized from them.

[53]Draft or contemporary copy in A.G.I., P. de C., leg. 2364, transcript in Library of Congress.

[54]Annex no. 2   Articles of Incorporation of the Missouri Company. Chapter II, document IX.

Annex no. 3.   Instructions to Truteau.   Chapter II, document XVIII.

405

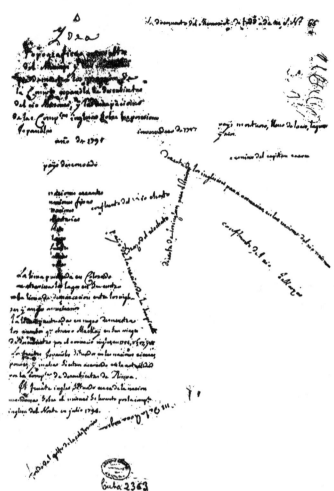

⁵⁵In the A.H.N., Est., leg. 3900 there is only an envelope of common paper with the following notation on it: "No. 4. A Map which goes under separate cover." I failed to locate this map in Madrid. There is a topographical map which I believe is the one, or a copy of the one, referred to here in A.G.I., P. de C., leg. 2363. It is enclosed in the French copy of the Instructions (annex no. 3) given by Clamorgan to Truteau. It is entitled:

Idea
Topográfica de los Altos del Mississippi y del Missouri que demuestra los progresos de la Compie. española de descubiertos del rio Missouri y las usurpaciones de los compias. inglesas sobre los posesiones españolas.

Año de 1795

Annex no. 5 is Chapter III, document XII.

[Annex no. 6.][56]

Señores: General-General and Intendant of the Army of these provinces

Don Andrés Todd, [formerly an][57] inhabitant of Canada, has the honor of representing to Your Excellencies that for many years he has managed the principal Indian trade in that province; but since according to the treaty recently concluded between His British Majesty and the United States of America, the posts and frontier forts of Michelimakinak, Detroit, and others which that province possesses must be delivered to the United States in the month of next June, the Americans will be in consequence absolute masters, with the power to prevent the traders of Canada from visiting the Indian nations of the west bank of the Mississippi. They will furnish these nations with whatever they need, attracting them to their devotion and alliance, and making them more and more attached to their cause, with the object that at any time when it may suit their plans and purposes, they can with the greatest facility not only destroy and ruin the establishments of Illinois, but also entirely annihilate the commerce of the Mississippi, unless they may be restrained for some time by garrisons and posts established in the upper part which is difficult and doubtful.

It is already at present an incontrovertible and indisputable truth that in spite of all the vigilance of the Spanish Government, the traders of Michelimakinak are the sole and only possessors of commerce on the upper part of the Mississippi. This they can maintain and increase by following the same plan which Great Britian wisely adopted of permitting the importation and exportation of goods free of duties from Canada, making it easy in this way for the traders, notwithstanding the length and difficulty of their journeys, not only to provide the Indian nations of Canada and the Upper Mississippi, but also to carry goods to the Spanish establishments themselves of St. Louis, Illinois, and to sell them at a price so small as compared with the cost of the merchandise which the Spanish traders carry up from New Orleans, that for some time there has scarcely been sent from this capital more than some brandy made of sugar cane, sugar and coffee, while all the ordinary and fine peltry of the country which naturally ought to come down here goes out of its proper channel and remounts by the lakes to Montreal and Quebec, where this single trade employs a considerable number of artificers and shopkeepers. This notably increases the imports of that colony, which now

---

[56]Also in A.G.I., Sto. Dom., 87-1-24 (old numbering), transcript in Bancroft Library. There is a draft in English in A.G.I., P. de C., leg. 2364 which varies slightly in its wording. This latter copy is cut at the top of the page.
[57]In draft in AG.I., P. de C., leg. 2364.

monopolizes the entire fur trade and furnishes at the same time a nursery of seamen for the squadrons of Great Britain.

This business may shortly fall into other hands through the posts from which the Indians receive the merchandise, for once they are delivered to the Americans, whose intentions are certainly well known to Your Excellencies, it is manifest that they, in order to promote their political interests, will spare neither trouble nor expense to attract the Indian tribes to their side; and if they succeed in doing it, solely upon them will depend the moderation of their encroachments and illicit commerce, prejudicial not only to this colony but even to the Spanish provinces adjacent to the west of the Mississippi.

For the reason that the suppliant has managed for many years the greater part of the commerce of Canada, by himself, by means of the traders whom he has employed, and through the connections which he consequently has formed with all the Indian chiefs, who personally profess much affection for him and have even aided him with their counsels, he solicits from the Spanish Government permission to trade and carry on commerce with it. This trade may bind those nations forever to the crown of Spain, and in place of having them as dangerous and irreconcilable enemies, this province might defend itself and put itself in safety in [the] future against the hostilities of the Americans, with whom the Indians have made peace solely because they saw themselves abandoned by Great Britain, [and] with whom they will surely not have the least connection after they can provide themselves in some other part.

The only means and channel which presents itself for the accomplishment of this important object is New Orleans, from which by way of the Mississippi and the rivers which empty into it, communication is opened to the very center of the possessions of the Indians; but at present, on account of the exorbitant duties charged, which amount at least to twenty-one percent on all articles of import, all idea of trade with them must be vain and useless, since the Americans, by way of the Ohio, which is the nearest to their villages, have the same advantage as was enjoyed by the English in Michelimakinak in importing merchandise nearly free of duties: what the merchants pay in America is returned to them as the recompense and reward [drawbacks and bounties] which they receive when they expend the goods among the Indians. This is done in the [same] manner which is practiced in their commerce with foreign posts, and cannot escape the attention of the chiefs of this colony.

It is useless to bring to the attention of Your Excellencies (who must be well informed) how important it is to attract to this province the friendship of the neighboring Indian tribes, and to considerably increase the trade by these known methods. In order to put it in execution [realize these aims] the petitioner promises to undertake to maintain good harmony among the Indians, to assure their friendship to the Crown, and to form for this purpose establishments in the places which Your Excellencies may judge necessary, under[58] the condition that he be permitted to import the goods absolutely indispensable for this commerce and to export the peltry and productions of the country which may result from the same without any more duty than the six percent established before the war. On this condition he will obligate himself to bring down in the course of the year 1796 by way of the Mississippi 4,000 pacquets of peltries, which, at the rate of forty-five *pesos* each will produce for the Royal Treasury an entrance fee of 10,800 [180,000] *pesos,* without counting the product of the exchanges, the increase in population, industry, consumption and navigation, and finally, the exclusion of the American traders, who would take possession of all this commerce to the great prejudice of this province of Louisiana and the internal provinces of New Spain.

The earnestness with which the petitioner has been recommended to this government by Lord Dorchester, Governor of Canada, is a testimony very much in favor of his character and the extensive business which he manages. If he is granted the privilege which he sollicits, just as soon as he has arranged his business up above, he will employ all his activities in putting into proper effect this interesting project.

This being a matter which requires a very prompt decision, since by the articles of the last treaty between England and the United States the forts of the Strait and the rest are to be delivered in the coming month of June, the interested party expects a very prompt and decisive answer, so that, if his offers are agreeable to Spain, he can arrange his commerce and relations in this capital, in order to go immediately afterward to Montreal and start on his trip to Europe. From there, he will return promptly with merchandise to prove to the Indians, before the Americans present themselves among them, that the Court of Spain is attentive to their needs, that it desires to protect them efficaciously, and that in order to make this clear, it has now permitted this importation. In consideration of this, the suppliant will take the most effective and quickest means to win the friendship of the Indians and to make sure of the traders, who are awaiting his return for their outfits, which he will order that they are not to get by way of Canada, and [as] has been their custom of doing, so that they shall not be under the necessity of taking the oath of fidelity to the United States, being certain that they will immediately take this oath to His Catholic Majesty when they receive information of the

---

[58]In the A.G.I., P. de C., leg. 2364 copy this paragraph is quite different. From here to the end of the paragraph it reads: "on being permitted to export and import the Goods absolutely necessary for this Trade duty free and that he may be able to enter into competition with the American Traders who otherwise must exclusively enjoy the whole of it to the whole prejudice of this Country".

success of this petition, that is, if no time is lost in the resolution and execution of this important project.

New Orleans, December 18, 1795. Andrés Todd.

DECREE:

New Orleans, December 21, 1795.

His petition is granted for a year, until His Majesty deigns to decide what he judges to be best for the good of the State and his Royal Services for the future. Baron de Carondelet, Francisco Rendón.

Baron de Carondelet [rubric][50].

---

[50]Annex no. 7. is Clamorgan and Reilhe's letter or report on the Missouri Company dated St. Louis, July 8, 1795. Chapter III document XIII.

IV

JAMES MACKAY TO JOHN EVANS, FORT CHARLES, JANUARY 28, 1796[1]

Instructions, given to Jean Evans for crossing the continent in order to discover a passage from the sources of the Missouri to the Pacific Ocean, following the orders of the Director of the company, Don St. Yago Clamorgan under the protection of His Excellency Mgr. le Baron de Carondelet, Governor-General of the Province of Louisiana, and Mr. Zenon Trudeau, Lieutenant-Governor of the Province of Illinois.

During the time of your absence from this place and during your journey to reach the Pacific or any other place, you will observe the following instructions:

Art. 1.

From the time of your departure from this fort until your return to the place where I will be living on the Missouri, you will keep a journal of each day and month of the year to avoid any error in the observations of the important journey which you are undertaking. In your journal you will place all that will be remarkable in the country that you will traverse; likewise the route, distance, latitude and longitude, when you can observe it, also the winds and weather. You will also keep another journal in which you will make note of all the minerals; vegetables; timber; rocks; flint-stone; territory; production; animals; game; reptiles; lakes; rivers; mountains; portages, with their extent and loca-

---

[1]Contemporary copy, written in French, in the Bancroft Library; edited and published in A. P. Nasatir, "John Evans: Explorer and Surveyor" in *Missouri Historical Review*, XXV (1931), 441-447. Several minor corrections have been made in this translation. This was sent, together with Mackay's "Journal," to Carondelet with Trudeau's letter to Carondelet, St. Louis, May 1, 1796, A.G.I., P. de C., leg. 193.

tion; and the different fish and shellfish which the waters may contain. You will insert in the same journal all that may be remarkable and interesting, particularly the different nations; their numbers, manners, customs, government, sentiments, language, religion, and all other circumstances relative to their manner of living.

Art. 2.

You will take care to mark down your route and distance each day, whether by land or water; in case you will be short of ink, use the powder, and for want of powder, in the summer you will surely find some fruit whose juice can replace both.

Art. 3.

In your route from here to the home of the Ponca, trace out as exactly as possible a general route and distance from the Missouri as well as the rivers which fall into it; and although you cannot take the direction of each turn and current of the Missouri, since you go by land, you can mark the general course of the mountains which will be parallel to each bank. You will observe the same thing for every other river [landmark] which you may see during your journey, whether river, lake, ocean, or chain of mountains which may effect your observations.

Art. 4.

Be very accurate in your observations concerning the nations, their size, their dwellings, their land, and their productions.

Art. 5.

Mr. Truteau, our private agent, whom you will find among the Ricara or Mandanes, will give you what you are bound to need. You will consult with him on the most practical route and he will give you guides that he will obtain from the nations where he will be.

Art. 6.

You will take for provisions on your route some well-skinned dried meat, which is very nourishing and a very little quantity of which satisfies your appetite as well as your fancy. Always lay up some provisions and keep them for a last resource.

Art. 7.

You will take heed not to fall in with some parties of savages, where there are neither women nor children, as they are almost always on the warpath. It would not be prudent to appear at any nation if you can avoid it, unless it be in their villages; and in spite of this be well on your guard. You will never fire any guns except in case of necessity; you will never cut wood except with a knife unless it should be strictly necessary; you will never build a fire without a true need, and you will avoid having the smoke seen from afar, camping if it is possible in the valleys. You will not camp too early and will always leave before daybreak; you will always be on guard against ambushes and will always have your arms in good condition, changing the tinder evening and morning, and you will never separate them from you or place them in the hands of the savages. When you will see some nations, raise your flag a long way off as a sign of peace, and never approach without speaking to them from a distance. When you will enter a village, stop and ground arms at a small distance until they come to receive and conduct you. Appear always on guard and never be fearful or timid, for the savages are not generally bold, but will act in a manner to make you afraid of them. If, however, they see that you are courageous and venturesome they will soon yield to your wishes. You will recollect that the pipe is the symbol of peace and that when they have smoked with you there is no longer any danger; nevertheless you must beware of treason.

On all occasions be reserved with your detachment as well as with the savages; always give to your conduct the air of importance and show good will toward everyone white or red.

You will carry with you some merchandise, consisting of various small articles suitable for new nations, in order to make presents to the savages which you will discover; but you must be careful of your generosity in this even as in all other things which you carry and bring with you, seeing that the time of your return is uncertain.

Say to the savages whom you will meet on your route that the white people, who come to meet them, speaking of our Company, still have many other kinds of merchandise for them. If they wish to trap some beaver and otter in order to give the skins in exchange for whatever they need, then it is necessary to show them the process of stretching and cleaning them in the same way as all other kinds of peltry are treated.

If you discover some animals which are unknown to us, you will see that you procure some of this kind, alive if possible. There is, they say, on the long chain of the Rockies which you will cross to go to the Pacific Ocean, an animal which has only one horn on its forehead. Be very particular in the description which you will make of it if you will be unable to procure one of this kind.

When you will have crossed the sources of the Missouri and will have gone beyond the Rockies, you will keep as far as possible within the bounds of the 40th degree of north latitude until you will find yourself nearly within the 111th to 112th degree of longitude west meridian of London. Then you will take a northerly direction to the 42nd degree of latitude always keeping the same longitude in order to avoid the waters which probably are destined to fall in California. This might induce you to take a route away from the Pacific Ocean. After all, you cannot travel over so great an expanse of land without finding some nations which can inform you about rivers which go toward the setting sun. Then you will build some canoes to descend these rivers, and will watch carefully since there may be some water falls on them which can carry you away, since the distance in longitude from the Rockies to the Pacific Ocean ought not to be above 290 leagues, perhaps less, which condition makes it necessary for the rivers to be very rapid or else to have great falls, in comparison with the distance which exists between the sources of the Missouri which runs over a space of about 1000 leagues to come to the sea by entering the Mississippi whose waters are very violent. This is so if it is true that this chain of mountains serves to divide the waters of the west from those of the east.

Mark your route in all places where there will be a portage to pass from one river to another or from one water-fall to another by cutting or notching some trees or by some piles of stones engraved and cut; and take care to place in large letters Charles IV King of Spain and below [that] Company of the Missouri, the day, the month, and the year when you do this in order to serve as unquestionable proof of the journey that you are going to make.

There is on the coast of the Pacific Ocean a Russian Settlement that they say is to the north of California, but there is reason to believe that it is not the only one and that the nations of the interior of the continent ought to have knowledge of it. Then, when you will have discovered the places that they inhabit, you will cease to make any sign of taking possession, for fear of having spring up with these foreigners any jealousy which would be prejudicial to the success of your journey. You will not neglect any interesting observation on the sea-shore and, although there may be some things which do not appear to merit the least attention, nevertheless, in a journey of this· nature, everything is sometimes of great importance. Do not fail to measure the rise of the sea in its ebb and flow.

As soon as you will have visited the sea-shore sufficiently, you will return from it immediately, with as much vigilance as you can to this place, or to the spot where I may be at the time, either among the Mandanes or elsewhere. You will take steps to return by a different route from that which you have taken on your way out if you believe it practical; but mind that if you find the route by which you will have passed rather straight and easy for traveling by water in a canoe or other craft, it will be wiser to return by the same route, and, in case there are portages to make from one river to another or from one rapids to another, see whether the place permits the forming of a settlement.

If, however, you are obliged to search for a new passage to return here from the sea-shore, you will return from any latitude where you may be when you will take your point of departure to forty-five degrees north

413

latitude; and on your entire route you will examine the most penetrable and practicable places for foreigners to the north country in order to give an account of the means of forming a settlement and fort there to prevent their communication [coming into this territory].

On your journey you will not forget to tell every nation that you discover, that their great father, Spain, who is protector of all the white and red men, has sent you to tell them that he has heard of them and their needs and that, desiring to make them happy, he wishes to open a communication to them in order to secure [provide] for them their necessities; that for this purpose, it is necessary that all the redskins be peaceful in order that the whites can come to see them; and that, instead of making war, it is better that they should slaughter game with which to feed their women and children.

In your orders be strict with your detachment and take care that no offense is committed against the nations through which you pass, especially by the connection that they may seek to have with the women, a thing which is ordinarily the origin of dissatisfaction and discord with the savages.

Whereas the journey is of very great importance not only to His Catholic Majesty, his subjects and the Company especially, but even [also] to the universe since it ought to open a communication of intercourse through this continent, it requires the clearest evidence to prove the truth of everything and to leave no doubt about the boldness of this discovery.

Take care, above all, to bring with you a collection of the products of the sea-shore: animals, vegetables, minerals, and other curious things that you can find, especially some skins of sea-otters and other sea animals and shell-fish which cannot be found in any fresh water. A portion of each will be an unquestionable proof of your journey to the sea-shore; but, if you can find there any civilized people who wish to give you an affidavit of your journey in whatever language they speak, this will be an additional proof of the validity of your journey.

If on your return, God has disposed of me or I have left the place of my residence on the Missouri, you will not deliver or show to anyone anything relative to your discoveries, but you will go immediately to St. Louis to deliver all your papers, plans, charts, and journals to *Monsieur* Clamorgan, Director of the Company. In case he is dead or absent, you will deliver them to whoever will represent him at the time, but in the presence of *Monsieur* Zenon Trudeau, Lieutenant-Governor or any other who should represent him, keeping in your possession a copy of each thing to be delivered and sent to the said *Monsieur* Zenon Trudeau by a safe means; this always in case *Messieurs* Zenon and Clamorgan should be dead or absent.

(Signed) Mackay.

Fort Charles, January 28, 1796.

Conjectural map based on James Mackay's instructions to John Evans (1796) to guide him to explore a route to the Pacific.

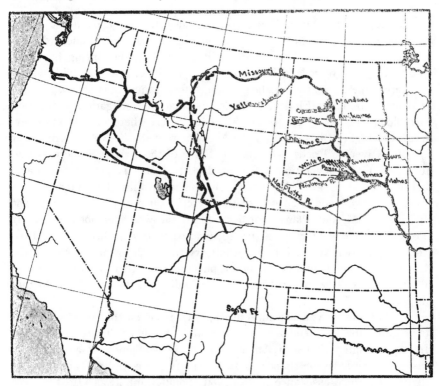

— — *Mackay's conception of the source of the Missouri.*
—— *Mackay's instructions for Evans to reach the Pacific.*
- - - - *Alternate route to avoid the Mandan villages.*

The routes beyond the Mandan villages, shown on the map, are to indicate the general and logical line that John Evans would have taken had he followed the instructions of his superior.

V

Mackay to Evans, Ft. Charles, Missouri
Feby 19th 1796[1]

Mr Evans

I have found the time tedious since you left this [*place*] notwithstanding my being constantly employed about some trip [?] or other,

---

[1] Original letter written in English found in A.G.I., P. de C., leg. 213. The side of this letter is torn or has been eaten by *polilla* worm. Question marks and letters in italics indicate those portions of the letter which have been torn or *polilla* eaten. Edited and printed in Nasatir, "John Evans: Explorer and Surveyor," *Missouri Historical Review*, XXV (1931), 447-449.

however, I begin to get accustomed to live Solletary² I dare say that in the course of some time hence I shall be happy alone as the Indian on the desert.

I suppose that by this time you are busy at your c[ommunic]ations & preparations for your voyage that is to say if the [?] Poncas do not prevent your writing—If you cannot ge[t there] in the Spring by water you will try to go by land & when you get to the ricaras you will inquire respecting the navigation of the [?] south fork Jaque³ tells me that it is— shallow at the m[outh] if you should find that the navigation of the fork is difficult you better go to the Mandans where there is a river a few leag[ues] higher that falls into the Missuri from the S West. This river is called River de Roche Jaune or the River of the Yellow Stone it is said to afford Good navigation & comes directly from the Stony mountains but it is hard to say whether it communicates with the waters of the west. I inclose you a Sketch of the Description given to Jacque by the Indians, reveal your Plans & projects to no one whatever not even to Mr Truteau except what is necessary to forward your expeditions & and for your information you will at all events try to see the white people on the Coast if it should answer no other purpose than that of corresponding by letters it will be of great service as it will open the way for a further discovery.

It is probable you will meet European vessels on the coast who trade to to [sic] the East Indians there are also vessels trading to that Coast from the United States of America, all these gentlemen or any of them that you may have the chance to meet, will (I am confident) oblige us by giving you some assistance in case you should want it, as also the most interesting news of the countries they have visited since they left their respective homes, & you will tell them that if they have letters to send to Europe or to America that I will take the greatest [care] in forwarding them with particular attention to their addr[ess]

Send me the particulars of what passes at the Poncas whatever you may learn from up the river

Tell I [or J.] & Scarlet & Tollibois [or Jollibois] [?] & any other that m[ay] go with you, that I hope they will not disappoint [me] in the confidence I have in their Conduct & persevera[nce?]

wishing you & them a prosperous voya[ge] & happy return
I am with the best wishes for your——
Your Sincere friend
J, Mackay [rubric]⁴

---

²Mackay did not marry until years later when he was *comandante* of the post of San André du Missouri.
³Jacques D'Eglise.
⁴On April 2, 1796, Trudeau wrote to Carondelet (A.G.I., P. de C., leg. 212A) :
"I received from M. Mackay the enclosed letter. He appears very content with the Mahas nation where he has been obliged to winter. I have not yet seen

I send you a letter for Dennis which I found the other day in my trunk Jaque Deglise's compliments to Mr. Truteau

[addressed to] Mr. John Evans

You will tell Mr. Truteau to send me an Inventory of what good remains with him this spring so that I may be able to judge what is best to take up & what Quantity. Tell him also to tell all the nations that I am coming up to that country to see them if the Sioux do not stop the passage.

You will give Jaque Deglise's compliments to Nourrow, who is at the ricaras & tell him that Jaque wants him to come down with the Company's cajons in the spring to help him up with his goods next summer.

J. M. [rubric]

As I mean to make Sunday (being a remarkable day) the day for observing the distance of the moon from the sun I wish you to do the same when convenient so that we may be the better able to compare them when you return. I will always make my observations when the sun is on the meridian which will of course give the just time of day. You may draw a meridian by the north star if you should be a couple of days in one place & if the sky be clear at night if this cannot be you may take it by the compass if you know exactly the variation.

---

the papers that he sent to the director of the Company and which need to be translated. I know only that he sent three men to advance the discovery of the South Sea. These expenditures have been considerable, which has obliged him to send six men to seek new merchandise which is to be prepared for him. In the month of June the Mahas chief, the man, the most despotic, like *Glorieux* of the establishment of the French and of [on account of] the immense presents he has received, should assemble all the nations which might put an obstacle to the navigation of the Missouri in order to harangue them in our favor, which cannot fail to produce very good effects." See Mackay's "Journal", Chapter III, document XX, and this Chapter, document VIII.

In the last paragraph of his letter dated St. Louis, May 1, 1796 (A.G.I., P. de C., leg. 193) Trudeau wrote Carondelet, "I am enclosing the translation of the journal and the last letters of *Monsieur* Mackay, agent of the Company of the Upper Missouri, to the director of same. You will see the instruction which he has given to those whom he has sent for the discovery of the Pacific Ocean. With time you will learn things, infinitely more interesting".

VI

Clamorgan to Carondelet, Ste. Genevieve, April 10, 1796[1]

Monseigneur:

I have had the very great honor of receiving your letter dated February 15th last, in which you had the kindness of conveying to me the interest which you take in the success of the Missouri company. The aid

[1]Written in French. Bancroft Library; edited and published in Nasatir, "John Evans: Explorer and Surveyor," *Missouri Historical Review*, XXV (1931), 454-458. This translation has been rechecked and a few minor errors corrected.

which Your Excellency has been so generous as to solicit from the Court[1] on our behalf will help us bear the immense expenditures entailed by our having to make frequent gifts to the various nations in order to obtain from them free passage for our boats. The militias which we shall maintain in our forts of the Missouri and beyond, being in the pay of the government, shall assist in preventing foreign raids on His Majesty's territory, where the bold ambition of these foreigners usurps from us our business and our property.

So far only the Maha and Ricara forts are in proper condition [are established]. Next June we hope to receive word of the construction of the forts of the Mandans and of the Poncas. Our agent-general, Mr. Mackay, during his passage among the Otoctatas promised them a fort[2] for next fall so that they might have protection against their enemies. This promise, which must be sacred, will be fulfilled in due time. Otherwise we should fall into the same discredit as the traders who were there before us. At that time we shall have five forts built which will require that the government give us some artillery and five royal standards to foster among the foreigners and the nations respect for His Majesty's flag.

Mr. Mackay would like to be commissioned Commandant of the forts we are establishing in the Missouri so that he will be clothed with greater authority in his mission to repulse all foreigners who may be so bold as to penetrate the territory of our government. I hope that you will deign to grant him this request.

We have need of medals for the five Mandan villages, for the two Ricara villages, for the Cheyenne village and for the Sioux who live with these last named. We should also like to have some medals for the Ponca village which we shall give only when the Chief of the Mahas deems it wise, because this Chief, who causes himself to be named "the Prince of the Nations," has a powerful influence over his neighbors. That is why we shower gifts on him in order to render him favorable to our views. Not satisfied with the presents which Mr. Mackay brought to him last fall, he has just caused the aforesaid Mackay to send us a boat to get the things which he needed.[5] Consequently, eight days ago, we sent a *voiture* armed with nine men for the fulfillment of his *mémoire* [with what he asked for]. This expedition, which is pure loss to us, adds a very cruel sum to our expenses; and besides, this will not excuse us from sending him the fine presents upon which he is counting next autumn. You will agree that it requires boldness and courage to use all

---

[2]See document III.
[3]See Mackay's "Journal", Chapter III, document XX.
[4]Carondelet's commission to Mackay is dated May 11, 1796 (document XII).
[5]See Mackay's "Journal", Chapter III, document XX, and this Chapter, document V, note 4.

means and stop at nothing in order to cause our western discoveries to succeed. As far as I am concerned, I shall be happy and satisfied if the perseverance which I have always encouraged in my partners can some day serve to attest to the purity of my zeal and the integrity [rectitude] of my principles.

The powerful House of Todd, established in England and Canada and with which you have contracted to form a branch of New Orleans,* has been, through my offices, a supply-house for the Company. The interests of both have always been very closely allied so that we need not apprehend that our plans [will] be thwarted. I have acted freely on behalf of some of my partners and myself concerning some advances which the house of Todd has lavished on me. I have exposed my reputation, my credit, and my fortune in causing each member to keep up his hopes so that we would not retrogress on a path which is so interesting to pursue; and today I hope more than ever to continue with glory a labor which will be useful to posterity, provided, however, that the Company be always fortunate enough to deserve your generous help.

To come back to the House of Todd, I should tell you that when Mr. Todd came here last fall he brought his interests into close relationship with mine. I have made engagements with his house in such a manner that I will never lack supplies. We are going to be known, beginning with the first of May next, under the trade name of Clamorgan and Loisel. This was put through at the time when I urged Mr. Todd to establish a branch at New Orleans in order to facilitate [fix the market for] our subsequent operations.

Today, in order for me to conform to your desires and to induce the House of Todd to be even more useful and favorable to the Missouri Company, I have tried to persuade several of our members to deal with the House of Todd in preference to the ones with which they have been dealing up to now in Canada for the merchandise which they needed in our expeditions of discovery. Several of them being opposed to this, I felt called upon to beg you to send me an order as Director of this Company, in order to require each member of the Company to secure his supplies from the branch house which Mr. Todd will establish either at New Orleans or St. Louis, so that the peltry which will result from this new commerce will cease being sent to Europe through foreign channels; for it is not proper to be ungrateful to our capital which henceforward will send us through the House of Todd and Company all the merchandise which we need at a reduced cost, but at the same time, we should be allowed to draw *engagés* and *voyageurs* from Canada. Otherwise we shall lack people here for our expeditions.

*See documents III and VII.

419

Also please send me an order to give[7] to Mr. Todd or his agents at this place an interest in the Company, since one of the articles of our constitution prohibits me from doing so on my own authority and since the opposition of one member alone is sufficient to prevent anybody from being admitted into the Company,[8] for it is certain that the reason for our going so slowly with our undertaking (if we have done so) was our inability in the beginning to make great sacrifices in order to open up through all the nations a free communication with others which are more distant. If you will please authorize me to make all the advances and disbursements necessary to the exploitation of this famous enterprise without having recourse to the purse of my colleagues, I will be answerable to you for speeding up our discoveries. I am not asking to be reimbursed for my advances by each member except from the future returns.

I have nothing to solicit of your kindness as far as the Des Moines River is concerned in view of the fact that your contract with Mr. Todd renders conditions for me and my Company almost the same as if you had granted my request. However, a fort is necessary at the mouth of the St. Pierre River; otherwise the House of Todd will suffer great injury from the traders who come from Michillimackinac to carry on their trade there.[9]

One important thing which I am sure Mr. Todd has not foreseen is that of obtaining from your kindness the exclusive trading privileges with the Sac and Fox nations who inhabit the eastern bank of the Mississippi about two hundred leagues from here to the north, and who can be induced to come on this bank to hunt, but as this hunt is likely to spread down below the Missouri, please be so kind as to grant to my *Société* the exclusive right to attract them to this bank and to trade exclusively with them, whether below or above and even in the interior of Missouri.[10]

---

[7]Or, "may have an interest."
[8]See articles of incorporation, Chapter II, document IX.
[9]See summary of Todd's contract document III note 44.
[10]The reply to this letter is Carondelet to Clamorgan, May 11, 1796, Missouri Historical Society, Clamorgan Collection; printed in *American State Papers: Public Lands*, VIII, 234, and is as follows:
"In consequence of what you wrote to me, Sir, in your letter of 10th April, I send to Mr. Trudeau some medals for the company [Document X], and among them a very fine gilt one which I intend for the great Maha chief, in order to flatter him most; I also send several commissions, leaving a blank for the names, so that Mr. Trudeau may have them filled up; but it is to be wished, as much for the company as for the king, that there should be but one single chief decorated with a great medal, one with a small one, and two captains in each nation; for hereafter, those chiefs will require compensations adequate to their grades. I send also by Mr. Chouteau five flags [Document X], and when, in execution of the treaty concluded with the United States [Pinckney's Treaty], we shall abandon the [Chicasaw] Bluffs, the Commandant will send to Mr. Trudeau ten swivels for the service of the Company's forts [Document VIII, note 9]. Mr. Chouteau is also bearer of a commission such as

A finger which I broke lately prevents me from having the honor of writing to you any more about it, but does not allow me to dispense with assuring you of the respectful sentiments with which I take the liberty of calling myself,

Monseigneur,

Your very humble, very obedient, and very obliged servant,

Jes. Clamorgan. [rubric]

Ste. Geneviève, April 10, 1796

---

you desired for Mr. Mackay [Document XII]. Finally, I have directed to Mr. Trudeau, the order to enable Mr. Todd to take an interest in the company of discoveries.

"There is not any difficulty to Mr. Todd's having the exclusive trade of the Sack and Fox nations in the country to the east of the Missouri and, even on the said Missouri, during the term of his contract; but it would not be proper to have it extended to the Western side before we positively know and are perfectly acquainted with the force and situation of the nations situated on the (last) above mentioned side of said river. Besides, I must avoid to have those nations at variance with the Osages whom Messrs. Chouteau are beginning to keep in subjection, and who will be an impediment to the progress of our settlements, as long as we cannot keep them in peace.

"I am concerned to see our settlers of Upper Mississippi, who might acquire true wealth by agriculture, prefer to devote themselves to the fur trade, which is as dangerous as it is precarious. The exploitation of the lead mines would also yield great profits, because we might furnish the Havana with this article, and yet we are constantly in want of it, for want of labour; and at this moment there is none either at the King's or in private warehouses".

VII

Clamorgan to Carondelet, St. Louis, April 15, 1796[1]

Monseigneur:

I have not had time to write you except very superficially from the village of Ste. Geneviève[2] where I received the honor of your gracious letter,[3] together with that which came to me from M. Todd through the kindness of M. Loisel,[4] in which he tells me of his success with you to furnish with merchandise the savage nations which are to the north of the Missouri.[5] Three excellent results will follow this continuation of your kindnesses for the prosperity of our *Illinois* and of our Company of Missouri: (1) [there will be] fewer rivals to combat and to expel from our territory; (2) distant nations whose trade belongs to us we will withdraw from seduction by foreigners in order to soften them or subject them; and (3) especially their abundant furs which are [will be] re-

[1]Written in French. A.G.I., P. de C., leg. 212B.
[2]Document VI.
[3]Of February 15, 1796.
[4]On Loisel see the excellent introduction by the late A. H. Abel in her edition of *Tabeau's Narrative of the Loisel Expedition to the Upper Missouri.*
[5]See documents III and VI.

421

ceived for our own industry in order to transport them to foreign markets; all these are hopes of a new branch of industry of which our colony will feel the effects. But I repeat once more; forts are necessary at the mouths of the Des Moines river and St. Peter's River. A population is necessary there which I reserve to my means [methods] and to my calculations.[6]

I must again inform you of the necessity of your sending me the order to draw upon the House of Todd, established at New Orleans or at this place, for all the needs of the Company during the entire time of its exclusive privilege; and furthermore to give to this House an interest in the above mentioned trade in the same manner in which each member of the Company enjoys, and of my being authorized to provide myself with men useful to our enterprise in whatever foreign places there may be.[7] [These steps must be taken] in the first place, to assure through my hands the passage of the furs to the capital; in the second place, to be assured of the zeal of the House of Todd by tying doubly its interests with those of our Company; in the third place, to draw from Canada men accustomed to the painful voyages which we could not procure for ourselves in all our dependencies.

In spite of our immense expenditures, if we have experienced and if we still experience slowness in our operations, it is on account of finance and the fear of my colleagues; expenses ceaselessly repeated without hope of a prompt return alarms the fortunes; but when I shall be authorized to make for the account of the Company all the necessary advances which I shall be able to do in [from] the House of Todd, I shall go with ease through the communication which we seek to the west, and I ask reimbursement only upon the product of the returns. Without this expedient, the prospect of our success is still far off.

[One necessary item of expense is] the number of men that it will be necessary to gather for an approaching expedition, to garrison our establishments in proportion as they are formed and to replace those which M. Mackay has sent by my order to the sources of the Missouri, to the summit of the chain of rocks [Rocky Mountains] and especially to the coast of the western sea. At the head of each party he has placed a man of distinction [homme de choix], among whom there is one capable of rendering geographically an account of his voyage, and of noting down all the latitudes of the route which he will have taken in order to reach the Pacific Ocean.[8] Furthermore [there is] the expense of the forts which it will be necessary to build from one place to another, that of the Octoctactas which it will be necessary to build this summer upon a

---

[6]See document III, note 44.
[7]Document VI.
[8]See Chapter III, document XX, and this Chapter, document IV.

promise which M. Mackay made to them of it.[6] [There are also] the ordinary presents for each nation to redouble and repeat each year, and those which will be necessary for those [nations] which we are seeking to discover. [All these expenses] weigh [heavily] upon each member of the Company in a disagreeable manner. Nevertheless it is necessary that it be so, and [it] must be accomplished if we do not wish to remain half way from our goal. How many obstacles there are to overcome when it is necessary to subject the success of an enterprise to the whim, to the ignorance, to the opinion or to the fear of each individual which makes up the mass of the association! A work of this nature must be entirely guided by the will of one single person and the decision of his judgement when his capacity is well known.

I dare to remind you here of my requests either for my commercial firm of Clamorgan and Loisel or for the firm of Todd concerning the trade of the Sac and Fox Indians who live on the east bank, two hundred leagues from this city. Their trade must be considered included in the contract of M. Todd,[10] and we are seeking to attract them to this bank in order to enjoy their furs and the advantages that their passage through our capital can bring us, whether they fix their hunts above, below, or in, the Missouri.

The establishment of the House of Todd in Louisiana already draws there a portion of the skins from the Mississippi which were destined for Canada.[11] The boat in which Loisel ascended to here must descend the river immediately upon his arrival in this place, loaded with packets of this nature [furs]—proceeding from the various correspondents of this firm. I imagine that next spring you will find already an importation of furs to the capital double that of the preceding years. Time will demonstrate the fortunate acquisition of this firm.

I am occupying your time in moments which perhaps are precious to you, but nothing else remains except to assure you of the sweet satisfaction that I shall experience next year in presenting to you as homage the exact map of the Missouri as far as its sources and the exact voyage of [to]

---

[9]Chapter III, documents XIX, and XX, and Chapter IV, document VI.
[10]Document III note 44 and document VI.
[11]"The contract which you have made with *Monsieur* Todd has already made to pass to New Orleans two hundred pacquets which would have taken the road to Mackinac. This gives me an unexpected occasion, of which I am taking advantage to thank you for the great welfare which you have made to the Illinois by the establishment of this *Maison* [House of Todd] which will not confine itself to commerce with Indians, but which will give a value to our flour, in order to spread [the flour] in this province by furnishing to our cultivators clothing and other means at better prices than those which our little merchants grant them". Trudeau to Carondelet, St. Louis, May 1, 1796, A.G.I., P. de C., leg. 193.

the western sea with all interesting remarks. That will be the time when I will be satisfied.

I have the honor of being, with the most respectful sentiments, *Monseigneur,*
Your very humble, very obedient, and very obligated servant.

Jaques Clamorgan [rubric][12]

St. Louis, April 15, 1796.
Monseigneur, le Baron de Carondelet.

---

[12]Carondelet wrote the Marqués de Branciforte on April 23, 1796 (certified copy enclosed in Branciforte to Prince of Peace, no. 228 *res.,* A.G.I., Estado Mexico, legajo 5, transcript in Bancroft Library; draft in A.G.I., P. de C., leg. 2364) of the extraordinary scarcity of flour in Louisiana which Carondelet believed was due to machinations of the United States, "to deceive Spain and hide from her its union with England." Carondelet asked for the remittance of 3000 barrels of fresh flour from Mexico and to charge the cost to the "two coming *situados"* because of the scarcity of money in Louisiana, and especially due to the expected incurrence of extraordinary expenses to defend Upper Louisiana against an expected British attack. Carondelet had certain news that England would carry out the provisions of Jay's treaty and deliver the posts of Detroit and others on June first. Carondelet feared an easy conquest of Louisiana by England and the United States jointly which would give to England an easy communication between the North Sea and the Gulf of Mexico and would extend her establishments "from Hudson Bay and Canada on the left of the Upper Missouri until meeting on the South Sea with Nootka Sound, so that the *Provincias Internas* would have as neighbors the Americans who would extend themselves along the Mississippi and the English along the Missouri, ambitious nations which undoubtedly would not limit themselves to the clandestine and easy commerce that they would immediately undertake with the vassals of the King in the said provinces and the Kingdom [of Mexico]". Carondelet asked for money and two regiments of artillery.

VIII

Clamorgan to Carondelet, St. Louis, April 30, 1796[1]

Monseigneur:

According to the letters which I have had the honor of addressing to you by the last boats,[2] I should perhaps stop interrupting your time; but Mr. Mackay's voyage as far as the Mahas[3] and his instructions given to the detachment which has left for the Western Sea,[4] in conformity with my orders of which I have just remitted a copy to M. Don Zenon[5] Trudeau, permit me to send you the present [letter]. You will see by it *de rechef* [sic] the obstacles that we have to combat and the costly means which we are using to overcome them or at least to lessen them [*adoucir*].

It seems very likely that a year from next June I shall be able to announce to you the discovery of the Pacific Ocean by crossing this vast continent and to offer to you an exact map[6] of the course of the Missouri

---

[1]Written in French. A.G.I., P. de C., leg. 212A.
[2]Documents VI and VII.
[3]Chapter III, document XX.
[4]Document IV.
[5]See document V, note 4.
[6]See document VII.

which hitherto I have been able to obtain only from vague reports of several *voyageurs*.

In order to tell you a few more things relative to the contract of Mr. Todd,[7] it is to be feared that there may be formed some league [alliance] among the merchants of Canada to exploit in competition with him the commerce of the Upper Mississippi and especially the commerce of the St. Pierre river. It is surprising that he has not made you perceive the need of being protected the first year especially by one of the *galères* of His Majesty. I am morally sure of a thorny opposition which the aforementioned *Sieur* Todd will not be able to overcome, and as it is to my private interest and to the interest of the Company to expose it to you, I need no longer worry myself about the means that your kindnesses will employ to surmount all the difficulties.

By the journal of Mackay[8] you will see that the English were on the point of building a fort among the *Mahas,* and that the traders have had the impudence to cross the Missouri in order to go to the Panis who inhabit the Platte River, a few leagues above the village of the Otos. It is time to close the doors to this nation if we do not wish them to kick us out.

While awaiting the honor of your response to the two preceding letters which I have sent to you, in order to regulate my operations and conduct towards the Company, at the time of the expedition which I propose to make at the end of the month of August, next, I remain always with the sentiments of a most respectful gratitude, *Monseigneur,*

Your very submissive, very dutiful and very
devoted servant,
J. Clamorgan [rubric]

St. Louis, April 30, 1796.

[To] *Monseigneur* Le Baron de Carondelet.

[On another page] P.S. [?] [Please send?] Some swivel-guns if it is possible. A fort without canon is a body without a soul.[9]

---

[7]See document III, note 44.
[8]Chapter III, document XX.
[9]Carondelet ordered Lieutenant-governor Folch of Barrancas to deliver to Chouteau ten swivel guns with their balls, arms and utensils, which he was in turn to deliver to Clamorgan for the Missouri Company with the order that two swivel-guns were to be placed in each fort. The Company was to be responsible for the guns. Carondelet to Trudeau, New Orleans, May 11, 1796, A.G.I., P. de C., leg 24. For reply see document XXI, note 5.

In a letter of Dehault de Lassus to Carondelet dated St. Louis, May 2, 1796, (A.G.I., P. de C., leg. 212A), the former asked the latter to give his son employment, an opportunity for which perhaps "will not delay in presenting itself if it is as they assure, a question of protecting the commerce of trade in the upper part of the river and in the Missouri in order to oppose the enterprises of the English," which would increase soon if England gave up Detroit and other posts to the United States in June.

IX

[CARONDELET] TO MORALES, NEW ORLEANS, MAY 11, 1796[1]

In order to animate more and more to our devotion the Big and Little Osages, the Kansas, Ricaras, Mandanas, Poncas and Octactas— among the latter four nations of whom the *Illinois Company* [sic][2] has already erected three forts and is to construct a fourth one this summer,[3] there are needed for the present: fifteen large medals, fifteen small ones with their corresponding ribbons and five flags with the Burgundy Cross.[4] I find them necessary and I shall be indebted to Your Excellency to dispose that they be delivered by the storekeeper of Indian effects to Don Augusto Chouteau who will deliver them to the Lieutenant Governor of Illinois, Lieutenant-Colonel Don Zenon Trudeau, who has my orders for their distribution.[5]

God, etc. New Orleans, May 11, 1796.

[draft]

Señor Don Ventura Morales[6]

---

[1]Written in Spanish. A.G.I., P. de C., leg. 89. See document X.
[2]Missouri company.
[3]Document VI.
[4]Document VI.
[5]See document X.
[6]Intendant of Louisiana.

X

CARONDELET TO TRUDEAU, NEW ORLEANS, MAY 11, 1796[1]

Answered

Don Augusto Chouteau is carrying ten large medals and ten small ones to distribute among the Big and Little Osages, Kansas, etc. nations; five large ones and five small ones, a large gilded one [*dorada*] (which he is to give to the Maha Chief), eleven commissions [*patentes*] in blank, which will be filled in as they are needed and five flags with the cross of Burgundy.

All the medals, commissions and flags with the exception of the first twenty medals are to be distributed among the nations of the Company, and you will inform me of their distribution, according to *informes* which the Director Clamorgan is going to give you.[2]

God keep you many years.

New Orleans, May 11, 1796.

El Baron de Carondelet [rubric]

Señor Don Zenon Trudeau.[3]

---

[1]Written in Spanish. A.G.I., P. de C., leg. 24. See document IX.
[2]See document VI.
[3]Reply is document XIV.

XI

CARONDELET TO TRUDEAU, NEW ORLEANS, MAY 11, 1796[1]

Under date of today I am telling literally the Director of the Company of Discoveries of the Missouri[2] the following:

The solidity of reasons which you have exposed to me[3] puts me in a position of warning you that in the future it will be convenient that you draw from the Maison Todd, established at New Orleans, or from that one which is to be established in these districts, all the needs of the Company during the entire time of its exclusive privilege. Moreover you will give to the said Maison Todd an interest in the commerce of the Company in the same manner as each member enjoys.

I am transmitting this to you for your government, and for fulfillment in that part which concerns you.

May God keep you many years.

New Orleans, May 11, 1796.

El Baron de Carondelet [rubric]

Señor Don Zenon Trudeau.

---

[1]Written in Spanish. A.G.I., P. de C., leg. 2364. Reply is document XXI.
[2]See document VI, note 10.
[3]Document VI.

XII

CARONDELET TO TRUDEAU, NEW ORLEANS, MAY 12, 1796[1]

I am sending to you the despatch as Commandant of the forts established by the Company, in favor of M. Mackay, so that after having

---

[1]Written in Spanish. A.G.I., P. de C., leg. 2364. Transcript in Library of Congress. The letter alone without the enclosed commission for Mackay is printed in Houck, *Spanish Régime in Missouri*, II, 192. I have retranslated this. The commission was asked for by Clamorgan (document VI).

In despatch no. 266 to Carondelet dated St. Louis, August 4, 1796 (A.G.I., P. de C., leg. 34) Trudeau acknowledged receipt of Mackay's commission and stated that he had delivered it to Clamorgan.

Long after Mackay's return and when he was soliciting a commission for Mackay as captain of the militia to be formed among the inhabitants of Bon Homme Creek, Trudeau stated that Mackay, "had already held from Your Excellency's predecessor [Carondelet] the title of Commandant of the forts *which were to be* constructed on the Upper Missouri". [my italics]. Trudeau to Gayoso de Lemos, no. 322, St. Louis, February 28, 1798, original in Bancroft Library, photostat in Missouri Historical Society.

examined [recognized] it, you may deliver it to the Director, Don Santiago Clamorgan.

May God keep you many years.

New Orleans, May 12, 1796.

El Baron de Carondelet [rubric]

Señor Don Zenon Trudeau.

[Enclosure]

Don Francisco Luis Hector, Baron de Carondelet, Caballero de la Religion de San Juan, Field Marshal of the Royal Armies, Governor General, Royal Vice-Patron of the Provinces of Louisiana and West Florida and Inspector of the Veteran Troops and Militias of them, etc.

Whereas it is of the greatest importance to keep subordination and good order in the various forts and establishments which the Company of Commerce and Discoveries of the Missouri has made in the Indian nations Mandans, Poncas, Ricaras and Octoctactas as likewise in those which in the future might be made in the different places into which they might penetrate:

Therefore, and desiring to conciliate the private interests of the Company with those of the state and those of the establishments of Illinois, in view of the good reports which I have had of the honesty, good conduct, good principles and fidelity of Mr. Mackay, agent of the cited Company, I have come to appoint him commandant of all the forts established and of those which might be established by the Company during the time of its exclusive privilege, with [and he shall be given] the power to appoint a lieutenant in each fort to whom, for the government, will be sent the corresponding *despacho* with the advice of the Lieutenant-governor of the Illinois, whoever he might be at that time.

I likewise order to this one as well as to the other commandants, adjutants of the lieutenant-governor, soldiers, settlers and inhabitants that they have [recognized] and hold [respect] the above mentioned Mr. Mackay as commandant of the said forts and establishments under the direction of the Company in all that which respects the economy and government of it; he having in all other matters to obtain power from and depend upon the governor-general of these provinces and the cited lieutenant-governor in the civil and military administration of the said posts; authorizing him likewise to drive away, impede, and even destroy every establishment or trade of foreign nations on the Missouri river and to the south of that river. The individuals of the Company and employees in the forts will obey all orders that he might give them in writing or by word or suffer the penalty thereof. And so that it may be so, I give the present document signed by my hand and sealed with the seal of my arms, and legalized [countersigned] by the undersigned secretary for his Majesty of this government in New Orleans, May 11, 1796.

XIII

Clamorgan to Carondelet, 1796[1]

I have received the honor of your two letters dated May eleven[2] concerning your intentions and orders to which I will conform attentively. I do not doubt the discontent of members of the Company towards me, when I will announce to them that *Monsieur* Todd would perhaps furnish a little of the merchandise of the Company and moreover there should be [given him] an interest equal to each member.[3] This step will be of inestimable value to the Company because of the money which he can furnish and this will be always a new sign of your kindness and of your encouragement.

The honor of your second letter which pays attention to everything that can contribute to the prosperity of the industry would require many things on my part in order to convince you concerning my sentiments of thankfulness for which I will be everlastingly indebted to you. But the departure of *Monsieur* François Collett, who is ready to leave, does not permit me at the present time to inform you sufficiently upon various important points. I will do that soon by another occasion, if I do not bore you too much by my writing.

Receive, *Monseigneur,* the sentiments which inspire me and which will convince you of the great satisfaction that I have had in learning of your advancement to the rank of Captain-General of Havana.[4] It will be for me a double motive in order that I will perhaps trouble you by soliciting your souvenir of this colony to which you had begun to give a fortunate impulse.

I have the honor of being very respectfully, *Monseigneur,*

Your very devoted and very obligated servant.

J. Clamorgan [rubric]

His Excellency, *Monseigneur* le Baron de Carondelet.

---

[1]Written in French. Undated but 1796, probably July. A.G.I., P. de C., leg. 215A.

[2]See document VI, note 10 for one of the two letters. These letters are printed in *American State Papers, Public Lands,* VIII, 234-236.

[3]Documents VI, VII, and XI.

[4]This proved to be premature.

429

XIV

TRUDEAU TO CARONDELET, ST. LOUIS, MAY 22, 1796[1]

Number 269

Upon the arrival of Don Augusto Chouteau's *lanchón*, he delivered to me the ten large medals and ten small ones to be distributed to the Big and Little Osage, Kansas, Octoctactas, Mahas and Ponca Nations; five other large medals and five small ones; one large golden medal with the corresponding commissions [*patentes*] in blank; and five flags with the cross of Burgundy, to be distributed among the nations with whom the Company of the Upper Missouri is going to trade. As soon as the director of the said Company, Don Santiago Clamorgan, advises me of the distribution, I will inform Your Excellency of it as you have informed me in your official letter of May 11, last,[2] to which I am answering.

May God keep Your Excellency many years.

St. Louis, May 22, 1796.

Zenon Trudeau [rubric]

Señor Baron de Carondelet.

---

[1]Written in Spanish. A.G.I., P. de C., leg. 33.
[2]Document X.

XV

CARONDELET TO MORALES, NEW ORLEANS, MAY 23, 1796[1]

In order to provide for the Indian nations of the Upper Missouri and San Pedro Rivers, separating them from their friendship with the English who are openly seducing them, going even to the point of taking the liberty to erect forts among our own nations and territories,[2] it is necessary to deliver to Don Daniel Clark, power of attorney of Don Andrés Todd, 2250 pounds of powder which he must pay for in cash.

I am advising you of this for your knowledge, since I decided to take this step, because powder is non-existent or at least very scarce in the city

---

[1]Written in Spanish. A.G.I., P. de C., leg. 2364, draft without marginal note in A.G.I., P. de C., leg. 89.
[2]These points are brought out many times in the documents printed in this volume. See Nasatir, "Anglo-Spanish Frontier on the Upper Mississippi 1786-1796," *Iowa Journal of History and Politics*, XXIX (1931), 155-232; and Nasatir, "Anglo-Spanish Rivalry in the Iowa Country 1797-1798," *Ibid.*, XXVIII (1930), 337-389.

[and] I am unable to hope that any will come to us from England or from France because of the circumstances of the present war.[3]

May God keep you many years.

New Orleans, May 23, 1796.[4]

El Baron de Carondelet [rubric]

Señor Don Juan Ventura Morales.

Note of the pounds of powder which are required for the Indian nations of the Upper part of the river.

San Pedro River	700
Sacs, Renards, Puants	400
Panis Loups	250
Maha	400
Hoacto	500
	2250

[Marginal notation] : To the *Contaduría* the following day

---

[3]War was declared between Spain and England on October 6, 1796. Among reasons for war, Spain asserted, were the contraband trade of the English with the Spanish colonies and English attacks upon Spanish possessions since the peace of Basle, especially "in the establishment of their [English] commercial companies, formed in North America on the shores of the Missouri river, with the purpose [*ánimo*] of penetrating by way of those regions as far as the South Sea". Royal decree of His Majesty declaring war on England, dated 14 Vendémaire, An V and translation published in *Moniteur* of 9 Brumaire, An V, in A. E., Corr. Pol., Espagne, vol. 643, folios 149-153; French translation is on folios 143-144.
[4]On May 13, 1796, Benito Vazquez petitioned for the trade of the Kansas Indians. In this petition, as was customary, Vazquez outlined his services to the government and the wretchedness of his financial position and large family. A.G.I., P. de C., leg. 2365. Bernardo Pratte also petitioned for a similar trade with the Pamis Indians in the Missouri. Trudeau forwarded these memorials or petitions to Carondelet. On May 24, 1796, Carondelet acknowledged receipt of the two memorials and asked Trudeau if the trades requested were "those for which lots were cast among the entire commerce in which case I cannot admit them nor will you send similar solicitations". Carondelet to Trudeau, New Orleans, May 24, 1796, A.G.I., P. de C., leg. 24. To this Trudeau replied in his letter no. 272 dated St. Louis, September 28, 1796 (A.G.I., P. de C., leg. 34). In it Trudeau stated that the Kansas and the Panis were the only nations for which at present lots are drawn annually among the merchants of St. Louis and that he would abide by Carondelet's orders.

XVI

CLAMORGAN TO CARONDELET, ST. LOUIS, MAY 26, 1796[1]

Très Excellent Gouverneur:

Nothing has astonished me more than the underhanded and unfaithful [disloyal] trickery of *Sieur* Robidou,[2] member of the Missouri Company,

---

[1]Written in French. A.G.I., P. de C., leg. 215A.
[2]See Robidoux' letter to Gayoso de Lemos, St. Louis, March 7, 1798. Bancroft Library, poorly translated in F. L. Billon, *Annals of St. Louis in its Early Days*

who has been shamelessly goaded by malicious envy. I have learned that he has villanously complained to you; that he has acted with the blackest and most evil artifice in order to make me hated by you. Most Excellent Governor, I would like to be openly accused if I am guilty of the slightest misconduct towards the Company or to him or to any private person, and I will justify without any trouble at all the purity of my sentiments. My actions are pure in every way. They do not fear the attacks of any ambitious, envious, or jealous enemy. When they will require of me an obvious and manifest justification concerning the slightest suspicion that wickedness will be able to cast upon my steps, I shall always be ready to convince [them or you] of the true loyalty of my feelings. My eyes fear the glances of no one. When the heart is without blemish the soul of man is serene. Most Excellent Governor, for the future impose silence on *Sieur* Robidou and his bitterness, just as your law imposes upon me never to harm my equals, especially those who, conjointly with me, have sought by new discoveries to render themselves useful to the prosperity of our colony. I shall be happy if this glorious desire can some day have its effect, and all the more happy if this truth can some day be understood and known in the eyes of His August Wisdom; and if this happy and future event may banish forever from the shelter of our hearths the banner of hate and animosity. May you be able to conjure them forever, and believe that the last of my days will be most glorious if I may see floating as far as you on our miry waters the industrial resources of the sources of the Missouri.

I have the honor to be very respectfully,

Most Excellent Governor,

Your very devoted and very affectionate servant

J. Clamorgan [rubric]

St. Louis, May 26, 1796

---

under the French and Spanish Dominations (St. Louis, 1886), 283ff. A poor, incomplete and incorrect copy taken from Billon is in O. M. Robidoux, *Memorial to the Robidoux Brothers* (Kansas City, 1924), 24-28, etc. See Chapter VI document V. See also this Chapter, document XIX, for an opinion of Trudeau.

XVII

Minutes of the Council of State, May 27, 1796[1]

*   *   *   *   *[2]

Also the governor of Louisiana having sent the money to General

---

[1]Written in Spanish. A.H.N., Papeles de Estado, printed in Nasatir and Liljegren, "Materials for the History of the Mississippi Valley," *Louisiana Historical Quarterly,* XXI (1938), reprint pp. 62, 64-71, where it is fully edited. The major portion of this document is based upon document III which I have edited more fully than this document.

[2]The omitted portions are translated and fully edited in Nasatir and Liljegren, *op. cit.,* reprint pp. 62-64.

Wilkinson was approved [by the Council of State], recognizing the merit of the subjects of whom Carondelet speaks; and His Excellency ordered collected all these notices in order that the King, Our Master, might see the result which the treaty was beginning to produce, and that its conclusion not only avoided the expenditure of the huge sums of money which would have been entailed by the consummation of the separation plan and the war which would then have been necessary against the United States; (the English had already conceded them the right of free navigation of the Mississippi in their treaty of 24 November, 1794[3]); but, it also facilitated to us the restraining and preventing of the usurpations of the English themselves in our North America, of which Carondelet speaks in letter no. 65 of January 8, last,[4] already mentioned.

In it the governor refers to the provisions he has made and the means which he has used in order to restrain the smuggling carried on by the English in the Spanish settlements of Illinois; and at the same time he proposes the measures which seem to him most efficacious for preventing further unsurpations on the part of the English and Americans.

Since the beginning of his administration Carondelet was informed of the fact that the Spanish establishments of St. Louis of Illinois were declining from day to day because of the competition of the English in the fur trade on the Missouri river, and because of the smuggling carried on by the same from Canada, purveying to our establishments whatever utensils were needed at better prices than those of New Orleans, distant 500 leagues from Illinois. He [therefore] ordered his lieutenant-governor to confiscate with energy all, even the smallest, English boats that he might find with goods in the territory on the west bank of the Mississippi.

Complying with this order, the Lieutenant Governor Don Zenon Trudeau, armed an expedition toward the end of October, 1793, and with it took possession, at forty-one leagues above St. Louis of Illinois, of various personal effects of Mr. Andrew Todd and other inhabitants of Michelimackinack.[5]

At the same time Carondelet persuaded the wealthy inhabitants of St. Louis to form a Company under the name of "Discoverers of the Missouri" under the direction of Don Santiago Clamorgan, an active and educated man; and he, Carondelet, approved the rules and by-laws [reglamento é instrucciones] which they presented to him in May, 1794,

---

[3]Jay's Treaty. See Bemis, Jay's Treaty.
[4]Document III.
[5]For an account of Todd and his relations with the Spaniards see Nasatir, "Anglo-Spanish Frontier on the Upper Mississippi 1786-1796," Iowa Journal of History and Politics, XXIX (1931). See also document III.

and which he now remits [enclosures] marked numbers two and three, conceding to the Company the exclusive privilege of trade with all the Indian Nations of the Missouri who live beyond the Poncas, and he offered furthermore a reward of three thousand *pesos* to the one who should first arrive at the South Sea. This discovery was very important because, aside from fixing its limits, it would undoubtedly be the proper place for a post capable of preventing both the English and Russians from settling on those remote coasts.

[One of] the greatest obstacles which the Company of the Missouri has encountered in its first two expeditions was the danger of passing through the nations of the Lower Missouri. These nations do not wish our traders to carry arms nor ammunition to their enemies who inhabit the shores of that river, not only because of the commercial interest they have in it but also because of the instigation of the English of Hudson Bay, who wish to embrace all that trade.

The passage through the nations of the Lower Missouri may be made safe without difficulty with the three forts which the Company has constructed in the nations of the Othos [Otos], Mahas and Poncas; and [it may be secured] with even greater advantages if His Majesty consents that one or two flat-bottomed boats [*galeotas-chatas*] armed with six two-pounders, some swivel guns and twenty sailors, ply the river protecting the expeditions at the most dangerous points.

These precautions, according to Carondelet, are the more indispensable as the English now leave no doubt as to their intentions toward Missouri, as is shown not only in the line of forts, marked in map [enclosure] number four, which they have established from Lake Superior to the mountains of the Black Rock [*Roca Negra*—Rocky Mountains], not very far, it seems, from the South Sea; but also particularly by the attempt of the English Company of the North, which according to two English deserters, a copy of whose testimony is included as (enclosure) no. five,[7] has established a fort on the Missouri itself, half a league from the village of the Mandans in the midst of the Spanish possessions.

In consideration of this, the governor of Louisiana believes that it is necessary to hasten by the quickest means to restrain the unsurpations of the English Companies of Montreal, Michelimakinak, and Hudson's Bay, and to prevent them from taking possession of the territory which is watered by the Missouri, and, passing through the mountains of *Roca Negra* and joining their posts with that of Nootka-Sound, taking over all the trade with the *Provincias Internas* and with the Californias.

---

[6]See document III, these annexes are given in full in Chapter II. documents IX and XVIII. See Nasatir, "Formation of the Missouri Company", *Missouri Historical Review*, XXV (1930) 10-22.
[7]Chapter III, document XII.

But considering that the Governor intends to dislodge the English from their posts adjoining the Mandans, distant more than 400 leagues from St. Louis of Illinois, from where the expedition ought to start, he would have to spend more than fifty thousand *pesos* (and perhaps fruitlessly, because the English Company could establish itself lower down or further up). Carondelet [therefore] proposes that ten thousand *pesos* be granted annually to the Company in order to maintain one hundred armed men in the forts which it has built and intends to build, until they reach the South Sea, adding that, when the ten years of exclusive rights are ended, it [Company] will not need this sum, and in the meantime the Royal Treasury will have gained more than 30,000 *pesos* annually from the duties upon the fur trade and from those upon the introduction of goods necessary for that trade.

Although the forts of the Company can contribute to the suppression of the hostile incursions of the nations of the Sioux, Sauteurs, Assiniboine, and others who live north of the Missouri, which is the second obstacle which presents itself to the settlement of the establishment of the former [the forts], the governor of Louisiana proposes as the only means of overcoming this difficulty, that His Majesty yield to the petition [enclosure number 6][8] of the English merchant, Mr. Andrew Todd, inhabitant of Michilimackinac, permitting him to introduce all goods needed to trade with the Indians and take out the furs and products of the country, under the six percent duty established before the war, upon which condition Todd offers not only to assure the friendship of the Indians, with whom he has very favorable relations because of the many years that he handled the greater part of the trade of Canada, but that he will cause to go down the Mississippi, during the course of the present year, four thousand *paquetes* of furs, which at the rate of forty-five *pesos* will produce for the Royal Treasury a sum of ten thousand, eight hundred *pesos,* without counting the product of the returns, nor the gains from increase in population, industry and consumption, and navigation, and above all, the exclusion of the American traders, who, if we do not do this, will take possession of all this trade with great damage to Louisiana and the *Provincias Internas* of New Spain. At the same time, Carondelet says that, in agreement with the Intendant, Don Francisco Rendón, he has conceded to Todd the favor of reduced duty on imports and exports from fifteen to six percent, for the term of one year and while His Majesty in consideration of all this, resolves the problem, keeping in mind for the solution not only the reasons explained here but many more of greater importance.

Whereas Mr. Andrew Todd, fearing to lose the rich fur trade which he was doing with the nations situated to the north of the Ohio, Mis-

⁸Document III.

435

sissippi, and Missouri rivers, because of the cession of the Forts of the Strait [Detroit] and others, agreed upon by the English and Americans by next June,[9] has offered to transfer his trade to Louisiana and to continue it under the conditions cited; and in this state of affairs, should his petition be denied or should he await His Majesty's decision, which could not arrive until July, it would be necessary for Todd, in order to avoid ruin, to side with the United States. That country has not yet ceased to regard him with anxiety, freeing his goods from all duty, for those duties which are paid in the said states are returned to the merchants when they lay out their goods among the Indians. Consequently lost would be the gains offered by a trader as intelligent as Todd, a man of sufficient means, one of the principal partners [interested] in the Company of the Missouri, for which he provided all the supplies needed for the three expeditions which it had made, and, most important, a friend of the Indians with whom he would trade.

The exemption from import duties enjoyed by the English Companies of Hudson's Bay, Michilimackinac, etc., has been the principal reason not only for their usurping all the fur trade of the north and of our own establishment of Illinois, but also for their being able to furnish to the latter whatever goods they have needed, at prices cheaper than those current in New Orleans, despite the great expenses and difficulties which the long distance by land and water causes them. And His Majesty has continued these precepts by conceding various privileges to the English house of Don Guillermo Panton, freeing it from all duty in the trade which it has with our Indians in the south, in order to keep his [their] friendship. Furthermore, says Carondelet, the reduction of duties in favor of Todd, does not harm in any way the rest of the trade of Louisiana or of the Company of the Missouri; due to the fact that his privileges do not extend beyond the particular trade with the savage nations to the north of the Ohio and of the Missouri; and with this motive, he recalls his previous statements and those of the Intendant, to the end that all export and import duties be reduced to the same six per cent as a sure means of augmenting the Royal Treasury, of promoting agriculture and commerce, of conciliating the will of the colonists, and of transforming Louisiana, which is today as grievous as it is uncultivated and deserted, into a settled, useful and fertile province.

Finally, Carondelet believes that upon accepting the propositions of Todd, English smuggling will cease; and consequently with it will cease a subject of complaint between our Court and that of England, as has occurred in the complaints directed by Lord Dorchester on the matter of the Todd confiscation. Enclosing Todd's memorial, he [Carondelet] recommends to the generosity of His Majesty, that he may deign to

[9] In pursuance of Jay's treaty.

436

order returned to him the 7,860 *pesos,* the value of the goods and properties taken by Don Zenón Trudeau.

His Majesty and the Council, informed in detail of all the occurrences in Louisiana and of the opportune provisions and dispositions that have been communicated successively through the Ministry of State to the Governor without the least delay, according to the situation in which were found the affairs of the United States, now these and now those meriting your sovereign approval, and commendation as most wise and convenient to consolidate permanently the good friendship between His Majesty and the United States of America, to the general good and reciprocal benefit of both countries, suppressing at the same time the incursions of the Indian nations allied to the English and the usurpations of the latter, who in the last year have arrived at the said extreme of constructing a fort in the nation of the Mandans, situated on the Mississippi [Missouri], 440 leagues from the town of St. Louis of Illinois, and 200 from *Nuevo Santa Fé* and consequently in the middle of the Spanish possessions:

Royal Resolution: finally, [with] His Majesty and the Council informed of the means by which the Governor (in accord with the Intendant and with the English merchant, Mr. Andrew Todd, established in Michilimackinac) proposes to suppress all those evils and to stop the growing contraband trade which the English carry on from Canada with the Sioux, Sauteurs, Assiniboine and other nations which inhabit the country north of the Missouri; in conformity with all the articles of the treaty of *Friendship, Boundaries and Navigation*[10] concluded between His Majesty and those States, read by me in this same Council; and as a result of the reflections connected and almost identical, which I presented, His Majesty deigned to grant the following points and concessions:[11]

First Approval of the Spanish Company formed in 1794 for the discoveries to the west of the Missouri River, under the constitution and *by-laws* [*Reglamentos é instrucciones*] with which the Governor permitted and conceded to it the exclusive privilege of trading with all the Indian nations of the said Missouri who live beyond the Poncas, offering the award of three thousand *pesos* to the first who should arrive at the South Sea.

Second: Permission for the Company to arm at its expense and maintain armed in the forts which it has and may have in the future, the one hundred armed men which are considered necessary, all under the

---

[10]Treaty of San Lorenzo el Real or Pinckney's Treaty.
[11]This decision and exerpts from it may be found in a number of letters some of which are as follows:
    Montarco to Prince of Peace, Aránjuez, May 29, 1796, A.G.I., Sto. Dom., 87-3-22 (old numbering) ; copy in *Ibid.* 86-7-17 (old numbering—new num-

orders of the Governor and with the object indicated, which will be fulfilled with the greatest care.

Third: That all export and import duties be reduced to six per cent as is proposed by the Governor and Intendant, both taking care to keep exact account and to report to His Majesty at the end of the first year the results which are hoped from such a beneficial measure.

Fourth: The permission which is solicited by the English merchant, Mr. Andrew Todd, to introduce all the goods necessary for his private trade with the savage nations to the north of the rivers Ohio and Missouri, and to take out the furs and other products of the country under the six per cent duty established before the war, and [upon] the conditions which he offers, and which must be preceded by his establishing himself in Louisiana.

Fifth: That in this same matter be effective the concession of the reduction from fifteen to six per cent import and export duty which the Governor, with the Intendant, conceded to Todd for a year, without prejudice to the royal resolution.

Sixth: That in order to excite anew the zeal with which Todd offers to realize the gains which he proposes, there be returned to him one third of the 7,860 *pesos*, which, it seems, is the value of the goods of which he was despoiled by Don Zenon Trudeau.

---

ber is legajo 2580) ; copy in Missouri Historical Society, Papers from Spain, no. 97.
Gardoqui to Governor of Louisiana, Aránjuez, June 11, 1796, A.G.I., P. de C., leg. 176B; copy in *Ibid.*, leg. 23.
Gardoqui to Intendant of Louisiana, Aránjuez, June 11, 1796, a copy in A.G.I., P. de C., leg. 129, certified copy to Morales in *Ibid.*, leg. 2364, translated in Houck, *Spanish Régime in Missouri*, II, 179-180.
Carondelet to Trudeau, New Orleans, September 16, 1796, A.G.I., P. de C., leg. 2364, draft in *Ibid.*, leg. 130. In letter no. 283 in reply to this letter, dated St. Louis, March 8, 1797 (A.G.I., P. de C., leg. 35), Trudeau acknowledged receipt and said that it gave to his inhabitants the immense benefits of Pinckney's treaty. In conformity to point six with regard to Vincent's capture of Todd's men and goods Trudeau forwarded a valuation of the goods seized, and costs of the expedition. See Nasatir, "Anglo-Spanish Frontier on the Upper Mississippi 1786-1796," *Iowa Journal of History and Politics* XXIX, (1931) 198, et. seq. Carondelet forwarded this letter and document to the Intendant on April 7.
Carondelet to Clamorgan, New Orleans, September 18 and October 26, 1796. Missouri Historical Society, Clamorgan Collection, translated in *American State Papers, Public Lands*, VIII, 235-236.
A copy of this royal order was also sent to Gayoso de Lemos in Carondelet's letter of September 16, 1796 (A.G.I., P. de C., leg. 23). In this letter Carondelet takes pride in winning the concessions from the court which he had solicited and brags about it to Gayoso. He says: "The approbation of the Company of the Missouri with the permission of maintaining one hundred men armed at the expense of the King, as I proposed it, at the rate of one hundred *pesos* per man per year, will produce a good effect and will place it in a position to oppose the English traders."

And, finally, that the Governor, making all understand the great importance of these concessions and immense benefits which the sovereign piety and magnificence of His Majesty has condescended to grant in the treaty of *Friendship, Boundaries and Navigation,* to the reciprocal benefit of his beloved vassals, of the United States, and of the Indian nations associated and subject to the two contracting parties, he hopes that all the important objects of these provisions may be speedily fulfilled.

XVIII

CARONDELET TO BRANCEFORTE, NEW ORLEANS, JUNE 7, 1796[1]

Most Excellent *Señor:*

I have had news that seems to merit complete confidence that the English companies of Canada which trade with the savage nations situated to the north of the Missouri river are beginning to form establishments on this [river], whose dominion belongs incontestably to His Majesty, and that lately crossing this same river at some three hundred leagues from its mouth in the Mississippi, they penetrated with twelve horses loaded with merchandise to the river which these colonists call the Plat River or Chato River to trade with the Panis, Abenaqui, and other nations. I was later informed through another party with information from the post of Natchitoches that not far from the mountains of Santa Fé in the vicinity of the Yambaricas Indians who are accustomed to live between the sources of the Colorado and Arkansas Rivers, the English or Americans have formed a fortified establishment with a *casafuerte.*[2] Finally, various travelers of these provinces assure me that in the Bay of St. Louis or San Bernardo on the Gulf of Mexico, there exists another American establishment of considerable consequence, which if allowed to grow, will cause much uneasiness to the *Provincias Internas* and to our Court.

I have prognosticated with much feeling the prompt invasion of the *Provincias Internas,* which will follow indubitably from the concession to the United States of the posts that we had on the eastern bank of the Mississippi. This must be [verified] carried out immediately in conformity with the Treaty of *Friendship, Boundaries, and Navigation* which the United States ratified in the month of March, it not being in my

[1]Written in Spanish. This is a certified copy enclosed in Branciforte to Prince of Peace, no. 288 *res.,* Mexico, May 27, 1796. A.G.I., Estado Mexico, legajo 6, transcript in Bancroft Library; draft in A.G.I., P. de C., leg. 2364 with the following prefix:

"He reflects on the dangerous situation of the *Provincias Internas* with [on account of] the new establishments of the Americans on the eastern side of the Mississippi". Printed in Nasatir, "Anglo-Spanish Frontier on the Upper Mississippi 1786-1796," *Iowa Journal of History and Politics,* XXIX (1931), 179-181.

[2]See Chapter III, document XX.

power any longer to restrain the eruption of the people from the western American States, who are approaching and are going to establish themselves on the eastern bank of the Mississippi in an expanse of territory of 400 leagues, opposite which we have nothing but deserts [unsettled territory]. This is from the Ohio River to 31 degrees, or 60 leagues from this capital. It follows that Your Excellency will see himself obliged to take beforehand the most active measures to oppose the introduction of those restless people, who are a sort of determined bandits, armed with carbines, who frequently cross the Mississippi in numbers, with the intention of reconnoitering, of hunting, and if they like the country, of establishing themselves in the *Provincias Internas,* whose Indians they will arm both to further their fur trade and to make the Spaniards uneasy. Five or six thousand of those ferocious men who know neither law nor subjection are those who are starting the American establishments and are attracting in their footsteps the prodigious emigration both from the Atlantic States and from Europe, which menaces the *Provincias Internas* which the Americans believe are very abundant in mines. A little bit of corn, gunpowder and balls suffices them, a house formed from the trunks of trees serves them as shelter; their corn crop finished, they raise camp and then go further inland, always fleeing from any subordination and law [justice].

In short, those provinces exposed to the hostile incursions of the Americans from the side of the Mississippi and to those of the English from the Missouri side, I consider will need for their conservation all the zeal, the activity and the talent that Your Excellency has always manifested and to the success of which I[you?] will be happy to contribute, if you consider that I can for my part contribute to the peace of these same provinces and of the kingdom which His Majesty has confided to your vigilance.

May God keep Your Excellency many years.

New Orleans, June 7, 1796

Most Excellent *Señor* El Baron de Carondelet—[to] Most Excellent *Señor* Marquis de Branceforte.

It is a copy—Mexico, August 26, 1796

Antonio Bonilla [rubric]

XIX

Trudeau to [Carondelet], St. Louis, July 3, 1796[1]

Mon Général:

I am sending to you with an official letter, all the papers concerning Dn. Buenava. Collell, whose brother has just definitely made arrange-

---

[1]Written in French. A.G.I., P. de C., leg. 212B. This document is partly damaged.

ments with the second wife who will be able to contribute to the hushing up of this miserable affair, if you wish to favor it.

I received by land from New Madrid the letter with which you have honored me dated April 16. At this time M. Chouteau was not able to go, his return greatly delayed; and I, impatient, am persuaded that if a courier arrived, you could inform me of what would become of us with our neighbors, who are more than ever persuaded that we will deliver to them the line of the 31 degree.

By some letters that I have received from my friends, it is a question that I should be relieved by M. Acosta. Although this unexpected disturbance is infinitely onerous to me, I shall conform thereto, persuaded that you have or will have no opportunity of being discontented with me and that I shall merit more than ever your confidence and protection.

Sr. Truteau, first agent of the Company of the Upper Missouri, who left here in the spring of 1794, was forced to abandon the Ricaras nation where he had been established for eighteen months in order to await there the [expected] help of the Company which the latter had sent out on two different occasions in 1795. The first of the two expeditions, under the conduct of one named Lecuyer was stopped (for its misconduct) by the Poncas nation which, without paying, consumed eight thousand *piastres* of merchandise. *Monsieur* Mackay who was not able to go in the second expedition except to the Mahas (where he perhaps still is) did some very bad business there among the savages, entirely lost on account of frequentation of the English. Finally Lecuyer, not having rejoined M. Truteau as he was supposed to do, [and thus leaving] the latter lacking help has retarded him and obliged him to winter there among the said Ricaras where the Sioux came several times in a body to attack. As a result of these attacks, as soon as the ice and snow melted, this nation decided to abandon the village and to go far away in the prairies, leaving Truteau with two other whites, abandoned to the fury of the enemies, without *voitures* and without trees to make them. Their situation determined them to embark in a canoe of cow-hide and to retreat to the others employed by the Company whom they found after much trouble and after escaping the enemies who pursued them to the Mahas nation. The total loss of all the merchandise, and the exorbitant wages paid to a number of men; all those things ruined the Company even to the point of reducing several members to beggary. Division reigned among them, indecision followed; they did not know what to do. Clamorgan [driven] by his ambition, wanted to usurp everything with the help of Todd, always combining and conducting these operations poorly. I do not pay any attention to anything that he proposes, and I rely more upon Srs.

441

Robidou[2] and Reilhe who, being more prudent through greater experience, beside meriting the confidence of everyone, have men agreed to direct and conduct the affairs and to use all their credit for it.

Sr. Truteau reported to me that the English are penetrating more than ever into the upper part of the Missouri; that all winter there has been a coming and going of men from their forts of the north among the nations who inhabit this river; and that they [nations] are infinitely and much more commonly armed than the nations further down which we frequent.

The curate St. Pierre of Ste. Geneviève arrived triumphant. The Abbé Maxwell[3] has been with me for a month. He is descending with M. Collell.

There is nothing new, *Mon Général,* at the Illinois where the harvest of wheat is superb. American families are coming to us daily. Marameck has thirty-two of them now and Marias des Liars twenty-three. This last place is especially well cultivated.

I again recommend myself, *Mon Général,* to your goodness, and I am with the most profound respect,

Mon Général,

Your very humble and very obedient servant,
Zenon Trudeau [rubric]

St. Louis; July 3, 1796

[2]See document XVI. Although on September 24, 1796, Trudeau wrote to Gayoso de Lemos (A.G.I., P. de C., leg. 212B) that Santiago [Clamorgan] was descending and he recommended him to Governor Gayoso who knows Clamorgan "to be an honest, active and intelligent man and associate of the commercial firm of Todd, who is descending in order to arrange matters which must be interesting for the fomentation of this western district of Illinois". Delassus Deluzières recommended Clamorgan to Carondelet as "honest, talented and of good principles". Deluzières to Carondelet, New Madrid, September 29, 1796, A.G.I., P. de C., leg. 48.
[3]J. Rothensteiner, "Father James Maxwell of Ste. Geneviève," *St. Louis Catholic Historical Review*, IV, 142-154; W. H. Hill [ed.] "Rev. James Maxwell, missionary at St. Geneviève by Firmen A. Rozier," *United States Catholic Historical Magazine*, (1887), 283-286.

XX

CARONDELET TO CLAMORGAN, JULY 9, 1796[1]

New Orleans, July 9, 1796

I have received, Sir, the account of Mr. Mackay's travels to the Maha nation, as also his instructions given to the party going to the discovery of the South Sea.[2] I shall be so much more flattered should his

[1]Missouri Historical Society, Clamorgan Collection, and quoted in letter of Mary Louise Dillon to Arthur Shelbourne Hardy, St. Louis, April 22, 1903, *Ibid.*, Papers from Spain; printed in *American State Papers, Public Lands,* VIII, 235.
[2]Chapter III, document XX.

last expedition succeed, as it is confidently reported that a Spanish squadron has sailed from Europe in order to go and dislodge the English from Nootka Sound; and it would be a curious fact if our people were to arrive at the same point at the same time.

I thought I had written to you that the establishment of a fort at the river St. Peter[3] had already been proposed to the Court, which is occupying itself of the means required to put Louisiana in a respectable state of defense; but time is needed, for all remains yet to be done and the political circumstances of Europe attract all the intention.

I have the honor of being with the most perfect consideration, *Monsieur,*

Your very humble and very obedient servant
Le Baron de Carondelet
[rubric]

Monsieur Chamorgan

---

[3]See document III and other documents in this collection.

XXI

TRUDEAU TO CARONDELET, ST. LOUIS, AUGUST 4, 1796[1]

Number 265

I have received Your Excellency's official letter dated May 11[2] of the present year in which you forewarn me that the members of the trading company of the Upper Missouri will be obliged to take their goods from the house that Don Andrés Todd is to establish in St. Louis. I do not doubt that you will receive representations concerning the matter from the traders interested in the Company who have suffered a considerable loss in the first engagements of its [Company's] commerce—a loss which has already obliged many to resign from the Company because of being ruined.[3]

Without consulting his companions, Morgan [Clamorgan] has solicited the obligation of necessarily taking from the store of Don Andrés Todd all the merchandise which his company might need, because he is associated with the aforementioned Todd or his *caxero* [agent] in Illinois. Also, by this obligation, he seeks to force his associates in the Company to resign from it in order alone to profit from the privileges already conceded and from the advantages of the ten thousand *pesos* which Your Excellency has solicited in favor of the same Company[4] which must serve

---

[1]Written in Spanish. A.G.I., P. de C., leg. 34. Reply is document XXXIV.
[2]Document XI.
[3]See documents XVI and XIX.

to maintain garrisons in the forts which are necessary to be established for the protection of their commerce.

May God keep Your Excellency many years.

St. Louis, August 4, 1796.[5]

Zenon Trudeau [rubric]

Señor Baron de Carondelet.

[4]*e.g.* Documents III and XVII. For Todd's activities see Nasatir, "Anglo-Spanish Frontier on the Upper Mississippi 1786-1796," *Iowa Journal of History and Politics*, XXIX (1931), 224ff.

[5]In number 263 of the same date (A.G.I., P. de C., leg. 34) Trudeau told Carondelet that by one of His Majesty's galliots the commandant of Barrancas had sent him the swivel guns, etc., which Carondelet had ordered and had advised Trudeau on May 11, 1796 (A.G.I., P. de C., leg. 24—Document VIII note 9). They were delivered by Chouteau to Trudeau for the Missouri company. Trudeau stated that he would deliver them to Clamorgan and advise.

XXII

CLAMORGAN TO CARONDELET, NEW ORLEANS, SEPTEMBER 15 [16?], 1796[1]

Very Respectable *Seigneur*:

As Director of a Company in the Missouri which you have never discontinued to honor with your protection and your favor, I have the honor of delivering myself up to your kindness to testify to you my sensibility regarding the delay of the projects of discovery and of commerce which have not until now ceased to be [being] obstructed in the different ways which have been put to use to realize its [Company's] objects.

On the one hand there have been continually opposing us a number of unmanageable nations which the indispensable preparation of a vigorous and important expedition ought to curb; while on the other hand, the slight means combined in the Company obliges me, in order to succeed, to take recourse in the creation of sufficient shares which might give it strength and capacity.

Author, if I dare thus explain myself, of an enterprise which will be important some day to the State, to the Commerce, and to Posterity: What greater satisfaction [can there be] to me, *Monseigneur*, than to contribute towards carrying it to its greatest success. Envious of this hope, I am taking the liberty of remitting to you below a supplement to the *reglement*[2] which was made to serve as a basis for the Company at the time of its creation.

[1]Written in French. A.G.I., P. de C., leg. 188C. Cp. document XXIV.
[2]Chapter II, document IX.

Article 1.

[Comments by Carondelet]

The Court alone can grant this grace which it will certainly not refuse if the Company has the success that it [Court] expects.

On account of the retardation of the enterprises of the Company of the Missouri, occasioned both by the different barbarous nations whose territory it is necessary to pass through, and by the losses and useless sacrifices which it has experienced up to now, the exclusive privilege granted to the Company will last and will be continued for two more years.

Article 2.

Granted in so far as this privilege does not include the trades which have been conserved up to now for inhabitants of the Illinois not interested in the Company.

The Company of the Missouri will have for its line of demarcation from north to south the degree of longitude which forms the entrance of the Platte River, the waters of which empty into the Missouri; and all the savage nations which will be discovered located west of this line extending as far as the Pacific Ocean including the nations Octoctata and that named Missouri, which might have their establishments outside of the abovementioned line, will only be frequented and furnished their needs by the Company to whom this commerce belongs.

Article 3.

Granted provided that the greater number [majority] of the present shareholders consent to it.

The present Director will create twenty shares of one thousand *piastres* each, where every shareholder will take the number of them which will be convenient for his means, in order thus to provide for the Company a base of more solid means.

Article 4.

Granted with the same reservation as in the preceding article.

Each share will be paid for in full to the present Director in cash or in merchandise suitable to the Company at the price that they are worth in St. Louis for cash.

Article 5.

Without the knowledge and the wish of the greatest number [majority] of the shareholders, t h a t would be unjust.

Notwithstanding article three above, the Director will be able, in the name of the Company, to make such loans as he will believe necessary for its needs, and the funds of the Company will be responsible for them.

Article 6.

Granted

Before the expiration of the privileges granted to the Company, the shareholders will not be able to withdraw or require [demand] the capital of [for] their shares from the total; but they can sell or alienate them whenever and to whomever they desire.

Article 7.

This cannot be without the assent of the majority of the shareholders.

The present Director will continue in charge for the term of the privilege granted to the Company in order to keep in the same hands the management and administration of the funds of the loan [loaned funds].

Article 8.

This is just.

The Director will enjoy the commission of two and one-half percent ($2\frac{1}{2}\%$) each year for administration; all that was granted to him at the time of the creation of the said Company.

Article 9.

The Company has to decide on this article.

In case of need, the present Director can be replaced or succeeded by such of the shareholders as he shall believe suitable.

Article 10.

This is just.

The deliberations [resolutions] of the assemblies of the Company will be made by the majority of shares and not by heads.

446

Article 11.

This is just.

The Director alone will have one vote in the deliberations [resolutions] of the assemblies in order to give the balance in case of an equal division of the voting shares. [The Director will cast a vote in case of a tie vote.]

Article 12.

Granted in so far as bringing *engagés* from Canada.

The Director will have the power to have *engagés* brought from [hired in] Canada for the use of the Company and will be empowered for this to send the necessary funds to procure them.

Article 13.

The King alone can grant upon the solicitation of the Company a decrease of duties, but it is useless to ask for less than three percent (3%).

The merchandise and the skins which will be for the account of the Company will pass through the Capital without paying any import or export duties during the time of its privilege.

Article 14.

No other flag can be raised.

The forts of the Company and its vessels will always raise the royal flag of His Majesty.

Article 15.

The Company will pay the price that it costs the King.

His Majesty will grant each year one thousand *livres* of powder both for the protection of the forts of the Company and to make His limits [boundaries] and flag respected.

Article 16.

That would be unjust.

The Director will be able to send forces to the Upper Missouri for the protection of the enterprises of the Company without any deliberation [resolution].

Article 17.

Granted.

The Director will have the right to attract and to form as much as it will be within his power to do so, a fixed establishment of a population [settlement] among the Mahas [nation] or elsewhere for the protection of its commerce of the Upper Missouri.

Article 18.

His Majesty will grant ten arpents in breadth by forty arpents in depth to every family which will establish itself in the environs of these forts, and in addition one l e a g u e square [one league on each side] of territory for the *commune* of the said establishment, dependency of the Company, as long as it will exist.

His Majesty will give and accord to the Company for itself or for its heirs or assigns, a square of territory six leagues on each side in the environs of the establishment of the Maha nation and the same in the environs of the establishment of the Ricara nation near the mouth of the Cheyenne River, and also the same amount of territory in the environs of the Mandan or Gros Ventres nation, all situated on the right bank of the Missouri—descending the current—in order to dispose of [the territory] as property belonging to it, [Company] its heirs or assigns.

Article 19.

Refer to the article above.

At every other fort that the Company might build in the future, there will belong a league square [one league on each side] of territory which will remain and continue in the hands [or as the property] of the Company, its heirs or its assigns.

Article 20.

Granted, conforming to the decree of His Majesty which approves of the said Company.

His Majesty will grant to the Company the levy of one hundred militiamen to accompany its next convoy to the Mandan nation. This militia will be maintained throughout the term of this privilege by His Majesty. The Company will feed, lodge and pay it [militia] in return for one hundred *piastres* per head for each year, in order to aid and protect the different forts of the Company.

448

Article 21.

Granted under the express conditions mentioned and with the prohibition to trade or sell on the right bank of the Missouri (descending) which the Company occupies, under penalty of confiscation and indemnification.

It will be permitted to *Sieur* Todd or his agents interested at St. Louis under the name of Clamorgan, Loisel and Company, to furnish the needs of the Sioux nation which frequents the Missouri, sending them merchandise by way of this river, in order to contribute towards familiarizing themselves with them, without however injuring the Company in its commerce.

Article 22.

Granted in as much as the Company will exploit them a year after their discovery, and in the future without interruption.

All the salt springs or mines, except those of gold and silver, that the Company will discover during the entire time of its privilege will belong to it—in ownership to it, its heirs or assigns, and the amount of land which will be attached thereto and dependent upon it, will be one-half league in circumference.

Article 23.

His Majesty reserves the permission of exploiting them if he judges it *à propos* at the time.

As for the gold and silver mines, His Majesty will grant to the Company the same advantages that he makes to all other of his subjects everywhere else.

Article 24.

This is just.

In the case where it will be more convenient to His Majesty to cede or remit to any other power his superb province of Illinois and dependencies during the course of the privilege accorded to the Company of the Missouri, then His Majesty is begged to reserve under the conditions of this arrangement, the rights, favors and immunities which it would have granted to the Company. Until then they will be guaranteed and conserved in their entirety to the full extent.

Article 25.

Granted.

His Excellency will please call attention to the kindnesses of His Majesty the special regard to Article 24 above, in order that it may please him to have regard and to stop by that the retarding of the prosperity of the Company in the midst of vast works which the Director is going to conduct henceforth; that the fear of finding himself some day separated from his beneficial flag might slow down its work.

Article 26.

No change can be made to the *reglement* already approved by the King without his sanction.

Every article of the *reglement* made for the creation of the Company or [and] all resolutions taken since then will become null and void if they will tend to alter or destroy a portion or any of the articles stipulated above.

In the firm hope in which I am that you will deign to continue your kindnesses in favor of the Company of the Missouri, it remains to me to beg you to give me the orders that you find best for the execution of my demands.

I have the honor of being very respectfully,

Monseigneur,

Your very obligated and very devoted servant.

Clamorgan [rubric]

His Excellency *Monseigneur* Le Baron de Carondelet.
New Orleans, September 15 [16?] 1796[3]

———

[3]See p. 451 for map traced from the original which is found on the back of the above document.

XXIII

CARONDELET TO CLAMORGAN, NEW ORLEANS, SEPTEMBER 18, 1796[1]

No. 5.

New Orleans, September 18th, 1796.

I have just received, Sir, the agreeable news of the approval of "the Spanish Company (these are the proper words of the Royal Decree,

———

[1]Missouri Historical Society, Clamorgan Collection, printed in *American State Papers, Public Lands,* VIII, 235; same although dated September 13, 1796 in *Ibid.,* III, 305.

450

Map of the Missouri Basin
Remarques

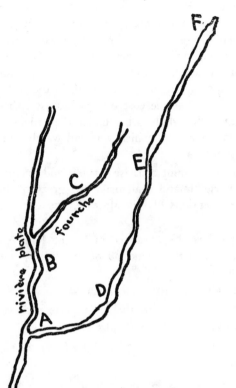

A. *Sejour des athoctata & Missouri entree de riviere plate*

B. *vilage des panis*
C. *vilage des loups*
D. *vilage des maha*
E. *vilage des ponca*
F. *vilage des ricara*
[*There is no G*]
H. *vilage des Cancés*
I. *Entrée de la rivière des Cancés*

Il est aisé de voir par la plan que Les Maha, les Othoctata, Les Missouri, les poncas & les ricara peuvent être continuelement frequenté par les traiteurs panis & loups qui sont comme au centre des autres nations qui n'ont discontinué De deranger & empecher la communication du haut missouri.

made in the Council of State held on the 27th of last May) formed in 1794,[2] in order to make discoveries to the Westward of the Missouri, with the regulations and instructions under which Your Lordship has sanctioned, and granted to the said company the exclusive privilege of the fur trade with all the nations of Indians on said Missouri who inhabit beyond the Nation of Ponca; offering three thousand Dollars as a reward to the first who shall reach the South Sea. 2$^{d.}$ the permission granted to the said company to arm and maintain armed, in the forts which it has or may have hereafter, and at the cost of His Majesty, the one hundred men thought necessary; the whole being under the orders of your Lordship and for the ends designated, which you will watch with the greatest care &c."

I hope, Sir, that on account of these favours and privileges, the company will derive new vigour and shall make the greatest efforts in order to correspond to the intentions of His Majesty, and exclude the English from those parts.

The house of Todd is also approved of by the King who has added to all those favours, that of the reduction of the duties from 15 to 6 p$^{r.}$ cent, for all the Colony.

We shall see if Léglise gets the prize of $3000.

I have the honour to be, with the most perfect consideration, Sir, your very humble and very obedient servant

Signed, Le Baron de Carondelet

Monsieur Clamorgan.

----

[2]Document XVII.

XXIV

CLAMORGAN TO CARONDELET, NEW ORLEANS, SEPTEMBER 20, 1796[1]

Very Illustrious Sir,

As Director of a Company of the Missouri which you have never ceased to honor with your protection and your favors, I have the honor to impose upon your goodness to testify my sensibility upon the retardation of the project of discovery and of commerce which till now has not ceased to be impeded or held back in the different ways which your goodness has used to realize them.

----

[1]Written in French. A.G.I., P. de C., leg. 2364. See document XXII. The marginal notations are by Carondelet.

These major hindrances which incessantly are putting the work of the Company in an opposition by malicious caprice of several savage nations which it is necessary to subject henceforth by an apparent *force majeure* only when all the resources of friendship and presents will be exhausted, have determined the Director to solicit from your goodness, the liberty to create a sufficient number of shares for the Company which will assure it a solid base and durable means.

It is for this purpose that I have the honor to expose to your wisdom a supplement to the *Reglement* of the company in order that it may please you to permit the execution of everything which would be convenient to its prosperity in the name of His Majesty.

Article 1.

The Company must solicit this grace by a memorial accepted by its shareholders and presented to His Majesty by way of the government.

Considering the obstacles that the Company has experienced up till now in its enterprises, His Excellency is supplicated to solicit for the said Company two years more prolongation of its privilege in the Missouri.

Article 2.

The article will be decided only after having heard the representations of the commerce of the Illinois and the advice of the Lieutenant-Governor.

The Company of the Missouri is incessantly experiencing insurmountable difficulties among the Octoctata and Missouri nations located at the mouth of the river Platte, whose waters fall into the Missouri, where the trader of the Panis and the Loups is obliged to pass in order to go to his post. The Company is obliged to solicit from Your Grace the power of exploiting the above mentioned nations by giving as a gift a sum of a hundred and fifty *piastres* in merchandise to those who, in consequence of drawing by lot in St. Louis will obtain the above mentioned trade and commerce with the said villages of Panis and Loups which are situated on branches of the river Platte approaching very near the abode of the Ricara

453

nation on the Missouri and drawing that trade away from the Company. Interests foreign to the commerce of the Company are doing harm and causing prejudice by penetrating there, both by the independence of their needs, and by knowledge contrary to the ties of friendship and of kindness which must reign between this nation and the Company.

Article 3.

Idem

Without the execution of the above article, the fort, which the Company is erecting at the entrance of the Platte river in order to restrain the Octoctata and Missouri nations, who have never ceased to disturb the passages of the routes and expeditions of the Company to the Upper Missouri, has become useless and the precautions taken to diminish the obstacles to a new commerce are continually subsisting. It is for this reason, therefore, His Excellency is supplicated to grant the demand of the Company.

Article 4.

Idem

The line of demarcation the Company of Missouri will have from north to south [shall be] the degree of longitude of the entrance of Platte River, in the interior of which line will be included the Octoctata and Missouri nations although they are established beyond that line near the fort of the said Company; and all other nations [to] in the west will belong to the Company. Then the individuals from the province of the Illinois, far from spreading themselves in the Indian trade of this portion of the Missouri and especially among the Panis and Loup nations located on the Platte river, will unfailingly turn back to agriculture each year, which is the inexhaustible source of prosperity, with the presents of the Company explained in article two above.

Article 5.

Idem. The Lieutenant-Governor will inform you upon this article, after all shareholders will have voted [accepted].

The present director will leave twenty shares of one thousand *piastres* each [one] to each shareholder and take his part of interest to assure to the Company a base of solid and durable means.

Article 6.

Each share will be paid for in cash-paid to the Director in money-or in merchandise suitable for

Idem

the Company at the sale price in St. Louis.

Article 7.

The shareholders will not be allowed to withdraw nor exact the capital of their shares, outside of the *masse,* before the expiration of the privilege accorded the Company, but they will be allowed to sell them at any time or to any person whosoever.

Idem

Article 8.

The Director will receive his commission of two and a half per cent commission in the future as it was granted at the time of the formation of the said Company, taking into consideration his trouble to make the Company prosperous.

Idem

Article 9.

The decisions in meetings of the Company will be by majority of shares and not by head.

Idem

Article 10.

The Director alone will have a deciding voice in assemblies in case of a tie vote.

Idem

Article 11.

The Director will have the power of obtaining from or of sending men to Canada, to make a

Granted

levy of men in Canada and to hire *engageés* of which the Company will have need for its commerce in the Missouri.

Article 12.

This article must be solicited from His Majesty by a memorial in the name of the Company and by way of the Governor-General.

The merchandise and furs which will be for the profit of the Company will pass to the capital by paying only three per cent during the time of its privilege: Thus His Excellency is supplicated to solicit it from His Majesty.

Article 13.

Granted

The forts and embarcations of the Company will fly the royal flag of His Majesty at all times, which His Majesty will be pleased to furnish them. The flags are to be of medium size.

Article 14.

Granted

It will be granted and delivered every year to the Company two thousand pounds of gun powder at a cash price to indemnify the said Company for presents which it is obliged to make to the various nations and also to protect its forts and flags.

Article 15.

Granted—if the Company will find it convenient.

The Director will form as much as will be in his power an establishment of population among the Maha nation and environs for the security of its remote commerce.

Article 16.

His Majesty will grant to the Company a title of property for it, its heirs or legitimate successors, the space of six square leagues of land, near the establishment of the Maha nation; as much near to the nation Ricara near the mouth of Cheyenne river; and as much near the Mandan or Gros Ventres nation—all being situated on the banks

456

of the Missouri on the right side, descending by stream, in order to enjoy this as a thing belonging properly to it.

Article 17.

Granted

Notwithstanding the above article, there shall belong to every other fort of the Company whenever it may be or wherever it may be erected in the future one square league of land upon each side, in order to enjoy and dispose of it as if it was a *title to property*.

Article 18.

By the first mail this representation will be made and strongly urged.[3]

According to the official letter which the Director has just received[2] concerning the one hundred militiamen which His Majesty has permitted him to raise in order to protect the convoys in the Upper Missouri and in order to maintain the defense of its forts against the attacks by foreign commerce which are introducing themselves with impunity upon the possessions of His Majesty; His Excellency is supplicated to solicit an explanation concerning the payment of the one hundred *piastres* per head which must be paid by His Majesty to the Company, in order to pay the soldiers and maintain the above militia each year.

Article 19.

Authorized by the Intendant.

While awaiting the explanation of His Majesty upon article 18 above, His Excellency is supplicated to order that the Director receive the sum which must serve to raise and pay the first year, the one hundred militiamen which the Company needs in order to escort its next convoy to the Upper Missouri, at the rate of one hundred *pias-*

---

[2] Document XXIII.
[3] In a draft to Morales dated October 1, 1796 (A.G.I., P. de C., leg. 1574) it is stated "I am sending you a memorial of Don Santiago Clamorgan, Director of the Spanish Company—From the treasury must be sent the ten thousand *pesos* amounting to the pay of the one hundred men which must be maintained in arms by the Company paid by His Majesty as he solicited, and which I recommended in my representation to the Minister of State" (documents III, XVII). See document XXIX. The Intendant refused to pay and it never was paid.

tres per head as it has solicited, from which sum the Director will furnish in this village and pay into the hands of the treasury of His Majesty, good and solvent security, from the lack of which the operations of the Company for next year will suffer.

Article 20.

Accorded under the expressed condition that the above merchandise will be confiscated for the profit of the Company if it happens that they should be found on sale at places destined to the exclusive commerce of the Company, when this permission will be *ipso facto* suppressed.

It will be permitted to *Sieur* Todd or his interested agents in St. Louis, under the denomination of Clamorgan, Loisel and Company, to furnish with merchandise the Sioux nations who frequent north of the banks of the Missouri and communicate with the Missouri at its mouth—and this with reservation that they will not trouble the privileged commerce of the Company.⁴

---

⁴Todd was granted the exclusive trade with the Indian nations to the west of the Mississippi and rivers which empty into it north of the Missouri. To prevent the English from trading there and to protect the agents of Todd on the Des Moines, Trudeau asked for permission to send along with Todd's men a corporal and two soldiers to remain there as a garrison and notify the British and Americans to keep out of Spanish territory. Todd was to pay all the expenses. This was approved by Carondelet and carried out. Trudeau to Carondelet, no. 270, St. Louis, September 22, 1796, A.G.I., P. de C., leg. 24; draft in leg. 34; and Carondelet to Trudeau, New Orleans, October 17, 1796, A.G.I., P. de C., leg. 24; draft also in *Ibid.* See Nasatir, "Anglo-Spanish Frontier on the Upper Mississippi 1786-1796," *Iowa Journal of History and Politics,* XXIX (1931), 224-230; Nasatir, "Anglo-Spanish Rivalry in the Iowa Country 1797-1798," *Ibid.,* XXVIII (1930), 337 *et. seq.* The small garrison which returned to St. Louis after two months stay, was wholly inadequate for the job which was assigned it to do. Todd's men asked for more protection for their commence. War had been declared and Carondelet sent Carlos Howard to St. Louis with instructions, Trudeau to Carondelet, no. 276, St. Louis, November 22, 1796, A.G.I., P. de C., leg. 1574; and reply dated February 15, 1797, A.G.I., P. de C., leg. 24. See Chapter V, document VII.

The granting of exclusive trades was not an unusual or unique feature of this era. Several others were proposed or/and granted. Chouteau had one for the Osages. Grandpré proposed one for Rapides, Avoyelles, and Natchitoches. The full documentation of the grant to Chouteau and of its history is given in Nasatir, *Imperial Osage.* For an example of the grant at Natchitoches see Grandpré to Carondelet, Avoyelles, September 27, 1796, no. 19, original with draft of reply by Carondelet in the latter's own handwriting and with his rubric is in the Bancroft Library; certified copy in A.G.I., P. de C., leg. 130.

Article 21.

Granted.

All the mineral sources and salt mines except gold and silver which the Company will discover during the time of its privilege will belong to the Company, its heirs, or legitimate successors, and the space of territory, which will be attached to it and dependent upon it shall be one-half league in circumference.

Article 22.

If that is convenient to His Majesty of which it is necessary to solicit permission to exploit them.

As to mines of gold and silver: His Majesty will grant to the Company the same advantages which he grants to all his subjects in any other place.

Article 23.

This petition should be made to His Majesty by the Company via the government.

In case it should please His Majesty to cede or to put in the hands of any other person [power?] his superb province of Illinois and dependencies during the time of the privilege conceded to the Missouri Company, then His Majesty is supplicated to reserve in his condition of arrangements that the rights, favors and immunities which have been granted to the Company until then will be granted to it and preserved in all its extensions.

Article 24.

Granted.

His Excellency will find it agreeable to obtain from the goodness of His Majesty the remembrance from the article twenty-four [sic] in order that it will please His Majesty to take into account and prevent by this the retardation of the prosperity of the Company in the midst of its vast work which the Director is about to conduct it [the Company], for fear of seeing it [him or Company] some day separated from its beneficial flag could retard it.

459

It is in this hope that I have the honor of
being
Your very respectfully
Monseigneur
Your very obliging and de-
voted servant
Pre Clamorgan
[rubric]

New Orleans, September 20, 1796.
To His Excellency Mr. le Baron de Carondelet

XXV

GRANT TO EVANS, OCTOBER 8, 1796[1]

RIVER TREMBLANTE
8 OCT 1796

Mr. Evans

Sir

As I find by Mr. James Mackay's[2] letter that the Missisourie
[*sic*] is Chartered by a Company I wish to withdraw what little property
the N. W. Co.[3] has their, indeed it has been my wish for some time past
as we have lost a good deal of money by Mr. Gousseaume [Jusseaume]
whome we have employed in that business. I therefore beg you will be
kind enough to deliver the bearer all the property of whatever kind belonging to the said Gousseaume that may be in your possesion, he has
wrote you himself to that effect he is to pass some time here himself to
settle his affairs but means to return to the Missisourie in course of next
month. I am very much obliged to you for your kindness in lending a
man to Mr. Mackay[4] as this is the last time any of our people will go
that way I hope you will be kind enough to give your assistance in getting
away the men who has deserted from us in that quarter and should any

[1]Sealed original letter written in English in A.G.I., P. de C., leg. 213. Edited and
printed in Nasatir, "John Evans: Explorer and Surveyor," *Missouri Historical
Review*, XXV (1931), 458-459. For a discussion of this letter see Nasatir, "Anglo-
Spanish Rivalry on the Upper Missouri," *Mississippi Valley Historical Review*,
XVI (1930), reprint pp. 32-33.
[2]This was perhaps Mackay's declaration to all British subjects, dated Fort
Charles, May 27, 1796, and delivered by McDonell to Brandon House. Brandon
House Journal, entry for October 25, 1796 in Hudson's Bay Company Archives.
See document XXVI.
[3]Northwest Company.
[4]Neil or Donald Mackay. See L. R. Masson, *Les Bourgeois de la Campagnie
du Nord Ouest* (Quebec, 1889), I, 282-295 *passim*. More light is shed on his
earlier career in Charles M. Gates [ed.], *Five Fur Traders of the Northwest*
(Minneapolis, 1933).

of your people ever come this way you may depend upon it they shall
be delivered up to you I hope you will be so good as send me an acct.
of everything you will deliver the men belonging to Gousseaume and you
will oblige.

Sir

Your most obedient
Humble servant
Cuthbert Grant⁵ [rubric]

Addressed to:
Mr Evans
at the Mandan Village
Missisourie

---

⁵On Cuthbert Grant see G. C. Davidson, *Northwest Company* (Berkeley, 1918),
and Gates, *Five Fur Traders*.

XXVI

Extracts from Brandon House Journal
(James Sutherland)¹

[*25th October, 1796.*]

Rec⁴· the following declaration from Mʳ· McDonnell, Just come from
the Mandals [Mandans]:

To All British Subjects Trading to the interior parts of N. America,
and all other persons of whatever description who may frequent the
said Country:

His Catholic Majesty having granted to his subjects (the Missurie
Company) that part of his dominions sitenated on both sides of the Missurie to its Westermost source and from its source to the coast of the
Pacific Ocean, and North to the hight of land, that divides the waters
that empties into the Missurie from those that falls into Hudson's Bay.

I am therefor commanded to forbid and prevent all foriners whatever (especiely all British subjects) who are or may be in the neigh-
bourhood of his Majestys dominions to enter any part of the said Chartered dominions on pain of confiscation of all such offenders property and
such punishment as the law of the land may inflict on the conveyers
of such property.

---

¹Hudon's Bay Company Archives. Publication is permitted by the Governor
and Committee of the Hudson's Bay Company. See Nasatir, "Anglo-Spanish
Rivalry on the Upper Missouri" *Mississippi Valley Historical Review*, XVI (1930),
reprint pp. 33ff. There were three Brandon Houses, see D. A. Stewart, *Early
Assiniboine Trading Posts of the Souris-Mouth Group 1785-1832*, 12-14; Gates, *Five
Fur Traders;* Davidson, *Northwest Company;* Masson, *Les Bourgeois*, etc. James
Southerland was the head of the Hudson's Bay Company post called Brandon House.
See Chapter V, document II.

Given under my hand at Fort Charles this Twenty-seventh day of May, Anno Domini One thousand Seven hundred and ninety six.
Signed
J. Makay

To all whom it may concern

Oct^br 26, Wednesday. Snowy weather. the men variously, Stept over to the other House to hear more news from the Mandals. M^r. McKay says the above Mr J. Makay has not yet arrived at the Missurie, only a party under a M^r. Evans, a Welsh Gentleman, who has come to explore the source of the River as far as the stoney mountains if not to the Pacific ocean in search of mines, some of which is already found, M^r. Evans permitted him to return for this time without confiscation of his property, but on promise of not returning again with any more goods.

[23rd November, 1796.]

As Canadians are going from the other House to the Mandals I sent the following Letter to M^r. Evans,[2] barly out of couriositey:
Dear Sir:
Your written decleration dated Fort Charles 27th of May last, has come to our hands, forbiding all British Subjects from Trading at the Missurie, this may effect the Traders from Canada,[3] but very little those from Hudsons Bay—I should be glad however to know if we may be permitted on any future ocasion to visit the Mandals and Trade Horses, Indian corn and Buffalo robes which articles we supose to be unconnected with the Fur Trade and consiquently expect you will have no objections to, with wishing to hear of your health and Success, I Remain,

Dear Sir,
Your Obedient Humble Servant
J. Sutherland

[16th January, 1797.]

Rec^d the following letter from Mr Evans in answer to mine of the 23^d of Nov^br last[4]
Fort Makay Dec^br. 20th 1796
Dear Sir

Yours of the 23^d of Nov^br. came to hand, and I thank you. The Trade from the N. to this place being prohibited I believe cannot effect

----

[2]Original in A.G.I., P. de C., leg. 213; printed in Nasatir, "John Evans; Explorer and Surveyor," *Missouri Historical Review*, XXV (1931), 459-460. There are a few differences from the original as printed.
[3]Referring to Northwest company traders.
[4]For reply see Chapter V, document IV.

neither the Hudson's Bay nor the N.W Company as they never met with anything but loss from this quarter.

As to your requist concerning admission to Trade Horses, Indian Corn and Buffalo Robes, it is not in my power to answer you on that head; But I have reason to believe the latter will not be permitted as it is the staple Trade of this Countrie, but however you will be propperly inform'd after the arrival of the Agent General and Lieutt. Mooroch at this Post, having no entertaining news of any kind to transfer to you,

I Remain
Dear Sir
Your Obt Servt.
J.T. EVANS

[25th Feb., 1797.][5]

Saturday Cloudy, cold weather, the men hauld home the Cattle kild yesterday, About 3, P. M., Slettar and Yorston arrived from the Mandals with 4 Sleds well loaded with Furs, Mr Evans was as cival to them as his wretched siteuation would admit, but would not permit them to Trade with the natives, he Traded all the goods they had and gave them furs for it, but would have bought it much cheaper had they dealt with the natives who was highly displeased with Evans on that account, and some thinks will endanger his siteuation, On thir arrival there they wer met by above 300 Indians who carried their Slids on their Shoulders into the village, so fond wer they of the English, Mr. Evans hoisted his Spanish flagg

---

[14th April, 1797.]

Friday (Good Friday) snow all day Watson and Easter making a bed place for the Master upstairs, 2 making a door for the flesh House, the door of which has been stolen either by the Indians or Canadians. News from the Mandals, Mr. Evans and the Canadians[6] was almost at fisticuffs in atempting to prevent them from Trading with the natives, and not having goods himself set all the Indians out against him, he was obliged to set off with himself and all his men down the River for Fort Charles, the Indians threatning to kill them if they refused being greatly exasperated against them for preventing the Subjects of G. Britain from comming to Trade with them, The Indians has plenty of Furs still

[5]See Nasatir, "Anglo-Spanish Rivalry on the Upper Missouri," *op. cit.*, reprint, pp. 33-37; also Chapter V, documents II and V.

[6]See *Ibid;* and documents printed in Nasatir, "John Evans: Explorer and Surveyor," *op. cit.;* Evans' "Journal" is Chapter V, document II.

among them particularly the Grovanders (or bigg bellys) and are determined to visit this place nixt fall or at least to meet Traders halfway, what a pitey there is not men and goods to encourage this Trade

XXVII

Agreement Between Todd and Clamorgan, New Orleans, October 26, 1796[1]

Agreement[1] between *Sieur* André Todd, merchant represented in this city by the firm of Mr. Daniel Clark, Jr., party of the first part and *Sieurs* Clamorgan, Loisel & Company merchants of the Illinois party of the second part—

To wit:

Article 1

The *liaison* of interest according to the articles stipulated hereinafter shall be continued and will last between the firm of Mr. André Todd and that of Clamorgan, Loisel & Company for the time and consecutive space of four years beginning with the first of August, last, of the present year.

Article 2

The firm of Todd established at New Orleans will sustain in the Illinois only the firm of Clamorgan, Loisel and Company with the exception of that of Mr. Chouteau and that of Sr. Arundel both situated at the said place.

Article 3

As a consequence of the above article the said *Sieurs* Clamorgan, Loisel and Company shall draw the merchandise which they will need for their commerce from the firm of Todd only, during the course of the four years stipulated in Article one, above.

Article 4

The interests and advantages which Clamorgan as Director of the Company of Missouri does or shall obtain from *Sieur* Todd in particular

---

[1]Written in French. Missouri Historical Society, St. Louis Archives number 2934. See Chapter VI, documents XIX, note 1. There are a number of promissary notes signed by Clamorgan, Loisel and Company and made out to Daniel Clark, Jr., in the Missouri Historical Society, Pierre Chouteau Collection.

Clamorgan, Loisel and Company petitioned Trudeau on June 19, 1798 that they wished to deposit the two documents which they enclosed (the contract containing 19 articles and the contract containing 9 articles) in the archives of the government. Trudeau agreed and ordered it done as well as copies made and collated. Missouri Historical Society St. Louis archives, no. 2934.

or which he shall obtain himself in the commerce of the Missouri shall remain the property of Clamorgan, Loisel and Company during the said term of four years.

Article 5

Sieur André Todd in so far as possible shall procure for *Sieurs* Clamorgan, Loisel and Company all men hired from [in] Canada that they shall need for their commerce each year on condition that the said Clamorgan, Loisel and Company reimburse *Sieur* André Todd for all the expenses and advances that he will have made for them.

Article 6

The merchandise demanded each year of the firm of Todd of New Orleans by Clamorgan, Loisel and Company in order to have them imported and drawn from England shall maintain on their arrival in this city a commission of twelve and one-half per cent which will be added at the foot of their European account, all of it payable three months after their arrival in this city; after which time the interest shall be carried at the rate of ten per cent upon the sums which will not be paid during that time.

Article 7

The *bateaux* or small vessels of which *Sieurs* Clamorgan, Loisel and Company shall have need for their commerce from this City to the Illinois shall be to the benefit of the mutual account [profits divided] between the two firms.

Article 8

All merchandise purchased in this city by the firm of Todd for the account and in accordance with the orders of Clamorgan, Loisel and Company shall maintain a commission of five per cent as well as all other disbursements which shall concern them in this city.

Article 9

Sieur André Todd shall make the disbursement of the price of the *bateaux* or vessels, and the repairs or rigging of ships which the commerce of the said Clamorgan, Loisel and Company will require, without charge of commission to them. In this consideration, the said Clamorgan, Loisel and Company shall receive in the Illinois for the account of the said *Sieur* Todd, the furs which shall belong to him; and they will send them to him for his account and risk and at his expense in [to] the hands of Mr. Daniel Clark, Jr., merchant of this city, without charge of commission to the said *Sieur* Todd.

Article 10

If the furs which Clamorgan, Loisel and Company shall receive in the Illinois for the account and risk of the said *Sieur* Todd, cannot be lodged in the *batteaux* or vessels which shall be at the mutual account for the commerce of the said Clamorgan, Loisel and Company, then the said furs shall be loaded as freight always at the expense, account and risk of the said *Sieur* Todd, on board any other vessel that the said Clamorgan, Loisel and Company shall be able to procure; and in case that they cannot be loaded as freight, the said Clamorgan, Loisel and Company shall procure for the said *Sieur* Todd any other means suitable to have them reach him without any charge, risk or expense to the said Clamorgan, Loisel and Company.

Article 11

Each year the voyages of the *batteaux* or vessels in the service and for the need of the commerce of Clamorgan, Loisel and Company in this city shall be balanced and shall carry a commission of five per cent by the firm of Todd, after which one-half of the resulting profits shall be carried to the credit of the account of Clamorgan, Loisel and Company.

Article 12

No advance shall be made at New Orleans by the firm of Todd to any of the hired men which Clamorgan, Loisel and Company shall send to it by the *batteaux* or vessels which they shall have descend to this city, except upon the advice which they shall give to it [firm of Todd].

Article 13

The price of the men hired will always be borne at the ordinary price in the voyage of the *batteaux* of the Illinois sent to this city for the commerce of the said Clamorgan, Loisel and Company.

Article 14

In so far as possible the merchandise demanded by Clamorgan, Loisel and Company are to arrive in New Orleans at the latest in the month of April and in the month of December to put the boats which they shall send to this city in a condition to return to the Illinois at a time convenient to their trading operations.

Article 15

Upon all the returns which the *Sieurs* Clamorgan, Loisel and Company shall send to *Sieur* Todd or to his firm of New Orleans, a commission of two and one-half per cent shall be allowed in the price of the sale which they will make for their account on this city; the cash or bills of exchange, excepting when they shall be made payable here, the *piastres* shall be at the rate of four and one-half shillings, English money.

Article 16

Articles twelve and thirteen above mentioned, appearing useless, shall remain null and of no effect.

Made and done in the presence of the undersigned witness at New Orleans the 26th of October, 1796.

Clamorgan, Loisel & Company
[rubric]

Andrew Todd   [rubric]
Daniel Clark, Junior   [rubric]

Richard Relf, Witness [rubric]

Articles relative to the voyage of the *batteau, Le Missouri,* under the conduct of Henri Duchoquet[2] sent from this city to the Illinois by Mr. Daniel Clark, Jr., in the month of [blank], last.

Article 1

The merchandise and cargo placed on board the said *batteau* shall be for the account of Clamorgan, Loisel and Company.

Article 2

The *facture* of the said merchandise shall be charged with seven and one half per cent in favor of the firm of Todd, represented by Mr. Daniel Clark, Jr., excepting the powder which shall be priced at the rate of four *livres* per pound.

---

[2]In a draft [Morales?] to Trudeau, New Orleans, September 15, 1796 (A.G.I., P. de C., leg. 261) the Intendant's office wrote that goods were being shipped in two *lanchones El Afortunado* and *Los Quatro Hermanos,* and Chouteau's *bercha,* the *patrones* of which were Luis Bordas, Pedro Lecont, Bautista Duchouquet, and he asked that Trudeau check over the goods brought in the vessels. He stated that the goods were allowed in New Orleans under a special lowering of duties granted temporarily by Carondelet and his predecessor, and to watch over the merchandise so that the people of Ste. Geneviève may not have complaints that the goods were sold for other than purposes of the Indian trade. Again on March 8, 1796, Trudeau was asked to do the same with respect to the *bercha* belonging to Todd named *El Succeso,* its *patrón* Francisco Caillau. A.G.I., P. de C., leg. 261B.

Article 3

Upon money disbursed and provisions there shall be carried five per cent.

Made and done in the presence of the undersigned witness in New Orleans this 26th day of October, 1796.

> Clamorgan, Loisel & Company [rubric]
> Andrew Todd [rubric]
> Daniel Clark, Junior [rubric]

Richd Relfe, witness [rubric]

Articles relative to the sending of two *batteaux,* one *patroné* by Pierre Lecompte, the other by Louison Barada [which] left from this city to go to the Illinois in the month of [blank] last.

Article 1

It is agreed between *Sieur* André Todd represented in this city by the firm of *Sieur* Daniel Clark, Jr., and *Sieurs* Clamorgan, Loisel and Company that the loading of the above mentioned *batteaux* are for the account and risk of the said Clamorgan, Loisel and Company to whom there shall be furnished a general account [*facture*] of the prices of Europe.

Article 2

The powder which is aboard the said *batteaux* shall be carried at one hundred *sols* per pound.

Article 3

The earthenware according to the *facture* number 29, shall be carried at the rate of one hundred fifty per cent on the prices of Europe.

Article 4

The iron and steel bar, stoves, pots and pans, lead in beads, pipes, glassware, window panes, scythes, kettles of white iron, corks, *les flots á peser,* and the articles of iron carried in *facture* number 28 will maintain a profit of one hundred per cent on the European prices.

Article 5

All other kinds of merchandise for the Indian trade as well as for the commerce with the whites, carried in the *factures* of Europe will maintain a benefit of fifty per cent.

Article 6

All merchandise purchased in this city shall be carried at cost price plus a commission of five per cent as well as on the expenses, money disbursed, provisions or hire of *batteaux*.

Article 7

There shall be carried by the firm of Todd an interest of seven and a half per cent upon the total for the first year to date from the day of the sending of the merchandise mentioned above, after which time the interest shall be carried at the rate of ten per cent for that which shall remain to be paid.

Article 8

On the arrival of the *batteaux* in the Illinois, *Sieurs* Clamorgan, Loisel and Company shall remit to Mr. Chouteau, merchant of St. Louis, the objects which they have loaned to *Sieur* Todd at the same price, same charge, interest and freight at which they were sent to the said *Sieurs* Clamorgan, Loisel and Company, since the risks are entirely for the account of *Sieur* Todd.

Article 9

Sieurs Clamorgan, Loisel and Company shall furnish on the arrival of the said *batteaux* in the Illinois and under the same conditions as to Mr. Chouteau, an assortment to *Sieur* Arundel, merchant at Cahokias, which shall not exceed the sum of 10,000 *livres*, which remains for the account and risk of the said *Sieur* Todd from this moment on.

Made and done in the presence of the undersigned witness this 26th of October, 1796, in the city of New Orleans.

Clamorgan, Loisel & Company
[rubric]

Andrew Todd   [rubric]
Daniel Clark   Junior
[rubric]

Richard Relfe, witness
[rubric]

469

XXVIII

CLAMORGAN TO CARONDELET, NEW ORLEANS, OCTOBER 27, 1796[1]

Most Excellent Sir:

I received the honor of your official letter dated day before yesterday[2] which informs me of the decree of His Majesty for the approbation of the Spanish Company of the Missouri created May 12, 179[?] as well as for the power of maintaining at His [its?] expense the one hundred militiamen for the protection of its [Company's] different forts established or to be established on the Missouri at the rate of one hundred *piastres* per head which the Company has solicited from His Majesty for the cost of their maintenance each year.[3] For all of this the Company thanks the generous cares that Your Excellency has deigned to lavish on it for the future prosperity of its discoveries. And it unceasingly begs His Majesty's good will, to welcome at the foot of the throne the most sincere wishes for the fullest glory and the most sacred oaths that duty, zeal, attachment and gratitude has ever imposed on it.

It is with these inexhaustible sentiments that I dare to call myself with truth, in the most respectful manner,

Most Excellent Sir,
Your very devoted and very obliged servant,
J. Clamorgan
[rubric]

New Orleans; October 27, 1796
His Excellency, *Monsieur* Le Baron de Carondelet.

___

[1]Written in French. A.G.I., P. de C., leg. 212B.
[2]Carondelet to Clamorgan, October 26, 1796, is in Missouri Historical Society, Clamorgan Collection, printed in *American State Papers, Public Lands*, VIII, 236.
[3]See document XVII.

XXIX

CARONDELET TO MORALES, NEW ORLEANS, OCTOBER 31, 1796[1]

I am enclosing to you a memorial of Don Santiago Clamorgan, Director of the Spanish Company of Discoveries to the West of the Missouri, in which he solicits by virtue of the Royal order of approbation of June 11 of this year that the Royal Treasury pay to him the 10,000 *pesos;*

___

[1]Written in Spanish. A.G.I., P. de C., leg. 2364; transcript in Library of Congress; annex no. 1, to Carondelet's letter no. 89 *res.* to Prince of Peace, A.H.N., Est. leg. 3900; Chapter V, document VII; annex no. 2 to Carondelet's letter no. 61 *res.* to Minister, A.G.I., P. de C., leg. 2343, and certified copy Morales to Gardoqui, no 61, New Orleans, December 1, 1796, annex no. 1, A.G.I., P. de C., leg. 2343, this Chapter document XXXVII. Reply is document XXXI.

which is the amount of the salary of the one hundred men which the Company must maintain armed, [and who are to be] paid for the account of His Majesty as I solicit [he solicited] and as I supported in my representation to the Minister of State.

May God keep you many years. New Orleans, October 31, 1796
Señor Don Juan Ventura Morales   El Baron de Carondelet   [rubric]

[Enclosure]

Señor Governador General.[2] Don Santiago Clamorgan, Director of the Spanish Company of Discoveries to the West of the Missouri, has the honor to inform Your Excellency that by the royal order of June 11 of the current year, His Majesty has been pleased to approve the said Company under the *Reglamento y Instrucción* with which Your Excellency permitted it and conceded to it the exclusive privilege of the traffic with all the Indian nations of the same Missouri who inhabit that river above the Poncas.

He likewise has the honor to inform Your Excellency that His Majesty was pleased to concede the license that the Company may arm at its [his] cost and maintained armed in the forts which it has and may have in the future the one hundred men which it considers necessary, for that purpose, all under the orders of Your Excellency.[3]

He begs Your Excellency to please send the official correspondence so that the Royal Treasury may pay to the petitioner the 10,000 *pesos,* — the annual amount of the salary of the one hundred men, in accordance with the proposition that he has made. This is a favor which he hopes to receive from the kindness of Your Excellency. New Orleans, October 27, 1796.
S. Clamorgan   [rubric]

Don[4] Santiago Clamorgan, Director of the Spanish Company of Discoveries to the West of the Missouri, has solicited 2000 pounds of powder, paying its just value; for he is unable to procure this article because of its scarcity in the city, and it must be used in the commerce or trade of the

---

[2]Also annex no. 1, Carondelet to Minister, no. 61 *res.* A.G.I., P. de C., leg. 2343. Document XXXVII.

[3]Document XVII. On November 8, 1796, Carondelet wrote Clamorgan that he could see no objection to the latter's raising one hundred militia men in the Illinois country which His Majesty had granted for the forts of the Missouri Company, but that he could not answer for the 10,000 *piastres* since that depended upon His Majesty's decision but that he was fully persuaded that His Majesty would grant that favor when he would read his representation on the matter sent to Spain. Original in Missouri Historical Society, Pierre Chouteau Collection; draft in A.G.I., P. de C., leg. 129; in Missouri Historical Society, Clamorgan Collection, printed in *American State Papers, Public Lands,* III, 305. See document XXXIII.

[4]Written in Spanish. Draft also in A.G.I., P. de C., leg. 89.

aforementioned Company which cannot make great progress without this requisite. I am advising you of this for your due knowledge.

God, etc. New Orleans, October 31, 1796.

[draft][5]

Señor Don Juan Ventura Morales.[6]

---

[5]Morales replied to Carondelet on the same date, October 31, 1796, (A.G.I., P. de C., leg. 89) that he has no objection to delivering the two thousand pounds of powder if a just price is paid.

[6]Also enclosed are: Copy of Morales to Carondelet, New Orleans, November 3, 1796 (Document XXXI); Copy of Gardoqui to Intendant of Louisiana, Aránjuez, June 11, 1796 (cited in Document XVII).

[At end of document] Decree: New Orleans, September 16, 1796. This was sent to the *Contaduría Principal de Exército* for its intelligence. Certified copy by Leonard [rubric]

XXX

MORALES TO GARDOQUI, NEW ORLEANS, OCTOBER 31, 1796[1]

Index of the representations which under this date the *Contador de Exércitos,* Don Juan Ventura Morales, temporarily charged with the Intendancy of the provinces of Louisiana and West Florida, sends to the Most Excellent *Señor* Don Diego de Gardoqui, *Secretario de Estado y del Despacho Universal* of the Treasury.

No. 49.

No. 53. He has communicated to that *administración de rentas* and that of the other districts that he has believed opportune the favor accorded by His Majesty to the commerce in general of that province, to the Company of Discoveries of the Missouri, and to Don Andrés Todd; and in observance of that which is forewarned to him, he will advise the results as soon as the first year is completed, and he will try to persuade to all the gratitude which they must profess to the Monarch for the particular favors which he pours out in that province.

New Orleans, 31 October, 1796.

Fragata-Mississippi, Captain Juan Luis Maroteau

No. 53. Most Excellent Sir:

Immediately upon receiving the letter which under date of June 11th, last, Your Excellency was pleased to send to this Intendancy, I circulated to the *administración-general de rentas* and other royal offices of this province for their intelligence, observance and fulfillment, the six points and favors which His Majesty with uniform *dictamen* of the *Consejo de*

---

[1]Written in Spanish. A.G.I., P. de C., leg. 584A, and an unsigned copy in A.G.I., P. de C., leg. 2343.

Estado has deigned to accord to his commerce in general, to the Spanish Company of Discoverers to the West of the Mississippi [*sic*], and to the English merchant, Don Andrés Todd, in particular, it remaining for me to inform His Majesty at the end of the first year of the result which the beneficient step of diminishing duties may produce; and to persuade all of the greatness of this and other concessions, and of the innumerable benefices which the sovereign piety of His Majesty has deigned to unite in the treaty of friendship, limits, and navigation in reciprocal utility of his beloved vassals, of the United States, and of the Indian nations allied and affected to the two contracting parties, as Your Excellency informs me by order of His Majesty in the cited letter to which I am answering.

May Our Lord prosper Your Excellency's Important life many years
New Orleans, October 31, 1796.
[draft]
Most Excellent *Señor* Don Diego Gardoqui.

XXXI

MORALES TO CARONDELET, NEW ORLEANS, NOVEMBER 3, 1796[1]

"The meaning which I give to the article of the Royal order of the 11th of June of this year,[2] upon which Dn. Santiago Clamorgan, Director of the Spanish Company of Discoveries to the Westward of the Missouri, bases the demand which Your Excellency has been pleased to inclose in your official letter of the 31st ultimo,[3] is, that the cost of arming and maintaining the one hundred men, whom the Company needs for the forts which it has or may have hereafter, must be on its own account. I am convinced of this not only by the literal interpretation of the said Article: *the permission that the company may arm at its cost and maintain armed,*[4] convinces but also on the one hand, by the circum-

---

[1]Written in Spanish. This translation is from the original in A.G.I., P. de C., leg. 2364; annex no. 2, Carondelet to Prince of Peace, no. 89 *res.* A.H.N., leg. 3900 (Chapter V, document VII); certified copy is annex no. 3., in Morales to Gardoqui, no. 61 (document XXXVII). Same in Carondelet to Clamorgan, New Orleans, November 5, 1796, Missouri Historical Society, Clamorgan Collection, and printed in *American State Papers, Public Lands,* VIII, 236.
[2]See document XVII.
[3]Document XXIX.
[4]A great deal of quibbling between Morales on the one hand and Carondelet and Clamorgan on the other took place over the meaning and interpretation of this phrase which involves the translation of the Spanish adjective "su" which may mean "his", "her" or "its". See Chapter V, document VII. There is a great deal of correspondence concerning this matter in the archives. The end result was that Clamorgan never collected the money. It is my belief that Clamorgan never had the one hundred armed men either. The matter was submitted by Morales (Document XXXVII) to Spain and also by Carondelet (Document XXIX note 3, and especially Chapter V, documents VII and VIII), for His Majesty's decision.

473

stance of the permission to arm having been granted; for, it appears to me that, had the appropriation been intended to be on the King's account, it would have been only necessary to notify that the one hundred men were to be furnished to the Company. On the other hand, I am convinced by the said Royal Order's not mentioning any sum, as it would have been indispensable in order to enable the Royal Treasury to make the disbursement. And finally, I am convinced by His Majesty's not having destined funds for this no small expenditure, which could not be supported by his royal coffers in this province, particularly in their present state of scarcity and embarrassment without being deprived of the means necessary for the subsistence of the troops, the civil officers, the squadron of galleys, the works at Pensacola, and other extraordinary contingencies which occur every day. In consequence of all this, I find myself under the obligation to oppose the delivery of the said sum of ten thousand *pesos,* and to beg of Your Excellency, that, in case my reasons should not appear well founded, to consult His Majesty on this matter, in order that, by his Royal Declaration, I shall be sheltered from the responsibility which would result to me, were I to accede to the demands of Dn. Santiago Clamorgan on the terms he has established."

May God keep Your Excellency many years. New Orleans, November 3, 1796.

Juan Ventura Morales [rubric]

Señor Baron de Carondelet

XXXII

JUSSEAUME TO EVANS, MANDAN VILLAGE, NOVEMBER 5, 1796[1]

Au Coude de Lomme[2] [?] of the Red River   November 5, 1796.

Monsieur:

After my accounts here with *Monsieur* Grand were examined, it was found that I still owe him a great amount. I beg you to have the goodness to deliver to the order of M. Grand all the pelts belonging to me that I have at the Missouri which I count for 50 [pt?] *de robe,* 150 more. If more are found you will deliver them all. If any are missing, you will do me the pleasure to complete the number of them. I will account with you upon my return. I cannot leave until next month when I will have the pleasure of seeing you. I beg you to look after my wife and

---

[1]Written in French. A.G.I., P. de C., leg. 213. This document is very difficult to decipher. For the surrounding facts and circumstances see Nasatir, "Anglo-Spanish Rivalry on the Upper Missouri", *Mississippi Valley Historical Review,* XVI (1930), reprint pp. 32 *et. seq.,* and Nasatir, "John Evans: Explorer and Surveyor," *Missouri Historical Review,* XXV (1931).
[2]At the elbow or bend.

children. I will be very obliged to you. I am not sending you a single pipe of tobacco; I do not have any. I am, *Monsieur*

Your very humble servant,
René Jussomne
[rubric]

My compliments to all the French
To M. Evans
At the Mandan Village
Missouri.

XXXIII

CLAMORGAN TO CARONDELET, [NEW ORLEANS?], NOVEMBER 8, 1796[1]

Very respectable Sir:

In consequence of the honor of your official letter dated the fifth,[2] instant, it appears that the *Seigneur* Intendant refuses the delivery of the 10,000 *piastres* that I solicited for the maintenance of the one hundred men needed by the Company of the Missouri in order to be always ready [*sur pied*] to protect the possessions of His Majesty in the remote places that have been discovered, where the foreigners from Hudson Bay are seeking to spread their commerce in spite of our laws. I am taking the liberty to beg Your Excellency to permit me in the name of the said Company to make from this moment [erased in original] in the dependencies of the Illinois, the levy of the one hundred militiamen that His Majesty grants the said Missouri Company, and to make to it the advance of 10,000 *piastres* that he has solicited for their maintenance until it may please you to obtain from His Majesty an exact order for the annual deliverance of the said sum conjointly with the reimbursement of that from the present year. I am asking this in order not to interrupt the important combination of the expensive operations of the said Company.[3]

I shall not cease in his name as in my own to be penetrated with the sentiments of the most lively gratitude, and with which I have the honor of calling myself, very respectfully,

Very respectable Sir,
Your very obliged and devoted servant,
J. Clamorgan
[rubric]

To His Excellency M. Le Baron de Carondelet
[No place but probably New Orleans.] November 8, 1796

---

[1]Written in French. A.G.I., P. de C., leg. 2364.
[2]Same as document XXXI.
[3]See document XXIX and especially note 3.

XXXIV

Carondelet to Trudeau, New Orleans, November 9, 1796[1]

When I arranged that the Company of Commerce of the Upper Missouri might take their merchandise from the firm of Don Andrés Todd—provided that they might be of equal [like] price and quality as the others—I had in mind the greater advantage for the royal treasury on whose duties the merchants of Upper Louisiana cheat, by taking their merchandise from the English of Michilimackinac as contraband; this practise moreover contributes to the enriching of that foreign establishment. At the same time, I realize that the Company needs the influence of the firm of Don Andrés Todd over the savage Sioux and other nations who are found to the north of the Missouri river in order to obtain free and peaceful passage for its expeditions on the same river. So it was very convenient to the interests of the Company to unite with the interests of the firm of Todd.[2]

I see by the official letter which you sent to me [dated] August 4, last,[3] that this step has displeased many members of the said Company; and I, not wishing that they may take this apparently unjust pretext to attribute their losses to that step, I annul it [that step or permission] immediately, but with the circumstance that you will stop all specie of commerce and trade with the English of Michilimackinac, confiscate all the effects which will be found as contraband, and proceed judicially against their masters, with all the rigor of the laws. You are and will be responsible for the infractions which will result against the royal treasury and [which] might reach my knowledge.

May Our Lord guard your life for many years,

New Orleans, November 9, 1796.

El Baron de Carondelet [rubric]

Señor Don Zenon Trudeau

---

[1]Written in Spanish. A.G.I., P. de C., leg. 23; parts printed in Nasatir, "Anglo-Spanish Frontier on the Upper Mississippi 1786-1796," *Iowa Journal of History and Politics*, XXIX, (1931), 229. This translation differs slightly from that printed text and is more literal. See Nasatir, "Anglo-Spanish Rivalry in Iowa Country 1797-1798," *Ibid.*, XXVIII (1930), 337 *et. seq.* for sequel and consequences to Carondelet's orders given in this letter.

[2]See documents XXII and XXIV.

[3]Document XXI.

476

XXXV

CLAMORGAN TO CARONDELET, NEW ORLEANS, NOVEMBER 12, 1796[1]

Très Respectable Seigneur:

Being informed that someone was soliciting from you the exclusive trade with the Otos and Panis nations[2] for the term of ten [*sic*] years under the condition of the solicitor paying to His Majesty the sum of one thousand *piastres* during the first three years and of constructing in the Otos village a fort armed with four cannons of which he [His Majesty] would dispose at the expiration of the aforementioned privilege, I must in the capacity of Director of the Spanish Company of the Missouri beg you to accept at this moment the essential remarks upon the demands which are being made to you.

Experience has continually shown that the mixture of private foreign interests with those of the Company spread over the routes which lead it [Company] to the Upper Missouri make its communication with the far distant nations thorny and difficult. [Therefore] it is important to expose to you the fact that the sacrifices of this same Company ceaselessly reiterated to make itself useful to important discoveries, permit it [Company] to solicit from your kindness the preference for the Oto and Panis posts, under the same conditions which are proposed to you by persons whose private interests consult only their one ambition. We solicit this favor especially at a time when the Company has already taken measures for the establishment of a fort at the post of the Otos, measures which I have had the honor of communicating to you in one of my last letters where I enumerated to you the forts which we had already built[3] and informed you of the construction of that one of the Oto which we are going [are about?] to undertake to be assured of the passage of our boats destined for the Mandans, and even more important to serve His Majesty's interest in uniting the needs of the different nations depending upon a single object in order to restrain them in their contrarities against us.

Cast down under the weight of a vast and important enterprise, you have not seen anyone seeking from you the desire to ease us and to aid us in the repeated losses which we have experienced at various times; but, on the other hand, if they have overwhelmed your kindness with importunities, it has only been in order to steal from us the small amount of assured trade which we have had reason to expect of which the advantages

---

Written in French. A.G.I., P. de C., leg. 212B.
[2]Pratte had petitioned for the Panis Indian trade. The Kansas and Panis trades were the only ones for which lots were cast among the merchants of St. Louis. Trudeau to Carondelet, no. 272, St. Louis, September 28, 1796, A.G.I., P. de C., leg. 34. See Document XV, note 4.
[3]See documents XXII and XXIV.

for ten years will not fill the void of losses and sacrifices which we have made elsewhere for the good of the state.

Furthermore, the entrance to the Platte river which leads to the west can perhaps become for the Company an indispensable passage when the Mahas and the Poncas will oppose our communication [lines]. This route, although more difficult than that directly by the Missouri, is precious to the Company if ever the Company is obliged to make use of it. That is why, *Monseigneur,* the Company hopes that you will deign to take into consideration the necessity of granting to it the preference of the Otos and Panis and the need of assuring to it [Company] this new district, *porte de communication,* if ever the Company is obliged to make use of it, the Company offering to His Majesty the same advantages which are made to him, if however [unless] His [Majesty's] kindness does not judge it *à propos* to make this remittance to it [Company] for it [advantage].

I have the honor of being very respectfully,

Très Excellent Seigneur
Your very humble and devoted servant.
Jacques Clamorgan [rubric]

New Orleans, 12 November, 1796
His Excellency *Monseigneur* le Baron de Carondelet.[4]

[4]On November 14, 1796 Carondelet wrote Gayoso de Lemos and on November 19, 1796 Carondelet wrote Trudeau (both letters in A.G.I., P. de C., leg. 23) that "Poor Andrés Todd is at present dying which I regret infinitely because of the harm which will result from his death to Upper Louisiana and to the Company of the Missouri". See document XXXVIII.

On November 19, 1796 (A.G.I., P. de C., leg. 24) Carondelet forwarded Clamorgan's memorial with his marginal notations to Trudeau for the latter's opinion on the matter based on impartiality. (Clamorgan's memorials are documents XXII and XXIV.

On November 22, 1796 (A.G.I., P. de C., leg. 23) Carondelet wrote Trudeau confidentially that, since war between England and Spain was certain, he should "immediately work hostilely against the British subjects either on the Missouri or on the Upper Mississippi without any declaration of war and the Company can do the same within the extent of its privilege". See Nasatir, "Anglo-Spanish Rivalry in the Iowa Country 1797-1798," *Iowa Journal of History and Politics,* XXVIII (1930), 337-389.

XXXVI

MCDONNELL TO EVANS, NOVEMBER 23, 1796[1]

Dear Sir

We are obliged to trouble you with another visit though infinitely against our wills in order to fetch the dearly acquired debt of M[r]

[1]Sealed original letter written in English. A.G.I., P. de C., leg. 213; edited and published in Nasatir, "John Evans: Explorer and Surveyor," *Missouri Historical Review,* XXV (1931), 585-586. This is discussed also in Nasatir, "Anglo-Spanish Rivalry on the Upper Missouri," *Mississippi Valley Historical Review,* XVI (1930), reprint pp. 33-35. See also Chapter V, document IV.

Jussaume, Desmairais Interpreter to the NWest Company is the person that has the little goods sent in charge. which I suppose will only be sufficient to purchase two Horses if requisite to transport the above-mentioned Peltries of Jussaumes' to the place. As you know the turbulent spirit of the French Canadians I will tell you that I found it impossible to get any of them to undertake the voyage at this severe season of the year without giving them some articles on credit to be paid in Robes, etc. upon their return but I had represented to them that their property ran risk of confiscation, they replied that they heard that Mr Evans was a *bon garçon* and hoped upon asking leave to trade what little they brought that you would not refuse them as they so little thot it would not injure your interest in the least—

I beg it of you as a particular favor that you would give Desmarais any information or assistance in your power for apprehending Chayé & conveying him back to his duty, as he has three years of his time to serve to the Company yet—

Garreau owes here the price of a horse say 42 king—besides the Horse he decoyed from Mr S. [?] Mackay & a slave girl he owes to my servant man—I hope if in your power you will help Desmarais to receive what he can out of his hands—Please accept as a Small token of my esteem a few trifles I forward you by Desmarais viz: Two European Magazines & a Guthrie's Geographical Grammar for your amusement, a Powder Horn & Shott Bag, 1 Bottle Turlington's Balsam; 1 Ditto Pepper-mint, ½ doz. vomits, ½ doz. Punges, 1 Lanut and the Compass you had the bonté to let Mr. McKay have the loan of. You will please return the Books by any favourable opportunity after perusal as they are not my own—

If the Horses are not two heavy loaded, I would be obliged to you for a little Corn, which is a great luxury with us in this quarter, and I hear is quite plenty your way—A propos I forgot to mention M^r La Grave I must inform you that that Gentleman ran away from me three years ago at the Riviere qui appelle with about 1800# or double money in Dette—a pretty sum you will say

1800#
2
———
3000# [*sic* 3600?]

479

Inclosed I send you Jussaumes will & power[2] to have his Peltries & little slave girl &c delivered to the bearer nothing further from D[t] Sir

Your Hubl Serv[t]
John McDonnell [rubric][2]

P. S. I cannot sufficiently thank you for your goodness in letting one of your own men accompany M[r] McKay in his distress

Yours while,
J M[c] Donnell

Addressed
> Mr. Evans
> Mandan Village
> Missouri

River La Sourie
Nov[r] 23rd 1796

---

[2]See document XXXII.

[3]John Macdonell was for a time leader of the Northwest Company's La Souris fort. Diaries of his are in Gates, *Five Fur Traders* and Masson, *Les Bourgeoisie.* See also Davidson, *Northwest Company*; J. B. Tyrell, *David Thompson's Narrative and His Explorations in Western America* (Toronto, 1916); and Stewart, *Early Assiniboine Trading Posts.*

XXXVII

Morales to Gardoqui, New Orleans, December 1, 1796[1]

[Marginal Notation]

The *ad Interim* [Intendant] of Louisiana, with copies of three documents, gives an account of his having resisted the delivery of ten thousand *pesos* solicited by the Director of the Company of Discoveries of the Missouri, which delivery the Governor approved; and he asks that in case the Royal Treasury must pay them, besides ordering it done, funds be sent with which to do so.

No. 61. Most Excellent Sir:—By the enclosed copy number one,[2] Your Excellency will be advised of the request made to this Government by Don Santiago Clamorgan, Director of the Spanish Company of Discoveries to the West of the Missouri, for the delivery to him of the 10,000 *pesos* which is the amount of the annual pay of the one hundred men which His Majesty permitted the said Company to arm and maintain armed in the forts which it has and may have in the future; and document number

---

[1]Written in Spanish. Original in A.H.N., Est., leg. 3902; certified copy in A.G.I., Sto. Dom., 87-1-23 (old numbering), drafts without enclosures in A.G.I., P. de C., legs. 584A and 2343, copy in Missouri Historical Society.

[2]Document XXIX.

two[3] will likewise advise Your Excellency that the Governor, sending me the petition, directed the delivery of the said sum, giving as a reason that the Company had asked that this expense be borne by His Majesty, and that he had supported it in his representation to the Ministry of State.

Since I had no final determination of this question, and since the terms of article two of the royal order of June eleventh of this year, upon which the demand is based, are, in my opinion, to be understood in the contrary sense, that is, that the cost of the hundred men should be borne by the Company, the reasons of the Baron de Carondelet seemed to me very weak to authorize a disbursement of such importance, and I resisted it in the terms set forth in copy number three.[4]

I do not know, Most Excellent Sir, whether by acting in this way, I have done right or have mistaken the intention of the King; but I do know, that if the said expense of ten thousand *pesos* annually has to be borne by the Treasury, unless His Majesty by a new declaration will indemnify the Intendancy by reason of the scarcity of funds which this royal depository suffers even for more useful objects and of greater urgency, provision will have to be made for the viceroy of New Spain to supply the funds to satisfy it.

I beg Your Excellency to please lay this whole matter before His Majesty, so that he may resolve it according to the Royal pleasure.

May Our Lord prosper the important life of Your Excellency for many years. New Orleans 1 December, 1796.

Most Excellent Sir
Juan Ventura Morales [rubric]

Most Excellent *Señor* Dn. Diego de Gardoqui

---

[3]Document XXIX.
[4]Document XXXI.

XXXVIII

Morales to Gardoqui, New Orleans, December 1, 1796[1]

[Marginal notation]

The *ad-interim* Intendant of Louisiana informs of the death of Don Andrés Todd to whom His Majesty conceded by royal order of June 11 of the present year, the exclusive commerce with the Indian nations to the north of the Ohio and the Missouri, and he adds some matters which

---

[1]Written in Spanish. A.H.N., Est., leg. 3902; draft in A.G.I., Sto. Dom. 87-1-23 (old numbering); draft in A.G.I., P. de C., leg. 2343; index only in A.G.I., P. de C., leg. 584A; parts printed in Nasatir, "Anglo-Spanish Frontier on the Upper Mississippi 1786-1796," *Iowa Journal of History and Politics*, XXIX, (1931), 230-231. Also in Missouri Historical Society, Spanish Archives, no. 99; published in *Missouri Historical Society Collections*, IV, 13-14.

he judges His Excellency may find it useful to be informed of for the arrangement [resolving] of his determination.

Most Excellent Sir:

No. 63. Among the individuals who have recently had the misfortune of being victims of the epidemic which in my letter of October 31, number 47, I informed Your Excellency was afflicting this province and which at this time, thanks to the Omnipotent, seems abated due to the light rain and cold weather which we are experiencing, fate struck Don Andrés Todd,[2] to whom His Majesty by royal order of June 11[3] was pleased to accord the exclusive commerce of the Indian nations established to the north of the Ohio and the Missouri. This young and robust Irishman had descended from Illinois in order to arrange his affairs with his correspondent in this capital, give his orders for the shipment from Europe of the effects necessary for his trade, and return immediately by way of the north; but before he had been in the city fifteen days, the contagion attacked him, and within five days he was buried.

In addition to the disappearance of the favorable results which were the cause for the conceding of the privilege if his heirs or associates do not obtain the same privilege or continue the same plans, his death is a mortal blow to the Spanish Company of the Discoverers to the West of the Missouri. It was Todd who had the majority [greatest number] of the shares and who moreover, because of his extensive views of gathering and assuring to himself all the peltries of those territories, had advanced to the Company to the value of 80,000 *pesos* in effects proper for the trade with the Indians; and should his heirs, creditors, or companions demand payment, undoubtedly the Company will remain without the means for continuing its operations.

I am notifying Your Excellency of this in fulfillment of my duty and in order that you may not lack the complete knowledge of the occurrences in these countries which you should have in order to facilitate the steps which you may judge opportune in fulfillment of the better service of the Sovereign.

May Our Lord prosper Your Excellency's important life many years. New Orleans, December 1, 1796.

Most Excellent Sir,

Juan Ventura Morales [rubric]

Most Excellent *Señor Don* Diego de Gardoqui

---

[2] The yellow fever epidemic struck New Orleans. Todd was stricken with the dreaded disease fifteen days after he arrived in New Orleans; in five days he was dead. Over 800 persons died of the yellow fever within a short time. Gratiot to Charles Buyon, April 18, 1798, Missouri Historical Society, Gratiot Letterbook, pp. 3-9.

[3] Document XVII.

XXXIX

Morales to Gardoqui, New Orleans, December 1, 1796[1]

[Marginal notation]

The *ad-intermin* intendant of Louisiana informs that, following the practice of his predecessors, he remitted to the *Tribunal de Cuentas* of Havana a certified copy of the royal order of June 11th, in which His Majesty was pleased to accord various favors to the Company of Discoverers of the Missouri, to that "commerce" in general, and in particular to the English merchant Don Andrés Todd; and that [when] the said Tribunal having asked him what it presented [in this letter] for his understanding of three articles of the Royal Resolution, he answered that he would not do so without the determination of the King for which he begs, based upon the reasons which he exposes.

Most Excellent Sir:

No. 79. Following the practice which my predecessor observed of remitting to the *Tribunal de Cuentas* of Havana a certified copy of the royal orders which are connected with matters of *cuenta y razon,* I sent to it on September 16th, last, the royal order of June 11th of this year[2] in which His Majesty with uniform *dictamen* of the *Consejo de Estado* was pleased to accord various favors to the Spanish Company of Discoveries to the West of the Missouri, to the commerce of this province in general and to the English merchant, Don Andrés Todd, in particular.

Acknowledging receipt of the previous document, the Tribunal manifests to me on November third, last, that since it was necessary for the due understanding of *capítulos* three, four, and five to have in view advanced by this intendancy to which the royal resolution refers, it was awaiting for a copy of them to be sent to it for the expressed effect.

For three reasons the preceding demand has seemed to me unfounded:

First—because of my believing that the Tribunal only needs what is granted in order to arrange its operations.

Second—because of it appearing to me that no one else must be given knowledge of what was represented to His Majesty secretly [*por la vía reservada*] and,

Third—because of its being clearly and distinctly explained in article three that it was the sovereign will that for the present all the import and export duties be reduced to the six per cent proposed by the government

---

[1]Written in Spanish. A.H.N., Est., leg. 3902; A.G.I., Sto. Dom., 87-1-23 (old numbering—leg. 2614 new numbering); draft and index only in A.G.I., P. de C., leg. 584A.

[2]Document XVII.

and intendancy; in article four that the English merchant Todd had permission from the King to introduce the effects necessary for his particular commerce and to extract the peltries and other products of the country under the same duty of six per cent; and in the fifth [article] that His Majesty made effective the favor of reduction or lowering of the import and export duties from fifteen per cent to the six per cent which the government in agreement with the Intendancy conceded to Todd for one year. Neither can the *informes* which my predecessor gave to His Majesty by way of Your Excellency, give more light than that which the literal explanation of the royal order facilitates in the said articles, nor can the solicitation of the former originate, in my opinion, from any other cause than an effect of pure curiosity.

Believing it thus, perhaps mistakenly, and availing myself of the second reason because I have expressed that the demand of the Tribunal seemed to me unfounded, I answered him under date of the twenty-third of the current month, that he should bring it to His Majesty's notice and that if, in consequence of that, he was pleased to order remitted copies of the representation which he was soliciting, I would have on my part the most exact fulfillment of that which concerns the Intendancy which I shall do if the King, finds the reasons which [I] have exposed, weak and unfounded. I beg Your Excellency to elevate this to His Royal notice for him to determine whether the Tribunal must have the knowledge which I have refused to give it.

May Our Lord prosper Your Excellency's important life many years. New Orleans, December 31, 1796.

Most Excellent Sir

Juan Ventura Morales [rubric]

To: Most Excellent *Señor Don* Diego de Gardoqui.

CHAPTER V

1797

I

Table of Distances Along the Missouri in Ascending
from the Mouth up to the White River,
Taken By James MacKay, 1797[1]

		Distances	
		Total	
		Leagues of 25	Description of
Names of Places	Leagues	to a Degree	Places and Remarks
St. Charles	7 1/2	7 1/2	Village upon the northern bank of the Missouri; containing families; site advantageous for commerce, for hunting, good land in the neighborhood.

---

[1]This document is admirably and scholarly edited with copious notes by the late Annie Heloise Abel in *Mississippi Valley Historical Review*, X (1923), 432-441. See also by same editor "A New Lewis and Clark Map" in *Geographical Review*, I (1916), 329-345. F. J. Teggart maintains that Mackay is the author of Perrin du Lac's map. See "Notes Supplementary to any Edition of Lewis and Clark" in *American Historical Association, Annual Report* 1908, I, 185-195. See also Mackay's "Journal," Collot, *Journey in North America*, and Perrin du Lac, *Voyages dans les Deux Amériques*. There is no doubt but that Mackay was one of the best informed men of the geography of the Upper Missouri. Only Truteau and perhaps some of the *voyageurs* like D'Eglise, Tabeau, or Loisel could dispute with Mackay the title of "best informed" man on the geography of the Upper Missouri. It might be well to compare this document with the *Original Journals of Lewis and Clark*. See also the discussion in the Introduction to A. H. Abel, *Tabeau's Narrative of the Loisel Expedition*, pp. 15-16. Dr. Abel's comparisons with Perrin du Lac and the Indian office map are omitted here.

Names of Places	Leagues	Total Leagues of 25 to a Degree	Description of Places and Remarks
Habitation	2	9 1/2	Two houses upon the northern bank
Good Man's island	3	12 1/2	Large.
American settlement	3	15 1/2	Upon the southern bank; begun this year
Wood river	4	19 1/2	Little river upon the southern bank.
River St. John	2	21 1/2	Small—the same
Shepherd's river	3 2/3	24 1/6	Little river—the same
Otter river	1 2/3	25 5/6	Little river—northern bank.
River Gasconade	4	30 5/6	Upon the south bank—40 fathoms broad; navigable for a considerable distance for pirogues: Good land and hunt abundant upon both banks—takes its source near the river des Argues
Montbrun's Cave	1 2/3	32 1/2	In a chain of hills on the north bank
Muddy river	2 2/3	35 1/6	Small—upon the north bank—
River of the Great Osages	4	39 1/6	Upon the south Bank—a beautiful river, navigable for almost 100 leagues for pirogues—the two villages of the Great and Little Osages are 80 leagues from the mouth: It has its source near the river des Argues
Moreau river	1 1/3	40 1/2	Small; there are some lead mines, but far from the Missouri
Little Manitou river	6 5/6	47 1/3	Small, upon the south bank—on this river and near the Missouri there is a lead mine.
River of the Split Rock	3 5/6	51 1/6	Small, upon the north bank.
Little Salt river	1/3	51 1/2	Id. Upon the south bank.
Big Manitou river	3	54 1/2	Id. Upon the north bank.
Mine river	4 1/3	58 5/6	Upon the southern bank—20 fathoms broad at the mouth—navigable for canoes for a considerable distance. There are mines on this river.

Names of Places	Leagues	Total Leagues of 25 to a Degree	Description of Places and Remarks
First Prairie	3	61 5/6	Small prairie upon the south bank.
Chariton rivers	2 1/6	64	Two rivers which empty into the Missouri at almost the same place on the north bank; the larger (which is) navigable for small boats for a considerable distance, and its waters come from good land and hunting.
Grand River	8	72	Beautiful river upon the north bank, width of 40 fathoms at the mouth. Navigable for pirogues for more than 100 leagues: it has its source in the country to the west of the sources of the river Des Moines which flows into the Mississippi: Good land and all kinds of hunting.
Snake Bluff	1 1/3	73 1/3	A hill upon the northern bank where are found many snakes.
Two old villages of the Little Osages and the Missourias	3 2/3	77	Upon the south bank, on a beautiful and very high plain: these two nations were forced to abandon this place because of constant war between them and the nations of the Mississippi; there are good lands and hunting there.
Flag Pond	6	83	Upon the southern bank.
Saukee Prairie	2	85	Large and high, upon the north bank.
Fire Prairie	5 1/3	90 1/3	High prairie—upon the south bank.
Kansas river	10 5/12	100 3/4	Beautiful river upon the south bank, width of 100 fathoms at the mouth, navigable for canoes for more than 60 leagues at all times; but not for more than 20 leagues for large boats in the autumn when the waters are low; the village of

Names of Places	Leagues	Total Leagues of 25 to a Degree	Description of Places and Remarks
			the Kansas is 80 leagues from this river.
Little Platte river	3 2/3	104 5/12	North—Navigable for canoes for about 25 leagues. Many deer, bears, beaver.
First old village of the Kansas nation	8	112 5/12	South—Situated upon the bare hills
Second old village of the Kansas	7 1/3	119 3/4	Upon the south bank, about a league lower and on the same side of the Missouri is an iron mine.
Prairie St. Michael	4 1/3	124 1/12	Beautiful high prairie on the north bank.
Nodaway river	8	132 1/12	Upon the north bank, about 16 fathoms broad at the mouth, navigable for small canoes for a considerable distance. There are many different kinds of animals in this river.
Wolf river	4 1/2	136 7/12	Small river on the south bank.
River of the Great Nemahas	4	141 1/4	Upon the south bank—width about 15 fathoms at the mouth, navigable some leagues for pirogues. It is upon this river that boats pass that carry on commerce with the nation of Republican Pawnee whose village is upon a branch of the Kansas river.
Nishnabotna river	6 1/3	147 7/12	Small, but deep, upon the north bank, navigable for canoes a considerable distance.
River of the Little Nemahas	2 5/6	150 5/12	Small river, on the south side.
Bald island	5 1/2	155 11/12	Point cut off on the south bank.
Weeping Water	9 1/3	165 1/4	Small river on the south side. From there there is a path which goes to a village of the Oto upon the River Platte.

Names of Places	Leagues	Total Leagues of 25 to a Degree	Description of Places and Remarks
Oeil de fer	3	168 1/4	Large hill upon the southern bank.
Post of the Oto	1	169 1/4	First building, or fort, belonging to the Company of the upper Missouri, upon the south bank.
River Platte	2	171 1/4	Upon the south bank—as large as the Missouri but so shallow and the course so rapid that navigation is very difficult for every kind of boat, excepting in the spring when the waters are high; then one can descend with large long-boats. It takes its waters near to the forks of the Santa Fe River.
Old village of the Iowa and Oto	7	178 1/4	Situated upon the southern bank on a high plain.
Boyer river	6	184 1/4	Small river on the north bank in which there are many beaver and other animals.
Iowa Bluff	3	187 1/4	About 40 feet high, south bank—
Soldier's river	11 1/2	198 3/4	Small, north bank, an island at the mouth.
First river of the Sioux	14 2/3	214 5/12	Upon the north bank, width about 15 fathoms at the mouth. Navigable some leagues for canoes: Takes its source near the forks of the river Des Moines.
Cedar Bluff	13 1/6	226 7/12	On the south bank.
Washcanda Nipishi	3 1/6	229 3/4	Idem.
The Two rivers	1 5/6	231 7/12	Idem, two small rivers which unite near to their mouth in the Missouri.
Yellow Bluff	7 5/6	239 5/12	On the south bank.
River & village of the Omaha	6	245 5/12	On the south bank—The village is situated in a beautiful Prairie near to the foot of the hills a league from the Missouri. There is a small river which flows near to the village.

489

Names of Places	Leagues	Total Leagues of 25 to a Degree		Description of Places and Remarks
Second River of the Sioux	6 5/12	251	5/6	North bank — Navigable some leagues for canoes.
Old Village of Petit Arc	7 1/3	278	7/12	South bank. Built by an Omaha chief, named Petit-arc.
James river	5 1/12	283	2/3	North bank. Navigable for canoes for a considerable distance.
Goodman's Island	6 3/4	290	5/12	Large island
Plum river	3	293	5/12	Small river, north bank.
Rapid river	3 2/3	297	1/12	Upon the south bank, width 70 fathoms at the mouth, very rapid and so shallow that a canoe can not navigate it. It takes its waters near to the forks of the White river, at the old village of the Padouca nation.
River & village of the Ponca	5/6	297	11/12	Upon the south bank, at a league and a half from the Missouri. There is a large island in front of the village.
Post of the Ponca nation	6 2/3	304	7/12	North bank. Third building belonging to the company.
Basque Island	2 1/3	306	11/12	
Cedar island	6 1/2	313	5/12	
Buffalo island	7 7/12	321		Upon the south bank.
Vieux	5 1/3	326	1/3	Large river, shallow and rapid, on
White river	1 2/3	328		the south bank. It takes its waters in the country far away to the southwest.

II

Captain McKay's Journal[1]

The Grand Portage situated on the north side of Lake Superior at 60 Leagues of the West Extremity of said Lake, and about 500 Leagues North West of the Town of Montreal, is the General *Rendevous* of his Britannic Majesties Subjects who carry on the Canada furr Trade with

---

[1]Extracts from Captain Mackay's Journal, edited by M. M. Quaife and printed in *Proceedings* of the Wisconsin State Historical Society, 1915, LXIII, pp. 190-195. Also in *Medical Repository*, Second Hexade, III, 27-36.

The events alluded to in this and Evans' "Journal" chiefly relate to 1795-1796. They are inserted here in the midst of documents relating to Mackay and Evans

the Interior Parts of Western America. It is there where the Merchants of Montreal assemble every spring to receive the furrs that are brought there, and deliver in turn the Goods necessary for the Indian Trade. It is with these merchandizes that the Traders get into the interior parts of the Country in Bark Canoes (birch) carrying about 2500 lb, with which they cross over many lakes, and Rivers that they have to ascend and descend, and when obstacles arise in their navigation they carry by land over their Shoulders, their Canoes, Goods Provisions &c that they contain, till they come to some lake or River nearest to their Route, of which is generally directed to the West.

The principal Lakes through which those Traders pass are Lakes Lapluie (or Rain[y] Lake) the Lake of the Woods (or lac du Bois) the Great Lake Ouinipique (Winnipeg), the latter is the most Westerly of the three and at the same time the most Considerable it extends in length from the 50th Deg: to the 56th Deg: Latitude north and in breadth from 104th deg: to 105th deg: 30 m. longitude West.

The Route from the Grand Portage to the Lake Ouinipique has near 250 leagues Contains 72 carrying places of which some are near a league in length and some not more than 60 feet.

The Greatest part of all that Country, from the Grand portage to the Lake Ouinipique is Barren, covered with Mountains & Rocks; it is inhabited by a savage nation, which they name Saulteuxs or Bungees, they have no fixed habitation, but they rove from place to place in search of a very precarious subsistance, which they procure by hunting and fishing, this hunt is one of their greatest occupations for the greatest part of the Year, excepting Summer, a season which they Consecrate to War, which they generally make with the Sioux nation which inhabit the upper Branches of the Mississippi. Many considerable Rivers empty themselves in the lake Ouinipique particularly those that Come from the West and take their Sources near the Rocky Mountains, Chain of Mountains that separate the Waters that fall in the Atlantic ocean from those that lose themselves in the *Pacific—*

One of the largest of those Rivers, is that which is called the River Assiniboine it take its source from the Rocky Montains where it Runs due East through immense plains and meadows, beautiful and fertile and

---

(Chapters IV and V). Mr. Hay's notes included in the Quaife edition are not included here. For a discussion of Mackay and Evans see Nasatir, "Anglo-Spanish Rivalry on the Upper Missouri," *Mississippi Valley Historical Review,* XVI (1930), 507-530, reprint, pp. 25-39; and Nasatir, "John Evans: Explorer and Surveyor," *Missouri Historical Review,* XXV, (1931) 219-239 [narrative account]; 432-460; and 585-607 (documents), a good many of which are here reproduced in Chapters IV and V.

Comes and Empties itself in Lake Ouinipique by the South West Corner of said Lake about 200 from the Mouth of the River Assiniboine, in going up to its Source and on one of its branches called River Catapoi, on the South West, we there find the furthermost wintering post of the English Traders from Canada. It is from this Post that the English Traders start to go and make their unlawful Trade on the Missouri with the Mandaines and other nations that inhabit the Territory of his Catholic Majesty.

The distance from this English Post to the Part of the Missouri on which the Mandaine Nation reside exceeds not 80 leagues, the Route going generally to the South, the greatest part of the Route is through plains and marshes of a Considerable extent, separated here and there by vallies and Runs bordered by Poplars of an inferior Quality. As there is no known Communication by Water from the Assiniboine (in the North) and the Missouri, the English Traders, during summer transport their Merchandizes and Peltries, on horses or mules, which they Buy or hire of the natives of the Country and in Winter they more often use Sledges drawn by one, two or more Dogs.

The Country situated between the North and upper Missouri is inhabited by a Savage nation that they call Assiniboines, those Indians generally keep or have their residence near Turtle Mountain which is formed by the heights of the land that separate the Waters of the Missouri with those of the River Assiniboine in the north. In the Beginning of the Year 1787[2] I made a Voyage in the River Catapoi in the North, to the Mandaines on the Upper Missouri, it took me Seventeen days to get there, but I believe in the Summer it might be done in ten days. On my arrival at the Mandaines, they received me with all the Affability possible, many of their Chiefs Came to Meet me, at some distance from their village, and would not permit me to enter their Village on foot, they carried me between four men in a Buffaloe Robe, to the Chiefs tents, When in a little time they prepared a feast for me and my men—I had brought with me some few Merchandizes to which they appeared to set a great value on, as they offered me in Exchange the best of what they had in Possession—I saw Some Guns and Ball in their Possession, which as they said, they had traded with other nations who according to their Report, had traded them from White People—I remained ten days with them, and when I satt off, they appeared to regret very much that I should leave them So soon. The Mandaines, jointly with the Manitouris [Minitaree] and Wattasoons live in five Villages, which are almost in sight of one another, three of those Villages are on the South of the Missouri and two on the North Side. The Situation of those five Villages is

---

[2]Mackay's voyages in 1784, 1786, 1787 and 1788 are delineated in a Spanish "plat" attached to Clamorgan's Instructions to Truteau, Chapter II, document XVIII.

charming they are built on an Elevated plaine, even and fertile, which extends on either Side to a considerable distance. Those Nations cultivate the Ground round about their Villages and sow Corn Beans, Pumpkins and Gourds; they also make earthen pots in which they Boil their Meats, these Pots resist to fire as well as if they were iron. The Mandaines, as well as all other Nations that inhabit to their West, near the Rocky Mountains, are in general people as good as they are mild who lay a great value on the friendship of the Whites. I perceived in my different voyages amongst these people that their Manners were more or less corrupted by reason of their more less Communication they had with the Whites, whilst to the Contrary those who had had but little or no Communication with them, are absolutely yet in a State of Nature and remain in their primitive Simplicity not being hardly able to distinguish good from Evil.

In the Course of the Year /93 & /94 the English Traders sent from their Post they have on the River Assiniboine, several of their hireling to the Mandaine Nation on the Missouri, but as these persons were sent by different Employers or Traders, and that in Consequence they found themselves on an opposition the one with the other, they paid Double the Value for their peltries they exchanged, which made the Indians think immediately, that Goods were not of that value which they had at first imagined; the immoderate desire that those unfit traders showed, to procure themselves pelteteries; convinced the Indians that it was not necessary to show so much friendship to the whites to entice them to return to them with goods, seeing that the only object that brought them was to procure pelteteries—

In 1795 authorized by Mr. Zenon Trudeau Lieut. Govr. of the Illinois by the River Missouri by the Mississippi. The object of this Voyage[9] was to open a commerce with those distant and Unknown Nations in the upper parts of the Missouri and to discover all the unknown parts of his Catholic Majesty's Dominions through that continent as far as the Pacific Ocean—I remained in the Missouri until the Year 1797 without any possibility of fulfilling this Object, the want of help and many other unexpected circumstances hindered me, nevertheless I explored the Country as far as the Mandaine Village about 5 or 6 hundred leagues above the Entrance of the Missoury by 47.48 latitude and about 111 deg: West longitude—After what I had seen and observed during my residence on the Missouri, I think, if the Mandaine nation and those nations around them were regularly furnished with merchandizes, in a sufficient Quantity for their Wants, as well as a Number of Men under the conduct of persons of as much Prudence as Experience, it would be the true Means of

---

[9]Mackay's "Journal" is Chapter III, document XX.

putting a Stop to the unjust progress of the English on that side of his Catholic Majesty's Dominions: but to have this operation on a Solid Basis, great Expenses must be made, for which funds would be required far more considerable than is generally possessed by the Majority of the Merchants of this Country, for the following reasons—Merchandizes are at an exorbitant price in the Illinois, Mens Wages and other Expences are too great, besides, there are several Nations from the Entrance of the Missouri to its upper parts, to whom Merchandizes must be furnished, not only for the Trade, but even for a Tributary present, without which they would never permit Traders to pass further up. These Nations would consume a great quantity of Goods, for which very uncertain Returns must be expected for the first Years at least until permanent posts or Forts were established at each of those Nations as far as the great fall, which falls from the Rocky Mountains and which from all the Information I could procure, I suppose to be about 200 leagues West above the Mandaines that is following the Meanders of the River, making near about 800 leagues from the Entrance of the Missouri.

The Indian Nations that reside as well on the Borders of the Missouri as in the Environs of this River are the *Attotactoes* or *Ottoes*, the *Mahas, the Poncas,* Siouxs of the *Grand Detour* or *Great Bend,* Sious of the Plains, Shivitauns and Corbeaus (crows), there are other nations who reside at the foot of the Rocky Mountains, of whom I could not procure any information, Many of these Nations cultivate the Earth and Sow Corn, Beans, Pumpkins and Gourds, I had brought with me from the Illinois several kinds of seed, such as Water and Musk Melon and of other Vegetables, I sowed them and they succeeded very well. I made a present of those Seeds to the Indians who also succeeded and reaped a harvest of them as in the Illinois and they preserve the seed with great care. The Earth on the Borders of the Missoury is in most parts a Rich and fertile Soil, capable of producing fruits and Vegetables as good as those that grow in any Country of the same temperature—These Countries are in general very healthy, in Consequence of which the Indians are not subject but to very few Diseases, and those generally the fruits of their intemperance, amongst those they reckon dysenteries and the Venereal, but of all those Scourges and Plagues, the most Terrible is the Small Pox, truly they are attacked of it but very rarely, but when it does visit them, it Strikes them with a Mortality as frightful as Universal.

Mr. Evans ascended the Missouri as high as the White River about 80 leagues above the Mahas their having been met by a Nation called *Sious of the Grand Detour,* who generally pass the Spring and Autumn on the borders of the White River, was obliged to Return to the Maha Post. Those Indians having discovered Mr. Evans near their Camp they pursued him near 4 leagues descending the River and Would have probably stopt him if the Weather and the Approach of the night had not favoured his Retreat. This Nation of Sious had never been as yet favorable to the Whites and although I had sent them a Parole the preceding winter, they refused to come and see me. As Soon as Mr. Evans had returned from this fruitless Expedition, I sent to those *Sious* Another Parole, accompanied with presents of Tobacco and Cloth, and I prevailed on some of the principal Chiefs, among them, to come and see me at the Maha Village, so that they might hear the Parole of their Great Father the Spaniard, that was sent them by the Commandant of the Illinois. One month had elapsed when four of the principal Chiefs of the said *sious* came to see me at the Maha Village, bringing Answers to my parole—I had a long Conference with them and gave them such Presents as I thought would be most acceptable to them, but as all negotiations of this kind that is entered upon with Indians are generally not only tiresome in their details, but even rarely can they be brought to a positive conclusion, without losing much time; I shall only say that this Conference served to open a communication more for the future—Nevertheless as those Chiefs appeared well satisfied when they left me I thought I could hazard a second trial for penetrating in the West, in consequence I prepared for a second Expedition, the command of which I again trusted to Mr. Evans.

In the Course of 1796 I sent an Expedition from the Maha Post under the command of Mr. John Evans a young man of an Upright Character on whose Perserverance and Ability I could entirely rely; the Instructions[4] that I gave him were to penetrate to the Western or Pacific Ocean by the Missouri or by any of its Branches, if he found any coming from the West. &c—I will here add what was most Essential in Mr. Evans Journal, so as to give an Idea of the Result of his Expedition.

EXTRACTS OF MR. EVANS JOURNAL[5]

8th June 1796 After having received from Mr. James McKay Agent of the Missouri Company the necessary Instructions, as well as men, Provisions and Merchandizes, I sat off from the Missouri Company's Establishment at the Maha Village, to ascend the Missouri as far as the Pacific Ocean—After a long and fatiguing voyage I arrived the 8th of August following at the Village of the *Rik,ka,ras* on the South Side of the Missouri, 250 leagues above the Mahas, I here met with some difficulties to get along, the *Rik,karas* would not permit me to pass their Village and

---

[4]Chapter III, document IV.
[5]Edited by M. M. Quaife and printed in *Proceedings* of the Wisconsin State Historical Society, 1915, LXIII, 195-200. See the accounts by A. P. Nasatir cited in note 1. See also Chapter IV, document XXVI.

carry my Goods to those nations that reside above them, they said, they were themselves in want of Goods &c. finding then that all my Efforts were in vain, to get on, I was obliged to stay among them. Some Weeks after my arrival, several Indians of different nations particularly the *Caneenawees* and *Shayenns* habitants of the Rocky Mountains, came to the village to see me their Chief in a very long and prolix discourse expressed to me the joy they felt to see the Whites, they assured me of their Love and Attachment for their Great father the Spaniard and for all his children who Came in their Country. Judging it necessary for the better insuring the success of my enterprise to take Possession of the fort built at the Mandaine Village by the English Traders of Canada, I succeeded in persuading the *Rikaras* to let me go so far as there with a few Goods. The 23 Sept. I arrived at the Mandaine Village which is situated about 10 leagues above the *Rikara* on the Same Side (south) of the Missouri, there I was visited by the *Munitarees* and *Wattassoons* whose villages are only a league above those of the Mandaines, those nations as well as the Mandaines received me very cordially. I gave their Chiefs in the name of their Great Father the Spaniard, who inhabits the other Side of the great lake and in the name of the Great Chief who inhabits this Side of the great Lake and also in the name of the Chief who resides at the Entrance of the Missouri, the Flags and Medals that were given me for that purpose by Mr. McKay. Besides those medals & flags I made some small presents, which were received with the greatest of Satisfaction, and testified their acknowledgment in the most expressive manner, promising to observe the most sincere attachment to their great father the Spaniard and his Chiefs, who have Sent to them from so far, their children the Whites with such great marks of their Esteem and of their Charity for the Red People; they added that they would hear what I had to say and had sent to all their Brothers, and hereafter they would follow my Counsels on all occasions—The 28th September in Conformity to the orders I had, I took possession of the English forts belonging to the Canada Traders, and I instantly hoisted the Spanish flag which seemed very much to please the Indians—

The 8.th of October arrived Several men at the Mandaine Village belonging to the Canada Traders that I have above mentioned, they had brought some Goods with them, not having a Sufficiency of men I did not strive to oppose their arrival, nor of their goods: I nevertheless found a means to hinder their Trade and some days after absolutely forced them to leave the Mandane Territory, I sent by them in the North the Declaration that I had received of Mr. McKay: forbidding all strangers whatever to enter on any part of his Catholic Majesty's Dominions in this Quarter under any pretext whatever—The 13th March 1797 Arrived at the Mandaine Village from the North, a man named *Jusson* accompanied by several

Engagees he was sent by the English traders, with Merchandizes as presents for the Mandaines and neighboring nations, so as to be able to break off the Attachment & fidelity they had promised to his Majesty and his Subjects, the said *Jussom* and those who Accompanied him advised the Indians to enter into my house under the Mask of Friendship, then to kill me and my men and pillage my property; several of the Good Chiefs who were my friends & to whom *Jussom* had offered presents; refused them with indignation and shuddered at the thought of such a horrid Design and came and informed me of the Whole. Nevertheless the presents that *Jussom* had made to the Indians had tempted some of the inferior class, who joined him to execute his abominable Design, happily for me his presents had not the same Effect with some of the Principal chiefs, to undertake Such an enormous crime, therefore many of those chiefs Came to my house to guard me and were resolved to die in the attack if any should be made; this Resolution disconcerted entirely my enemies and totally put an End to their infamous Design. Some days after *Jussom* came to my house with a number of his Men, and seizing the moment that my Back was turned to him, tried to discharge a Pistol at my head loaded with Deer Shot but my Interpreter having perceived his design hindered the Execution—The Indians immediately dragged him out of my house and would have killed him, had not I prevented them—this man having refused me Satisfaction for all the Insults he had given me, Moreover disgusted on the ill success of the Execution of his Black Designs, left the Mandanes with his men some days after and returned to his people in the north and bring them the News of his Ill success—I found out by all I could learn that the Intentions of the British Traders were Not to spare trouble or Expence to maintain a Fort at the Mandaine Village Not that they see the least appearance of a Benefit with the Mandanes but carry their views further, they wish to open a trade by the Missouri with Nations who inhabit the Rocky Mountains, a Trade, that at this Moment is Supposed to be the best on the Continent of America.—The general Course of the Missouri from the Maha Nation to the Mandaines is near about North West, it runs for the greatest part of this space, on a Rocky Bottom & Gravel, it is Shut up like in Each side by a chain of Rocky Mountains and of Sand, which in some places coming so near to one another reduces the Breadth of the River to about 500 toises. The Land on both sides of the River is at one time Mountainous & barren and at other times even & fertile, but in the Back part a tree can hardly be found. The best Quality of Land is found in the Mandaine Country, this quality of Land Extends itself on the West as far as the East chain of the Rocky Mountains which are about 170 league to the West of the Mandaines, it is at these Mountains where the great Meadows and Prairies terminate the Country then begins to be Absolutely Covered with trees, even upon the Rocky Mountains and it is probable these woods extend to the Pacific Ocean—The Country from the Mandaines to the Rocky Mountains is well watered by different Rivers that empty themselves in the Missouri, particularly from the South West, many of these Rivers are navigable for Boats of one or two tons burthen, The largest of these Rivers is the Rivière Blanche (White River) Whose mouth is About 80 leagues above the Mahas the River *Shayenn* 70 leagues higher— The River LaBombe about 65 leagues higher and the Yellow Stone River, (Rivière des Roches Jaunes) about 120 leagues further and about 80 leagues above the Mandaines, all these Rivers Come from S. W. of Missouri and there is also a River that comes from the N. W. and which joins the Missouri near the mouth of the Yellow Stone River, they call it Riviere dufoin (hay river) they say it is a large and fine River in which there is More Beaver and Otters than in any other part of the Continent.

Mr. Evans measured the Missouri near the Village of the Mandaines And he found it 500 toises large, which confirms me in my Opinion that the Sources of the Missouri is much further off than what it is imagined, although the Indians who inhabit at the foot of the Rocky Mountains have but a Confused Idea of the upper parts of the Missouri; Nevertheless after all the Information I could collect, it appears that the Missouri takes it source in abt. the 40th deg. North latitude from Whence it Runs to the North (between the chains of the Rocky Mountains) as far as the 49th deg. Latitude that thence running East, it falls over the East chain of the Mountains in the great plains across which it runs to the East till it reaches the Maindaines—There is no other fall, in the whole Course of the Missouri, but where it falls over the Rocky Mountains, in the plains, as I have said before. This fall it is Said, is of an astonishing height, from the Situation of the Country and the Meanders of the River I suppose this fall to be 200 leagues West of the Mandaines. Among the innumerable Numbers of different animals found on the Rocky Mountains, there is one that is really an Object of curiosity, it is near about the height of an Elk, its hair is like to that of a fallow Deer or Buck, it carries its horn like those of a Ram, but turned in a spiral form like a trumpet and of an immense size, some have been found of 8 inches Diameter in their thickest part. This Animal lives but about 10 or 12 years, by reason of their horns, that advance foremost, as to hinder the Animal from eating Grass, which is its only food, so that he becomes obliged to die for hunger; The Indians make spoons, cups &c of the horns, some of the latter are so large as to contain a Sufficiency to satisfy the Appetite of 4 men at a meal—There are also found on the Rocky Mountains, Ermines, and a kind of Wild Cat, whose skin is of a great Beauty, it is spotted as that of a Leopard; it is probable there are in those unknown Regions many other kinds of Animals which are not found in the other different parts of America. As to the manners and Customs of the Indians I found they differ but little one from the other, In the different parts of the Continent across which I voyaged, all that I could remark was, that the nations who had but an imperfect knowledge of the Whites (being yet in a State of Nature) were of a softer and better Character. Whilst those who have frequent Communications with the Whites appeared to have contracted their vices Without having taken any of their virtues.

III

CLAMORGAN TO ———————[1]

Very excellent Sir

In consequence of the power to raise the royal flag over the forts and on its embarcations,[2] granted to the Missouri Company by His Majesty, His [Your] Excellency is begged to have some of these flags delivered to the director of said Company so that he may put his intentions into execution and thus render the places that it [the Company] oversees more respectable to its neighbors [?]

I have the honor of being respectfully,
        Very excellent Sir,
                Your very obliged and very devoted servant
                        Clamorgan [?]

[1]Written in French. A.G.I., P. de C., leg. 201. This is undated.
[2]See Chapter IV, documents X, XII, XXIV, etc. On January 10, 1797 Carondelet wrote to Bernardo Fernández (draft in A.G.I., P. de C., leg. 124) that the English were ambitious to extend their trade and "are already attempting to introduce themselves into the *Provincias Internas* by way of the Missouri river, on which and its environs they have built a fort." He was without answer as to how to guard the expanded frontier (due to Pinckney's treaty) of over 800 leagues, and asked Fernández if he had any suggestions as to how to stop the evil among the nations.

IV

SUTHERLAND TO EVANS, JANUARY 21, 1797[1]

Brandon House, 21st Jany 1797

Dear Sir

By the arrival of M^r De Murier[2] and men the 16th Ins^t from your place, I was favoured with yours of the 20th of Dec. b^r last,[3] and although

[1]Original sealed letter written in English in A.G.I., P. de C., leg. 213; edited and published in Nasatir, "John Evans: Explorer and Surveyor" in *Missouri Historical Review*, XXV (1931) 587-588.
[2]Desmarais. See Chapter IV, document XXXV. On him see E!!iott Coues [ed.], *New Light on the Early History of the Greater Northwest* (New York, 1897) vol. I; Gates, *Five Fur Traders;* Masson, *Les Bourgeois;* Davidson, *Northwest Company,* etc.
[3]In Chapter IV, document XXVI.

personaly unknown to me, as a Country man I was pleased to hear of your wellfare.

It is not my business to enquire into the causes of your exposing yourself to such dangers and difficulties which from hearsay attends your situateion [?], it is sufficient for me to suppose that your future views doubtless are adequate to your present hardships.

The Canadians,[4] having lost their Horses the first or 2d night from the Missourie obliged them to leave their property behind, which they now return for, two of my men out of curiosity accompanys them to see the Mandan Villages and to try if they can purchase a Slave girl, they bring with them no goods of any consequence—I send by them 6 lbs. of Flour, two cakes of chocolate, and a little sugar as a small present, supposing you to be none [run?] out of such articles I am only sorry I have not any thing more worthy of your acceptance as my stock is near out, but hope you will take the will for the deed—all the news from this quarter you can hear from our men, a little from you would be very acceptable such as when you expect the gentlemen from below to your post, what your future Intentions are with regards to exploring further up the River &, if your agent general be the same M*r* James Makay who was formerly a trader here in Red River. These perhaps you will say are tedious enquiries, but I suppose a gentleman of your abilitys can have no objection to any communication which does not immediately concern the Companys affairs in so remote a country I remain with Respect

> Dear Sir
>
> Your Obedient H*ble* Servant[5]
>
> James Sutherland [rubric]

Addressed

> Mr J Evans
> Trader at Fort Makay[6]

---

[4]Traders of the Northwest company. Their horses fell into the hands of the Pawnees, see document VI.

[5]John Sutherland was in charge for a while of the Hudson's Bay Company post at the Elbow of the Assiniboine river. See Gates, *Five Fur Traders,* especially the diaries of John MacDonnell and McLeod; Davidson, *Northwest Company;* Masson, *Les Bourqeois;* G. Bryce, *Remarkable History of the Hudson Bay Company;* Stewart, *Early Assiniboine Trading Posts,* etc. Document V is also written by Sutherland.

[6]Fort Mackay was the name sometimes applied to the fort which Evans constructed among the Mandans.

V

Brandon House 26th Feby 1797

Dear Sir

I was favoured with yours, of the 6th Inst., by the arrival of my two men last night,[2] and cannot omit returning you my thanks for your kindness to them during their stay with you. I have also received the Indian kettle and what you call Cannon ball, which shall be deposited among the archives of my kingdom, with a medal pendant, declaring from whence & from whom they came—The Canadians[3] are again on another visit to your place, by whom I send this, and by whos return I shall be happy to hear of your wellfare. I hear you have complaints against some of them and possibe'ly not without reason, and I could say more on that hand, had I the pleasure of seeing you, there is no harm however on your being on your guard against designing people; a word is enough to the wise————You d need be under no apprehension of any more of our men visiting the Missourie, the exclusive trade to which being now in the hands of a foreign nation, nor are we permitted to act on [our] own account without the direct orders of our Company, who never as yet has been known to violate any law either foreign or domestic—I am obliged to you for the little information you have given me, your correspondence would be highly acceptable. I was far from meaning to dive or enquire into your affairs any further than you was pleased to intimate only such a sensible man in such a remote quarter of the world is a rare thing and your letters will appear with pleasure before our Governor and Council, as I shall leave this place about the 10th or 12th of May to proceed for Ernest House, near Albany Fort where we receive our supplies, I should be extremely happy to have the pleasure of seeing you in this or any other country, wher[e] perhaps something better than we can command at present would cheer our Souls and make us forgit our past cares, and each relate the adventure of the wandering Sailor (or rather Soldier) for as well as you I have been appointed by providence to

---

[1]Sealed original letter written in English in A.G.I., P. de C., leg. 213. Printed and edited in Nasatir, "John Evans: Explorer and Surveyor" in *Missouri Historical Review*, XXV (1931), 588-589. A long quotation from this letter is printed in Nasatir, "Anglo-Spanish Rivalry on the Upper Missouri," *Mississippi Valley Historical Review*, XVI (1930), reprint pp. 35-36, where it is discussed.

[2]Sletter and Yorston. See entry in Brandon House Journal for February 25, 1797—Chapter IV, document XXVI. Evans' letter was not transcribed in the extracts from the Brandon House Journal which the Hudson's Bay Company was so kind as to send to me in 1930.

[3]Nor'westers. See document VI.

traverse the wild regions of America for several years past—I shall only
add my wishes for your prosperity and remain

Dear Sir
Your Ob^t H^{ble} Servant
J Sutherland
[Rubric]

Addressed
    J T Evans
    Trader at the Missourie

VI

McDonnell to Evans, February 26, 1797[1]

River La Souris Feby
26th 1797

Dear Sir

I recd. your very acceptable favor by the two English Lads yesterday,[2] & note the contents—As you mention that the men inform'd you of the cause of my not writing you I shall be silent on that head—I'm soray [sic] to find that the Horses are fallen in the hands of the Panees—they could not have gone to a worse place—as for ye Books be so kind as to deliver them to Jussoume.[3]

As you speak much of La France[4] in your letter I have ventured to send him with Jussome, he could not be in better company, as you seem to be as inveterated against the one as the other; they have an opportunity of vindicating themselves from your aspersions in your own presence—Let

---

[1]Sealed original letter written in English in A.G.I., P. de C., leg. 213; edited and published in Nasatir, "John Evans: Explorer and Surveyor" in *Missouri Historical Review,* XXV (1931), 590-591; a long extract is printed also in Nasatir, "Anglo-Spanish Rivalry on the Upper Missouri," *Mississippi Valley Historical Review,* XVI (1930), reprint p. 36, where it is discussed.

[2]In Sutherland's employ—see document V.

[3]Rene Jusseaumé was an interpreter to Thompson and Lewis and Clark. There are numerous references to his career: Davidson, *Northwest Company,* 47, 93; L. J. Burpee, *Search for the Western Sea* (London, 1908 [New edition, two volumes]), 353-358; Thwaites, *Original Journals of Lewis and Clark;* a letter of his to President Jefferson is printed in *Missouri Historical Society Collections,* IV, 234-236; several references to Jusseaume are contained in documents in Chapters III. IV and V. See Nasatir, "Anglo-Spanish Rivalry on the Upper Missouri"; Tyrell, *David Thompson's Narrative:* Nasatir, "Spanish Exploration of the Upper Missouri"; and Nasatir, "Jacques D'Eglise on the Upper Missouri," *Mississippi Valley Historical Review,* XIV (1927), 47-71; Coues, *New Light,* etc. etc.

[4]Jean Baptiste La France accompanied Jusseaume to the Mandans in 1793-1794 and again as indicated in the text in 1797. On La France see Masson, *Les Bourgeois;* Gates. *Five Fur Traders:* Coues. *New Light,* I, 301, 302, 329, 332, 345; Thwaites, *Original Journals of Lewis and Clark;* Nasatir, "Anglo-Spanish Rivalry on the Upper Missouri."

their conduct be what it will you would expose yourself in acting agreeable to your letter—British subjects are not to be tried by Spanish laws, nor do I look upon you as an officer commissioned to apprehend oth[er] people's servants, if you serve a chartered Comy. why not show the Spanish Governors Orders, declarations, denounciations or manifestoes, prohibiting others from frequenting that country—Then shall we leave you in peace— Be at bottom of it who will most certain I am [of the belief] that there is most complicated vilainy carried on this year at the Missouri in many respects witness the debauching of Chaye last fall, and the offering 200 dollars to the English men arrived yesterday—If we were nearer neighbours than we are we could easily come to an explanation.

It must give any sensible person no grand idea of your Missouri Company making use of such *Canaille* as I have reason to think many of your *Engagees* are by judging of the remainder by La Grave[5] Garreau[6] Chayé &c Such as are not run aways from here[7] are Deserters from La prairie du Chien & other places in the Mississippi La France goes with Jussaume to help the latter in bringing his family [I am]—Dr Sir Your very Humble Servt

John McDonnell [rubric]   Addressed to Mr. J. T. Evans Missourie

---

[5]La Grave was with Jusseaume on the latter's trip to the Mandans in 1793-1794, Masson, *Les Bourgeois*, I, 286 and compare *Ibid.*, I, 294.
[6]There are many references to Garreau. See Nasatir, "Anglo-Spanish Rivalry on the Upper Missouri"; Truteau's "Journal" in Chapter II of this volume; Thwaites, *Original Journals*, I, 272-274, and V, 355. A sketch of Garreau is given in S. M. Drumm [ed.] *Journal of a Fur Trading Expedition on the Upper Missouri* 1812-1813, by John C. Luttig (St. Louis, 1920), 64; Houck, *Spanish Régime in Missouri*, II, 356 ff. See also Abel, *Tabeau's Narrative;* and Masson, *Les Bourgeois*.
[7]See *e.g.* Chapter III, document XII.

VII

CARONDELET TO PRINCE OF PEACE, NEW ORLEANS, MARCH 20, 1797[1]

No. 89 *Reservada*

The Baron of Carondelet says that the Director of the Spanish Company of Discoveries of the Missouri has demanded that, through the Royal Treasury, he be given the 10,000 *pesos* annually which he solicited for the daily pay of the one hundred men that he must have armed in his forts in conformity with Article 2 of the Royal Decree of the 11th of June, 1796,[2] which approves the aforementioned Company. The *ad interim* Intendant has absolutely refused [payment of this sum] until

---

[1]Written in Spanish. A.H.N., Est., leg. 3900; index and draft in A.G.I., P. de C., leg. 1574. The first four enclosures [annexes] are given under the original dates and are here cited only
[2]Chapter IV, document XVII.

the final resolution of His Majesty for which he asks, because it is in conformity with the *instancia* he made and with the very approbation of His Majesty himself since all the propositions and advantages of the Company are based upon this economic favor for the Royal Treasury itself and proper for the defense of those countries, which without defense will make it easy for the English to enter the Kingdom of New Spain.

Resolution:

August 17, 1797—Consolidate the *expediente* but enquire of the Treasury how the Resolution of the King was expressed in this matter.

Most Excellent Sir:

The Director of the Spanish Company of Discoveries of the Missouri has previously solicited the 10,000 *pesos* [from the Royal Treasury]. This sum is required to cover the daily pay of the hundred men which the Company must maintain armed in the forts it now has and may have in the future, in conformity with the second Article of the Royal Decree of June 11, 1796, which decree approves the said Company in the same terms that I solicited of Your Excellency in my official letter *reservada,* number 65,[3] dated January 8, 1796. The *ad-interim* Intendant, Don Juan Ventura Morales, has replied to the official letter which I sent to him concerning this matter, a copy of which is enclosed herewith, [under] number one,[4] with which I also enclosed number two,[5] completely refusing to issue the 10,000 *pesos* to the Company until I consulted His Majesty concerning this doubt.

The motives given by the *ad-interim* Intendant for his refusal to pay, will, no doubt, seem very apparent to anyone who may not bear in mind the aforementioned Representation, the same which was brought to His Majesty's attention in the [meeting of the] *Consejo de Estado* of May 27, 1796.[6] But one must remember that all the propositions made by that Company and all the advantages that can be expected of it are based upon the supposition that His Majesty would deign to concede to it the sum of 10,000 *pesos* annually, to cover the maintenance of one hundred armed men in the line of forts that it proposes to establish on the Missouri as far as the South Sea. [And one must also remember] that the words, *to arm at his cost* and *maintained armed,* refers to the antecedents that are to be read in the introduction to the Royal order: *"His Majesty has deigned to accord, with uniform dictamen of the said Consejo, the following points and favors: the permission that the Company will be able to arm at his cost* (that is, of His Majesty's) *and to maintain armed, in the forts that it now has and may have in the future the one hundred men that are*

---

[3]Chapter IV, document III.
[4]Chapter IV, document XXIX.
[5]Chapter IV, document XXXI.
[6]Chapter IV, document XVII.

considered necessary for it, all under Your Excellency's orders, and with the object already indicated, the fulfillment of which you will watch with the greatest of care.[7] From this it is deduced that if the royal intention had not been that these one hundred men should be paid from his Royal Treasury, I would not have been charged with watching with care over the Company's ineffectual existence with such care. [It is also to be deduced] that, [since] His Majesty has deigned to accede to all the other petitions that I solicited on the strength of the previously mentioned official letter *reservada* in favor of the Company, he would not have been refused the primary one upon which all the others are based, especially when an infantry soldier costs the Royal Treasury more than one hundred *pesos* annually; [that] he is very difficult to replace at so great a distance from the capital; [and that] he is not suited for service among the savages, who scorn him because of his vices and he is even less suited to fight against them, since he has little dexterity in the use of the gun, and no knowledge of their manner of fighting.

One hundred Canadians whom the Company would recruit at its own cost and maintain armed in its forts with the 10,000 *pesos* annually for which it asks, would be more useful than 200 army men and could be replaced without any difficulty; they are suited to live among the Indians, to endure fatigue and the excessive cold of the north, and to eat whatever they find. Because of their imposing stature, they command the respect of the savage. They shoot with great dexterity, and they row and paddle with the same skill.

The new difficulties experienced by the Company because of the unfortunate death of the merchant Don Andrés Todd,[8] whose activities, which were to contribute to opening the passage of the Missouri to it, were delayed by the difficulties stirred up for it by the *ad-interim* Intendant, Don Juan Ventura Morales, are made evident in representation *number 90*[9] which accompanies this. The losses that the Company has just sustained because of the failure of the first two expeditions that it has undertaken; the efforts which are being made by the English companies of Hudson Bay and Canada to incite the Sioux and other Indian nations inhabiting north of the same river [Sioux River] against our Company are made evident in document number 3.[10] The competition into which it [Missouri Company] is about to enter with a new company which the United States had just established for the trade in peltries to the north of the Missouri and Mississippi Rivers, etc.: All these things argue the necessity of sustaining

[7] Underlined in original.
[8] Chapter IV, document XXXVIII.
[9] Document VIII.
[10] Trudeau to Carondelet, no. 276, St. Louis, November 22, 1796 (A.G.I., P. de C., leg. 1574) see note 4 to document XXIV in Chapter IV; and annex no. 4 was Carondelet's reply dated February 15, 1797, A.G.I., P. de C., leg. 24, see also *Ibid.* Annexes 3 and 4, are omitted here.

the Company with the 10,000 *pesos* for which it asks, in order to conserve the dominion of Missouri in the possession of Spain, as well as to protect by means of the line of forts which it proposes to establish from the Mississippi [*sic*-Missouri] to the South Sea, the *provincias internas* and California.

May God, Our Lord, Keep Your Excellency many years
New Orleans March 20, 1797,
Most Excellent Sir,
El Baron de Carondelet
[rubric]
Most Excellent *Señor* Príncipe de Paz

Annex:

Most Excellent Sir[11]

In answer to Your Excellency's official letter of the 21st of this month,—in which you are pleased to ask me how one should understand the resolution of His Majesty, communicated to the governor and intendant of Louisiana, concerning the pay of the one hundred men that must be maintained armed in the forts of the Spanish Company of Discoveries on the Missouri in conformity with the Royal order of June 11, 1796,—I must manifest to Your Excellency that the said order is an exact copy of the resolution which the King deigned to take in the *Consejo de Estado*,[12] and which was communicated to the *Ministerio de Indias* in my charge, by the Cónde de Montarco, on May 29 of the same year, 1796, in Aránjuez. There is nothing else about the interpretation of this order in Louisiana but what the Intendant said, both concerning the point relative to the 10,000 *pesos* requested of the Royal Treasury by the Baron de Carondelet for the said Company, and concerning the other matters in his letters of the October 31 and January 21 last, which, with numbers 3, 43, 60, 61, 63, and 85, were sent to Your Excellency on June 5th of this year, so that in view of them you might be pleased to decide, according to the will of His Majesty.

May God, etc. San Ildefonso, Aug. 26, 1797
Marqués de las Hormazas to
Señor Príncipe de la Paz
[in original handwriting]

Note in margin
August 27, 1797
join this to the *expediente* and ask the *minuta del Acta del Consejo de Estado*

---

[11]In original handwriting.
[12]Chapter IV, document XVII.

506

VIII

Carondelet to Prince of Peace, New Orleans, March 20, 1797[1]

No. 90 *Reservada*

Baron de Carondelet, political and military governor of the provinces of Louisiana and West Florida sends an *instancia* of Don Daniel Clark, resident and merchant, associate of the deceased Don Andrés Todd, to whom, by the Royal Order of May 27, 1796, was conceded the exclusive privilege to trade with the Indian nations to the north of the Missouri, considering him [Clark] creditor of the favor for which he is soliciting that he be relieved of the security which he gave for the disembarkment and introduction of the merchandise, which he brought from London in the ship "El Antilope", for this commerce and that the said cargo shall not pay more than six percent duty for the just reasons supported in his *informe*.

[Note of the resolution (minister's note) August, 1797—Join to its *expediente* and send with the referred to letter number 89.[2]]

Most Excellent Sir:

I am sending to Your Excellency the enclosed petition of the merchant and resident of this city, Don Daniel Clark, so that, informed of its justice and fairness, you will deign to entreat His Majesty to grant the favor which he solicits through the Ministry of Your Excellency. [In this connection, it will be necessary to] bear in mind the permission granted his associate, Don Andrés Todd, to carry on business with the savage nations situated to the north of the Missouri River, as well as to sever these nations from their connections with the English, all of which was resolved in [the meeting of] the *Consejo de Estado* of May 27, 1796,[3] and which has an intimate connection with the official letter *reservada* number 89[4] which too, under date of today, I am sending to Your Excellency.

Since the above mentioned Clark having shown himself to be constantly zealous as regards the Royal Service and a sympathizer with Spain, both during the last war against France—and the present, I cannot but

---

[1] Written in Spanish. A.H.N., Est., leg. 3900; index and draft in A.G.I., P. de C., leg. 1574.
[2] Document VII.
[3] Chapter IV, document XVII.
[4] Document VII.

support his petition and beg Your Excellency to uphold it with your powerful influence.

May God Our Lord guard Your Excellency many years.
New Orleans, March 20, 1797.
Most Excellent Sir
El Baron de Carondelet [rubric]
Most Excellent *Señor* Príncipe de la Paz.
[Enclosure]

Don Daniel Clark resident and merchant of this city, associate and testamentary executor of Don Andrés Todd, to the royal feet of Your Majesty with the most profound respect, says:

That a proposal was made by the said Todd to this government and to the Intendancy-General on the 21st of December, 1795,⁵ which was accepted and Your Majesty deigned to approve under date of June 11, 1796, to have goods brought here suitable for supplying and trading with the Indian nations coterminus in the Upper Mississippi with the territories of Canada and the United States of America. [Such trade was intended] for the purpose of attracting the commerce of the said nations to the dominion of His Majesty, which previously had been enjoyed exclusively by the English and Americans, who were taking out the furs via the north, to the prejudice of your royal interests, thus evading payment of export duties via this river (their natural highway), as well as import duties on the merchandise for the said trade, thus preventing the Spanish merchants from enjoying an important branch of commerce, so essential to the development of these provinces, whose triple advantage the project of the said Todd offers the State. In consequence of the acceptance of his proposal, the latter sent from London, in his ship "El Antilope", which reached here in the latter part of July, a shipment destined for the same object by virtue of the said permission.

Now, since there had not been any restriction whatever prescribed to him [Clark] pertaining to the manner in which he should conduct and introduce his merchandise here, he had legitimate reasons for believing himself, as Todd believed himself, free of any impediments not stipulated nor indicated in the acceptance of his proposition, although this was made clear by original letters of [to] his correspondents in London, who in consequence of the orders which he [Clark] communicated for the quick accomplishment of it, they made [nevertheless they took the precaution of making] the said shipment in agreement with His Majesty's Ambassador in that court, whom they consulted as to the most secure way of executing it for the most prompt and brief achievement of the goal to which it was

---
⁵Chapter IV, document III.

508

directed. Despite all this, he experienced serious contradictions in its admission from the new *ad-interim* Intendant, on the pretext that the said ship came without a passport from the Spanish consul in London, and that it was bringing some articles not proper for trade with the Indians.

As to the lack of a passport, although a requisite established for the general use of this commerce, Todd should have been considered to be expected because of the privileged nature of his particular permission, in which no mention of such formality was made, according to the copy of a letter certified by him which is herewith enclosed.

Neither was it a point made clear in his proposition, and it is a well-known axiom that one cannot demand more than to what he pledged himself.

Concerning the merchandise which he brought, which was not [intended] for the trade with the Indians, he should have been considered authorized for it, just as is any one of the other colonists, to whom it is [such imports are] permitted by His Majesty. For I must tell you that it is true that, for this purpose and for the purpose of taking up his domicile in the Province, he naturalized himself, taking the proper oath of fidelity, a certified copy of which also is enclosed.

These truthful reasons were represented by the exponent, adding the no less true facts that Todd absolutely ignored all formalities that rule in this *comercio*, since he knew no others than those contained in the permission that he obtained for the execution of his project, because, immediately on having proposed it and having been licensed, he went to inform the Indian tribes of it, and to prepare them to prefer the traffic and friendship which this government granted them. The delicate state of the political affairs in London, at the time that Todd's orders to send him the said shipment arrived there made it absolutely essential for him to hide his purpose, since it was as contrary to the interests of that Power [England] as it was favorable to those of His Majesty. Because of this state of affairs the agents of Todd communicated it [information] only to your Ambassador, without which precaution the undertaking probably would have failed.

Finally, this contract is so much more to the advantage of the country than the contract of the House of Panton, Leslie and Company, established in Pensacola, with your royal permission to supply numerous Indians tribes, which brings in its merchandise under the English flag and enjoys complete freedom of duties both in the importation of them as well as in the exportation of furs, since Todd agreed to contribute six percent both on imports and on exports. Those were [are] also worthy motives for excusing him, for the said unforewarned requisite as well as also not to demand of him greater duties on the other merchandise above indicated which he had brought, since they are for lawful commerce, [yet another reason for excusing him] is that, without the help of his products — barely sufficient to defray the indispensable and increased expenses of duties on the said cargo and [the expense of] shipment of the goods for trade with the Indians at their distant destinations (expenses which have amounted to 33,570 *pesos* as the enclosed *estado* of the goods demonstrates)—it would have been impossible to supply the said nations with the promised promptness necessary to prevent their being provided by our rivals, the English and the Americans.

All these powerful considerations did not make an impression upon the new intendant, and only after much delay did he permit the unloading of the said cargo, (which has occasioned considerable expense in salaries, as well as in the maintainance of the crew and judicial costs). This permission was granted under the strict conditions that the exponent should guarantee with collateral the amount of the said merchandise that was not to be used in the trade with the Indians, and that he should pay a duty of fifteen percent on their value pending the decision of His Majesty. Without the receipt and publication here (at the time that they were clearing the goods in this custom house) of the cited Royal Order in which Your Majesty deigned to reduce in general the import duties on merchandise imported into these provinces to the six percent stipulated by Todd, having been sufficient to revoke such a rigorous decree. This was a circumstance sufficient in itself to be recognized within the said grace, as the exponent solicited it with so many and such serious fundamental reasons.

The aforementioned decree allowed me no other alternative than that of yielding to the said harsh conditions, or the very grave one—because of the expenses and dangers involved—of re-exporting the said merchandise in the face of the critical circumstances of an approaching break with England, feared at that time and verified soon afterwards. Necessity, on one hand, and the desire of realizing Todd's project for Your Majesty, on the other, stimulated me to pass through that hard way [to accept the first hard alternative] in the blind persuasion that Your Majesty's good heart will deign to order the release of the said bond, and to have returned to me the nine percent that has been charged me in excess of the six percent stipulated by Todd, which duty alone has been contributed by the other vassals of Your Majesty in these dominions, ever since the time that this *Administración de Rentas* cleared the cargo of that person.

To the stated reasons which weigh in favor of this respectful solicitation, is added, *Señor*, the serious injury which resulted from the long delay of his [the petitioner's] trading merchandise in passing through the Royal Customs, and which has just been exposed. This delay impeded the expedition's arrival in time to supply the Indians and forestall the

English, the latter, persuading the savages that Todd had deceived them with false promises, made them drive away their [our] traders from the Mongoina River, located forty leagues above St. Louis of Illinois, and fire upon the troop that accompanied them [traders], as your commandant general will be able to verify. And finally [may be added] the no less meritorious reason that, in addition to having risked large sums of money to supply the said Indian nations, the petitioner gave merchandise on credit, at lower prices, and on longer terms than did the previous traders. This was done for the purpose of separating the Indians from our rivals and re-affirming their friendship with us. It was done [only] with grave risks of considerable losses, which will be greater if the present war continues because it prevents the supplicant from renewing his supplies, as is customary in order to collect the credits that have been given to the Indians. And now the activity and influence of Todd to stimulate the Indians to pay is lacking, because he, having descended to this capital to accelerate the promised supplies, unfortunately died. Todd died filled with painful dejection because the controversies which he experienced in his undertaking were as little expected as the utility of the enterprise to the state was clear, a circumstance which made him a creditor to all equity and indulgence.

Because of Todd's early and unexpected death,[6] the suppliant has remained in the greatest embarrassment, on account of having supplied all the money employed in this enterprise, and on account of the fact that I was forced to entrust its management to foreigners, who, not being interested, as was Todd, in managing it in the best manner to assure success, it is probable that it may occasion my ruin.

Because of all the accumulated hardships which I have suffered up to the present time, in order to pay the mortgage of 33,175 *pesos,* 24 *reales* for which he [Todd] obligated himself for merchandise not [used] in the trade with the Indians, I have been forced to pay more than 12,000 *pesos* out of my own pocket, in order to free the buildings, with which I guaranteed that quantity [loan], from debt. These vexations, because they were caused with little reason, are therefore far more painful to the supplicant, who is one of Your Majesty's most useful vassals in this city, because of the great amount of duties which he has contributed by virtue of his vast commerce, and because of the loyalty and love which he has already demonstrated to Your Majesty, as this government can well inform you.

In consideration of all these true expositions and in consideration of all the serious injuries which have been caused him,—as well as the losses of wealth from which he is beginning to suffer, because the dispersal of his wealth is exposed to fluctuations in the said enterprise, which,

6See Chapter IV, document XXXVIII.

together with the guarantee of the said loan, not only deprived him of the means for making other speculations of greater security and less uncertain profit, but also lessen his credit,—the supplicant is forced to an almost complete inactivity in his mercantile business, [at least] so long as the said last inconvenience shall endure.

In consideration of all these things, the supplicant humbly begs Your Majesty, because of your innate beneficence, to deign, with the greatest possible brevity to order the lifting of the referred to bond [mortgage] and that there be returned to him the nine percent overcharged on the 31,176 *pesos, 2½ reales,* total of the said merchandise on which he should have paid only six percent in conformity with the declaration approved by Your Majesty, these things are to be hoped for from Your Majesty's kingly benignity, and whose precious life may God preserve the many years that He can and may.

New Orleans, March 10, 1797
At the Royal feet of Your Majesty.

Daniel Clark [rubric]

[In the margin and in Carondelet's writing[7]]

Señor: The damage which resulted to the supplicant from the delay which he experienced in the unloading of the merchandise destined for the Indian nations north of the Missouri River, at the hands of the Royal Treasury—an injury perhaps irreparable both as concerns the State and the interested party, is in the present circumstances, true. It is also a fact that the valuation of the merchandise of the ship "El Antilope"[8] was made in the custom house twenty-four days after the publication of the reduction of Royal duties. I therefore consider the suppliant deserving of the grace which he is soliciting for the release of the bond, and that the merchandise brought in the said brigantine reap the benefit of the said reduction of duties, by way of reimbursement.

New Orleans, March 20, 1797.

El Baron de Carondelet [rubric]

---

[7]Also draft in A.G.I., P. de C., leg. 1574.
[8]See in this connection Chapter IV, document XXVII. For this see Nasatir, "Anglo-Spanish Frontier on the Upper Mississippi, 1786-1796," *Iowa Journal of History and Politics,* XXIX, (1931), 222-224. There is a lengthy correspondence over the merchandise brought in on the "Antelope." Most of it is contained in letters and enclosures of Morales to Pedro Varela y Ulloa, no. 115, New Orleans, March 31, 1797, A.G.I., Sto. Dom., leg. 2614 (87-1-24 old numbering); draft (without enclosures) in A.G.I., P. de C., leg. 2343; transcript in Bancroft Library. Carondelet supported Clark's contention as is here noted. Included among the many enclosures (the document contains 133 folios) are the petitions of Todd of December, 1795, letters of Todd, Brickwood, Clark, etc. See also Trudeau to Morales, no. 11, St. Louis, April 14, 1797, A.G.I., P. de C., leg. 261; and Morales to Varela y Ulloa no. 107, New Orleans, March 31, 1797, in A.H.N., Est., leg. 3902 [also in A.G.I., P. de C., leg. 2343] and enclosing copy of Trudeau to Carondelet, no. 282, St. Louis, February 11, 1797 [original in A.G.I., P. de C., leg. 351] and Carondelet to Morales, New Orleans, March 14, 1797 and Morales to Carondelet, New Orleans, March 16, 1797; draft of reply to no. 107 is in A.G.I., Sto. Dom., leg. 2579.

IX

GRAND PRÉ TO CARONDELET[1] [NOTE ONLY]
AVOYELLES, APRIL 27, 1797

Forwards three original documents from Nicholas Lamothe in which he speaks of having received news that Americans have penetrated into some of the interior provinces of New Spain through the nations of the Great Missouri. He refers to the injurious traffic of certain traders with the Indian nations of that dependency, suggesting the suppression of such commerce, and offering to seek out and expel the foreigners lodged in those dominions which he says he can do because of his experience in those regions.

Believes he could complete successfully the commission and could also conciliate and establish harmony among the Indians of this dependency, etc. Such action is necessary for the peace of these establishments, which are exceedingly disturbed by repeated hostilities of the Choctaws against many towns of these nations and by their insolent acts against the inhabitants.

---

[1]Bancroft Library. These are notes only and not the entire document. See Chapter IV, document XXIV, note 4. *Cp.* Houck, *Spanish Régime in Missouri*, II, 192. The originals of several of Grandpré's long letters to Carondelet are in the Bancroft Library; many more are in A.G.I., P. de C.

X

CHOUTEAU TO GRANT, ST. LOUIS, MAY 8, 1797[1]

St. Louis, Illinois, May 8, 1797

Monsieur:

I learned of your departure only just now, and I wish you a good and happy voyage. I pray you to sell among the Sioux to my best advantage, the two boat loads of furs which I have directed to Mackinac and of which I place you in charge. I rely completely on your good doing [beneficence] in this matter, having been persuaded that you will

---

[1]Written in French. Missouri Historical Society, Auguste Chouteau Collection. This is but an excerpt of one example of Chouteau's interests and dealings with the merchants of Canada. He was not a member of the Missouri Company and in fact acted as Daniel Clark, Jr.'s, power of attorney in dealings against Clamorgan. This was during the time of war between England and Spain and St. Louis was fearful of an attack from Canada. The story of these events is as yet not told in print. See A. P. Nasatir, "Anglo-Spanish Rivalry in the Iowa Country, 1797-1798," *Iowa Journal of History and Politics*, XXVIII (1930), 337-389. Gayoso writing to Carondelet from Natchez on May 8, 1797 (no. 670, A.G.I., P. de C., leg. 43) said that reports reaching him from St. Louis indicated confidence of not being molested by the English and "that in Michilimackinac there were many boats from St. Louis which upon the first news of an expedition from Canada some one of them would come to communicate the news, since all were subjects interested in the preservation of their own property in St. Louis."

act for the best. It is for this reason that I approve in advance whatever you may do concerning this transaction.

You will place to my credit the amount yielded by the sale of the above-mentioned furs. Please have the kindness to advise me [of this] on the first occasion, so that I may know the state of our affairs between us. I hope that you will have the goodness to do the favor of taking charge of this matter, and if I, on my part, can be of some service to you here, please take advantage of one who is desirous of finding an occasion to prove his esteem for you.

I pray you to purchase at Mackinac on my account about 2000 pounds of maple sugar [*sucre d'erable*], for which you may pay up to twenty-five *sols*, if it is not possible to buy it cheaper. I will send you this sum by the canoe of M. Reaves, and you may send me the above mentioned maple sugar by the boat which Tourville and François Lariviere are conducting.

XI

CARLOS HOWARD TO CARONDELET, ST. LOUIS, MAY 13, 1797[1]

[I am writing to Your Excellency] concerning the instructions you were pleased to give me in your letter of November twenty-sixth[2] last concerning managing to destroy English commerce as far as possible not only on the Upper Mississippi but on the Missouri; for this purpose arranging an expedition to the San Pedro River; sending another to capture the post of San Joseph on the river of the same name which empties into Lake Michigan; but first of all to destroy (since His Majesty's orders are positive on this point) a fort which it is believed has been built by the English among the Mandans on the Missouri;[3] and [the said instructions] ending that Lieutenant-Colonel Zenon Trudeau, and the captain of the militia, Don Carlos Tayon, would inform me on all the above-mentioned points in general concerning the expedition against San Joseph and the active traders on the Missouri. With regard to the Mandan nation, from the best information that I have been able to secure

---

[1]Written in Spanish. Original in Bancroft Library; printed in Nasatir, "Anglo-Spanish Rivalry in the Iowa Country 1797-1798," *Iowa Journal of History and Politics*, XXVIII (1930), 358-361. In the introduction to the documents printed therein, I have discussed the problems involved, *Ibid.*, XXVIII, 337-389. My former student, Ernest R. Liljegren, has written an excellent account of Carlos Howard (ms. unpublished M. A. thesis). See his "Jacobinism in Spanish Louisiana 1792-1797," *Louisiana Historical Quarterly*, XXII (1939), 46-97.

[2]Draft in A.G.I., P. de C., leg. 2364, printed in *Missouri Historical Society Collections*, III, 71-91, and in Houck, *Spanish Régime in Missouri*, II, 123-132 with incorrect date, and excerpts are also printed in *Wisconsin Historical Society Collections*, XVIII, 449-452.

[3]See document II. This is discussed in Nasatir, "Anglo-Spanish Rivalry on the Upper Missouri," *Mississippi Valley Historical Review*, XVI (1930).

from the above-mentioned persons, as well as from several others and particularly Don Diego McCay,[4] who returned a few days ago from the Missouri which he has been exploring since the month of July of '95, it turns out that the said post of San Joseph as well as the post of Michilimakinak was [were] turned over to the Americans last year.[5] Thus the English post nearest this place (which seems to be Tessalon, an island in Lake Huron)[6] is more than three hundred leagues distant. In order to get to this post one must first secure the permission of the United States, or rather violate their neutrality, all of which is made clear in the enclosed official note to Don Zenon Trudeau.

As to the trading-post or small English fort in the Mandan nation, it appears that there is no doubt of its existence, according to the assurances of the above-mentioned McCay, who has given me an explicit report of the route taken by the English, both from Canada and from Hudson Bay, in reaching that Indian nation. I will send you a translation of this report as soon as time permits.

McCay also informed me that, before he came down the Missouri, he had definite information that Don Juan Evans, who had been sent to explore a route to the Pacific Ocean, had crossed the Mandan nation successfully on his way to the Shining Mountains [montañas relucientes]— alias [Blancos] the White Mountains, alias [Pedrejosas] the Rocky Mountains—and that once they were traversed, he believed it would be easy to reach the sea.

According to what McCay has led me to believe, although it would be difficult, it would not be impossible to dislodge the English from among the Mandans. But, in order to accomplish that, I should have to be supplied with more aid than I now have, and it would have to be begun before they have advanced beyond their present position. Moreover, I would seriously devote myself to discussing the most desirable measures for the enterprise, if I were not restrained by the fact that at present suspicions have been cast on the good faith of my immediate neighbors.

May God keep you for many years! St. Louis, Illinois, May 13, 1797.

Carlos Howard [rubric]

To the Baron de Carondelet.[7]

---

[4]See Ibid. Mackay's "Journal" is Chapter III, document XX; and see also this Chapter, document II.

[5]In accordance with Jay's treaty.

[6]When the English gave up Michilimackinac they went to St. Joseph's Island.

[7]Carondelet acknowledged receipt of the contents of this letter on July 18, 1797 (original in A.G.I., P. de C., leg. 24 and draft in Ibid., leg. 131A). Carondelet approved Howard's action and urged him to fulfill his orders.

515

XII

Missouri Company-Expedition to Octoctata Indians in 1796

Zenon Trudeau-Examination of Derouin, St. Louis, May 14, 1797[1]

In the city of St. Louis, Illinois, on the fourteenth day of the month of May in the year one thousand seven hundred ninety-seven, I, Don Zenon Trudeau, Brevet Lieutenant-Colonel, Captain of the Regiment of Louisiana and Lieutenant Governor of the West District of the Illinois, in fulfillment of the verbal order of Don Carlos Howard, Lieutenant-Colonel of the same regiment and Military Commander of Upper Louisiana, I had appear before me in the presence of two witnesses, lieutenant of the Grenadiers, Don Joseph de Ville Degoutin and the Second Lieutenant, Don Frederico Autman, the one named Francisco Derouin, a trader who had just come from the Indian tribes of the Missouri River in order to question him concerning what he has seen and heard among those nations that might be of interest to the government and trade of these settlements. After he had taken the proper oath and promised to tell the truth, I asked him how long it had been since he left this city, among what nations he had gone to trade, if he were well received by the Indians he had seen and if they had traded with him at the usual prices and without [subjecting him to] any violence or rough treatment?

He replied that he had left this city on the twenty-fourth day of August of last year, in charge of the interests of the Trading Company of the Upper Missouri, bound for the Octotacta nation with an outfit of goods sufficient for the use of that nation. He had arrived there the twenty-second of the month of October of the same year, and found the tribe assembled. He gave them the gifts that the commandant of St. Louis had given him for them. Among other things there was a keg of brandy for the head chief, who gave it to his worst subjects to drink, for the purpose of annoying the deponent and his aids, as happened that same night when they came to his camp with arms to kill him, others preventing them in order to exact payment for their apparent protection. This [similar annoyances] continued during the whole winter, first one group appearing, followed by another in the same way, some appearing ill-disposed and others favorably disposed [towards the traders], so as to secure a reward for their good-will and protection. This used up a large part of their [Derouin's] merchandise, and he scarcely received a quarter part of the payment for the remainder, which was sold on credit (as was the custom). All during the winter this tribe and that of the

---

[1]Written in Spanish. Original in Bancroft Library.

Kance sent first one and then another war party so that several men were killed. This kept up a discord, which was still continuing when the deponent left, so that the head chiefs requested him to inform the governor of the bad conduct of their people, begging him as a favor not to send traders during the present year, so that they might be deprived of the things they needed, and thus punished for the future.[2]

I asked him if he had any knowledge as to whether the Octotacta or any other near-by nation had had communication with the English traders of the Mississippi, and if they had received from them any gifts or had traded with them. He replied that he did not know anything about the matters with which the question concerned, but that he had heard it said by the Indians that the Sioux had come in a band of about four hundred men to the Mahas to whom they had presented a gift of a hundred and fifty rifles and six kegs of brandy. That nation, the Mahas, were keeping the brandy to come [until they would be able to] join the Octotactas in order to go and make war upon the Kance, the brandy being intended to give courage to the warriors in battle.

I asked him to tell me the distance that one may reckon from this city to the Octotacta nation, which he had mentioned, and if the time he had spent on his last trip was the usual time taken to reach there. He replied that the distance asked for was reckoned by all travelers at two hundred leagues, and that the trips generally take about fifty days unless one meets with bad weather or has sickness among the rowers.

When this statement was read to him, he said that it was the same that he had made, and that he had nothing to add or delete, and that he affirmed and approved it in all its contents under the oath he had sworn. He also said that he is twenty-four years old, and that since he does not know how to write he is making the mark of a cross. The above-mentioned witnesses signed with me, the said lieutenant-governor, who testifies to the truth of the above.

Frederico Auteman [rubric]

Josef Deville Degoutin [rubric]

Mark of the

X

Witness

Zenon Trudeau [rubric]

---

[2]See Document XIII. Benito Vasquez said that he had been notified that the trade of the Kansas for which he had asked had been conceded to him and he, therefore, purchased on credit the merchandise necessary for that trade. Evidently that was not true, for on May 28, 1797, Vasquez again petitioned for it. Carondelet sent the "poorly considered and poorly thought out" letter of Vasquez to Carlos Howard asking that if some use could be had of Vasquez's services Howard should recommend him to Trudeau. Carondelet to Howard, New Orleans, July 28, 1797, A.G.I., P. de C., leg. 24.

á los *Tescazena en el Combate*

Preg.do quales la distancia que se puede contar desde esta *villa*
hasta la Nacion Octotacta que ha citado y si el tiempo q.
ha puesto en este su ultimo para llegar a ella es el Regular
que se acostumbra. Dixo que la distancia que se pregunta la
cuenta por todos los viageros de docientas leguas y que
los viages son lo mas regularmente de cinquenta dias quan.
do no se experimenta mal tiempo, ni enfermedades en las
Remesas y haviendole leido esta declaracion dixo que es
lo mismo que havia dicho que no tiene que añadir ni quitar en
ella, que se afirma y Ratifica en todo su contenido baxo el
Juramento que ha Prestado, y que es de edad de veinte y quatro
años, y por no saver escrivir hizo una marca de Cruz y
lo firmaron los expresados testigos de asistencia Comigo el
enunciado Theniente Governador, que da fe.

XIII

TRUDEAU TO CARONDELET, ST. LOUIS, MAY 26, 1797[1]

Mon Général:

Monsieur Howard arrived here the twenty-seventh of last month[2] and remitted to me the letter with which you honored me dated November twenty-seventh[3] and from which, believe me, I was greatly affected to learn that a man so fastidious and attached to these duties [as I am] can be found to have been suspected of having failed in his duties there. Nevertheless, the presence of this respectable chief cheered me up, and I regard it as a good favor which Providence has been willing to use to justify my conduct in an unequivocal manner and therefore still dare to hope for your confidence and your goodness. Moreover, *Mon Général,* should I not have [had] confidence in General Collot, since he was recommended by the Minister of the King at Philadelphia? In the circumstances in which we find ourselves as regards France, should I not have treated this officer with regard? Should I have been persuaded that, provided with such good papers, I had to deal with a profligate? Despite everything, *Mon Général,* believe that I have dealt with him with reflection, and that if I made some mistakes, in which all of my honor was at stake, as was also the honor of all the *militaires* of the nation and more particularly that of those who were commandants such as I, I had to represent the good will of the King in some manner. Everything not withstanding, this general saw nothing but what I wished to allow him to see, and proof of this is the false plan which you found on him, entirely contrary to the true one which I had, and which I abstained from showing him despite these instances.

Monsieur Mackay, agent of the Company of the Upper Missouri, has just arrived, having been recalled by the Director who has attributed to him the considerable losses which the said Company suffered in his [its] expedition in 1794 [*sic*]. The expedition of 1796 was not more fortunate, although managed by another, and gave absolutely proof of

---

[1]Written in French. A.G.I., P. de C., leg. 206. The problems described in this letter are fully recounted in Nasatir, "Anglo-Spanish Rivalry in the Iowa Country 1797-1798" *Iowa Journal of History and Politics,* XXVIII (1930), 337-389; Nasatir, "Anglo-Spanish Rivalry on the Upper Missouri," *Mississippi Valley Historical Review,* XVI (1930); Liljegren, "Jacobinism in Spanish Louisiana 1792-1797" *Louisiana Historical Quarterly,* XXII (1939), 1-53, see *esp.* pp 47 ff. See also Carondelet's letter of Instructions to Howard, *res.,* New Orleans, November 26. 1796. cited in note 2 to document XI: Carondelet to Prince of Peace no. 85 *res.,* New Orleans, December 1. 1796. A.H.N., Est., leg. 3900: Carondelet to Azanza. no. 1 *res.,* A.H.N., Est., leg. 3900 and translated in Houck, *Spanish Régime in Missouri,* II. 133-138: and draft of a letter of Carondelet to Las Casas, New Orleans, December 1, 1796, A.G.I., P. de C., leg. 178B.
[2]See document XI.
[3]A.G.I., P. de C., leg. 2364, and printed in Houck, *Spanish Régime in Missouri,* II, 122.

519

the vice [treachery] of the Mahas and Octoctata, who have not been any wiser since. This prevented the Company from sending merchandise to them this year, and seems to me to agree infinitely, and more particularly since we have now a galliot on the Upper Mississippi, which will intercept the entrance of foreign merchandise in the Moingoina river, and in this manner completely deprive the two said nations of all aid. The Chief Hockastas solicited me earnestly not to send them anything at all, since without that expedient they could not answer for the abuses of their young men.[4] I believe it prudent to accord them their demand for if we do not the disorder can only grow, and the Company will find themselves in the absolute necessity of abandoning all their [its] projects, for which it [Company] has no means with which to undertake this year— the season now being well advanced. Last year, *Monsieur* Mackay sent from the Mahas [where he then was] to the Upper Missouri a well-educated young man, whom he had taken with him to aid him in making discoveries.[5] At the time of his [Mackay's] departure from the said Mahas, he knew that this young man had reached the Mandan, from whence he will start [again], when the snow melts, to search for the Sea and seek out the different nations to which it will be possible to go to trade. Moreover we have our former discoverer Jacques D'Eglise, who, as we know, also went to the Mandans, and who, according to his plan, should return only after having earned the three thousand *piastres* promised by the government to the first one who should bring evident marks [indisputable proof] of having found the said sea. *Monsieur* Mackay made a very good map of the Missouri from its mouth as far as the *rivière Blanche* which includes about three hundred and fifty leagues.[6] You will receive this map as soon as it is *distinct*.

Doubtless *Monsieur* Howard will have written you concerning the two Osage partisans whom we have in irons in St. Louis—the one be-

[4]See document XII. This had an effect on the trade. By June 4 no beaver had come down from the Upper Missouri. Chouteau to Wm. Grant, St. Louis June 4, 1797, Missouri Historical Society, Auguste Chouteau Collection.

[5]Evans. See Chapter IV, document IV, and this Chapter, document II.

[6]See in this connection discussions of Mackay's maps in Abel, *Tabeau's Narrative*, introduction; and by same author, "A New Lewis and Clark Map," *Geographical Review* I, (1916), and "Mackay's Table of Distances," which is document I in this chapter, but see pages 442-446 in vol. X (1923) of *Mississippi Valley Historical Review* (which pages are not included in document I); Teggart, "Notes Supplementary to any edition of Lewis and Clark," *American Historical Association, Annual Report* 1908, I. Collot and Perrin du Lac apparently had access to Mackay's information and map.

On October 14, 1797, Clamorgan wrote to André López (A.G.I., P. de C., leg. 213). "I am sending to *Monsieur* the Governor the map of the Missouri well drawn up at the cost and expenses of the Company. I hope that it [the Company] will recover its usual vigor shortly and that in the future by its zeal and activity in making discoveries it will merit the bounties of the government." See the excellent discussion of maps in Aubrey Diller, "Maps of the Missouri River Before Lewis and Clark" in M. F. Ashley Montagu, [ed.], *Studies and Essays—to George Sarton* (New York, 1946) 503-519.

cause it is certain that his party killed a hunter on the *rivière des Arcs,* and the other because he too killed another man on the Washita, though we do not know whether he was a white or a savage. I do not know whether these two savages will be executed.[7] That would contribute to the continuation of tranquillity, of which we have need in the present circumstances because our establishments are increasing in good cultivators—which could be, it appears to me, *à propos* to allow to strengthen (in) their establishments before troubling the way by which we have obtained the calm of three years which has made all the Illinois prosperous so advantageously. If, after having punished these two men by keeping them in irons, as they now are, they were to be returned to their chiefs, I believe that it would be better than acting with extreme vigor, and that we would gain a great deal by letting our population prosper until it is sufficient to restrain this same nation. It seems to me that a handful of hunters of the *rivière des Arcs* might be better forgotten for an instant in order to let prosper a country which is going to become, perhaps, the most consequential in the province.

Monsieur Howard has very kindly found satisfactory the small accomodations which I had prepared in my house to receive him, and in which I have the satisfaction of seeing him pleased. I dare to affirm that as for himself, he would have been hard to please in this country, where there is as yet no market, and where it is necessary to store up— a year in advance—the most ordinary small provisions, to have a garden, a poultry-yard, cows, etc., without which one would die of hunger. The increase of two hundred and ninety men more at St. Louis would soon effect our consumption of all of our last year's grain, and this year's harvest of wheat promises nothing favorable. The abundant rains which we have had constantly for three months have ruined the greater part of what there was planted, and it has been absolutely impossible to do any work in regard to the maize, which, it is already evident, we shall lack entirely. Moreover an inundation is to be feared for Ste. Geneviève, and if it ensues, as it apparently will, we will find ourselves in a state of famine before the end of October. *Monsieur* Howard wanted me to remain in charge of the King's storehouse, and I inform you that I accepted it only in self-defense and in the persuasion that that would not last long. My family has already been scalded ["in hot water" with] by the *Real Hacienda,* and I fear it more than the Tribunal of the Inquisition. Moreover I am so little instructed in the manner of rendering such accounts and they are so exacting as to form that I only fear to fail, since I do not have anything with which to bribe them, I should like to be able to avoid their chicanery.

---

[7]See [Chouteau] to Gayoso de Lemos, St. Louis, July 29, 1797, in Missouri Historical Society, Vasquez Collection.

Our commandant informs you definitely of our positions, and of the news of the day, which is alarming enough for this Upper district. However, one does not yet need to believe it entirely just as it is told or spread about, considering that most of it consists of very equivocal sayings, which might truly have some reports [connections] with what concerns the taking possession of the posts, but not with the war.

If I am always too lengthy when I have the honor of writing to you, it is because I know your indulgence for those who, like myself, have difficulty in expressing themselves, and because I know that for the sake of the zeal which drives me to instruct you of some of the peculiarities of this post you will kindly excuse me, and pardon the one who is with the most respectful attachment,

Mon Général
Your very humble obedient servant
Zenon Trudeau [rubric]

St. Louis, May 26, 1797

XIV

TRUDEAU TO CARONDELET, ST. LOUIS, JULY 21, 1797[1]

No. 191.

I herewith enclose to Your Excellency a letter written in English[2] (and its translation) which was written to me by Don Isaac Todd, uncle of Don Andrés Todd, who passed away in New Orleans.[3] Your Excellency, with His Majesty's approval, had conceded to him [Andrés Todd] the exclusive trade with the Indians of the Upper Mississippi, including those along the rivers on its western shore above the Missouri.[4] It appears that this merchant, according to advices which I have received from Mr. Swan,[5] representative of the deceased, was under instructions

---

[1]Written in Spanish. Original in Bancroft Library; edited and published in Nasatir, "Anglo-Spanish Rivalry in the Iowa Country 1797-1798," *Iowa Journal of History and Politics,* XXVIII (1930), 380-382, reprint pp. 46-48.
[2]Herewith enclosed and printed *below.*
[3]Todd died from an attack of yellow fever in the fall of 1796. See Chapter IV, document XXXVI, note 4, and document XXXVIII, note 2.
[4]See the letter of Todd to Carondelet, New Orleans, December 18, 1795, annex no. 6 to Carondelet's letter no. 65 *res.* to Prince of Peace New Orleans, January 8, 1796 (Chapter IV, document III) which is in A.H.N., Est., leg. 3900 and also in A.G.I., Sto. Dom., 87-1-24 (old numbering). A draft of this same letter written in English is in A.G.I., P. de C., leg. 2364. See also Todd to Carondelet, New Orleans, December 21, 1795 (See Chapter IV, document III). The letter referred to is also found in A.G.I., P. de C., leg. 129 and in A.G.I., Sto. Dom., 87-1-24 (old numbering). See also Carondelet's letters nos. 65 and 66 *res.,* both dated January 8, 1796, in A.H.N., Est., leg. 3900 (see Chapter IV, document III). The official decree was given in the *Consejo de Estado* meeting on May 27, 1796, Chapter IV, document XVII.
[5]Swan went to St. Louis in 1798 to attempt to recover for Todd payment of debts owing by the firm of Clamorgan, Loisel and Company. M. M. Quaife [ed.], *John Askin Papers* (Detroit, 1928), I, 375. Swan, however, was unsuccessful in this undertaking.

from Your Excellency to make no changes in the trade but rather to facilitate it, and that he now has the intention of sending a nephew[6] of the aforementioned deceased, who has already been in St. Louis, to continue the management and government of the said interests.

It would appear to me that in order to carry out Your Excellency's ideas, I should proffer no support to his pretension[s]. But, as it is my wish to be governed in accordance with present conditions, which every moment change in aspect, I place before Your Excellency that which occurs to me, so that you may prescribe to me whatever new instruction may pertain to the matter.

May God preserve Your Excellency many years. St. Louis, July 21, 1797.

Zenon Trudeau [rubric]

Señor Baron de Carondelet.

[Enclosure]

Isaac Todd to Trudeau[7]
Michilimacka: 27th June 1797

Sir

The unfortunate death of my nephew Andrew Todd[8] has called me to this Post to attend to his concerns. Mr. Swan[9] & my Grand Nephew Mr. Merry[10] is very sensible of your kind & polite attention to them at St. Louis for which I beg leave to return you my best thanks, also for a letter you were so kind to write Mr. Swan the 27th April on his leaving St. Louis wherein you say there is no change in the commerce & ex-

---

[6]Mr. Merry. See *below.*
[7]Original in Bancroft Library, edited and published in Nasatir, "Anglo-Spanish Rivalry in the Iowa County," *op. cit.,* XVIII, 378-380, reprint, pp. 44-46. This is written in English but a Spanish translation was enclosed in Trudeau's letter, *above.*
[8]Andrew Todd was a British subject and merchant, who turned to Spanish Louisiana and became a Spanish subject when the fulfillment of the provisions of Jay's Treaty threatened his business. See many references and documents relating to him in this volume, especially in Chapters III, IV, and V.
[9]James Swan was Isaac Todd's agent at Michilimackinac. Quaife, *John Askin Papers,* I, 375. Swan was sent by Todd, McGill and Company to see about Todd's contract. He left St. Louis the day after Howard arrived. Howard to Carondelet, St. Louis, June 9, 1797, A.G.I., P. de C., leg. 35.
[10]Mr. Merry, nephew of Andrew Todd, arrived in St. Louis before August 30, for on that day Trudeau advised Howard of the arrival of Mr. Merry. Draft of a letter of Carondelet [?] to Trudeau, New Orleans, October 17, 1797 (A.G.I., P. de C., leg. 131). Trudeau wrote as follows:
"By your letter of August 30, you advise Lieutenant Colonel Don Carlos Howard of the arrival at your place of Mr. Merry, nephew of the defunct Don Andrés Todd, the unrest in Canada, and the construction in Tessalon on Lake Ontario [Huron?] of a fort by the English; and finally of the loyalty of the Indians of the Upper Mississippi, they not permitting any introduction [of men or materials] against our establishments.
It is best that you maintain them in such good disposition with the little forces and powers and provisions which you have." See also Trudeau to Howard, St. Louis, August 30, 1797, A.G.I., P. de C., leg. 48.

clusive privileges granted my late Nephew by Government in Louisiana, among which was the river de Moin. Messr: Mongrain & Co. who wintred there could not benefit by the exclusive privileges Granted them as other Traders came thru to Trade and occasioned difficultys with the Indians, so that Messr. Mongrain & Co did not bring out of the River Peltry sufficient to pay within 30,000 Livres of their outfitt—as I believe this Year no Traders from hence will attempt going to that River without your permission and as I trust the Trade of this River will this year—be continued to my Nephews Representatives for the benefit of his Estate, I intend soon to send my Grand Nephew to St. Louis in order to arrange this business and obtain your permission & orders as I propose that he will winter in the River de Moin, by him I will have the honor of writing you and sending you some Tea & other things that may be acceptable at St. Louis.

I was at New York this Spring and sent from thence a Gentleman to New Orleans to attend to my Nephews Interest there and to assist Mr Clark[11] & Doctr: Don his Executors there. I took the Liberty of writing his Excellency the Baron de Carondelet representing that as it was under his Auspices and his particular incouragement & protection that our Nephew embarked so largely in Business in Louisiane and was Naturalized a Spanish Subject, I had no doubt that his Excelly would continue the same protection to his Representatives, the property my Nephew had at New Orleans, (independent of what is owing for Goods Taken from this Post) exceeded 40,000 pounds Sterling, and to support my Nephews Credit in this business I became his Security.

I have the honor to be with Respect Sir
        Your much obliged Debt Sir
                Issac Todd[12] [rubric]
Zenon Trudeau Esquire.

[Reply]

In[13] your official letter number 191, you enclosed for me a letter from Don Isaac Todd, uncle of the defunct Don Andrés, concerning which I can offer only one observation just at present—one, which, in my opinion, is most important—and that is that the nephew, whom Don Isaac may send, will not realize the same good effects that might have been expected from Don Andrés, a man whom the Indians trusted and

[11]Daniel Clark, Jr., was a merchant in New Orleans with whom the merchants of St. Louis dealt.
[12]Isaac Todd of Todd, McGill and Company. There are many references to this company in Davidson, *Northwest Company;* Quaife, *John Askin Papers;* Stevens, *Northwest Fur Trade;* Wisconsin Historical Society Collections, etc.
[13]This is the reply to the above letter. It is in A.G.I., P. de C., leg. 44; draft in *Ibid.*, leg. 131A. This is not printed in Nasatir, "Anglo-Spanish Rivalry in the Iowa Country 1797-1798" cited in note 1.

loved, while they perhaps do not know the other. The gentle disposition and agreeable character of Don Andrés attracted all of them to him, and the latter may perhaps turn them aside or even repel them. The war which we are having with England is still an obstacle which must be very embarassing. In view of this proceed with circumspection and vigilance, conserve Todd's privilege for him, maintain for him the just use of his advantages, but take care that this condescension be not prejudicial to the interests of the King or the tranquility of this colony. Be careful that he pursue his commerce at an opportune time, but wherever it prove adverse to the two objects which I have just mentioned, it must cease. This must not have further interpretation and this line of conduct is the one we must follow in this case and others similar to it.

May God keep you many years.

New Orleans, August 15, 1797

Manuel Gayoso de Lemos
[rubric]

Señor Don Zenon Trudeau

XV

Trudeau to Gayoso de Lemos, St. Louis December 20, 1797[1]

My Dear Sir and My Most Esteemed Governor: I shall not fail in the trust which you have placed in me of informing you of the method which has been followed up to the present with the permits to trade with the nations of the country.[2] As soon as I was appointed to take charge of this command the Baron delivered some instructions to me, by which he authorized me to select for myself the nation which best suited me, leaving the others free for all the merchants of St. Louis, without demanding the least recompense.[3] Trusting in the favor which you granted me, I took steps for the benefit of my interests. After eight days you asked me for the aforesaid instructions, in order to substitute others, which were delivered to me on my departure. By them I was deprived of the nation which I was to have selected, in order that all might be left free to the

---

[1]This is an original document in the Bancroft Library but with the middle folio missing. I found the missing folio in A.G.I., P. de C., leg. 124 where undoubtedly the parts now in the Bancroft Library were before reaching the Bancroft Library. This letter as well as many others from the Bancroft Library, some of which are published in this volume, have been used by Teggart in his "Notes Supplementary to any Edition of Lewis and Clark" in *American Historical Association Annual Report 1908*, I, 185-195.

[2]See document XVI.

[3]See Chapter I, documents XII, XIV, XIX, XXXII; Chapter III, document XIV, etc.

merchants, on condition that they should pay to the commandant twenty *pesos* for each passport.

The charge for each in the first year, 1792, was seventeen *pesos*. The ambition of each trader and the different interests in the same nation in this way caused the ruin of all. And the Indians, after providing themselves with their necessities at a low price, became so insolent that very little hope was left of continuing to trade with them on this new basis. I do not know what merchant proposed it [this procedure] to the governor-general and thus caused the regulation,⁴ to be issued, a copy of which I enclose to Your Excellency. It has been strictly followed up to the present in all cases in which it has not been annulled by the exclusive agreements granted later.

In 1793 a representation by the inhabitants of Ste. Geneviève and by Don Luis Lorimier (the latter in the name of the Chavanon [Shawnee] and Loup nations) caused the governor-general to declare war on the Little and Great Osages. The publication of it was scarcely made when extreme terror seized on all of our settlements, and the inhabitants did not venture to go out except in armed parties of twenty or thirty men. Having on my part not the smallest recourse for this war, which was ordered to be made without any expense, my principal and only effort was to try to deprive the enemy nations entirely of arms and ammunition. In order to accomplish the desired object, I prohibited the entrance of the Missouri to traders and hunters, and as a result none of the other Indian nations on this river had merchants [traders] in that year; for otherwise there would have been the danger that the Osages would intercept what was destined for others.⁵

In the month of January, 1794, the Osages, to the number of one hundred [200?] men, presented themselves at the village of Ste. Geneviève with hostile intent and finding a man alone killed him. This was enough to throw the whole settlement into despair and caused the inhabitants to clamour for the solicitation of peace, which they did. At this time Don Augusto Chouteau went down to the capital, where he made proposals to the governor-general for subjugating the Osage nations by means of a fort, which he obligated himself to construct on condition that he should be allowed the exclusive trade with them. These proposals were accepted by a contract for six years, to be concluded at the end of 1799.⁶

The merchants of St. Louis made as loud an outcry as they could over this concession. It deprived me personally of sixteen passports at twenty-five *pesos* each, but my desire for the general good always makes me admit that this contract has done a great deal of good for Illinois, and

---

⁴Chapter I, document XXXII.
⁵Full documentation and narrative in Nasatir, *Imperial Osage.*
⁶*Ibid.* The contract is printed in Houck, *Spanish Régime in Missouri,* II 100-110.

526

that from the moment when Don Augusto Chouteau put his plans into execution we have enjoyed the greatest peace and tranquility in all our settlements. I also admit that with this motive, excepting for the envy of some of the merchants, all the rest of the inhabitants commended this measure. I do not know whether Don Augusto Chouteau has paid or contributed anything. Personally I give my word of honor that, far from having received anything, I have lost to the amount of four hundred *pesos* annually in the privilege of issuing passports which had been previously granted to me.

You are not ignorant of the fact that, with the approval of this general government, there was formed at St. Louis in 1794 a trading company under the name of that of the Upper Missouri,[7] and that there was granted to it for ten years thence exclusive trade of all the nations that it might discover above the Poncas. This Company,[8] composed of eight shareholders and as many members, in the first year aforesaid made an expedition in a pirogue, in charge of the person named Juan Bautista Truteau,[9] an intelligent and prudent man. Having but a few men with whom to face a party of Sioux whom he encountered a good way up, he was compelled to sacrifice the greater part of his goods as presents, in order to retreat to the village of the Poncas. The latter also consumed something.

Nevertheless, in the following year of 1795, he [Truteau] set out to continue his journey in the expectation that he would be overtaken by another and larger expedition which the Company was to send.[10] This was done, but it was entrusted to a man without experience and of bad behavior, who detained the expedition purposely among the Poncas nation, where it was broken up, with the loss of 8000 *pesos* in merchandise in addition to heavy expenses. Truteau, awaiting these resources in order to continue his journey, in which he had already overcome the greatest obstacles, had gone to the Ricara nation, where he occupied himself in calling together the surrounding nations, in order to cultivate friendship with them and establish the beginning of his commerce, for which he had great hopes.

Then in the month of May, 1796, the Sioux came in force to attack the Ricaras, who abandoned their village by night. Truteau, in order to escape with his life, was compelled to do the same, leaving behind his goods and skins. He took the road to fall back upon the Mahas nation,

---

[7] See documents in Chapter II.
[8] Trudeau gives a brief but excellent account herein of the Company. The documents are published in this volume. They have been summarized and narrated in Nasatir, "Anglo-Spanish Rivalry on the Upper Missouri," *Mississippi Valley Historical Review*, XVI (1929-1930), 359-382; 507-530.
[9] See Truteau's "Journal"—Chapter II, document XXII.
[10] End of copy in Bancroft Library. From here until a later indicated point the letter is taken from A.G.I., P. de C., leg. 124

where he found a third expedition of the company. In charge of this [was] *Monsieur* James Mackay, a new agent of the Company appointed by the Baron de Carondelet as commandant of all the posts of the Upper Missouri.[11] The said Mackay was forced to winter among the aforesaid Mahas nation, where he was to form an establishment. His trade during the winter was very unfortunate, because of the despotic way in which he was treated by those Indians, and for the following year there was nothing left to him for the journey farther up. This necessitated his waiting for new goods, which the Company determined to despatch in charge of a new agent called Breda, who, as unfortunate as the first two through the perversity of the Indians, returned with them in June of the present year, without having brought enough to pay the expenses.

All the blame should be placed on those Indians, and not on the agents, whose honesty and experience is [are] well known to me. The members of the Company accuse their director, Clamorgan, of bad management and infidelity. This has caused division between them all, and has caused some of them to abandon their shares, while others have tried to sell to Clamorgan, who has collected seven of the eight shares, the eighth remaining with Don Joseph Robidou. This year no attempt has been made to do anything, and I believe the death of Todd has broken up all the projects of the aforesaid Clamorgan. The two were to have formed a company, and the deceased was to have taken the office of administrator of the funds. Now I am absolutely ignorant of what Clamorgan will do with his exclusive privilege. If he does not meet some other rich merchant, it remains to be seen whether his intentions are to continue in the spring of the coming year.

For more than twenty years the trade of the Indians of the Mississippi above St. Louis has been in the hands of the English, and now it is in the hands of the Americans. It has never been seen that our merchants have tried to enter into anything with them, and the reason is that they pay dearer for the merchandise and sell their skins cheaper than in Canada. It seems that this having been seen by Your Excellency's predecessor in this government, it caused him to form a contract with the deceased Andrés Todd, to whom he granted exclusive trade with all the Indians of the Upper Mississippi, including the rivers on our side which discharge into the first-named. Last year the house of Todd began this trade, which was not at all favorable to him because many Englishmen had begun it at the same time. As a result, it was necessary for him to sell his goods at a price which displeased the others and ruined them. The representative of the

---

[11]Mackay's "Journal" is Chapter III, document XX and see this Chapter, document II; Mackay's commission is Chapter IV, document XII.

deceased went up the Mississippi this year with the goods which came to him from the capital, but nothing is known today of the results.[12]

Small parties of the Chavanones [Shawnees], Loups, Peorias, Illinois, Miamia, Otave, Mascutin, Kikapoux, and Pouteatamia nations are scattered over our territory. Many of them, encamped close to our settlements, carry on commerce or exchange as best pleases them. Most often they bring their skins to the different villages, and the same is done with us by the nations of the American side when they find that goods are sold to them cheaply.[13]

The trade in skins in Illinois does not go beyond the value of 75,000 a year; and, as it is visibly diminishing, it cannot be more than twenty years before it will disappear entirely, as has been the case for some time in Lower Louisiana. There will then be left only the regions remote from [far regions of] the Missouri to obtain them from, and these inhabitants will then be reduced to the obligation of all applying themselves to the cultivation of the land, which will be fortunate for them.

I am sending Your Excellency an exact report of the income produced for me by the passports of trade of which I have spoken.[14] I can assure you that I have only made use of a fourth part of it, and the rest was spent in relieving some families more unfortunate than mine. I have no fear that Your Excellency will withdraw this emolument from me, which is the only one produced for me by my command, and, on the contrary, I am confident that if it is in Your Excellency's power to better my lot, you will do so gladly. I am assured of this by the generosity of your heart which is inclined to bestow favors and which has always merited my love and respect. I pray God to preserve the life of Your Excellency many years. St. Louis, Illinois, December 20, 1797.

I kiss Your Excellency's hands. Your most attentive and respectful servant.

Zenon Trudeau [rubric].

Señor Don Manuel Gayoso de Lemos.

[12]See Nasatir, "Anglo-Spanish Frontier on the Upper Mississippi 1786-1796," *Iowa Journal of History and Politics*, XXIX (1931), 155-232; *Ibid.*, XXVIII (1930) 337-389.
[13]End of fragment in A.G.I., P. de C., leg. 124. The remainder of this letter is in the Bancroft Library.
[14]See document XVI.

XVI

Trudeau to [Gayoso de Lemos?], St. Louis, December 20, 1797[1]

Brief demonstration of the method with which by order and superior rule the trade with the Indian nations of the Missouri from the year 1792 to the present one, 1797, inclusive, has been divided.

[1]A.G.I., P. de C., leg., 131A. Most likely enclosed with document XV.

1792

In this year all the trades of the Missouri were free and seventeen traders who paid twenty *pesos* each to the commandant for the passport entered its trade.

1793

In this year the *Reglamento* was remitted,[2] a copy of which I am enclosing, and on account of the war which was ordered declared on the Osages, the step was taken of not permitting entrance into the Missouri to the traders, and thus all the nations were without trade.

1794

	Division of each nation	Value of each share	Total for each nation
Big Osages	12	@1000 *pesos*	12,000
Little Osages	4	1000	4,000
Kansas	4	1000	4,000
Otos	2	1400	2,800
Mahas	3	1333	3,999
Panis Republic	1	1000	1,000
Panis Tapage	1	1000	1,000
Panis Loups	1	1000	1,000
Panis Bonchef	1	1000	1,000
	29		30,799

In the referred to year of 1794, after lots had been drawn in conformity with the *reglamento* of the preceding year, Mr. Chouteau arrived from the capital with orders and concession of the exclusive trade[3] with the two Osage nations, thereby frustrating the sixteen merchants to whom these nations belonged by virtue of the said drawing of lots. Therefore, there remained thirteen who used their trade and paid the twenty-five *pesos* passport fee.

Year 1795

Kansas	6	@800	4800 *pesos*
Otos	3	935	2805
Mahas	4	1000	4000
Panis Republic	2	600	1200

[2]Chapter I, document XXXII.
[3]Houck, *Spanish Régime in Missouri*, II, 100-110.

Panis bon chef	1	1000	1000
Panis Tapage	1	1000	1000
Panis Loups	1	1000	1000
	18		15805

Year 1796

Kansas	6	@800	4800
Panis Republic	2	600	1200
Panis Bonchef	1	1000	1000
Panis Tapage	1	1000	1000
Panis Loups	1	1000	1000
	11		9000

In the said year of 1796 the Commercial Company of the Upper Missouri obtained from the *Señor* Baron de Carondelet the exclusive trade of the Otos, Mahas and Poncas nations[4] and there remained for the drawing of lots eleven shares of the remaining nations, the recipients of which paid the same passport fee of twenty-five *pesos* each.

Year 1797

Kansas .... 6 shares   @ 800 pesos   4800

The other nations have had no traders during the present year, because in the previous years they have comported themselves very badly with the whites who went to trade with them, the latter having incurred losses of fifty per cent on their effects of their commercial ventures. It was the desire of all the merchants to punish these nations by depriving them of their needs. Due to the present war, the English cannot introduce merchandise into the Missouri at low prices, as they have done in previous years, and so the merchants have taken advantage of the circumstances to make known to the Indians whose conduct was irregular that they must depend upon this government. I hope this step will have the best effect.

---

[4] See Chapter IV, documents XXIV and XXXVI: Pratte and Vasquez petitioned for the exclusive trades of the Pani and Kansas, respectively, but did not obtain them. Again on May 28, 1797, Vasquez in a "poorly considered and poorly thought out letter" asked for the Kansas trade. Carondelet to Howard, New Orleans, July 28, 1797 enclosing Vasquez to Carondelet, St. Louis, May 28, 1797, A.G.I., P. de C., leg. 24.

Emoluments which the commandant has received, the product of the passports paid for by the merchants who have engaged in trade with the Indian nations of the Missouri, from the year 1792 to 1797, inclusive.

	Number of Passports	Value	Total
Year 1792 17		@ 20 *pesos*	340
1793 There was no trade			
1794 13		25 *pesos*	325
1795 18		25 *pesos*	450
1796 11		25 *pesos*	275
1797 6		25 *pesos*	150
		Total	1540

St. Louis, December 20, 1797

Zenon Trudeau   [rubric]

Dear Evans

The Severety of the winter & the want of opportunity prevented my leaving this place hitherto & I suppose that I Shall remain here until Sometime in the New Year

I have taken some lands & wish you were here to survey them so as to take the Certificate to N. Orleans to get a deed, but do not leave any part of your business undone at Cap Gerardeau on any account whatever —

No news since you left this place except that Gaihard & Dupon is making much load & that the Navigation is stoped here owing to the Ice —

yours Sincerely

St Louis Dec 23
1797

James Mackay

Cuba 217

CHAPTER VI

1798

I

TRUDEAU TO GOVERNOR, ST. LOUIS, JANUARY 15, 1798[1]

The settlements of His Catholic Majesty in Illinois form part of Upper Louisiana and are located on the western bank of the Mississippi River between 37 and 39 degrees of latitude, between the two confluents which the above river forms with the Ohio and the Missouri. These settlements are Cape Girardeau, New Bourdon, Ste. Geneviève, Carondelet, St. Louis, San Fernando, and San Carlos del Misury.

The first settlement which one meets on ascending the Mississippi is Cape Girardeau, fifteen leagues above the junction of the Ohio. That place was occupied already for some years by Don Louis Lorimier, who, some time ago, was appointed Commandant of it by Baron de Carondelet. About thirty families, attracted by the advances offered by our Government in granting lands free of charge, having emigrated from the United States of America, have settled there. This country is yet without a clearing and that seems truly a pity, because on considering the beauty of its situation, the healthfulness of its climate, the amenity, strength, and fertility of its land, the abundance of various creeks and springs which water it, the many good woods for construction, and all the rest that can be desired by the planters in said site, as well as in all Illinois; one cannot be less than astonished at seeing that instead of finding flourishing settlements with most abundant harvests, according to the promise of the fertility

---

[1]Written in Spanish. A.G.I., P. de C., leg. 2365; printed in Houck, *Spanish Régime in Missouri*, II, 247-258.

of the land, nothing but small settlements, which are beginning to spring up, and wild mountains, are found.

Twelve leagues from Cape Girardeau, in the interior of the country, there is a branch of the river San Francisco, which empties into the Mississippi. The lands located on the shores of the said branches are as beautiful and fertile as those of the above-mentioned Cape Girardeau. Already some habitants desire and are thinking of settling there, since they find the same advantages of being able to transport their products by said branch to the Mississippi and thence to the capital, as the other settlers located on the shore of the first-named river.

Twenty leagues from Cape Girardeau is found New Bourbon, located on a hill which commands a low point, about one league broad, between the Mississippi and said hill. It is on that low point that the habitants carry on their principal cultivation, in spite of the fact that the freshets of the river frequently inundate it, destroying in an instant the fruit of a year of toil. The most notable habitants have assured me that they are accustomed to lose two out of five harvests regularly, but such is the power of custom and of preoccupation that they always persist in cultivating there, for they believe that they find it more fertile than the other lands, in spite of the example presented by the Americans newly settled among them, who, more experienced and prudent, sow on the heights in that neighborhood, where they gain an abundant harvest of grain of a superior quality, and do not fear to lose it by the rising of the river.

That village, whose population consists of 461 persons of both sexes, including the plantations of La Salina and others, has separated from the village of Ste. Geneviève, in order to give its command to *Monsier* de Luzière. The village of Ste. Geneviève, which follows immediately within half [a league], is situated on the same hill. The habitants of this latter village cultivate the same low point as those of New Bourbon. It is not yet more than seven years since they settled the said hill, although they have been settled on said low point (so subject to frequent inundations) for more than sixty years. But, warned by so many reiterated occasions, they finally decided to seek a position where they might place the houses under shelter. The inhabitants of this district are united by the most narrow bonds. Nearly all of them being related, blood binds them to maintain the fast friendship and harmony which has always existed among them. Don Francisco Vallé, who is their Commandant at present, is, at the same time, the head of the most numerous and notable families. The personal qualities which this man possesses make him one of the most to be recommended of that country, for not only is he esteemed by those habitants, but he is their true friend and protector.

The city of St. Louis, located forty leagues from Cape Girardeau, and twenty from New Bourbon and Ste. Geneviève, is the principal settlement of Illinois. Like the city of New Orleans, it is located on the banks of the Mississippi River. It has a population of 948 persons of all ages and sexes. It is in this city where the very limited commerce of these settlements is carried on, and whence the merchandise is sent out for the purpose of trade with the Indians of the Missouri. It has very few farmers and those who follow that calling cultivate blindly without the least knowledge except what custom teaches, as is shown by the abuse of enclosing in common the farm lands which are separated one from another by a great distance, in order to prevent the sheep and other domestic animals from entering the cultivated parts. It is true that, in the beginning, necessity may have obliged them to follow that method, which experience ought to make them abandon at this present day, for, since the stockade which they have to make annually is extremely extended, and since the interest of all is not the same, in order that the stockade be kept up, the most exact vigilance is not sufficient to restrain the animals and in attending in time to its repair. Therefore, the crops are destroyed most years by said animals, and it will continue so in the future, if that vicious custom is persisted in. Already the good habitants desire to abandon it, present circumstances also demand that it be done away with, in order to further the prosperity of the inland plantations. And their animals abandoned to themselves, as in Natchez, they will begin (each one) to enclose their farms.

The village of Carondelet is some two leagues below, being also located on the shores of the Mississippi River. Its population consists of persons of both sexes and all ages. Its habitants are poor and the greater part Canadians and Creoles. The married men cultivate their fields and the young men are employed in the voyages of the Mississippi and Missouri. It is two years since they have abandoned the stockade which they made in common with those of Saint Louis for the safety of their fields. That has proved very advantageous to them, for in the above-mentioned two years they have gathered very abundant harvests; and the lands, that had no value in the beginning, as they were slow in building the stockades, are today sold at an excellent price.

The village of San Fernando is located west of this city inland and distant from it about five leagues.[2] Its population consists of persons of

---

[2]In 1783, Fr. Dunégant left St. Louis to establish himself in St. Ferdinand. It became a village of cultivators and they were able to resist the insults of the savages. Zenon Trudeau proposed Dunegant for captain of the militia which was granted by Carondelet. In 1798 he asked for the annual salary of 100 *piastres* which was the customary salary for such positions. Petition of Dunegant to Gayoso de Lemos (1798), A.G.I., P. de C., leg. 91. See also Gilbert J. Garraghan, *Saint Ferdinand de Florissant* (Chicago, 1923). Gayoso ordered that Dunegant be paid the salary of civil and mili-

both sexes, including some American plantations. Its cultivation has resulted quite advantageously for some years back, and said habitants are very attentive to work, which gives hopes that their children will be good planters. There is no parish priest in this village, which has plantations in its neighborhood. It would not be a bad thing to send them a priest of the Irish nation. He could also serve the small village of Marais de Liars [*i.e.,* Cottonwood Swamp], which is near by, and whose population consists of [*no number given in MS.*] persons. All the young men of this last settlement are hunters, although there are also good planters. It is about eleven years since the villages of San Fernando and Carondelet have been settled by the people of Saint Louis, who at the present time get a great part of their provisions from these two towns.

For one year back and, even today, plantations have been made, and are being made in the neighborhood of these villages. Their population at the present time is composed of persons of both sexes and all ages, as appears by the general register of this year which I enclose. I ask the Governor-General to please cast his eyes on it so that he may easily obtain a correct idea of all the population in these settlements, whose district offers, in general, lands abounding in mountains and unappropriated prairies. Almost all of these lands are cut by various springs in all parts. Few countries unite so many advantages as this under one sky and in a very delightful climate. Nevertheless, the cold is severe some years, but there is no winter which the fine moderation of the spring does not allow the farmer the opportune time to do his plowing.

This country is also abundant in lead mines and salt deposits scattered a certain distance one from another. They can easily supply their products to numerous settlements. There are also iron mines in abundance, and they abound as well at intervals in navigable rivers, which makes their excavation and transportation easy. It is in the working and settlement of these mines that the hope of the population and cultivation of this country depends. The establishment of an excellent foundry and forge for the reduction of the minerals into bars would be very convenient. It would be of great encouragement for all the people, since the farmer who pays at present four or five *reales* a pound for this metal has to get along perforce without the most useful tools for his calling. Others would willingly devote themselves to farming, but hesitate to do so because of the great expenses which said instruments would cause them. Consequently, the first object of encouragement that I must present to the Royal Governor is to favor the working of some of these mines.

---

tary commandant of the post of San Carlos de Florisante from January 1, 1794. Gayoso to Trudeau, April 13, 1798, A.G.I., P. de C., leg. 44 and Morales to Gayoso, April 14, 1798—*Ibid.,* leg. 91.

The Indian tribes who inhabit the territory of Illinois have always been the greatest obstacle to the progress of the settlement of the country. For, obliged to unite in masses in the villages in order to be able to oppose and to resist the raids and vexations of every kind committed by those barbarians, there have been times in which they did not dare to go to their farms. That introduced among them a passive idleness which gave them over to the tasting of spirituous liquors and drunkenness, a taste fatal to all the villages, and which has caused the total ruin in these new settlements of the greater part of the best families, upon which was placed the hope of prosperity of this country. Since the three years the Government has granted Don Augusto Chouteau exclusive trade with the two Osage tribes, these two tribes have been restrained in their piracies on these settlements, because said Don Augusto Chouteau found the means of diverting and dissuading them by good counsels and by means of the accredited ascendancy which he has among both tribes. But there are still other tribes which frequently steal horses, and treat very badly the whites who are isolated. It is an evil which it is still necessary to endure, and which it is not possible to avoid, since most times it is not known what tribes are the aggressors, and because if we used harshness we should find ourselves in the sad necessity of making war on some men quite distant from here, of whom the greater part live outside of our territory. That would make their punishment more difficult.

Without doubt the Osages have been harmful in the river of Arkansas, but I do not know whether it would be prudent to break with them in a point in which they leave the important district of Illinois at peace, which is beginning to be settled by a large emigration of foreigners who can be attracted only by tranquility and quietness, which said settlements enjoy at the present time. It is, therefore, desirable that the Governor-General regard and consider for a moment the prosperity of Illinois, and the slight evil suffered by the hunters and wanderers of the Arkansas River. That class of people is the scum of the posts. Let the Governor attempt to restrain said Osages by way of gentleness and patience, until these settlements, having been assured by a numerous population, may themselves lend to the Government aid and a strong hand to punish this tribe and any other which transgresses order.

The trade of Illinois is sufficiently limited in comparison with its population. What goes up annually from the Capital for the consumption of the habitants is very little, for it consists in brandy, sugar, coffee, soap, iron, some ordinary cloth for the Indians, and all kinds of goods for trade. In exchange for these goods the merchants receive wheat, corn, tobacco, and different kinds of furs. These latter consist of the skins of deer, bears, beavers, and otters. The annual amount of all this barter may be about eighty thousand *pesos,* which converted into skins are taken down to New Orleans annually.

The private trade of the two Osage tribes belongs exclusively to Don Augusto Chouteau. Among these two tribes can be counted one thousand two hundred men, who have their villages on the shores of the river named for them. During good years, they trade in both villages about six hundred packs of furs at the rate of forty *pesos* a piece, which amounts to 24,000 *pesos.* It is toward the furtherance of this trade that the merchants of this district direct all their ambition. It is often very damaging to them, since a slight reason causes the Indians to leave the hunt and nothing at all makes them abandon their traders, after having received from them the best of their goods, leaving the rest to the discretion of their enemies, who generally rob them. On many occasions they compel the traders to an unequal and unjust exchange, maltreating them if they resist. But these vexations do not prevent the traders from returning next year to seek others like them.

The Kance tribe has its village located on the banks of the river of that name. They number about 400 men, and are all better hunters than the Osages, and at the least as great rogues as they. This tribe would have an easy entrance to the river of Arkansas if it were not for the Osages who prevent them, and certainly they would commit more acts of piracy and roguery than these latter. This is the only tribe whose trade is not exclusive. It is usually divided into six equal parts, each one valued at the sum of eight hundred *pesos.* These six parts are distributed by lot among all the merchants of Saint Louis and Sainte Geneviève. Those which have drawn the lot one year are excluded from it the next year, and until all have shared in this advantage. From this tribe 180 packs of furs are obtained annually.

The village of the Octatacta tribe is located about 200 leagues above the entrance of the Missouri, between the confluence of the latter river and the Plate. Their number is 400 men. Thirty leagues inland from said river Plate is the Panis tribe, consisting of 800 men. Eighty leagues from the entrance of the Plate River, ascending by the Missouri, are found the Mahas, consisting of 600 men. The trade of those four nations belongs exclusively to a company established in 1794, under the approval of the general Government. This Company, which must go to the source of the Missouri, caused one Juan Bautista Truteau, prudent, intelligent and experienced, who was sent from here the same year of the Company's formation, to penetrate to the Mandana tribe. The Mandana tribe is supposed to be distant from Saint Louis some five hundred leagues. The great obstacles and difficulties which had to be conquered on the part of the wandering tribe of the Sioux, whom he found in the path of his navigation, compelled him to go back to winter among the Poncas tribe. That tribe consumed for him half of the few goods which he took. He returned the following spring to acomplish his voyage and reached the Ricaras tribe, which he found settled on the south shore of the Missouri River, to the number of about 800 men. There he decided to await some reinforcements which were to be sent to him by the above-mentioned Company. The latter really sent him a second expedition, but unfortunately the one in charge of it managed it so badly that he was captured and detained by the Poncas tribe, who used up for him almost all the goods he carried.[3]

In the year 1795 said Company sent out a third expedition in charge of Mr. Mackay, an intelligent and prudent man.[4] In his charge, were placed all the interests which he carried. Since the season of the year was already advanced at the time of his departure, he was only to penetrate that first year as far as the Mahas tribe, and form there a post, in order to send thence every year the effects which it was necessary to send farther up. Winter had already begun when he reached the village of this perverse tribe, whose chief is so arbitary, despotic, cruel, and implacable a tyrant toward the whites, that one cannot hope that the hunt from this tribe, nor the traffic and barter which can be carried on among them, can compensate for the excessive expenses which it causes in the long and toilsome voyages made thither.

The above-mentioned Mackay established his settlement immediately upon his arrival, which he succeeded in doing during the rest of the winter. But he used up almost all his goods in the various presents which he had to give to the Indians to gain their friendship, and in the support of his employees. While awaiting the following spring for new reinforcements from the company, he despatched to the Mandana tribe up the Missouri, one Mr. Evans.[5] The latter encountered, as did Truteau, the Sioux tribe who persecuted him, and forced him to go back to the Mahas, whence he again undertook the said voyage after a short time. Finally, he reached a new village of the Ricaras which that tribe had established near the Mandanas. There he found a fort built by the merchants of Montreal. He took possession of it for an instant [only], as a short time after that he had to descend to this city.

It is three years since that fort was built, and it was continually occupied by the English traders of Canada. I know also that the traders of

[3]The essential documents relating to Truteau's expedition are given in Chapters II and III. An extensive account of his explorations is given in Nasatir, "Anglo-Spanish Rivalry on the Upper Missouri," *Mississippi Valley Historical Review,* XVI (1929), 359-382.

[4]Essential documents given in Chapters III and IV. Narrative in Nasatir, "Anglo-Spanish Rivalry on the Upper Missouri," *Ibid.,* XVI (1930), 507-530, and Nasatir, "John Evans: Explorer and Surveyor," *Missouri Historical Review,* XXV (1931), 219-239; 432-460; 585-608.

[5]*Ibid.*

the Hudson Bay also penetrate as far as the Missouri. Their voyages are, like those of Montreal, immense, because both the length of the journey and the transports and supplies which they must have in order to reach the Missouri are double those of ours; nevertheless, they have anticipated us in reaching that district belonging to us, by a river navigable from its mouth to its source. Men, although of different countries, all make the same struggle to achieve wealth; and I am of the opinion that, if our traders of Illinois possessed the same faculties as those of Canada for the carrying of goods, these English traders would see themselves very quickly driven out of our territory, and by this means, quantities of fine furs would be sent down to New Orleans which those men get in spite of a long and expensive journey.[6]

This Company consisted at the beginning of eight members or associates who risked an equal sum.[7] The greater part of them resigned, ruined, and the Company is today represented by the house of [Cla]Morgan, Loisel and Company, which has acquired the shares through the resignation of some and the purchase of the rest. This house was established for its operations in that of Don Andrés Todd, who died in New Orleans. This event can do no less than destroy the plans of the Company, which cannot be carried on without the support of another rich house. On the contrary, it is probable that these plans will have no effect, and will be buried in oblivion. Said Company not having risked another enterprise the past year, I determined to make use of this means for the punishment of the Octoctatas, Panis, Mahas, and Poncas tribes, by depriving them of goods in order to show them and convince them that they depend upon us and to reduce them to obedience.

Besides the Indian tribes of the Missouri, whose number is considerable, there are many others on the Upper Mississippi, as well as on the other rivers which empty into it from our territory. Those tribes have no trade with Illinois, for they have no other traders than the merchants of Montreal who have traded there this year under an American passport, which they got from Michilimakinac. The goods that they bring are superior to those brought us from the Capital, and they give them at better bargains. In order to supersede the English in this trade, Baron Carondelet has granted the exclusive trade of all the Upper Mississippi to Don

---

[6]There is an abundance of documentation on British penetration of the Upper Mississippi in the A.G.I., P. de C. See Nasatir, "Anglo-Spanish Frontier on the Upper Mississippi 1786-1796," *Iowa Journal of History and Politics* XXIX (1931), 155-232, and Nasatir, "Anglo-Spanish Rivalry in the Iowa Country, 1797-1798," *Ibid.*, XXVIII (1930), 337-389.

[7]See Nasatir, "Jacques Clamorgan: Colonial Promoter of the Northeastern Border of Colonial New Spain", *New Mexico Historical Review*, XVII (1942), 101-112. I have collected a mine of material for writing the life of this most interesting character.

Andrés Todd whose operations I believe prudent. Already that trader has caused a great quantity of goods, suitable for his operations, to be sent up from New Orleans, but his death and the war have frustrated this enterprise. It would have been immediately so useful and advantageous, that skins of all kinds to the value of one hundred [thousand ?] *pesos* more would have been sent down annually to the capital, besides the profit which another plan of Todd, namely, to cause all the young men whom he needed, to come down from Canada, would have produced for us. These pledged to his service for a limited time, the greater part would have remained, as happens, at the end of that service, and this settlement would have advanced by this means much more rapidly.[8]

His Majesty's settlements in Illinois have opposite them, on the east bank of the Mississippi, settlements to the same number, belonging to the United States of America. Their population is at the present time slightly greater or less than ours, but the United States have powerful means for their increase, namely, the eye of a good Government on whatever can bring its population from such to such a point, on this account depending the so rapid advances which Ohio has made in a very short time. If Congress will open up subscriptions for the sales of land for which Ohio already has the most ardent desires, the American Illinois will be seen to be covered with inhabitants. At the present time, it has a population of three thousand souls and at this rate, it is probable that they will reckon a hundred thousand ten years from now.

The more I consider the location of these settlements, and seek the possible means for increasing their population, I see no other means than that of the United States, who alone can supply a great number of families. The voyage from New Orleans is too great and costly. Canada also needs population. I do not see then only Ohio in which our Government must found its hopes. As I have heard said, the United States have many Catholics and French emigrants and Germans, and many Americans who are today disgusted with their Government. In order to attract these people, I am of the opinion that it would be advisable to form a settlement near the Ohio, so that the migrators might find an assylum to aid them in disembarking effects and furnishing food and aid to the most needy. Besides this settlement, another could be formed higher up, and so successively, until finding a district whose soil promised a good fertility for the establishment of numerous population. It would then be necessary for the government to grant some food to the most needy and those who have families, an essential point which would attract more families.

---

[8]A few of the many documents on Todd are given in Chapter V. See articles cited in note 6.

The few Americans who have migrated to this district the past year have behaved very well, for since they have found lands superior to those of the Ohio, they are earnestly beginning to improve them. Almost all of them desire to obtain good sites for mills. Those who have obtained them are earnest in increasing this industry; already they have constructed two small water-power mills [for flour] and one saw mill in distinct places where no one would have imagined even that one could really work. Their houses are already better than those of the Creoles and Canadians, who were settled in villages thirty years ago. In spite of all the advantages which our Government has given them, they have always present in their minds the difference of sect as regards our religion. This point occupies them so much that worthy and rich families have returned to the other district, because they are obliged to celebrate their marriages and baptisms by means of our Catholic priests.

It is a fact (and experience itself has shown its strength) that the soil of this country is extremely fertile in all kinds of grains, since whenever the old and new inhabitants wish to pay attention to their work they can make from here an output of very fine flour, so good, indeed, that I believe it would exceed in anyway the flour of Europe. The soil produces hemp of its own accord, since it is a natural product, and of so superior a quality, that it can be compared with that of Russia. Already several Americans have begun to cultivate it, and this very year many have resolved to begin its cultivation in real earnest. This means that it will not be slow in extending itself; and on that account, I beg the Governor-General to please devote himself to furnishing a suitable outlet for the cordage which can be manufactured here in a short time throughout Illinois, whose increase will become considerable, if the Government assists it with some spirit.

The Spanish settlements of Illinois and those of the United States are, as I have said, separated by the Mississippi River, and the villages are but very little distance apart, while the population of both districts is about equal. There are certain rumors in these last villages [i.e., the American] that they are going to construct forts in various posts and that they are to be garrisoned with troops. That is quite likely and will make it necessary for us to increase the garrison of Saint Louis. Since Spain has had possession of this province, the garrison has never exceeded fifty men, although we ought at the present time to have at least two hundred young men, strong and active, so they could overrun the mountains, and conduct and know how to journey in small boats. Without that requisite, the King will never be well served in a country where people must know how to make war in the manner of the Indians, either against them or against the whites.

The command of the abovesaid settlement has always been under charge of a Captain of the Regiment of this Province, both in regard to civil and military matters. In each village of these districts there is a Commandant, whose employment is regularly as Captain of Militia, under the orders of the Commandant-in-Chief. The Commandants of Ste. Geneviève, New Bourbon, and Cape Girardeau are assigned one hundred *pesos* annually, while all the others have no pay, although they have the same duty, and are even more exposed to seeing and receiving Indians. Consequently, they are entitled to the same pay. Each Commandant has the public archives under his charge, as well as the drawing up of all the documents of their affairs in the French idiom, as they do not know Spanish. It is the duty of the Commandant-in-Chief to go to any of those villages when any summary or criminal process is to be pursued. That causes them very heavy expense, to the detriment of their pay, in voyages and support. They have no other means of standing this expense than by their intrinsic pay as Captain. Consequenty, all the Commandants who have preceded me obtained from the Governors of their time concesssion of trade with the Big Osages, by which they could live decently. In order to furnish me a like relief, Baron de Carondelet authorized me to take twenty-five *pesos* for each passport, which I signed for the traders, who went hence to the Missouri. That gave me a regular income to the number of twenty-eight passports, which allowed me to support myself decently. But this emolument lasted only one year and I am today reduced to only one hundred and fifty *pesos* by reason of the various privileges of exclusive trade granted to Chouteau and to the Company of the Upper Missouri.

The Governor has no room to doubt that I have always endeavored to act honorably in the charge which has been conferred on me in this command, and, in particular, with the foreigners whom we have at our boundaries, since officials of all kinds, even generals and judges, etc., have come to visit me. The expenses of that, as can be seen, can not be supplied by the sole pay of a Captain, if he wishes to sustain the honor and splendor due his nation.

If the said Commandant-in-Chief needs greater emolument at the present day, the multiplicity of the affairs which he has to despatch demands also that he keep a secretary; the settlement requires a notary public who is honorable and intelligent; the Americans, an interpreter; and affairs of justice, an assessor. All of the above is indispensable and I bring it to the consideration of the Governor-General for a country which is five hundred leagues away from the Capital, whose situation, both politically and rurally, announce that it must within a short time become the most valuable that His Majesty possesses in Louisiana.

St. Louis, Illinois, January 15, 1798.

Zenon Trudeau [rubric].

II

TRUDEAU TO GAYOSO DE LEMOS, ST. LOUIS, JANUARY, 16, 1798[1]

Number 316

I am enclosing to Your Excellency a *relación* of a voyage[2] which M. Mackay has made in the Upper Missouri, and the map of the said river, as far as the Mandan nation, made by the same person,[3] which I believe to be the most exact of those which have have been formed up to the present, since M. Mackay was instructed in the matter and knew that he had pledged himself to procure this map with careful attention for the government. Up to the present time the government had only [information] intellectually based upon the simple *relaciónes* of the hunters.

May God keep Your Excellency many years.

St. Louis, January 16, 1798.

Zenon Trudeau [rubric]

Señor Don Manuel Gayoso de Lemos.

---

[1]Written in Spanish. A.G.I., P. de C., leg. 2365.

[2]Chapter III, document XX.

[3]Mackay stated that he made a map (*American State Papers, Public Lands*, VI, 718, 720; and VIII, 868). That Mackay made a map is inferred also from Thwaites, *Original Journal of Lewis and Clark*, I, 50; VI, 125 and see also I, 147. Teggart believes that Perrin du Lac's map was the work of Mackay. "Notes Supplementary to any Edition of Lewis and Clark" in *American Historical Association, Annual Report,* 1908, I, 188-189. Writing to Andrés López [de Armesto] on October 14, 1797, Clamorgan said that he was sending the governor "the map of the Missouri well drawn up at the cost and expenses of the Company. I hope that it [Company] will recover its usual vigor shortly and that it will merit in the future by its zeal and activity in making discoveries, the bounties of the government". A.G.I., P. de C., leg. 213.

Trudeau highly recommended Mackay to Gayoso de Lemos upon his going to New Orleans to present himself to the governor. He [Mackay] was quite conversant about the Missouri. "He is the author of the map which Mr. Chouteau will deliver to you, and he still has the ambition to continue to form another entire one but the expense would be too considerable to propose to Your Excellency." Trudeau to Gayoso de Lemos, St. Louis, March 5, 1798, A.G.I., P. de C., leg. 49.

Perhaps in reply to this on May 1, 1798, Gayoso appointed Mackay captain of militia and commandant of San André del Misuri, in compensation "for the activity and zeal which he manifested while he was employed by the Missouri Company". A.G.I., P. de C., leg. 44; draft in *Ibid.*, leg. 133. *Cp* and *cf.* Houck, *Spanish Régime in Missouri*, II, 245. Mackay's appointment as taken from a draft or copy in A.G.I., P. de C., leg. 2365 is in Houck, *Spanish Régime in Missouri*, II, 245-246. Mackay did visit New Orleans and returned, taking possession of his new command of San André on October 1, 1798. Trudeau to Gayoso, no. 28, St. Louis, November 15, 1798, A.G.I., P. de C., leg. 2365, which is in reply to Gayoso's letter of May 1, 1798. Same in Gayoso de Lemos to Morales, New Orleans, April 2, 1799, A.G.I., P. de C., leg 2366 and draft in *Ibid.*, leg. 92.

III

Vasquez to Gayoso de Lemos, St. Louis, March 5, 1798[1]

My Dear Sir and Most Venerated Chief and Master:

I do not believe that there is in this entire province a person who has experienced more jubilation and satisfaction than I, when the happy news was announced that you were remaining as governor-general of this province: This has animated me so much, that it has brought the most profound hope in my painful situation, with the heavy burden of family which I have on my hands. I live with sure confidence that Your Excellency will not forget the offers of your important protection which you have made to me when you were in these settlements—assured that Your Excellency will set me right, if you cannot support my requests, giving me some more secure light from Your Excellency's opinion in order to again expose what it may please you to indicate to me.

On May 13, 1796, I presented the enclosed memorial to the *Señor* Baron de Carondelet, soliciting the exclusive trade of the Kansas nation in the Missouri, and the latter assured me that he was sending the said memorial decreed [for the concession of the said trade] to the lieutenant-governor of these establishments, so that he might put me in possession of the trade of the mentioned nation. With that I left your city very contented, persuaded by the firmness of the *Señor* Baron's reasons, [and] after having made many attentions and courtesies to persons whom I had begged to interest themselves in my behalf for the success of my pretention, which in fact I believed that they had done. But as soon as I returned here, having spoken concerning this matter to the *Señor* Don Zenon Trudeau, he answered me that the *Señor* Governor ordered him nothing concerning this matter, and that on the contrary, the memorial came without a decree, and the official letter which was enclosed to him said in express terms that the solicitation could not be allowed. This has

---

[1]Written in Spanish. A.G.I., P. de C., leg. 2365. Benito Vasquez had on at least two previous occasions in two different years asked for the trade of the Kansas Indians and had been turned down. I did not include Vasquez' earlier memorial or petition in this volume. See Chapter IV, documents XXIV and XXXVI, Chapter V, document XVI, note 4.

Enclosed with this letter was Vasquez' petition which was dated St. Louis, March 5, 1798. The letter summarizes the contents of Vasquez' petition which was addressed to the governor general.

Vasquez' earlier petition and letter was, said Howard, "poorly worded and poorly thought out." Vasquez was held under arrest for thirty-five days for having made some improper remarks against Carondelet while under the influence of "wine." Vasquez said that Carondelet, *"havia obrado como un picaro ladron y usurpador . . . . que havia usurpado los empleos que havia obtenido"*. Trudeau to Gayoso, no. 303, St. Louis, December 28, 1797 and enclosed written statement of Francisco Garrell dated St. Louis, November, 2, 1797, A.G.I., P. de C., leg. 48.

put me in great debt, because I had provided myself in your capital with the merchandise proper for this nation, having taken on credit a sum equivalent to its premises; being, as I was, frustrated, I could neither sell the said merchandise, placing them at the most moderate price (because of the great competition of the merchants of this post), nor even less pay the debt which I had contracted, as I have said, in the capital. If the *Señor* Baron had not undeceived me, I would not see today the loss of my small interests, for I can assure Your Excellency that I find myself at the end of my resources, and have never seen myself in such a straightened condition.

In view of this, having trusted in the offers which Your Excellency made to me when you visited these establishments, I am daring to importune you, by supplicating that you deign to concede to me the trade of the Kansas nation for the time which you may judge conducent for indemnifying myself for my losses, without which support I see no other alternative that to deliver myself over to great poverty. If Your Excellency fears that this may occasion some complaint or murmur among the public, I will annually give a certain sum to aid in the re-building of a church in this *villa*, which example must shut the mouth of anyone who may wish to speak, seeing that it redounds to the general good.

If I obtain this petition from the great benevolence of Your Excellency, you will be able to flatter yourself that you have succored a father of a family, and one weighted down with years by the sea of misery, assuring you that I will employ all means in order to give the most passionate proofs of my gratitude, with which I remain begging of the all powerful [to guard] Your life infinite years, and to exalt you in greater undertakings.

St. Louis, Illinois, March 5, 1798.

Your most affectionate servant kisses
Your Excellency's hand.

Benito Vasquez [rubric]

Señor Don Manuel Gayoso de Lemos.[2]

---

[2]Gayoso de Lemos replied on April 24, 1798 (A.G.I., P. de C., leg. 44) telling Vasquez to go to the lieutenant governor to obtain the trade which he desired, but that he (Gayoso) was strongly opposed to conceding such trades for a longer period than one year. Vasqeuz presented that letter to Trudeau who, because of the fact that the Panis trade alone remained, granted Vasquez three out of the four parts (each part amounting to 1000 *pesos* merchandise) and reserved the fourth part for himself, permission for which Carondelet had granted him. Trudeau to Gayoso de Lemos, no. 15, St. Louis, July 17, 1798, A.G.I., P. de C., leg. 50. Gayoso on August 8, 1798 replied approving Trudeau's action, A.G.I., P. de C., leg. 44.

IV

ROBIDOU TO [GAYOSO DE LEMOS], ST. LOUIS, MARCH 7, 1798[1]

Monseigneur

Since your sojourn in our city,[2] you have had the goodness to offer your services to us, and more particularly to me, *Monseigneur;* consequently, I dare from this generous offer to beg you to kindly grant me the post of the Kansas nation to trade there exclusively for several years. This post will redeem for me the immense losses which I have suffered from time to time. It will furnish me with the means of honoring my creditors and raising my numerous family. Due to the manner in which this post is exploited today, it is pure loss to the country because of the manner in which it is distributed; it is divided into ten portions. It is necessary that a trader who goes to the Kansas pay a sum to these ten persons, who have the permission [that he may then] take there a modest equipment which he never takes; so that neither the trader nor the equipper can make their returns [profits]; thus causing the commerce to languish.

The request, which I have the honor of making to you, will only harm very slightly a few individuals while it will open to me a branch of commerce sufficient for my position, and will place the trader in the happy position of not risking his life, without being sure of a real benefit.

I dare to await, *Monseigneur,* this grace from your bounty, and beg you to believe me to be with a profound respect, *Monseigneur,*

> Your Excellency's very humble, very respectful
> and always devoted servant
> J. H. Robidou [rubric]

St. Louis, Illinois, March 7, 1798[3]

[1]Written in French. A ʔ.I., P. de C., leg. 215A.
[2]In 1795.
[3]Unaddressed but to Gayoso de Lemos. See document V.

V

ROBIDOU TO GAYOSO DE LEMOS, ST. LOUIS, MARCH 7, 1798[1]

To Monseigneur Don Emmanuel Gayoso de Lemos, Brigadier of the armies of His Catholic Majesty, Governor General of the Province of Louisiana.

Your humble petitioner, Joseph Robidou, merchant, lieutenant of militia, has the honor again to expose to you that he had been peacefully

[1]Written in French. I have translated this from the original in the Bancroft Library. It is very incorrectly translated in F. L. Billon, *Annals of St. Louis in its Early Days under the French and Spanish Dominations.* (St. Louis, 1886) 283-288. A poor, incomplete and incorrect copy taken from Billon is to be found in O. M. Robidoux, *Memorial to the Robidoux Brothers* (Kansas City, 1924), 24-28.

and advantageously pursuing his trade with the Indian nations, in the vicinity of his dwelling in St. Louis, where he is a resident, when on May 12, 1794, *Monsieur* Zenon Trudeau, Lieutenant-Governor of the western part of the Illinois, desirous of extending the knowledge of the places under his jurisdiction, promote commerce, and wrest from the English nation a portion of the riches they fraudulently acquired from the dominions of His Catholic Majesty, assembled together all the traders of St. Louis, and proposed to them to unite in co-partnership, consolidating their capitals, that they might make themselves masters of this branch of the trade in peltries, existing in the Upper Missouri. *Monsieur* Zenon Trudeau in suggesting this enterprise, [also] explained to them, that his purpose was, at the same time, to enlighten the age, in regard to that portion of the globe, as yet so little known.

For that purpose he required that in pursuing this commerce, the interested parties should pay attention to join to the traders whom they might send to those countries, enlightened persons, who would use every exerting force to penetrate to the sources of the Missouri, and beyond if possible to the Southern Ocean—take observations and heights of the localities; who would make notations of the tribes that inhabit them; their customs, the kind of trade that might be established with them—note the establishments to which the places would be susceptible; indicate them [carefully] in order to be able to [later] establish their entrepôts, [and even] forts to protect the commerce; in a word, to acquire a correct knowledge of a country which thus far has been inhabited solely by Indian tribes, and consequently entirely unknown. Your petitioner was one of the first to eagerly embrace a project so wisely conceived, and which was some day to cause the colony to flourish, enrich all the members, and add to the glory of the Monarchy. It is unnecessary to enumerate to Your Excellency, the name[s] and the number of traders, who co-operated with your petitioner, and who perceived as the supplicant, the good fortune and wealth attached to this enterprise, [for] they are known to Your Excellency. They are [were] but two of them who, after having agreed, withdrew, and renounced the partnership. More enlightened that your petitioner, they perceived their future ruin in the understanding, which he [the supplicant] has since found out, but too late, and which would not have occurred, had it been managed by an honest man. In fact, *Monseigneur,* the *acte* had no sooner been resolved, when by a blindness at which the supplicant and his associates are still amazed, they selected to place at the head of this enterprise, the man who was the least proper to its success. It was *Sr.* Clamorgan, whose private business affairs were in the greatest disorder and confusion, whose probity was violently suspected, [who engaged in] intriguing, great talking, com-

549

placency, affability, and even servility, when it was politic to deceive, in order to exhalt himself, or to injure others. Such was the man that the supplicant and his associates chose, believing him to be the most competent to conduct great operations, which he said he had done all his life.

All the associates have always known *Sr.* Clamorgan, as I have just depicted him to Your Excellency. They feared that he might not act justly toward them and that he might trick them. In order to prevent his succeeding in these ends, they associated *Sr.* Reilhe with him as assistant. [*Sr.* Reihe was] a man of established probity, whom they thought was in a proper position to watch over their greatly suspected chief, but this honest man became the dupe for Clamorgan [who] deceived and ruined him as he did the others.

Your Excellency will be surprised that a *société* placed at its head a chief whom they did not esteem and in whom they had no confidence. Your Excellency will recover from this surprise when he will realize that the associates did not believe themselves sufficiently competent to conduct so extensive an enterprise. They feared that in assuming it, they might jeopardize their fortune and that of their co-associates. The *société* persuaded themselves that by honoring *Sr.* Clamorgan, as head of the concern, this man would bear in mind the true principles of integrity, and that he would manage this affair more honorably, than he had up to that day managed his own, and being ambitious to merit the good esteem of his co-citizens, or to regain it, if forfeited unjustly, he would strive to employ all the light and knowledge he possessed to conduct with disinterested nobleness and magnanimity an enterprise, which would manage his fortune and that of his co-associates, to the general advantage of the colony, and add to the glory and prosperity of the Monarchy. Their hopes were deceived, and far from having opened to them the road to fortune, he led them to the abyss of misfortune. Despite all the trust that his associates placed in the ability of *Sr.* Clamorgan and the little they had in his probity, they believed that it was to their interest to make some laws or regulations regulating the *société*. Consequently under the auspices, and aided by the intelligence of Mr. Zenon Trudeau, the before mentioned *acte,*[2] which is in Your Excellency's custody, was drawn up. This *acte,* after having been maturely examined, was signed and sent to the government for approval. This *acte* was not at all respected by *Sr.* Clamorgan. He transgressed it, whenever he believed it to his interest to do so.

---

[2]Chapter II, document IX.

Sr. Clamorgan, chosen and placed at the head of the *société,* began his work. He was then entirely unprovided with merchandise, as were also several of the associates. The supplicant, in order not to delay the operations of the Company, opened his store and loaned to *Sr.* Clamorgan, and to some of the co-partners, the articles which they lacked. It was believed that *Sr.* Clamorgan was going to select from amongst the traders, men of integrity, skilled in this kind of trade, and speaking various Indian dialects. The associates were surprised that he selected only those who were known to be the most worthless and corrupt, and for the sole reason that they had long been in his debt. [True,] he selected a few honest ones among the number, but so ignorant and of such little experience in his kind of commerce, that it is not surprising he did not succeed. He needed men of this sort, who, having eyes might see nothing, thus allowing him without fearing objections to alter the invoice that each co-associate furnished for his share. From that moment it was doubted that he was not going right, but it was only suspicion.

If *Sr.* Clamorgan had really had at heart the success of the Company, he would have selected intelligent, prudent, economical men, to manage an undertaking which required wisdom, system and economy to accomplish success for the benefit of the *société* and the government. A conduct so lacking in honesty on the part of *Sr.* Clamorgan caused the loss of the first outfit [*envois*]'. Men poorly selected, goods in bad condition, damaged, and even changed necessarily caused this loss.

A second and third outfit' were not more successful, because nothing was done properly. Several of the associates backed out after the first loss, not because they had a glimpse of the adventure (good in itself), but rather because they perceived the faithlessness of the principal agent, which would occasion the loss of all other outfits that they might make. At the last outfit, there remained only the supplicant.

Sr. Clamorgan in contempt of the articles of association [*reglement*], had acquired the shares of two of the associates, so that he was in himself Agent and Company, and the supplicant, having but one vote, could neither oversee nor have the slightest influence in the expeditions which were made. Thus, he [Clamorgan] succeeded in consummating the ruin of the supplicant who lost in the three adventures, ten thousand *piastres.* The supplicant would not have complained of this loss. had he had no fault to find with *Sr.* Clamorgan and if he had acted like an honest man, but the supplicant will not forgive him for not only having mismanaged, but also for having abused the credit with the government that the *société* had mistakenly confided to him. That is the one thing that it is proper

---

'Referring to Truteau's expedition.
'Under Lecuyer and Mackay or possibly Breda.

to expose to Your Excellency in order that you may know the cunning of *Sr.* Clamorgan.

Sr. Clamorgan perceiving that the Missouri Company was necessarily going to fail for lack of means, since he had succeeded in nearly ruining the members; no longer finding the means of making dupes, and unwilling also to lose the reputation that he flattered himself he had acquired by the crafty letters he had written to the government, and because he had inserted in the papers 'that he was the soul of an enterprise that would immortalize its projector': He forestalled a rich English merchant of Canada who was intent upon extending his trade as all the English are; he exhibited to him the great means he had in hand to promptly realize a great fortune; he succeeded in gaining his confidence to such an extent that he put in his hands a large capital, solicited for him the exclusive trade of the Mississippi, hoping by this means to re-unite some day, this privilege to the one of the Missouri, and to forestall all the trade of the Illinois country.[5] He was upon the point of succeeding, when death carried off this merchant at New Orleans, who had been duped as the supplicant. The heirs will soon learn to what a man their relative had surrendered himself.

Your Excellency must perceive in this brief exposé that *Sr.* Clamorgan's aim was, after having destroyed the fortunes of some of the merchants, to monopolize all the trade of the country, and to carry it on alone, on the ruins of these same fortunes which he had the ability to appropriate to himself.

Your Excellency may perhaps imagine that the object of the supplicant is to demand from *Sr.* Clamorgan damages and interest on the losses he sustained. He is not so fond of litigation as to attempt such an enterprise. Moreover, it would necessitate lifting of the curtain which hides all the fraudulent tricks of *Sr.* Clamorgan; and probing an almost impenetrable abyss; and the supplicant's life would not be long enough to travel over the ground [and] this pursuit would impair the tranquillity of the soul of the supplicant. He does not intend to call *Sr.* Clamorgan to account for his depredations. He ventures only to pray you first: to withdraw from *Sr.* Clamorgan the exclusive privilege of the trade of the Mississippi, which he exercises under the name of Todd and Company a privilege which, in changing the trade of the Illinois, brings no advantage to New Orleans, the center of all the commerce of this country, inasmuch as all the peltries from this river are transported to Canada, and never are seen at the place which should be their true destination, such as it was agreed on when the privilege was granted, Second: To allow the applicant to continue in the Missouri Company which he does

---

[5]Referring to Todd.

not regard as a chimera, although he lost heavily, begging you at the same time to order the said *société* to be reformed; also that *Sr.* Clamorgan, who by his manipulations has made himself the perpetual head, be, not only excluded from all management, but also to be obliged to relinquish his stock and all those he bought or traded for, to the end that the said Company, remodelled and re-created under the auspices of Your Excellency, and [be put] under the direction of Mr. Zenon Trudeau, the most sagacious, prudent, and zealous of commandants who has made his appearance in the colony. If Your Excellency deigns to entertain the request of the supplicant, he might recover his losses, and again try the enterprise, risking the remainder of his fortune, to attain the object which the *société* and the government had proposed. He dares to expect that grace from your kindness and your justice.[6]

> The supplicant has the honor of calling himself with respect,
> your very humble and very obedient servant,
>
> Joseph   Robidou   [rubric]

St. Louis, Illinois, March 7, 1798[7]

[6]In April, 1798, Gayoso de Lemos wrote Trudeau that Robidou's claims should have the prompt attention of the government and a remedy. Therefore, he was sending Robidou's letter to Trudeau who was to draw up an *informe* with regard to it and if his [Robidou's] accusations were discovered to be well-founded, Trudeau was to take the necessary but not violent steps in the case. (Gayoso de Lemos to Trudeau, New Orleans, April 24 1798, A.G.I., P. de C., leg. 44. See also document VIII). However, Robidou and Reilhe refused to appear against Clamorgan on account of fear of "incurring his ill-will and strategy". Trudeau annulled the exclusive privilege of the Company. (Trudeau to Gayoso de Lemos, November 15, 1798, document XX). But Clamorgan was saved after all and Robidou failed in his efforts to overthrow him and was even denied his request for the trade of the Otos, Mahas and Poncas, and Panis. (Robidou to Gayoso de Lemos, St. Louis, March 15, 1799, Chapter VII, documents II and IV). Other attempts were made to overthrow Clamorgan, and Robidou joined with Lisa and others against him, but even that opposition was overcome by Clamorgan. See Nasatir, "Jacques Clamorgan: Promoter of the Northeastern Border of Colonial New Spain". *New Mexico Historical Review*, XVII (1942), 101-112.

[7]Clamorgan wrote two letters to Gayoso de Lemos "representing against *Sieur* Robidou concerning the reports which he has given to me on the Company of the Missouri and having taken my dispositions in the matter [see documents VII, XIII, XIV, etc.]. I shall communicate them opportunely to whom it may concern." Draft to Clamorgan, New Orleans, July 13, 1798, A.G.I., P. de C., leg. 215.

VI

Gayoso de Lemos to Trudeau, New Orleans, March 10, 1798[1]

You will oblige the persons who are in debt to the Company of the Missouri to clear their accounts with it as soon as possible, so that they can continue their business, [you?] collecting the immense credits which

[1]Written in Spanish. A.G.I., P. de C., leg. 44.

the Company has wasted in the Illinois because of the different cargos which it sold, and which proceeded from the advances[2] of the defunct Don Andrés Todd and Don Daniel Clark.

I charge you not to lose sight of this matter, as it is just.

May God, Our Lord, keep you many years.

New Orleans, March 10, 1798.

Manuel Gayoso de Lemos [rubric]

Señor Don Zenon Trudeau

---

[2]There are many letters, accounts, and documents in the Missouri Historical Society which show that advances were made.

VII

DRAFT [GAYOSO DE LEMOS?] TO MORALES, NEW ORLEANS, APRIL 16, 1798[1]

It is of the greatest consequence to maintain the inhabitants of our establishment of Illinois in subordination, to inspire respect in the innumerable and war-like nations which concur there, and to restrain both the incursions of the latter, as well as the usurpations which our residents make of the commerce, repressing at the same time the boldness and daring of the British nation which has already reached the point of forming factories in the Mandan nation on the Missouri and others [factories], aspiring to nothing less than taking entire possession of all that trade; it is of the greatest consequence that there be in St. Louis respectable forces which may supply that Lieutenant-Governor at the same time [the means] for restraining the clandestine commerce which the said English are making, introducing themselves by the Moingona and San Pedro rivers; and these are reasons why I communicated to you in the official letter of the fourth, instant, the thought which I had of sending the *galera* upstream as soon as circumstances might permit it. I am informing you of this, in view of the reflections which it pleased you to reproduce to me under date of the thirteenth of [- -], thinking, out of respect to the greater economy of the royal interests, that it would be sufficient to charter a *lanchón* for the remittance of the effects and presents which you express.[2]

God, etc. New Orleans, 16 April, 1798

[draft]

Señor Don Francisco Morales

---

[1]Written in Spanish. A.G.I., P. de C., leg. 91.

[2]Gayoso de Lemos asked Morales to deliver 3000 pounds of powder, to be paid for at the established rate, to meet the urgency for heeding the commerce and trade of the Indians in Illinois. Morales agreed. Draft [Gayoso de Lemos] to Morales, New Orleans, March 31, 1798, A.G.I., P. de C., leg. 91; and Morales to Gayoso de Lemos, same day, *Ibid.*

VIII

GAYOSO DE LEMOS TO TRUDEAU, NEW ORLEANS, APRIL 16, 1798[1]

If the Company of Discovery of the Missouri does not continue its operations, whether it be because of a lack of funds or because of motives of particular convenience, the government cannot, nor must not, remain exposed, and regard with patience the fatal consequences which must result from the savage nations, [who], seeing themselves without trade on the part of Spain, will commit extortions against the vassals of Spain and its establishments; and, exasperated, [will] deliver themselves up to the discretion of the English and Americans, who, though unjustly and without the slightest right, are trying to attract them with flattering and brilliant hopes, even regaling them with gifts and presents. Circumstances being in such a state, neither must the Company conveniently expect that, while it is so visibly failing in the conditions of its institution [contract], the government must conserve to them, its privileges, so notably harmful to the state, to the residents, and [even] to the Indian nations, whose defense and protection is so strictly recommended to me.

In view of this supposition, as soon as you receive this, you will call the Director of the Company and you will inform him on my part that if he does not immediately remedy those inconveniences, the government will be obliged to give permission to trade freely with the nations to those who present themselves with means to do so, in spite of the fact that the Company has the exlusive privilege, and you will communicate your resolution to me, so that I may take my disposition.

Should the formal reply in writing indicate that the Company is not in a state to continue its commerce, you are authorized by this to divide equally the permissions among the inhabitants most worthy of this favor.[2]

May God keep you many years.

New Orleans, April 16, 1798

Manuel Gayoso de Lemos [rubric]

Señor Don Zenon Trudeau

---

[1] Written in Spanish. A.G.I., P. de C., leg. 44; draft in A.G.I., P. de C., leg. 132. See documents XIII, XIV, etc.

[2] See document V and especially note 6.

Gayoso de Lemos to Trudeau, New Orleans, April 16, 1798[1]

Since I took possession of the general government of these provinces, continuing my desires and eagerness to see them prosper in their population, agriculture and commerce, I have taken as many steps and dispositions that have seemed to me adaptable to the attainment and success of these desires.[2] To these I have always joined the most decided intention to do everything possible in favor of those individuals whose accredited conduct and laborious industry have made them deserving of the protection of the government, provided that no prejudice may result to a third party and without trying to make changes in the dispositions of my predecessor unless powerful reasons of justice require the convenience of giving another disposition.

Under these suppositions, and with the desire to make the Sarpy family see the respect and esteem which the government has for it, I have promised to take care of it, supplying to him the trade of the Kansas nation. If it can conveniently be done and is not prejudicial to good order, you will give him a license in the customary terms, beause of the promise I have given to him to serve him, provided that there might be no notable prejudice to a third party, and under which [promise] he has perhaps made his preparations and expenses.

To the reasons and powerful causes which present themselves for serving Sarpy is added how much the house [firm] has suffered in the two fires of the capital,[3] the many credits it has in its favor as a result of the very extensive commerce which it has done with these establishments. One must also take into consideration the preference which it

---

[1]A.G.I., P. de C., leg. 44; draft in A.G.I., P. de C., leg. 133.

[2]In another letter of the same date, Gayoso de Lemos proposed to aid the colony by having Trudeau call Cerré and other important men in St. Louis who have trade with Canada in order for them to attract good families of French emigrants from Canada to locate themselves "in your districts in the points most advantageous and adapted for the reciprocal defense and protection of all". Gayoso de Lemos offered ten arpents of land for each 1000 arpents settled by the families that each one would bring in. (A.G.I., P. de C., leg. 132). Trudeau replied in his dispatch no. 14, dated St. Louis, July 17, 1798, (A.G.I., P. de C., leg. 50). He talked to Cerré who said it was difficult to attract Canadians as settlers; (it was easier to attract them) only as *engagés* in the trade.

[3]1788 and 1794.

seems must naturally be accorded to those who at their own expense make armaments from the capital.

May God keep you many years.

New Orleans, April 16, 1798.[4]

Manuel Gayoso de Lemos [rubric]

Señor Don Zenon Trudeau

---

[4]Reply is document XV.

X

TRUDEAU TO GAYOSO DE LEMOS, ST. LOUIS, MAY 6, 1798[1]

My Dear Sir and Most Venerated Governor:

In a confidential letter of the seventeenth of October[2] of last year, Your Excellency recommends that I give you information on various points on which you are desirous of being informed, so that you might efficaciously manage this country, regulate its commerce and foster the good administration of justice, etc. Through Mr. Chouteau I sent Your Excellency the memoranda that I considered most conducive to this, in which I spoke of the House of Todd and of the Company of the Upper Missouri.[3] I may now add that since the death of Todd, his heirs and representatives occupy themselves solely in securing what was his.[4] The exclusive trade of the Mississippi which was granted to the deceased[5] is now in the hands of Clamorgan.[6] This has not harmed in any way nor could it harm our settlements, for on the contrary it is greatly to their advantage. The English, for years in control of the Mississippi trade, and now the Americans added to them have resources which prevent the meager resources of the Illinois from competing with them in the said trade. Todd, as an intelligent merchant, and one who was backed by a strong London house, had the intention of establishing himself at St. Louis, having sent via New Orleans the necessary goods to suffice to supply all the Upper Mississippi. This could have been done in large boats, without the need of any of those supplies coming from Montreal,

---

[1]Written in Spanish. Original in Bancroft Library.
[2]Gayoso de Lemos took over the governor-generalship of Louisiana on August 1, 1797.
[3]Possibly referring to document I.
[4]See Nasatir, "Anglo-Spanish Rivalry in the Iowa Country 1797-1798," *Iowa Journal of History and Politics*, XXVIII (1930), 337-389, for discussion and some documents.
[5]Among other grants to Todd see Clamorgan to Carondelet, New Orleans, May 11, 1796, Missouri Historical Society, Clamorgan Collection, printed in *American State Papers, Public Lands*, VIII, 234.
[6]See Chapter IV, document XXVII.

by which route they would have saved on the expense of transportation, and which would have put them in a position to sell at an advantage over others who, accustomed to this trade, would have been obliged to come to St. Louis to get the supplies in the same way that they still do at Michilimakinac. Todd would have also brought from Canada all the boatmen that he needed for his trips to New Orleans and for all his trade. This would have left people in the country every year, and a large amount of provisions would have been consumed to the benefit of the inhabitants. Now that Todd is gone, I do not think that his enterprise can last beyond the time necessary to collect the amount which he had brought up of his own to this place.

As I have already informed Your Excellency, all the shares of the Trading Company of the Upper Missouri are in the possession of the firm of Clamorgan and Loiselle. They were to form a company with Todd who was to provide the merchandise, and bring Canadians trained to follow this trade with untiring determination. Now that Todd is dead, the great project has gone to the four winds. Clamorgan has neither the experience nor the means to carry it out; Your Excellency may [thus] consider it ended.

There is no doubt that the nations that inhabit the Upper Missouri are many, and that others could be attracted to it from those who at present trade with the English of the Northwest; also, that a firm, with means, well managed, could handle the trade with them with one-half the expense and labor of the Canadian merchants. This country does not offer anyone who can undertake such an enterprise. Your Excellency is the only one who can find a firm such as is needed, or, if peace permits at the time, I will write to Canada to see if one can be found there for the task.

As Your Excellency must have seen (now that the Big and Little Osages are eliminated) that our present trade on the Missouri is very limited, [and] it is still the ambition of more than forty, who call themselves merchants, and who beg, petition, and clamor for the method of division in the manner which I have sent to Your Excellency, [which is] all in their favor.' This gives rise to a monopoly which the latter form with the traders who are the ones having the risks and the work. In regards to the said merchants, the portions of the trade, for which they cast lots, they sell them to the traders, and, in addition, they oblige them to purchase their supplies in their stores, so that the said traders have to pay for the privilege, the merchandise, and the passport. Therefore it seems to me that it would be better to give the traders the license to trade

---

'See Chapter V, document XVI.

since, not having merchandise, the merchants would still get their profit by selling it to them, which seems to me to be enough for them.

Some years ago I suggested to Your Excellency's predecessor another method which he rejected: That was to put on sale each year separately [by individual nations] the privilege of these trades for the benefit of the construction of a church which St. Louis needs. I think that this method would be beneficial to the majority of the inhabitants. The said trades by individual nations would produce each year the following amounts: the Kance, 500 *pesos;* the Otos, 350; the Panis, 300; the Mahas, 200; and the Poncas, 100.[8] In three years with these sums, and the materials and labor that the citizens would be able to furnish, we could build a church[9] as fine as the country requires. Your Excellency will determine, if it is advisable to do so. However, it can not be put into effect this year since I do not expect to have a reply from Your Excellency in time to do this for the present year.

Your Excellency will easily be able to imagine the effect which has been produced by the new *reglamento* which you sent me, which limits the admission of immigrants to Catholics alone.[10] At once, all the projects for large settlements that were founded on a mixed population vanished. On the other hand, there is little hope that those who have begun homes will be left in peaceful possession of them. The Indians, seeing our weakness, will continue their outrages. We shall therefore be kept constantly in our wretched villages, without any other industry than that which hunger and sheer necessity forces upon us. I do not doubt that politics and the security of the province demand it, but I hope to heaven it does not last long. For if, on the contrary, it should last, in a few years all the American side of the Mississippi will be so well populated that we shall be very much like a child [minority] in these remote districts, which are so hard for the capital to aid.

---

[8]See *Ibid.*

[9]Speaking of building or reconstructing the church from what amounted to a tax on the Indian trade had long been under discussion at times. In several petitions for exclusive trades (such as Vasquez) the petitioners offered to raise or grant money for building or reconstructing a church. Money will be necessary for the reconstruction of the church said Father Didier "and there is none. Your Excellency has been asked for some posts on the Missouri, taxes on retailers of liquor or billiards, and on the companies that have exclusive privileges It seems that all these means are impracticable to Your Excellency, since you have not adopted them." Didier suggested that since the conditions of war existed, cash was not to be had and that "hardly fifteen citizens can be considered in easy circumstances," all should contribute their work and the government supply what would be lacking which would be considered as a loan and repaid. Gayoso de Lemos ordered Vandenbemden to draw up a plan for a church with his evaluation and remit it to the governor. Didier to *Monseigneur* [Carondelet?] St. Louis, April 15, 1797, A.G.I., P. de C., leg. 213. See further on the church, Trudeau to Gayoso de Lemos, no 44, St. Louis, April 12, 1799, A.G.I., P. de C., leg. 51, etc.

[10]See Gayarré *History of Louisiana, Spanish Domination;* Cp. document IX, especially note 2.

Your Excellency will see from my brief reflections that I have not wished to enlarge upon them, since I am persuaded that Your Excellency has done what has seemed best to you for the welfare of the state in the present circumstances, which are truly critical, and, more so, for this district of Illinois than for the rest of the province. The citizens are complaining; as they rightly fear war between them and the French, our allies, and are certain that we shall have our role to play and that it will be first to begin it. It will be fortunate if I can obtain a capitulation, which will permit me to join you in order to serve at Your Excellency's side, which I plan to do in the last extremity of necessity, in which I shall see myself unable to await aid against a neighboring enemy, who will be able to recruit whenever it may wish and can not help, but discourage the inhabitants upon whom I depend for defense.

Today my wife gave birth to a son, leaving your God-son in the arms of death.[11] In the despair which we find ourselves at the irreparable loss of the strongest and most beautiful son of all those whom I have, we offer you our most profound respects, and I beg the all powerful to preserve Your Excellency's life many years.

St. Louis, May 6, 1798.

Your most attentive and affectionate servant kisses Your Excellency's hand.

Zenon Trudeau [rubric]

Señor Don Manuel Gayoso de Lemos.

---

[11]This boy gained in health and Chouteau held him over the font during his baptism. [August Chouteau] to [Gayoso de Lemos], April 14, 1799, Missouri Historical Society, Pierre Chouteau Collection, no. 1.

XI

CLAMORGAN TO GOVERNOR, ST. LOUIS, MAY 26, 1798[1]

Very Excellent Governor:

I have the honor to remit to you herewith enclosed, a request in the name of the the Missouri Company to grant to it a portion of land in the Missouri, which can defray the expenses and losses that it has experienced so far in the different enterprises of discoveries that it has made

---

[1]Written in French. A.G.I., P. de C., leg. 215A.

The versatile promoter, Clamorgan, had at various times unhesitatingly asked for large land grants in return for his claimed services. For example among many the following may be mentioned:

In August, 1796 (Clamorgan to Delassus, New Madrid, August 1, 1796, Missouri Historical Society, Clamorgan Collection, printed in *American State Papers,*

to procure knowledge of the nations which are existing there, and for which the said Company proposes to renew its attempts and to defy the dangerous events by new ways and new means that it proposes to use this autumn.

As a protector, zealous with industry and with all that can contribute to the prosperity of our colony, I have a right to believe that you will be good enough to grant the request that I have the honor to make you in the name of the Missouri Company.

I have the honor of being

Very excellent governor.

Your very humble and very obedient servant,

J. Clamorgan

[rubric]

St. Louis, May 26, 1798.[2]

Public Lands, VIII, 230, 231) he asked for a large grant of land to establish a rope factory and encourage the raising of hemp—536,904 arpents (458,936 acres).

On March 1, 1797, he petitioned Trudeau for 500,000 arpents of land to recompense him for the refusal of the Intendant to pay the 10,000 *piastres* annually granted him for the support of 100 militia men. The land was to be used for a saw and grist mills and slaughter houses. Clamorgan to Trudeau, St. Louis, March 1, 1800, Missouri Historical Society Clamorgan Collection, printed in *American State Papers, Public Lands* VIII, 233 and *et. seq.* (233-242); *United States Supreme Court Reports* (volume 101), XI Otto, 822.

Trudeau in a letter to Gayoso de Lemos, no. 29, dated St. Louis, November 15, 1798 (A.G.I., P. de C., leg. 49) mentions nine memorials sent to him by Clamorgan, all claiming land. (draft [Gayoso de Lemos] to Trudeau, New Orleans, August 10, 1798, A.G.I., P. de C., leg. 215A).

[2]Gayoso de Lemos replied to this and to two other letters of Clamorgan on July 13, 1798 (draft in A.G.I., P. de C., leg. 215): "Concerning the 3000 arpents of land which you solicit in favor of the Company of the Missouri, thirty leagues from its mouth, it is impossible for me to concede them for the reason which is made evident in the margin of the *instancia* of May 26th, which I am returning."

XII

MACKAY TO GAYOSO DE LEMOS, NEW ORLEANS, JUNE 8, 1798[1]

His Excellency, Manuel de Lemos, Brigadier General of His Majesty's armies, Governor General in and over the Provinces of Louisiana and Florida etc.

Sir—

As I wish to discharge my duty properly and agreeable to the commission with which you were pleased to honor me, and as my present appoint-

---

[1]Written in English. A.G.I., P. de C., leg. 2365; copy in Missouri Historical Society. Parts of this letter are quoted in Nasatir, "Anglo-Spanish Rivalry on the

ment is so very small that it is impossible for me to do justice to my trust, being dependent on small and uncertain resources (having lost and expended my property in my enterprise) I hope that Your Excellency will be pleased to extend your bounty in employing me to the service going up the Mississippi to the Illinois or as long as you may be pleased to continue such an employ, meantime that you may have the goodness to take the earliest opportunity to make application to His Gracious Majesty for such an appointment in his armies as Your Excellency may think proper to bestow on me and which may render me so far independent as to enable me to employ all my time and capacity for the service of my sovereign, and those of Your Excellency who has been pleased to bestow on me already distinguished marks of your confidence favor and goodness.

I have but little merit to recommend me to my Sovereign or to your Excellency excepting that of being a Traveler from my youth, principally through the wild & unknown Deserts of this Continent. Especially through that part of His Majesty's domains watered by the Missouri & its Branches, & agreeable to my Commission from Baron de Carondelet, the then Governor Gen[1] of these Provinces I omitted nothing in my Power to render my Services useful to my Sovereign & to my fellow subjects.

My Chief objects were, to pave the way for the discovery & Commerce of that vast Country on both sides of the Missouri & across the Continent to the Pacific ocean. In this enterprise I succeeded as much as could be expected from the resources & support I hade.

I Brought the Indian nations who were then at war to peace with each other & those of them who were at enmity with the white people of Louisiana (the Sioux of Grand Detour) I brought to a sense of their Duty by Convincing them, how much it would be [to] their Interest to Traffic & live in perpetual friendship with the white children of their Great Spanish Father [the King] to whom they owed the strictest alliance & attachment as well as to the Great Spanish Chief residing near the mouth of the Mississippi, who from pity & regard for his red children wished to have the roads Clear for the purpose of sending the white people among them with the necessaries of life, etc. To convince them of the reality & sincerity of my message I presented them (in the name

Upper Missouri" in *Mississippi Valley Historical Review*, XVI (1930), 507-530; quotation printed on pp. 38-39 of the reprint.

Mackay considered the work of Evans as part of his own. Mackay was appointed commandant of San André. On May 1, 1798 (Gayoso to Trudeau, May 1, 1798, A.G.I., P. de C., leg. 44. A draft of the appointment is in *Ibid.*, leg. 2365, and is printed in Houck, *Spanish Régime in Missouri*, II, 245). Gayoso de Lemos proposed to use both Mackay and Evans in defining the land claims of Spain, England and the United States in the north. Gayoso de Lemos to Saavedra, New Orleans, November 22, 1798, document XXI.

of their Great Spanish father & the Great Spanish Chiefs) with medals and pavillions for their principal chiefs and tobacco and other goods for them all.

I also found means to drive the English out of His Majesty's Territories & took possession of a Fort which they built at the Mandan nation on the upper part of the Missouri & broke off the Alliance that existed then between the said English & the nations of that Country. I also took a Chart of the Missouri from its mouth to the wanutaries nation, which following the windings of the river is a little short of 1800 miles.

I will not tire your Excellency with any further relation of my transactions but I hope that you will not forget me, I rely wholly on your Excellency's goodness and I am persuaded that I will not be disappointed and I flatter myself that the more you know of my conduct the more I will be honored with your confidence, which honor I will make my continual study to deserve.

I have the honor to be with the most profound respect and Esteem, Your Excellency's most obedient and most humble servant.

James Mackay [rubric]

New Orleans June 8th, 1798.

XIII

CLAMORGAN TO [TRUDEAU],
ST. LOUIS, JUNE 18, 1798[1]

Monsieur:

In reply to your letter of today by which you informed me of the intentions of the general government towards the Missouri Company,[2] I am obliged to tell you that despite the support of the late André Todd, upon whose resources we laid the foundation for the quick success of our enterprises for the discovery of the Pacific Ocean, we are still none the less moved by the same zeal and the same ambition that we have always had to continue the course, which should carry our business beyond the very sources of the Missouri.

If the communication that M. le Baron de Carondelet gave us, concerning His Majesty's intentions to grant our Company the sum of ten thousand *pesos* annually for the maintenance of a hundred militiamen in the forts[2] that we have built and are to build at various places on the Upper Missouri, should some day bring results, there is nothing we will not dare to attempt to repulse vigorously foreigners who dare to violate

---

[1]Written in French. Original in the Bancroft Library. See documents V, VII, and VIII. Enclosed with document XIV.
[2]See document VIII.

the boundaries of our possessions. We shall march with our guns [*la foudre en main*] in hand, to place, in spite of our enemies, the standard of our empire in the midst of the most distant savage nations; even though we have been deprived up to the present of this powerful help, and in spite of the smallness of our fortunes, we have never spared anything to further this brilliant enterprise, although it is true that we have continually had to maintain at our own expense and in our pay some men on the Upper Missouri to win over to us the different nations which live there, and to repel, as far as it lay in our power, the ambition of our neighbors. We have done better. *Monsieur*, we sent one of the members of our Company last spring into the Upper Missouri to attract to us the sacred confidence [*confiden sacre*] of all the Sioux nations, who [to] controls and leads them at his pleasure. We have spared nothing to win over to our interests, this man [who is] so important to the safety of our boats on the Upper Missouri where this nation is wandering about at all times. We have recruited strong, brave men whom we are going to have sent into the midst of danger in the different nations which one must pass through, in order to reach the sources of the Missouri.

The loss of the late André Todd deprived us of the means and resources which his wealth promised us, but it did not destroy the zeal, ambition and the glory which we desire to have in making ourselves useful to posterity.

This is the reason, *Monsieur,* why we are going to send out a strong expedition, being stimulated by sentiments of boldness, courage, and ambition; however, His Majesty's help will be necessary for us, especially now that we find ourselves deprived of the right to count upon the promises and the resources of the late André Todd to maintain the burden of our enterprises, after we made great sacrifices at his urging to buy from most of the members of the Missouri Company their rights of ownership in the hope of furthering our discoveries with more vigor and activity; all the more so as aid would have been generously granted us by the agents of the late André Todd, but at the very moment when we were going to stretch the most active thread of our business among the distant nations, we suddenly saw our best calculated plans broken. We not only made great sacrifices, contracted great expenses, and went to great trouble to secure the resources which our ties of interest with the house of the late André Todd promised in the future, but what is even worse is that we have been obliged to interrupt the course of our customary discoveries from lack of merchandise, munitions, and wealth [men?] on whom we had the right to count for the difficult voyages. The representatives of the late André Todd do not pay the least attention to this.

---

⁵Chapter IV, document XVII.

We should like, *Monsieur*, to have you willing to aid in making the governor-general see the truth of all these important things, and at the same time set before him the necessity, now greater than ever, of His Majesty's aid of ten thousand *pesos* a year, which he seems to have promised the Company for the maintenance of a hundred men to be employed in the defense and protection of our boundaries, and for which the Company had paid the larger part of the expense from the beginning of its foundation, always in the hope of being favored by His Majesty's kindness for aid in carrying out its burden.[4]

The expenses, losses and sacrifices that the Company has experienced up to the present have already amounted to more than a hundred thousand *piastres*, since its foundation. Most of the members have been disheartened, or have been unable to support it [the Company,] were forced to yield their interests to our house after the late André Todd formed it, thus assuring us of the advantages that the resources of his means would permit us.

It is important to tell you also, *Monsieur,* that the agents of the heirs of the late André Todd have not been satisfied with breaking the agreement of the late André Todd with the firm of Clamorgan, Loisel and Company, the chief share-holders in the Missouri Company, but they have, in addition, by means of the canoe[s] of their agents, introduced merchandise in the Des Moines and St. Pierre rivers[5] with which they have underhandidly obtained the nations that live on the Missouri, such as the Mahas, the Otos, and the Missouris; [this was] probably [accomplished] by insinuating to them all that they could so that they might seduce and corrupt them, and then draw their trade into their own hands to the prejudice of the Company, while the house of Clamorgan, Loisel and Company, at the same time, found itself deprived of the necessary means to supply the needs of those nations, just as if the occasion had been prepared in advance to take advantage of these means, in order to harm the Missouri Company and to make use to their advantage of all that circumstance might offer them for their gain. [They did all this] without any regard for the rights of the said Company, and without paying any attention to the fact that it was abusing His Majesty's intentions, by making use of the privilege he had granted to the late André Todd to trade with the nations of the Western part of the Upper Mississippi, in order to entice beyond the boundaries of the Missouri the commerce of the nations that live there, doubtless by every means ambition and personal interest are able to suggest.

---

[4] See Chapter IV, document XXXVII.

[5] See Nasatir, "Anglo-Spanish Rivalry in the Iowa Country 1797-1798," *Iowa Journal of History and Politics,* XXVIII, (1930), 337-389.

Only His Majesty's forces are capable of stopping this pernicious abuse of our trade and of the docility of the nations. Otherwise, the foreigners will always be destroying, by way of the Upper Mississippi,[6] the enterprises and ventures of the Company in the Lower Missouri, in spite of His Majesty's most complete protection.

It is enough for the Company to have to combat the Hudson Bay trade and that of Lake Superior, both of which encroach upon the possessions of His Majesty, and only occupy themselves in turning the nations of the Upper Missouri from their affection towards us by their enticing speeches and by repeated presents, so that we will be obliged to surpass them in the matter of generosity to retain the affection and friendship of the nations which live there. But it would be too much for a company, just starting, to have to drive back all the trade of the Upper Mississippi which might penetrate to the Missouri by streams which obviate the distance and make transportation easy.

This is why, *Monsieur,* the Company wishes His Excellency the governor-general not only to explain to His Majesty the necessity of his supplying the ten thousand *pesos* annually, that were promised it for the purpose of maintaining a hundred men in several posts on the Upper Missouri to protect them, as was granted by a decree of His Majesty still not enforced, but it also requests that he please grant to the Missouri Company the quantity of two thousand pounds of powder annually, for the maintenance of the forts and posts,[7] but [and] especially that His Majesty be begged to oppose with all his power the introduction of foreign traders who introduce themselves in the Missouri, especially by way of the Des Moines and St. Pierre rivers. There would then be left to the Company only the need of resisting and pushing back that [the trade] of Hudson Bay and Lake Superior, which it hopes to be able eventually to accomplish with success.

The Company wishes that it may please you to inform the governor-general of all these matters, in order that it may be agreeable to him to take them all into consideration, and acquaint His Majesty with them.

God keep you in His Holy Keeping.

J. Clamorgan [rubric]

Director of the Missouri Company

St. Louis, June 18, 1798.

---

[6]Something was done by the government, such as sending garrisons and war vessels to patrol and guard entrances to Spanish territory on the Upper Mississippi. See *Ibid.* for some cases.

[7]See document VII and especially note 2.

XIV

TRUDEAU TO GAYOSO DE LEMOS, ST. LOUIS, JUNE 20, 1798[1]

Number 8

Having transcribed to Don Santiago Clamorgan, Director of the Trading Company of the Upper Missouri, Your Excellency's official letter of April 16, last,[2] which orders the said Director to explain in writing whether the Company is in a position to continue its commerce, etc., he answered me with the letter which I am enclosing to Your Excellency,[3] which is made up of the absurdities of a veritable madman, who enriches himself with dreams. All of his propositions, complaints, and plans are the effect of either the most daring knavery or the most complete madness, since it is as clear as day that the Company has not done a fourth of what he says, being 74,000 *pesos* in debt with the house of Don Daniel Clark,[4] and 25,000 *pesos* with that of the defunct Todd in Canada; and that in addition, to being in arrears for many years in paying these sums, it will be in bankruptcy for more than 40,000 *pesos,* this makes him anxiously desire the *10,000 pesos* which he expects from the government in order to maintain the 100 men in the forts, [?] which he has only imaginarily constructed; moreover, all the money possible could not make him succeed because of the bad way he manages.

In spite of everthing, I am forewarned that only in case of a formal reply in writing that the Company cannot continue its commerce, am I permitted to divide equally among the inhabitants the permissions to trade which were conceded to the said Company, which offers the contrary, as is evident from its official letter. I am informing Your Excellency of this, in order that you may determine,[5] in view of the fact that more than a month ago the Company was to have begun its outfitting and expeditions, which I see will not be done, except for those well known nations as the Hotos and Mahas[6] whose trade was conceded to the Company as a sure

---

[1]Written in Spanish. A.G.I., P. de C., leg. 49.

[2]Document VIII.

[3]Document XIII.

[4]There is a large correspondence with regard to these debts chiefly in the Missouri Historical Society, Pierre Chouteau Collection, etc. A very few are given in this chapter, e.g. document XVII.

[5]See Gayoso de Lemos' reply, document XVIII.

[6]Granted by Carondelet in 1796. See Chapter V, document XVI, and also Chapter IV, documents XXIV and XXXVI.

benefice in order to help support the expenses of the more remote nations [yet] to be discovered and civilized [and] which I do not think will be undertaken.

May God keep Your Excellency many years
St. Louis, June 20, 1798
Zenon Trudeau [rubric]

Señor Don Manuel Gayoso de Lemos

XV

TRUDEAU TO GAYOSO DE LEMOS, ST. LOUIS, JUNE 21, 1798[1]

Number 11

In accordance with the desires of Your Excellency to favor the firm of the Sarpy brothers, for the reasons which you were kind enough to express in your official letter dated April 16,[2] last, I have forewarned the one that is in St. Louis of the favor, which you have conceded to them, namely, the trade of the Kances nation[3] for which trade he is preparing himself. And as Your Excellency does not explain for how many years the said commerce is to be conceded to them, I beg Your Excellency to advise me how long it should be, in order for me to serve my government.

My God keep Your Excellency many years.

St. Louis, June 21, 1798[4]
Zenon Trudeau [rubric]

Señor Don Manuel Gayoso de Lemos.

---

[1]Written in Spanish. A.G.I., P. de C., leg. 49.
[2]Document IX.
[3]Trudeau stated that the trade with the Kansas was the only one open to the traders lots for which were to be drawn. It was divided into six shares. Chapter V, document XVI.
[4]Reply is document XVI.

XVI

GAYOSO DE LEMOS TO TRUDEAU, NEW ORLEANS, JULY 9, 1798[1]

My official letter of April 16[2] which had for its purpose that the trade of the Kansas nation be facilitated to the Sarpy brothers, if it is without prejudice to a third [person], without my having explained whether one part should be given or all. It is well that you have given

---

[1]Written in Spanish. A.G.I., P. de C., leg. 44.
[2]Document XIII.

it, but it must not be for more than one year, since all are waiting for it. There are many persons who solicit [it] and who also have a right to this favor. But it is best to have as a maxim the distribution of these same favors with the greatest possible equity, having as an object making the greatest possible number happy or at least content. This is the way to avoid slanders and complaints.

This does not mean that at the same time you must cease watching over the well being of the Indians, since you must not lose sight of the fact that they be satisfied with the traders who are sent to them.

These are the rules with which you must invariably surround your conduct in this very important part of your command. This is in reply to your official letter number 11.[a]

May God keep you many years.
New Orleans, July 9, 1798.

Manuel Gayoso de Lemos [rubric]

Señor Don Zenon Trudeau

----

[a]Document XV.

XVII

Clamorgan, Loisel and Company to Clark, New Orleans, July 13, 1798[1]

New Orleans, July 13, 1798

M. Daniel Clark, Junior
Merchant, New Orleans

You have been informed and we ourselves have given you knowledge of the rigorous movements of your power-of-attorney towards our firm. We desire to know in which way you wish to terminate with us. We have nothing more at heart than to liquidate with you that which we owe you, by offering to remit to you in kind the properties, whatever they might consist of, resulting from the operations of the *Société* and coming from the merchandise for which we have given our obligations in proportion to the remittance in merchandise which shall be counted with the same charges of profit, commissions, expenses, interest which it cost us.

We do not believe we were making you an unjust proposition, all the more so since we are no longer in a condition to continue our firm, while the continuation of furnishing, which was expected from the *Maison* Todd represented by you, in conformity with the respective engagements, has been interrupted.

----

[1]Written in French. Missouri Historical Society, Pierre Chouteau Collection, no. 1.

We no longer being sustained, we absolutely cannot hold out any longer since the greatest expenses and immense interests which we would be obliged to pay in the end, would make a big void, and would place us in the impossibility of paying the entire total; and from that, there would follow a real loss, since we have nothing with which to pay our creditors except the funds which have been [he has] advanced to us, or the product of the said funds.

The rigorous resolutions that your power-of-attorney have shown by demanding judicial proceedings, engages us again to make you this proposition—finding ourselves in the impossibility of being able to liquidate otherwise.

Your powers-of-attorney have a perfect knowledge of the property which we have on hand; please give them the orders which you shall judge to be most suitable, in order to terminate [the matter] as promptly as possible. By doing this, you will infinitely oblige those who have the honor of being with the most profound respect,

Monsieur,
Your very humble servants
Clamorgan, Loisel & Company[2]
[rubric]

Addressed :

> A *Monsieur*
> *Monsieur* Daniel Clark
> Merchant,
> at New Orleans.

---

[2]This was one of the lowest ebb times of Clamorgan, Loisel and Company. Bankruptcy was staring Clamorgan in the face; he was being harassed by the heirs of Todd; and he had many enemies jealous of his exclusive trade privileges. Auguste Chouteau was appointed by Clark to press his claims against Clamorgan. Clamorgan salvaged himself out of this "bad mess" and by 1800 Daniel Clark, Jr., was representing Clamorgan and Company in New Orleans. But this was the beginning of the real downfall of Clamorgan, Loisel and Company. The correspondence and documentation with regard to these matters is very large, especially in the Missouri Historical Society, Pierre Chouteau Collection, and in A.G.I., P. de C.

In a letter to Chouteau, Daniel Clark, Jr., told him, after having received authority to proceed without obstacles against Clamorgan in the collection of money owed to him, that he [Clark] did not have any desire to do the least injury to Clamorgan, Loisel and Company, and he asked Chouteau to proceed but to have regard for that company, but to go against "Todd for the true wrongs, injuries and prejudices which I shall suffer". New Orleans, July 28, 1798, Missouri Historical Society, Pierre Chouteau Collection.

On May 11, 1799, Clark wrote Auguste Chouteau of Clamorgan's desire to terminate his business with him (Clark had held Clamorgan in New Orleans by judicial means) and an agreement was made between them and he [Clark] asked Chouteau to use "moderation towards Mr. Clamorgan". "I have not been motivated except by compassion for his position and if on his part he does not fulfill the promise which he has made to me or if he shall not follow the orders which you will give to him, you will please consider the stipulation on my part as null and you will exercise against him all the rigor of the law". Missouri Historical Society, Pierre Chouteau Collection.

XVIII

[GAYOSO DE LEMOS] TO TRUDEAU,
NEW ORLEANS, AUGUST 14, 1798[1]

I have read with attention the answer which Don Santiago Clamorgan,[2] Director of the Commercial Company of the Upper Missouri made to you regarding the question which you asked him, as to whether the former was in a position to carry on its commerce, as well as the just reflections which you make concerning his diffuse *memoria*. The latter in fact, only contains illusory contrarities of dreams which never can be realized with Morgan's [sic] powers [*facultades*] alone. And, as it may not be just that the beneficent intentions of His Majesty remain without effect, because of the interests and private caprice of one man alone, and in order to avoid contestations which may hamper and retard the fullfillment of the dispositions of the government, you will positively tell Clamorgan who has my order so that whenever a year passes that the Company does not fulfill the conditions to which it has bound itself by its *institutos* approved by the King, you may distribute the Indian trades which the Company has exclusively among those who suffered most by its [the Company's] establishment. You will in fact do so, informing me in detail of what you might have done, in whose favor, and the expenses they might have incurred, both for equipping themselves, as well as for the management of this trade, and the profit that they might have realized from it.[3]

God, etc. New Orleans, August 14, 1798.

[draft] to Zenon Trudeau.

_____

[1]Written in Spanish. Draft in A.G.I., P. de C., leg. 132.
[2]Document XIII.
[3]Document XIV.

XIX

MEMORIAL OF CLAMORGAN TO TRUDEAU,
ST. LOUIS, SEPTEMBER 27, 1798[1]

Memorial:

To Mr. Don Zenon Trudeau, Breveted Lieutenant-Colonel, Lieutenant Governor and Commander-in-Chief of this western district and dependencies of Illinois.

Sir: Santiago Clamorgan, a merchant in this city of St. Louis and with due respect before Your Excellency, declares that Mr. John Hay,

_____

[1]Missouri Historical Society, St. Louis Archives, no. 2934. This interesting, long, incomplete series of documents illustrates the financial workings of Clamorgan,

agent with substitute power of attorney [is] to represent in this dependency the heirs of the defunct Andrés Todd, according to the legal act passed in your archives dated the 2nd of June of this present year. According to the attached copy, folio 19 of the procedure, these powers have been made known to the business firm of the supplicant, known by the name of Clamorgan, Loisel and Company, so that it can not be ignorant of it, from the 13th of June of this present year, according to the document attached to folio 21 of the procedure. After this time, the said substitute has taken note of all that could be owed to the same firm, and of all the effects that belong to it, whether in money, accounts or notes that the same has extended in the books of its business, which he maintained and administered in his private home, it being more convenient for him to get a more perfect knowledge. After this trust, it has not surprised the supplicant at all to know that the said Mr. John Hay in his said capacity had become a fugitive yesterday night, 26th of this present month, with his whole family, and crossed over to the American side. This has caused the supplicant to suspect that the said Mr. John Hay might not have taken away with him the business books of his firm; which obliged him [the supplicant] to go immediately to his home to verify the conviction. When the above supplicant arrived there his suspicions were verified. Immediately he then gathered and took away the said business books, wherein, after having inspected all the accounts that the said Mr. Hay had established, he noticed that that of Mr. Hay amounted to the sum of 22952 #19s. 1 d. which debit he has charged to his account, without paying back anything of what he owed before his departure; it can be conjectured that it is probably to deprive the firm of Daniel Clark in New Orleans of the sum, and pass it over to that of Isaac Todd of Canada. In consequence of this irregular conduct on the part of Mr. Hay, in his capacity, as is specified by what is fitting to the rights of Mr. Daniel Clark, to which he had made an attempt, he seized his property: the supplicant has the honor of requesting of your Justice that he give him a legal act of the flight of the aforesaid Mr. John Hay, substitute agent of Mr. Isaac Todd, heir of the defunct Andrés Todd who died in New Orleans, in order to verify not only about the flight, but also concerning the injury he has done to the good faith and confidence of the supplicant to whom

---

Loisel and Company and of their connections with Todd. I have a photostatic copy of this document and have translated it. I hope to edit and publish this in its entirety in the near future. I have selected these documents as illustrative of the Company. See also Chapter IV, document XXVII, which is also from this same source. A good many other documents relating to Daniel Clark, Jr.'s, efforts to collect money due him from Todd are in the Missouri Historical Society, Chouteau Collections, and the A.G.I., P. de C., which repositories contain the surrounding official letters and documents, e.g. letter of Daniel Clark, Jr., New Orleans, July 28, 1798, Missouri Historical Society, Pierre Chouteau Collection.

he has not given an accounting for the sum that he himself seized, as it appears by the books of the firm of Mr. Clamorgan which he had in his possession, a thing that the supplicant asks Your Excellency to inspect, and take cognizance of it in order to verify in a legal manner, and demand, by way of restitution of funds, all the property of the estate of the defunct Andrés Todd, which may exist in the extent of the province of [for] the total amount with expenses, arrears and interests; that would be justice.

St. Louis, Illinois, 27 September 1798.—Jacques Clamorgan.—St. Louis, 27th September 1798.

As presented, and at the same time I made it known to Don Santiago Clamorgan, giving to him his writ for the right that he claims.

Zenon Trudeau

To *Señor* Don Zenon Trudeau, Breveted Lieutenant Colonel and Commander-in-Chief of this western part and Dependencies of Illinois.

Sir: Santiago Clamorgan, merchant in this city of St. Louis, has the honor of showing you that he desires to legally verify the deposition of Messrs. Antonio Reilhe, Josef Motard and Lorenzo Durocher, concerning the Missouri Company for which the supplicant has worked, both in his name and in that of his associates, for the account of the defunct Andrés Todd. The latter has declared the same to the Baron de Carondelet, which the supplicant offers to prove, if it is necessary, by a letter that has been addressed to him and that exists in his power, in order to claim the disbursements that have been made with interest and commission on the funds of the said Todd estate in the hands of the person on whom they may be found. Consequently, the supplicant desires that Your Justice accord him a legal act of the deposition that has been made by the said Messrs. Antonio Reilhe, Joseph Motard and Lorenzo Durocher, in order to add it to the procedure, and stamp it X to legally verify the truth, making any use of it that may be needed.

St. Louis, Illinois, 28th of October, 1798.—Jacques Clamorgan.

Decree
As he asks for it and let there be delivered the original declarations on the matter and I made it known to the interested party.—Zenon Trudeau

Document stamped X

Sir:

To Mr. Don Zenon Trudeau, Lieutenant Governor and Commander-in-Chief of the western part of Illinois. The supplicants have the honor of showing you that they are the owners of three shares of the Company of Missouri, coming from Messrs. Antonio Reilhe, Lorenzo Durocher, and Josef Motard, totaling considerable sums, which they have paid them for the account of the late Andrés Todd, deceased at New Orleans, who had charged the supplicants to acquire them without having his name appear, in order to enjoy clandestinely the fruits and advantages that could result in the future from the business of the said Company. In this circumstance, Sir, the supplicants are obliged to have recourse to your justice that it might please you to have the said Messrs. Antonio Reilhe, Lorenzo Durocher and Josef Motard give evidence to legally verify that the supplicants have only been the agents of the late Andrés Todd and that it was for him alone that the said supplicants acquired the said shares in the said Company; and so they have given evidence of the disbursements they made and remitted the said shares into the hands of the agent of the said estate that would be justice.—at St. Louis 27th of September, 1798.

Jaque Clamorgan   Regis Loisel

Decree

St. Louis, October 4, 1798

Let it be done, as it is requested for the depositions and as has been demanded.—Zenon Trudeau

We, Zenon Trudeau, Breveted Lieutenant Colonel, Captain in the regiment of Louisiana and Lieutenant Governor, commanding the Western part of Illinois, and in the presence of the undersigned attending witnesses have made appear before us Mr. Lorenzo Durocher, merchant residing in the village of St. Charles of Missouri, to whom we have given a reading of the above request. Having taken an oath to tell the truth, he declared to us that he has in effect sold his part and portion, as well as his share in the business Company of the Upper Missouri to Mr. Regis Loisel for the late André Todd, who dealt with him and that at the same time was to buy from him also his firm; that he also says he does not know the reasons the said Mr. André Todd had in making use of the name of Mr. Regis Loisel to transfer the act of the cession that he made of his interest [?] in the said Company of Upper Missouri, for which there was paid to him by the said Mr. Loisel a sum of 11,279 pounds, 11 sols which the document mentions; another sum of 435 pounds, by omission made in the said document that he always understood to have made the transfer of his interest in the above mentioned Company of Upper Missouri to the said late Todd; and regards Mr. Loisel as agent in this affair, which is what

574

he can affirm: in witness of the truth, and under oath taken by him, he has signed with Mr. François Vallé and Jean Baptiste Bellier our attending witnesses with us.

Lieutenant Governor; St. Louis, October 4, 1798.—Laurent Durocher—Jean Baptiste Bellier—Zenon Trudeau.

We, the above mentioned, Lieutenant Governor, the same day and year have made appear before us, and the same attending witnesses, Mr. Josef Motard; After an oath was made by him to tell the truth, we gave him a reading of the request above presented to us by Messrs. Jaque Clamorgan and Regis Loisel. He declared to us that, being uneasy about the results of the interests that he had in the business Company of the Upper Missouri, he told these fears to Mr. Andrés Todd, who told him, "be calm, I am going to buy your share in the said Company, but I do not wish to appear to deal with you, and I am going to have it done by my associates;" that some time after declaring this to him, he had entrusted Mr. Auguste Chouteau, to whom he owed the greatest part of the merchandise that he had furnished for his share in the Company, to take care of this business for him, which he did with Messrs. Clamorgan and Loisel, by passing over to them a legal act of cession which was signed by the declarant; that Mr. Todd confided to him the secret of this affair, and that he had never spoken of it until this day, when he is under obligation to give testimony under oath which he has made and which he affirms by his signing the said sale.—Josef Motard—François Vallé—Jean Baptiste Bellier—Zenon Trudeau—.

At St. Louis of Illinois the 5th day of October, 1798. We, Zenon Trudeau, Lieutenant Governor of Western part of Illinois have had appear before us and the undersigned attending witnesses, Mr. Antoine Reilhe, and, after he had taken an oath to tell the truth, we gave him a reading of the request above presented to us by Mr. Jaque Clamorgan. He declared that he does not know whether the said Messrs. Clamorgan and Loisel were agents of Mr. Andrés Todd in the cession, but has abandoned to them his interest and share in the commercial firm of Missouri, and that that affair was taken care of for him by Mr. Auguste Chouteau whom he had entrusted with his interests in that affair. He can only say that on the day it was terminated, he met in the street the said Mr. Andrés Todd, when he was leaving the commandant's house, [and] that the latter asked him summarily, if his business of the cession was finished; that answering him, Mr. Chouteau gave his word, assuring him, yes, and the said declarant replied, "very well, he has mine and I will not put up any opposition." This business ended, a sum of 8682 pounds and diverse objects were handed over *en nature* to him by Messrs. Clamorgan and Loiselle.

This is all he can declare in witness of the truth and under the oath taken by him, and [he] Mr. François Duquet and Jean Baptiste Bellier signed with us and we Lieutenant Governor—Antoine Reilhe—François Duquet—Jean Baptiste Bellier—Zenon Trudeau.

Let the original be remitted to serve the owner—Zenon Trudeau.

To Mr. Don Zenon Trudeau, Lieutenant Governor and Commander-in-Chief at St. Louis. The supplicant being informed that Mr. Motard had not mentioned the sum which was paid to him for the total of his share that the firm Clamorgan, Loiselle, and Company bought from him for the account of the late Andrés Todd, he begs you to have the said Mr. Motard declare the price that he received for the total of the said share, which he sold, in order to verify it to obtain the reimbursement for the succession of the late Andrés Todd, thus doing justice. St. Louis 26th October 1798—Jaque Clamorgan—St. Louis 26th October, 1798. Let this be done as is requested. Zenon Trudeau.

At St. Louis of Illinois, the 27th day of the month of October, 1798, we, Zenon Trudeau, Lieutenant Governor of the Western part of the said Illinois, and accompanied by Messrs. Jean Baptiste Bellier, and François Vallé, Jr. as attending witnesses, we caused to appear before us, Mr. Josef Motard, resident in this city of St. Louis and after having made him take an oath to tell the truth, and having instructed him of the above as to the content of the request presented to us by Mr. Jaque Clamorgan, he declared to us that the total sum paid to him by Messrs. Clamorgan Loiselle, and Company for the cession of his share and interest in the Company of the Upper Missouri is 10,182 pounds, both for what belonged to himself, and for what was paid to Mr. Auguste Chouteau for diverse merchandise which had been advanced to him, for his part and placed in the said Company of Upper Missouri, that he ratifies what he has just declared under oath and in witness of the truth, he signed with the above attending witnesses named with us, the Lieutenant Governor. —Josef Motard—François Vallé—Jean Baptiste Bellier—Zenon Trudeau.

Memorial

Monsier Don Zenon Trudeau, Lieutenant Colonel of the fixed regiment of Louisiana and Lieutenant Governor of the western part of Illinois,

Sir, Auguste Chouteau very humbly begs, as trustee of the firm of Mr. Daniel Clark, junior, following his legal authorization stated in the preceding documents relative to the affairs of the firm of Messrs. Clamorgan Loisel and Company [and] has the honor of showing you, sir, that the firm of Messrs. Clamorgan Loisel and Company is indebted to the firm of Mr. Daniel Clark, Junior, according to the account settled this day of 68211 *piastres,* one *dénier,* 3 *maravedis.* In consequence of the transactions made up to this day by the supplicant and which are known by you, sir, the result of it has been: first, the seizure of the account books of the said firm of Messrs. Clamorgan and Company, by which books it is found that there is owed to the aforesaid firm, by various individuals, a sum of 53862# 2S. The supplicant has the honor of calling to your attention, that this sum cannot be considered settled, while the debtors, in coming to a settlement, can set up counter accounts, and the supplicant knows that Mr. Louis Courtois, who has bought merchandise for the payment of which he still owes 4010# 19s. has the right invoice to send back the merchandise that he will not have sold when the payment which he must make falls due; these will probably be the articles of less demand, to add, sir, to those the sums payable in commodities; all that will necessarily diminish the total of the said sum of 53862# 2S. owed by current account. The supplicant has divided it into three types, (to) which it summarized at this time, because one can establish nothing very positive for this said sum, until after the accounts will have been settled.

Sum total of good debts
Sum total of dubious debts
Sum total of debts on which very little
    faith can be laid

53862#   2 S.

2nd.

The seizure of the various promissory notes totaling the sum of 118117# 16/9—which notes the supplicant divides again in four types, following his manner of seeing, in which however, he can be mistaken.

Sum total—the solvent and those payable on demand	35941....1 1/7
Sum total—the notes which can be paid during the course of time	48574....1 1/8
Sum total—the notes on which very little faith can be laid	24593....5
Sum total—the notes that one can regard as lost	9008....1 8/6

118117....1 6/9

3rd.

The sales of the stock in store after the seizure, inventory and the appraisal made by you, sir, in the course of the present month, which sale has come to the amount of 9781 *piastres* six *escalins*; and the seizure made also on a portion of furs, that after the receipt made and the estimation at the price current of this country, gave a sum of 2266#....5/. All which sums above-mentioned total together

for the total of the standing accounts established on the books of the said firm	53862....	2/
for the sum total of all the promissary notes	118117....1	6/.9
for the sum total of the legal sale-piastres 9781,6ᵗ, which equals	48908....1	5/
for the sum total of various furs	2266....	5/
	223154#	18/.9

4th.

The firm of Messrs. Clamorgan Loisel and Company will be perhaps astonished that the supplicant has not put in the total of their assets sums owned by them privately—first, a sum of 41290# 5/ owed by Mr. Clamorgan; second of another sum of 9550#....18/ owed by Mr. Loisel; third, of another sum of 22952# 19/ owed by Mr. John Hay; the supplicant believed he had to do so, considering that the said Messrs. Clamorgan, Loisel and Hay make up the company against which Mr. Daniel Clark, Junior, has an immediate suit, and that to omit these would not be showing their present assets.

5th.

The said firm of Messrs. Clamorgan Loisel and Company will be similarly astonished that the supplicant has not put in the total of its assets another sum of 20064# 15/ owed by the Company of Missouri; the supplicant believes himself again justified in not putting this sum in the said total, considering that he is not acquainted with the members who make up this company; the supplicant will not refuse to all to admit it when the firm of Messrs. Clamorgan Loisel and Company will have made them known to him; according to the requests that the supplicant has had the honor of making to you, sir, by his petition of the 27th of the current [month], if there are found in the number of that company some persons who could answer for it, he will sue them in order to obtain the payment of the said account.

You will see, sir, by the transactions made by the supplicant up to this day that he has scrutinized with care the assets of the firm of Messrs. Clamorgan Loisel and Company, and that by means of his work [and] of his scrupulous investigations, the supplicant finds that the assets of this firm seem to increase, if one adds to them what the three above-mentioned associates owe in their own and private name, to the total of their company, as well as the sum owed by the Company of Missoury, the whole amounting to—

for the total of the 4 sums established above	223154# . . 1 8./9
for the sum owed by Mr. Cla- morgan, mentioned above	41290# . . 5./
for idem by Mr. Loisel	9550# . . 1 8./
for idem by Mr. John Hay	22952# . . 1 9./
for idem by Company of Missoury	20064# . . 1 5./
	317013# . . 1 5./9

On this sum of 317013# .... 15/ . . 9, the supplicant does not believe he will receive from now, until the end of next April, (as far as his knowledge permits him to judge) anything except approximately 17 to 20 thousand *piastres,* considering the nature of the various debts mentioned above.

According to this rough estimate, the supplicant finds himself obliged, sir, to again have recourse to your authority, begging you to kindly order the firm of Messrs. Clamorgan Loisel and Company to make known to the supplicant the members who make up the said company; by imparting to him its act of association, and, consequently, to authorize the said supplicant, if you find his requests in conformity with the orders that the said Mr. Daniel Clark, Junior, has obtained from the government, against the said firm of Messrs. Clamorgan Loisel and Company, to carry out the seizure, inventory and sale of the effects belonging to each of the said members, taken collectively or separately, until the settlement of the balance of the sum owed to Mr. Daniel Clark, junior. Doing this you will do justice— at St. Louis of Illinois, the 28th of October, 1798.—Auguste Chouteau.

Decree:

St. Louis, November 2, 1798—It being of record that not enough has been attached and sold [of the assets] of the business firm of Clamorgan Loisel and Company to cover the debt of sixty-eight thousand two hundred and eleven *pesos,* one *real* and three *maravedis* that it owes Mr. Daniel Clark of New Orleans, let there be attached and judicially seized a settlement, made with the separation of the private property from the property of the aforesaid Clamorgan and Loisel, as likewise that of Mr. John Hay, member of the same firm, if he has it in this town and jurisdiction. Let them be deposited with a bonded person, in order that it may be sold in favor of the creditor, and since there is no constable nor scrivener, the above will be carried out by me. M. Santiago Clamorgan and Loisel will make known who the members of the business company of Upper Missouri are, and will surrender the documents that establish to whom one must apply for the collection of the twenty thousand sixty-four *livres,* fifteen *sueldos* that the said company owes in the books that have been attached.—Zenon Trudeau.

Notification:

The third day of October [*sic*], 1798, I made it known to Mr. Augusto Chouteau, whom I called to my home for the purpose.—Zenon Trudeau.

Memorial—

To Señor Don Zenon Trudeau, breveted Lieutenant Colonel, Lieutenant Governor and Commander-in-chief of this western part and dependencies of Illinois.

Sir, Santiago Clamorgan, merchant in this town of St. Louis, in the best form for which there is occasion by law, before Your Excellency reveals in the name of his business firm that, after having searched in his said firm, among all his correspondence of letters of the defunct Andrés Todd, and of Mr. Isaac Todd, merchant in Canada, relative to the business of his said firm, he was very much surprised to perceive that they had been removed from his house with the exception of one letter alone, dated the first of May of this present year that was found by chance, and which I present enclosed, fearing perhaps that the supplicant does not make use of those that could serve him for the reclamation of losses which he has the right to seek from the inheritance. This is a thing which is very easy to suppose, for by document Y attached, it is known that the agent of the said Andrés Todd in Illinois has declared that he regretted not having taken with him the business books of the Clamorgan Loisel and Company, from which it is concluded that, if the business books of the supplicant have been forgotten, the correspondence has not been. First, a letter that is missing to the supplicant which is of the month of June or July 1796, written by the defunct Andrés Todd of Makinak in which he asked and ordered the said supplicant *not to neglect to procure from himself the business of the Missouri Company, of which he had spoken to him, and that the supplicant could count on him; and other things along the same lines, and that after a short time he would arrive in Illinois.* 2nd.

Another letter of Mr. Isaac Todd, as heir, written in the winter of 1796 to 1797, in which he told the supplicant that his business firm could count on the merchandise that it might need to supply itself with, and that it could immediately have a statement passed to Makinak, that it [where he?] would have it carried out, a favor that was only a courtesy to attract to Canada the skins that the Clamorgan Loisel and Company firm owed Mr. Daniel Clark, merchant in New Orleans. The conduct of the agents of the Todd succession in Illinois has manifested this truth.

3rd. By another letter of the beginning of this present year, Mr. Isaac Todd ordered the said Clamorgan Loisel and Company firm to have sent to Canada all the funds that were owed to that of Mr. Clark of New Orleans. There were means taken, concerning this affair between the Canada firm and that of New Orleans, and the said Mr. Isaac Todd answered for everything. [On the other hand,] the conduct of Mr. Daniel Clark with the firm of the supplicant has evidently demonstrated to the contrary, proving that the Canada firm only seeks to withdraw the funds of that of New Orleans, via that [firm] of the supplicant, which they have abused, tricked, and conducted into an abyss of error; all of which the firm of the supplicant intends to render responsible to the succession of the defunct Andrés Todd, for reparations, losses and deviation from justice, wherever it can persecute it. In the same way [do they hope to get] the reimbursements of different sums in double employ that the agents of the succession in Illinois will have paid to the firm of the supplicant, according to the accounts that it will make, having value when suitable, for which it makes its protests and reservations as is by law. For all of this supplicant asks for an *Acte* from your justice to add to the legal procedure and to serve as needed. St. Louis 30th of October, 1798.

Jaque Clamorgan.

St. Louis October 31, 1798.

As presented, and may it serve as it is needed. Trudeau. On the same day I made it known to Don Santiago Clamorgan.—Trudeau.

XX

Trudeau to Gayoso de Lemos, St. Louis, November 15, 1798[1]

Señor Governor-General

I have seen Don Joseph Robidou the party who is presenting this memorial[2] and who has begged and supplicated me not to *ponerle en*

---

[1]Written in Spanish. Bancroft Library. This is not complete, extract only.

[2]Document V. See also document VIII. In another letter of same date carrying similar information (Bancroft Library) Trudeau said that he was returning the

proceso abierto against Don Santiago Clamorgan, whose malice and schemes he fears. He says that he is willing to sacrifice his losses in order to conserve tranquillity. Don Antonio Reilhe who for the same reason could also make a complaint against Clamorgan—thinks the same as Robidou, and absolutely does not wish to enter into difficulties with him, so that not knowing any other persons than the two cited persons, it is not possible for me to give Your Excellency a report [*informe*] supported by documents which could convince Clamorgan of what he is being accused of and of which nevertheless I do not have the least doubt.

The downfall of his commercial firm and his total ruin, notwithstanding all his schemes, must make Your Excellency see that the exclusive privilege which he holds for the commerce of the Upper Missouri ought to be annulled. And I so consider it, although I am sure that he will speak to Your Excellency, as if he had all the means possible for its continuation.

St. Louis, November 15, 1798.

Zenon Trudeau [rubric]

---

memorial of Robidou which Your Excellency sent to me for my information. "Clamorgan being entirely ruined surely cannot indemnify the losses he has caused the said Robidou and Antonio Reilhe who are so fond of their peace that they prefer it to a lawsuit with a man so keen and rascally as Clamorgan."

XXI

GAYOSO DE LEMOS TO FRANCISCO SAAVEDRA
NEW ORLEANS, NOVEMBER 22, 1798[1]

Index of the *carta reservada* which under this date Brigadier Don Manuel Gayoso de Lemos, political and military governor of the provinces of Louisiana and West Florida remits to the most Excellent *Señor* Don Francisco de Saavedra first Secretary of State y del despacho Universal.

Number 1. Sends copies of two replies and documents which he has remitted to the Most Excellent *Señor* Conde de Santa Clara, his captain-general, acknowledging the receipt of the royal order of June 26, concerning fear of hostilities from the Americans. He manifests the precarious military situation of those provinces upon whose conservation the Kingdom of Mexico depends.

He makes evident how much he is interested in the knowledge of the limits between Spain, Great Britain and the United States towards the origin of the Mississippi, New Mexico, and Pacific Ocean.

He proposes and indicates what they must be, he having conserved in our service, for that purpose, two famous travellers, Don Jayme Macay

---

[1]Written in Spanish. This index is from A.G.I., P. de C., leg. 2365

and Don Juan Evans, who served in the English Companies and in our Company of the Missouri, and can accompany the commissioned astronomer who is to be sent, and for whom *con instancia* he asks.

He treats the operations of the divisory line of the recent treaty of limits, and of the bad dispositions which on the part of the Americans is observed in the fulfillment of articles two and five of the said treaty. He enlarges upon their operations, designs and necessities; and the urgency of continuing the already begun connection with Kentucky concluding by soliciting the approval of His Majesty.

New Orleans, November 22, 1798.

By the Frigate of War, *La Serena* stationed in Pensacola.

Duplicate by goleta, *Amaia Ysnard.*

To His Most Excellent Sir, Don Francisco de Saavedra
New Orleans, November 22, 1798.

No. 1 *reservada*[2]

Most Excellent Sir:

My Captain-General, the most Excellent *Señor* Conde de Santa Clara: Under date of September twenty-first, last, you transcribed to me what under date of June twenty-sixth,[3] the Most Excellent *Señor* Minister of War communicated to you, relative to the hostile intentions on the part of the United States against this province.

As this matter concerns not only the minister of War, but has its origin essentially in the political influence of Europe, I consider it my obligation to inform Your Excellency of the state of affairs between this province and the United States.

In order that Your Excellency may be informed of my military situation, enclosed are copies of my official letters, *reservadas,* numbers twenty and twenty-one, in answer to the last ones from my captain-general of which it is best that Your Excellency have knowledge.

The few safe occasions which offer themselves have increased the difficulty of informing Your Excellency regularly of all the occurrences which would be very *à propos* that Your Excellency not be ignorant of, not only to provide what is best, but in order to possess certain data, which it will be well to bear in mind at the time of the general peace, which I do not consider very remote, at that time a general congress might be held in which a new arrangement of the political interests of all the nations will be treated.

---

[2]Complete with enclosures in A.H.N., Est., leg. 3900; draft [without enclosures] in A.G.I., P. de C., leg. 2365, and copy in Missouri Historical Society, Papers from Spain, no. 98.

[3]Royal order of June 26—concerning fears of hostilities on the part of the Americans.

The local situation of this province merits Your Excellency's most particular attention. Upon it depends the security of the Kingdom of Mexico and the preservation of the greater part of His Majesty's dominions in North America.

The English nation and the United States are our frontier neighbors from latitude thirty-one degrees to the highest latitude known and in discoveries which may be made in the future.

From the thirty-first [parallel] to the source of the Mississippi, the treaties clearly express what the limits must be; but ascending farther to the north it is a matter which requires the most scrupulous arrangement. The English and the United States have provided what is best to produce this arrangement, but have feigned not to know the intention of Spain, for the indication of some limits which border upon their territory.

It is probable that the differences and difficulties which the English commissaries and those of United States will find may be settled by agreeing to compensation on the territory of His Majesty, whose interests no one defends, because of his not having a commissary for our part in those remote districts.

Supposing that the operations between the English and the United States are justified, it is an indispensable necessity to arrange the limit which fixes the territory of His Majesty and that of the King of Great Britain from the latitude of Lake of the Woods to the north.

Up to the present this operation has not been essential because of those climes being frequented little or not at all known, although in the last few years in this district the English traders solicitous of arriving in the country where they would benefit from the fine skins, have introduced themselves via the San Pedro river, which enters into the Mississippi, and have reached as far as the Missouri. Others from the Lake of the Woods have passed to the lake called Winnipeg, and by it, entering the Colorado river, [marginal notation: there is another river of this same name which traverses the territory of Natchitoches and empties into the Mississippi a little to the north of the thirty-first parallel] have reached its source which is at a very short distance from that of the Missouri. Other English traders from the river of Los Osmoboines [Assiniboine], travelling 120 leagues southward have arrived at the villages of the Mandanas on the Missouri. By these three routes they have been making the referred to trade in fine skins, until recently when they were interrupted by the Illinois companies, and also due, in no smaller manner, to Fort Carondelet on the Missouri in charge of Don Augusto Chouteau, merchant of Illinois, and who, being a man of greatest confidence completely possesses the [confidence of the] entire Osage nation.

The object of the English will naturally be to pretend or, more specifically, claim all the territory to the north of a line which runs west, directly from the Lake of the Woods to the Pacific Ocean, which will come out with a very small difference at Nootka Sound. They will [also] allege reasons for it, founded upon our last agreement, concerning the coast which runs towards the north from Nootka Sound; but if this action is reasonable, and is not in a position of requiring advantages which our situation cannot deny them, it seems to me that the divisory line between the territories of His Majesty and His Britannic Majesty in the northern part of North America should be as follows:

Supposing that the angle from the northwest of the limits between the United States and Great Britain may be in some part of the Mississippi, further to the north in a communication by water, leading to Lake Winnipeg, and from there following, also by water, where it approximates most closely a northwesterly direction to Slave Lake, entering it by the river of the same name, and following from its mouth by means of the said Lake to its western extremity, and from there by the McKenzie River to the district where the traveller McKenzie reconnoitred the sea in 1789, near to the Island of *La Ballena*.

Also on the side of the Pacific Ocean it will be best to establish our limit, drawing a line from east to west, straight from Nootka Sound to the chain of mountains, which the English know under the name of Stoney Mountains, until arriving at the peak of the principal range of the said chain of mountains, where following from peak to peak, more or less, to the north-northwest until arriving at the latitude of the district in Slave Lake where the McKenzie River begins. From this latitude in the mountain range the line is to run straight east until it cuts the referred to river.

In this manner the Colorado river would remain within the territory of the King, and the peace and good faith between our Indians and the merchants of Illinois would be reestablished, resulting to our favor, the rich traffic of fine skins which would be exported, via the mouth of the Mississippi.

It is very important to divert [drive out] the English from the Missouri, all the more so, since that is the only way to prevent their penetrating into the Kingdom of Mexico, which otherwise would be very easy for them. It is probable that [this] favorite object towards which the combined policy of the United States and England is directed does not escape their ambitious designs.

Foreseeing the importance of this matter, I tried to keep to our cause the two most famous travelers of the northern countries of this continent; one Don Jayme Macay and the other Don Juan Evans, both natives of the

Island of Great Britain, who, displeased with the Canadian companies, entered the service of our Missouri Company. But when this company failed due to its poor management and great losses, I knew that necessity would oblige these two valuable subjects to solicit employment among the referred to Canadian Companies to our own very great loss. In order to avoid this inconvenience, after having had Macay at my side for some time, in order to assure myself of his principles, I have decided to locate him at San Andrés, a new establishment near the entrance of the Missouri, naming him commandant of that post, under the dependency of the Lieutenant-Governor of Illinois.[4] Not having any position to give Evans, I have preferred to maintain him at my cost, keeping him in my own house, in order to prevent his returning to his own country, or for his own convenience, to embrace another cause.

These two subjects are most important to accompany the astronomical commissioner [surveyor], whom His Majesty may appoint to arrange in the north of this province and the Kingdom of Mexico the limits between His territory and that of His Britannic Majesty and to ratify or supervise those between this Sovereign and those of the United States.

Complying with my honor, I can only inform Your Excellency that if such an operation should be to His Majesty's approval, that he deign to appoint an eminent astronomer, as commissioner, and that from Europe there be sent the implements and [astronomical] tables, necessary for this object. Having been named commissioner for boundaries indicated by the treaty with the United States, I am discussing the difficulties which present themselves to me, in order that the operation be made scientifically on our part, and, even in order, to provide myself with the instruments proper for such an important operation, which necessarily might have been delayed, much to our discredit, if I had not had some instruments and purchased for the account of the King an astronomical compass which a friend of mine in Natchez had just received from London, via the United States for his own amusement. This instrument is of the most modern construction and I had to pay 840 *pesos* for it, [I] not charging anything for my instruments . . . .[5]

New Orleans, November 22, 1798[6]
Manuel Gayoso de Lemos [rubric]

Most Excellent *Señor* Don Francisco de Saavedra

---

[4] Document II, note 3, and document XII. Mackay's appointment is in Houck, *Spanish Régime in Missouri*, II, 245.

[5] The remainder of this long letter deals with Wm. Dunbar and Ellicot; the boundary line between the United States and the Spanish possessions; problems arising out of the treaty of San Lorenzo el Real; etc. etc. See A. P. Whitaker,

586

The Mississippi Question (New York, 1934), Gayarré, History of Louisiana: Spanish Domination; etc.

Fear of a rupture with England and consequent invasion of the Spanish Illinois from Canada caused the Spanish officials in the Mississippi Valley to confine the greater part of their attention to effecting a better military defense for the Spanish settlements and to a military patrol of the Mississippi. More than one military reconnaissance was made of the Upper Mississippi, while spies were also sent into the interior, which, although technically belonging to the United States, was really in the hands of the British fur traders, and to the United States and Canada. There was fear also of war between the United States and France. Merchandise was scarce on account of these war scares and little merchandise came to St. Louis from Canada. England also feared an attack upon Canada from the Spanish settlements. See Nasatir, "Anglo-Spanish Rivalry in the Iowa Country 1797-1798," Iowa Journal of History and Politics, XXVIII (1930), 337-389. There is a veritable mine of documentation upon these matters still in manuscript form, e.g., document V. of Chapter VII. Trudeau to [Gayoso de Lemos] no. 18, St. Louis, August 6, 1798, A.G.I., P. de C., leg. 188B; Trudeau to Gayoso de Lemos, no. 14, St. Louis, July, 1798, A.G.I., P. de C., leg. 50; letter of Daniel Clark, Jr., New Orleans, July 28, 1798, Missouri Historical Society, Pierre Chouteau Collection, etc. etc. For some printed references see Houck, Spanish Régime in Missouri, II, 259, 285; Wisconsin Historical Society Collections, XVIII, 449, 456; Missouri Historical Society Collections, III, 71; Peter Russell Papers; etc. For some time past I have been translating and editing some of this vast documentation for a volume on the Upper Mississippi Frontier similar to this one on the Upper Missouri Frontier.

[6]The following enclosures, all certified copies, are in A.H.N., Est., leg. 3900:

1. Gayoso de Lemos to Santa Clara, res. New Orleans, November 20, 1798 [American attacks upon Spanish Louisiana; galliots, Wilkinson.] Two letters of same date.
2. José Vidal to Gayoso de Lemos, no. 4 res., Natchez, October 8, 1798.
3. José Vidal to Gayoso de Lemos, no. 5 res., Natchez, October 8, 1798.
4. José Vidal to Gayoso de Lemos, no. 6 res., Natchez, October 10, 1798.
5. José Vidal to Gayoso de Lemos, no. 7 res., Natchez, October 11, 1798.
6. Two letters of Gayoso to Santa Clara, dated November 20, 1798.

XXII

MACKAY TO GAYOSO DE LEMOS, ST. ANDREWS, NOVEMBER 28, 1798[1]

St. Andrew du Missouri Nov. 28, 1798

Excellent Sir:

I avail myself on [of] the opportunity (being the first since my arrival here)[2] to acknowledge the many obligations that I am under to you & thank your Excellency in the most sincere manner for all the civillity & goodness with which you was pleased to honour me, during my residence at New Orleans which I will ever remember with Gratitude.

---

[1]Written in English. A.G.I., P. de C., leg. 215B.
[2]Mackay took possession of the command of San André on October 1, 1798, cited in note 3 to document II.
On November 28, 1798, the same date as the text, Mackay wrote another letter to Gayoso de Lemos in English (original in A.G.I., P. de C., leg. 2365; copy, in Missouri Historical Society, Papers from Spain, no. 99) complaining that his written instructions given him by Trudeau were not the same that he had from Gayoso de Lemos verbally. Mackay complained aga:nst the governor's edict stopping emigration which was a mortal blow to Upper Louisiana and made the Indians bold to steal and plunder "our weak and new settlements on the frontier". Mackay

On my arrival at my Post, I found all the people living in peace and plenty; indeed, it is surprising to See the Great Clearing of land & the quantity of Grain raised by so smal a number of inhabitants, & I am persuaded that if there were about Two hundred Families more permitted to emigrate to this district it would be one of the most Flourishing settlements in Louisiana & in a short time would be able to furnish lower Louisiana with Flower & Hemp & other articles for which we are at present indebted to a foreign country, while our own vast countries lays waste & its rich soil left to be frequented only by a few mischievous savages & the wild beasts of the forest.

Since my arrival here several families came with all their property to this country in expectation of getting lands as usual, some of them came from the most distant parts of the United States even from the Limits between the state of vermount & Canada, but finding themselves disappointed they remain on the American side. Some have bought lands & settled opposite to us & others is going to remain camped in the woods, until (they) your Excellency takes pity on them—as they say—

I assure your Excellency that the American side of the Illinois gains a great advantages by the Stoppage of the Emigration on our side, which, if it should continue the American Illinois will soon become too powerful a neighbor & consequently Dangerous in case of a war.

I am now beginning to make the King's Road from the upper extremity of the inhabited part of St. Andre to Communicate with St. Louis which project, I hope Your Excellency will approve of, I am in hopes of finishing the whole of it before the beginning of the Spring, that is to say if the winter be favourable. The only Obstacle I met with, in this project is a Doctor Renalle [Reynal] who lived & practiced a number of years at St. Louis, & who (I believe) possesses about Twelve Thousand acres of land in this District, he is well known to be of a mutinous disposition & a leader of the Rabble. As to the americans, they are all ready to turn out at minutes warning to any thing that they are ordered to do; even those who could not obtain land but is laboring for others are willing to assist, they say all, that they will make a Good road so that when Gover^r Gayoso honours them with a visit, he may ride in a Coach in safety. [and] they

said it was impossible to people the country with Roman Catholics alone except at great expense to the government. Canada, which is Roman Catholic, only gave them *engagés* and *voyageurs* and not farmers. In the United States there was not one Catholic in a thousand inhabitants and due to Gayoso de Lemos' edict restricting emigration to Spanish Louisiana to Catholics alone it practically put a stop to that emigration. Mackay asked to be permitted to allow good and honest farmers, regardless of religion, to come to settle until San André would be strong enough to protect itself and serve as a barrier "for the upper part of the Illinois". The reply to both of these letters is dated May 20, 1799 and is printed in *United States Documents*, 24th Congress 1st Session Document number 59, (serial 288) p. 33 and also in *American State Papers, Public Lands*, VI, 719.

hope that his Excellency will find their conduct at all time to be such as will entitle them to the same protection, as any other Class of people of their fellow subjects.

As the Missouri Company seems to be incapable of continuing any longer & as it is probable that your Excellency will order the posts that was occupied by the Company to be Given to other Individuals, I beg that your Excellency may Have the Goodness to reserve for me my share that I hold at present in the Said Posts which is the fifth part, being in all but four parteners, besides myself. If it Should be your pleasure to Grant me this privilege untill the expiration of the privilege which was Given to the Company, it may perhaps make up in some degree for my losses & for the toil & Dangers that I suffered in that wild country, besides it is probable that my Knowledge of that Country may enable me to render Services to All those who may engage in the Commerce or Discovery of that Immense Country.

I hope your Excellency has not forgot to forward the permission for a Billiard Table in the Town of St. Charles to Mr. Lawrence deroche which you was pleased to promise when I was at N^w Orleans he has a small family, very Decent & very little to Support them.

I have the honor to be with every sentiment of esteem & respect

your Excellency's Most Hum^e and Most obedient serv^t

Santiago Mackay

[rubric]

To His Excellency the Govr General

Addressed) His Excellency Manuel Gayoso Bridagier Genl of his majesties armies, Governor General & Commander in Chief of the Province of Louisiana and Florida &c &c. N. Orleans.

CHAPTER VII

1799

I

Summary by Delassus of Trade Licenses Issued at St. Louis, 1799-1804[1]

The year 1799. The trades have been accorded as follows, by order of *Monseigneur* Gayoso de Lemos, Governor-General of these provinces: The Big and Little Osages[2] to *Monsieur* Auguste Chouteau according to his contract with the government.

The Kansas to *Monsieur* Gregoire Sarpy, according to the order of the governor.[3]

---

[1]Written in French and also in Spanish. Missouri Historical Society, Bundle "Indian Trade and Fur Companies."

In Jerome C. Smiley's, *Semi-Centennial History of the State of Colorado* (Chicago, 1913), I, 163, the following is written but upon what authority is not stated:

"The far-upper reaches of the Missouri River became very well known by French fur-gatherers from the French settlements in Illinois and from St. Louis in the last half of the eighteenth century, and many miles of the courses of the Platte and Arkansas rivers were equally familiar to them. While it is probable that some of these energetic adventurers had seen the Colorado section of the Rocky Mountains at various times in the last quarter of that century, the earliest definite account known to the present writer of a trading expedition to our mountains in that period is that of the enterprise of Jean de la Maissonneuve and a Swiss associate named Preneloupe.

"These men, in 1799, with fifteen or twenty engagées, leaving St. Louis in the spring of that year, ascended the Missouri River in boats, laden with trading-goods, to the mouth of the Platte, where they had immediately an active trade with the Indians of that part of the country.

"Having started their boats back to St. Louis with cargoes of furs and in the charge of some of their men, Maisonneuve and Preneloupe, with ten of their French Canadian engagées, six Indian guides, and twenty pack animals well burdened, set out, near the middle of June, for the Western Mountains. Proceeding up the course of the Platte, they reached the confluence of the North Platte and South Platte

The Panis to *Monsieur* Benito Vasquez,[4] according to the said order and including my share.

The Otos to *Messieurs* Chauvin and Ortiz, according to the said order.

The Mahas to *Messieurs* Mackay and St. Cire, according to the said order.

The Poncas to *Monsieur* Goth [Hosty] according to the said order.

St. Louis, Illinois, This 31st December, 1799

Charles Dehault Delassus[5] [rubric]

The year 1800,[6] the trades have been distributed as follows by order of the Marqués de Casa Calvo in that which was changed from those of *Monsieur* Gayoso de Lemos.

The Big and Little Osages to *Monsieur* Auguste Chouteau, according to his contract.

The Kansas and Panis République to *Monsieur* Bernal, according to the said order.

The Otos, Mahas and Poncas to *Monsieur* Clamorgan, according to the said order.

The Panis to Don Benito Basquez, including my share.

St. Louis, this fourth December 1800.

Year 1801[7]

Exclusive Trades [granted] by order of the Marqués de Casa Calvo, governor of these provinces.

The Big and Little Osages for four years to *Monsieur* Chouteau.

The Mahas and Poncas to *Monsieur* Charles Sanguinet for two years dated from March fourteenth.[8]

To *Monsieur* Clamorgan the Panis Republic dated from January twenty-sixth.[9]

---

rivers in seventeen days. Turning up the way of [the] South Platte, they came within sight of the mountains in ten more days of travel, and on July 20th arrived at the site of Denver. Here they saw arrayed upon the lowland between them and the foot-hills the encampment of a great body of Indians; and here, also they fell in with a passing party of Spanish dragoons, from Santa Fe. These were commanded by Don Bernardo Burro, and were upon their homeward way from a scouting expedition that had taken them to the North Platte River."

I have found no corroborative evidence of these activities.

[2]Chouteau's contract was for six years. See Nasatir, *Imperial Osage*. The contract is given in Houck, *Spanish Régime in Missouri*, II, 100-110.

[3]See Chapter VI, documents IX, XV, and XVI.

[4]See Chapter VI, document II, especially note 2.

[5]Several of the requests and permits listed hereinafter in this document will appear in the documents and notes in this and succeeding chapters. The Osage documents and narrative are in Nasatir, *Imperial Osage*.

[6]Delassus succeeded Zenon Trudeau as lieutenant governor on August 29, 1799.

[7]Another copy in Delassus' handwriting containing from here to the end is also in Missouri Historical Society, Bundle "Indian Trade and Fur Companies."

[8]Chapter IX, document III.

[9]Chapter IX, document I.

To *Monsieur* Chauvin the Panis-bon chef and Topage, dated from February twenty-sixth.[10]

To *Monsieur* Bernard Pratte the Des Moines River for four years.[11]

To *Monsieur* Benito [Vasquez] the Loups and Missouris.[12]

To *Messieurs* Gre Sarpy and Cabanne, the Kansas and Otos.[13]

St. Louis, this July 11, 1801.

Delassus [rubric]

Year *1802*

This year Colonel M*l* *Salcedo,* governor, has changed all, as follows: The Big and Little Osages accorded for five years to *Messieurs* Lisa, *Gre* Sarpy, Sanguinet and Benoît.

The entire Missouri accorded to *Monsieur* Clamorgan for two years except the Panis for *Monsieur* Chauvin.

Delassus [rubric]

Year *1803*

In the same manner as last year, except that *Monsieur* Sanguinet has arranged with *Monsieur* Lisa not to take his share in the trade this year, and *Monsieur Gre* Sarpy has sold him [Lisa] his share for this year. Thus the Osages remain exploited by *Messieurs* Benoît and Lisa.

Delassus [rubric]

Year *1804*

The Devil may take all![14]

---

[10]Chapter IX, document II.
[11]The other copy says "five" years but see Chapter IX, document X, and especially note 5.
[12]See Chapter VIII, documents IX and XI.
[13]See Chapter VIII, documents IX, XI, etc.
[14]This entire document is in Delassus' handwriting.

II

Robidoux to Gayoso de Lemos [St. Louis], March 15, 1799[1]

M. Gayoso de Lemos, Brigadier of the armies of the King and Governor General of the Western Provinces of Louisiana, Florida, etc.

Sir:

Joseph Robidoux, merchant of St. Louis, Illinois, has the honor of informing you that, at the beginning of the year 1794, there was formed in this city a trading company, under the auspices and protection of the govern-

---

[1]Written in Spanish. Original in Bancroft Library; copy in Missouri Historical Society, Bundle: Indian Trade and Fur Companies. It is enclosed with document IV.

ment, for the purpose of undertaking the discovery of the nations who inhabit the Upper Missouri and to go as far as the Pacific Ocean if that were possible, with the purpose of extending the commerce of the settlements and making known to the government a country which, up to that time, had remained unknown.

The petitioner, animated by a desire for the general prosperity of this province, as well as by a desire to make himself useful to the government, has never for a single moment hesitated to take part in the said Company nor to risk his fortune—as he has indeed done—in expeditions poorly organized by the Director and managed in a still worse manner by the employees—all facts of which Your Excellency is cognizant.[2]

The government, always ready to protect when it is a question of something profitable to the trade and prosperity of the province, has been willing to grant the Company, of which the petitioner is still a member, the privilege of the exclusive rights to trade with the Octoctacta, Mahas, and Ponca nations, who inhabit the banks of the Missouri River. This trade was granted both for the purpose of facilitating passage of the Company's *voitures* and for that of assuring it a compensation for the expenses which it was necessary for it to undergo among those same nations, in order to secure their consent to go beyond them.

The Company, today ruined by the discredit cast upon it by M. Clamorgan [Clamorgan's loss of credit], can not be continued in the same form or for the same purposes or by the same persons by whom it was started, because, of all the original members, only the petitioner remains, and he, in truth, is without fortune. But he still retains (he dares to say this and offers, as witness to what he asserts, M. Zenon Trudeau, whose integrity is as well known to Your Excellency as to the entire country, whose happiness he insures by the wisdom of his good government and his personal honor), —he still retains his credit, his youth, and his experience, on which he yet dares to base the hope that he will recover from the losses he has experienced. Since he is inspired by the boldness of this desire deign, Your Excellency, to cast a benevolent glance upon him and have regard for his losses by granting to him alone the exclusive right to trade with the above-mentioned nations, the Octoctacta, Mahas, and Ponca,[3] and to join to it the trade of the Panis, up to the time of the expiration of the license previously granted to the Company by your predecessor in the government.[4] The petitioner will then be enabled to undertake with better means, more wisely and carefully planned, all that the Company had pur-

[2]See Chapter III, document V.
[3]Robidou did not get this request. See document I for list of those who received the trades for 1800.
[4]See Chapter IV, document XXIV.

posed to do, as well as to see his fortune restored to him once more. Thus he can make known to the government a river and its surrounding country, in which up to the present time, nothing has been discovered except some nations, and these of no use either to commerce or to the government.

The petitioner dares to expect the granting of this favor from Your Excellency and he will not cease to make his prayers to Heaven for your prosperity.

March 15, 1799   J. H. Robidoux   [rubric]

To the Governor-General:

I agree with everything that the person concerned has said, and I consider it important to the government to find a person who will undertake to inform the government of the progress that is made by the merchants, and that it know those established on the Upper Missouri of whom it has heard nothing for two years. For these reasons and because I have found the petitioner to be a man of his word, Your Excellency should decide what you consider best.

Zenon Trudeau   [rubric]

III

Trudeau to Saucier, St. Louis, March 15, 1799[1]

I have already informed you that several creole inhabitants from the neighboring American bank have expressed to me their desire to form a village at the place called *Le Portage des Sioux,* which is situated above the

---

[1]Certified copy in French, enclosed in Saucier to governor-general, March 28, 1799, also accompanying Saucier to Governor-General, March 28, 1803 in Bancroft Library; Missouri Historical Society; Bundle: St. Charles Papers. It is printed in *American State Papers, Public Lands,* VI, 741 and in United States Documents, 24 Congress, 1 Session, *House Document 59* (serial 288), p. 76. See and *cp.* with document VIII. The translation here given is from the French.

On May 6, 1800, Delassus wrote to Casa Calvo (no. 36, A.G.I., P. de C., leg. 71B) in general reciting the contents of this letter, saying that on October 11, 1798, Trudeau wrote to Saucier proposing Portage des Sioux and choosing Saucier to command it, which the latter accepted. Delassus told of the advantages of Portage des Sioux and proposed Saucier for the position of commandant with the office of captain of the militia with an annual salary of 100 *pesos.* Casa Calvo answered on July 10 and sent the documents to the Intendancy. Casa Calvo replied on July 9, 1800 in which he stated that he would assist and support Trudeau's petition explained in Delassus' letter no. 36 for the establishment of a post at Portages des Sioux and choosing Saucier to establish it. Certified copy in Bancroft Library, draft in A.G.I., P. de C., leg. 69. On July 10, 1800, Casa Calvo wrote to the Intendant López y Ángulo transmitting the documents. The latter approved and forwarded the petition to Spain, calling the place San Ysidro de los Sioux. He approved the payment of the annual gratification of 100 *pesos.* Draft in A.G.I., P. de C., leg. 94. On April 2, 1801, Delassus wrote Casa Calvo (no. 76-A.G.I., P. de C., leg. 72) that he had received on March 8, 1801, the governor's reply dated July 9, 1800, and by it Saucier was creditor of the pay of 100 *pesos,* as other special commandants from the time that the governor sent the official letters to the Intendancy. (In the margin was stated "from the day of possession".)

Missouri at a short distance from the Illinois river. I consider this settlement very advantageous for us, for it will attract the sort of population that we need in this country. Moreover it will be located almost in view [opposite] of the military post which the Americans have planned to form at a place called *Paysa*. This is an advantage which it is prudent to foresee, and which will be one of the most important in the future.

Moreover, I consider that this same establishment will be a very respectable one, and that it will be able to put an end to the disorders which the savage nations of the Illinois and Upper Mississippi rivers often commit against the habitations of the interior of this country. In accordance with these considerations, and knowing your principles and the confidence and respect which you enjoy among the people in question—and whom you know and with whom you have lived for a long time — I beg you and urge you in the name of the government to busy yourself with secretly encouraging the said inhabitants to carry out their project, and to place yourself at their head, if it is possible, and to act with them as if you were their commandant. I give you all the authority which I might have to establish them in the most suitable [favorable] place to establish their village, and to assign to them lands for cultivation in proportion to the means [abilities] of each one, in such a way as to be able to bring together the greatest possible number of people. You should, however, give them just what is necessary for them to maintain a comfortable living and to remain always content [faithful].

Monsieur, since in accordance with your verbal promise, I do not doubt that you will concern yourself with carrying out what I am proposing to you to the greatest advantage of the government, I have given orders to M. Antonio Soulard, the commissioned surveyor, to go with you to the place where it is intended to establish the village in question as soon as you request it. He will go for the purpose of marking out the boundaries and making a plan thereof in duplicate, in conformity, as far as it is possible, with the instructions which he has from me, one copy of which plan shall be remitted to you, and the other will remain deposited in the archives of this commandancy.

I think, *Monsieur,* that if you succeed, as I hope you will, in accomplishing this plan which I am suggesting to you, you may have confidence in the generosity of a government which has never allowed anyone's service to it to go without reward. This place [or service] of which it is a question is important to it [government], and I flatter myself that you have only to praise yourself for having been employed for it.

May God keep you in His Holy Keeping.

St. Louis, 15 March, 1799

Zenon Trudeau [rubric]

Monsieur François Saucier

I, Don Carlos Dehault Delassus, Lieutenant-Colonel of the Armies and Lieutenant-Governor of the Illinois, certify that the above is a true copy of the original. St. Louis, Illinois, March 29, 1803.

Delassus [rubric]

IV

TRUDEAU TO GAYOSO DE LEMOS, ST. LOUIS, MARCH 19, 1799[1]

Number 41:

I am sending you herewith a memorial of Don Joseph Robidou,[2] who solicits the continuation of the exclusive trade with the Octoctactas, Mahas, and Poncas nations, which trade the governor who preceded Your Excellency had conceded to a trading Company formed in this town for the exploration and commerce of the Upper Missouri. The object of this memorial is to indemnify the said Company for the heavy expense which it has incurred through the benefactions which must have been made to those nations by Clamorgan (a person sufficiently well-known to you). The latter is today the only partner of the said Robidou in the above-mentioned trade, and it would be a pity for the bad conduct of one to have an influence on the interests of the other. For this reason I hope that Robidou may secure what he asks for two or three years at least, so that he may reimburse himself for the very great losses which he has suffered through his determination not to abandon the Company, as was done by many of its members in the first years of its existence. I have no doubt that he will undertake to make some discoveries, for his own interests will cause him to go to trade with the distant nations, first with those already known, such as the Aricaras and Mandans, and from these two nations gradually to others further up. I see no difficulty in granting him the exclusive trade with the Mahas and Poncas, for it has been three years since they have seen any white men from our district, as no one dared to go to trade with them on account of their bad conduct. The Octoctacta trade may yield some advantages and [if they are given some presents they may] arouse the envy of the other nations, but for five years their needs have been supplied by the same Company, and [now] no one pays any attention to them.

Don Joseph Robidou asks also that the Pani nation be added to the exclusive privilege in which he has certain rights at present. This

---

[1]Written in Spanish. Original in Bancroft Library; photostatic copy in Missouri Historical Society, Bundle: Indian Trade. Reply is document VI.
[2]Document III.

596

nation and the Kansas are the only two that are left to be divided among the rest of the merchants of this city, and it is rather small for all of them. By this method of distribution, this privilege, ever since it was granted to the merchants in preference to the traders, who are, after all, the ones who risk their lives, has only succeeded in creating a monopoly against them. But by so granting the exclusive trade with this nation, the government loses its means and opportunity to favor or reward a deserving person. Knowing Your Excellency's generous heart, it is not my opinion that it should be granted to him unless you think it desirable.

May God keep Your Excellency many years. St. Louis, March 19, 1799.

Zenon Trudeau [rubric]

To *Señor* Don Manuel Gayoso de Lemos.

V

GAYOSO DE LEMOS TO DELASSUS, NEW ORLEANS, MAY 16, 1799[1]

Answered

The accumulation of matters requiring my executive resolution in the circumstances of the present war do not permit me to make decisions on various *instancias* of individuals of your territory. Therefore, you shall determine in my name in all urgent matters which may arise, informing me [of your actions] afterwards.

Since last year I offered the *Señores* Sarpy the continuation for the present year of the same branch of trade which they enjoyed last year, therefore, with respect to all the rest, you will heed some letters of recommendation which I have made in favor of Don Benito Vazquez, Ortiz and one Mr. Pratt, the husband of an Indian godchild of mine, who resides in San Carlos de Missouri.[2] To all the rest you shall distribute justice equitably, favoring the most worthy, among whose number you shall consider Don Augusto Chouteau and Mr. Cerré, in consideration that they have actually had occasions of proving their zeal for the service of the King and the good of the country.[3]

I most especially recommend to your consideration Don Antonio Soulard, whose name has been, since the time of my predecessor, before

---

[1]Written in Spanish. A.G.I., P. de C., leg. 27B; draft dated May 12 is in A.G.I., P. de C., leg 134A

[2]In official letter to Gayoso de Lemos, no 10, dated St. Louis, November 15, 1798 (A.G.I., P. de C., leg. 50) Trudeau speaks of Gavoso de Lemos' god-child married to the hunter Gascon living in San Carlos del Misuri. Gayoso de Lemos had written to Trudeau previously recommending them to him, in a letter dated August 10, to which this letter was a reply.

[3]See document I for list of trading licenses granted.

the court for the position of Adjutant of the lieutenant-governor of that territory, but the present circumstances of the war have delayed his *despacho*.[4]

I have appointed Captain of the Army, Don Enrique Peyroux de la Coudrenière, as commandant of New Madrid.[5] He shall remain dependent upon you in matters of military jurisdiction. In civil affairs his people may appeal to your tribunal in cases amounting to no more than 100 *pesos;* cases involving more than that sum shall recur to me. In criminal cases not involving crimes which merit corporal punishment or banishment that commandant shall be recognized, and will be able to sentence with the proviso that the parties concerned may appeal to you if they so demand. But in cases of grave crimes he shall try the case and he shall take it upon himself to use whatever prompt steps he may judge best. If it be an urgent case, he shall refer it to you, who will immediately decide what corresponds, and you will inform me of your action later, whether for my knowledge or for my final determination.

In all disputes between interested parties or claims between residents, when they are not matters that might be injurious to the government or to the general public, it is best for the parties concerned to leave such cases to the decision of the arbitral judges and friendly arbitrators. All the judges must try to prevent the residents from becoming entangled in lawsuits and *por decontados* [if] the sum in a dispute does not amount to 100 *pesos,* formal judicial proceedings shall not be taken; and it is only necessary for the judge to inform himself summarily and decide according to equity. Similar procedure will be used in disputes between residents who usually proceed to court more out of caprice that for any other reason. But if it be a case which involves appraisement, and which may have some consequences, you shall proceed with all formality [of a law court].

---

[4]See Houck, *Spanish Régime in Missouri,* II, 327-330.

[5]Henri Peyroux de la Coudrenière was born in France and came to Louisiana in 1784 as interpreter for the Acadians. He was appointed commandant of Ste. Geneviève, succeeding Antonio de Oro on August 5, 1787. In 1793 he made a trip to the United States, where he became imbued with the democratic spirit of France and the United States. He became acquainted with André Michaux and was recommended by him to Genêt. He was suspected and was replaced as Commandant at Ste. Geneviève by François Vallé in 1794. Neither Carondelet nor Gayoso de Lemos could prove Peyroux' disloyalty and he was returned to Ste. Geneviève as captain of the militia after promising Carondelet that he would move from the post as soon as possible. Carondelet continued to distrust him and suggested to Carlos Howard in 1796 that he remove him if an excuse could be found. When Delassus became lieutenant-governor. Peyroux was transferred to New Madrid and was commandant there until 1803. In May of that year he was replaced because of insubordination and was ordered not to attempt to take part in the government of the post on the threat that if he did he would have to face formal charges.

These same regulations shall be observed in all the posts of your jurisdiction.

The commandant of San Andrés, Don Juan Mackay, deserves special consideration of the government. I recommend him to you so that you may help him and even facilitate to him some branch of trade.[6]

You will be especially careful to acquire the most exact and prompt advices concerning the intrusion of Canadian traders into His Majesty's territory, and you will take whatever measures in this matter that prudence may dictate to you.

You will be zealous that no injustice be done to the Indians. Instead, let the best harmony be cultivated with the friendly nations, and try to win the good-will of those who are indifferent or inimical to us.

Punctually upon the return of the traders let them give you whatever report on these Indians which each one has acquired, whether it be relative to new discoveries or respecting commerce.

Every year you shall form a very exact report of everything and you shall remit it to me, so that I may be informed of the progress or decadence of the commerce and of the causes which produce these effects in order to promote them or to remedy them, as well as matters regarding our relations with the Indian nations and new discoveries.

With the United States your neighbors you shall cultivate the best harmony, since it is by all means best to assure our reciprocal good understanding for the benefit of both nations.

Under these general rules you shall proceed until more tranquil times may permit me to dedicate myself entirely to these important objects, as I am especially interested in the prosperity of all your inhabitants, for whom I desire the greatest good.

May God keep you many years.

New Orleans, May 16, 1799

Manuel Gayoso de Lemos [rubric]

Señor Don Carlos Dehault Delassus.

---

[6]Mackay had a share of the trade of the Mahas in 1799 (Document I). He said he owned a fifth share in the Missouri Company. See Chapter VI, document XXII.

In a letter to Mackay, dated New Orleans, May 20, 1799, (*American State Papers, Public Lands*, VI, 719 and in *United States Documents 24 Congress, 1 Session, House Document* 59 (serial 288) p. 33), Gayoso de Lemos wrote: "Poor Evans is very ill; between us, I have perceived that he deranged himself when out of my sight, but I have perceived it too late; the strength of liquor has deranged his head; he has been out of his senses for several days, but, with care, he is doing better; and I hope he will get well enough to be able to send him to his country. I have proposed to Court a very important project, in which you shall be employed". This is quoted in various places, *e.g.* see Nasatir, "Anglo-Spanish Rivalry on the Upper Missouri," *Mississippi Valley Historical Review*, XVI (1930), reprint p. 39; Nasatir, "John Evans: Explorer and Surveyor," *Missouri Historical Review*, XXV (1931), 238-239.

VI

Gayoso de Lemos to Delassus, New Orleans, May 21, 1799[1]

Without Answer

Dated March 19 and under number 41,[2] your predecessor in your command sent me a memorial of Don Joseph Robidou, soliciting the continuance of the exclusive trade of the Octoctacta, Mahas, and Poncas nations, which was conceded to the Trading Company of the Upper Missouri. Although I am taking into consideration all that you or your aforementioned predecessor have told me concerning this matter, I must not deviate from what I manifested to you in my official letter dated the sixteenth of the current month,[3] and you must confine yourself to it in all its parts.

May God keep you many years.

New Orleans, May 21, 1799

Manuel Gayoso de Lemos [rubric]

Señor Don Carlos de Lassus.

[1]Written in Spanish. A.G.I., P. de C., leg. 27B; draft in A.G.I., P. de C., leg. 134A.
[2]Document IV.
[3]Document V.

VII

[Gayoso de Lemos] to Delassus, New Orleans, May 29, 1799[1]

Emiliano Yosty, formerly a soldier in the regiment of Louisiana, [who] has served his time and after his release established himself there, observing a regular conduct and earning his livelihood in an honorable way. By virtue of this he is a creditor of the attentions of the government, and I am recommending him to you, so that you look out for him, giving him each year some trade of the small [trades] of the Missouri,[2] in order that he may exist in some comfort.

May God keep you many years.

New Orleans, May 29, 1799[3]

[draft] [Gayoso de Lemos]

Señor Don Carlos Dehault de Lassus.

[1]Written in Spanish. This is a draft in A.G.I., P. de C., leg. 134A.
[2]Yosty was given the trade of the Poncas in 1799. See documents I and X.
[3]Delassus replied on October [September?] 5, 1799 (dispatch no. 7, A.G.I., P. de C., leg. 66) stating that in accordance with Gayoso de Lemos' letter he had given Yosty a share of the trade of the Missouri for this year.

VIII

SAUCIER TO DELASSUS, ST. LOUIS,
SEPTEMBER 10, 1799

To Don Charles Dehault Delassus, Lieutenant Colonel, attached to the stationary regiment of Louisiana, and Lieutenant Governor of the upper part of the same province:[1]

Francis Saucier,[2] appointed by Your predecessor, Don Zenon Trudeau, commandant of the new settlement of Portage de Sioux,[3] formerly an officer in the reformed French troops of the navy, and father of fifteen children, having not received, to this date, any concessions from the Government, and having been obliged to make great sacrifices to correspond to the confidence of your predecessor, when he (the petitioner) left the village of St. Charles, to go and take the command of that of Portage des Sioux, has the honor to supplicate you to have the goodness to grant to him, in full property, a concession of 8,800 arpens of land in superficie, which will be divided as follows: 600 arpens for each of his children, to the number of thirteen, under his charge, which makes 7,800 arpens, and 1,000 for him and his wife: this will complete the above stated quantity of 8,800 arpens, to be taken in vacant places of the domain, as follows: 1,000 arpens in the point formed by the rivers Mississippi and Missouri, to the eastward of the land of Lewis Labeaume; 1,000 arpens to the westward of the small lakes, distant about forty of fifty arpens from the village of Portage des Sioux; and finally, the remaining quantity of 6,800 arpens, to be taken in a vacant place of the domain, at the choice of your petitioner, who hopes that you will be pleased to take his demand into consideration, and that his years, the numerous family which he has to maintain, and the laborious task he fills, without any remuneration from the Government, will be strong motives, in your opinion, to obtain the justice which he presumes to deserve.

St. Louis, September 10, 1799

F. SAUCIER

---

[1] *United States Executive Documents,* 24 *Congress,* 1 *Session, House Document* 59, (serial 288) pp. 75-80; also *American States Papers, Public Lands,* VI, 741.

[2] François Saucier, senior [J. B. Saucier ?] was a young French officer who came with the first French troops to Fort Chartres. After the transfer of Illinois to England, 1765, he went to Cahokia where he died, leaving three sons, one of whom François, Jr., afterwards founded Portage des Sioux, long known from the earliest days as the portage or carrying place of the Sioux Indians in passing from the Mississippi to the Missouri, thereby cutting off a long detour. Notes from a folder on Portage des Sioux in the Missouri Historical Society, Delassus Collection, no. 3.

[3] Document III.

Considering the numerous family of the petitioner, and examining the generous sacrifices made by him in order to answer the views of the Government, when he was appointed commandant of the new settlement of Portage des Sioux, where he commands and performs his duties with the greatest zeal, without enjoying the annual salary granted by His Majesty to all civil commandants of posts; as much for these motives, as in consideration of his great age, I do grant to him, and his heirs, the land he solicits, if it is not prejudicial to any person; and the surveyor, Don Antonio Soulard, shall put the interested party in possession of the quantity of eight thousand eight hundred arpens of land in superficie, solicited for, in the places indicated; which being done, he shall draw a plat of survey, to be delivered to the interested party, with his certificate, to enable him to obtain the concession and title in form from the Intendant General, to whom alone corresponds the distributing and granting all classes of land of the royal domain.

CARLOS DEHAULT DELASSUS.

Registered by request of the interested party. Book No. 2, Pages 21, 22, and 23, No. B.   SOULARD.

The deputy surveyor, Don Santiago Mackay, will survey the quantity of six thousand eight hundred arpens of land, which remains to be taken to complete the total of the above title, in a vacant place of the domain called La Pointe Basse de la Riviere au Se, (Salt River Bottom) situated at, at least, one hundred and eighty miles from the town; which tract of land is evidently in the domain of His Majesty, and consequently can be prejudicial to no one.

St. Louis, 5th December, 1803.   ANTONIO SOULARD.

I' have already made known to you, that several creole inhabitants of the neighboring American side had manifested to me the wish of forming a village at the place called Le Portage des Sioux, situated above the Missouri, and at a little distance from Illinois river; considering this settlement as very dangerous in drawing to us a population analogous to the one wanted in this country, besides being almost in view of the military post which the Americans intend to form at the place called Paysa. This is an advantage which it is prudent to foresee, and which must be most important for the future. Furthermore, I do consider that this same settlement will be a respectable guard, which may put a stop to the depredations often committed by the nations of Indians of

---

'Compare with document III.

the rivers Illinois and Upper Mississippi, upon the plantations in the interior of the country. Owing to these considerations, and knowing that you enjoy the esteem and confidence of the people in question, that you know them, and have lived a long time with them, I do entreat you, and recommend to you, in the name of Government, to employ yourself in encouraging, silently, the said inhabitants to execute their project, and put yourself at their head, if it is possible to you, and act as their commandant, giving you all the facilities in my power to place them on the most convenient spot to form their village, and assign lands to them for cultivation, in proportion to the faculties, of each of them, in such a manner as to collect the greatest number of people possible, giving to them, however, just what is necessary to live with ease, and be forever contented.

Having no doubt, sir, after your verbal promise, that you will employ yourself to fulfil, for the greatest advantage of the Government, what I propose to you, I have given orders to Mr. Antonio Soulard, commissioned surveyor, to be ready at your first command to go with you on the spot where it is fit the village in question would be, to have the lines marked, and to execute two plats of survey, conformably, as much as possible, to the instructions he has received from me, for the one to be delivered to you, and the other to remain deposited in the archives of this Government.

I think, sir, that if, as I hope, you succeed in accomplishing what I have proposed, you will have confidence in the generosity of a Government which has never left without reward any service rendered. The service in question is important, and I do flatter myself that you will have but to congratualate yourself for having employed yourself to it.

May God Keep you under his Holy Guard.

St. Louis, 15th March, 1799

Zenon Trudeau

To Mr. Francois Saucier

IX

Petition of Mackay, October 18, 1799[1]

James Mackay, Captain commandant of the settlement of St. Andre of Missouri, has the honor to represent, that during the years 1795 and 1796, he made (in consequence of the commission sent to him to this effect by his Excellency the Baron de Carondelet, Governor General of these provinces, which document is here annexed,) a voyage of discovery to the upper and unknown parts of Missouri, from which voyage he had

---

[1]*United States Documents,* 1 *Session* 24 *Congress, House Document* 59, Serial 288, pp. 31-32.

brought memoirs, and particularly a map, such as never appeared before, of this unknown part of the world; which papers he has himself delivered to his Excellency Don Manuel Gayoso de Lemos, Governor General of these provinces, who, in consequence of his services, has granted to him the rank he holds now, and that of Commandant of St. André, with the permission to make choice of a considerable quantity of land in this Upper Louisiana, and the assurance, as a reward for his services, that he should be proposed to the King for a grade in the army; this could not be effected on account of the war. Therefore, your petitioner being willing to establish himself, and not having enjoyed any of the favors which have been promised to him, commandant, with a very small salary, of a settlement which gives him a great deal of occupations, he hopes of your justice that you will be pleased to grant to him, in full property, for the establishment of farms, and considerable stock farms, thirty thousand arpens of land, in superficie, to be taken on the vacant lands of his Majesty's domain, in one or several parts, at his choice. The distance of said lands from the settlements, and their known little value, are reasons which will lessen, in your opinion, the importance of the favor which your petitioner expects of your justice, which favor cannot give him any hopes of utility but at a very remote time. Full of confidence in the information which must have been given to you upon his services and conduct, by his Excellency the Governor General of these provinces, and by your predecessor, Don Zenon Trudeau, to whom your petitioner has delayed, by divers reasons, to submit his demand, he hopes to obtain the fulfilment of it, of your equity and justice.

James Mackay

St. Louis, 12th October, 1799.

St. Louis of Illinois, 13th October, 1799

Cognizance being taken of the foregoing petition, presented by the captain of mounted dragoons of militia, James Mackay, commandant of the settlement of St. Andre of this dependency; being well satisfied of the truth of what he advances, and due regard being paid to the respectable recommendations which have been made to me of this officer by Don Manuel Gayoso de Lemos, Ex- Governor General of these provinces, and by my predecessor, Don Zenon Trudeau, I do grant, as a reward for his good services, for him, his heirs, or others that may represent his right, the land which he solicits, if it is not prejudicial to any person, and the surveyor, Don Ant. Soulard, shall put the petitioner in possession of the quantity of land which he asks for, in different (various) parts of the royal domain; and when this is done, he shall draw a plat, which he shall deliver to the party, with his certificate, that said party may use it to obtain the concession and title in due form from the Intendant General, to whom alone corresponds, by royal order, the distributing and granting of all classes of lands belonging to the royal domain.

CARLOS DEHAULT DELASSUS.

X
DELASSUS TO GAYOSO DE LEMOS, ST. LOUIS, OCTOBER 28, 1799[1]

Number 14

Consequent to your Excellency's official letters, in which you forewarn me of what corresponds to the trade of the Missouri, I have taken care of the following persons for this year:

The Big and Little Osages to Don Augusto Chouteau, according to his contract with the government.

The Kansas to Don Beral Sarpy, as Your Excellency has forewarned me. I have conceded it to him for this year.

The Panis to Don Benito Bazquez, and the commandant for his share, as Your Excellency forewarns me; the former granted for this year, and my share as is customary in the post each year.

The Otoes to Don Santiago Chauvin and Don Joseph Ortiz: to the former because he is a respectable and poor inhabitant and to the latter, as Your Excellency forewarns me, for his merits and his state of poverty.

The Mahas to Don Santiago McKay, as Your Excellency forewarns me in your letter of instruction to take care of him by giving him some trade.[2]

The Poncas to the former soldier Emiliano Yosty,[3] as Your Excellency forewarns me.

I am informing Your Excellency of all this for your knowledge. For the present I cannot say what I think concerning the *ramos de treta,* since I have not had time to observe the result myself, other than what Don Zenon Trudeau told me and informed Your Excellency. I find it necessary to ask Your Excellency to do me the favor, (if it is not contrary to what you have already arranged,) to forewarn me in an official letter, concerning this year, when these inhabitants solicit from Your Excellency to grant them a branch [*ramo*] of trade for an entire nation,

---

[1]Written in Spanish. A.G.I., P. de C., leg. 48.
[2]For these names and recommendations of Gayoso de Lemos see document V. For the grants as made see document I.
[3]See document VII.

which Your Excellency deigns to concede them, that they should not be exempted from paying for their passports. It has long been the custom that all the traders generally have to pay for their passports, (it being understood that "traders" refer to those who go to trade in the Missouri and Upper Mississippi), this [revenue] being the sole and only means which the commandant of this post has to maintain his decorum which his office indispensably requires and this means . . . .[4]

For the future distribution, for the year 1800, I shall make this distribution of trade as Your Excellency forewarns me in your official letter dated May 16th of this year,[5] with instructions for my conduct in this post.

God keep Your Excellency many years.

St. Louis, Illinois, October 28, 1799.

Carlos Dehault Delassus [rubric]

Señor Don Manuel Gayoso de Lemos.

---

[4]This document is torn and the rest of the sentence is illegible.
[5]Document V.

CHAPTER VIII

1800

I

COUR QUI BRULE TO DELASSUS [1800?][1]

Monsieur le Commandant des Illinois [De Lassus]

My Father

I received your letter which I have had read before my whole village, to show that, although you do not know me, nevertheless you have written to me personally, and you have recommended your children to me, because you learned that, for a long time, I was the hand and sole support of the French.

Since you have thus written me, I take it that you wish me, doubtlessly, to listen to your parole and that I may know you. Yes, My Father, I wish to listen to your parole, and to prove this desire to ycu at the melting of the ice, at which time I wish to descend with my comrade.

For a long time I have wished to see the city. If you consent to my coming there, I shall not ask you for any presents, for I have the heart of a Frenchman, and I am not like those chiefs who come to see you to

---

[1] Written in French. Undated but perhaps 1800? Missouri Historical Society, Pierre Chouteau Collection.

Stephen Ayres made a trip in 1800 on which he gathered specimens of limestone in the Mississippi Valley. He kept a manuscript journal. He says: "We understand the Missouri is considered by the Spanish and British governments as the territorial line defining the limits where the dominions of the former, extending from Canada and Hudson's Bay, and of the latter reaching from Florida and New Spain, meet, and circumscribe and compress the United States. The policy of the two powerful and hostile nations has not, that we know, given rise to any expedition whereby the sources of this vast river might be visited, and the adjacent regions explored". *Medical Repository*, IV, 304.

obtain presents. Consent, my father, to my request, and be persuaded that I will always continue to defend your children from the brutality of my young men, and that I shall pray to the Master of life for you.

Cour qui Brule
Chief of the Kansas

II

PETITION OF CLAMORGAN, NEW ORLEANS, JANUARY 15, 1800[1]

To *Messieurs* the Generals and Intendant of Upper and Lower Louisiana.

His Majesty, having considered agreeable the creation of a Company formed in the Illinois for the purpose of making the discovery of savage nations which are scattered in the Missouri from the Maha Nation to the Pacific Ocean, accorded to it [the Company] in 1796 [*sic*] the exclusive trade for ten years that might be carried on there. At this [that] time the Director sent out great expeditions and expensive armaments, which actions were repeated. The first expedition reached a point about 450 leagues distant from the Illinois; the second was pillaged and destroyed; the third went about 150 leagues further than the first; and the fourth was obliged to stop at the village of the Maha nation, where the Company formed a fort, *entrepôt,* for two reasons: first, because it is [was] necessary to pass the winter there in order to continue its route the following spring, and second, because this same Maha nation does [did] not wish to permit communication with the distant nations, who might sooner or later start a war.

It was by surprise that the first armaments had the good fortune to pass the nations Othos, Maha and Poncas, but the second expedition did not escape them. The passage of the third expedition was purchased very dearly from the great chief of the Mahas who rules over all the nations with whom he communicates. Despite the fact that his will was respected among the Oto and Poncas nations, nevertheless, it was found necessary to make considerable sacrifices not only to the Big and Little Chiefs but also to the entire nation, of which even the least of its individuals could obstruct communication because they are situated on the banks of the Missouri river. This is what obliged M. Le Baron de Carondelet to give orders to M. Don Zeon Trudeau—at that time Lieutenant-Governor of Illinois—to abandon to the Company of the Upper Missouri the special trade with the three nations mentioned, which it was

---

[1]Written in French. Missouri Historical Society, Clamorgan Collection. The narrative here recited has been documented in the previous chapters of this volume. For a short summary see Nasatir, "Anglo-Spanish Rivalry on the Upper Missouri," *Mississippi Valley Historical Review,* XVI (1929-1930).

absolutely necessary to restrain on the one hand by fear of being deprived of merchandise in the future if they interrupt henceforth the ex-peditions to the Western Sea, and on the other by the hope of the continuation of presents which it is necessary to give them unceasingly. It is [was] then that the Company saw itself in the necessity of establishing a fort among the Maha nation in order to render it there a little respectable.

These different expeditions have cost the Company, up to the present, more than 40,000 *piastres* in losses and sacrifices, which its zeal and ambition will never recover for it as long as the administration shall refuse it its support. Therefore, it is necessary to say this, certainly, since last year at the time for a new expedition, the Director was not able to obtain from the present M. the Lieutenant-Governor the trade of the three nations: Otos, Mahas, and Poncas, which M. Le Baron de Carondelet had abandoned to the Company as much out of necessity for the passage of its distant armaments as well as to ease its sacrifices a little. The Director was also forced to postpone his armament until next spring, or at least until he shall know whether the governor-general will or will not honor it with his support any longer, be it to give to this enterprise all the extension of discovery which His Majesty is expecting or otherwise to renounce and abandon with regret the first steps of a bold enterprise, which cannot go to too great limits to hasten to become useful in the communication between the two seas.

After having smoothed out the route which must transport the Company to unknown lands, other obstacles yet remain to be overcome. The necessity to expose them to you in a convincing manner would entail a vast detail to paint the picture. It will suffice to warn you that the English, continually surveillant and ambitious, are trying to win over the savage nations on the Upper Missouri in order to manage, when it will be time, the sureness of an invasion. A detailed *mémoire* on this matter was addressed to M. le Baron de Carondelet by the Director, supported by M. Zenon Trudeau, Lieutenant-Governor of the Illinois, in consideration of which the Company asks that His Majesty be pleased to accord to it 10,000 *piastres* per year to provide the pay for 100 militia men. These latter it offers to maintain in the various forts, especially among the Mandan nation, 600 leagues distant from the Illinois, where the Company has established and is maintaining a fort to this day, in order to repel the advances of the commerce of the English, which is being brought there by way of the Bay of Hudson and the lakes of the north. It has pleased His Majesty by his decree to permit the Company to raise the 100 militia men, without, however, explaining himself clearly at whose expense they would be. However, it is to be presumed that His Majesty was of the sentiment to accord to the Company the wish that it had exposed, since the decree states in one of its articles, "His Majesty permits the Company to raise 100 militiamen at his pay." True, this expression leaves doubt as to exactly upon whom, His Majesty or the Company, payment for their support must fall. But, in another article, His Majesty said that the Lieutenant-Governor shall be careful to watch that "the number of 100 militia men be there briefly [*courtamente—sic*] maintained." Therefore, what interest did His Majesty have in such a remark unless it were to be assured of the number which must be maintained for the defense of the fort against the incursion or invasion of the enemy, to the extent of paying the expense himself. But, up to the present time, far from having obtained support in the critical crisis in [that attends] the beginning of a discovery,—when it is necessary to fight, to push back and destroy dangerous enemies who not only invade the commerce in fine peltries of the Upper Missouri, but also by their false, deceiving, and seditious discourses try to arm against us the nations who do not even know us, although living in the territory of His Majesty, but who still are trying to make them believe that the branch of peace, tranquillity and harmony which we offer them is rather a rod or iron which must subject them under a yoke *d'erain* [*sic*]—far, I say, from having obtained the slightest support up to the present time, it seems, on the contrary, that all the disadvantageous circumstances have leagued themselves together to choke, destroy and nullify all the happy hope of a discovery which would prove forever useful to the future race, even though it may not be for that of the present race.

Whatever has happened, it is certain that after the oft-repeated sacrifices and losses which the Company has been obliged to undergo up to now, it must at least expect not to be deprived of aid from His Majesty, nor to be further deprived of that of the post of the Othos, Maha and Poncas nations, which the Baron de Carondelet had known to be indispensable to the Company as much to assure to it the passage of its expeditions as well as to indemnify it in small measure for its expenses.

This, then, is the consideration which the Director of the Company has the honor of soliciting from your bounties—the restitution of the three posts of the savage nations, Othos, Mahas and Poncas;[2] that the said Company may continue its *entrepôt* there and subject these same nations to the docility of a free communication with the most distant places of the Upper Missouri. [The Director begs that] it may be your desire to be pleased to tell His Majesty of the reason which has caused the suspension of the payment for the 100 militiamen at the rate of 100 *piastres* per year, [the same being necessary] for the protection of its [Company's] forts, and especially for those of the Mandan nations situated to the northwest of the Illinois at a distance of 600 leagues. These latter are too near those places which the English occupy on the rivers which flow

---

[2]See Chpter VII, document I, and this Chapter, document IV.

into Lake Winnipeg for them not to have to fear future incursions of this latter nation which has communication with Upper Canada by water to this point. But meanwhile it is nevertheless ever important [that the Company] continue communication via the Missouri with all the nations who are found along its extent. For this reason the Director desires that there be restored to him the possession of the savage posts, Othos, Mahas and Poncas, which he here solicits. May it please you likewise to have delivered to him six flags, six big medals and six small medals, accompanied by commissions, the names of the chiefs being left blank, as well as a passport in the three different languages for the person whom the Director must have march at the head of an armament next summer, so that if he should fall [sic] into California, he will be protected and aided if there is need for it, authorizing him by the said passport to take possession of English properties which he might encounter along his route when they happen to be in the territories of His Majesty.

New Orleans, January 15, 1800.
Jaques Clamorgan [rubric]
Director of the Company of the Upper Missouri.

New Orleans, 29 January, 1800.[3]

Whenever the Company of the Missouri follows the expeditions and projects of its *Instituto* the Lieutenant-Governor of Illinois will proportion to it the exclusive trade with the Otos, Mahas and Poncas nations.

Casa Calvo [rubric]

[3]In 1800 the Marqués de Casa Calvo became governor-general of Spanish Louisiana, and Clamorgan ever ready to seize an advantage immediately petitioned the new official for a renewal of the Company's privilege with the Otos, Mahas and Poncas. Casa Calvo replied that the trade went with the Company grant. In 1800, therefore, Clamorgan regained the trade of these tribes (see Chapter VII, document I). His courage renewed, Clamorgan petitioned on March 15th for the exclusive grant of the Kansas. The governor about faced on the Mahas and Poncas trade and hence Clamorgan in 1801 made a plea for more of the trade of the Upper Missouri and got it from Salcedo (see Chapter VII, document I).

III

PETITION OF LOISEL, ST. LOUIS MARCH 20, 1800[1]

To Mr. Charles Dehault Delassus, Lieutenant Colonel of the stationary regiment of Louisiana, and Lieutenant Governor of Upper Louisiana, etc.

Sir:

Regis Loisel has the honor to submit that, having made considerable sacrifices in the Upper Missouri Company, in aiding to the discovery of

[1]*American State Papers, Public Lands*, VIII, 117-118. See also *United States Executive Documents, 24 Congress, 1 Session, House Document* 59 (serial 288) p. 7; and *American State Papers, Public Lands*, II, 567. On Loisel and this grant of land and Loisel's fort see Abel, *Tabeau's Narrative*, 22-27; pages 227-230 reprints the document from the same source as given here.

Indian nations in that quarter, in order to increase commerce hereafter, as also to inculcate to those different nations favorable sentiments towards the Government, and have them devoted to the service of his Majesty, so as to be able to put a stop to the contraband trade of foreigners, who, scattering themselves among those Indians, employ all imaginable means to make them adopt principles contrary to the attachment they owe to the Government. The petitioner has also furnished, with zeal, presents, in order to gain the friendship of those different nations, for the purpose to disabuse them of the errors insinuated to them, and to obtain a free passage through their lands, and a durable peace. The petitioner, intending to continue on his own account the commerce which his partners have abandoned in that quarter, hopes that you will be pleased to grant to him, for the convenience of his trade, permission to form an establishment in Upper Missouri, where he will build a fort,[2] about seven leagues higher up than the great bend, (*grand détour*), distant about four hundred leagues from this town, and which shall be situated on the said Missouri, between the river known under the name of *Rivière du vieux Anglais* (river of the old Englishman) which empties itself into the said Missouri, on the right side of it, in descending the stream, and lower down than Cedar Island, and the river known under the name of *Rivière de la Côté de Medecine,* (river of the medicine bluff,) which is on the left side in descending the stream, and higher up than Cedar island; which island is at equal distance from each of the two rivers above named. That place being the most convenient for his operations, as well in the upper as in the lower Missouri, and it being indispensable to secure to himself the timber in an indisputable manner, he is obliged to have recourse to your goodness, praying that you will be pleased to grant to him a title of concession in full property for him, his heirs or assigns, for the extent of land situated along the banks of the said Missouri, and comprised between the river called the Old Englishman's, and the one called the Medicine bluff, here above mentioned, by the depth of one league in the interior, on each side of the Missouri, and including the island known by the name of Cedar Island, as also other small timbered islands. In granting this demand, he shall never cease to render thanks to your goodness.

St. Louis of Illinois, March 20, 1800.   REGIS LOISEL

St. Louis of Illinois, March 25, 1800.

Whereas it is notorious that the petitioner has made great losses, when in the company he mentions, and as he continues his voyages of

---

[2]See Abel, *Tabeau's Narrative; cp.* H. M. Chittenden, *History of the American Fur Trade of the Far West* (New York, 1902), III, 954; and Thwaites, *Original Journals of Lewis and Clark,* I, 160; VI, 59; and also *Wisconsin Historical Society Collections,* XXII, 135. For geographical identifications see Abel, "A New Lewis and Clark Map" in *Geographical Review,* I, (1916), 329-349; and *Mississippi Valley Historical Review,* X (1923), 432-441.

discoveries conformably to the desire of the Government, which are the cause of great expenses to him; and it being necessary, for the commerce of peltries with the Indians, that forts should be constructed among those remote nations, as much to impress them with respect, as to have places of deposit for the goods and other articles which merchants carry to them, and particularly for those of the petitioner; for these reasons I do grant to him and his successors the land which he solicits, in the same place where he asks, provided it is not to the prejudice of anybody; and the said land being very far from this post, he is not obliged to have it surveyed at present; but however, he must apply to the Intendant General, in order to obtain the title in form from said Intendant, because to him belongs, by order of His Majesty, the granting of all classes of lands belonging to the royal domain.

Carlos Dehault Delassus.

IV

DELASSUS TO CASA CALVO, ST. LOUIS, APRIL 24, 1800[1]

Number 32

To the *Señor*
Intendente on
July 9th.

As I have had certain information that many parties of various Indian nations of the Mississippi and Missouri rivers are going to war against the Osage nations, in order to prevent their committing excesses and to prevent the Osages from again committing incursions in this vicinity, I have ordered that, from the twenty-eighth of March of this year, the commandant of San Carlos, Don Carlos Tayon, have thirty men of his militia on army rations, continually ready for use to watch and impede the excesses that these Indians are accustomed to committing when they go to war. I would also have sent the galliot of His Majesty *La Flecha* at that date, had it not been indispensable to send it to be repaired because of its being very deteriorated, and therefore it has been impossible for me to send it up until now. I am going to order its commandant, Captain of Militia Don Santiago de San Vrain, to ascend the river to cruise at the entrance of the Des Moines river, also in order to avoid and stop the entrance into the said river of some contraband traders from the district of the United States, who are accustomed to coming

---

[1]Written in Spanish. A.G.I., P. de C., leg. 71B.

thither to incommode the commerce of these inhabitants.[2] As I have been informed that they had gone with the Mahas nation and obstructed the trader of this post, having done evil to him by giving merchandise to the Indians at such a low price that he could scarcely make his expenses, and because I am informed that perhaps he has not yet left the said Des Moines river, I shall forewarn the said Captain to arrest him [them] and conduct them [him] to this post, if he presents himself during his cruise, as well as any others that he may find without my passport, who are extracting furs from this territory to the United States, which is causing a noticeable injury to this trade.

I am informing Your Excellency of all this for your knowledge.

God keep Your Excellency many years. St. Louis, Illinois, April 24, 1800

Carlos Dehault Delassus [rubric]

Señor Marqués de Casa Calvo[3]

[2]This was done because of extremely low water in the Mississippi. Delassus to Casa Calvo, no. 64. St. Louis, December 20, 1800, A.G.I., P. de C., leg. 71A. The *galliot* was sent up the river in 1801, etc.

During 1800 there was another war scare and fear of a British invasion of Spanish Louisiana. Casa Calvo ordered maintaining Upper Louisiana in a good condition; for it was unprotected on the upper part of the river and the English traders were penetrating it via the San Pedro river as far as the nations of New Spain. Spies were again sent to the United States and to Canada. Casa Calvo to Somuerlos, no. 12 *res.*, New Orleans, May 20, 1800, A.G.I., P. de C., leg. 1573; draft in A.G.I., P. de C., leg. 154C. Casa Calvo's numbers 7, 9, and 10 also treat of the fear of a British invasion. See also Cornel to Saavedra, Palacio, December 31, 1800, A.H.N., Est., leg. 3889 bis. More especially see copies of twelve letters, most of them addressed to Delassus in 1800, in A.G.I., P. de C., leg. 135; including Delassus' proclamation and orders to the various post commandants for militia preparations; Mackay to Delassus, San André, July 12, 1800, in A.G.I., P. de C., leg. 217.

Noting the intrusion of foreign traders and their influence over the Indians of the Iowa country and even extending to the nations of the Upper Missouri, Bernardo Pratte offered to stop this by erecting a fort at the mouth of the Des Moines river in return for the exclusive trade of that river for six years. Delassus supported Pratte's petition and referred to it in his letter to the governor—document IX. Pratte to Delassus, St. Louis, December 1, 1800, A.G.I., P. de C., leg. 71A. Casa Calvo granted Pratte that trade for four years including 1801 under certain conditions which Delassus said he would watch to see that Pratte fulfilled the conditions. Delassus to Casa Calvo, no. 81, St. Louis, April 3, 1800, A.G.I., P. de C., leg. 72. See Chapter VII, document I.

[3]Casa Calvo replied on July 9, 1800, approving Delassus' measures and transmitting his letter to the Intendancy to approve army rations for Tayon's men. Missouri Historical Society, Pierre Chouteau Collection, Spanish Archives of St. Louis, Box II, Envelope VI. Álvarez to López y Ángulo, St. Louis, December 4, 1800. A.G.I., P. de C., leg. 581B. This service lasted from July, 1800, until May 16, 1801. Álvarez to Morales, no. 65, St. Louis, May 13, 1802, A.G.I., P. de C., leg. 581B.

V

SARPY AND CABANNÉ TO CASA CALVO, NEW ORLEANS, [APRIL 26, 1800][1]

To His Excellency the Marquis of Casa Calvo, Lieutenant-Colonel of the Regiment of Cuba, Brigadier of the Armies of His Majesty, Military governor of the Provinces of Louisiana and West Florida.

[1]Written in French. Missouri Historical Society, Bundle: Indian Trade and Fur Companies.

Monseigneur:

The protection with which it has pleased this government to favor our company, and the grace which it recently has granted us allowing us to enjoy the exploitation of the post of the Kansas,[2] excite our lively gratitude, which naturally should spur us to make every effort to render ourselves useful and agreeable to this same government. It is thus that we address ourselves to you with complete confidence, *Monseigneur,* asking that you kindly look favorably upon this exposé, and may it please Your Excellency to grant us the protection and the [propitious] view which we need for the success of the project which we have the honor to place before you.

The post of Kansas, which we have been exploiting for two years, is neighbored by the Panis nation, a nation for a long time enemies and always at war with the Kansas. Their disagreements have occasioned us considerable expense in maintaining ourselves in this post: To place our *comptoir* [factory] under protection from all insults and restraining the Kansas nation, as much as is within our power inspiring them with peaceful sentiments towards their brothers and friends, the misintelligence and the reciprocal fear that these two nations have for each other, — all these considerably hinder the commerce of furs. This reciprocal fear prevents them from hunting, and forces them to abandon several rivers rich in furs, which these two nations have never been able to frequent for the above reason. We think, *Monseigneur,* that it would be possible to bring these two nations together to make a solid peace. From this many great advantages would result. Good harmony which one might establish among them would soften their manners; in case of need, the government could find faithful and bellicose subjects among them; and commerce would benefit by a considerable increase in furs. Consequently, uniting a much larger consummation of merchandise which are [would be] necessary for them to succeed in peace, always desirable for the welfare of humanity, it is indispensable that these two posts be exploited by one and the same firm. The rivalry of the traders is always an obstacle to the reunion of the savages; sooner or later it brings disorder or dissension among them. The credit that our conduct has merited among the Kansas nation makes us presume with reason that we will easily bring them to make peace with the Panis. No doubt it would be necessary to make presents to these two nations, and to continue such presents for some time until good understanding is perfectly established between them. We offer you, *Monseigneur,* to be the mediator between these two nations, and to make for them a solid peace at our cost and expense, asking you for the favor of the exclusive exploitation of these two posts for whatever number of years it may please you to fix—an exploitation necessary to unite these two nations,

---

[2]See Chapter VII, documents I, V, and X.

an exploitation upon which depends the success of the project which we
have the honor of offering you. We will be careful, *Monseigneur,* in
case it would please you to acquiesce to our demands, to establish several
posts of intelligence [*postes de intelligence*] so that we may be in a
position to watch over the diverse parties of the two nations, and always
to restrain them within peaceful and amicable limits in whatever direction we wish to take them, until, knowing the welfare of the country and
their true respective interests, they might make a gentle practise [*douce
habitude*].

> We are with the most respectful sentiments
>> Your Excellency's
>>> *Monseigneur*
>>> Your very humble and
>>> very obedient servants
>>> Gre[goire] Sarpy and
>>> Cabanné [rubric][9]

New Orleans, May 27, 1800
> granted
>> Casa Calvo [rubric]

[*Delassus' marginal note*]
Señor Comandante General:

I must inform Your Excellency that it seems to me that the
solicitor is worthy of the favor which he solicits of Your Excellency,
by virtue of the good and prudent manner, with which he has proven
to me, in which he has conducted himself and managed in the two
years in which he has held the exclusive trade of the Kansas nation,
as well as by reason of the expenditures that he discloses. And I believe
that he will not omit any step, however costly it may be, in order
to fulfill what he is offering to Your Excellency in regard to the peace
between the two nations, Kansas and Panis. And if this can be effected, according to what I have learned, it would be very advantageous
to the prosperity of the other traders who have to pass through those
two nations.

These are the motives which spur me to inform Your Excellency,
and solicit these exclusive trades from your goodness for the solicitor
on whatever terms Your Excellency may find convenient.

Your Excellency will order whatever may please you.

St. Louis, Illinois, April 26, 1800

> Carlos Dehault Delassus [rubric]

---

[9]This is most likely dated April 26, 1800.

VI

LETTER OF MACKAY, ST. ANDRÉ, MAY 25, 1800[1]

Answered

The bearer, William Belliaur, has just accused the one named Butler of having stolen his horse. As I do not have a prison here in which to imprison him [Butler] immediately, and as the witnesses are not here, I am sending him to you, so that you may order done with regard to him as you see fit.

The said Butler has been hunting in the Missouri and among the Kansas nation and other savages for a long time. And although he may not be guilty of the crime that he has been accused, I believe that it will be very necessary to prevent him from entering in the Missouri, and all the more so, because many whites are being lost [killed] there, due to the considerable length of time that they are remaining among the barbarians.

May God keep you in His Holy keeping.
St. André, May 25, 1800.

Santiago Mackay [rubric]

---

[1]Written in French. A.G.I., P. de C., leg. 217.

VII

CASA CALVO TO DE LASSUS, NEW ORLEANS, JUNE 28, 1800[1]

Answered

I have conceded to Don José Cruzat, lieutenant of the regiment of Louisiana, the trade with the Otos Indians for one year. I am advising you of this for your knowledge, in the intelligence that if this permission should not arrive in time for the present year you will see that it be granted next year.

May God keep you many years.
New Orleans, June 28, 1800.

El Marqués de Casa-Calvo. [rubric]

Señor Don Carlos De Lassus

---

[1]Written in Spanish. A.G.I., P. de C., leg. 69; draft in A.G.I., P. de C., leg. 136. This was not received by Delassus until March 8, 1801. He replied to it on April 2, 1801 acknowledging receipt of the information and saying that Cruzat would enjoy the trade of the Otos for this year (1801). Delassus to Casa Calvo, no. 72, St. Louis, April 2, 1801, A.G.I., P. de C., leg. 72. See also Chapter VII, document I.

VIII

CLAMORGAN TO DELASSUS, ST. LOUIS, NOVEMBER 24, 1800[1]

To *Monsieur*:

Monsieur Don Charles Dehault Delassus, lieutenant-colonel of the Fixed Regiment of Louisiana and lieutenant-governor at the Illinois. When a courageous Company was formed in the vast country of Upper Louisiana to undertake to navigate the rapid waters of the Missouri and even beyond its sources, there to seek the means of a useful industry for this colony, when this same Company was bold enough to hazard the ambition of rendering itself useful to posterity by making important discoveries, when it became inflamed with the courage to seek out unknown peoples who inhabit the territory of His Majesty, when it displayed there, in the name of Our Kind Monarch, the standard of peace, friendship, union, and kindness in order to open, via the channel of the vast Missouri, a communication with the Pacific Ocean, it received at the same time a portion of the recompense for its painful labours by contributing to the future happiness of the colony.

But when His Majesty tried to accelerate the progress of this same Company by granting to it a levy of 100 militiamen to protect its commerce against the foreigners who border its limits, could one fail to discover his intention and to foresee his will without causing harm to the advancement and to the prosperity of the extensive industry?

The permission granted by His Majesty to put this militia on foot implied a tacit explanation regarding the payment of 100 *piastres* per militia head, which the Company should receive each year for the costs of its maintenance

If His Majesty had not intended to sustain the expenditure for this militia himself, in order to protect his vast limits against usurpation and the infraction of his rights, had he the right to grant this grace with the strict condition which is carried in article 2 [?] of his royal order sent June 11, 1796,[2] to His Excellency the Baron de Carondelet, wherein is stated at the end of the preamble:

---

[1]Written in French. A.G.I., P. de C., leg. 2366. Clamorgan was no longer the director of a prosperous and secure organization; he was now a man who was staring failure in the face. He was doggedly fighting to maintain himself and the Company which was his creation. In this letter Clamorgan uses his waning talents of a brilliant imagination, but his bluster is all gone. His arguments were meaningful, written persuasively, almost frantically. Needless to say, Clamorgan never received the money payments.

[2]Chapter IV, document XVII. This problem and quarrel over the paying of the 10.000 *pesos* has been mentioned on several occasions in the documents presented in the previous chapters in this volume. Clamorgan in part attributed to this fail-

"SE HA DIGNADO S. M. ACCORDAR CON UNIFORME DICTAMEN DE DICHO CONSEJO LOS PUNTOS Y GRACIAS SIGUIENTES." [His Majesty has deigned to grant with uniform *dictamen* of the said *Consejo,* the following points and favors]. Article two of the royal order: LA LICENCIA DE QUE LA COMPANIA PUEDA ARMAR A SU COSTA, [Permission that the Company can arm at its (his) cost] signified either at the expense of the Company or at the expense of His Majesty. But it is necessary to observe that this second article speaks in the name of His Majesty, and that the words "DE SU COSTA" are entirely relative to him, since His Excellency Don Diego de Gardo[qui] explains the double sense of these words contained in the same article, and he says: MANTENER ARMADOS LOS CIEN HOMBRES CUYO CUMPLIMIENTO CELARÁ CON EL MAYOR CUIDADO. [to maintain armed the 100 men, the carrying out of which he will oversee with the greatest care]. Would it not do injury to the literal sense of this article to give it an interpretation contrary to the motives which have given birth to this article? Of what importance is it to His Majesty that he might have [to keep] more or less of a militia maintained in the forts of the Company, if he had not intended to pay the expenses of it himself according to the conditions which were proposed to him? That is all the more evident, for this great favor was only granted the Company by virtue of its representations concerning the necessity of being assisted against the usurpations of the foreigners who try to invade the territory of His Majesty and [appropriate] the commerce in rich skins with all the savage nations who inhabit there, to the injury of the advantages which must be some day felt by the chief city.

These critical circumstances being as well known as the losses and the continual sacrifices into which the Company has been so deeply plunged without ever being disheartened in its enterprise, His Majesty has judged it best to base his kindnesses on these considerations, but the double sense [interpretation] given to the desires of His Majesty so far has retarded the progress and advancement of the Company, and has increased the influence and temerity of the neighbors who surround us in this part of the globe. It is high time to repress it, and maintain them [neighbors] within the limits of their spheres [of interest] by the fright of a vigorous militia and by the rampart of canons which we must multiply there in order to render our frontiers respectable to their audacity. And by these means we must at the same time prevent the corruption of the opinions of the savages, which our neighbors spread among them and strive vigorously to destroy the less equivocal indications of our friendship for them, a friendship which we have always cemented by presents unceasingly repeated.

---

ure to receive the money the downfall of his plans and of the Missouri Company. Among the many documents relating to this problem see Chapter IV, documents XVII, XXVIII, XXIX, XXXI, XXXVII; Chapter V, document VII, etc.

These expenditures, which are becoming enormous as they continue to increase, are imperceptibly undermining the means of the Company. Hope alone consoles it and maintains it. But, *Monsieur,* if in the midst of our career our weakened means cease to sustain our hopes to what shall we take recourse? Although we are devoted to perseverance on this thorny way, should we conduct ourselves toward the glory of a fortunate success, or be swallowed up under the ruins of our fortunes? But whatever the turn of events may be, we shall consider ourselves satisfied if we can contribute to opening a career [path] useful to posterity.

In such circumstances, there is no doubt that His Majesty, jealous of his rights, of his properties, and of his commerce, will support the Company in a portion of its sacrifices, if you deign to inform the general government of the resulting consequences, and to supplicate at the feet of the throne as to the need for repelling the intolerable ambition of a neighbor who anticipates possessions which it will claim the right to enjoy—that it will have usurped without formal opposition. You know that the reiterated enterprises of the various English companies of Hudson's Bay, Lake Winnipeg, and that known under the name of the North West Company, are all approaching the sources of our Missouri by expeditions, which they are all abetting with presents, flags, and insinuating discourses, deceitful and contrary to our rights and interests. Their forts erected on the *rivière des Osseniboines,* which is only four days' journey form the Missouri, have already menaced the establishment of the Company situated among the Mandan nation for two years. Soon the enormous expanse which separates us from the Pacific Ocean will be inundated under the flag of Britain, and the nations which surround California and New Mexico will not delay being corrupted by the venom of English industry. We have already destroyed a fort that they had the audacity to erect among the Gros Ventres nation, and have lowered the British flag which was raised there, but we are afraid that we have forced them within their boundaries only for a short time. We fear their return. It is necessary for us to have a local militia consecrated to the protection of our forts, to which we will unite a sufficient number of *engagés,* men which the Company is obliged to maintain. This must be done in order to impose respect to the line of demarcation formed by our establishments situated in the upper part of the Missouri, and especially in the places most penetrable to foreigners, where ramparts must soon be erected in order to prevent the savage nations from receiving information dangerous and pernicious to the tranquillity and the security of the possessions of His Majesty, and to repulse with violence the seditions which they are triumphantly carrying on in the territory of Our Monarch under the protection of the British flag.

It is in these circumstances, *Monsieur,* that the Company devoted to a project which must some day be a source of abundance for the capital that His Majesty had been supplicated by His Excellency the Baron de Carondelet to grant permission for the levy of 100 militiamen, whom the Company would maintain on condition that it be paid 100 *piastres* for each one annually, under the orders and command of the *agent-general* of the Company, in order to have respected the rights and properties of Our Sovereign, and to repulse the venomous insinuations of the foreigners upon those nations which we have overwhelmed only by means of kindnesses and presents in order to purchase their apparent friendship. This friendship is [has been] maintained only by the generosities incessantly spread among these nations, and even despite this, how many times have the expeditions of the Company not been ravaged and destroyed during the régime of M. Dn Zenon Trudeau, your predecessor! We know very well that we have not deserved those losses which we have experienced solely because of the jealous industry of our neighbors, but we can only remedy this situation by forcing them to withdraw to beyond our borders. Under your very eyes, *Monsieur,* and at this very moment, we receive the news that the last expedition of the Company made in the month of June, last, was found to have been totally sacrificed. The circumstantial details of this loss have not yet reached us, but we know that the chief of this *armement* disappeared and that the merchandise of the Company was pillaged by the nation in which the expedition was at the time.

In accordance with our remarks, *Monsieur,* the Company supplicates you to make the most lively entreaties to the general-government, in order that it may be pleased to solicit from His Majesty payment for the 100 militiamen at the rate of 100 *piastres* per head, as the Company had previously requested, in order to make it respected in the eyes of the savage and civilized nations and to establish [a regular government] the rights and properties of our Sovereign. The Company also solicits that His Majesty include the arrears of the said pay from June 11, 1796, at which time His Majesty pronounced the decree in favor of the Company and addressed immediately to His Excellency the Baron de Carondelet, who was disposed to execute His Majesty's intentions, had it not been for the badly-founded opposition to which *Monsieur* the *ad-interim Intendant,* Don Morales, devoted himself,[3] against which opposition, however, His Excellency the Baron de Carondelet sent to His Majesty[4] an estimate of the wrongs which the delay of this favor occasioned to the industry and peaceful possession of his domains. This will be one more favor for

---

[3]Chapter IV, document XXXVII.
[4]Chapter V, document VII.

which the Company will be accountable to its protectors, if you deign to favor it with your support.

St. Louis, Illinois; November 24, 1800.

J. Clamorgan [rubric]

St. Louis, Illinois; December 1, 1800.

The exponent will present himself to the *Señor* Governor-General of these provinces.

Carlos Dehault Delassus [rubric]

IX

DELASSUS TO CASA CALVO, ST. LOUIS, NOVEMBER 29, 1800[1]

Number 61

I have distributed the posts of the Indian trade for the present year as follows :[2]

By order of Your Excellency, the Otos, the Mahas, and the Poncas to Don Santiago Clamorgan since it seemed best to me in accordance with Your Excellency's wishes.[3] He [Clamorgan] has informed me that he has sent men to continue his discoveries, and that he has just received word that the discoverer, M *Éné*,[4] has been driven out and assassinated, and his goods given up to plunder. Some of his men have returned but it is not known yet whether it was they or the Indians that committed the crime, a fact I shall try to find out in the proper time with great thoroughness.

By order of Your Excellency the Kansas and the Panis Republic to Don Gregorio Sarpy. Because of a dispute, of which I have been informed, and because of the fact that the Kansas are arming themselves, he runs the risk of having very bad trade. Therefore I think it would be advisable to grant him the same nation for the coming year.[5]

The remaining Panis to Captain Benito Bazquez. He is very loyal to our government, is the father of a large family, and is hampered by the small means that his industry supplies. For all these reasons, it is my

---

[1]Written in Spanish. Original in Bancroft Library. Reply is document XI.
[2]See Chapter VII, documents I, V and X.
[3]Document II.
[4]This information proved later to be false. See Chapter IX, document X. On Heney see *post*, e.g. Loisel-Heney Convention du Commerce, Missouri Historical Society, Auguste Chouteau Collection: Accounts of Clamorgan on equipment given to Loisel and Heney, July, 1801—June 20, 1805, *Ibid.*; Clamorgan to Salcedo, April 18, 1801—Chapter IX, document V. See also Abel, *Tabeau's Narrative*, 24-26, 49, 79-81. 112-113; 162, 231-234; Thwaites, *Original Journals*, consult index, *e.g.*, V, 282-286; Coues, *New Light On the Early History of the Greater Northwest* (New York, 1897), I, 101-102; F. A. Laroque's "JOURNAL" in Masson, *Les Bourgeois de La Compagnie du Nord - Ouest*, etc.
[5]See document IV.

intention to keep him in the same place every year, so that it will serve as some relief to his wretchedness.

The Osages to Don Augusto Chouteau, according to his contract which ends this year, and which permits him to withdraw his capital and stores next year.

As Your Excellency's predecessor, Don Manuel Gayoso de Lemos, told me to give my observations on the condition of this country as regards trade after I had been employed at these posts for four years, having busied myself, as part of my duty and as far as my poor understanding would permit, with observing the improvement in prosperity in this upper part of Louisiana which is now entrusted to me. [I wish to state that] I believe, from the results that I have noticed, that, at least until agriculture and the lead mines are exploited to a much greater degree than they are now, we should not spare any means of attracting the Indians with their furs, since that is the one and only branch of trade that is producing a livelihood for the larger part of this town and its dependencies.

In order that this essential division of commerce may be continued with profit, and avoid the harm which experience has always shown to result from having many traders go at one time to the Indians—since from jealousy of one another they sell their goods at cheap prices in the lodges, and are afterwards often unable to pay their outfitters, as was experienced by this post when trade was free, for this reason and since their disputes have often been the cause for the savages killing people of the towns when they found themselves involved in these quarrels—I am of the opinion that it is very essential and vital that all trading with nations worth considering should be exclusive and granted to persons of means, or to persons who have relations with such people. This should be done so that they may know them and not look askance in case they spend something to avoid harm, and so that they may deserve their respect, a thing which is accomplished only by acts which seem generous to them [Indians], and which can not be done by a trader limited in his equipment, since with the greatest economy he can scarcely earn enough to pay his frugal annual expenses.

An example has just occurred which proves what I have just said. Since Don Augusto and Pedro Chouteau have had the privilege of trading with the Osage nations, they have employed a large number of persons who earn their living there. From the time they took over the trade, it is agreed that that nation has greatly lessened its raids against the rest of us, and they can really be said to be nothing in comparison to what they were before. Now, when anything happens, the Osage nation gives satisfaction for it in every way that can be expected. For example, when Mr. Chouteau had the greater part of his horses stolen, they were returned. Two murders occurred; twice they handed over the *partidarios*, one to the orders of Lieutenant-Colonel Carlos Howard,[6] and the other to me this last summer, the latter being at present in chains.

In the years before this trade was limited, all who engaged in it were ruined as a result of it; some were killed or wounded, and the rest at least injured by that nation, and because of the jealousy which I mentioned above. Experience and the desire to preserve this quieting influence on that nation, which consists of more than fifteen hundred belligerent and savage warriors, urge me to beg Your Excellency to be pleased to extend the contract to the above-mentioned *Messieurs* Chouteau on the same terms that they enjoy at present, at least for a period of six years, so that this district may keep its quietude. I desire this favor all the more in this case, because if that nation is laid open to the rumors of the people as it was before, and if the unwelcome English get to them, they will be capable of making their way even into the very houses of those villages. And I should not omit the fact that, aside from these reasons which are a concern of the general welfare, I know of no one who deserves this great favor more than Don Augusto Chouteau both for his loyalty toward the government and for his ability, and likewise his brother Don Pedro Chouteau, who alone carried with him to that nation the greatest daring that was possible, as I informed Your Excellency in my official letter number 51, dated September 25. I repeat to Your Excellency that if the occasion occurs, I expect to send him with a party against whatever enemies happen to present themselves.

I present the above to Your Excellency so that you may order whatever you may consider best.

May God keep Your Excellency for many years; St. Louis, Illinois, November 29, 1800.

Carlos Dehault Delassus [rubric]
Señor Marqués de Casa Calvo

---

[6]See documents in Nasatir, "Anglo-Spanish Rivalry in the Iowa Country, 1797-1798," *Iowa Journal of History and Politics*, XXVIII (1930), 337-389.

X

Robidoux and others to Governor of Louisiana, St. Louis, December 8, 1800[1]

To *Monseigneur* The Governor General of the Provinces of Louisiana and Dependencies.

Monseigneur:

It is with the most profound respect and with the most complete confidence that we dare to tender you our just claims. Faithful and sub-

---

[1]Written in French. A.G.I., P. de C., leg. 217. See Delassus' comment in Chapter IX, document IX. Compare this with another petition in 1801, Chapter IX, document XIII.

missive subjects, Spanish citizens for more than twenty years, we make bold to claim our rights. Of you, *Monseigneur*, the representative of His Catholic Majesty, we beg that we be allowed to enjoy the prerogatives that his bountiful and paternal soul grants indiscriminately to all his subjects. Our fate is frightful, and we have before us only a most unhappy future. Nearly all of us, fathers of large families, are on the eve of being ruined. The trade in furs, the one and only unique resource for supplying the commerce of Illinois, is forbidden to us. The exclusion of this trade[2] threatens us with imminent poverty, a poverty all the harder to endure, since we see every day how easy it would be to make us all happy and the commerce flourishing. We are far from claiming the exclusion of this trade; our old men limit themselves to sharing it with our co-citizens, merchants like ourselves. All children of the same father, we desire to participate in his benefits.

We are quite convinced that this just and kindly government never had intended to make miserable wretches of us; but let us be permitted to say this, *Monseigneur:* the exclusion of the trade in a country where there is no other commerce must necessarily bring about the ruin of all the merchants who do not participate in it. The merchant who alone enjoys this privilege monopolizes all the furs; he allows only whatever part of them he so desires to circulate; thus, he makes a brilliant fortune, while the trade of his colleagues languishes, is in jeopardy, and ends by dragging them into the abyss. It is a well-known truth that the circulation of specie or of a valuable product which represents it, makes the wealth of the merchant, tests the abundance in the country, regenerates it, makes it flourish, and makes in general for the happiness of all the individuals who live in it.

The commerce of the metropole must by this exclusion lose a considerable sum. In 1793, ten laden vessels were sent out from New Orleans for the Illinois. Cargoes valued at 200,000 *piastres* were entirely consumed in the country, and the returns were all made in furs. From that time to the time of the exclusion, the commerce drew annually a value of 150,000 to 180,000 *piastres*. What is the value which the commerce is drawing today from the *Metropole?* Setting aside what is drawn for the exclusive privileges, it does not amount here to the value of 30,000 *piastres* annually. The merchant is forced to abandon the commerce of this Metropole because he cannot promise returns in the sole value [commodity] which may have a market price.

Permit us, *Monseigneur*, to place before you the statement of the furs which can derive annually from the various trading posts exploited in the Missouri, the Mississippi, and the adjacent rivers, furs which are almost all going into two houses [firms] of this city. These dif-

[2]See document IX.

ferent posts yield an annual total of 3500 packets calculated at the lowest number, because this number can be made to increase greatly. This quantity of packets, evaluated at the sum of 140,000 *piastres,* widely spread among all the commercial firms of this city, to each in proportion to its commercial means, would make it [city] prosper; there would be a great increase of business, circulation becoming general and abundant; consumption would increase in proportion, and the country itself would feel the better effects.

Let us glance rapidly over the first period of this establishment. Mr. Piernas, the first Spanish commandant, the first person who established rules for the commerce of furs and of trade,[3] rules which are still in force, Mr. Piernas never permitted the exclusion of the trade. He distributed the posts equally; each found his account there and felt the good effects of this administration. Some good traders were equipped by the entire commerce. In general, each merchant furnished according to his means, and withdrew his share of the furs in proportion to the funds that he had invested. Thus, the people were happy; the merchant comfortable, and no one was reduced to [feared] poverty.

How flattering and consoling it would be for us if this example should again be followed. You alone, *Monseigneur,* can put it into force. Be so kind as to abolish the privileges which are dragging down and necessitating the ruin of a number of honest families; privileges which are restraining the industry of a number of faithful subjects of His Majesty. We are far from demanding the general liberty of the trade. Perhaps from that there would result an even greater evil than has come from the exclusion. We beg you only to order, *Monseigneur,* that the trade in furs be made generally by the body of commerce of this city by forming a *société* in which each merchant will furnish merchandise in proportion to his commercial means and the total in proportion to the number of posts which they can exploit; demanding that this association be ruled and directed by a Syndic, who will be the Syndic of all the commerce, and who will be named by the merchants assembled, with the authorization of and in the presence of Mr. the Lieutenant Governor; [and to order] that some commercial regulations be established, to which regulations the commerce will be subjected and which it will not be able to derogate.[4]

This way appears to us the best, *Monseigneur,* in order that all the merchants without complaining can enjoy an advantage which will make for the well being of them all. The posts being better exploited, there will be an increase of furs. The savages, supported by the general in-

---

[3] See the Introduction, part II, *infra.*

[4] Quite similar to what took place in 1793-1794. See documents in Chapters I and II. See also Nasatir, "Formation of the Missouri Company," *Missouri Historical Review,* XXV (1931), 10-22; and Nasatir, "Anglo-Spanish Rivalry on the Upper Missouri, part I," *Mississippi Valley Historical Review,* XVI (1929), 359-382; see especially reprint pp. 9-13.

terest, will not be induced so easily to commit their depredations. The traders, equipped, one might say, by the same firm, will not have any jealousy among themselves. There being no rivalry [competition], they will support each other, and will be less exposed than ever to the insults of these barbarians.

Deign, *Monseigneur*, to accede to our claims. They are just. They are founded on the right that our August Monarch has freely granted to all his subjects. With a single word *Monseigneur*, you can restore peace to many fathers of families, and overwhelm them with satisfaction. By doing the good that your heart inspires in you, by making for the happiness of faithful subjects of His Majesty, you will be able only to anticipate and accomplish his paternal intentions.

St. Louis, December 8, 1800.

Jh. Robidou[5]	Chles. Sanguinet
[rubric]	[rubric]
F. N. Benoît	Patrice Lee
[rubric]	[rubric]
A. Reilhe	Jacque Chauvin
[rubric]	[rubric]

---

[5]These were the men who were envious and desirous of overthrowing Clamorgan's privileges as well. Robidou had attempted to overthrow Clamorgan and the Company—see Chapter VI, document V. Failing in his effort he got these men to join with him and attempted it by means of pleading for free trade. In 1801 he joined with still others to overthrow Clamorgan's privileges. See Chapter IX, document XIII.

On December 1, 1800, Bernardo Pratte wrote Delassus telling the lieutenant-governor that the foreigners in commerce in Spain's Upper Mississippi territory had placed so many shackles on the industry of the inhabitants of the Illinois and that it was even beginning to extend to the Indian nations inhabiting the Upper Missouri. To aid in repelling such moves Pratte offered to establish a fort at the entrance of the Des Moines river in order to put a stop to the entrance of foreign traders into Spanish territory. For doing that Pratte asked for the exclusive trade of the Des Moines river. On the following day Delassus wrote on the bottom of Pratte's petition that Pratte was telling true facts and if he could fulfill what he offered to do, it would be one of the most certain means of cutting the route of contraband which the English and Americans were making via that river. Delassus stated that Pratte was possessed of sufficient means to carry out his offer and considered him "worthy of the grace which he solicits". (A.G.I., P. de C., leg. 71A) and referred the governor to Document IX.

XI

CASA CALVO TO DELASSUS, NEW ORLEANS, DECEMBER 30, 1800[1]

Answered

In your official letter number 61[2] you inform me of the distribution which you made last year of the trades with the Indians, dependent on

---

[1]Written in Spanish. A.G.I., P. de C., leg. 69.
[2]Document IX.

your jurisdiction, but I have noticed that some are lacking. It is best for the dispositions which must be taken, that each year you send me a general note of the trades granted,[3] as well as those who solicited for the vacant ones for the next year, informing me as to who is worthy of this favor, and who is not, it being well understood that you must always preserve one trade for your benefit, so that you may be able to support the indispensable expenditures which are incurred.

In this manner the government will also be able to take its precautions, and to recompense prudently the fidelity and affection of those who may distinguish themselves.

In this supposition, it seems well to me that you have given the trade of the Otos, Poncas, and Mahas to Don Santiago Clamorgan and I hope that you will inform me of the assassination of Mr. Éné.[4]

To Captain Don Benito Vazquez, bearing in mind the good reports which you give me of him and those which I have from other sources, he shall be given the trade of the rest of the Panis, as you propose.

I have conceded the Osage trade for four years to Don Augusto Chouteau, because he is really worthy of it.

Finally, I agree with you that it is very essential that all the trades of some consequence and considerations be made exclusive, and be conceded to opulent persons, or to those who are maintained by such persons, in order to support in case of necessity some expenses which they can offer to them. Under this rule you will resolve in the future, at the same time procuring that those who profit from them employ good men which are required. I say "good men", because it is necessary to make a strict law that no one take part in this benefit who has not previously made worthy his love and fidelity to his sovereign, and who does not give signs of having a moderately well regulated moral conduct.

God keep you many years. New Orleans, December 30, 1800

El Marqués de Casa Calvo   [rubric]

Señor Don Carlos Lassus.

---

[3]See Chapter VII, document I.
[4]See document IX and Chapter IX, document X.

CHAPTER IX

1801

I

CASA CALVO TO DELASSUS, NEW ORLEANS, JANUARY 26, 1801[1]

Answered

I have conceded to Don Santiago Clamorgan the trade of the Panis Republic[2]. I am advising you of this for your government.[3]

May God keep you many years.

New Orleans, January 26, 1801.

El Marqués de Casa-Calvo [rubric]

Señor Don Carlos Lassus.

[1]Written in Spanish. A.G.I., P. de C., leg. 70B.
[2]See Chapter VII, document I.
[3]Delassus acknowledged receipt of this in his dispatch no. 80, dated St Louis April 3, 1801, A.G.I., P. de C., leg. 72. Delassus significantly added the word "for this year". Casa Calvo granted the Oto trade to Josef Cruzat—Delassus to Casa Calvo, number 72, St. Louis, April 2, 1801, A.G.I., P. de C., leg. 72.

II

CASA CALVO TO DELASSUS, NEW ORLEANS, FEBRUARY 26, 1801[1]

I have conceded the trade with the Panis nations to Don Santiago Chauvin[2] in view of the solicitude which he gave to me and the large family which he has.

[1]Written in Spanish. A.G.I., P. de C., leg. 70B.
[2]See Chapter VII, document I.

I am advising you of this for your intelligence and government.[a]

May God Keep you many years.

New Orleans, Febraury 26, 1801

El Marqués de Casa-Calvo

[rubric]

Señor Don Carlos de Lassus

Marginal note: R[answered]

---

[a]In official dispatch no. 94 to Casa Calvo, dated St. Louis, August 3, 1801, Delassus acknowledged receipt of the information that Casa Calvo had granted the trade of the Panis to Chauvin, as well as "by the decree attached to the memorial of the said person." A.G.I., P. de C., leg. 72. See also Chapter X, document VIII.

III

PETITION OF SANGUINET, NEW ORLEANS, MARCH 14, 1801[1]

Señor Governor

Don Carlos Sanguinet, resident and of the commerce of St. Louis, Illinois, with due respect to Your Excellency, presents himself and says:

That he has been established in that post for twenty-three years in which he has suffered many losses in the various speculations which he has undertaken with the Indian nations, and particularly in the Missouri Company of which he was a member, as is well known. He now finds himself favored by various subjects who are advancing to him sufficient funds for re-undertaking the commerce and placing him in a position to recover the enormous losses which he has sustained. He is taking recourse to the well known kindness of Your Excellency, begging you to deign to concede to him for the term of three years the exclusive trade of the Mahas and Poncas Nations, notwithstanding the fact that the supplicant is informed that this last [trade] is conceded to Don Santiago Clamorgan for one year.[2] It will be easy for the supplicant to come to an agreement with Clamorgan for the time which remains to him for his profit.

Therefore:

He humbly begs Your Excellency to please accord to him this grace and it is a favor which he hopes from the well known kindness of Your Excellency.

New Orleans, March 14, 1801

Ch[le] Sanguinet [rubric]

---

[1]Written in Spanish. Missouri Historical Society, Bundle: Indian Trade and Fur Companies. See Delassus' comment in document IX.

[2]See Document I, and Chapter VIII, documents IX and XI, and Chapter VII, document I. See also this Chapter documents VI and V.

630

New Orleans, March 14, 1801

I concede to the supplicant the trade of the Maha Indians for two years. With regard to the trade of the Poncas which he also solicits for a like term of years, it is already conceded for one year to Don Santiago Clamorgan. In regard to the proposition which he makes for making an agreement with him, I am leaving the action free to him so that he may take what steps he can by associating himself with him or in some other way. And in case such does not take place the Lieutenant-Governor by my order will permit him to engage in the said trade of the Poncas for two years.

Casa Calvo [rubric]

IV

DELASSUS TO CASA CALVO, ST. LOUIS, APRIL 3, 1801[1]

No. 84 Marginal note:[2] Approved

It having come to my notice that the Mahas, Ayoas, and other Indians of that [my] district suffered last winter from smallpox and that the *enganchados* of the traders had [been?] pillaged [in] it, I believed it my duty to take prudent precaution in order to avoid the contagious disease being introduced into these establishments where at present it is not known. And in order to avoid the ravages it could occasion, I have ordered that Don Carlos Tayon[3] and Don Francisco Saussier[4] do not permit anyone at all to approach their posts, and that they choose a place quite distant from it in order to oblige those who may be returning from trading with those nations to be placed in quarantine, and during the quarantine they must air their peltries and pass them through smoke. The traders of the Otos, Mahas, and Poncas nations, having arrived within a league of here, I ordered them to unite on the *Isla á Cabaret,* one league distant from here, in order to go through quarantine, where they have been under the same specified rules since March twentieth of this year, with a guard of three men in order to avoid all communication with this post until the quarantine is over.

---

[1]Written in Spanish. A.G.I., P. de C., leg. 72.
[2]On May 7, 1801, Casa Calvo replied to this letter approving the steps taken by Delassus as stated in this official letter. Missouri Historical Society, Pierre Chouteau Collection, Spanish Archives of St. Louis, Box II, Envelope VI; draft in A.G.I., P. de C., leg. 137A.
[3]Commandant of San Carlos del Misuri.
[4]Commandant of Portage des Sioux.

I am communicating all this to Your Excellency for your due knowledge.

May God keep Your Excellency many years.

St. Louis, Illinois, April 3, 1801.

Carlos Dehault Delassus [rubric]

Señor Marqués de Casa Calvo.

V

CLAMORGAN TO SALCEDO, ST. LOUIS, APRIL 18, 1801[1]

To His Excellency Don Manuel Juan de Salcedo, Governor-General of the Province of Louisiana.

The members of the Company of the Missouri, being informed of the disasters which are ravaging its operations feel that it is most urgent to place before your eyes the calamities which pursue it without interruption. The Director of this same Company has already taken the liberty of making known to the government the unfortunate loss of *Sieur* Héné, its agent,[2] who had been sent last year into the Upper Missouri where he seems to have been carried off [captured] and destroyed by the savage nations who live there. These nations have entirely pillaged the merchandise of the Company and have threatened to forbid the traders to pass beyond.

Never, *Monseigneur*, have circumstances offered anything similar: All of this is due to the fact that the English merchants from Canada have had their commerce take the route to the Upper Missouri, passing through Lake Superior, via Lake Winnipeg, and via the Upper Mississippi, in order to envelope and to take possession by these three different channels of the rich and precious commerce of fine furs. Our capital finds itself deprived of these furs because of the small strength which the Company can oppose to foreigners whose jealousy, rivalry, and ambition leave nothing to desire. They undertake everything and dare everything to the prejudice of honor and equity.

The frightful plot of the English, to cause the destruction of *Sieur* Héné, agent of the Company of the Upper Missouri, in the course of his voyage, is not the only one which these foreigners seem to have caused

[1]Written in French. A.G.I., P. de C., leg. 218. See reply referred to in Chapter X, document I. and note 1. Clamorgan, always ready to take advantage of the occasion of a new governor (Salcedo became governor general in June, 1801) and also angry because of what had happened to his agent, Heney [Éné], and the governor's [Casa Calvo's] about face and sudden granting of the Maha and Ponca trade to Sanguinet, expressed his feelings in this lengthy petition to Salcedo. See document VI.

[2]See Chapter VIII, documents IX and XI.

to be exercised at the same moment and at the same time in order to ruin the interests of the Company.

The Maha nation, through whom it is necessary to pass by water, after we leave the Octoctata nation, has declared open war on the Company, by presenting themselves, weapons in hand, to pillage the merchandise which was actually destined for their usage and consumption.[3] This nation, sustained and subsidized by the English who furnish them all that they need, no longer wish to permit the passage by water for transporting any effects to the nations of the Upper Missouri. They declared themselves by a combat and have fired upon the whites attached to the service of the Company who have been obliged to withdraw to the Octoctata nation in a fort established for the protection of its commerce, where, nevertheless, here and there, there were persons killed and wounded.

This is the moment to make known to you, *Monseigneur,* the powerful impression made on the Maha nation by the English in a council where all the chiefs of this nation had been assembled by invitations which the agents of Great Britain had had sent to them, accompanied by presents, medals and flags. This council has been held at the place called Prairie du Chien and the journal of what occurred there is at present found in the hands of the one named Dubuque,[4] established on the Upper Mississippi, serving as an interpreter for the various nations who live there. From all this that I have said, it is easy to discover the secret intrigue of the government of England which through seduction, cleverly conducted, and manipulated by artifice, seeks only to capture the spirit [*génie*—character] of our savage nations in order to attach them to the English under guise of interests [commerce].

A conduct so dangerous on the part of foreigners requires not only that the Company take measures suitable for the security of its commerce, but requires also that the general government be attentive to the steps of a powerful and dangerous enemy in this far distant district in order to prevent an usurpation which it seems to wish to have carried out in silence.

Now is the time, *Monseigneur,* when more than ever the Company must call to its aid the support of the one hundred militiamen for whom the Director of the Company has already had the honor of soliciting from your predecessor[5] in order to obtain them and have them under the pay of His Majesty to which it appears consent was given during the administration of His Excellency the Baron de Carondelet. *Monseigneur,* please honor this same Company with your new protection when not only its

[3]See *e.g.,* Chapter VIII, document IV. These problems are treated in my former student, L. R. Devlin's manuscript study entitled "Upper Louisiana 1796-1804" See Nasatir, "Anglo-Spanish Frontier on the Upper Mississippi 1786-1796," *Iowa Journal of History and Politics,* (1931), XXIX, 227-228.

[4]M. M. Hoffman, *Antique Dubuque* (Dubuque, 1930) ; *American State Papers, Public Lands,* III. 678.

[5]See Chapter VIII, document II.

prosperity is attached to it [Your new protection] but also when the properties [prosperity] of His Majesty are dependent on it.

Surrounded by circumstances always more or less fatal the Company no longer has the power to have its convoys pass through the lands of the Maha nation or through the lands of the Ponca nation, and it sees itself in the necessity of routing them via the Platte river in order to reach the Upper Missouri by other routes.

Therefore, *Monseigneur*, it is indispensable to the Company not to be at all opposed [thwarted] on its way to becoming mistress of furnishing or depriving merchandise in the future to the nations who are found or will be found in the dependency of the Platte river by which the said Company is forced to open a new route of communication by depriving, (if it is convenient to its interest), the Maha and Ponca nations of all commerce with the whites in order to have them re-enter within the limits of submission and of friendship. But in order to prevent the dangers of the pillage of merchandise of the Company, so often repeated, the supplicant desires that he be permitted to form his *entrepôt* in the Kansas river in order to enjoy the commerce which is made there with the nation which inhabits it and to force it by pacific means to the most perfect harmony and sincere friendship so often scorned by the other nations.

In this consideration the supplicant, Director of the Company, desires that it may please Your Excellency to grant to him for the term of five full and consecutive years to date from the next year of 1802, a brevet in order that he (or any other who would be able to represent him), may enjoy the exclusive trade, commerce, and hunt of the Kansas River and its dependencies, as well as the exclusive trade, commerce and hunt of the Platte river and dependencies, with the nations who frequent or inhabit one and the other river such as the Kansas, Octoctactas, and the three different Panis nations or [and] others.[6] If it is agreed to build on both [one and another of the] rivers fortifications at the expense of the Company in order to keep good order and restrain the frequentations of the enemies, such fortifications shall remain the property of His Majesty at the expiration of the privilege, reserving to the said Company the right to furnish or deprive the Maha and Ponca nations of their needs in accordance with the circumstances in order to recall them to peace. And the supplicant will not cease to give thanks for your kindnesses.

Jacques Clamorgan [rubric]

St. Louis, Illinois, 18 April, 1801.

---

[6]See Chapter VII, document I. Salcedo favored Clamorgan consistently and rescinded the grant to Sanguinet. He approved the grant to Clamorgan of the exclusive trade of the Kansas and other nations above the mouth of the Kansas River, Platte River and dependencies, on February 2, 1802, (February 3—Chapter X, document I). See Delassus to Salcedo, number 142, St. Louis, May 13, 1802, A.G.I., P. de C., leg. 77. See Chapter X document I etc. and this Chapter document VIII.

VI

Clamorgan to Casa Calvo, New Orleans, April 27, 1801[1]

To His Excellency
The Marqués de Casa Calvo
Governor General of the Province of Louisiana

The suppliant has the honor of exposing to you that it pleased your kindness to continue to the Company of the Upper Missouri the enjoyment of the posts of the Octoctatas, Mahas, and Poncas during the duration of the time which the exclusive privilege of His Majesty is to last, but since that time Your Excellency had disposed differently this year of the post of the Octoctatas of which the Company finds itself deprived at this moment[2]—although it is of the greatest importance to the Company to enjoy it, in order to render easy the passage of its boats destined for the Upper Missouri, as well as to establish there the seat of a convocation of the Maha nation, in order to take steps with that nation for the re-establishment of the union which was completely broken last winter by a war openly declared against the agents of the said Company[3] who suffered a battle in which there were killed and wounded on both sides. It appears that a continuation of hostilities was stimulated by the commerce of the English nation which filters in there profusely.

In this unfortunate circumstance the suppliant desires that it please you to accord him the trade of the Kansas nation and dependencies as well as the trade of the Pani-Loups in order to enjoy it jointly with the trade of the Mahas and Poncas and to take the place of the loss that the Company is undergoing in the Octoctata nation, of whose trade it is deprived this year.[4] The suppliant renders thanks to you for your kindness.

New Orleans, April 27, 1801.

Jacques Clamorgan   [rubric]

New Orleans, May 2, 1801.

Conceded to this party for one year the trade which he solicits of the Kansas and Loup-Pani nations.[5]

Casa Calvo   [rubric]

---

[1] Written in French. Missouri Historical Society, Clamorgan Collection and in Pierre Chouteau Collection.
[2] See document III and Chapter VII document I.
[3] See document V and, *e.g.*, Chapter VIII, document IV.
[4] See Chapter VII, document I.
[5] This together with requests in document V having been granted to him, Clamorgan had practically the entire trade of the Missouri with the exception of the Osages and some of the Panis. See Delassus to Salcedo, no. 142, St. Louis, May 13, 1802, A.G.I., P. de C., leg. 77. But it should be noted that these grants were made or rather conceded to him in his name and not in the name of the company.

635

VII

ARTICLES OF AGREEMENT BETWEEN LOISEL AND HENEY, ST. LOUIS, JULY 6, 1801[1]

Convention de Commerce with the nations of the Upper Missouri drawn up according to the articles hereinafter stipulated, between S*r* Regis Loisel, merchant living in St. Louis, as party of the first part and S*r* Hugh Heney, at present in this city, as the party of the second part. To Wit:

Article 1.

There shall be between the two parties a *Société en portions d'interest* for S*r* Loisel 2/3 [and] Sr. Hugh Heney 1/3 both of the expenses, losses, as well as of the profits which will result from all the operations of their commerce which is to last for the term and entire and consecutive period of two years dating from today and ending at a similar day of the year 1803, and in the case that there should remain of the merchandise unsold belonging to the said *Société* at the end of the said term of two years, the one of the two who shall remain in the said posts for his private account shall be obliged to keep them for himself upon paying to the said *Société* what they will have cost delivered on the upper part.

Article 2

Since neither of the abovementioned associates places any capital in the present *Société*, at present belonging to them, they will make use of the advances which Mr. Auguste Chouteau, merchant of this city, offers to them to open the commerce which they propose to undertake.

Article 3

The merchandise necessary for the commerce of the above mentioned associates for two years only and no longer, will be demanded by a note signed by the said associates or by one alone authorized by the other under the denomination of Loisel and Heney.

Article 4

All the merchandise, furs and other effects belonging or being for the account of the said associates shall be marked with the following mark "L. H."

---

[1]Written in French. Missouri Historical Society, Auguste Chouteau Collection. Also printed from the same source in Abel, *Tabeau's Narrative*, 231-233. I have translated this from my own photostat and it is slightly different from that published by Abel. For a discussion of this partnership and venture see Abel, *Tabeau's Narrative*, 24-26; 233-234.

Article 5

None of the associates shall be able to take from the bulk [capital] of the business any funds or any sum to be reckoned as deduction on the share of the future profits in the business of the present *Société*.

Article 6

Each associate shall have the right to take from the storehouse of the present *Société* that which he will need for his personal use at the price of the equipment and, if he wishes to take any thing in addition to his share, it shall be charged against his account at the same price as for the *engagés*.

Article 7

There shall be kept account books for credit and debit [intake and outgo] so that each associate may know the balance of the operations of the said *Société*. This shall be made each year at the most convenient time.

Article 8

All the hiring of *engagés*, agents [*commis*] and interpreters as well as all other kinds of agreements made by Sr. Loisel and in his own and private name, relative to the present expedition and *Société* are to the profit, charge and account of the said *Société*.

Article 9

None of the associates shall be responsible to the other for the debts incurred before or during the course of the present *Société*, in his own and private name.

Article 10

At the expiration of the two years that the present *Société* is to last, the liquidation shall be made by the above mentioned associates for all which might have been contracted, decayed, disappeared or expired [lost]

Article 11

In case or at the dissolution of the present *Société* there will be found a void [deficit] in the business through any unexpected event then each associate will give reciprocal security for the balance of what the said *Société* might owe up to the time of its complete liquidation.

Article 12

In case of the death of one of the associates before the complete conversion of all the merchandise, demanded or purchased for the account of the present *Société,* the survivor will terminate by converting them for the expense, account and profit of it [*Société*] and will be obliged to render account to the heirs or representatives of the deceased when it shall be required of him, remitting to them the share and portion of benefit that could result from all the operations of their *Société.*

Thus granted and agreed upon between the said Sr. Regis Loisel, party of the first part, and Sr. Hugh Heney, party of the second part, who respectively obligate themselves to execute each one of the articles hereinabove drawn up in their form and tenor. In testimony of which the said associates above named have signed in the presence of witnesses, likewise undersigned. At St. Louis, this sixth day of July, 1801. Made in duplicate and in good faith. Article 8 one word struck out—[is] nothing.

Witness:

Auguste Chouteau	Regis Loisel
[rubric]	[rubric]
	Hugh Heney
	[rubric]

VIII

Delassus to Casa Calvo, St. Louis, August 3, 1801[1]

No. 101

Don Santiago Clamorgan having arrived at this post after the posts of trade with the Indian nations had been distributed, I have not been able to fulfill Your Excellency's order of conceding to him for this year the trade of the Kansas and Loups-Panis nations,[2] since the traders, Don Gregorio Sarpy for the Kansas and Don Benito Vasquez with the Loups-Panis, to whom I had conceded them as I forewarned Your Excellency in my official letter Number 61, dated November 29,[3] had already left. Not having had a contrary order from Your Excellency in reply to the cited official letter[4] I ordered this and I have not been able to countermand this order because a ruinous harm would result to the aforementioned Sarpy and Vasquez, while such would not to Clamorgan by his not

---

[1]Written in Spanish. A.G.I., P. de C., leg. 72.
[2]See document VI. See also document V and Chapter VII, document I.
[3]Chapter VIII, document IX and XI.
[4]Chapter VIII, document XI.

going. The latter will suffer no loss by waiting until next year in order to enjoy his privilege, as I have forewarned him and he is informed.

May God keep Your Excellency many years.

St. Louis, Illinois, August 3, 1801.

Carlos Dehault Delassus   [rubric]

Señor Marqués de Casa Calvo.[5]

---

[5]On August 23, 1801, Salcedo acknowledged receipt of this letter and of its contents. Draft to Delassus on that date, A.G.I., P. de C., leg. 137A.

IX

DELASSUS TO CASA CALVO, ST. LOUIS, AUGUST 3, 1801[1]

Number 95

By the memorial which Don Carlos Sanguinet has presented to Your Excellency and by the decree which Your Excellency has attached thereto,[2] I am informed of your having conceded to him the trade of the Mahas and Poncas for two years.

I can do no less than observe to Your Excellency how much the claim of Don Carlos Sanguinet has surprised me, he being one of the inhabitants of this post who shouts so much and so loudly against the exclusive trades[3] and to such a degree that I have been informed that before making his trip to your city he solicited various traders here to sign a memorial[4] for the purpose of representing to Your Excellency the harm that they claim was resulting to him from the exclusive trades and with the intention of having recourse to the *Sindico del Commercio* [*Syndic* of Commerce] of New Orleans in order to represent it to the *Cabildo*.

Of this a person of confidence secretly forewarned me, but not until after Sanguinet had left for your city. And he also told me that after having reflected they tore up that memorial and made another simpler one to present only to Your Excellency.

I am exposing this to Your Excellency for your due knowledge, believing it necessary because of the local knowledge that I have of this post and of the methods of each inhabitant, merchant, and trader. Your Excellency will be pleased to require my *informe* from them when they claim some branch of trade.

May God keep Your Excellency many years.

St. Louis, Illinois, August 3, 1801.

Carlos Dehault Delassus   [rubric]

---

[1]Written in Spanish. A.G.I., P. de C., leg. 72.
[2]Document III.
[3]*E.g.* see Chapter VIII, document X.
[4]Chapter VIII, document X.

Señor Marqués de Casa Calvo.

[Draft of Reply][5]

I have seen what you tell me in official letter number 95 concerning the memorial of Don Carlos Sanguinet to whom my predecessor the Marqués de Casa Calvo conceded the trade of the Mahas and Poncas for two years.

What you tell me concerning this particular gives rise to my idea of warning you to inform me, in all truth and sincerity, what you think of a particular individual in view of the experience which you have acquired regarding various advantages and inconveniences. [You should tell me] who the subjects are to whom trades might be conceded and to which ones they should not be granted, together with a true relation of the nations; the product of each one, and all other information which may contribute to forming a concept on this matter, bearing in mind what you told my predecessor in official letter number 29, of November, 1800[6] as well as the concession of the Osages made in favor of Don Augusto Chouteau for his services.

It will be best that I have this information as soon as possible so that I may plan the dispositions which seem to me consequent to the best arrangement and satisfaction of your inhabitants.

God keep you many years. New Orleans, August 22, 1801. [to] *Señor* Carlos de Lassus.

---

[5]A.G.I., P. de C., leg. 137A.
[6]Chapter VIII, document IX.

X

Delassus to Casa Calvo, St. Louis, September 29, 1801[1]
Number 108

By Your Excellency's orders dated December thirtieth, last year,[2] the duplicate of which it pleased you to send me under date of May seventh of this year, I am informed that Your Excellency approves my opinion concerning the exclusive trades,[3] and the other matters of which it warns me for my exact fulfillment; and on the first occasion that presents itself I shall remit to Your Excellency the *estado* of how they have been distributed this year by your order, proposing also the subjects who appear to me apt and worthy of enjoying this privilege, reserving one [trade or share] for myself, according to and for the reasons which Your Excellency forewarns me and which it has pleased Your Excellency to concede to me for the expenses which I am incurring here which truly are excessive.

---

[1]Written in Spanish. A.G.I., P. de C., leg. 72.
[2]See Chapter VIII, document XI
[3]See Chapter VIII, document IX.

Your Excellency has been badly informed, since in the *estado* which I remitted to you[4] there are included all the trades which I found exclusive and I have proposed to Your Excellency one more which up to the present has not existed, that is, the trade of the Moingona river which Your Excellency has conceded to Don Bernardo Pratte for the term of four years.[5]

And the report of the murder which was said to have been committed on the person of *Héné*[6] has been proved false, the latter having presented himself here after some extraordinary work in escaping from the different Indian nations who pursued him, and, at the present time is again *en route* following the same undertaking, the *señores* Chouteau and Clamorgan having equipped him again.[7] Notwithstanding the loss which they suffered last year they persist in their project of continuing the discoveries and they have given him an intelligent traveling companion,[8] also for the undertaking, with orders to go as far as possible up the Missouri.

I am informing Your Excellency of all this for your intelligence.

May God keep Your Excellency many years. St. Louis, Illinois. September 29, 1801.

Carlos Dehault Delassus [rubric]

Señor Marqués de Casa Calvo.

---

[4]Chapter VIII, document IX.
[5]Pratte's memorial, dated St. Louis, December 1, 1800, in which he asked for the trade of the Des Moines river for six years, is in A.G.I., P. de C., leg. 71A. Casa Calvo granted it to him for four years. Delassus to Casa Calvo, no. 81, St. Louis, April 3, 1801, is in A.G.I., P. de C., leg. 72. Cited in Chapter VII, document IV, note 2.
[6]Chapter VIII, documents IX and XI, and this Chapter document V.
[7]Document VII.
[8]Loisel. See *American State Papers, Public Lands*, II, 567, and Abel, *Tabeau's Narrative*, 24-26.

XI

DELASSUS TO CASA CALVO, ST. LOUIS, OCTOBER 7, 1801[1]

Number 114

Enclosed I am remitting to Your Excellency three representations signed by various inhabitants of all classes of this post and of that of San Carlos of Missouri, which Manuel Lisa (a merchant established in this post for two years) remitted to me with the memorial, also enclosed, and having informed myself of its contents I have believed it prudent and my duty to remit them to Your Excellency immediately, as I have ordered signified to the said Lisa by my decree to the said memorial.

---

[1]Written in Spanish. A.G.I., P. de C., leg. 70B. See documents XII and XIII. The three representations refer to three copies of Document XIII: 1) for the *regidores of the Cabildo* of New Orleans; 2) for the governor-general; and 3) for the Intendant-general. Documents XII and XIV.

Although I have nothing to add to what I have already informed Your Excellency in my official letter number 61, dated November 29, 1800,[2] I would desire that Your Excellency inform himself from Lieutenant-Colonel Zenon Trudeau, my predecessor, who knows by experience the prejudicial abuse which the liberty of the trades of the Missouri caused both to the public tranquility and to each individual trader in the year 1792.[3] There are many now petitioning who should still remember having lost their funds in that year. The following year a company was formed from among some merchants, some of whom are the ones who have signed it.[4]

I could answer and represent against all that is contained in this long representation but I find it useless, considering that Your Excellency, better than anyone else, will see how absurd it is, and I shall restrict myself to observing to Your Excellency only that the greater part of those who have agreed to it are not notable inhabitants as the enclosed explanatory list shows and among the few who are, are some fathers of honorable families who by their small talent or bad turn in their business are like so many in this world with only the bare necessities for living and very envious of the advantages which their neighbors have obtained through their perseverance in what they undertake with talent and conduct, and they have surely signed this representation without being informed of its contents, influenced alone by the insinuations of the said Lisa who since his return from your post here has concocted this scheme, spreading rumors sufficient to remove the confidence which these inhabitants (docile but credulous and ignorant) have in our government.

The following are, as I have been informed indirectly, the rumors: "that Your Excellency does not have the privilege nor authority to concede the exclusive commerce of the Indian trades; and that in representing that his brother-in-law, Don Juan de Castañedo, *regidor perpetual* and Don—Argote in your post had assured him [Lisa] that the trade would be free; that the *ramo de Indias* would pass to the direction of the Intendancy, that the representations in case of necessity would even go to Madrid, etc."

That Lisa is doing all possible perhaps in order that his creditors in your post believe that the failure of his payments originate from the exclusive trades, is very credible, because he is making a false show here of the very many expenses which he is continually making. I believe that he is selling very little because few inhabitants like to trade with him because many times it ends in disputes on his part and in view of this it seems credible that he may be looking for all means to gain time.

---

[2] Chapter VIII, document IX.
[3] See documents in Chapters I and II.
[4] Documents on the founding of the Company are in Chapter II.

But the inconsistency of the *señores* Carlos Sanguinet, Don Santiago Chauvin[5] and Gregorio Sarpy is incredible, since the first named has merited from Your Excellency's goodness the exclusive trade of the Mahas and Poncas nations for two years, counting from this year.[6] The second has also merited from Your Excellency the Panis for this year.[7] And Sarpy has reaped profit from the Kansas nation exclusively for three successive years[8] and this year, in view of the losses which he suffered last year, I have conceded it to him which resulted in damage to Don Santiago Clamorgan as I have informed Your Excellency.

What then are the motives which could have incited these three men to sign the representations, (in my opinion, false in all their points) which are against their personal interests because it is notorious that if they achieve what they ask, commerce being free there is no doubt that except possibly by chance they will not reap a 1/100th part of what they can obtain by having the exclusive trade which they are at present enjoying.

How can it be presumed that it is through public generosity when Sanguinet is the father of a numerous family which he has to maintain or perhaps is it because he sees that effectively he is not wealthy enough to risk an entire equipment by himself, having equipped one-half with Robidou in the trades of the Mahas and Poncas which are conceded to him?

Chauvin and Sarpy [are] heavily obligated—will it also be for the public good? No. Immediately it is seen that it is a lack of reflection on their part in having allowed themselves to be influenced by Lisa's reasons, because I should not like to accuse them of being of a perturbing nature or envious persons, comprehending that they finishing the time of their privilege may wish to impede others from taking advantage of the same grace from which they reaped profit, ruining the little which remains from this productive branch of commerce because there is no doubt that if the liberty of commerce is effected as they ask, by trading with the few nations which remain in the Missouri, from the instant that it is published, they will all run to their ruin to the envy of each other and from this will result disputes with the Indians, battles, murders, resulting in the inhabitants who are cultivators, who are quiet in their habitations, being exposed as victims of the vengeance of the Indians,

---

[5]Sanguinet and Chauvin had joined Robidou and others in such a plea earlier. See Chapter VIII, document X.

[6]See Chapter VII, document I, and other documents in this and the preceding Chapter, *e.g.* Chapter VIII, documents IX and XI and this Chapter documents III, V, and VI.

[7]Document II.

[8]See Chapter VII, documents V and X, and this Chapter, document VI.

643

and the latter will receive bad advice from the traders who by chance will be with them.

Your Excellency will dispose what you consider best.

May God keep Your Excellency many years.

St. Louis, Illinois, October 7, 1801.

Carlos Dehault Delassus [rubric]

Señor Marqués de Casa Calvo.

[enclosure]

List of the individuals who have signed the three representations against the exclusive trades which are remitted under this date to the disposition of the governor of Louisiana with official letter number 114.

Of the town of St. Louis.

The Gentlemen from St. Louis[9]	*Observations*
Manuel de Lisa	Merchant. Came to this town from the post of Vincennes two years ago.
Gregorio Sarpy	Established in this town and merchant here. Has been favored with the privilege against which he is representing and at present enjoys the trade of the Kansas nation.
Carlos Sanguinet	Also resident of this commerce and represents against the privilege which he has solicited and obtained from the government for two years of the trade with the Mahas and Poncas nations.
Patricio Lee	Resident of this commerce.
Don Santiago Chauvin	Very honorable man; father of a large family and in consideration of this he obtained from the government this year the post of the Panis.
Antonio Reilhe	Resident of this trade, very honorable, father of a family and ruined.
F. M. Benoît	Traveller by commissions, [Commission Salesman] who is beginning to trade.
Don Joseph Robidou	Resident of this commerce, father of a large family and ruined because of his envy and undertaking too much.
Jacinto Egliz	Merchant of flour and salt pork.
Francisco Vallois	Ironsmith who cannot give enough to his business for the large amount of work which comes to him from all sides. He is the owner of a billiard table.

---

[9]The memorials (documents XII and XIII) contained all the names listed here by Delassus.

The Gentlemen from St. Louis	Observations
Geronimo Hebert alias Lecomt	Honorable inhabitant with a billiard table. He also sells drinks.
André Landréville	Sutler [*Cantinero*]
Emiliano Yosty	Former soldier of the Louisiana regiment, married here, very honorable man. Sutler.
Juan Bautista Monier	Enlisted by Beral Sarpy as well as Sanguinet, at present by Robidou. Sutler. Saloon keeper.
José Motard	An old Frenchman whom my predecessors have put up with because of pity and besides being a bad subject he is scorned generally by the honest class.

San Carlos de Missouri The Gentlemen	Observations
Antonio Janis	Inhabitant and cultivator.
Piché	Sutler. commissioned by Robidou and sometimes by Sarpy.
Basilio Proulx	Ruined merchant.
Carbonneaux	A poor old man who was master of the *primeras letras* [school teacher].
Joseph Marié	Equipped by various merchants. Sutler.
Antonio Reynal	Surgeon, known by my predecessor.
Joseph Lacroix	Ruined inhabitant.
G. Robt. Spencer	Currier.
Makay Wherry	Merchant.
Prieur	Parish priest.

XII

LISA AND OTHERS TO DELASSUS, ST. LOUIS, OCTOBER 7, 1801[1]

To Don Charles Dehault Delassus, Lieutenant-Governor of Upper Louisiana:

Monsieur:

The undersigned inhabitants of Illinois have the honor of sending to you a *mémoire*[2] which should be presented to the *regidores* of the *Cabildo* of New Orleans, to *Monsieur* the Governor General, and to *Monsieur* the Intendant General of this province. This *mémoire* carries our claims against the exclusive privilege of the trade of peltries. We have the honor of communicating it to you so that in making it known to you, we beg you

---

[1]A.G.I., P. de C., leg. 192. Enclosed with document XI. The original petition is written in French, the latter two parts are written in Spanish.

[2]See Document XIII.

to attest to the general government the justice of the demand, and to certify that this is the unanimous *vocus* of the citizens of this city.

Manuel de Lisa—Gr^e Sarpy—Ch^les Sanguinet—J. H. Robidoux—F. M. Benoît — Patrice Lee — André Landréville — Jacinto Egliz — J. Reilhe—Emiliano Yosti—Carbonneaux—Joseph Mostard—A. Janis—Piché—Jh. Marié—Prieur—Mak. Wherry—J. Robt Spencer—Antoine Reynal—J. Bte. Monier—Lacroix—Chauvin—Fcois. Valois—Gre Hebert dit Le Comte. [One signature illegible.][3]

Don Carlos Dehault Delassus, Lieutenant Colonel of the Royal Armies and Lieutenant-Governor of Upper Louisiana and its Dependencies, etc.

Having seen the present memorial and the three which accompany it,[4] the ones which *Señor* Manuel de Lisa has remitted to me requesting that they be sent on to the disposition of the *Señor* Governor by the first occasion so that Your Excellency may order or dispose what you might find most convenient or best. Thus I did In the city of St. Louis, the seventh of October of the year 1801.

Carlos Dehault Delassus [rubric]

To Don Joseph Hortiz, performing the function of public scrivener in this city of St. Louis, Illinois, by order of the *Señor* Lieutenant Governor of this Upper Louisiana: I notified the preceding decree to Don Manuel Lisa in his domicile and speaking to him in person in the presence of Don Francisco Valois and Don Pedro Laffillard. In truth of which they as assisting witnesses signed it together with me.

St. Louis, October 7, 1801.

Joseph Hortiz [rubric] Frcois Valois [rubric] P. Laffillard [rubric]

---

[3] Basil Proulx.
[4] Document XIII.

XIII

Memorial by Lisa and Others to the Governor, St. Louis, October 8, 1801[1]

Copy of a memorial addressed to His Excellency by various persons in Illinois.

Señor Gobernador General

The inhabitants of Illinois, who have been suffering for a long time through being excluded from the trade in peltries, the exclusive privilege

---

[1] The original of the French copy is in A.G.I., P. de C., leg. 218, where it is addressed to the governor-general and where it has an N.B. "We believe we should inform you that we have presented this *mémoire* to *Messieurs* the *Regidores* of the *Cabildo and to Monsieur* the Intendant General of this province." There is a copy in A.G.I., P. de C., leg. 178 B, from which the translation here given was made; and a torn copy is in A.G.I., P. de C., leg. 2366, from which was made the translation printed

of which has been given to certain individuals of this town,[2] venture, with the fullest confidence, to present before you their just demands; and they are persuaded, *Monseigneur*, that you will direct all your attention to cause the end and suppression of the privileges which discourage all classes of the citizens, and cause many to fear approaching poverty.

The trade in peltries, the sole and only resource which for a long time has supported the commerce of Upper Louisiana, being forbidden to the greater part of the citizens must necessarily involve the ruin of the merchants, who cannot hope to make returns to the metropolis since they are deprived of the only valuable commodity which they could introduce there.

By these exclusions from trading, the commerce of this metropolis must suffer a considerable loss in the fact that, besides the peltries which are no longer received and which go to support the foreign commerce, its storehouses are no longer drawn upon for the same amount as formerly.

In[3] 1783 there were sent from New Orleans for the Illinois ten cargoes valued at 200,000 *piastres;* all was consumed in the country, and the returns were made entirely in peltries. From that period until the

---

in Houck, *Spanish Régime in Missouri*, II, 194-97. I have corrected this printed translation. The heading is "To *Monseigneur* the Governor-General of the Provinces of Lousiana and Dependencies. *Monseigneur.*"

This document translated from French into Spanish was presented to the governor-general and to the Intendant-general (in neither case is Manuel Lisa's name on the list of signatures, although there are 33 or 34 signatures). The translation for the governor-general was certified to as being an "accurate translation in conformity with the original memorial written in French which Don Manuel de Lisa has exhibited to me." Pedro Derbigny [rubric]. New Orleans, October 30, 1801, A.G.I., P. de C., leg. 178B. The same to the Intendant-general certified in the same manner and signed by Pedro Derbigny [rubric], New Orleans, November 5, 1801, is in A.G.I., P. de C., leg. 600.

Clamorgan had been attacked by jealous men at the height of his success and when the decline of the Company became obvious, greed motivated the same group in its attempt to destroy his reputation and obtain his privileges. Joseph Robidou was the foremost early one of those attackers. See Clamorgan to Governor [Carondelet], St. Louis, May 26, 1796, A.G.I., P. de C., leg. 215; Robidou to Gayoso de Lemos, St. Louis, March 7, 1798, Bancroft Library; Gayoso de Lemos to Trudeau, New Orleans, April 24, 1798, A.G.I., P. de C., leg. 44; Trudeau to Gayoso de Lemos, St. Louis, November 15, 1798, Bancroft Library. Robidou joined with Reilhe and a few others in a petition or memorial dated December 8, 1800, A.G.I., P. de C., leg. 217. Having failed in these efforts Robidou gained a formidable ally in his schemes in the person of Manuel de Lisa, long a trader and troublemaker in St. Louis. Together with Sarpy and Benoît they sought approval of Delassus in an effort to gain the power of attorney for all the inhabitants, but Delassus refused (Delassus to Salcedo, no. 116, St. Louis, October 15, 1800, A.G.I., P. de C., leg. 77). Lisa was not stopped, however. Now in October Lisa remitted the three memorials (document XIII) signed by persons of St. Louis and St. Charles. Delassus disapproved but forwarded to New Orleans the memorials together with his arguments and characterizations of the signers (documents XI and XII). This mighty effort only resulted in a reply which was a poetic exhortation to the people to return to the blessings of agriculture, in reality a curt and decisive refusal to the petition.

[2]See Chapter VII, document I, and various other documents in Chapters VII, VIII, and IX.

[3]This and the following paragraph are strikingly similar to two paragraphs in document X in Chapter VIII.

time when the exclusive privileges were given, the commerce of this city drew annually from the metropolis a value of 150,000 to 180,000 *piastres.* But what is the value that the commerce draws from it to-day? It does not amount here annually to 30,000 *piastres,* not counting what is obtained from the metropolis by those holding exclusive privileges.

It is true, there is no doubt that the commerce in peltries has greatly diminished: but enough of it still remains to secure the welfare of all those who could participate in it. The posts on the Missouri alone yield annually a total of 2,500 packs [of furs] at the lowest calculation—for they can produce more. The peltries, which can be valued at the sum of 100,000 *piastres,*[4] if distributed and put into circulation would encourage all the inhabitants. The trader, stimulated by eagerness for gain, and restrained by fear of losing the confidence of the merchant, [would make a fortune for his family] [and he] would give all his attention to curbing the savages, and to securing the most important parts of the exploitation entrusted to him. The *engagé,* sure of receiving his salary in current money, would become more careful and economical, in the hope of acquiring some landed property.

The tiller of the soil, assured of selling his products and of receiving a price at their current value, would increase his means [of production], and would give all his attention to agriculture. We would see industry revive; speculations would quickly follow one another; and various enterprises would be formed which would tend to regenerate the country and make it flourish.

If commerce were free, and every individual could have a claim on the trade, there would be a much greater consumption of merchandise. With the peltries reverting to all, there would be abundance of business; the circulation being general and plentiful, consumption would increase in proportion; and the metropolis, from which the people would be obliged to obtain their merchandise, would find therein a great benefit.

Exclusion from the commerce is the worst scourge which this country can experience. This country demands all the encouragement possible, in order to bring it to the degree of splendor of which it is capable.

Exclusion enervates courage, withers imagination, and ruins industry; and, without mentioning the particular evils to which it gives birth, we shall say that exclusive privileges are contrary to all laws, civil and political, and wound natural equity.

Monseigneur, you probably know that peltry is the only article of merchandise which represents here specie money; and if it is owned exclusively by a few private persons, what hope is there for other individuals, what resource for the merchants? Checked in all their plans, their com-

---

[4] Chapter VIII, document X, says 3500 packs and 140,000 *piastres,* the base figure per pack being the same.

merce languishes, their invested capital remains shut up in their warehouses; all is ruined or damaged. The time for payment arrives and the unfortunate man does not know where to look for his first *sueldo* with which to meet his obligations; pursued by his creditors, he makes a great sacrifice, and his innocent family, stripped, suffer losses which could not be foreseen.

The distressed farmer no longer can place his commodities, being entirely dependent on those who alone possess the privileges, and is obliged to furnish his produce at the prices which they are willing to allow to him for it—fortunate, besides, in receiving articles of merchandise, which given in payment, are sold to him by their weight in gold. Despair in his heart, he is most often left in inaction and does no more work than is enough for the existence of his family.

It would be a great mistake to suppose that it is a matter of indifference, and even greater to think that it is advantageous to the public welfare, that the trading-posts should be operated by a single man exclusively. Not only are the savages not restrained either more or less, but the advantage is found entirely with him who enjoys the privilege; all the produce of the trade remains with him, and all the expenses of the trade besides. Still more the wages of the employees do not go out of his house, for he takes great care to pay them in merchandise—so that, as he receives all the peltries, the other merchants can obtain from the *engagés* only such outlay as he cannot prevent from going outside, and it is always the smallest quantity possible. No advantage, then, remains for the public, since nothing is put into circulation; and it is only fully recognized that the circulation of money, or that of a valuable article which represents it, makes the wealth of business men, procures abundance and prosperity in the country, and in general secures the welfare of all the individuals who inhabit it.

With exclusion [from the trade] abolished, every one would try to procure for himself a part of the money so necessary to the extension of commerce. Then would be seen many persons employed in carrying on operations at the various trading-posts; the traders, vying with one another to make their way into the interior of the country, would seek out the Indian tribes in the hope of conducting a more prosperous business and they would stimulate [attempt to make] new discoveries [of tribes], which, while increasing the consumption of merchandise, would yield an immense product, and distribute considerable value in this province. The Indians, surrounded by a crowd of white men that were maintained by the general interest, would no longer turn so easily to commit their depredations; and the traders, combined together, would be less exposed to insults from the barbarians.

Fearing lest we weary Your Excellency's attention, it is not in this brief statement that all the disadvantages of the exclusive privileges can be depicted and proved. In whatever way one chooses to consider them, they tend only to cause and hasten the ruin of the country in which they are tolerated. You will find us ready to answer and explain all objections which can be raised in regard to this subject, and to prove more fully how the exclusive privileges have been and always will be injurious especially to these towns.

Your Excellency will therefore be pleased to abolish those privileges, to restore general freedom of commerce in peltries and do justice to our claims. We believe them to be just; they are founded upon the right which our August Monarch has accorded to all his subjects without distinction. In rendering justice to us, in doing the good to which Your Excellency's heart inspires, in facilitating the welfare of the faithful subjects of His Majesty, Your Excellency will cause peace and happiness to spring up again in the hearts of the fathers of families; and Your Excellency will heap up the prayers of an entire people, who will not cease to offer them for you preservation and the prosperity of the kingdom.

Saint Louís, October 8, 1801.

P.S. We think we ought to inform you that we have presented the same memorial to the *Regidores* of the *Cabildo* and to *Monseigneur* the Intendant-General of this province.

[Signed—all rubrics][5]

Manuel de Lisa[6]	Hiacinthe Egliz [Église]
Benito Vazquez	A. Reilhe
Chles Sanguinet	J. Montan [Motard][8]
Gre Sarpy	Emileon Yostie [Yosti]
Jh Robidoux	François Duquette [or Doquelt]
Patrice Lee	Juan Batiste Pujol, fils
F. M. Benoît	J. Bta Piepez
André Landréville[7]	Gabriel Constant

---

[5]The original and copies contain 34 (or 33) signatures. Houck (*Spanish Régime in Missouri*, II, 197) gives but 22. Delassus gives 25 names (document XI). Add: Landréville; Motard, Hébert; Cabil (Gabriel Proulx); Piepez; File; Christoval Seitz.

[6]In the Spanish copies in A.G.I., P. de C., leg. 178B the name of Manuel de Lisa is not included. It is, however, included in the copies in A.G.I., P. de C., legs. 2366 and 600. Delassus headed his list with Manuel de Lisa (document XI). Undoubtedly this petition was presented to others for their signatures and were refused. e.g., see document XIV.

[7]Landréville is not included in the original French in A.G.I., P. de C., leg. 218. He is included in Delassus' list (document XI).

[8]Motard is not included in the original French in A.G.I., P. de C., leg. 218. He is included in Delassus' list (document XI)

L. Lajoye
Jean Leroy
File
Piché
Chauvin
Guillaume Herbert[9] [dit Lecomte
  Carbonneau de Caspiché]
Alexis Marié
Antoine Reynal
Fcois Valois [Vallé]
Basille Proulx
Cabil [sic. Gabriel] Proulx[10]
G. Robt Spencer

Mackey Wherry
J. Bte. Lacroix.
Prieur [Noel Antoine?][11]
J. B^{te} Monier
J. Janis
——Visieltz [?]
Chistoval Seitz
Pier Trogs
V^t Lagotenee
Carbonneaux
T. S. Cerré
Laurent Durocher
Charles Tayon

[On the margin of the preceding document is the following:]

"To *Messieurs* the memoralists for the commerce of the other side. Sirs: You have asked for my opinion; I give it to you.

"I remain, etc."

[The following vehement reply to the memorial is unsigned.][12]

The Government, enlightened as to the necessity of keeping the savage tribes of Missouri in a dependence advantageous to the preservation of the territory, has believed that it ought to grant the privileges of the Indian trade to certain persons rather than to others, in order to avoid the corruption of the tribes which is and always has been entailed in their being frequented by all sorts of white men. Scarcely has experience made the Government understand which of the two modes of conducting the trade, the free or the exclusive, has been more or less favorable to the interests of His Majesty; it has doubtless pleased him by adopting that of exclusion. Where are you, Don Zenon Trudeau—you who have so well known how to secure the attachment of the savage tribes to the banner of His Majesty, you who have led and directed them to suit the interests of the Government? Had you adopted the foolish system of freedom for the Indian commerce in the Missouri, you would certainly have kept

---

[9]Hébert is not included in the original French in A.G.I., P. de C., leg. 218. He is included in Delassus' list (document XI).

[10]Not included in the original French in A.G.I., P. de C., leg. 218. These four must have been signatures to the petition for they are all on the list of men who presented the memorial. Document XII.

[11]François, Antoine and Noel Jean François Prieur were brothers who for over four years had lived in St. Charles. Petition to Delassus for the concession of some land near Portage des Sioux, St. Charles, December 15, 1799 Missouri Historical Society, Clark Collection, No. V.

[12]A.G.I., P. de C. leg., 2366. Contained in the margin. This is printed in Houck, *Spanish Régime in Missouri*, II, 197-208. I have rechecked this translation with the A.G.I., P. de C., leg. 2366 copy only. Delassus' opinion of the memorial is in document XI. His views are also given in Chapter VIII, document IX.

it in check, because your experience had made you understand the necessity of the opposite [policy].

And you, Don Carlos de Lassus, who have followed in the same path, because you have seen that it was useful for the preservation of his Majesty's property, tell me: when your predecessors adopted the [policy] of exclusion from the trade of the Missouri, were they mistaken? Your political lights, your discretion and your accomplishments have without doubt made you recognize the truth of this.

The trade in peltries is precarious; that of the former is founded on solid bases. It would be desirable that the Indian trade give place to agriculture; for then fruitful sources would nourish a commerce which would steadily expand, and with success, in the heart of the capital. Look at your neighbors established on the *Belle Rivière* [Ohio River]; is it peltries or agriculture which is steadily enriching them? Already you see that these new inhabitants, who are hardly emerging from their [political] infancy, no longer recognize the weapon which they employed to make a living when they formed their first settlement in Kentucky; there it is everywhere replaced by the plow, which digs long furrows under the ox, weighted down by his yoke, and the fertile soil rewards amply the generous cares of the farmer. Behold the true source of prosperity and abundance. It is also that which the beneficient government rigorously protects in order to enrich its subjects. So that the authors of the memorial may no longer occupy themselves, then, in insinuating that the fortune of the business men of the capital depends on the skin of the deer that runs in the woods—for which is longing the merchant of the Illinois, who has need to borrow the industry of his neighbors in order to furnish to his family a livelihood less doubtful than that which the trade with the savages procures for them; it must, besides, be believed that it is the policy of the Government to prefer the exclusion of the trade in the Missouri, which is the route to Mexico. This is in order to avoid the pernicious counsels of all the classes and sorts of white men who would enter that trade, as well as to avoid the seductions of foreigners who would thrust themselves into it under feigned names, in order to favor, with the allurement of reward, their commerce and their ambitions, when they are only longing for the means for proceeding over the boundaries of New Mexico. Two advantages apparently ought to result at the present time from the secret views of the Government: first, that of preserving for His Majesty a territory which would soon be invaded by foreigners; second, that of obliging every class of citizens to attach themselves to the source of true good fortune by embracing the industry which recourse to agriculture furnishes them.

If the commerce of the metropolis were suffering, as you, Sirs, who are the authors of the memorial say, a considerable loss, not only from this exclusion from the trade with the savages, but also from the loss which the capital suffers of the peltries which go among the foreigners, then the merchant of the Illinois would find himself overstocked with merchandise which he had obtained from the capital. But on the contrary, *Messieurs* the signers, there is not one of you who has not obtained and who is not still obtaining goods from the foreigners for maintaining his trade not only with the whites, but with all the tribes of the Mississippi, and with those that surround you, without there being the least hindrance to it on the part of the Government; because there is not any dangers from the foreigners to the estates of His Majesty, which the Government is always vigilant to preserve from the approach of their ambition. To the Government alone does it pertain to understand the most effective means for the prosperity of its subjects, because it is against the natural order that it should apply itself to its own destruction.

In 1783 the ten cargoes of which you, *Messieurs* the memorialists, speak were distributed as much on the American side of the Mississippi River as on your own; and, notwithstanding that it has been eighteen or nineteen years since the sale of those goods was made, a very large part of the returns is still unpaid. You know that *Monsieur* so-an-so and *Monsieur* so-and-so doing business in New Orleans, and *Monsieur* so-and-so and *Monsieur* so-and-so at St. Louis, are still unprotected for these outstanding debts—which they have charged to "profit and loss," because the balances due will never be paid, for lack of means. If the cargoes amounted to 200,000 *piastres* as you, Sirs, say, it amounted to at least the value of the revenue of the Illinois for at least five years which Illinois must yield in order to meet its obligations; for it is well known that the returns from Missouri do not yield above 40,000 *piastres* in value for all the peltries which come thence, and with that sum it is necessary to pay for the merchandise outside and the *engagés* inside, and the expenses of equipment—without including therein the risks, which he himself must guarantee without any assurance of profit. According to these facts, which, Sirs, are contained in your archives (for the Lieutenant-Governors have always made, every year, a recapitulation of the returns from the Missouri,)[18] it is evident that the demands which you have represented as flowing from the capital since the year 1783 have anticipated, each successive year, the returns from the Missouris, which were absorbed in advance for five consecutive years by the excessive amount of merchandise which was imported for the consumption of 1783. The adjustment of this ill-advised combination necessarily involved the Illinois in bankruptcy or in an excessive delay of the payment, since the income of five years was necessary to meet their obligations. What has been and what is yet to be the result of this, *Messieurs* the memorialists? This:

---

[18]Some of these are given in the documents in this volume.

that, through the little knowledge which you have of the locality, in the commercial exchanges which exist there, the advances that you have made to the greater number serve in part to liquidate the arrearages of old creditors; and that with you there appears a chasm which your new debtor cannot fill. You make new advances to him the following year, in the hope of breaking away from his clutch; but another, an old creditor, more shrewd, more adroit, or more tricky than you, makes part of your funds avail to pay himself, sometimes for sums which he had believed to be quite lost. Thus, Sirs, the latest comers in the business of the Illinois will always pay those who came earlier; and every shopkeeper will cause the merchant in the capital, in his turn, to complain, the latter being absolutely ignorant that it needs at least the incomes of ten consecutive years in the Illinois to pay his claims. In order to establish a system of prosperity, we must go to the source of the means which oppose it or which conduce to it; and with a guide, Sirs, you will not proceed blindly in the fruitful path the entrance of which you seek. Up to the present, Sirs, the prudent conduct of the Government has kept you back from the sacrifices to which you all would be exposed if every individual had been free to furnish unlimited merchandise to the savage tribes of the Missouri—sacrifices which three times the amount of peltries which come thence could never have recompensed. The Government, since its first organized beginning in the Illinois, knowing well that the fortune of each merchant would not permit him to endure the interruption in his business that was certain if competing shipments of goods entered the Missouri country, has always set limits to that trade. But, Sirs, when one has very little to lose in business one is usually willing to risk much to make a fortune; and this is to be, at the time, neither judicious nor prudent. It is not thus that you tell him the means that it is necessary to adopt "in order to regenerate the country and bring it to a degree of splendor." I say, on the contrary, that this [notion of free trade] would lead the country to eternal ruin. Your demand, Sirs, would be admissible anywhere else than in the traffic with the savage tribes, where industry has no scope; while here the share of talents of each citizen can have no extension, since it is true that the interests of the Government demand that at one time the savages shall receive merchandise and at another be deprived of them, according to the greater or less pressure that it is expedient to exert in order to reduce them to fidelity. After having demonstrated to you the falsity of your principles, it is necessary also to make you understand the rash error into which you have fallen in making the statement that the output of the Missouri region is 2,050 packs of peltries.[14] You can have recourse to all the recapitulations of the Lieutenant-Governors of the Illinois, and you will find that the enumeration has never ex-

---

[14] See note 4.

ceeded 1,200 packs, for usually it is only 1,000 to 1,100. It is, as you see, to carry matters beyond the extreme to put forth the idea that the peltry of the Missouri, if placed in circulation, "would encourage the inhabitant and secure the welfare of the family of every trader"—whereas the trader is usually only a ragamuffin, who has neither hearthstone nor abode, nor wife nor children, save those which the commercial venture entrusted to him induces him to procure among the savages with whom he trades. Therefore, Sirs, not to assert myself longer so harshly to persons who are 500 leagues away, who cannot see things as they really are, as I can who am close by, in reading your statement, Sirs, I cannot fail to see that you are continually imposing on the good faith of your readers. You ignore, or try to ignore, that it is the white men who have corrupted the savage tribes, and that the latter, before the whites went among them, were pliable and docile. Why, then, say in your memorial that the trader would give all care to restraining the savages, when precisely the opposite is known to be the fact? as also that the merchant needs to make choice of the least worthless of the traders in order to entrust to him his venture, if he would not sacrifice the whole of it?

To hear you argue, *Messieurs* the memorialists, one would say that you were not citizens of the Illinois. Has not the farmer of Upper Louisiana the same right as foreigners to carry to the capital the surplus of his consumption in grain, if he has it, and to receive for it its actual value? Answer me, *Messieurs* the memorialists; for I imagine that you were absent-minded in reasoning out this false idea when you set it down in your memorial. So it depends on you, as on every other citizen of the Illinois, to regenerate your country after the example of your neighbors. For it is now 150 years during which you have been sowing wheat, and you have not yet had even the little ability to furnish your capital with that grain, in order to pay for the clothing that you are obliged to ask from it; your new neighbors on the contrary, more industrious, more active, more vigilant than you are or ever will be, go there to seek, under your very eyes, the gold and silver which the treasures of Mexico are obliged to lavish in order to serve as exchange for all the wants of your capital. Do they, like you, call to their aid the deer's back to supply them with bread? In truth, *Messieurs* the memorialists, you are blind to your own interests when you abandon the branch of industry that is certain of prosperity, to run after the exchanges that are made with the savages.

It is useless to disprove anew the [arguments for the] system of liberty for the Indian trade for each individual in the Illinois. "The consumption of merchandise would be great." it is true; but the goods, or at least the greater part of them, would never be paid for, or the payment would remain in arrears, because the limits of the hunting are well known. The exploitation of the Missouri would always be the injury of the merchant, and without question would recoil upon the capital, which would have no hope of making its collections if the dealer who next handles the goods lacks funds to fill the gap therein.

Still again it must be repeated, "Go, draw from the lap of agriculture, which is the true prosperity and the inexhaustible source of happiness;" for then I will listen to you. If at this time the Government, prudent and economical in the distribution of its bounties, places obstacles and hindrances to your general industry, let it be permitted to act thus from legitimate representations; but until that time you will incur derision if you establish the prosperity of the colony on the deer that runs in the woods, for whose skin you long in order to exchange it for goods which you have obtained from the capital—without being able to consume them, you say. You deceive yourselves, *Messieurs* the memorialists. Excuse my frankness; but I know that *Monsieur* so-and-so, *Monsieur* so-and-so, and *Monsieur* so-and-so go themselves or sometimes send others to buy goods at the capital on their credit. But *Monsieur* so-and-so, *Monsieur* so-and-so, *Monsieur* so-and-so, *Monsieur* so-and-so, *Monsieur* so-and-so, *Monsieur* so-and-so, *Monsieur* so-and-so, *Monsieur* so-and-so, and *Monsieur* so-and-so[15] are not farmers and do not transact business at the capital or anywhere; why, then did you ask for some useless signatures? It is true they keep a tavern or a billiard room,[16] and that the more *engagés* there are dependent on you, or negroes robbing their master, the more their trade will be profitable and showy. But, *Messieurs,* enlighten me, I pray you, in regard to the reckoning of *Monsieur* so-and-so, *Monsieur* so-and-so, *Monsieur* so-and-so, *Monsieur* so-and-so, and *Monsieur* so-and-so;[17] do you take them for Merchants of the Illinois? At this place I protest, Sirs, and I openly declare to you that you confound, in a contemptible manner, qualities and titles which I believed you more capable of appreciating. In fine, of a man who is useless to society of the first comer, who has neither ability nor industry nor capacity nor talent nor reputation, you immediately make of him a man who has entrance among your select class of merchants. In this manner, Sirs, you have forgotten those who are in the woods in the pursuit of wild animals, whom equally you ought to include in your demands. Ah! I promise you on my faith that if it is necessary to use their names twice, they will take part in it with pleasure. But what the devil will you do with the signature of *Monsieur* so-and-so? Do you fear some colic in the contents of your memorial? And *Monsieur* so-and-so, with his anvil; what are you doing with him among the crowd? His signature ought without doubt to have weight, on account of his calling. On my word, I am obliged to tell you that you are sinking into

[15]There are only three "*Monsieur* so-and-so" in the A.G.I., P. de C., leg. 2366 copy.
[16]See the list in document XI.
[17]There are only three "*Monsieur so-and-so*" in the A.G.I., P. de C., leg 2366 copy.

dotage. Do not be offended if I am sincere; for I am only trying to make you see your error, and that in which you will involve all your readers. You see very well, *Messieurs,* the memorialists, that it was useless to state in your memorial that your invested funds "remain shut up in your warehouses, and that everything is ruined and damaged." Another time, give currency to the truth in a manner more shrewd and adroit, if you wish people to have confidence in it. Take care, then; for if you continually deceive yourself it will become necessary to stop believing you.

Have the goodness, *Messieurs* the memorialists, not to speak of the farmers of your Illinois; for they are slothful enough in general, not to produce enough for their own living. You all know it, Sirs, why deceive yourselves? So let the farmer take pattern by his neighbors on the opposite bank of the Mississippi; he will see their fields producing hemp and flax in abundance; he will see the sheep abounding to offer each year its fleece to its master, in order to shelter him from the inclemencies of climate; he will see the wheat waving at the will of the breeze which tosses it, and promising the farmer a rich harvest, which he conveys, much to your shame, into your own capital, where they draw your treasures from Mexico. Is this branch of prosperity prohibited to your farmers? Answer me, *Messieurs* the memorialists.

Why do you, Sirs, who have drawn up the memorial, bring the public upon the scene? You confound the farmer with the merchant, and the merchant with the trader, while each calling has its separate industry. The welfare of the farmer depends on his plow; that of the merchant depends on his activity in supplying the market of his capital city at times when it is in need of abundance, in order to reap with interest all the advantage of a well-calculated speculation. The trader, who is born and naturally lives in the mire [?] ought to be devoted to the exchanges which are made with the savage tribes, with suitable precautions for the interests and the tranquillity of the tribes, which ought to be kept in ignorance and in subordination by all gentle means, such as continual presents to attach them to us. The Indian trade, in order to conduct it according to the wishes of the Government, can belong to only a very few persons. Besides one must be glad to be able to make sacrifices and act liberally in their behalf; otherwise, there are no connections, no attachment, and no friendship for you. If it ever occurs that the Government shall become weary of possessing its territory, it has only to give up its Missouri to a general freedom of trade. Then the English will soon be the masters of that region, and the Government will have the misfortune of seeing its possessions there taken away from it, through having listened to the demands which are hostile not only to the safety of His Majesty's possessions, but even to local prosperity. In view of the effeminancy, idleness, the sloth of nearly all your Illinois people, it is probable that your young men would allow themselves to be drawn into the foul voluptuousness of the tribes to whom they would fly at a rapid pace, in order to find there a shameful mode of existence in a dissolute life. This would be so many hands the less for agriculture in the next generation, for which the Government ought always to foresee. It might well be desired, Sirs, for the advantage of each individual that there had been no Indian trade; perhaps in that case agriculture would have made the progress that it ought to have attained in these many years. But consider, Sirs, that at the extremities of the rampart which defines your boundaries the Government must be viligant with the savage tribes, and with them embrace all politic means which must tend to dissipate the fears that result from the ambitious desires of your neighbors. You are very lavish in erroneous speculations, Sirs; but it is necessary to know how to reserve something for the future, and not to dissipate in imaginary calculations a prosperity which the Government is under obligation to preserve for your coming generations.

Ah![18] *Messieurs* the memorialists, for the present moment you are declaiming against your own actions and against yourselves. You have without doubt forgotten that in the year 1794 all those who are assuming the title of "merchants to the Illinois," in whose number you, Sirs, are, formed an assembly under the auspices of Don Zenon Trudeau, formerly Lieutenant-Governor of your Upper Louisiana, in order to obtain from the general Government the exclusive right of discoveries on the Upper Missouri, in order to carry on the Indian trade there during twelve consecutive years. You have, moreover, forgotten the general Government— which kindly obtained from His Majesty the ratification of your claims, by a decree which exists in your archives.[19] What gratitude did you return to the zeal of the Government to be useful to you? It saw all those who have at this time signed your memorial hand in their resignations to the manager of that very Company, in the fear of incurring much expense and making little profit; and that same manager was obliged to depend upon new stockholders to support the enterprise of discovering the tribes permitted by His Majesty. And you dare to present yourselves before the Government to demand favors, after having betrayed and deceived it with impunity! It is for those same stockholders to implore the kindness of the Government to sustain them by some lucrative means in the expenses and repeated losses which they must continually experience—and to which they submit with docile zeal to render themselves useful to the success of a discovery which may become important for the future—and not for you, *Messieurs,* the memorialists, who have feared to sacrifice your own in-

---

[18]From here until the beginning of the last paragraph is not in my copy from A.G.I., P. de C., leg. 2366.

[19]See documents in Chapter II.

terests for the prosperity of future generations, in return for which course you would have the Government sacrifice its political views for your benefit. You are straying from the path of reason. Remember the immense losses which have been incurred by this same Company for the Upper Missouri, when, going among the tribes below, with equipments which were plundered, they gave law to vessels and forbade them to go any farther, under penalty of death. How many presents has it not been necessary to promise for the future, and how many has it not been necessary to give to the very savages among whom you would desire that all the whites should have freedom to thrust themselves in! Ah! they are already sufficiently wicked, without giving them masters to teach them to be worse. To hear you speak, Sirs, it would appear that the Indian trade of the Missouri is the general key to your prosperity; you have, notwithstanding, only five different tribes there, and outside of the Missouri you have five times as many of them, with whom every individual can trade without hindrance, because they are not, like the tribes of the Missouri, on the routes which lead to Mexico. Believe me, then, Sirs, the Government is wise not to permit every one to rush in there. There is another reason, Sirs, against which the Company of the Upper Missouri would cry out if this regulation were changed; it is the danger of continually seeing their expeditions stopped, cut off, plundered by the tribes of the Lower Missouri, if these latter did not remain dependent for receiving the things they need on those very stockholders who are risking their fortunes and their credit in order to go exploring.[20] I conclude by telling you, *Messieurs* the memorialists, that it would have been quite in the order of things to have not excluded you from partnership in the privileged commerce that was granted by His Majesty; and that you would, like the actual stockholders, have borne the losses that the Company has suffered every year on the Upper Missouri, and would equally have profited by the mediocrity of the advantages that are furnished by the trade of the Lower Missouri—which His Excellency Baron de Carondelet believed must necessarily be granted to some proprietors, in order to facilitate the passage of the company's supplies. But you, Sirs, have tried to select the business of the trade; that is not just. Remember that the savages have plundered on the Missouri, at the instigation of the English, four complete expeditions of this same Company, which amount to considerable sums; and that it needs many years and great success to restore to the level the funds which have supplied this enterprise. Do you not know, Sirs, that if the Company should unfortunately cease to procure for the tribes of the Upper Missouri the necessary articles to which they are accustomed, the English would not delay to overrun that country again, by way of Hudson Bay and Lake Onepik—[Winnepeg] to which

[20]These arguments reflect the influence of Clamorgan.

the river of the Osseniboines, [Assiniboine.] which falls into the lake, approaches exceedingly close. You know, Sirs, the contest of *Sieur* Evans, agent of the Company, in 1796 to cause the British flag to be lowered among the Mandan tribe, when he caused that of His Catholic Majesty to be hoisted, while on his expedition to find the Western Sea.[21] In this the English were repulsed, with the aid of the savage tribes, who from that hour acknowledged the standard of His Majesty, by means of the presents which the Company carried to them in order to secure their friendship and affection—in the expense of which, *Messieurs* the memoralists, you would have been obliged to share in order to be somewhat justified in your demands.

Believe me, Sirs, believe me: leave the political administration of the Missouri to the wisdom of the Government; and if you positively will make your industry stagnate in the traffic confined to savages, take flight among the tribes of Upper Louisiana who surround you, and you will find there the means to display your talents. For the Government, far from ever having placed any obstacle in your way, has, on the contrary, favored your enterprises with all its power; but you would rather leave the usufruct of them to the foreigner who comes from five hundred leagues away to despoil you, without saying a word. Doubtless, that does not please you, because there is no hindrance to it on the part of the Government; but if the latter wishes you to do a thing, it has only to oppose it, and I will stake my head that by the next day you begin to cry, "An attempt against our rights!" Believe me Sirs; undertake to incite the farmers—whose name you sometimes utter without knowing what the qualifications of one are—to plow deep furrows, and you will find there the treasure that you desire; and you will be convinced of the wisdom of my opinion.

[21]See documents in Chapter IV, and Chapter V, document II.

XIV

MORO TO ARMESTO, ST. LOUIS, OCTOBER 13, 1801[1]

My Dear and Most Venerated Master:

The information which I am going to submit to your thought arises from the faith which your wonderful heart has inspired in me, and out of respect I beg you to observe secrecy, if by chance I merit this attention. You should not doubt that if this information leaks out you will see me very much hated in this country.

It is then the case that by this opportunity of Don Manuel de Lisa are being sent three petitions from the commerce [merchants][2] of this place, the first directed to that *Señor* governor, the second to the *Señor*

[1]Written in Spanish. A.G.I., P. de C., leg. 188B.
[2]Document XIII. See also documents XI and XII.

Intendant and the last to the *Ayuntamiento* of your city; soliciting that the exclusive rights of the fur trade with the Indians of this country be revoked and for that purpose the said Lisa is going clothed with powers of attorneys. Lisa is authorized to carry their representations to other tribunals.[3] In spite of all the steps which have been practised, I strongly doubt that the purposes will be achieved, because, although I believe the petition just, I know also the abuse of liberty in the said trade, because the competition of the traders who might meet in each nation establishes a jealous rivalry in the prices of mercantile goods; that most of them will not bring back one-half of the capital which they will have taken from here. Therefore it is true that discord is going to give rise to an unexpected number of pamphlets and more writings, beginning as formerly to molest the attention of the government, taking precautions, ways and means regulated by articles, all of which will be reduced to begging with voluminous notebooks [*quadernos*] that each one be obliged by himself to dispatch his goods at a price agreed to by all, by a tariff of duties, which for this purpose they will present to the government in order that it sanction it and give it the force of law.

It is to be noted that the merchants who make their purchases by cash obtain their merchandise at least fifty per cent cheaper than those who trade on credit. The former say: We wish to give our goods at the price which we choose and no one may order our pocketbook! The others say: Gentlemen, you are ruining us and it is best to make a unanimous price in order to avoid bankrupting us! The others answer that they do not agree because then they would not be able to send all of their cargoes, and that the essential point of business consists in reducing goods promptly into cash, in order to buy others and in this manner keep the ball rolling. Who is right? I do not know any text that I may quote, but I am of the opinion that each one is to decide for himself if he is to give his birthright for a platter of lentils!

I have not forgotten yet that the *Señor* Baron de Carondelet made all these trades free, upon his arrival to this post. This gave rise to meetings and more meetings, agreements and more agreements, until they agreed to name, as syndic of this branch, the worthy and never sufficiently praised Mr. Clamorgan whom they begged to exercise his fecund imagination and produce for them adequate rules so that, obliging them all and individually to submit to them, they would not suffer grave losses, which undoubtedly some would, and their small earnings would redound in favor of the others.[4] Nothing daunted the fearlessness of this illustrious Lycurgus, since within a few days he convoked a gathering, placed himself on his syndical throne, coughed and said in an intelligible voice:

---

[3] Document XII.
[4] Documents in Chapters I and II.

"Gentlemen: Since I have been elected and elevated to this syndicate I have not ceased to work, doing my best with that vigilance which is best for the success and certainty of all the precautions which the matter questioned at my election requires, and to fulfill all that you have exposed to me." Grasping a notebook which contained about a half ream of paper he repeated to them: "Gentlemen: I flatter myself beforehand that I will win the very appreciable support of all, as all that I have put in writing which I am going to submit to your sagacity concerns the welfare of all and every one of you individually." After this preface he read to them the contents of that enormous pamphlet without omitting corrolaries, connections, and alphabetic notes, and, it being heard and understood that it was for all, they divided in opinion and each one found his fault, and in the end each one found some pretext for reviling the troubled syndic. One said that such and such an article would cause by its ambiguity such and such damage; another said that such and such an article was only favorable to a small number of individuals which occasioned the overturning of the system of the unappreciated syndic who remained by this time without applause and his provident sagacity and sanity frustrated.

He again set about to stipulate the errors which they had pointed out to him and for that purpose he employed a councillor who served him as a clerk, he not being able to do it by himself, and the poor man had to investigate and thoroughly revise the provident views of this learned legislator. His work finished the assembly was again convoked and all were, just as formerly, of varying opinions; no one understood the other and it approached a *miniature republic*. But nothing dismayed the syndic. He sent them to trade and on their returns there was much misunderstanding.

This happened in 1792. In 1793, there was war with the Osages and no traders were sent to that nation; and in 1794, the *Señor* Baron de Carondelet cut short all these difficulties with his wise sanity conceding the trade of that nation for six years to Don Augusto Chouteau,[5] a young man of talents and merited for his fine personal qualities. He has continued it up to the present.

I am telling you all this because it is a basis for my believing that you are not influenced a little in favor of the exclusive trades which the government conceded at times to some and at times to others and I do not doubt that you will oppose the pretentions of the solicitor, Lisa. I must also inform you that they brought the pamphlets to my house in order that I sign them. I read them and returned them to them saying that it seemed to me that their pretention was just, but I did not sign them because there were articles which did not suit me. They asked me

---

[5]Houck, *Spanish Régime in Missouri*, II, 100-110. Chapter VII, document I.

which ones they were and I told them the objections which occurred to me. These they did not find well founded because in truth I did not tell them all of my opinion since there is a delicate matter of which I did not wish to inform them.

Begging you again not to give out the slightest hint of this, I am reiterating to you that upon my departure from your city last March, you told me in your *secretaría:* Next year I shall remember Moro! I am trusting that you will verify it, since in addition to being a good Spaniard, I have served His Majesty fifteen years with all honor, love and zeal. I shall add frankly that my beloved father, grandfathers, great grandfathers, and great-great grandfathers [may they rest in peace] have contributed with their forces and wealth in favor of the state, which I do not think can be said of Mr. Chouteau or of many other prosperous people here. You will say but Monsieur Chouteau————I am already inferring it; let us not explain ourselves. I cannot do it because the little that I ask is only to support my family and be able to live, and if some day *I am elevated* [?] I shall prove to you physically that I am speaking as a Christian. Do not send me incense which turns into smoke when I need food. And I believe I am somewhat of a creditor of the pity of the government and for this purpose I am enclosing to you with all confidence a memorial for the governor trusting that you will have him decree it favorably to me, for which moreover I will remain thankful to you. I shall look for all occasions which may facilitate me the pleasure to accomodate you, without requiring you to do me the pleasure and honor of a reply because I know the many occupations of your *secretaría* do not give you time for these details. And so I remain reduced to only awaiting the aid for which I am asking, and I beg God to prolong your life many years and aggrandize you to greater employments.

St. Louis, Illinois, October 13, 1801.

Your most faithful and humble servant kisses your hand.

Manuel Gonzalez Moro [rubric]

Señor Don Andrés López Armesto

[enclosure]

Señor Governor General[6]

Don Manuel Gonzalez Moro, resident and merchant of this town of St. Louis, Illinois, with the greatest respect for Your Excellency, exposes that for the alleviation of his family he desires that the merciful benignity of Your Excellency favor him with a post of the fur trade of those which the compassion of the government distributes annually to these fathers of families among the various Indian nations of the Mis-

---

[6]Original with Moro's signature is in A.G.I., P. de C., leg. 188B.

souri river. From this grace the suppliant has not yet profited. He has moreover served His Majesty with distinction for fifteen years in the Regiment of Louisiana with all love and zeal. His merit is well known by almost all the persons of character in your capital.

In consideration of this: He humbly begs Your Excellency to deign to concede to him for the coming year, 1802, the trade in furs of the Panis nation, situated on the said Missouri river or another equivalent [nation] from the many which there are in the said district. For this you will receive the greatest thanks, and he will not cease to beg God to prolong your life many years. St. Louis, Illinois, October 13, 1801.

Manuel Gonzalez Moro [rubric]

[In Margin⁷]
Señor Governor-General

The supplicant is accreditor of the grace for which he solicits, there being present in him the qualities required by the contents of the official letter of the *Señor* Marquéz de Casa Calvo dated December thirtieth of last year, 1800,⁸ relative to the exclusive trades.

Your Excellency will dispose what may be your pleasure.

Delassus [rubric]

---

⁷In margin of original in A.G.I., P. de C., leg. 188B with Delassus' signature.
⁸Chapter VIII, document XI.

XV

DELASSUS TO SALCEDO, ST. LOUIS, OCTOBER 15, 1801¹

Number 116

Since I sent my official letter number 114,² dated October 7, to the *Señor comandante militar* of these provinces, the Marqués de Casa Calvo, the *Señores* Manuel Lisa, Gregorio Sarpy, Don Josef Robidou, and *Señor* Benoît presented themselves before me with two powers-of-attorney written in Lisa's handwriting to be passed and agreed to by me. The first stated that the latter three in the name of all these inhabitants were giving to Manuel Lisa a power-of-attorney in order to present the case in your [city] against the privileges of the exclusive trades that Your Excellency's aforementioned predecessor disposed in favor of some private individuals of this city.³ The second was one that Lisa was sending to his brother-in-law, Don Juan de Castañedo, by virtue of the first, in order to obtain the same end.

I observed to them that I could not grant these powers-of-attorney, because, in addition to the number of notables of these posts being in-

---

¹Written in Spanish. A.G.I., P. de C., leg. 77.
²Document XI.
³Document XII.

sufficient, they [petitioners] had no power from them [notables?] and that the representations that those present and the rest had signed were made without my permission having previously been granted to them to meet, with knowledge of all the commerce of this town and other notables. I also observed to them that the method they were taking was not regular and that I could not grant them those means which may be directed against the prudent and wise orders of this government.⁴ To this Lisa answered me that my determination was forcing him to abandon his business in this post in order to continue his undertaking in the city and today he asked me for his passport which I gave to him on the same date. I am warning Your Excellency to be pleased to wait in order to end the claim of Manuel Lisa in case the latter arrives before the arrival in your city of the sure occasion bearing my cited official letter number 114,⁵ by which Your Excellency will be informed of the matter, reiterating that Manuel Lisa is solely responsible for these representations.

May God keep Your Excellency many years.

St. Louis, Illinois, October 15, 1801.

Carlos Dehault Delassus [rubric]

Señor Don Juan Manuel de Salcedo

---

⁴Document XVI.
⁵Document XI.

XVI

Robidou and Others, Power of Attorney to Lisa, St. Louis, October 7, 1801¹

Don Manuel de Lisa, resident of the post of Illinois and at present residing in this city, before you as the highest legal authority, [*Como mas haya lugar en derecho*] I appear and say: That according to my rights it is best that the present scrivener make authentic copies of the testimonies which I may ask of him for the power-of-attorney which I am duly presenting. In virtue of this I beg Your Excellency to please, it having been presented to you formally, to order that it be carried out as I solicit it, and once fulfilled, to deliver to me the original. For that I am ready to pay its just and due fees.

Therefore I beg Your Excellency to please decide as I beg, with justice, costs, and I swear to whatever is necessary, etc.

Manuel de Lisa [rubric]

As he asks [rubric]

Señor Don Nicholas Fortall; *regidor perpetual and alcalde ordinario* of the first vote [highest voting rank?] of this city and of the jurisdic-

---

¹Written in Spanish. A.G.I., P. de C., leg. 600. This was presented to the Intendant-General on November 6, 1801. Document XVII.

tion of this town—for His Majesty decided it, and signed it in the City of New Orleans October 30, 1801

Nar^{so} Broutin
Public Scrivener [rubric]

On the same day I made it known to Don Manuel de Lisa. I certify.

Broutin
Scrivener [rubric]

In the city of Saint Louis, Illinois, October 7, 1801, in default of a public scrivener, before me, Don Carlos Dehault de Lassus, Lieutenant Colonel of the Royal Armies, *con agregación* to the fixed regiment of Louisiana and Lieutenant-Governor of the Western District of Illinois and dependencies and in the presence of my assisting witnesses, Don Eugenio Álvarez and Don Pedro Lafilar, the undersigned merchants and inhabitants appeared who authorize and give all their power, sufficiently ample as required by law, to permit Don Manuel de Lisa in their names and representing their rights and shares to ask and claim from the Governor-General of these provinces and from any other tribunals concerned the common and general right to the trade in furs with the various Indian nations of the Mississippi and Missouri rivers and in other various districts of the territory of His Majesty in this Upper Louisiana, authorizing him to ask and demand the revocation, abrogation and absolution of the exclusive rights enjoyed at the present time by various individuals here, who monopolize by special grace all the trade in furs in the said districts whose exclusive exceptions frustrate and deprive the community of this commerce [merchants of this town] from participating in the favors which this locale grants. In the capacity of vassals of His Majesty to whom all in genera! are accreditors and if some obstacle may appear to their claims, the said Don Manuel de Lisa, they authorize him to bring [continue] judicial action against any person who might oppose his just right in hearing *autos* and give sentences and continue appeals, supplications, appeals, and conclusions, present documents and proof [evidence], to make the required petitions, and sworn statements and everything that these granting parties might do if they were present because for all that is required and is dependent on them. They give him full power with general administration and faculty to prosecute [bring suit], to substitute and to revoke substitutes, and to appoint others if he finds it best to do so and by his signature obligate their persons and their property which they possess or which they will possess and gives power to the justices of His Majesty and in particular to those of the city of New Orleans to whose Tribunal he submits himself so that it may oblige by sentence passed in the adjudicated cause and agreed to by them.

In virtue of this they signed it with my above mentioned assisting witnesses, which I certify. I, the Lieutenant Governor—J. H. Robidou—Charles Sanguinet—Gre Sarpy—F. M. Benoît—Gme Herbert dit Le Comte—Patrice Lee—Lendresill [Landréville]—Fco Valoi—Hiacente Eglisse—Emilio Yosti—Joseph Molave [Motard]—A. Reilhe—Lovejoye, Fils—Mackay Wherry—Charles Tayon—Alexis Marié—Charles Noy—Jean Baptiste Pujol—Gabriel Constant—L. *frix* Roy and Fult—Basille Proulx—La Croix Kaydesce—Char Bonneaux—Janis—Antoine Reynal—G. Robt. Spencer—Laurent Duroche—Ceré—J. Bte Marié—Prieur—Piché—Fois. Cayne—Uguitate—Chauvin—Piertrog.[2]

Don Joseph Robidou, lieutenant of the militia of this city of Saint Louis: I certify that today the foregoing power of attorney of the notable persons herewith signed was presented to *Señor* Don Carlos Dehault Delassus, Lieutenant Governor of this Upper Louisiana, so that in default of a public scrivener he would legalize it and certify the authorization which the said *Señor* Delassus denied without our knowing what motives there were for his doing so. Because of his having refused it[3]—which I certify, and heedful of the objects which may be best, I beg the *Señor* Governor and Justices in the name of all the undersigned it may please them to add and certify and give credence to the present power-of-attorney since all remain and make themselves responsible with their persons and property for the security of the contract without their being induced or compelled [to make it] for they protest that the said authorization is an act of their own volition.

In virtue of this I signed in this said city, October 8, 1801.

Jh. Robidou.

It is in accord with its original which I returned to the party who remitted it to me, and by virtue of what was ordered by the preceding decree I give the present in the city of New Orleans, October 30, 1801.

Narso Broutin
Public Scrivener [rubric]

[2]See the names given in documents XII, XIII and also XI.
[3]Document XV.

XVII

Manuel de lisa to Intendant-General, New Orleans, November 6, 1801[1]

Señor Intendant-General:

Don Manuel de Lisa, resident and of the commerce of the town of St. Louis, Illinois, residing in this city as proxy [power-of-attorney]

[1]Written in Spanish. A.G.I., P. de C., leg. 600

for various merchants and inhabitants of that post, does present to Your Excellency with due solemnity, the enclosed power-of-attorney and copy of a representation, (the original in French, which was translated into Spanish by the public interpreter), sent to Your Excellency by the above-mentioned inhabitants, like the one they have made to the *Señor* Governor-General, to the end that Your Excellency for your part be pleased to interpose your authority with the said *Señor* Governor, or with whom-ever might have the capacity by the law so that he be pleased to listen to the honest plaints of some faithful subjects of His Majesty, residents of this province, and that he may be pleased to exempt them from the exclusions from the fur trade which today only a few individuals carry on, to the prejudice of the rest, with the Indian nations of the upper posts, as Your Excellency will see by the said representation,[2] and he [you?] may be pleased to declare free to each citizen the right to be able to trade freely as he best can and his wealth permits him, Your Excellency being so kind as to interpose equally that His Excellency be pleased to solicit from His Majesty the declaration of the said freedom of commerce, in order that hereafter it may not be innovated with prej-udice [brought in again to harm anyone] and that Your Excellency will elevate it on your part to His Majesty, you being pleased to inform him of the prejudice that like exclusions are, and the rest, that Your Ex-cellency will be pleased to inform him in favor of the settlers and locale of the province. [This] is a favor that we hope for in the name of all of us, of Your Excellency's sense of justice.

New Orleans, November 6, 1801.

Manuel de Lisa [rubric].

[2]Document XVI.
[3]Document XIII.

XVIII

Victor Collot, Général de Brigade, to Citizen Talley-rand, Minister of Foreign Relations, Paris, 15 Brumaire, An X [November 6, 1801][1]

Citizen Minister:

At the time when the session of the Congress of Amiens is going to regulate definitely the great interests of France and of England,[2] I believe it my duty to send you some observations concerning the fixation of limits which should separate the Spanish possessions in Louisiana which have become French[3] from those of England and of the United States.

[1]Written in French. Archives du Ministère des Affaires Étrangéres Correspond-ance Politique, États-Unis, Supplément, Volume VII, folios 174-176 *verso*.
[2]Peace or Truce of Amiens.
[3]By treaty of San Ildefonso, October, 1800.

One[4] of the principal objects of the treaties of peace between the wise and sincere powers is to avoid future wars or at least to retard their return as long as human foresight can permit.

According[5] to this unquestionable principle the care of positively determining in a clear manner the lines of demarcation which should serve as limits for the territories of the different empires is without contradiction one of the points which should be most forcibly brought to the attention of the government; this wise foresight makes itself felt even more by the countries distant and almost totally unknown in Europe.

At[6] the peace of 1783, [there was] no man, even slightly instructed [no well informed man] inhabiting Canada or the states of the West [but who] knew that the sources of the Mississippi *are situated more than two degrees below the most southern part of the Lake of the Woods.* And moreover it has been established by article two of the treaty between England and the United States that the division of the possessions of these two powers should be a line drawn at the extremity of the Lake of the Woods running due west until it meets the Mississippi.[7] In this article, therefore, we see the capital disadvantage of a fictitious line, of which no point takes or determines the direction, adding to the most complete inaccuracy, the greatest ignorance of the locality; but by following this imaginary line in its direction one would reach the South Sea before meeting with any of the branches of the Mississippi.

Also, it is upon the appearance of this error that England was seen, since the treaty of 1783, to take possession with an audacity which impunity alone can justify—all of which might arouse their cupidity to establish posts and *comptoirs* upon the rivers—*Oupas* [?], and *Catupe,* Red, St. Pierre and Des Moines; rendering herself mistress of commerce of the nations: Sioux, Mandan, Ponca, Sauteux, Panisses, and invade the most populated portion, the richest of Upper Louisiana belonging to His Catholic Majesty and today to France.[8] This violation of international law has been *à la fin* [lately] actively felt by the court of Madrid, since it has been one of the most forcibly expressed griefs in its last manifesto, since the declaration[9] of war against Great Britain.

The necessity then of establishing fixed lines of demarcation in a country today almost unknown but which will soon become of great interest to Europe is evident and it will be necessary in taking possession of this colony that England evacuate the entire immense country which

---

[4]See Collot, *Journey in North America,* II, 252.
[5]Compare, *Ibid.,* II, 252.
[6]See Collot, *Journey in North America,* II, 254.
[7]See treaty of peace of 1783. See also Bemis, *Jay's Treaty.*
[8]See Chapter VII, document II.
[9]Declaration of war, October, 1796.

they have usurped. This would not have occurred had the limits been fixed and determined.

In supposing this state of things unknown to the government, I believe that in order to forewarn the difficulties which might henceforth bring forth jealousy or bad faith, it would be prudent to specify in a special article of the treaty of peace which is going to be concluded between France and England—"That there shall be named on both sides *commissaires* charged with definitely regulating the limits of the territory of the contracting parties in North America." I shall even add that the United States should be invited as an interested party to send such commissioners.

Let it be permitted me, Citizen Minister, to add to these first observations some ideas which might not be useless; those concerning the organization of this precious colony.[10] Upper Louisiana—better known under the name of Illinois Country separated from Lower [Louisiana] by a desert of more than four hundred and fifty leagues, requires on the part of the government the most serious attention.

Every year the heaviest immigration to Louisiana comes from that part of the United States which borders Louisiana. It is of the greatest importance to encourage it but with prudence while watching that it does not become too numerous for then it would be feared that it would stifle [suffocate] the French germs and succeed in changing there the manners, tastes, and even the language: that, according to the commercial and political *rapports,* we have so much interest to conserve. In a word, there should be observed such a proportion between the emigrants of the United States and our French colonies that they could be *forced to incorporate with us and not we with them.*

It is also in Upper Louisiana that there are found the most numerous savage nations. These peoples who while we possessed these countries, were most affectionate to us, detached from our alliance by the intrigues of England and our long absence, have scarcely preserved the memory of the French name. It is necessary to awaken it. It is necessary to re-attach to us, those who already know us only by tradition.

Moreover it is from a point in Illinois, in Upper Louisiana [France], where the immense communication with the South Sea—should be opened, by following the noble course of the Missouri, whose sources, according to all information which I obtained from the places on my last trip,[11] interrupted by the loss of my aide-de-camp,[12] should be separated—from the

---

[10]Collot made many such documents and sent them to the French government or/and its agents. His reports show information obviously given to him by Truteau and/or Mackay. He may have had access to such information through Auguste Chouteau who entertained Collot when he visited in St. Louis.

[11]See Collot, *Journey in North America.*

[12]Warin who died at Arkansas.

waters which flow into the Bay of Don Juan de Fuca and from there into the South Sea—only by a *portage* which I estimate to be at most thirty leagues. It is believed that it will be of the greatest service [utility] that the government have this voyage continued.

Add, Citizen Minister, to this collection of political and military advantages [the fact] that Upper Louisiana contains the richest mines of copper, iron, lead and tin—what an immense exploitation! If, as it is to be preserved, the government established founderies there, immediately.

So many advantages assembled according to so many *rapports* indicate the necessity for an administration which, without ceasing to be linked to the general administration, should be however, totally distinct. The government will understand, then, how to apply so much attention to the choice of the individuals who must compose it, and it will feel that it is indispensable for them to know the language, the men, and the localities.

There, Citizen Minister, is what my zeal and my devotion have suggested to me. You know both. They are without limits.

Salut and respect.

V. Collot [rubric]

XIX

MORALES TO SALCEDO, NEW ORLEANS, NOVEMBER 17, 1801[1]

On the part of the inhabitants of St. Louis, Illinois, there has been a memorial[2] sent to me demonstrating the damages and injuries that they are suffering because of the exclusion with which the *Señores* predecessors of Your Excellency, have distributed the commerce with the Indians, and asking me to serve them as a mediator with you, so that ending the evil from which is proceeding the decadence of that establishment, its inhabitants may find means of subsisting and of assisting [providing] for the maintenance of their families. It appears to me that Your Excellency acceding to their supplications, settling this matter to what may be considered best both to the inhabitants themselves as well as to the Indians, upon whose friendship depends the tranquility of these establishments, would result in its development and by it the increased income of the royal treasury. I am taking the liberty of recommending to Your Excellency the favorable determination of the said *instancias* which I am not enclosing because of stating in the letter of their having sent to Your Excellency another one similar to it.

May God keep Your Excellency many years. New Orleans, November 17, 1801.

Juan Ventura Morales [rubric]

Señor Don Manuel de Salcedo.

[1]Written in Spanish. A.G.I., P. de C., leg. 94.
[2]Document XIII.

CHAPTER X

1802

I

SALCEDO TO DELASSUS, NEW ORLEANS, FEBRUARY 3, 1802[1]

Desiring to give the Company of Discoverers of the Missouri, a further proof of the inclination of the government to further its operations and to guarantee the commerce for our nationals, placing the Company in a position to resist the designs and incursions fomented by the English Companies of Canada: following the system of my predecessors I have agreed to concede for two years, counting from this date, to its Director Don Santiago Clamorgan for the Company and in his name the exclusive trade of the Kansas and other nations from the mouth of the river of that name, Platte River and dependencies, ascending the Missouri, so that by this means its expeditions may have free and prompt passage to the other nations of the Upper part of the said Missouri river, opposing and destroying the designs of the English and in this way recompensing the innumerable losses it [Company] has suffered.[2]

I am advising you of this for your fulfillment in the part which concerns you, having provided the interested party with the corresponding document which accredits it.[3]

May God keep you many years.

New Orleans, February 3, 1802.

Manuel de Salcedo [rubric]

Señor Don Carlos de Lassus[4]

---

[1]Written in Spanish. A.G.I., P. de C., leg. 2367; draft in A.G.I., P. de C., leg. 11 which carries the following note, "Under the same date the document was given to Clamorgan, confined to the same text as the official letter, minus the last page."
[2]See Chapter IX, document V, and Chapter VII, document I.
[3]See note 1 to this document.
[4]Delassus in his official letter no. 142 to Salcedo, dated May 13, 1802, acknowledged receipt of this letter and of its contents. Clamorgan probably carried

this letter on his trip up the river but did not arrive in St. Louis until the end of April, due to a shipwreck which occurrred to him twelve leagues below New Madrid in which he lost all of the ship's cargo. Delassus to Salcedo, no. 137, St. Louis, May 13, 1802, A.G.I., P. de C., leg. 137.

Perrin du Lac says that the "nations inhabiting the banks of the Missouri, with whom alone the merchants of Louisiana trade with advantage," are the Osages, Kansas, Republicans, Octoctatas, Great Panis, Loup, Mahas, Poncas and Ricaras. "The Mandannes, Chaguyennes, and Maniataris partake very little of trade. They carry it on by means of other nations, that buy their furs to sell to the Whites". Perrin du Lac gives figures as to the number of men bearing arms among those tribes and the number of bundles of furs obtained from them. All the nations which he lists, united form a mass of about five thousand hunters. The Paducas yield about fifty and six bundles of fine skins, "and the Ricaras, fifty, almost all fine, and of a superior quality, on account of the animals being taken very far north. Thus the commerce with the people of the Missouri amounts to about 20,000 French livres annually." Perrin du Lac also gives some facts and figures concerning the trade on the Mississippi and of the English. Perrin du Lac, *Voyages dans Les Deux Amériques*—Chapter X, document XII.

II

Delassus to Salcedo, St. Louis, May 13, 1802[1]

Number 143

Don Carlos Sanguinet, inhabitant of this post, presented himself to me and observed to me that the posts of the Mahas and Poncas had been conceded to him for two years,[2] including last year, and as they are included in the exclusive trade which Your Excellency has conceded to Don Santiago Clamorgan, I gave him to understand that Your Excellency had surely and perhaps [*sic*] disposed it thus because you were surprised at seeing his signature on the memorial which they presented in order to obtain that free commerce,[3] and that Your Excellency had seen by this that he did not crave that favor, and he answered me to this that if he was in favor of it, he would do it.

I am forewarning Your Excellency of this in case the aforementioned person presents himself to Your Excellency with some similar claim since he must descend to your city one of these days.

May God keep Your Excellency many years.

St. Louis, Illinois, May 13, 1802

Carlos Dehault Delassus
[rubric]

Señor Don J. Manuel de Salcedo.

---

[1]Written in Spanish. A.G.I., P. de C., leg. 77.
[2]See Chapter IX,, document III.
[3]See Chapter IX, documents XI and XIII.

III

Delassus to Salcedo, St. Louis, May 13, 1802[1]

Number 144

It is with the greatest regret that I see myself forced to inform Your Excellency of the imprudent and seditious conduct of Don Manuel de Lisa, resident and of this trade. In addition to what I forewarned Your Excellency in my official letter number 114,[2] under date of October 7 of last year, he came from your post to this post in January of last year. Upon arriving he began loudly to proclaim in all the billiard halls and other public places that he had been successful in his claims, that he had been very well received by Your Excellency in his representation,[3] but that upon the arrival of Mr. Provencher's *lanchón*, which was carrying my letters, everything was changed; but that he had certain word that the fur trade would be free[4] and that everyone would be able to count on it, he using several indecent words to explain himself which I neither can nor must express. He had proclaimed the same thing in the posts further down through which he had passed, and when the letters which Boyau was bringing from New Madrid arrived, Lisa presented himself here saying to me that they were writing him that they had won the free trades. The same day in the afternoon, upon going into a house to be present at an auction, I found him under a gallery reading a letter. The instant he saw me coming he closed it and said in a loud voice to the person to whom he was reading it "Do you think that I would have come here to deceive everyone, if I had not been sure of the news I was bringing" and that he knew for certain that the trades would be free and shouting the fact which he had strongly expressed that neither I nor my predecessors were to be consulted in this because we were paid for it, even Don Andrés, the secretary himself, who drew the red ball against his claim. [*que tirava a bala Roxa contra pretención*].

Since the arrival of Don Santiago Clamorgan it is rumored that he and several individuals upon his advice are proposing to take other steps in order to obtain that liberty, and if they do not obtain it, they say that they are going to trade with the Indians anyway, which trades are exclusive.

I do not know this last for certain, and as Lisa in a few days is to descend from here with his friend Carlos Sanguinet, it seems to me that it is very convenient for the tranquillity of these inhabitants that Your

---

[1]Written in Spanish. A.G.I., P. de C., leg. 77.

[2]Chapter IX, document XI and XVI.

[3]Chapter IX, document XIII.

[4]Morales had supported the memorial and had urged Salcedo to take favorable action on it. Chapter IX, document XIX.

Excellency be pleased to trouble him in your city and forewarn him that you are sending me the order to observe his conduct and investigate his conversations in order to have him descend at the first similar conversation that he should have, whether in public and with his friends or with those whom he is inducing to error. I hope, since he is the principal motivating influence that when he will learn that he is known by Your Excellency and that the others will know that he is reprimanded, these inhabitants who are generally submissive and of good disposition, but credulous, will be quiet.

I would have sought a method for investigating with more certainty the last point, but perhaps it would become a very delicate cause against him, and in consideration of his family in your post, who are respectable citizens, it seems to me that a reproach from Your Excellency would perhaps suffice to restrain him. In addition I do not ignore that he has proclaimed that my relief would soon come since he had made it known that I did not know how to command, and that perhaps his malice may not think that it may be vengeance on my part, but that he has been persuaded that this precaution originates from *informes* that Your Excellency has had. Since they are public, I can moreover propose to prove what I am advancing by declarations here. He can verify it by the oarsmen of the *lanchones* that descend from here, if you find it best to order his declarations to be taken impartially concerning the contents of this official letter, with the exception of the last article of which I am not certain, but there probably was something to it.

Your Excellency will dispose what you may find best.

May God keep Your Excellency many years.

St. Louis, Illinois, May 13, 1802.

Carlos Dehault Delassus
[rubric]

Señor Don J. Manuel de Salcedo

IV

DELASSUS TO MORALES, ST. LOUIS,
MAY 14, 1802[1]

No. 49

He[3] has no other answer than to manifest to him that he is informed, again charge him to watch that no frauds be committed to the injury of the Royal interests.

Informed of the official letter of Your Excellency of January 21[2] of the present year, I must inform you that furs are at the bottom of all and accordingly more than can be imagined, since the traders who went last winter

---

[1]Written in Spanish. A.G.I., P. de C., leg. 608A.
[2]Copy in Missouri Historical Society; a badly torn draft is in A.G.I., P. de C., 608A. It is illegible. In it Morales speaks of the fur trade and of the sending of

675

and fall to trade with the Indian nations, most of them now find themselves back from their wintering places and most of them have lost so much in this enterprise that they haven't made enough with which to pay for the expenses of their expeditions. All that I have been able to learn concerning the clandestine imports and exports is that some Americans present themselves here against these inhabitants with obligations made more than ten and five years behind, and if they had received their corresponding payments these furs would not have gone to the capital.

It is very possible that the crowd of Americans who come to seek provisions in these establishments may introduce mercantile effects, which will be very difficult to impede, as much because of the proximity of this village with the Pueblo of Kas[4]—[torn] the navigation—[torn] Mississippi—[torn] by virtue of the treaty made in San Lorenzo el Real on October 27, 1795.[5]

Neither can it be denied them to be heard in justice, since the said treaty provided in its article 20 that the subjects of both districts will be admitted in the tribunals to bring suit and make reclamations of their properties. And here there is no other money other than furs.

To stop the introduction of merchandise in this post it would be necessary to establish a certain number of guards,[6] twenty would not be enough, because of all the passes being open, and I believe that the salaries of the guards exceed the amount of the duties received; besides that the fur trade in these countries is in such decadence that it can be said, it is already on its last breath.

The abundance of merchants who are in this land is very prejudicial because—[torn] if they put seriously—[torn] [to the practice of agri-] culture they would draw a greater advantage.

It has come to my notice that in past times, there has here been made a proof, planting hemp, and that it resulted in [the raising of hemp of] a superior quality. I am of the feeling that if, to kindle with passion and animate this branch of agriculture and commerce, Your Excellency would think it well to initiate a price for the account of the royal treasury, whether it be quintals, raw hemp or bundles of a certain size, etc., and that these inhabitants see that their work was paid for, perhaps they

---

goods from New Orleans to St. Louis, the results of which exchange of products had been bad for the commerce of New Orleans and therefore injurious to the royal interests. Morales compared the figures with those for 1781-1782. Morales admits that the fur trade had declined and did not produce now what it had in years before. This was due in part also to clandestine import and export of goods and furs made by the English and Americans. He ordered Delassus to stop such injurious practices, without however incurring expenses. He asked for Delassus' opinions not only for action on his part but also to send to Spain for decision.
[3]Marginal notation.
[4]Kaskaskia.
[5]Pinckney's treaty.
[6]Or garrisons.

would undertake it with ardor and perhaps these establishments would prosper.

This is what it occurs to me to tell you in reply to your cited official letter, except the better counsel of Your Excellency to which I shall submit myself with all zeal, and especially if it is for the good of these countries, and the benefit of the State.

May God keep Your Excellency many years. St. Louis, Illinois, May 14, 1802.[7]

Carlos Dehault Delassus
[rubric]

---

[7]Morales replied on June 2, 1802 (original in Missouri Historical Society, Pierre Chouteau Collection, Spanish Archives of St. Louis, Box I, Envelope I). Morales said that he saw the impossibility of stopping the disorders in Upper Louisiana, "which are being committed on account of the proximity of the foreigners"; he bewailed the lack of assistance on the part of the localities, and told Delassus to use his customary and well known zeal to deal with the problem.

V

LISA AND OTHERS TO SALCEDO, NEW ORLEANS, JUNE 4, 1802[1]

New Orleans—June 12, 1802[2]
granted and correspond-
ing dispatch issued by
the secretary of the
government.

Salcedo [rubric]   *Señor* Governor General

Don Manuel de Lisa, Don Carlos Sanguinet for himself and representing his son-in-law Don Francisco María Benoît, and Don Juan Bautista Sarpy in the name of his brother Don Gregorio Sarpy, all residents and inhabitants of the town of St. Louis, Illinois, expose to Your Excellency with due respect: That impelled by the laudable intentions of obviating the repeated public wrongs occasioned to these representatives and their fellow citizens by the exclusive privilege of fur trade granted to Don Augusto Chouteau,[3] because of this individual alone reaping the benefit from a branch of trade in the promotion of which all the inhabitants are interested, or, rather, in which they are interested for their subsistence. The inhabitants instructed in conjunction with these [memorialists] the corresponding representation in October, last,[4] presenting it to Your

---

[1]Written in Spanish. A.G.I., P. de C., leg. 77; copy in A.G.I., P. de C., leg. 76.
[2]Marginal notation. See Chapter VII, document I, where the grant was made and listed.
[3]Of the Osage Indians.
[4]Chapter IX, document XIII.

Excellency and to the *M.Y.A.*[5] so that through the interposition of this respectable body you might be pleased to restore to them the former general liberty of the said trade with absolute extinction of the exclusive grants. But they have not been successful up to the present time in having any step ordered. This inactivity in a matter of such import has engaged the attention of the present representatives. They confess with the greatest satisfaction the well-known justice of Your Excellency and your zeal for the public good, and they have been prudently persuaded that the government probably has found some difficulties, perhaps insuperable or that require judicious examination and much time for the pending resolution; and persuaded that these just causes can retard it noticeably to the harm of that town, whose interest and common happiness they regard with the greatest love: [Persuaded of all this] they have agreed to a means which, diminishing considerably the common evil or rather exterminating it, can conciliate their own interests and those of almost all the inhabitants of those districts with the right which the privileged ones might have acquired to the commerce in question. It is, that Your Excellency concede to the exponents the exclusive trade corresponding to the post of the Big and Little Osages situated at a half day's journey from the Missouri river about forty or fifty leagues from its mouth, with power to equip the hunters who might wish to enter that river.

This solicitude can only excite sentiments of the pity and justice of which Your Excellency has given unequivocal proofs from the first moment of his taking over the reigns of this government. If it pleases you, harken to the rules of humanity which clamor in favor of the said Don Gregorio Sarpy in view of the destructive fire which last May, consumed a *Tahona de arina* [flour mill?] and a storehouse belonging to him, the value of which and of the articles which were included in it amounted to twenty thousand *pesos* after having maintained commerce since the establishment of St. Louis, due to his cares and the cares of his older brother Don Juan Bautista, now deceased. And moreover your beneficent mind will be moved in the presence of the good which results to the greater part of the said inhabitants because of their being bound by ties of blood and affinity with the exponents to the number of sixty odd families who, reduced to one [family] through good union and harmony which they keep among themselves, should participate in the benefit which results from the exclusive trade.

It is however not the mind of the supplicants to require from Your Excellency a favor which might be prejudicial or painful to the royal interests; rather than that, they are compromising themselves henceforth

---

[5]The representations were presented to the Intendant-General and to the *Cabildo*. See Chapter IX, documents XII, XIII, XV, XVI, XVII, XIX.

in all form to maintain at their expense the redoubt of the Osages, making a donation to the King of two thousand *pesos* which up to the present has been paid annually by the royal treasury for that purpose in order that His Majesty may not have any expense and generally to fulfill the same conditions stipulated by Don Augustin Chouteau in virtue of the same privilege which he obtained up to last year and in order that you may see that the present solicitude involves the common interest of that town and even that of the colony: they obligate themselves also to construct a water-mill with two millstones with which to make flour as good as the flour of the Anglo-Americans.

There is no necessity for lengthening this discourse in order to pursuade you of the public advantages which this proposition offers. The fertile lands of St. Louis are uncultivated because the farmers lack the means to manufacture the wheat which they could produce, and fleeing from an unfruitful work they search for their subsistence elsewhere, from which it results that agriculture is approaching a complete condition of decadence; a decadence which will extend to all the population which because of the circumstances, local and others, can not find in industry and commerce recourse for their maintenance. This capital is provided with the flour which the Americans introduce and they extract all the money that they can collect, accelerating by this means the scarcity which ordinarily causes the retardation of the *situados*. And on the contrary the plan of the representatives carried out, the inhabitants of St. Louis will work their lands in competition to the Americans; that small colony will progress with the development of this branch so protected by laws and profitable to the state; this city will eat the bread made by those vassals of the King without begging it from the foreigners; money will circulate without leaving the province and other things useful to the public good will result.

The commendable proposals of dividing the benefit of the exclusive trade which is solicited among the four representatives and their vast families also offers to the state an advantage of consideration in the greater facility of restraining and subjecting the incursions [*inovaciones—sic*] of the Indians, it being verified that they will do so because of their own interest, as they promise it with greater security and force than if the privilege were to be conceded to one individual alone. For this purpose they will sacrifice their lives and estates for the sake of an object so plausible and interesting to His Majesty no less than to the common and individual welfare of those inhabitants.

It can be affirmed without temerity that the foregoing propositions assure to the exponents the public esteem for honor and patriotism which has led them to this representation, and which could confer upon them grave injury by considering them ambitious and clothing themselves in the name of common happiness.

And in view of all this they beg Your Excellency that through your kindness you may be pleased to concede them the aforesaid exclusive trade in the stated terms for the period of five years and in consequence to issue strict orders to the commandant of the city of St. Louis, in order that for no reason may he forbid the representatives to have the use of the said privilege as soon as they return to that post, which will be about August or September in view of the fact that it is within the appointed time for making commerce and the suspension of this trade is necessary at the beginning of November on account of the considerable cold and ice which is frequent in that climate. Therefore they are hoping for it from Your Excellency's bountiful beneficence.[6]

May God guard Your Excellency's important life many years for the happiness of the colony.

New Orleans, June 4, 1802.

Manuel de Lisa,

Charles Sanguinet, for Gregoire Sarpy, Lille Sarpy[7] [all three rubrics]

---

[6]The complete history and documentation of the Osage trade is given in Nasatir, *Imperial Osage*. Chouteau did not yield his Osage Indian trade without a struggle and in fact held on to it indirectly. For example: On April 30, 1803, Chouteau petitioned Delassus to collect a note for 1500 *livres* agreed to by the associates for the Osage trade. Lisa refused payment. Chouteau entered suit and as soon as this was done Benoît, Sarpy, and Sanguinet agreed to pay each one-fourth of the note—375 each. Lisa refused and Chouteau asked for an attachment on Lisa's funds in the company. Delassus ordered Lisa to pay his share of the note and if he refused to attach his funds and pay expenses. Lisa finally agreed to pay. Documents in the Missouri Historical Society, Lisa Collection; Billon, *St. Louis under French and Spanish Domination*, 336-338. These documents are given in full and edited in Nasatir, *Imperial Osage*. Lisa, however, appealed to New Orleans. There was a good deal of bickering over the matter of the Osage Fort in 1804. E. g. Moro to Delassus, St. Louis, May 18, 1804 summarizing the matter. A.G.I., P. de C., leg. 142A. Full documentation in Nasatir, *Imperial Osage*. The partnership that took over the Osage trade from Chouteau was not a happy one. Sanguinet protested the actions of his partners while he was away in the drawing up of the contract or agreement for the Osage trade. See documents in Missouri Historical Society, St. Louis archives, no. 2927. Full documentation in Nasatir, *Imperial Osage*.

[7]Lille Sarpy held a power of attorney for his brother. See petition of Lille Sarpy dated New Orleans, June 1, 1802. A.G.I., P. de C., leg. 76.

VI

VILEMONT TO MINISTER, SEDAN, FRANCE, 17 PRAIRIAL AN X [JUNE 6, 1802][1]

No. 75 [Duplicate?]

28 Pr [airial]

Citizen Minister: during the administration of the Directory,[2] I was the first one to represent to my court the inconveniences of the cession

---

[1]Written in French. A.E., Corr. Pol., États-Unis Supplément, vol. VII, folios 186 *et. seq.* See Chapter IX, document XVIII.

[2]Directory period, 1795-1799.

of Louisiana to France. Today when an enlighted, wise, and energetic government has replaced an effervescent, arbitary, [and] subversive system, I shall employ the same zeal in praising the reunion of my fatherland to a metropolis which assures its splender. This apparent contradiction of principles on my part, tends to an invariable end, the welfare of my country. I have always been an ardent philosopher and shall never be a low *palinodiste*.

This preliminary information proper to justify my past actions, once admitted, permit, Citizen Minister, that I take from another [datum] to reassure you of my ulterior intentions. It is that I have renounced all sorts of honors and employment from any other sovereigns of this globe. I have in the fortune of my fathers in my own mind enough domains to provide for my needs and the use of my time. I cease speaking of myself and come to the subject.

The new colony which France has just acquired is surely too interesting from a political, mercantile and military aspect not to warrant that the government does not accord to it a serious solicitude. It is under this triple consideration, Citizen Minister, that I would desire to speak with you. The trips which I have made by order of His Catholic Majesty between 1794 and 1796 across the United States, Canada, New Mexico, and Upper Louisiana,[8] have placed me in a position to acquire some knowledge about the localities the report of which would perhaps not be without interest to you. The remarks especially which I was able to make about the inhabited regions from east to west of the western bank of the Mississippi and Missouri to beyond the St. Pierre river might be of some use to you. I advanced myself in this zone several degrees further than that which had been recognized by any other civilized traveler known to me. Of course, I am far from having gathered in proportion to the immensity of the riches which were paraded under my eyes. I leave this glorious task to more learned observers than I, who will follow me in this career, but at least I have gleaned from this

[8]Louis Vilemont. E. W. Lyon, *Louisiana in French Diplomacy* (Norman, 1934.) Louis Vilemont travelled in the United States to Philadelphia, Virginia, and Pennsylvania and proposed plans to the Spanish court to improve and populate Louisiana. He urged emigration of German, Fleming, and Dutch colonists, agriculturalists, and artisans to Louisiana, and permission for other religions than Catholicism to be exercised. Spain should financially aid that emigration. Spain turned down Vilemont's plans. Original and correspondence with Carondelet dated July 30, 1795, concerning Vilemont's plans are in A.H.N., Est., leg. 3890 *bis.*, *expediente* 34. It was discussed and rejected by the *Supremo Consejo de Estado* in its session of March 13, 1795 wherein Vilemont's plan is discussed. Nasatir and Liljegren, "Materials Relating to the History of the Mississippi Valley," *Louisiana Historical Quarterly*, (1938), XXI, reprint pp. 55-61. Vilemont visited in St. Louis, New Madrid, Cape Girardeau, Arkansas, etc. Lorimier to *Monsieur*, Cape Girardeau, April 1, 1795, A.G.I., P. de C., leg. 211; Trudeau to Vallé, St. Louis, March 11 [?], 1795, Missouri Historical Society, Vallé Collection #7; [Portell?] to François Vallé, New Madrid, April 6, 1795, *Ibid.*

large harvest several particles which no one had yet discovered, and I can render an account one day of the employment of my time without being forced to blush at my uselessness. The topographical relief [map] and the three *mémoires*[4] which I deposited at the Secretariat of the Indies at Madrid; the samples of minerals and plants which I remitted to the Intendant of Louisiana will prove if not the profoundness of my knowledge at least my zeal and some happiness in my researches. Having in other trips, visited Lower Louisiana and a part of Florida, I could, Citizen Minister, give you at your first demand a statistical outline to be taken from La Mobile and Pasachola [Pensacola] in the south to the nation of the Mandanes and the Cataract of St. Antoine between 45 to 46° north and from the East to West, from Kentucky and Georgia to the river, New Santa Fé, Texas, New Leon, etc.

The population of some tribes of natives can have diminished since my statements because of their wars and the excess of strong liquors. Their produce in skins can well have suffered some modifications but there will always exist a basis of population and commercial reports upon which to base approximate data, and the French Ministry will surely not regard with the same indifference as the Spanish Ministry the fact that the *comptoirs* and the traders of Montreal and Quebec carry away each year from the territory of Louisiana from 120 to 130 thousand *piastres* of skins whose exchange suppose the illicit entrance of a quantity of foreign merchandise of like value. The French Ministry will surely not regard with the same apathy as the Spanish Ministry a communication so simple, so well traced among the *peuplades* [villages] of the North-West of Louisiana and those of several points of the Pacific Ocean. It will not be so long in convincing itself that the Mississippi must be the reflector of all kinds of commercial operations of almost all of North America, and that nature serves as fully as *politique* to disturb the commerce of England in China. It is a very great ignorance to permit to escape so sure a way of diminishing the power of such a dangerous rival.

This consideration, which I would not permit myself to follow freely without your agreement, Citizen Minister, merits to be developed aside from others and with some care. I will wait to the end that you may send me your intentions. Several other points of prime importance would demand a similar attention. They would be:

The *reglemens* to be observed with the new populations which shall be sent from Europe so as to render their dissemination as useful as possible to agriculture, commerce, and defense of the country by placing [*jettant*] the colonists in the localities most proper for fulfilling this

---

[4]In 1764, A.H.N., Est., leg. 3882, *expediente* 12. These are *memorias y representaciones de* Mr. Jean Pierre [?] de Vilemont, *oficial Francés al Servicio de España, en la Luisiana.*

triple object. The mouths of the rivers, the streams, [are] the most important to fortify or [and] to populate. The more sure and less onerous means to make use of in order to prevent ruptures and to be able to act either on the side of the United States or of Canada or of the Spanish possessions. The resources which Louisiana offers in its spruce, cypress, [and] its green oak trees for the construction of war vessels and merchant marine. The means of making this possession the granary of all the colonies of France, of the West Indies who would no longer depend upon the United States for the provisioning of their flour; to encourage there the most essential territorial productions because of their relations with such and such locality; the known mines more or less rich which it is most convenient to exploit such as those of gold of the Arkansas river, those of silver of the Marameck, those of lead of Ste. Geneviève, etc. etc.

Here are, Citizen Minister, several questions which seem to me worthy of your solicitude and which I shall have the honor to approach separately whenever you will desire it whether it be in writing or verbally. Being absolute master of my time today it will be easy for me some day after your desire is known to transport myself to Paris. In confiding some part of my zeal in hands as wise and as able [as yours], it is very sweet for me to presage the splendor reserved to my country under such favorable auspices!

What a vast field is open to you, Citizen Minister, in which to leisurely spread the machinery [ronages] of invigorating and consolating arts! Suffer that for a moment I bring your attention to some details of this majestic *tableau*. Suppose for an instant yourself elevated in an aëro-static chariot above the mouth of the Ohio in the Mississippi (36 degrees north). This shall be about the middle of the vast horizon which you are going to be charged to embellish: cast your glance over the sites which surround you.

There (to the East) is the beautiful river of Ohio which receives in its bosom at least forty large navigable rivers which water the fertile territories of the western division of the states of the Union. Here (to the North) are the Lakes Superior, Erie, Ontario, Michigan, etc. which offer communications with the northern sea and the famous St. Lawrence river. Further on, always towards the north, are the mountains of Canada whose immense reservoirs of snow give water to the country of that name, to the Lakes, to all of North America. In projecting your views towards the West successively—from the chain of mountains which bar this continent from Canada to the South Sea, to beyond Nootka Sound, you will arrive at that incalculable reservoir of ice heaped up since the beginning of the globe. From there drawing a lateral line you will discover the source of the Mississippi situated in the environs of White Bear Lake. If afterwards you will examine the chain of mountains which goes straight to the West after having followed it for about a thousand leagues you will meet the source of the impetuous Missouri. March along its course which after 900 leagues of circulation will come to terminate at St. Louis at 39 degrees north (latitude). You will see on the right bank New Mexico and the rich metals which are exploited there; on the left [bank] prairies from 200 to 300 leagues in extent which in order to render the most fertile harvest await only the moment to be ploughed by the first plows.

Now, Citizen Minister, that you have under your aërostatic view the spectacle of two of the most beautiful rivers of the world, form a triangle, beginning with 40 degrees, a bit above their junction, drawing a line which would go to the source of the Mississippi, due north; and another [line] to the source of the Missouri due west. Take as a base for this triangle the cordillera situated higher, which will be fixed only by 49 degrees of latitude north instead of the 50 and more which they are conjectured to be, and you will have a superficie of 22,458 square leagues suitable for all kinds of agriculture, at the same time joined to the large villages of Indians, of *républiques,* of beavers, martins, and large quantities of other fine furs of the most precious [sort].

If afterwards, turning your head about, Citizen Minister, you project your view towards the south, beginning with the St. Francis River to the Red [or Vermillion] river you will see a diameter of about 400 leagues which waters besides these two beautiful *canaux,* the Ouachita, the Black River, the rivers of the *boeufs,* of Arkansas, White River, etc. All are navigable over 300 leagues; all tend to their source which takes rise in the mountains of New Mexico; the one towards the other as rays which one would draw from a center of a circle to its circumference, very advantageous to cultivators, miners who would establish themselves in this fertile and vast area for their commercial communications, [and] at the same time in order to help each other against the incursions of the Indians.

Now from 40 degrees latitude north, a point adopted by general examination, deign, Citizen Minister, to follow the course of the Mississippi to its mouth in the Atlantic Ocean in 29 degrees and some minutes, and for an instant throw your attention on the eastern bank in possession today of the Americans from Fort Natchez in 31 degrees north latitude to Canada.

Fifty leagues below the junction of the Ohio and the Mississippi you will note a cordon which abuts this river having an extent of 20 leagues, known under the name of *Écors à Margot*[5] and which seems to be a ramification of the Alleghanies. This natural fort which the Spanish government has had the complaisance to embellish for the Americans will infallibly, in later times, [be] one of the principal *entrepôts* and one of the most important ramparts of the new continent. How many beautiful *canaux* opened from this promontory to New Orleans! There is the river of the *Chits* which enters the interior and reascends to near the Alleghanies. Further down is the Tasous [Yazoo?] which furnishes for Florida and the Sea a direct communication; then comes the Chafalaya, arm of the Mississippi, which communicates again with the ocean by the large lakes of which it forms a part.

But the beauties too greatly multiplied of the two banks leave uncertain the choice. If one transports himself to the western bank, one sees the *Théchis* water all the pleasant plain of the Attakapas; very near the Vermillion separating this district from Opelousas. Then comes the *Mémentan* which serpentines the plains, the charming hills [slopes] which border the sea as well as the Cascacious [Calcasieu], the Sabine river, etc., etc.

Lower Louisiana which includes from the *hauteur* of the mouth of the Mississippi to Natchez, shows off just as well as Upper Louisiana; there is everywhere natural riches of all kinds as well as *canaux* to transport them but if the difference that there is between them concerning their territorial *rapports* is difficult to calculate because of the embarrassment of counter-balancing their immense *bénéfices* there is not however any difference to be made, politically speaking. The contrast of the localities is then so striking that it brings by itself distinctions in the judgement of the observer. The province is defended by itself [if] attacked by the sea; it has everything to fear from a descent from the north: Lower Louisiana being then irresistibly dependent upon Upper Louisiana, all the means which will tend towards belligerent views must be carried to the first named point. But this is not the place to approach this question. I again take up the thread of my material:

I have already by one method of reckoning measured a part of the rich and vast possession which France has just acquired. I shall examine the other side in the same manner.

Represent to yourself, Citizen Minister, a plane the bases of which lie, from Florida to 100 leagues beyond the Bay of St. Bernard, which

[5]Chicasaw Bluffs, Memphis, Tennessee, was obtained from the Indians and fortified by Gayoso de Lemos in 1795; demolished by Carlos Howard and ceded to the United States under Pinckney's treaty. The story is to be found briefly narrated in print in several places, viz: Whitaker, *Spanish American Frontier;* Whitaker, *Mississippi Question;* Bemis, *Pinckney's Treaty,* Gayarré, *History of Louisiana: Spanish Domination.* The present editor is now editing the diaries and writing a narrative of the galleys and life on the Mississippi, 1792-1796, which will give the story and citations to and for Chicasaw Bluffs.

will comprehend a diameter of about 300 leagues; draw then the perpendicular line to above the Illinois only, thus adding 500 leagues to the first product, and you will have a superficie of 190,000 square leagues situated between 30 and 39 degrees north latitude, everywhere watered by rivers, streams, bayous, all navigable, under the most beautiful sky, the most healthful climate, the interior part of which territory can surely be counted among the most fertile in the world and its productions the most voluminous can be transported in eight or ten days from one extremity to another.

In this immense field to be established, the administrator is not narrowed in his views as in Europe. The men of all countries find by analogy the temperature suited to the needs of their physique; it suffices that one ascend 20 leagues or that he descend as many to find just the equilibrium which agrees to his constitution. Here one can engage in the culture of indigo, coffee, sugar, cotton, etc.; higher up it will be the culture of wheat, flax, grapes; everywhere wood suitable to the construction of ships of all sizes is paraded with profusion.

The course of the Missouri which always goes westward causes that this river spread its *rapports* all at once with Louisiana, New Mexico, California; and finally on a large section of one of the most rich continents, the most vast in the universe. To this remark so interesting for commerce and the progress of the arts of agriculture, it is necessary to add that continuing to ascend the Mississippi immediately after the mouth of the Missouri in its bosom one meets at each 30 to 40 leagues successively on the left, large rivers navigable for the largest ships whose course is always directed from the Northwest; while the eastern bank is watered by only the single Illinois river which disembogues at two leagues above St. Louis and has no other communication. From this point to the source of the Mississippi one does not meet in ascending it any torrent of water to which one might give the name of creek, a circumstance entirely in favor of the transactors of the western bank.

Louisiana since the cession to Spain has only been for its metropole a continual object of contentions, cares, and sacrifices. By returning it to its first dependency, it must promptly *changer de face*. This beautiful and vast province only brought in annually to the *fisc* [treasury] 70 to 80,000 *piastres* and cost for its administration from 500 to 550,000 *piastres*. In the hands of a vigilant and liberal minister it would do very differently. There would be necessary for Louisiana, population and more population. Now the Spanish *metropole* has [been] deprived of the territory, it having been far from providing for the deficit of its colonies. I flatter myself that it will not be so with France. Four [twenty-seven?] thousand whites and 48,000 slaves[6] are all there are today scattered from the mouth of the Mississippi (exception made of the savages) to the *Petites Côtés du Missouri*. What a beautiful country lost to industry! How many rich territories tired of being idle!

Here is, Citizen Minister, a grand and glorious metamorphosis which is reserved to you to operate. Oh that I could in my capacity of a Louisianian see you soon begin it! May the wise and liberal views of an energetic minister, substitute soon for the *Hidre* of distress and inertia which are consuming my country, the horn of abundance which nature seems to have bestowed upon this beautiful region for its distinguished *coat of arms*.

Deign, Citizen Minister, to receive the assurances of my respect.

Louis Vilemont [rubric]
former Captain in the Regiment of Louisiana
at Sedan—*Département des Ardennes*

P. S. I do not believe that I shall now make a long sojourn in Europe. Citizen Minister, in case you might have some information to ask of me, I beg you not to delay too long a time in doing so.
Sedan, 17 Prairial An X

---

[6]See Stoddard, *Sketches Historical and Descriptive of Louisiana* (Philadelphia, 1802); and [Burguin Duvallon], *Vue de La Colonie Espagnole du Mississippi— en l' anée 1802* (Paris, 1803,) chapter XIX.

VII

Concession by Salcedo to Lisa and Others, New Orleans, June 12, 1802[1]

Don Manuel de Salcedo, Colonel of the Royal Army, political and military governor of the provinces of Louisiana and West Florida, Inspector of the veteran troops and militia there, Royal Vice Patron, and Judge, subdelegate of the general superintendency of mails, etc.

Bearing in mind the various remonstrances which have been made to the government concerning the exclusion of traffic with the Indian nations of the dependency of Illinois;[2] considering how important it is to have them friendly and under the protection of Spain; reflecting how much better it is to restrain effectively the progress of the English companies of Hudson Bay, Canada and Michilimackinac; having listened to the *informes* of the former Lieutenant-governors of the said post, the Lieutenant-colonels Don Manuel Perez and Don Zenon Trudeau, and particularly those given by the *Sindico procurador general,* Don Pablo

---

[1]Written in Spanish. A.G.I., P. de C., leg. 76; copy or draft in A.G.I., P. de C., leg. 138. Copy in Missouri Historical Society. Enclosed with document VIII.
[2]See Chapter IX, document XIII, etc.

Lanusse, and various individuals of this trade, after a conference held in the government house attended by the *Señor* Intendant and Lieutenant-Governor of these provinces; having read with attention the various documents which exist in this government [archive] on this matter, and finally, desiring to conciliate with the political views of this government the desires of the inhabitants in order that the profit from the said trades be divided among all; as well as even experimenting to indicate the conduct which may be most favorable to the public good of the province, to the quietude of those establishments, and to the prosperity and growth of them; bearing in mind that it is just that all the honorable and powerful residents profit from trade with the Indians, I have come to yield to the reiterated solicitations which under date of the fourth, instant,[3] the inhabitants of the town of St. Louis, Illinois, Don Manuel de Lisa, Don Carlos Sanguinet for himself and for his son-in-law Don Francisco María Benoît, and Don Juan Bautista Sarpy in the name of his brother Don Gregorio made to me, conceding to them for the precise term of five years, to all four in common, the trade with the Osage Indians under the same precise conditions which they promise and are verified in the certified copy of their memorial which is enclosed.[4] This concession is made in view of the fact that in addition to the good circumstances of fidelity, zeal and love for the Sovereign, they proportion advantages to the state, since they are obliged in due form to provide at their cost, without any expense to the royal treasury, for their defense and for the preservation of the redoubt of the Osages under the other [same?] conditions which Don Augusto Chouteau observed when he held this privilege.[5] Neither am I neglecting the public utility since they are to construct a water mill to make flour as fine as that of the Anglo-Americans.[6]

Therefore, I am ordering the Lieutenant-Governor of the Establishments of Illinois as soon as this is presented to [by] the memorialists, Don Manuel de Lisa, Don Carlos Sanguinet, Don Francisco Maria Benoît and Don Gregorio Sarpy, to place them immediately in possession of the re-

---

[3]See Chapter IX, document XIII, etc.
[4]Document V.
[5]The full narrative and documentation is contained in Nasatir, *Imperial Osage.*
[6]The question of building this mill was still in the air in 1803. Sarpy said that he alone built the mill and that his partners refused to share in the expense, and he petitioned that the Osage trade be given to him alone. This petition was dated May 4, 1803. Delassus certified to the truth of Sarpy's allegations on May 18, 1803. On August 26, 1803, Salcedo ordered that Lisa, Sanguinet, and Benoît be forced to pay their share of the expenses of the building of the mill or grant the exclusive trade to Sarpy alone or to those "who will contribute to the building of the said mill." Missouri Historical Society. William Dunn, a millwright by trade, and resident of the United States, was brought in by B. Sarpy and A. Rutgers to build watermills for them. Petition of William Dunn, St. Louis, June 15, 1802, *American State Papers, Public Lands,* VIII, 899-900.

doubt and trade of the Osage Indians, removing from the plan any obstacle and hindrance which might be formed; taking care that this privilege be completely fulfilled on the part of the government as well as on the part of those favored persons, and giving a detailed account every six months of the conditions and progress of the matter for the purpose of arranging my steps. The present is given and signed by my hand, sealed with the seal of my arms, and countersigned by the undersigned honorary commissary of war, secretary for His Majesty in this government house in New Orleans, June 15, 1802.

Manuel de Salcedo
Andrés López Armesto

This is a copy of the original which I certify. New Orleans, June 19, 1802   Andrés López Armesto [rubric]

VIII

SALCEDO TO DELASSUS, NEW ORLEANS, JUNE 19, 1802[1]

Answered

Anxiously desiring to do all the good possible, after having taken all the time necessary for examining the frequent reclamations which at all times have been presented; using all the resources imaginable; and listening to the *informes* of the *Procurador Síndico,* of the commerce and Lieutenant-governors who have been of these posts, and finally heeding the verbal and written recommendations which have been made to the government by the Intendancy and by the Lieutenant-Governor of these provinces; I have thought that I should pay attention to public clamors and to conciliate in all possible the political view of the government with the general well being of these establishments and with the personal interest of these inhabitants; and with this object in view I have conceded for five years the trade or commerce with the Osage nations in the precise terms which are verified in the enclosed copy to Don Manuel Lisa, Don Carlos Sanguinet, Don Francisco Benoît and Don Gregorio Sarpy and I charge you with the complete fulfillment of all that is expressed and ordered in the concession,[2] avoiding firmly all discussion and embarrassment and informing with precision what is ordered concerning the condition and progress of the said trade in order

---

[1]Written in Spanish. A.G.I., P. de C., leg. 76, draft in A.G.I., P. de C., leg. 138.
[2]Document VII.

to take the steps which the nature of the information and the exigency of the case requires.

These same beginnings place me in a position of forewarning you that although the trade of the Panis Indians is among those included in the general concession granted to Don Santiago Clamorgan as director of the Company of Discoverers on the Missouri,[3] as it was conceded to Don Santiago Chauvin[4] at the instance of the *ad-interim intendant* in order to assist him in the support of his family, it is my intention that he shall have the use of it for the same precise *termino* [for] which my predecessor *Señor* Marqués granted it.[5]

The same foundation places me in a position to order you to arrange or have compromised without judicial bustle the difference which originated between Don Carlos Sanguinet and Don Santiago Clamorgan or Loisel concerning a part of the peltry belonging to the former which the latter took or had taken by his traders.[6]

The well known zeal which animates you to the best service of the King does not leave me the slightest doubt that you will use all the means which your influence and prudence suggests to you for eliminating animosities and disputes, conciliating uniformly the good harmony and intelligence which must subsist if the general welfare of the state and the personal interest of the inhabitants is to be promoted as is just.

May God keep you many years.

New Orleans, June 19, 1802.

Manuel de Salcedo [rubric]

Señor Don Carlos de Lassus.

---

[3]See Chapter IX, documents V, VI, VIII.
[4]Chapter IX, document II.
[5]See Chapter VII, document I.
[6]See Chapter IX, Document III.

IX

Vilemont to Minister, Sedan, France, 14 messidor An 10 [July 3, 1802][1]

Copy

Citizen Minister:

In order to obey the desire which you deign to manifest to me by your letter of the *27 Prairial,* last, I am going to approach separately, as I had the

---

[1]Written in French, A.E., Corr. Pol., États-Unis, Supplément, vol. VII, folios 189-200 *verso.* Parts in B.N., n.a., vol. 9286—see note 9.

honor of offering you in my first note,[2] some questions which I believed to be most worthy of your solicitude relative to the administration of Louisiana and to the splendor to be given to this beautiful colony.

Far be it from me [to impart] hypotheses, hearsay, and idle reasoning. That which I shall quote I will have seen; that which I will discuss will always be of palpable and prompt execution. The mania for abstractions is passed and it certainly will not be me who will make it live again.

At the moment when you are going to set yourself to the decoration of the vast domains whose embellishment has just been confided to you, Citizen Minister, it is very natural that you take pleasure in familiarizing yourself with your hosts. Suffer, then, that I begin to tell you about the natives of Louisiana in regard to politics, war, and commerce.

The principle of all the digressions, of the projects which I shall have the honor to submit to you about this nation [*sic*] will always tie up to this great goal to be attained: *The gradual civilization of the villages by the use of agriculture which is to be introduced among them.*

The administrators whom the government will send into this colony will meet there a very favorable prerogative to be welcomed by the natives and turn it to good account; it is the tender memory which they have never ceased to bear to the French and the well pronounced partiality which they have always accorded them in their transactions in all the rivalry of other nations. It has never occurred to me during my trips to harangue a village chief without having him end by asking me *"When will the brothers of the great country return? who had left to their red children the province as a hostage and had well promised them to reappear some day in order to live together."*

The conduct of the governors and intendants of Louisiana, the Comte de Gálvez excepted, during 36 years toward the savages is the height of absurdity. The villages, although overwhelmed with kind deeds from Spain, have always given to these subjects exclusion in time of peace in their commerce and preference in time of war in order to scalp them. Considerable presents were annually distributed among the allies. The government guaranteed them a haven, protected them against the attack of white powers; and the colonists received as a recompense continual insults, pillages, and death. If this conduct was constant among these singular men, if they exercised thus on all whites indifferently, it would be necessary to think about any means to free oneself. But it was altogether different.

The deference which they bear toward the English who trade with them is known. One is astounded, as I have just said, at the venerable

---

[2] See document VI.

attachment which they have always accorded to the memory of the French whom they have ceased to see in possession of the country since 1767. From whither comes this so shocking contrast? It is that the French had the custom which the English observe with great care today; that of sending agents, honest and of a certain character, to visit the hordes, learn what was going on and make them affectionate to their protectors; while Spain had, amongst her to make her interests valuable, only rude and inept men [who were] much more suitable to excite among the Indians scorn for their sovereign whom they represented near them, than to attract the slightest regard.

If it did not suit the French government to maintain these interesting hosts on its new territory, in order to use them defensively and offensively in time of war, if there was not any commercial speculation to derive from it, one might by breaking all communication with them, cut short the various expenses which their relations necessarily incur, but the locality of Louisiana, but the moral of the events of the day, obliges one to act differently.

The occupation of this interesting colony by France must necessarily act in opposition the United States[8] to their former metropolis.

This consequence which (was almost repeated several times by the new opposition) has been approaching several new beginnings by the new opposition in parliament, Citizen Minister, will surely not have escaped your foresight and merits a serious attention. In fact, one cannot deny that if in case of rupture with France, England succeeded in interesting the United States; the arms of these two powers united would occasion annoying diversions in the domains of the Republic and its new ally in the new continent. Now until the government has had organized regular armies on the Mississippi what would be more suitable to defend its passage and the immense territories which it waters than the bands of Indians so easy to raise with the help of their customs and predilections?

To these ulterior considerations I shall join present ones which also bring with them the necessity to improve relations with the natives of the colony.

The astonishing increase of the American population, their enterprising genius, has excited the ambition or the cupidity in turn, of the new inhabitants of the Lakes,[4] some to attempt more ample discoveries, others

---

[8]Or, "bring again the United States closer to the former metropolis."
[4]Note in document: "Since the cession in 1795 [sic] by England to the United States of Detroit and Michilimackinac, the Americans have been able to open a new branch of commerce with the Indians and follow in the footsteps of the merchants of Montreal and Quebec."

to open their trade of furs personally or by the medium of the Indians. In either case all their footsteps are exercised on the dependencies of Louisiana and New Mexico according to the example of the English. In these two cases, they have encroached and will encroach all the more on both territories. Now, how to immediately undermine these anticipations or at least to weaken them as well as their tragic results? Because of lack of the necessary population in the country or of any army in temporary station there is only one way; it is by the aid of the savages. How can one hope to combine the forces and make them act with success? There is only one way; it is by creating *commissaires* to influence and divide them and to weaken their predilection for the English.

It surely is not difficult to conceive that some active and intelligent agents which the government would send amongst them would prove to them that they have more good deeds, security, to expect from the French at this very hour, than from the Americans, which experience itself proves to them, that they have in the future many good things to hope for from the former and many bad things to fear from the latter; that the territories upon which the hunters procure their skins belong to France and so they must then give preference to her traders rather than to those of England, the rivalry of which violates international law. But what is very easy to imagine is how one would restrain, in the way in which things are regulated in these countries, the smallest military party of Englishmen or Americans who escaping from the *Rivière des Renards* [Fox river] or from the Wisconsin, would conceive the project of penetrating to New Mexico via the *Mongoina* River [Des Moines river] or any other way.

However, setting aside the forces which the evacuation of Detroit and Michilimackinac have caused to flow back to Louisiana, let us calculate a bit those of which one could dispose with some ingenious measures from St. Louis to 45 or 46 degrees north latitude only, if not totally at least in a large part, and of which all the products can and must naturally end at this post owing to the course traced by the rivers. I shall profit by this same picture to establish the general enumeration of the trade of the natives with the whites. The most populated nations such as the Sauteurs and the Sioux, living as nomads, cannot be assigned a fixed abode. They camp and decamp because of the migration of herds of bisons and wild oxen which leisurely spread in the prairies from 200 to 300 leagues in extent.

Nomenclature of the Nations	Men Bearing Arms	Residence of the Nations. (The post of St. Louis at 36° north latitude on the Mississippi, the base of the evaluation of the residences)	Commercial Reports Received in Merchandise the following values valued in *piastres*	Sold in skins the following quantities; each paquet is worth 40 *piastres*
Western Bank of Mississippi			Piastres	Paquets
The Sacks and the Renards	1.200	1400 leagues west	15.000	1.200
The Sioux	8.000	from 200 to 300 leagues west and north	78.000	2.500
The Aowias	300	80 leagues west	33.000	500
Eastern Bank of Mississippi				
A detachment of Sauteurs	1.500	from 200 to 300 leagues north	60.000	1.500
The Puankaskas	300	250 leagues north	55.000	790
The Pouwatoumis	1.000	100 leagues north	60.000	2.000
The Maskoutins and Kapouk	700	idem	8.000	200
The Sauteurs (situated between the Lake Inférieur and the Mississippi)	12.000	from 300 to 500 leagues north	84.000	3.000
The Sauks	150	Base of Michigan	10.000	290
The Otawouas	800	200 leagues north	22.000	500
Banks of the Missouri				
The Grand Osages	1.200	150 leagues west	72.000	780
The Cannes	180	250 leagues west	24.000	460
The Petit Osages	800	150 leagues west	24.000	480
The République	50	300 leagues west	6.000	150
The Othos	120	300 leagues west	14.000	300
The Mahas	180	330 leagues west	20.000	240
The Panis	90	320 leagues west	10.000	160
The Panis Mahas	40	330 leagues west of St. Louis	5.000	140
The Poncas	50	390 leagues idem	6.000	140

Whatever there may be in this exposé what can Spain promise herself with so many warriors to give battle to? Around 300 men in cases of necessity.[5] What has she been able to gather from all the hunters living on her territory under her hospitality? 600 to 700 *pacquets* of skins annually. It is up to the French Ministry and up to the new chiefs who are going to be sent into Louisiana to make valuable these mercantile resources and these military forces. It is for a government which joins nerve to knowledge to rectify the indolence and the crying abuses which leave only in a country so suitable to realize the reign of Rhéa, linden and cypress trees to paint its languor! Yes, Louisiana changing masters will also change her face. Its productions are too precious for industry not to be encouraged by the active administration which is going to preside over the development of the riches of this beautiful colony. The importance of these integral [alliances] affinities is too large not to be seized upon by the vigilant eye who from the Tuilleries plans the destinies of the entire world. However little one considers the topography of the United States, of Louisiana and of New Mexico and the relations of these countries amongst themselves, one immediately sees the communications of all traced by the hands of nature. Now, human instinct and political combinations have joined together to determine the movement of rotation from east to west. The time must not be very far away when the same vibration will resound from the Mississippi to the Gulf of Mexico and shall cause to move all the energy of this immense surface uniformly.

Let us come now, Citizen Minister, to the organization of the *commissaires* of which I had the honor to point out to you the necessity. But before proposing to you the means which I believe most useful [and] the least expensive to this effect I shall take up again this observation which I only touched upon in passing, "The great goal to obtain from the natives of Louisiana is the introduction of agriculture amongst them."[6] President Jefferson has well felt this necessity and has only been able to maintain peace with the several nations of the western bank of the Ohio after having sent farming utensils amongst them. Orthodox abstractions are nothing for the savages of these regions. To capture their goodwill and maintain their interest, when one has succeeded in destroying their prejudice for labor of the soil, the result of a plow will do much more to the spirit of a Tala-

---

[5]Note in document: "At the time of the project to descend the Ohio into Louisiana planned in 1794 between the French envoy Genêt at Philadelphia and the American General Clark from Kentucky, the Baron de Carondelet who then commanded the province did not have any more savage warriors at his orders to defend Upper Louisiana." See Nasatir, "Anglo-Spanish Frontier on the Upper Mississippi 1786-1796," *Iowa Journal of History and Politics*, XXIX (1931).

[6]Note in document: "The chauvonanons [Shawnee] established about Cape Girardeau are already passible cultivators".

pouche or an Abenakis than the result of an explanation of the transfiguration of Jesus Christ, with all respect to the parable. A people, still new, who inhabit sterile localities is naturally superstitious. Hunger gives them vision. Each time their sufferings cease, they cast their eyes on the empyrean and make into beneficient deity the first constellation which strikes their eyes. Each time they reenter into the tortures of the needy, they look around them and also transform into an evil spirit the first animal which they see. This is the reason for the numberless divinities of the Thebaid. A people on the contrary who finds it easy to satisfy their needs enjoys them without greatly informing themselves from whence they come. Such is the case of the savages of Louisiana whose whole cult responses in a *Welcé or Watchi-Manitou* to whom they rarely have recourse, having an abundance of all kinds of game, [and] fish at hand. They profit indifferently without thinking of thanking the Good Spirit or evoking the Bad Spirit.

Christianity is very useful in maintaining negroes among the workshops. It helps them to keep a moral restraint, especially indispensable in the colonies because of the proportion of whites and blacks. It [Christianity] could even serve them as a comfort; but it surely would be harmful to introduce it among the natives of Louisiana all at once. In order to pretend to possess these restless and untamed men it is not enough to chain their spirit as much as one is able to, one must occupy their bodies as well. Many of the quarrels of the villages amongst themselves and even the villages with the European establishments are occasioned by unemployment. Now, religion, as it is attested by the attempts of missionaries from several governments in America and elsewhere, ordinarily increases rather than diminishes this vice amongst them. It would then be proper for the French administrators in Louisiana to think about making good laborers of these natives before making neophytes of them.

Property will make the savage lose his unsteadiness, the introduction of useful arts in his camp will soften his habits and will necessarily attach him to the hand which shall have taught him the use of it. This first step made towards industry and civilization, the exchanges will multiply with the products of new occupations, and the same tribes instead of being as it often happens onerous to the government which protects them, will participate in causing to shine the manufactures of the metropolis and will be the most sound ramparts of its distant establishments.

But I shall leave the calculation of this ulterior progress which is so dear to me to invoke for my country, but which time only, aided by a wise administration, can introduce, in order to cast your eyes, Citizen Minister, on existing conditions which need be only improved to obtain immediately powerful benefits.

These are not hypothetical speculations which I am going to present to you but advantages calculated on results which powerful rivals used against the interests of a Sovereign, but which have become yours by the acquisition which the Consulate has just made.

Louisiana presents on all its surfaces, at distances more or less large, Indian villages valuable and independent to which it is necessary to make presents or have war. Either decision is costly. But the experience of fifty-four years proves that besides the sparing [spilling] of human blood, the least rupture maintained with arms against these singular men is very much dearer to the government than all the losses which the commercial balance might suffer in the most unfavorable lapse [state] of peace with them.

Thus since a state of peace with the savages is most profitable to humanity as well as to *politique,* it is important while maintaining it, to increase as much as possible its benefits.

Louisiana has for a long time found, the same as New Mexico, its conservation in its own isolation. This situation was more suitable in mastering the natives, who too distant from civilized contacts, which might attract them and furnish them arms, were easily calmed at the sight of a few presents of which they felt the lack. But this state of things is changed; it is also necessary to change the mode of *liaisons.* To the East, fierce torrents threaten to inundate these countries; to the north, avid companies increase each day the encroachments which they have already made.

Now, under this double point of view, the union of France with the Indians must be fortified and active.

In regard to the Americans, not only because they are the most solid ramparts, which in case of rupture, the government might oppose until they have had pass in the districts the necessary regular troops, but again because it is urgent to counterbalance the influence of their most recent measures.

It is known that since Congress has acquired the Forts of Natchez, Nogales or Walnut Hill, Écores à Margot on the eastern side of the Mississippi, those of Detroit and Michilimakinac on the frontiers of Canada, the president has spared nothing to become attached to the villages even of the born enemies of the Americans and he has used the most powerful allurements to attract them into these posts.[7] Not only do the influential chiefs who go there receive presents but the hunters, ordinary warriors, still find in the stores maintained by the public administration all kinds of objects for exchange at the most modest prices. This generosity, these services which are greatly boosted by the skillful harangues

---

[7] By the treaties with England in 1794 and with Spain in 1795. See Whitaker, *Spanish—American Frontier* and *Mississippi Question,* and other printed works.

of the agents which the executive power hires for this service, have besides the pressing reasons of the moment a very marked ulterior end, that of first making the distant tribes, friends of the factories of Louisiana and then to indispose them by degrees against its traders and colonists in order to more easily travel [*parcourir*—survey] over the dependencies of this province and New Mexico and take possession of all the skins.

The audacity till today unpunished of the Canadian Companies who crush under foot all international law, and who have displayed their factors as absolute masters in all the Spanish possessions from the Falls of St. Anthony to New Santa Fé and robbed them of all the products, is another abuse too crying for the French government not to establish order there in whatever concerns it now.[8]

Now, what is there more suitable to enlighten the villages on the injustice of this monopoly, to protect the Louisiana traders, to stop the progress of the Canadians and the Americans on the possessions of France and her ally, to baffle the intrigues, the influence of the British and Congressional agents, than *commissaires* sent in the name of the Consulate who, living in the districts and furnished with some zeal, will have, near the Indians whom they will have rendered attached, [ways] means always ready to foresee or stop these blows? And still again why does England, which allows much less for expenses than Spain in its relations with the villages, receive more fidelity in political contracts and monopolize all their commerce? It is as I have already observed that the British government maintains amongst the Indians agents of a certain character to exalt them and attract their goodwill by dint of harangues; while on the other hand, the Spanish Government, has only miserable vagabonds, without any logic or quality to make valuable its interests.

Now it is not knack alone which attaches these proud and belligerent men but the method of distributing it. *"Quid expectat, qui offendit, dum obligat? Satis adversus illum gratus est si quis beneficio ejus ignoscit"*. The oratorical prestige is infinite on the soul of the savage, a good haranguer entices all wills. Mack-Ilbie on the shores of the Atlantic disposed as he pleased of 15,000 warriors. Lorimier, in the north, a simple trader as the other one, could move more than 20,000.

Till[9] now I have only shown the utility of my plan in respect to *politique*, war, and commerce. I shall leave for a moment the picture

---

[8]See in this connection Perrin du Lac, *Voyages dans les Deux Amériques,* and *per contra* Collot, *A Journey in North America.*

[9]Copy in Bibliothèque Nationale begins here. Extract from Vilemont's second *memoire,* Bibliothèque Nationale, Nouvelles Acquisitions, vol. 9986, folios 298-298 *verso.*

of dangers to which I opposed it as a remedy in order to substitute for it a more suitable use: that of the sciences.

In fact, why could not these same agents who would be employed to improve the relations of France with the Indians of the most Western section or in the North West of the country, occupy themselves in the important discovery of the communication of the Southern Sea with the new continent? Once so far advanced on the way, aided by the information of the Indians, the imagination stretched toward large things as it will be impossible for those who are greatly sensitive and who will go across these magnificent countries to keep from this [stretching the imagination], why would they not verify with exactitude the multiple conjectures which there already are about this discovery? It follows from rude tales and attestations of several Canadian hunters and savages that they have often gone on foot from the Missouri to the sea in a north-westerly direction in less than two and one-half months. The furs which they brought as proof of their declarations and which are never found in places already practiced of the new continent are found to be identical with the properties of those which Captain Cook[10] and M. de la Peyrouse[11] describe as found on the coasts of Nootka Sound and Monterey.

It is time to pertinently reveal all the advantages that this great discovery will show. But if it be permitted to me to calculate its full potentialities [fonds] by its accessories, what riches in all kingdoms could one not promise himself. Each step which one takes from East to West, the size of all kinds of objects increases ten fold in volume. It seems that nature has made this corner of the terrestrial globe the most favorite of its immense sphere. The products which one discovers there in proportion as one goes into the interior are more majestic, more beautiful than elsewhere. The rivers have courses there from 400 to 900 leagues. The unfolding of plants is prodigious. Men who are born there resemble rather the descendants of Alcide and Pirithous[12] than the brothers of the worshippers of Manitou.

The opaque veil which covered the bosom of these precious treasures has greatly expanded itself in seven years. It depends on the wisdom of the French Minister to entirely dissolve it. He can do so very easily; this will be the effect of Phoebus substituting for the darkness of night, the brilliant twilight of a beautiful day.

---

[10]Cook, *Voyage to the Pacific Ocean,* (London, 1785).

[11]J.F.G. de La Pérouse, *Voyage de la Pérouse autour de Monde* (Paris, An V); English translation, London 1798; Boston, 1811, etc.

[12]Note in document: "Such are the Mandannes the last nation which I have visited, till then, almost unknown and who live between 48 and 49 degrees north latitude."

Thus at the same time when sciences find vast harvest, in case the attempt to be made to methodically prove the projected communications—[be successful], *la politique* and commerce will acquire precious benefits. If on the contrary success does not answer the enterprise the slightest sketch which will be made of it will always procure for the French rich speculations with the villages such as those of the untouched regions, for whom the first elements of exchange and traffic are yet to be born.[13]

Moreover it is to be remarked that the very simple organization of a sole plan suffices to the mechanism of several considerations which we submit to the examination of your wisdom. It is not a question in this project, Citizen Minister, of either great disbursements or of large forces to be employed to support its march. Everything consists in a good choice of some several intelligent individuals whom dangers and fatigues do not frighten and who are familiar with the customs of the Indians. This kind of man can be found among the Creoles either at New Orleans or in the interior posts.

These same agents while advancing their careers could serve humanity. In fact besides the necessity of crossing, in all senses of that word, the vast territories where they would be employed, would make it necessary for them [to make] excellent topographical maps.[14] The habit of seeing the application which the Indians make of so many simple things unknown to the whites, would familiarize them with their properties and would make [of them] practical botanists, in case the study of some exact principles do not make them penetrate further. Let us indicate now a little something of the spirit to be given to this organization.

First. At least eight persons in the beginning, the fidelity of whom can be counted upon and who would be attached to the State by some powerful link of nature or of fortune, would be sent with the title of *commissaires* among the tribes.

Second. This corps would be divided into two divisions of four members each which would be called the *commissariat* of the north and that of the south. The employees in the north will have under their supervision all the villages which are located between Louisiana and New

---

[13]Here ends the extract in B. N., n. a vol. 9986, folios 298-298 *verso*.

[14]See "Instructions relative to the works of the geographers of Louisiana," number 3, Paris, Frimaire, An XI, in Archives Nationales, Colonies, C13A, vol. LI, folio 133. Sixth article: Until circumstances permit making the reconnoitring of the parts of the interior of Louisiana which return to the possession of France, and which are still little known, such as the upper part of the Mississippi, the greater part of the Missouri, which is said to be much longer than the Mississippi, and the other principal branches of these rivers, it would be useful to get busy as soon as possible in assembling the observations, notes, and individual information that inhabitants of the country or Indian travelers may have". Citizen Pitot a New Orleans merchant, made such a map. Many were gathered especially from Collot which are in the French archives.

Mexico from 36 degrees north latitude to about 45 degrees. Those of the south would have from the Atlantic Coast at 28 degree to 36 degrees north latitude.

Third. A *commissaire en chef* to whom would be attributed superior powers would be charged to supervise the conduct of the eight others and to observe that the data of the two divisions always be in the greatest possible concordance. He would periodically abstract the newspapers which it would be enjoined to each *commissaire* in particular to watch concerning the political situation of the nations of his section towards France, concerning their habits, customs, general character, commerce in order to afterwards collate them and to inform either the Captain General or the Minister directly.

Fourth. Besides the ordinances which would regulate the conduct of the *commissaires,* there shall be given to them by the Ministry or by the Captain General, instructions and a plan of work in which would be forecast [*prévis*] the state of peace and the state of war of France with the Indians or with the neighboring civilized powers. The spirit of these resolutions would be their political guide. These resolutions would always serve as a set of guide lines for their enterprises. There would be remitted to them in addition formulae for uniform harangues in order to be able to proceed from the various corners of their destinations on a regular march.

Fifth. The eight ordinary *commissaires* should especially obey in everything the *commissaire en chef* who would have power to cause them to be sent from one destination to the other, according to what he should judge proper for the interests of the government and the country.

Sixth. The agents would be obliged to reside in the camps of the Indians. Eventual necessities either of health or of *politique* would alone excuse their momentary sojourn in the establishments of the government.

Seventh. There should be promptly remitted to the *commissaire en chef* a determined quantity of presents,[15] or rather he shall be authorized to make some levies upon those which are sent to the commandants of

---

[15]The prefect Laussat was ordered to assemble ideas and information about presents to the Indians. He received his information from Fornerel, who was interpreter for the English from 1761 to 1782 and for Spain from 1782 to 1800. In 1794 Carondelet distributed 90,000 *piastres*. His predecessors distributed from 40 to 50,000 *piastres* per year. The English in Canada distribute 100,000 *livres* annually. There will descend to New Orleans two to three thousand savages per year, others say from three to four hundred chiefs. Under French rule this will increase to about 4000 and from 4 to 500 chiefs. Laussat therefore suggested 500,000 francs for the first year at least. Laussat lists twenty Indian nations who visit New Orleans, and the Illinois, Kickapoo, Puants, Osages, etc., about whom the upper establishments will have to report, since they rarely visited New Orleans, Laussat to Minister of Marine, Paris, 5 Vendemaire. An XI [September 27, 1802]. Archives Nationales, Colonies, C13A, vol. LI, folios 192-193.

the interior posts, because without this aid the most prime talents of the most zealous orator will always be useless or at least very cold near the savages.

Eighth. A salary of ...... per month would be assigned to each particular *commissaire;* something more to the *commissaire en chef.*

Ninth. There should be made first of all a general census of the nations which it interests France the most to trade and influence in order to more methodically propagate the new policy to be introduced amongst them, and that the greatest possible equal division be made among the respective *commissaires.*

Tenth. With things thus regulated, each agent would be responsible for his jurisdiction and the advices, and the aids of one to another would be passed all the more regularly, if one would be sure, from a short distance, of the dwelling place of each one.

Eleventh. If, as one must believe, the march of the furs extracted by the Mississippi and the Missouri for Canada and the United States is broken and if they [furs] return to New Orleans, their true *comptoir,* the *commissaires* would be very careful to forbid the entrance of merchandise from Montreal and Michilimackinac into the French domains; they would stop the delinquent traders and confiscate their goods, or they would simply protest against their conduct following the more or less strict instructions which they should receive, etc.

It follows from this sketch, First, that the only force, until new orders, which France can oppose to the irruptions which will be made against her properties in the new continent, resides in the employment of natives; that if one does not restrain immediately their predilection they will escape to join dangerous rivals. Second, that the state of good harmony with them costs less to the finances of the government than the state of war, while the ramparts which can be formed will be more solid and cheaper than the greater part of the fortresses skillfully built in these regions. Third, that their skins instead of passing to foreign lands can and must reflow into the *comptoirs* of France. Fourth, that more affectionate treatment, better understanding rendered to men often irritated, often misguided, will infallibly make them see in their new protectors brothers to cherish, instead of former victims which they were unceasingly ready to sacrifice to blind antipathy. Fifth, finally that the methodical discovery of the connections of the Pacific Ocean with the new continent, all revealing a brilliant supplement to the geographical riches, gives to the naturalist, the chemist, the most fertile harvest to collect.

Thus, according to the reports of *politique,* of economy, of treasury, of interests of business, of humanity, finally in reference to the sciences, it is best for France to ameliorate, to deepen her relations with the savages of the new continent. Several means are offered to attain this more or less promptly.

The choice of the one which I have the honor of presenting to you, Citizen Minister, is founded on the benefits that a laborious, practical study of the material has made me recognize; it reunites a double advantage materially proven: the great simplicity of its scope and the little expense which it entails.

Besides, the ardour, the purity of the vows of the author will serve in all cases to the justification of his plan. He thinks it is not altering the honorable debt which all good *philopolite* [philosophers] owe *à ses penatés*, that of transmitting with submission to an enlightened minister some ideas from which some utility for the fatherland can be reflected, once confided to his so capable hands.

Receive, Citizen Minister, with indulgence, the assurance of my profound respect

[Signed] Louis Vilemont
former Captain of the Regiment of
Louisiana
Sedan, département des Ardennes

X

Promissory Note by D'Église in Favor of Clamorgan, St. Louis, July 6, 1802[1]

In the spring of next year I promise and obligate myself to pay to the order of M. Clamorgan the sum of 12,278 *Livres* 10 *sols* in roebuck skins and in other furs *a poil* coming from the savage trade, all of it at the current price of this place, for a similar sum which I received from the said *Sieur*.

Made and passed at St. Louis, July 6, 1802.

I, Jacque D'Eglise not knowing how to write, I have made my usual mark in the presence of witnesses.

X mark of Jacques D'Église
Regis Loisel, witness
François M. Benoît-witness.

Amos Stoddard, Captain of Artillery, United States, First Civil Commandant of Upper Louisiana, I certify that the present copy is in con-

---

[1]Written in French. Missouri Historical Society, Stoddard Collection. There are two certified copies.

formity with the original remitted in the hands of *Sieur* Jacques Clamorgan.

St. Louis, Illinois—July 5, 1804.

Amos Stoddard [rubric]

I,[2] the undersigned Jacques D'Eglise, under my usual mark in the presence of witnesses promise to pay in the month of May, next, of the year 1803 to the order of M. Clamorgan the sum of 25,122 *livres,* 15 *sols* in money [25,122——15] for that sum which I have received from the said *Sieur* in merchandise to go to trade in the Missouri, in conformity with the passport of M. the Lieutenant-Governor[3] and in case I may not be able to satisfy entirely the above mentioned sum at maturity I obligate myself to pay 10% interest on the *viude* [?] for each year beginning with the month of June of next year, 1803. St. Louis, August 2, 1802.

X mark of Jacques D'Eglise.

Regis Loisel—witness

Pierre Labbadie

Amos Stoddard, captain of artillery of the United States and first Civil Commandant of Upper Louisiana.

I certify that the present copy is in conformity with the original placed in the hands of *Sieur* Jacques Clamorgan.

St. Louis, Illinois, July 5, 1804.

Amos Stoddard [rubric]

Clamorgan petitions Stoddard July 5, 1814 [sic-1804?] to sell territory of about 20×40 arpents in St. Charles. Petitions granted by Stoddard, and Mackay, commandant in St. Andrew and St. Charles is directed to carry it into effect.

Sale—July 8—Adjudication

15-2nd   "

22-3rd   "

sold to Clamorgan for 402 *piastres*

---

[2]There is also a copy in the Missouri Historical Society, St. Charles Archives: Concessions, no. 12.

[3]This seems to indicate that D'Eglise probably went up the Missouri. In 1804 he again ascended the Missouri.

XI

DELASSUS TO SALCEDO, ST. LOUIS, AUGUST 28, 1802[1]

No. 158.

On the third or fourth day of this month, Don Manuel Lisa arrived at this post coming by land; and he has given me your official letter, dated the nineteenth of June last,[2] by which Your Excellency has conceded to him for five years the trade of commerce of the Osage Indians on the exact terms that are evident in the enclosed copy to Don Manuel de Lisa, Don Carlos Sanguinet, Don Francisco Benoît and Don Gregorio Sarpy.

Acquainted with the contents, the next day I summoned Don Augusto Chouteau and Don Manuel Lisa and Francisco María Benoît, the only ones present in the city, and before them I notified Your Excellency's disposition to Don Augusto Chouteau who immediately agreed with the message, I giving to him a copy of Your Excellency's orders.

I should not fail to inform you that it has been brought to my attention that Chouteau is disposed to make the most lively representation of prejudice and impairment that has resulted to him from the merchandise that remains in his warehouse and that he had purchased, confident in the belief that it had been obtained[3] from the Government for four years, with a formal title from *Señor* Marqués de Casa Calvo, your predecessor, of which he reaped the benefit for only last year.

I have also notified Don Santiago Clamorgan of the order which permits Don Santiago Chauvin to trade with the Panis Indians which has already been agreed upon.[4]

With respect to the difficulty between the latter and Carlos Sanguinet,[5] I have had no knowledge of it nor that it even has existed, notwithstanding that it is true that Sanguinet's trader left last year to trade at the posts of others.

I shall employ all my zeal and prudence with justice in order to cut short all animosity and disputes as you forewarned me and I shall advise you concerning the results, as I am also forewarned, and I desire that it

---

[1]Written in Spanish. A.G.I., P. de C., leg. 77.

[2]Document VIII. See also document VII.

[3]See Chapter VII, document I. The full documentation and narrative is given in Nasatir, *Imperial Osage.*

[4]See document VIII.

[5]See document VIII.

should result as you see fit, so that what my predecessors and I have informed this government concerning this branch of trade, shall not [?] be verified.

May God keep Your Excellency many years.

St. Louis, Illinois, August 28, 1802.

Carlos Dehault Delassus [rubric]

Señor Don J. Manuel de Salcedo.

XII

Extract from the Travels of Perrin du Lac, 1802[1]

The chief commerce of Upper Louisiana is carried on with the savages, who inhabit the parts contiguous to the Missouri. The principal rendezvous of the Canadian merchants on the Mississippi are the Dog-field [Prairie-du-Chien], which is distant about five hundred miles from Saint Louis, and Saint Peter's River, which is three hundred miles farther. The Sioux who assemble here every year, bring with them skins, for which they receive in exchange gunpowder, guns, lead, vermilions, and trinkets. Being desirous to be acquainted with the manners of these uncivilized

---

[1] Perrin du Lac's account of the trade of Louisiana and of the Missouri, the furs furnished by each nation, the English trade and advantages of the French over the English in the fur trade and the difficulties experienced by the English in reaching the Mississippi are contained in chapter X of his *Voyages dans les Deux Amériques* (English edition, London, 1807, pp. 49-57). Perrin du Lac says that he left St. Louis on May 18, 1802, ascending the Missouri to the White River. His account in fact is perhaps taken literally from Truteau's "Description" (Chapter V, document I). See A. H. Abel's comments in *Mississippi Valley Historical Review*, VIII, 153-157, where parallel passages are given in extenso; and by same author in *Ibid.*, X, 441-446, and in *Tabeau's Narrative*, 15. See also Abel, "A New Lewis and Clark Map," wherein Perrin du Lac's map is analyzed, *Geographical Review*, I, 341ff. See also Mackay's "Table of Distances" (Chapter VI, document I).

Perrin du Lac's list of Indian nations and the amount of trade is as follows:

	men using arms			
Osages	1200	800 bundles of squirrel skins, and 150 of fine furs.		
Kansas	450	200	150	
Republicans	300	140	of which	10 are fine
Ototactas	350	160		20
Great Panis	500	140		10
Loups	200	80		
Mahas	600	310	of which	40 are fine
Poncas	300	70		6
Ricaras	1000			

Mandanes, Cheyenes, Minitarees
partake very little in the trade
All together they form a mass of about 5000 hunters

Paducas		50 bundles of which 6 are fine
Ricaras		50 almost all of which are fine and of a superior quality.

nations and the mode of their dealings with the Whites, I fitted out a boat, and took on board an old trader[2] of the Illinois river. He had formerly been employed by the Company of Upper Missouri, and had ascended this river farther than any one in the country, and was well acquainted with the different dialects of the savages. He informed me of their manners, customs, and ceremonies.

During his residence in these distant parts, the king of Spain offered rewards to those traders that would give him the best account of these then unknown nations. But notwithstanding these, the government have done nothing for the advancement of trade or public information. All these *mémoirs* are kept in the archives, from which I have made some curious and interesting extracts.

On the 18th of May, 1802, having received ten men on board, and loaded my boat with everything required for the savages, viz. woolen clothing, blue and scarlet cloths, guns, gunpowder, lead, vermilion, copper cauldrons, knives, wines, and silver trinkets, I proceeded on my passage. The banks of the Missouri, for six miles, contain neither villages nor houses; but the lands appear of an excellent quality. At 117 miles from the mouth of the Missouri, is seen the river of the Great Os or Osages. Having ascended it 240 miles, we saw two villages, which were the most populous on the south bank. Thirty miles farther we found their old villages, which are now almost entirely destroyed. They were forced by the Sioux to abandon them, and to retire into the interior.

At a little distance from the old villages, on the opposite bank, is seen the Great River. It is above forty fathoms wide at its mouth, and navigable with boats above 300 miles. We remained here twenty-four

---

Thus the commerce with the people of the Missouri amounts to about 20,000 French *livres* annually.
    The English trade with nations on the Mississippi
Sioux—2500 bundles of skins, one-fourth of the finest quality
Sacs and Foxes—1000 bundles of squirrel skins

Monis [Des Moines]	— about 300 hunters	} barter about 800 bundles, most of
Iowa	450	which are fine.
Perans	300	

The continuation of Chapter X giving his account of his trip up the Missouri follows.
    François Perrin du Lac was a young French *littérateur* who came to the United States to visit especially the Indian tribes of the Missouri, and to relate about them to his eager countrymen. France had just acquired Louisiana from Spain and was hungry for information about it. He landed at New York, went overland through Mt. Vernon, Lancaster, Pittsburg and Gallipolis, and arrived at St. Louis.
    [2]*Ancien traitteur.* Teggart says it might have been Mackay. Abel says Truteau. See citations in note 1. I agree with the latter, although it is possible that D'Eglise could have been the one. See document X. Although D'Eglise declined to join the Missouri Company, nevertheless his work was closely associated with it and he was outfitted at times by men belonging to the Company.

hours, in order to renew our stock of provisions, which was now nearly exhausted. Two or three miles from the Great River is a place, called by the savages Wachanto (harbour of Serpents). I was desirous of knowing whether it deserved the name, and therefore walked with my interpreter to the place. But on this point I was in a short time perfectly satisfied. We embarked next morning, and arrived in three days at the river of the Kanses. This river is navigable at all seasons to the extent of 500 miles.

The Kanses are tall, handsome, vigorous, and brave. They are active and good hunters, and trade is carried on with them by the Whites without danger.

When a trader arrives at a village belonging to these nations, his first business is to make presents to the chiefs, before he lands his merchandise. He is then permitted to construct his cabin in any part of the village which he pleases, and to open his shop. When the prices of the articles which he brings for sale are once fixed, no variations whatsoever are afterwards permitted. When a savage enters the trader's cabin, he lays down the skins which he has to dispose of, and fixes on the articles which he prefers. Each skin has a conventional value. What they call a *plu,* is equal in value to a dollar. Thus, two goatskins make a *plu,* an otter's skin two *plu.* As the prices are regulated by the *plu,* there is never any difficulty in the traffic.

All the persons of distinction seemed anxious to show their regard for me. They feasted me by turns; and, according to their customs, offered me their daughters. I accepted those of the great chief, whom I was afraid of displeasing by a refusal, and made presents to the rest. Among the questions which this people put to me was the following: "Are the people of your country slaves to their wives like the Whites with whom we trade?" Being fearful of losing my credit if I did not appear superior to the other Whites, I replied, that they loved their wives without being their slaves; and that they abandoned them when they were deficient in their duty. The trifling presents that I made to the chief's daughters gained me great reputation for generosity, which in no country can be obtained at a cheaper rate.

After remaining here twelve days, I departed for the mouth of the river Kanses, where we dug a hole, in which we deposited our skins, so that they might not incommode us in our voyage. Thirty-five miles farther we found one of the old villages of the Kanses, and twenty-two miles beyond the other. Three miles before we arrived at the last village we perceived some iron ore. I intended to have assayed it on my return, but an accident unfortunately happening, prevented me. The savannah of St. Michael commences a little higher up, extending to a great distance into the country, and occupying an extent of twenty-four miles on the river. From thence to the Weeping River, (which is one hundred and forty miles distant) nothing is found worthy the attention of a traveler. As I proposed visiting the *Ototatoes,* and afterwards the Great Panis, I left the boat, accompanied by my interpreter and a sailor, and pursued a path along the forest as far as the river. The following evening we arrived at the old villages of the Ototatoes. There were scarce any remains of this nation existing. The Sioux have forced them to retire to the north, where they have fixed their residence for many years. We saw some of them, who received us with kindness, and supplied us with fresh provisions in exchange for trinkets, etc.

If I may judge of the rest of this nation by those that I saw, they are ugly and ill-formed. The Platte River, on which their village is built, is nearly as large as the Missouri; but it is so shallow, and its current so rapid, that it can only be navigated from spring to the beginning of summer. Its sources are in the mountains of Upper Mexico, not far from that of the Santa Fe. We only remained thirty-six hours with Ototatoes, and continued our voyage on the Platte River to the Great Panis, where we arrived in three days. As there was very little water, the sailors were obliged to raise up the boat, and haul it thirty or forty fathoms on the gravel. We were better received by the Great Panis than we had been by the Kanses. They were at war with the nation called Republicans, and had only a small number of fire-arms, without any powder. We supplied them with some in exchange for beavers', wolves' and squirrels' skins. When any one arrives among those nations that are engaged in war, he must be careful not to shew any arms except those he intends to sell, otherwise he will be in danger of having them seized. The Great Panis are not so tall as the Kanses. They are active, and good hunters; and they would kill more game if the Whites came more frequently to trade with them, Their manners very closely resemble those of the Kanses. I was present at the burial of a person of distinction among them; but as this ceremony is the same among all the savage nations, I shall defer the account of it for the present. We only remained eight days among the Great Panis. On our return to the Missouri, we landed at the mouth of the Plate River, at a fort built by the company of the Upper Missouri, in the year 1792.[3] We left there some furs, and proceeded on our voyage. Twenty-six miles higher up is seen the first river of the Sioux. It is navigable only to a

---

[3]Truteau's or Mackay's fort.
Obviously a wrong date, for the Company's first expedition was not made until 1794.

small distance, and derives its source near to the Monis [Des Moines], which flows into the Mississippi.

Ninety miles beyond the first river of the Sioux, seven hundred and thirty-five miles beyond the mouth of the Missouri, is the Mahas river and villages. This nation suffered exceedingly in 1801 by the smallpox.' The village is situated in the fine plain, one league from the Missouri. The Mahas have nothing to distinguish them from the other savages. They have few fire-arms, and are therefore obliged to restrain their love of war. Although I had no personal motives for complaint, yet I found them less affable than the Kanses and the Great Panis. We supplied them with gunpowder, bullets, vermilion, and trinkets, in exchange for some buffaloes' flesh, of which we salted about three hundred pounds weight.

Two days previous to my departure I was present at their preparations for a war expedition which they were going to make against the Miamis nations. I ate there, for the first time in my life, dog's flesh, with which they always regale themselves on these occasions. Although this food was extremely disagreeable to me, I was obliged to commend and praise it. I frequently enquired of them the reason of this custom, but could never obtain any thing satisfactory; they said that they derived the custom from their ancestors, and that, if they omitted it, they would fail in their undertaking.

Twenty miles from the Mahas River, is the second river of the Sioux, and sixty miles farther, the remains of the village Petit-Arc. It was built by a Mahas chief of the same name, who in consequence of a dispute with some of his tribe, came with his family and friends, and formed an establishment. These, after his death, finding themselves too weak to resist the Sioux, who came to lay them under contribution, joined themselves to this nation, from which they are no longer separated. Three miles below the Poncas Village is the Rapid River, which is at its mouth seventy fathoms wide. It is so rapid and shallow, that it cannot even be navigated by a boat. The Poncas nation, to which I walked from the Running River, contains three hundred and fifty warriors, notwithstanding the ravages of the smallpox. One of my crew had a pair of silver ear-rings, on which a young savage appeared to have fixed his heart. He offered him in exchange furs of more than twenty times their value. But no offer seemed sufficient, and no importunity could prevail. He waylaid the possessor, shot him in the neck with an arrow, and left him for dead. He stripped off the ear-rings, and proceeded with an air of satisfaction to me, and presented what he had before offered for the trinkets, which were then suspended from his ears. As soon as I was informed of what had happened, I hastened

'See Chapter IX, document IV.

710

to the spot, and found the sailor motionless, and almost dead; the arrow still remained in the neck. One of the savages extracted it from the wound, on which he laid a plant which he had previously masticated, and made some signs to implore, as he said, the aid of the great Manitou.

On my return I found the whole crew under arms, preparing to revenge themselves on the supposed murderer. I assured them that the wounded man would recover, and by this means rendered them more calm. The next day he was perfectly recovered, and therefore we judged it proper to embark, and ascended the Missouri as far as the White River, which I had fixed as the boundary of my voyage. We here found a part of the Chaguyenne nation, composed of about one hundred and twenty men. The greatest part of them having never seen a white man, looked at us and our clothing with the greatest astonishment.

At a little distance from the mouth of the White River, I perceived a mountain, more elevated than any of those on the banks of the Missouri. The weather being extremely fine, I took with me two hunters, my interpreter, and a young savage for a guide. When we had ascended it half way, the cold became very sensible, and we had brought nothing to defend us from it. My companions lighted a large fire, near to which we slept during the night. At day-break we continued, and before sun-rise had gained the summit. The green which surrounded us, presented the appearance of a calm sea. Some of my companions having shot a calf and some squirrels, we regaled ourselves on them.

I proposed to employ some little time in raising a monument, which might one day attract the attention of travelers in those distant countries. For want of stone I used wood, and having cut some cedars, 20 inches in diameter, cleared the trunks, and made them square; these we fixed in the ground, so that each side was turned towards one of the four cardinal points. On one side I engraved my name, with this inscription, *Sitis cognoscendi;* on another, those of all my companions; on another, *Deo et Naturae;* and on the fourth the date of our arrival.

On the 26th of August we set out to return to St. Louis; from which we had been absent three months. When we reached the river of the Kanses, and were occupied in taking on board the furs that we had deposited there, we saw a party of the Sioux approaching; we therefore immediately reimbarked, leaving some of the least valuable furs behind. We had hardly gained the opposite shore when we were saluted with a discharge of musquetry; but night coming on, the savages abandoned their pursuit.

This was the only act of hostility that we experienced on our return to St. Louis, where we arrived on the 20th of September. It is unnecessary for me to say, that after a voyage of four months, during which time I had no other bed but the ground, no other drink but water, I required some rest.

XIII

Yrujo to Cevallos, Washington, December 2, 1802[1]

No. 313—

"Notice of a project communicated by the President to send travelers to explore the course of the Missouri River, and for them to penetrate as far as the Southern Ocean."

Most Excellent *Señor*

My Dear Sir: The President[2] asked me the other day in a frank and confident tone, if our Court would take it badly, that the Congress decree the formation of a group of travelers, who would form a small caravan and go and explore the course of the Missouri River in which they would nominally have the objective of investigating everything which might contribute to the progress of commerce; but that in reality it would have no other view than the advancement of the geography. He said they would give it the denomination of mercantile, inasmuch as only in this way would the Congress have the power of voting the necessary funds; it not being possible to appropriate funds for a society, or a purely literary expedition, since there does not exist in the constitution any clause which would give it the authority for this effect. I replied to him that making use of the same frankness with which he honored me, I would take the liberty of telling him, that I persuaded myself that an expedition of this nature could not fail to give umbrage to our Government. Then he replied to me that he did not see the motive why they [our government] should have the least fear, inasmuch as its object would not be other than to observe the territories which are found between 40° and 60° [north latitude] from the mouth of the Missouri to the Pacific Ocean, and unite the discoveries that these men would make with those which the celebrated Makensi made in 1793,[3] and be sure if it were possible in that district to establish a continual communication, or little interrupted, by water as far as the South Sea. I told him then that this was already a determined point, as

---

[1]Written in Spanish. A.H.N. Est. leg. 5630, *apartado 2.*

[2]Jefferson's early interest in the west and a route to the Pacific is well known. See J. C. Parish's excellent paper entitled "Emergence of the Idea of Manifest Destiny" in his *Persistence of the Westward Movement and other Essays,* (Berkeley, 1943) 44-77, esp. pp. 68-75.

[3]Alexander MacKenzie, *Voyages from Montreal on the River St. Lawrence Through the Continent of North America to the Frozen and Pacific Oceans* (London, 1801). See also Burpee, *Search for the Western Sea.*

much by the fruitless attempts made with this objective by the Jesuits in Northern California,[4] as by the particular surveys later made by the Captains Cook,[5] Maurelle,[6] Martinez,[7] Vancouver,[8] Cuadra,[9] and lately by the *Señores* Malespina,[10] and Bustamente,[11] who had reconnoitered in the most careful and scrupulous manner all that coast, from the south of the famous strait of Juan de Fucca, situated at 45° latitude, up to the Bucareli River, which the English call Cook River situated at 60° north latitude, and that all these examinations and attempts evidently prove there does not exist this passage of the Northwest, sought with so much anxiety by the most famous navigators of all the nations in the last two centuries, and that it has not existed except in the most exalted imaginations of our Ferrer Maldonado,[12] and Mr. Basq, French geographer. I added that although Miers[13] in these later times had inclined to believe in the existence of this passage, his error had been later demonstrated by the surveys which had been made of the points where it was supposed to exist. Finally that Mackinsee's second trip, in which he penetrated in 1793 up to the Pacific Ocean, shows that there does not exist such a communication by water, since although he arrived in his canoe up to the river of la Paz [Peace river] and not very far from a considerable cordillera of mountains which runs north and south parallel to the ocean coast between 50° and 60° he found himself later in the necessity of traveling by land a very great distance, and the practical [experienced] Indians of the country could not

---

[4]On Jesuits in California explorations see, *e.g.*, H. E. Bolton, *Rim of Christendom* (New York 1936) : Wagner, *Cartography*, I, 152-154, etc.

[5]Cook, *A Voyage to the Pacific* (London, 1785). There are many works relating to Cook's third voyage. See H. R. Wagner, *Cartography of the Northwest Coast of America to the Year 1800*, two volumes (Berkeley, 1943), I, 183-186, 179, 189-190.

[6]Antonio Francisco Mourelle. See Wagner, *Cartography*, I, 175-179, 192-216 *passim*, 231. Concerning the men listed here see in addition to Wagner, *Cartography;* W. R. Manning, *Nootka Sound Controversy;* H. H. Bancroft, *History of the Northwest Coast*, vol. I. (San Francisco, 1884) ; H. R. Wagner, *Spanish Exploration in the Strait of Juan de Fuca* (Santa Ana, 1933) ; etc. A good many manuscripts relating to these men are given in A. P. Nasatir, *French Activities in California: An Archival Calendar-Guide*, (Stanford University, 1945). W. Lowery, *A Descriptive List of Maps of the Spanish Possessions*, ed. by P. C. Phillips (Washington, 1912).

[7]Esteban José Martínez. See Manning, *Nootka Sound Controversy;* Wagner, *Cartography*, I, 172-173 ; 197-200 ; and esp. 202-219.

[8]Capt. George Vancouver, *A Voyage of Discovery to the North Pacific Ocean and Round the World*, (three volumes, London, 1798). See Wagner, *Cartography*, I, 239-249.

[9]Juan Francisco de la Bodega y Cuadra. See H. R. Wagner, *Spanish Explorations, op. cit.* and Wagner, *Cartography*, I, 175-177, 183.

[10]Alejandro Malespina. See Wagner, Cartography, I, 225-229, 236, 252.

[11]Carlos María de Bustamente, *Resúmen de Viaje Hecho por las Goletas Sutil y Mexicana en el año de 1792 para reconocer el estrecho de Fuca* (Madrid, 1802).

[12]Lorenzo Ferrer Maldonado. See Wagner, *Cartography*, I, 162, 226. See H. R. Wagner, "Apocryphal Voyages to the Northwest Coast of America," *Proceedings, American Antiquarian Society*, new series, XLI, 179-234.

[13]John Meares, *Voyages 1789-1790 from China to the Northwest Coast of America . . . Observations on the possible existence of a Northwest Passage*—(London, 1790). See Wagner, *Cartography*, I, 205-213; and *Spanish Voyages, op. cit.*

give him news of any considerable river whatsoever which from those mountains, which must be without doubt the source of the waters of the west in that vicinity, empties into the Pacific Ocean. This account of useless and fruitless attempts it seems to me calmed his spirit with which he began to talk to me of the subject.

The President has been all his life a man of letters, very speculative and a lover of glory, and it would be possible he might attempt to perpetuate the fame of his administration not only by the measures of frugality and economy which characterize him, but also by discovering or attempting at least to discover the way by which the Americans may some day extend their population and their influence up to the coasts of the South Sea.

I do not know what might be his final decision concerning this point, but I shall be on the lookout to see if it is attempted to realize or not this idea by the Congress, and in case of trying to carry it into effect I shall notify Your Excellency in order that it may please you to communicate to me His Majesty's orders concerning this issue.

May God keep Your Excellency many years.

Washington December 2, 1802

Most Excellent *Señor*

Your most attentive and constant servant, kisses the hand of

Your Excellency

Carlos Martínez de Yrujo [rubric]

Most Excellent *Señor* Don Pedro Cevallos

[Decree] "That His Majesty has seen with satisfaction that by their erudite reflections the President's project has been abandoned.

February 19, 1803.

CHAPTER XI

1803

I

YRUJO TO CEVALLOS, WASHINGTON, JANUARY 31, 1803[1]

No. 320

The Marqués de Casa Yrujo to Most Excellent *Señor* Don Pedro Cevallos.

"Gives notice of the President having passed to the Senate the project of sending travelers to explore the course of the Missouri, of which he gave account in the letter no. 313".[2]

Most Excellent *Señor*

Dear Sir:

In my letter No. 313 I notified Your Excellency that the President of the United States had a project directed to send travelers in order to explore the course of the Missouri River, who continuing their expedition up to the North West Coast, they were to examine the possibility or impossibility of communications by water, between the Atlantic Ocean and the Southern Ocean, and contribute to advance the geography of the North of America. I also told Your Excellency the conversation which pertaining to this project, the President had with me concerning this plan, he desiring to know whether our Court would refuse to grant the necessary passports to the travelers, and all of which I judged opportune to reply to you concerning the particular. I thought that in consequence

---

[1]Written in Spanish. A.H.N., Est., leg. 5630 apartado 3.
[2]Chapter X, document XIII.

he would desist in his attempt, and in this way I hinted this to Your Excellency, but later I have learned that he has communicated his design to the Senate, which has already taken a step towards the execution. Nevertheless I have understood that the good judgment of the Senate does not see the advantages that the President proposes in this expedition, and that on the contrary, they feared it might offend one of the European nations, and consequently it is very probable that the project will not proceed. But since I promised to give to Your Excellency news of any latest occurrence, I thought I should communicate this to you for your intelligence.

May God keep Your Excellency many years.

Washington, January 31, 1803.
Most Excellent *Señor*.

Your most attentive and constant servant kisses Your Excellency's Hand.
The Marqués de Casa Yrujo
[rubric]
Most Excellent *Señor* Don Pedro Cevallos.

II

LISA TO DELASSUS, ST. LOUIS, MARCH 14, 1803[1]

Don Manuel de Lisa and Company, residents and merchants of this Village of St. Louis, come before you to say, that last year a petition was presented to the Governor General of this Province earnestly requesting him to grant us an exclusive trade privilege for a term of five consecutive years,[2] stating in said document that we would build at our expense a water mill to make flour, this mill to have two runs of stones being as well equipped as those of the Anglo-Americans; at the same time we stated in the mentioned petition that we would make a donation of one thousand dollars to the King; at that time same was credited to the Royal Treasury for the expenses and repairs of a Fort. For this generous offer and calling to the attention of the Governor that this would be a general good and would be of mutual benefit to all the people, he has granted us the exclusive privilege of trade, which we requested, with the great and little Osages, who are located at mid-distance [*medio del Río Misuri*] of the Missouri River, about forty leagues from its mouth,

Presented on the 14th day of March, 1803[3]

---

[1]Written in Spanish. Missouri Historical Society, Pierre Chouteau Collection, Spanish Archives of St. Louis [and Lisa Collection].
[2]Chapter X, documents V, VII, VIII and XI.
[3]Marginal notation.

with power to equip, trade and facilitate by [every] means our commerce with the savages of that river; in consequence thereof among other orders that were sent you, the one for this purpose was included and we see with a great deal of sorrow that such high orders are in a way disregarded, because instead of giving us the assistance as it is ordered, we are provoked and insulted with censure (which we ignore), this was done largely when Don Manuel de Lisa arrived at New Orleans taking with him the document granting the exclusive privilege of trade.

Our intention is not to demand from Your Excellency any justice, because we are confident that you will not stand for one insult after the other, though it is true that Don Manuel de Lisa appeared before you with due submission as a subject should to complain about certain disorder originated by a resident of this place named José Ortiz, in fitting out a canoe which was taken by one of his sons and two men with direction to the River of the Osages to sell brandy to our traders and hunters who were in that place. He obtained his object and he brought with him some skins from our markets; this man returned here and Don Manuel de Lisa obtained all the information about him and found that he had taken advantage of some repugnant and scandalous act. He brought this before you, to which you answered *Esté vous Juge pour prendre des Informations* [are you Judge to take information?]. This unexpected answer from a judge shows indeed without the least doubt the little or no justice that we are to receive in the future from you, which statement we can assure you we make without fear, more so knowing that your intention at all times has been to ignore us and give us sufficient and equivocal proofs of the antagonism which you have towards us in matters pertaining to the trade of the Missouri; therefore we are impelled to appeal to the General Judge for our well founded justice so that through his pious intentions and generous Spanish soul he will grant us justice and what has been offered us. We can affirm with certainty, and we leave not the slightest doubt of, our zeal for the public good in the construction of the above mentioned mill, which is as well equipped as we have offered the Governor General in our petition dated last July, which mill is completed. It is also well known that our good intentions are well proven in dividing by our efforts a party of 60 warriors of the Kickapoo nations, who lately were going out upon a war against the Osages with the intention of surprising and attacking them, and in order to please them we were obliged to make them presents of goods and merchandise watching that they did not capture and destroy (if they had carried out their intended end) many white men who might have been victims of their voracity.

Not wishing to require more of your Excellency's attention, we have overlooked the personal offenses, which only our zeal and Spanish patriotism prompts us to bury, but we beg of you to decree whatever you judge necessary, protesting with every form of justice and appealing for the halting of these insults to the Highest Tribunal of these Provinces which is in New Orleans, and for this purpose please order to have a full testimony made of this writing and state that I am ready to give oath of same and to satisfy their just claims with costs; I swear.

Manuel de Lisa Y Compañía.
[Signed]'

'For presenting this document, which Lisa denied having written and having uttered the words, since he had personal grievances against the lieutenant-governor, Lisa was put in jail. He repented and was released to his own house still under arrest. Lisa retracted his statements and expressed his regrets for what he had said and written. Delassus released him. Petitions of Lisa to Delassus, St. Louis, March 12 and 17, 1803; decrees of Delassus, same date. Delassus' actions were approved by Salcedo and the *Auditor de Guerra,* New Orleans, May 3, 1803. Missouri Historical Society, Lisa Collection. Letter of Salcedo to Delassus, New Orleans, May 3, 1803, is in Missouri Historical Society, Pierre Chouteau Collection, Spanish Archives of St. Louis, Box II, Envelope VII. See Judge Douglas' excellently written biographical sketch of Manuel Lisa in *Missouri Historical Society Collections,* vol. IV.

III

NOTE OF ROBIDOUX TO CLAMORGAN, ST. LOUIS, AUGUST 27, 1803[1]

Jh. Robidoux à Jacques Clamorgan pour les avances faittes pour l'expedition des parte [de porter] du haut Missouri.

17681—19—6

St. Louis 27 August, 1803

pr. Jh. Robidoux
Agte. Chouteau [?]

Jq. Clamorgan
[rubric]

[1]Missouri Historical Society, Auguste Chouteau Collection, V. This document is included here because of the bitter hostility of Robidoux to Clamorgan and to show his activities in 1803. See Chapter X and other previous ones for documents.

IV

HARRISON TO JEFFERSON, VINCENNES, NOVEMBER 26, 1803[1]

Vincennes, Nov. 26, 1803

Governor of Indiana territory presents his respectful compliments to the President of the United States and requests his acceptance of the

[1]Library of Congress, Jefferson Papers, 136, printed in "Messages and Papers of William Henry Harrison", *Indiana Historical Collections,* I, 90. This is unsigned.

718

enclosed map which is a copy of the manuscript map of Mr. Evans' who ascended the Missouri river by order of the Spanish government further than any other person.

[unsigned]

²See Abel, "A New Lewis and Clark Map," *Geographical Review*, I, 329-345; Teggart, "Notes Supplementary to any Edition of Lewis and Clark," *American Historical Association Annual Report, 1908*, I, 185-195. In the Missouri Historical Society, Clark Collection, VI, package IV, under file at the end of the year 1803, is written, "Mr. Evins' sketches of the Missouri, presented by Mr. Mackay." This is the entire contents. See Thwaites, *Original Journals*, I and VIII; and maps.

V

DELASSUS TO SALCEDO AND CASA CALVO, ST. LOUIS, DECEMBER 9, 1803.¹

No. 213

The 7th of this month Mr. Merryweather Lewis, Captain of the United States army and former secretary of the President of them presented himself at this post.

He has given me a *carta avertoria* [*sic*] a copy of which I am enclosing telling me that the president thought that it was Captain Don Enrique Peyroux who commanded this Upper Louisiana but that he was presenting it to me so that I might become acquainted with it as well as with the passports, copies of which he also enclosed adding also that his intention was to continue his trip penetrating the Missouri in order to fulfill his mission of discoveries and observations. I have hinted to him that my orders did not permit me to consent to his passing to enter the Missouri River and that I was opposing it in the name of the King, my master.

¹Written in Spanish. A.G.I., P. de C., leg. 2368. Reply is Chapter XII, document III. This information was transmitted to Spain. On December 29 Salcedo and Casa Calvo reported that the French officials had turned over Louisiana to the United States. Previously on August 20, 1803, the New Orleans Spanish officials warned Cevallos that the Americans wanted to become master of the Missouri and its navigation and commerce and of the riches of Sonora and Sinaloa—that was the purpose of the Lewis and Clark expedition. Draft to Cevallos, New Orleans, January 13, 1804, A.G.I., P. de C., leg. 2356.

In discussing the differences and difficulties regarding the western and northern boundaries of the United States, Merry, the British *Chargé d'Affaires* at Washington, wrote to Hawkesbury (no. 10 January 2, 1804—Public Record Office (London) Foreign Office Papers, Series 5, volume 41) that the Spaniards said that the Missouri river was the boundary and Spain had ordered its officials not to give up the posts on the Missouri. The United States, on the other hand, said that it had a right to call all the territory as far west as Santa Fé and north to the source of the Mississippi river its own. See I. J. Cox, *Early Explorations of Louisiana* (Cincinnati, 1906) : and by same author, "Louisiana-Texas Frontier," *Texas State Historical Association Quarterly* X, 1-75; *Southwestern Historical Quarterly* XVII, 1-42; 140-187: T. M. Marshall, *History of the Western Boundary of the Louisiana Purchase* (Berkeley, 1914).

He then told me my opinion sufficed and that from now he would not go to the said river, I having observed to him that he surprised me for not having provided himself with a passport from our Spanish Minister in Philadelphia;[2] that if he had had a passport in the name of the King my master, he could have removed all difficulty. He answered me that when he left Philadelphia that it was already at the beginning of July, that he thought he would find here the French, that for that reason, he had not believed it necessary to carry a passport from *Señor* Marqués de Yrujo; that he thought that then it would be useless, but that during his trip he had learned that even though the delivery to France had not been carried out, he well supposed that I would not allow him to continue on, and especially with the news of the day; and that in order not to lose any time and so that his men might hunt he would continue in the Mississippi maintaining himself on the American side.

And I have forewarned him that I was going to inform Your Excellencies of the matter and that before spring I would surely have an answer from Your Excellencies which would inform me if they determine who may pass. The said man with his committee, which according to the information he has given me consists of twenty five men (which truly cannot be less so as to be able to be somewhat secure among the nations and cannot be larger because of the difficulty of the provisions in such an expedition), in view of my proposition has agreed to wait for Your Excellencies' determination and he is going to spend the winter on the Dubois River.[3]

Your Excellencies will determine what you think best.

I should inform Your Excellencies that according to advices, I believe that his mission has no other object than to discover the Pacific Ocean, following the Missouri, and to make intelligent observations, because he has the reputation of being a very well educated man and of many talents.

I have offered to serve him, in view of the cited letter, in all that I might be useful to him in so far as my orders did not oppose.

All of which I am informing Your Excellencies for your due knowledge. May God keep Your Excellencies many years.

St. Louis, Illinois, December 9, 1803

Carlos Dehault Delassus [rubric]

Señores Brigadiers of the Royal Armies
Don J. Manuel de Salcedo and Marqués de Casa Calvo.

---

[2]He had and showed Delassus passports from the British *Chargé d'Affaires* Edward Thornton dated Washington, February 8, 1803 and the French *Chargé d'Affaires* L. A. Pichon dated Georgetown 10 Ventôse an X (March 1, 1803). Certified copies in A.G.I., P. de C., leg. 2368.

[3]See *Original Journals of the Lewis and Clark Expedition.*

Washington July 3, 1803

[Enclosure]⁴

Copy

Dear Sir:

Since I had the pleasure of your acquaintance in Philidelphia in 1791,⁵ I had supposed you were returned to Europe. I have lately however been told that you preside at present at Ste. Genevieve & St. Louis. I cannot therefore omit the satisfaction of writing to you by Capᵗ Lewis, an officer in our army, and for some time past my secretary, as our former acquaintance was a mixt one of Science and business, so is the occasion of renewing it. You know that the geography of the Missoury and the most convenient water communication from the head of that to the Pacific Ocean is a desideretum not yet satisfied. Since coming to the administration of the U. S. I have taken the earliest opportunity in my power to have that communication explored, and Capᵗ Lewis with a party of twelve or fifteen men is authorized to do it, his journey being merely literary, to inform us of the geography and natural history of the country, I have procured a passport for him and his party, from the Minister of France here, it being agreed between him and the Spanish Minister, that the country having been ceded to France her minister may most properly give authority for the journey. This was the state of things when the passport was given, which was some time since. but before Capᵗ Lewis's actual departure We learn through a channel of unquestionable information that France has ceded the whole contry of Louisiana to the U. S. by a treaty concluded in the first days of May, but for an object as innocent and useful as this I am sure you will not be scrupulous as to the authorities on which the journey is undertaken; and that you will give all the protection you can to Capᵗ Lewis and his party in going and returning— I have no doubt you can be particularly useful to him, and it is to sollicit your patronage that I trouble you with the present letter, praying you at the same time to accept my friendly salutations and assurances of my high respect and consideration— *Th* Jefferson —

Mr. Peyroux Commandant of Upper Louisiana

This is a copy

Delassus [rubric]

---

⁴This is written in English—a copy certified by Delassus.
⁵Peyroux visited the United States in 1793. See Liljegren, "Jacobinism in Spanish Louisiana 1792-1797," *Louisiana Historical Quarterly,* XXII (1939), reprint, p. 41.

CHAPTER XII

1804-1806

I

Morales to Cayetano Soler, New Orleans, January 14, 1804[1]

No. 281

Most Excellent *Señor:* The enclosed copy of the official letter which on the fifth of the current month these commissioners of delivery directed to me, will inform Your Excellency of the motives which obliged the lieutenant-governor of St. Louis, Illinois, to direct to this capital an express notifying that there was approaching those establishments a body of five hundred armed Americans; of the steps which he took of placing the militia under arms; and of the arrival of Captain Wheather with the object of making discoveries in the Missouri.[2] [Enclosure] No. 2 is the agreement which by virtue of my order this Ministry drew up in order to liquidate the credit of 122 *pesos* which belong to the cited express, Josef Verdon, and to his two companions. I am directing all this to Your Excellency in order that you may bring this expense to the notice of His Majesty so that it may merit the royal approval. May God keep Your Excellency many years. New Orleans, January 14, 1804.

—Juan Ventura Morales

[To] Most Excellent *Señor*—Don Miguel Cayetano Soler

---

[1] Written in Spanish. A.G.I., P. de C., leg. 638.
[2] Chapter XI, document V.

[Enclosures]^a

No. 1 Official letter from the commissioners
January 5. "Lt. Governor of Illinois tells us, etc.
No. 2 Adjustment of this expense formed by the Ministry of the Royal
Hacienda.

---

^aEnclosures not here.

II

YRUJO TO CEVALLOS, WASHINGTON, JANUARY 17, 1804[1]

[Marginal notations]

He gives account of the President of the United States having received the news by an express of the delivery of Louisiana by the prefect Laussat to the American commissioners named for that purpose. Encloses the extraordinary issue of the newspaper which with this motive
is circulated in this city in which paper can be seen the proclamation made
by the *ad-interim* governor, and he advises of an act which congress has
passed, authorizing the president to treat with the Indians concerning an
exchange of land, which authorization would agree infinitely to the wishes
of Spain.

Most Excellent *Señor:*

My Dear Sir: Yesterday the president of the United States received by an express the notice of Louisiana having been delivered by the
prefect Laussat to the American commissioners named for this purpose.
And immediately circulated the extraordinary gazette, a copy of which
I have the honor of enclosing to Your Excellency, in which you will find
the proclamation made by the *ad-interim* governor and that of General
Wilkinson, Brigadier General and commander of the army.[2] Thus this
negotiation is concluded and there only remains to us to make a treaty
of limits in the future.[3] The government and the greater part of the
persons of influence and character in this country are more and more confirmed in the necessity that the American population should not cross the
Mississippi and establish themselves and extend on its right bank and it

---

[1]Written in Spanish. A.H.N., Est., leg. 5540, *expediente* 1.
[2]See documents printed in Alcée Fortier, *History of Louisiana*, (New York, 1904),
II, 295-301; J. A. Robertson, *Louisiana under France, Spain and the United States*,
Vol. II., Baron Marc de Villiers du Terrage, *Les Dernières Années de la Louisiane
Français* (Paris, 1904) etc.
[3]See, P. C. Brooks, *Diplomacy and the Borderlands* (Berkeley, 1939), and Marshall, *History of Western Boundary of Louisiana Purchase*. Also Cox's articles cited
in Chapter XI, document 5, note 1.

is probable that Congress before adjourning may pass an act authorizing the president to evict the Americans who may try to make establishments on the western side of the river.

It has already passed one authorizing the President for the purpose of treating with the numerous nations of Indians who inhabit within the limits of the United States and he may propose to them an exchange of the lands which they possess for an equal portion, or even a greater portion than they possess now. In a word, the just conviction that this country is threatened by the evils of which I have informed Your Excellency if the American population passes the natural line of that copious river has suggested to them the idea of removing, if it is possible, all the Indians who at present live in the territory of the United States to the opposite bank of the Mississippi. This plan if it can be put into practice will completely join together [reconcile] the interests of the Americans with those of the King our Sovereign. The former will succeed in confining its population in a territory already too extended for the number of its inhabitants and [by] removing the Indians not only will the United States acquire the large amount of lands which they possess within its bosom but also [in] stopping the friction and immediate collision with them they will also stop the motives of war which are so frequent and which in many cases have cost the United States much blood and money.

For our part we will obtain a natural and powerful barrier between the population of the American citizens and our possessions of New Mexico, a barrier which will be all the more solid in as much as there will result from this wise policy of the United States, in addition to the settlements of the Indians, an immense desert which will serve us equally for protection. From these bases of common interest should result a conformity of political ideas between Spain and this country which without doubt will facilitate the boundary treaty which must follow; but I repeat, it is, in my opinion, [to] our interests that our government should attract to Madrid the negotiation which must precede it. May God Keep Your Excellency many years, Washington, January 17, 1804.

Most Excellent *Señor,* Your most attentive and grateful servant kisses

Your Excellency's hand.

El Marqués de Casa Yrujo [rubric]

Most Excellent *Señor* Don Pedro Cevallos

III

[GOVERNOR OF LOUISIANA?] TO DELASSUS, NEW ORLEANS, JANUARY 28, 1804[1]

If upon the receipt of this Your Excellency finds himself commanding that post, without someone having presented himself, who would take charge in behalf of the United States, which took possession of this capital and province the 20th of December last:[2] you will not put any obstacle to impede Capt. Merry Weather Lewis' entrance in the Missouri whenever he wishes; nevertheless Your Excellency did right in taking the dispositions of which your official letter no. 213[3] treats; since you had no order from your government.

Your Excellency should try to conform at the capital to the terms which have been prescribed to you by our order, which you should have received in duplicate, as soon as you deliver your posts to the official or agent of the United States, who will present himself to that purpose.[4]

God keep Your Excellency many years.

New Orleans, January 28, 1804

[draft]

Señor Don Carlos de Lassus

---

[1]Written in Spanish. This is a draft in A.G.I., P. de C., leg. 141.
[2]See document II and references there cited.
[3]Chapter XI, document V.
[4]The transfer of Upper Louisiana took place on March 9 and 10, 1804. Billon, *Annals of St. Louis—under French and Spanish Dominations*, 339-363; Houck, *History of Missouri*, II, chapters XX-XXI; Stoddard, *Sketches of Louisiana;* Gayarré; *History of Louisiana*, vol. III; Fortier, *History of Louisiana*, II, 317-318, etc. On March 6, 1804, Delassus gave Stoddard a list and characterizations of the men in his employ. Printed in Billon, *op. cit.,* 365-371.

IV

FR. FRANCISCO GIL AND OTHERS, MADRID, MARCH 17, 1804[1]

Copy

Señor:

In view of the Royal Order communicated by the *Señor* Don Pedro Cevallos on February 12, last, with the doubts and replies which occurred between the commander general of the *Provincias Internas* and the Com-

---

[1]Written in Spanish. A.G.I., P. de C., leg. 176B. Cited by I. J. Cox, "Louisiana-Texas Frontier," *Southwestern Historical Quarterly*, XVII 20-21. See documents printed in Robertson, *Louisiana under Spain*, vol II, 139-214 relating to boundaries. See also *Pichardo's Treatise on the Limits of Louisiana and Texas* edited by C. W. Hackett, 4 vols., (Austin, 1931-1946.)

missioners for the demarcation of limits of Louisiana on the North and West of this Province; the committee of Fortifications and Defense of the Indies has examined very attentively, this *expediente* which Don Nemesio Salcedo remitted by the most direct route on October 4th last via *reservada,* by which is marked off the boundary between the Provinces of Texas and Louisiana, by a line which flowing out into the Mexican Gulf between the rivers Caricut or Calcasiu, and Armenta or Mermenta, rises towards the North through the vicinity of Nachitoches up to the Río Rojo or Colorado, which disembogues into the Mississippi. The northern limits of Louisiana are left undetermined, and it is said only that in that part the confines of Texas and New Mexico extend beyond the Missouri River. His Majesty, therefore, wishes to hear the judgment of the Committee concerning the referred-to-doubts. Although the latter lacks the information necessary to proceed in this important affair with the ability that it would wish, it is nevertheless of the opinion that the line of demarcation, before mentioned, to the West of Louisiana as far up as Nachitoches and Presidio *reformado* de Adaes, should be adjusted, because of being the safest and free of doubts that can be pointed out, and if the Commissioners of both Powers agree that this line be a neutral border of land of a few leagues in width, it would be very conducive to better strengthen these limits, and avoid in the future the inevitable disputes and controversies which the sly and fraudulent usurpation of lands of the neighboring Nations occasions; in this the Governor of Texas or *Nuevas Filipinas* must be very zealous especially in the beginning, in order to better consolidate the indicated limits to the West of Louisiana. Since the ones that should be surveyed in the northern part are so doubtful and little known, they should be entrusted to the prudent discretion and wise inquiries of our Commissioners, charging them that they should try to take in their demarcation all the advantage possible, and that it be more in conformity to fair reason, that the confluence of the Missouri and the Mississippi should belong without controversy to Spain. Thus among other reasons it can be deduced from some of the fundamentals which the committee indicated in its meeting of January 19 last, and moreover there belonging to Spain the two borders of the Missouri, the neighboring power is prevented from having any pretex to navigate on this large river, whose course encircles New Mexico to the north, previously penetrating part of the Province of Texas. The Governor of Texas, given the instructions and help which are judged necessary, should fulfill this point with particular care, to avoid not only the contraband which the neighboring power can make in that part, but also to impede their penetrating by that River and beginning to associate themselves with the nations and tribes of Gentile

Indians who inhabit its borders, to the very grave and irreparable harm of Your Excellency's possessions in all of New Spain, as they will do, ambitiously by the broad expanses of the Mississippi, as the public newspapers already are beginning to indicate. But the course of this river penetrating at greater distances toward the north, for the present the attempts which they are committing on it are not so feared or harmful as those they might venture upon on the Missouri, although such enterprises must in all cases arouse greatly our attention and vigilant observation.

This is, *Señor*, what seems proper for the Committee to state in fulfillment of the cited Royal Order, and of the efficacious desires which aid it to work with utility to the best service of His Majesty, who will decide concerning all that which may be to his sovereign will.

Madrid. March 17, 1804. Fr. Francisco Gil.

>Fernando Daoiz
>Josef Vasallo
>Francisco Requena
>Josef Betegon
>Pedro de Cortes
>Geronimo de la Rocha y Figueroa
>   It is a Copy
>   [there is one rubric]

V

CASA CALVO TO CEVALLOS, NEW ORLEANS, MARCH 30, 1804[1]

No. 5 *Reservada*

[Marginal note] The Brigadier of the Royal Army, Marqués de Casa Calvo, His Majesty's commissioner for the retrocession and limits of the province of Louisiana, communicates the steps that he has taken to detain the progress of the discoveries, that a subject sent by the president of the United States is making on the Missouri River towards the direction of the South Sea, where they are thinking of having a port within

---

[1]Written in Spanish. A.H.N., Est., leg. 5542; draft in A.G.I., P. de C., leg. 2356. Certified copy is in A.H.N., Est., leg. 5542, *expediente* 2 and A.G.I., P. de C., leg. 2368. Also in Archivo General y Público (Mexico), Sección Historia, volume 200; transcript in Bancroft Library.

five years; writing to the Commandant-general of the *Provincias Internas* to arrest and detain him.

Received—July 18, 1804

Most Excellent Sir.

With the idea of detaining the hasty and gigantic steps which our neighbors are taking towards the South Sea, entering by way of the Missouri river and other rivers of the west bank of the Mississippi; furthering their discoveries in that district; I have written to the Commandant-General of the *Provincias Internas,* Brigadier Don Nemesio Salcedo the letter, a copy of which is enclosed. I hope this step will merit the approbation of Your Excellency, with all the more reason in that it proceeds from the intimation made in [letter] number 13, that he believes and assures that it is of the greatest importance to restrain in that area the progress of the discoverers, who are directing towards that district all their views and voyages, not losing from sight the forming from the interior [*fondo*] of their states a chain of establishments, making themselves masters of our rich possessions, which they desire.

It is painful to acknowledge it and to experience it, but it will be much more painful not to use all our forces, while there is still time to remedy it, even though it be at the cost of continual vigilance and no small expense.

The duty of a vassal zealous for the glory of the King and nation impels my pen with irresistible force to write and to assure that the moment is a critical one and it is best to take advantage of it, for otherwise the rich possessions of the Kingdom of New Spain remain exposed. Therefore I urgently beg Your Excellency to call the attention of His Majesty to these dominions if he does not wish to be a witness of their impending ruin and destruction.

May God Our Lord keep Your Excellency many years

New Orleans, March 30, 1804

Most Excellent Sir,

El Marqués de Casa Calvo [rubric]

Most Excellent *Señor* Don Pedro Cavallos.

Most Excellent Sir:[2]

I am sending to Your Excellency a copy of the official letter in which Brigadier Marqués de Casa Calvo advises me of Mr. Merry, Cap-

-----

[2]Original in A.G.M., Historia, vol. 200; transcript in Bancroft Library. This covering letter is not in A.H.N.

tain of the United States Army having presented himself in the establishments of Illinois, with the solicitation of penetrating the Missouri river in order to make observations and discoveries, so that with that object in mind, with the notices included in the letter and those included in my reply, a copy of which is also enclosed, Your Excellency may be able to make whatever use of them that you judge.

May God keep Your Excellency many years.

Chihuahua, May 3, 1804

Most Excellent Sir

Nemesio Salcedo [rubric]

Most Excellent *Señor* Don Joseph de Yturrigaray

[Marginal note] acknowledge receipt and reply that His Excellency hopes that you will advise him of all results.

[draft of reply]

I have received Your Excellency's letter ot May 3, last, the two copies which are enclosed in it relative to the intentions of Mr. Merry, Captain of the United States Army regarding penetrating the Missouri river for the purpose of making observations and discoveries. I am informed myself of all and hope Your Excellency will be pleased to give me advice of the results because of it being very important to the service of the King.

May God, etc.

June 2, 1804.

[draft]

Señor Don Nemesio de Salcedo.*

---

*Enclosures are: Casa Calvo to N. Salcedo, New Orleans, March 5, 1804, and N. Salcedo to Casa Calvo, Chihuahua, May 3, 1804.

VI

NEMESIO SALCEDO TO CEVALLOS, NEW ORLEANS, MAY 8, 1804[1]

No. 4.

[Marginal notation]

The commandant-general of the *Provincias Internas* of New Spain relates that the governor of Louisiana has notified him that Captain Merry, commissioned by the United States for the purpose of making observations

---

[1]Written in Spanish. Original in A.H.N., Est., leg. 5542 *expediente* 2. All except the last enclosure is in A.G.M. Historia, vol. 200; transcript in Bancroft Library. Original of enclosure no. 2 is in A.G.I., P. de C., leg. 2368.

and discoveries, presented himself in Illinois. He also states what he answered to the said governor concerning the matter.

Most Excellent Sir:

I am remitting to Your Excellency under number one a copy of an official letter in which the Marqués de Casa Calvo notified me of Captain Merry having presented himself in Illinois soliciting to penetrate the Missouri River in order to carry out the commission which has been conferred upon him by the United States of America concerning observations and discoveries; and likewise is enclosed under number two a copy of the answer which I have given to the referred to Marqués concerning the matter.

By both papers Your Excellency will recognize that that expedition is directed to territories under my command and that it is a step of the said United States which indicates its ambitious views in the same act of taking possession of the province of Louisiana. I am unable to dictate any other precautionary step than the orders already communicated to the governors of Texas and New Mexico relative to their preventing the introduction of foreigners in the districts of both provinces, and to their refusing permission to such foreigners, and relative to their not allowing the boundaries of Louisiana to be marked out [set up] along their frontiers [borders of Texas and New Mexico], as I informed Your Excellency in my letter number three of October 4, last.

Even though these steps taken with all anticipation and the charge which the principal Indian nations have of giving advice of any news which they learn are the only ones in this case and for which cause I now repeat their observance to the cited governors, it has seemed to me well to augment those relative to New Mexico in the terms verified in copy number three.

I am informing you in it that in the present circumstances the limited forces of that province should be used to restrain one of the barbarous nations which has become restless [getting out of hand]. I sent a party of Comanche Indians or others of those who are affected to us to reconnoitre the country as far as the banks of the Missouri river in order to examine if the expedition of Merry has penetrated into these territories, to acquire all possible knowledge of its progress, and even to stop them, making efforts to apprehend it.

Nothwithstanding, as I have insinuated to the Marqués de Casa Calvo, I judge that through the Chief of Louisiana, you may have called the attention of the governor of the United States to this suspicious conduct. I am sending an official letter to the Minister of the King in Philadelphia instructing him of the present case for the conduct of the better service, and thus I hope it may please Your Excellency to inform His Majesty of it for his sovereign intelligence.

May God keep Your Excellency many years.

Chihuahua, 8 May, 1804

Most Excellent Sir

Nemesio Salcedo [rubric]

Most Excellent *Señor* Don Pedro Ceballos

[Enclosures with dispatch no. 4]

No. 1[2] Colonel Don Carlos Dehault Delassus, Lieutenant-Governor of the establishment of Illinois gave information under date of December 9[3] of last year that on the seventh of the same month Mr. Merry Weather Lewis, Captain of the Army of the United States and former secretary of the president of those states, presented himself in that post, intending to penetrate the Missouri River in order to fulfill the commission which he has of making discoveries and observations. The same commandant advises that he was opposed to his entrance until receiving the corresponding permission from the general government.

This step on the part of the United States at the same time that it took possession of the province of Louisiana; its haste to instruct itself and to explore the course of the Missouri whose origin they claim belongs to them,[4] extending their designs as far as the South Sea, forces us necessarily to become active and to hasten our steps in order to cut off the gigantic steps of our neighbors if we wish, as it is our duty, to preserve undamaged [intact] the dominions of the King and to prevent ruin and destruction of the *Provincias Internas* and of the Kingdom of New Spain.

The only means which presents itself is to arrest Captain Merry Weather and his party, which cannot help but pass through the nations neighboring New Mexico, its presidios or *rancherías*.

A decisive and vigorous blow will prevent immense expenditures and even countless disagreeable replies which must originate between the respective governments, and immediately we are impelled to act out of the necessity of the moment. The public claims which they manifest concerning the extensions of the province of Louisiana which the French Republic has sold to them dictate it. No less do they claim as their western limits than the mouth of the Río Bravo up to 30 degrees north latitude, and from there the line of demarcation penetrates [undetermined] far

---

[2]Draft in A.G.I., P. de C., leg. 2368; copy in A.G.M.. Historia, Vol. 200, transcript in Bancroft Library; Copy enclosed in draft to Cevallos, no. 5, March 30, 1804. Document V. A.G.I., P. de C., leg. 2356.

[3]Chapter XI, document V.

[4]See Chapter XI, document V, note 1.

to the north west as well as to the north, until it loses itself in the immense forests and wilderness, even though they are not [as yet] inhabited by Europeans.

What other end can the repeated designs and incursions of the Americans have, designs seen even earlier in the unfortunate one, for them, of Philip Nolan.[5]

We must not lose time, and the slightest omission can be of great consequence for the orders and confidential instruction with which I find myself. The greatest responsibility would fall upon us if we should not take, without losing a moment, steps to put a stop to these dispositions and give time for measures to be taken so that the limits of Louisiana may be arranged without compromising the interest of Spain or endangering its vast and rich possessions.

In view of what has been said above I do not doubt that Your Excellency will give orders that the most efficacious steps be taken to arrest the referred to Captain Merry and his followers, who, according to notices, number twenty-five men, and to seize their papers and instruments that may be found on them. This action may be based upon the fact that without permission of the Spanish government they have entered its territory. Since the line of demarcation has not been determined as yet, they cannot infer that it already belongs to the United States. It is fitting to the confidential intentions of the ministry, by which I am instructed to stop the progress of these investigations, that although there be no motive or pretext whatsoever, nevertheless it is absolutely necessary for reasons of state to carry out the arrest of the said captain, and in order to exonerate Your Excellency of whatever responsibility I am immediately giving an account of it to the Court including a copy of this official letter.

May God keep Your Excellency many years.

New Orleans, March 5, 1804, El Marqués de Casa

Calvo [and Manuel de Salcedo] to *Señor* Don Nemesio Salcedo.

This is a copy. Chihuahua, May 8, 1804

Francisco Xav[r] de Truxillo [rubric]

No. 2[6] I received today Your Excellency's official letter of March 5, last, in which you inform me of the Lieutenant-Governor of Illinois having in-

---

[5]Philip Nolan made several horse-trading ventures into Spanish territory and Texas, 1797-1801. He was captured and killed by the Spaniards. As a protégé of Wilkinson it appears that he probably had other motives than that of a horse trader. Although a good many references to Nolan can be cited an account of his activities and life based upon archival sources remains to be done.

[6]A.H.N., Est., leg. 5542 *expediente* 2. The original of this letter is in A.G.I., P. de C., leg. 2368.

formed you under date of December 9, last, that Mr. Merry, Captain of the United States Army, presented himself to him requesting permission to penetrate the Missouri river in order to carry out the commission which he has to make discoveries and observations.

With this motive Your Excellency reflects upon the ambitious views of the said United States, and in justification, your view concerning how important it will be to prevent Mr. Merry from carrying out his commission. But the *noticias* of the situation of demarcations which Your Excellency includes in your official letter, not agreeing completely with the only maps of the territories to which they relate and which I have before me, and noting among other things that since the date of the dispatch of the Lieutenant of Illinois five months have elapsed, I am notifying you regretfully that this concurrence of circumstances makes it difficult for me to take steps, the success of which will be as fortunate as I desire.

Eight months ago I communicated to the governors of the border provinces of your province the orders that I judged opportune not only to excite their care and vigilance but also for the purpose of forewarning their dispositions in every event, and they being quite opportune even in the very case that Your Excellency speaks of, I see with satisfaction that until I receive more exact news, the notices that I now have will suffice and I am protecting myself by repeating to you the punctual observance of my cited orders.

As concerning the expedition of Merry it is customary that Your Excellency might have called the attention of the United States by means of the chief or general who commands that province, I must commend your zeal, which may please you to communicate to me the reply which you must have received, for you must know already how useful must be any constancy of the manner of thinking of the referred to government in the present circumstances.

Likewise I ask Your Excellency that when you retire from that province to please give me knowledge of some person of confidence who resides in it with whom I may correspond in order to acquire the news which is necessary for the best service.

I am sending this official letter to Your Excellency by way of Havana, considering that course more convenient and secure on account of the delay to Your Excellency's letter to which I am answering, for having taken eight days from Texas to this residence, it took fifty-one in the remainder of the trip. Moreover, the direction by the indicated route of important letters prevents the inevitable contingencies of sending by land from your capital.

May God keep Your Excellency many years.

Chihuahua, May 3, 1804,

Nemesio Salcedo [to] *Señor* Marqués de Casa Calbo,

This is a copy, Chihuahua, May 8, 1804

Francisco Xav^r de Truxillo   [rubric]

No. 3[7]

The Brigadier, Marqués de Casa Calvo, commissioned for the delivery of the province of Louisiana has sent me by extraordinary [express] the official letter a copy of which is enclosed, including the notice that on December 7, last, Mr. Merry, Captain in the United States army, presented himself in Illinois with a solicitude to penetrate the Missouri river in order to make some discoveries and observations.

As the views of this expedition may be directed to the ends which the said Marqués affirms, it is very prudent and necessary that on our part they may be impeded and [if] it may not be possible, either on account of the weather which they have had since the cited date, or on account of the considerable distances, let us take at least some knowledge of its progress and state of being.

To this end, it is important under the circumstances that the force of that province occupy itself in continuing to punish the barbarous Navajo nation;[8] that Your Excellency, making use of the friendship and difference towards us in which the other gentile nations find themselves, come to an agreement with the chief of the Comanches or with the Chief of any other [nation] which you judge more *à propos*, [to] send a party of individuals which you may collect to reconnoitre the country which lies between those villages as far as the right bank of the Missouri, with instructions and necessary provisions so that they examine if there are traces or other vestiges of the expedition of Merry and so that they acquaint themselves with the direction that it has taken and of their operations upon the territory, if they do not succeed in finding any other Indian village which may have seen it and may be able to give these notices.

If it appears to you opportune to give to the Indians that Your Excellency destines to such an important service one or two soldier-interpreters, [you may do so for] I am leaving to your judgment to order

---

[7]A.H.N., Est., leg. 5542 [5443?], *expediente 2*. This enclosure does not seem to be in A.G.M., Historia, vol. 200, transcript in Bancroft Library.
[8]This was done.

it, as likewise that Your Excellency inform Don Pedro Vial of the object of this voyage in case he may desire to join the expedition, as he is the most experienced in those territories, and in this case you may provide him with whatever may be necessary for his maintenance, forewarning him that he must keep an exact diary which he must present to Your Excellency upon his return.

Nothing would be more useful than the apprehension of Merry, and even though I realize it is not an easy undertaking, chance might proportion things in such a way that it might be successful, for which reason it will not be superfluous for Your Excellency to give notice of this matter to the Indians, interesting their friendship and notions of generosity, telling them that they will be well compensated.

May God keep Your Excellency many years.

Chihuahua, May 3, 1804

Nemesio Salcedo [to] *Señor Gobernado* of
New Mexico

This is a copy. Chihuahua, May 8, 1804.

Francisco Xav^r de Truxillo [rubric]

To Don Nemesio Salcedo, San Ildefonso, September 24, 1804.

I have given account to the King of the contents of Your Excellency's letter No. 4 in which you give an account that the Governor of Louisiana had given notice, etc. [same as the index of his letter—Document V] and informed of all this His Majesty has given his royal approbation to Your Excellency's reply.

VII

LOISEL TO DELASSUS, ST. LOUIS,
MAY 28, 1804[1]

To Don Carlos de Hault de Lassus, Colonel of the Infantry Regiment of Louisiana and its dependencies, etc.

In accordance with the instructions with which Your Excellency was pleased to honor me on the 15th of April of last year, 1803, I must inform you of what I have been able to learn on my last voyage for the

---

[1]In French and in Spanish in A.G.I., P. de C., leg. 2368. The French copy is in good condition; the Spanish copy is not so good. Duplicate in A.G.I., Sto. Dom., leg. 200 (87-1-10 old numbering). Also in British Museum, Additional Manuscripts, volume 17569, folios 119-125. Certified copy enclosed in Casa Calvo to Cevallos, no. 47 *res.*, New Orleans, September 30, 1804, draft in A.G.I., P. de C., leg. 2368. and both enclosed in Casa Calvo to Prince of Peace, New Orleans, September 30, 1804, A.G.I., P. de C., leg. 2361, and duplicate in A.G.I., Sto. Dom., leg. 2600. Printed in Houck, *Spanish Régime in Missouri*, II, 359-364, and reprinted from this source in Abel,

trade and exploration of the Upper Missouri, with relation to the Indian nations whom I have frequented, their political status, commerce, etc.

I shall say nothing, *Señor* Lieutenant-Governor, of the customs of these nations, which differ but little if any from those of other savages.' But I shall inform Your Excellency in writing of the geographical location of the districts which are of interest to the government. Your Excellency will see therefrom and very distinctly how exposed the domains of His Majesty are to the undertakings of the foreigners who have for a long time been introducing themselves into the Upper Missouri, bribing the nations by holding large assemblies among them in which they reveal propositions most harmful to our government, taking away the richest furs.

They accompany all their insidious steps with presents, which are the [prime] mover and the delight of these tribes, who will do whatever one may ask of them, by virtue of the merchandise. The presents or gifts incite them to peace or war, and decide the preference of their affection towards one or the other government. The gifts, in a word. are the great mainspring which moves them with the greatest facility.

Not having taken two years on my voyage,' as I had promised myself, I have not had time to acquire all the information that I had proposed

Tabeau's Narrative, 231-240. I have retranslated this document. See also Loisel's petition in *American State Papers, Public Lands*, VIII, 117-118 and in *United States Documents*, 34 *Congress, 3 Session, House Report no. 79* (Serial 912) ; Billon, *Annals of St. Louis, op. cit.*, 465-466.

"Enclosed I am sending to Your Excellency a memorial which Don Regis Loisel has just presented to me and I can inform Your Excellency that he is the only one who has continued by himself the discoveries in the Missouri in spite of the losses which he has suffered on each voyage.

"He desires to follow the flag. I believe he can be of some use concerning the nations which he cites and he will be able to serve to maintain them affected to the government.

"He is one of those who has gone the most far distant in the Missouri according to appearances.

"Your Excellency will be able to inform yourself from the man himself who will be the bearer of this and dispose.

"May God keep Your Excellency many years. St. Louis, September 1, 1804. Carlos Dehault Delassus [rubric] [to] *Señor* Marqués de Casa Calvo." A.G.I., P. de C., leg. 73. There is an unsigned draft of this in Delassus' handwriting in Missouri Historical Society, Delassus Collection, no. 7.

'Extensively quoted in Abel, *Tabeau's Narrative, op. cit.*

'Abel, *Tabeau's Narrative*, 25-31. It was a short trip but another was contemplated, for on August 22, 1804, Regis Loisel signed a note promising to pay to Manuel Lisa 115 *livres*, 12 *sols*. And on August 27, 1804, he signed a note payable to Jean Munié in which he says, "During the course of June of next year, 1805, or at the arrival of my *cajeux* from the Upper Missouri, I will pay to the order of Mr. Jean Munié the sum of 250 *livres* and 6 *sols* in *argent courant en pelleterie de recette aux pris du cours de ce jour—pour solde & [and] parfait payement de les gages provenan de la Société de Loisel e Heney"*. Missouri Historical Society, Lisa Collection, I.

Loisel died in October. Billon, *Annals of St. Louis, op. cit.*, 466. There is a copy of Loisel's will in the St. Louis Mercantile Library Manuscripts and in the Missouri Historical Society.

to myself, because of having been detained in the Island of Cedros [*fort aux Cedres*] by the Sioux tribe, who kept me in sight all through the past winter. That, besides having caused me a great loss, has made it necessary for me to descend the river in order to be supplied with merchandise. I would have again ascended, however, had it not been for the change which the government has experienced; nevertheless, in order to satisfy the intentions of our government and satisfy the confidence that it has reposed in me, I have sent M. Tabeau, my agent and man of affairs, with seven men under his orders, at my expense, with instructions to continue the undertaking in my name.[4]

Nevertheless, I have discovered, *Señor* Lieutenant-Governor, that one may travel by water in a certain manner, from Husdon Bay to the chain of mountains in Mexico which surrounds Santa Fé, with the exception of a small portage overland of one-half league, in order to cross the small tongue or isthmus which separates the river Bois Blanc [White Wood—James or Dakota] from the River Qui Parle [Who Speaks—the Cheyenne], which empties into the Colorado [Red River of the North], which in turn empties into Lake Ouanipik [Winnipeg].

I must tell Your Excellency at this point of the principal known tributaries that flow into the Missouri. The Río Chato [Rivière Platte], which empties into the Missouri at a distance of two hundred leagues from the Mississippi must not be passed by in silence. It rises west of Santa Fé, and flows between two mountains bordering the New Kingdom of Mexico in order to discharge its waters into the Missouri under the well known name of Río Chato. It is impossible[5] to open navigation with the Mexican territory by means of its channel, but there is no necessity for it, for transportation overland is easy and the distance but slight, and the road which is open so far as the savages are concerned, assures the Americans of the ease of penetrating without any trouble. In order to stop that, no other means present themselves than the resistance of the tribes. It is important that they be not allowed to be bribed by a new people of whom they know nothing more than the name; for they will always respect the word that Your Excellency has passed them, so long as they do not abandon themselves to a new master entirely. Let the government cultivate their affection by the means by which men of all sorts may not be separated if they are employed suitably, and it may then immediately count on their fidelity. Benefits diffused and received for the sake of friendship and confidence, however slight they be, exceed in merit those which are scattered by fear and distrust although abundantly and

---

[4]See Abel, *Tabeau's Narrative, op. cit.*, and also *Ibid.*, 236, and notes 3 and 4.
[5]French copy says "*possible*".

profusely. Such is the political situation and general opinion of the nations whom I have visited and with whom I have traded.

Ascending the Missouri one hundred and thirty leagues above the mouth of the Río Chato one comes to the Río Que Corre [Niobrara ?]. Its direction likewise is from the west, and it rises in the first mountains known under the name of Costa Negra [Black Hills], a name which was doubtless given those mountains because of the color of the earth. Under that earth are hidden precious minerals, as is declared by the nations who frequent them. They are so abundant that they are found in nuggets, scattered here and there both in various places upon the Río Chato and upon this river [Que Corre].

Although my purpose has been to fix my attention upon the rivers which empty into the Missouri, and rise on the side of the Spanish possessions or in Mexico, I must not fail to inform Your Excellency of the river Bois Blanc, which is also called the River Jacques [James], whose mouth is on the north side of the Missouri fifteen leagues below [sic, above] the Río Que Corre [Rivière Qui Court], of which we have just spoken.

This river, which is about two hundred leagues in length, and runs towards the [north] northwest, rises very near the other which is called Río Que Habla [Rivière Qui Parle]. The latter flows into another river called Colorado, and empties in the north into Lake Oanipik. Consequently, in order to reach from there to the Missouri by way of these last three rivers, one need make an overland portage of only one-half league.

The waters of Lake Oanipik communicate with the Hudson Bay by means of the small river called York [Nelson] which unites them. That allows one to believe that communication by water would be very possible from Hudson Bay to the Gulf of Mexico by means of a small portage one-half league in length between the River Que Habla and the River Jacques, and a second one at the costas [hills or mountains] of Santa Fé.

Hudson Bay communicates with Lake Oanipik by means of the York river. The said lake communicates also with the Colorado river, which unites with the River Que Habla, whose waters it receives. Here there is a small portage in order to reach the River Jacques which empties into the Missouri, and thence ascending the Río Chato or the River Que Corre, one may reach the mountains of Santa Fé, where are found the branches of the Río del Norte, which empties into the Gulf of Mexico.

Reascending the Missouri to a distance of 450 leagues from St. Louis, one comes to the River Chayennes, or as it is also called, the Fourche or Braso. It offers the same means of communication with New Mexico to

738

the west by crossing the Costa Negra of which we have spoken above. It rises in the chain of mountains in which are found settlements of New Mexico.

Continuing to ascend the Missouri, one comes to the River of Rocas Pagizas [*Roches Jaunes*—Yellowstone], which leads also to the western region, and rises in the mountains of New Mexico, which extend farthest to the west.

Upon the banks of all these rivers as well as upon the banks of all that empty into them, are found an infinite number of different wandering tribes, who are as ready for war as for peace with the nations who reside along the mountain chain of New Mexico; and who are settled in fixed villages. The latter are the Ricaras, the Mandanas, the Ventrudos or Gros Ventres, and the Souliers [*Zapatos*], and they are the only ones who are fixed on the Missouri. The wandering nations are the Chayennes, Cayouva, Caninanbiches, Catakas, Otomies, Chaoines, Sioux, Bois Brulé, Saoñes, Oncpapas, Ockendanne, Siriton, Ynctan, Ynctoannan, Waepiton, and Minikaojoup. There are also other nations whom I have not visited and whom I only know by name, who are also wandering. Such are the Cuerbos, Serpientes, Ventrudos Volantes, Les gens des Feuille, Salcy, Pieds Ganes, and Pieds Negros, all very numerous.

At the present time when the United States of America have negotiated for this province of Louisiana, their undertakings are so much more to be feared, for they believe that their boundaries ought to be considered as the sources of the various rivers which empty by different branches into the Mississippi, although many of those rivers take their rise in the midst of Spanish settlements. The Americans are enterprising and ambitious, and there is no doubt but that they will avail themselves of any means in their power to win the minds of the savage nations, and will endeavour to erase by cunning arguments the fine impressions of our government that they have received. In spite of the deep rooted affection of the Indians towards us, it is quite easy to bribe them, by means of presents, as I have remarked, and I am of the opinion that the government ought to watch over this so important matter. We have examples that these barbarous nations have fallen upon various Spanish settlements which they have devastated after having murdered a portion of their inhabitants, and carried the remainder off as slaves. The Spanish Government has kept them from making such raids for many years by winning and captivating their good will by making enormous expenditures so that today they venerate His Majesty's banner, and the name of their great Spanish father. But if with the lapse of time they hear no more talk of it, they will forget about it, and the Americans will captivate their minds with much less difficulty, and will make use of the Indians for their ambitious designs. Already do they talk of making the Mexican *pesos* descend the Missouri by proposing to begin contraband trade with that kingdom. With that object in mind they are proposing to establish great merchandise magazines on the frontiers. Some men have already set out in order to prepare the way and to assure communication from the side of Santa Fé. I shall not dwell further on the consequences which Your Excellency can judge for yourself. I have privately undertaken the continuation of the explorations that were commenced by the Company of the Missouri. I have made great sacrifices in the presents which I have had to make to the savages in the name of the government especially on this last journey, in order to cover the foreign flags and medals, as Your Excellency had ordered me,[6] by making gifts to the chiefs. In this way I have succeeded with the Chayennes, Caninambiches, Sioux, Sabines or Sahonas, and Ricaras.

There is no one here who knows as much as I do of the distant tribes nor anyone who has penetrated farther than I. In view of this exposition, and as I am desirous of following Your Excellency's banners, since it is probable that the government intends to employ some trustworthy person to restrain these nations, and dissuade them from heeding all the persuasions and prejudicial impressions with which the Americans will endeavor to imbue them against the government, and perhaps against the Spanish settlements, whether by trade or by arms, I offer myself voluntarily, promising my good services as a faithful vassal, and the one best fitted for the undertaking, if the government desires to honor me with its confidence, by giving me some employment on the frontier, such as that of agent of the nations, with the object of preserving their friendship with us[7] and avoiding the result of the persuasions of the Americans, etc. etc.

St. Louis, Illinois, May 28, 1804.

Regis Loisel.[8]

It is a copy. El Marqués de Casa Calvo [rubric]

---

[6]See *American State Papers, Public Lands,* VIII, 117-118.
[7]French copy says "towards our government".
[8]French copy has Loisel, rubric.

VIII

STODDARD TO DEARBORN, ST. LOUIS, JUNE 3d. 1804.[1]

I have the pleasure to inform you, that Captain Lewis, with his party, began to ascend the Missouri from the village of St. Charles on the

---

[1]This is a draft in the Missouri Historical Society, Stoddard Collection; printed in *Glimpses of the Past,* II, 110-111. Endorsed "Account Capt. Lewis Journey over the mountains and about retaining the Catholic clergy in the territory".

21 Ultimo. I accompanied him to that village; and he was also attended by most of the principal Gentlemen in this place and vicinity. He began his expedition with a Barge of 18 oars, attended by two large perogues; all of which were deeply laden, and well manned. I have heard from him about 60 miles on his route, and it appears, that he proceeds about 15 miles per day—a velocity seldom witnessed on the Missouri; and this is the more extraordinary as the time required to ascertain the courses of the river and to make the other necessary observations, must considerably retard his progress.

A few weeks before he left this, he intrusted an Indian trader by the name of Crawford[2] with a parole and speech addressed to the Ayowas and Scioux, who dwell on the banks of the river Demoine. The effects of that parole may be known by a letter from Mr. Crawford to his partners in this place—a copy of which I enclose you.

The Demoine is an extensive river. It joins the Mississippi from the west about 240 miles above this. It is navigable for light craft to some distance above the falls of St. Anthony; and the distance from the head of navigation on this river to the Mississippi, is usually traveled in two days. The Sioux inhabit the upper parts of the Demoine, and the Ayowas the lower part of it. These two nations are generally at peace with each other, and speak nearly the same language.

The needs [?] on the Demoine are inferior to none in this quarter, if the traders may be believed.

I presume that Capt. Lewis has mentioned to you the fate of some Osages Indians, who were on their way to this place in a boat belonging to Mess*rs.* Manuel & Benoit.[3] The boat was fired on by the Saucks and some of the Osage killed, and the others made prisoners. These Saucks were headed by the *Pauxblanche,* a chief of bad fame, who was on his way to intercept the Osage chiefs under the care of M[r] Chouteau, and accidentally fell in with the boat already mentioned. The Saucks are the implacable enemies of the Osages, and I suspect it will be difficult to reconcile them. They certainly do not pay that respect to the United States, which is entertained by the other Indians—and in some instances they have

---

[2]On Crawford see Nasatir, "Anglo-Spanish Rivalry in the Iowa Country 1797-1798," *Iowa Journal of History and Politics,* XXVIII (1930), reprint, pp. 30, 37-39; Coues. *Expeditions of Zebulon Montgomery Pike,* (New York, 1895) vol. I; *American State Papers: Indian Affairs,* I, 711, 712, 714; *Iowa Journal of History and Politics,* XII, 170, 171, 487-491. A note of Auguste Chouteau in favor of L. Crawford, dated June 6, 1803, is in the Missouri Historical Society, Auguste Chouteau Collection, V.
[3]There was a war on between the Sac and Osage nations. Benoit's boat was fired on. See letter of Lisa to Moro, *n.p., n.d.* [1804?], in A.G.I., P. de C., leg. 142A. More documents are given on this war in Nasatir, *Imperial Osage.* See also [Stoddard] to [Dearborn], St. Louis, June 22, 1804, and June 16, 1804, in Missouri Historical Society, Stoddard Collection, printed in *Glimpses of the Past,* II, 114-115.

assumed a pretty elevated tone. At this time most of them together with the Reynards or Foxes reside on the west side of the Mississippi.[4]

[I believe an opinion has generally prevailed, that the Saucks mostly resided on the East side of the Mississippi—whereas the contrary appears to be the fact. A trader, who has resided among them for upwards of 20 years, lately informed me, that he now resides among them on the west side of that river—and that they can raise 3000 warriors from some villages contiguous to each other. He further states, that they have only a few straggling villages in Indiana, and no chiefs of any consequence. I do not implicitly credit this account—but I give it as I receive it.] [Crossed out in original].[5]

Several applications have been made to me on a subject—which I conceive it my duty to explain. Under the Spanish Government, three Catholic clergymen were established in Upper Louisiana (one at St. Geneviève,[6] one at St. Louis, and one at St. Charles[7]) with an annual salary from the crown of about 370 Dollars each. As the people are unacquainted with contributions or taxes for the support of religion the clergymen will follow the Spanish flag, unless some provision be made for them. If they could be put on the Missionary establishment, with a salary of about 300 Dollars per year cash, they would not leave the country; and this is what the people, particularly the French, are anxious for. I know these clergymen well; they are learned, and liberal in their principles; they have great influence among the Catholic people, and speak the English as well as the French and Spanish languages.

[4]See "Notes of Auguste Chouteau on Boundaries of Various Indian Nations" edited by Grant Foreman and printed in *Glimpses of the Past*, VII, 119-140.

[5]Some of this material was sent by Stoddard to Dearborn on June 22, wherein he mentions the trader as Mr. Tesson. (*Glimpses of the Past*, II, 114-115).

[6]Diego Maxwell. Delassus to Casa Calvo, St. Louis, October 3, 1804. A.G.I., P. de C., leg. 73.

[7]Pedro Janin—*Ibid.*

IX

DELASSUS TO CASA CALVO, ST. LOUIS, AUGUST 10, 1804[1]

Reservada.

I do not regret that circumstances require me to remain in this post much longer than I expected since it facilitates my observing the move-

[1]Written in Spanish. A.G.I., P. de C., leg. 141. There is an autograph draft, entirely written in Delassus' handwriting, in Missouri Historical Society, Delassus Collection. This letter was delivered by Loisel. Delassus to Casa Calvo, St. Louis, October 3, 1804, A.G.I., P. de C., leg. 73.

ments and listening to the conversations of the Americans as a result of the retrocession of this province to France and the cession by the latter to the United States.

It is clearly to be seen that the general opinion of this latter named nation is that its limits will extend to Mexico itself, extending their boundary lines to the Río Bravo, penetrating into the said kingdom at different points adding [following] other small rivers. So general is this persuasion that I believe that beforehand many are thinking of obtaining a great advantage from those lands, and, as I see it, they are already calculating the profit which they will obtain from the mines. Their conversations support this belief.[2]

I am informed that they are disposed to send troops to the Upper Missouri, although at this moment I am not very certain of this information. There is no doubt that this news is rumored here and if they do not carry out this plan soon it will be because of the few troops which they have now, but it is not necessary to overlook that they will approach that Kingdom as soon as it is possible. At least appearances indicate that.

The officials who are commanding here are continually informing themselves from the Indians of the Missouri and the white hunters and traders, whether they know the shortest routes to New Mexico or to Santa Fé. I know positively that in the month of July of this year merchants left here in some embarcations for that purpose. The one named Jeanot Meteyer in company with another named Batiste La Lande have left here carrying merchandise advanced to them by a merchant of the post of Kaskaskias, named William Morrisson, a sufficiently rich person to risk such undertakings. The former two are going with the idea of meeting another, named Josef Gervaes who they say is waiting for them in the nations and is to guide them to Mexico. This Gervaes, it is said, knows the road very well. He is the same one who last year conducted the Panis

---

[2]Casa Calvo writing to Ceballos on July 25, 1804 (draft in A.G.I., P. de C., leg. 2368) gives a lengthy discussion of the historical boundaries of Louisiana. He argues that *presidios* already existing must be reinforced and new towns must be added on the frontiers of the *Provincias Internas* to keep the Americans out. He protests against the United States claims to territory as far as the Río Bravo and gives an historical account of the French and English in the Mississippi Valley, especially the lower part and Texas, based chiefly upon the correspondence of Athanase De Mézières and Ripperdá. The line should be drawn from north to south approximately on a parallel between Los Adaes and Natchitoches. The Spaniards cannot therefore stop the Americans from ascending the Missouri as far as that undefined boundary. C. W. Hacket [ed.], *Pichardo: Limits of Louisiana and Texas* (Austin, 1931-1946, 4 vols.) ; T. M. Marshall, *History of the Western Boundary of the Louisiana Purchase* (Berkeley, 1914) ; P. Brooks, *Diplomacy and the Borderlands* (Berkeley, 1939); I. J. Cox, "Louisiana-Texas Frontier," *Texas State Historical Society Quarterly*, X, 1-75, continued in *Southwestern Historical Quarterly*, XVII, 1-42; 140-187. See also Amended and enlarged report of the Engineer Don José Martinez showing that the Americans own the mouth of the Missouri, explorations of Dr. Hunter, etc., New Orleans, August 20, 1804, Missouri Historical Society, Papers from Spain, no. 82A.

nation to make peace with the governor of Santa Fé or with the commandant of the frontiers and it seems that he has also conducted them this spring. He is returning from this latter trip and is waiting for the said Meteyer.[3] Likewise an inhabitant from here named Laurent Durocher[4] has undertaken this same voyage and in the same manner. The latter, although somewhat old knows a little [about the route] and he will be able to facilitate the march for the others who will go later and [who I believe] will not delay. I understand that these commandants have knowledge of the trip of Durocher. It has come to my notice that it is believed that he is carrying special instructions from Captain Stoddard. The one named Jacques D'Eglise,[5] who for many years has gone on reconnoitering expeditions[6] and who was employed last year by Don J. Clamorgan to trade with the nations of the Missouri has also left. He has not returned this year and I have been assured that he has also gone to Mexico with the remainder of his merchandise.

I believe that Your Excellency knows that one can go from here to Mexico in less than two months. This can be done it is true with hard work and is exposed to meeting with various Indian Nations who are making war and exposed to being defeated by those parties, but by taking arms and some presents one can succeed in pacifying them and with continually seeing the Americans pass through those districts they [those barbarians] will very soon accustom themselves to trading with them and will facilitate them on their voyages. Perhaps it will result that those Indians who are friends of the Spaniards [now] will become enemies, incited by the Americans. This may be presumed from a report of a conversation, which surprised me greatly, which this civil commandant, Captain Stoddard, and the military commandant, Major Bruff, had with two Osages who related, in answer to various questions which the two commandants put to them, that

---

[3]See H. M. Chittenden, *History of the American Fur Trade of the Far West* (New York, 1901), II, 401; Coues, *Pike*, II, 602-603; 604; 623-624; 756ff.; I. J. Cox, *Early Exploration of Louisiana* (Cincinnati, 1906), 116ff.; L. Bloom, "Death of Jacques D'Eglise," *New Mexico Historical Review*, II, 370ff; H. A. Bierck, Jr., "Doctor John Robinson," *Louisiana Historical Quarterly*, XXV, 644-669; H. G. Warren. *The Sword Was Their Passport* (Baton Rouge, 1943), Cox, "Opening of the Santa Fé Trail," *Missouri Historical Review*, XXV, 30-66.

[4]*Missouri Historical Society Collections*, IV, 10.

[5]See Bloom, "Death of Jacques D'Eglise", *op. cit.* On August 2, 1802, D'Eglise signed [made a cross on] a promissory note for 25,122 *livres*, 15 *sols* payable to Clamorgan for which he received goods to trade on the Upper Missouri under a passport issued by Delassus. In 1804 Clamorgan petitioned to sell D'Eglise's land since this debt was not paid. The land was sold to Clamorgan for 402 *piastres*.. There is another note of Jacques D'Eglise payable to Clamorgan for 12,278 *livres*, 10 *sols*, dated St. Louis, July 6, 1802. Certified copies in Missouri Historical Society, St. Louis archives, concessions, no. 12.

[6]The copy in the Missouri Historical Society says: "Likewise the one named Jacques D'Eglise, who for many years has been going on discovery trips without gain because of being an absolutely ignorant man [has also left]".

744

several years ago a party from their nation went to Mexico and surprised a caravan; that the troop submitted and they pillaged horses and mules loaded with that *white metal* (silver) (the deed is verified as Your Excellency knows) and they counselled the said chiefs to go in search of that metal and bring here as much as they could. This deed came to my notice through a friend whose name I cannot give, I having pledged my word [not to do so], which has stopped me from asking for an explanation from the said gentlemen concerning this seditious indication apparently against Spain.

At present this post abounds in dry goods of all sorts and many of the finest. There is a surplus here of more than three-fourths for the consumption of this district, and more are arriving every day. I do not doubt that it is for the purpose of sending them to the frontiers of Mexico. I am of the opinion that if the greatest precautions are not taken to stop this contraband, within a short time, one will see descending the Missouri, instead of furs, silver from the Mexican mines [which will] arrive in this post in abundance.

It is also said that the voyage of Captain Lewis (of which I have informed Your Excellency at the time) is directing itself towards New Mexico; that his plan to discover the Pacific Ocean was no more than a pretext. This I doubt because the preparations which he made here before leaving did not indicate any other object than a very long voyage such as was announced, although it would not be impossible to verify it [what was said].

This is all that my duty obliges me at present to inform Your Excellency, advising you that while I remain here I shall not cease to inform myself of all that this nation will dispose and inform Your Excellency of what may appear to me to be against Spain, communicating it to Your Excellency by express in case it is necessary.

May God Keep Your Excellency many years.

St. Louis, Illinois, August 10, 1804.

Carlos Dehault Delassus   [rubric]

Señor Marqués de Casa Calvo, etc.

X

[Salcedo] to Cevallos, New Orleans, August 20, 1804[1]
[In margin: April 17, official Letter of Salcedo, no. 2]

No. 2.

Most Excellent Sir:

We have received the Royal Order of April seventeenth, last, in which Your Excellency was pleased to communicate to us His Majesty's resolution

---

[1]Written in Spanish. A.G.I., P. de C., leg. 2368.

concerning the *informe* which the commandant-general of the *Provincias Internas,* Don Nemesio de Salcedo, sent to the commission on September twenty-sixth[2] of last year concerning the matter of the demarcation of the limits between Louisiana and those provinces.

In the scarcity of news with which we find ourselves, not having been able to obtain any either from the Viceroyalty nor from the commandancy-general which could satisfy us; there remained to us no means other than that of taking recourse to the correspondence of the neighboring posts of Natchitoches, Atakapas, and Opelousas with the province of Texas. These latter have furnished us with little information, which is not to be wondered at since the beginning of their villages dates back only to a few years before Louisiana was ceded to Our Sovereign; but that of Natchitoches which runs parallel with that of the establishment of Louisiana, is the one which, supplying abundant knowledge, opens for us some avenue; having had a commandant of the greatest instruction, activity, enterprise, and zealous for the best service of the King and at the same time desirous of glory, who was Lieutenant-Colonel Don Athanasio de Mézières y de Clugni, Chevalier of the Royal and military order of St. Louis and Lieutenant Governor of the post of Natchitoches.[3] This correspondence we say is the one which lends the most solid foundations for our purposes. Nor have we been able to find others with the exception of the verbal *informes* of old people who witnessed many things and deeds which illustrate the material. All agree, generally, in assuring that the *San Francisco de Sabinas* River is the true boundary, its current ascending from the sea until meeting the *Río de Adaes* or even the bayou of this name, between which presidio and the post of Natchitoches, according to what they say, are to be found supposedly the arms of Spain buried at the foot of a laurel.

From this point up crossing the Colorado river is the difficulty as we have shown, but we always have to keep in view the treaty of peace celebrated in Paris in 1763.

Through a long and continued experience the English in this continent feared greatly the proximity of the French. All the Indians below Hudson Bay declared openly in favor of the latter. The English colonies were continually alarmed, and unceasingly exposed to new incursions. This was without doubt one of the principal causes why they restored Martinique, forcing them to cede the part of Louisiana contiguous to their possessions. France on the other hand had employed abundant sums in the preservation and maintenance of this province which they had already looked upon as

[2] See N. Salcedo to M. Salcedo and Casa Calvo, Chihuahua, September 26, 1803, A.G.I., P. de C., leg. 2355; and document IV.
[3] Concerning De Mézières see H. E. Bolton, *Athanase De Mézières and the Louisiana-Texas Frontier* (Cleveland, 1914). See also document IX, note 2.

a heavy burden; believing at the same time the possession of Martinique as more useful and advantageous, and thus it ceded to England all that part of Louisiana on the left bank of the Mississippi from its source to its mouth in the Sea, establishing as limits between the possessions of both powers a line drawn in the middle of the Mississippi River, reserving to itself nevertheless on the same bank, New Orleans and the island on which it is situated.

In the same year by an agreement made with Spain, France ceded to the latter all of Louisiana in the same manner as it possessed it.

It is then clear and evident that all the right bank of the Mississippi from its source to the sea, by the last treaty which France made with England, belonged to the province of Louisiana and the copious Missouri emptying into the Mississippi on the same right or west bank. We cannot [sic] claim the absolute dominion of that river nor its exclusive navigation since, as we have manifested, there are dependent possessions of Illinois on the banks of that river itself, and therefore it is unquestionable that they are lands belonging to the United States, which have acquired the entire possession of the province by the agreement of April 30, 1803.[4] But nevertheless by the said treaty the restriction of navigation will afterwards take place since the divisory line which must be marked will cut the said river and will fix the part navigable by the Americans, it remaining to us to take care to stop them from ascending or introducing themselves into territories of His Majesty or altering in any manner the good intelligence and friendship with the Indians.

For greater clarity of what we have exposed it is necessary for you to bear in mind that as early as in 1684, the French descending via the Lakes of Canada formed their first establishment in Louisiana among the Illinois Indians far above the Missouri, on whose banks there were known among others, the Missouri and Kansas tribes of Indians who seem to have a common origin with the Arkansas, Octohues, Big and Little Osage, White Panis and black Panis-mahas, Ayaguis [Iowas?], Paducas and wandering Sioux who inhabit both banks of the Upper Missouri as well as those of the Mississippi, famous warriors who intercept the traffic and [knowledge or contact] with the nations further up, and who, up to the present time have impeded the exploration and reconnoitering of the source of the said Missouri river, although the Indians agree in saying that it comes from some mountains of stones on the other side of which and at a not very great distance is the great water or the sea.

---

[4] Purchasing Louisiana. Text of treaty published in many places, *e.g.* Hunter Miller, *Treaties,* II; Fortier, *History of Louisiana,* II, 335-339, etc.

The wandering life of the Sioux, their number and extension to a considerable distance to the north in districts still not yet explored by any European make very difficult any expedition of discovery in that district.

It must not be forgotten that the French had among the Missouri Indians at eighty leagues from the mouth [?disemboguement] of the river of that name, which empties into the Mississippi, an establishment commanded by the Caballero de Bourmont [sic];[5] that they had another among the Osages and that they have traded with various Indian nations since the beginning of last century at two hundred leagues upstream on both banks of the Missouri and other rivers which empty into it.

Finally, it is best to have in view that on July 18, 1794, the Field Marshall Baron de Carondelet, commanding this province, approved the "Company of Discoverers of the Missouri" created on May twelfth of the same year. One of the first objects of this corps was to form factories among the Ricaras nations at 393 leagues, and the Mandanas 100 leagues farther up, that is to say at 493 leagues from where the Missouri empties into the Mississippi, not very far from Santa Fé in the Kingdom of New Mexico; and it may be observed in passing that French traders from Illinois had been among these same nations and that also the merchants of the English companies of Canada, Hudson Bay and Michilimackinac have penetrated among them.

It results from all this that the United States of America will have a right to claim at most that part of the Missouri in which the French already had establishments, that is, at a point beginning eighty leagues along its course from the Missouri nation and below, and that indisputably from there above will belong to us because of the formal discoveries undertaken in the time of the domination of His Catholic Majesty without serving as obstacles the entries which the French have been able to make in the Upper Missouri to trade with the nations which belong to New Mexico, for if this traffic or commerce would have legal foundation, the Spaniards would have no less, it being verified by history that at the beginning of last century or some years before there left from Santa Fé a caravan composed of men, women and soldiers, with cattle and beasts of burden, under the command of an Engineer with the idea of forming an alliance with the Osages, afterwards destroying the Missouris and forming an establishment on their lands. This expedition succeeded badly and does not seem to have been repeated, although probably about ten years later on different occasions a discoverer was sent from Santa Fé who made his trip to St. Louis, Illinois, in twenty days and later another trip to Natchitoches[6] in which he took almost the same amount of time.

---

[5]See "Introduction", part I.
[6]Referring undoubtedly to Pedro Vial but his dates are not accurate.

Therefore it will be one of our principal cares to advance nearer the limits from the San Francisco de Natchitoches River to the Missouri, either by a straight line or a curved line as close as possible to the Mississippi, disputing the land inch by inch; since it is always of the greatest moment to keep the Americans as far as possible from the *Provincias Internas,* capturing by all means the benevolence and friendship of the Indians in the Upper Missouri, a charge which it seems to us should be made to the governor of New Mexico with respect to the Mandans, Ricaras, Poncas, and Panimahas.

In this supposition in order that Your Excellency may base a possible concept in such an interesting matter (and in our manner of seeing things one of the most difficult, intricate and laborious which Spain has to discuss in this America) respecting the security and possession of the richest and most fertile part of the *Provincias Internas,* [which] I say [are] co-terminous with Louisiana, we are remitting to Your Excellency copies of three documents which are found in the correspondence of the Lieutenant Colonel Don Athanasio de Mézières, former Lieutenant-Governor of the Post of Natchitoches for the great information which they shed upon the Indian nations dependent upon the Province of Texas and this one of Louisiana, and because they lend much knowledge in settling inevitable difficulties which will probably arise in the first operations of the demarcation of limits.

Copy enclosure Number 1—is a treaty of peace with the Indians, formerly enemies, Quitsais, Yscanis, Caniones, Tahuacanas, Tankahueis, and Tabuayases, celebrated in Natchitoches on July 30, 1771.[7]

[Enclosure] Number 2 is an *informe* which the Lieutenant-Governor of Natchitoches gave Colonel Baron de Ripperdá concerning the consent of the Tahuacanes Indians to establish a presidio in their territories and the importance of this.[8]

[Enclosure] Number 3 is another *informe* to the said Baron de Ripperdá concerning the voyage undertaken to the nations by virtue of the order of the governor-general of Louisiana.[9]

We must also here observe to Your Excellency that although it is almost eight months since the United States of America took possession of this province, they are maintaining themselves in the greatest inaction and are guarding a most profound silence concerning the time when they are to begin the marking of the boundaries. Meanwhile with great activity and care they are sending expeditions to the Upper Mississippi, Missouri, Arkansas and Red Rivers[10] in order to reconnoitre their sources and courses,

---

[7]See Bolton, *De Mézières,* I, 93.
[8]See *Ibid.,* I, 97.
[9]See *Ibid.* See also document IX, note 2.
[10]Pike, Lewis and Clark, Dunbar, Freeman and Hunter made the voyages mentioned. See Cox, *Early Explorations of Louisiana.*

examine the lands, and attract and conciliate the Indian nations to them, which with study and with cautious skill they will separate from our friendship with their extended trade and presents.

In hand we have a very recent proof of what we have just assured. On the twenty-sixth of last July Dr. Hunter arrived at Natchez with all the necessary apparatus to explore the west bank of the Mississippi. He is a botanist and mineralogist. He is to accompany the expedition which is to ascend to reconnoitre the Red River as far as its origin, descending afterwards with the same motive from the source of the San Francisco de Arkansas river to its mouth—in the Mississippi.

In this situation we find ourselves perplexed and confused without knowing what action [measures] to take, although if commissioners from the United States present themselves to commence the demarcation of limits, we shall not separate ourselves from the San Francisco de Sabinas river, endeavoring always, if it should appear obtainable, to place the demarcation line between the Calcusiac and Nementao rivers, notwithstanding that for it we have no more foundation than what the commandant-general of the *Provincias Internas,* Don Nemesio de Salcedo, advances in his letter of September twenty-sixth of last year[11] which alludes to the royal order of April seventeenth of the same year to which we are replying.

In any case we shall use all our endeavours and forces to promote the best service of the King and restrain the Americans to as close to the bank of the Mississippi as the former establishments of the French on the Ouachita, Arkansas and Missouri rivers permit, unless His Majesty's orders prescribe other conduct for us. However our forces and means will be in vain if the aid asked from the Viceroy of Mexico does not arrive, because on account of the lack of funds we have not yet reconnoitred various points important for the object of our commission. It is necessary to inform Your Excellency that all the existing capital in these treasuries is reduced to the sum of twelve thousand *pesos.* For this reason we shall be on one-half salary from the first of September, next. May God keep, etc. New Orleans, August 20, 1804. [draft] [to] Most Excellent *Señor,* Don Pedro Cevallos.

---

[11]Cited in note 2.

XI.

[Draft] to Cevallos, September 18, 1804[1]

September 15, 1804

No. 41   To His Most Excellent *Señor,* Pedro Cevallos

I am enclosing to Your Excellency a copy of the answer of the *Comandante-General* of the *Provincias Internas,* dated May 3rd, which is in

---

[1]Written in Spanish. Draft in A.G.I., P. de C., leg. 2368.

reply to my letter of March 5th.[2] With it I also enclose my intention to record that my message's only object was the reconnaissance which the American Captain Merry Whether was going to make of the origin and course of the Missouri, recalling to mind the pretensions of the French over the limits of this Province, which the Colonial Prefect manifested, and in which I had no other object than to hasten with doubled fears the news and excite the dispositions which must be taken to contain the ambitious designs and extraordinary intentions of our neighbors.

In these parallel documents Your Excellency will surely observe the indifference with which so important a message has been treated and therefore since there will have remained obscure in their meaning the efficacious and prompt measures which might have been followed upon receipt of my letter in order to compensate for the time and the distance. I say to compensate for time and distance because, the notice being from the Lieutenant Governor of Illinois, in the month of December on the 20th of which month the Americans took possession of the province.[3] Since that time Merry has had time to undertake and to advance his expedition, and the *Comandante-General* is unable to know the district in which the expedition is at present, due to Spain's not having establishments on the Upper Missouri. Consequently I think that before writing the second paragraph of his answer, he should have [had] examined and inquired all that was possible about the immediate roads, [surrounding passageways] in order to see if he could acquire news as to his stopping place, not having had notice of his stopping place at the time he was writing because the expedition was enroute to the Upper Missouri. This having been done there would have been left no object which would delay another message as long as five months.

It is impossible for me to procure any news as to the course of the voyage since I have no plans [*planos*] of the upper part of that river, since we only calculate its proximity to the New Kingdom of Mexico from the news of travelers, from the voyages recently made, from what the Indians tell us, and from the landmarks and the signs which are observed among the Indians of the Upper Missouri, which manifest clearly their traffic with Spaniards. From a summing up of these facts the writers have decided that the origin of that river is to the northwest. This in the general plan of the maps should bring it very near to the capital of the aforementioned Kingdom of New Mexico.

I cannot understand the idea of the *Comandante-General,* nor on what basis he can uphold himself, nor to what expression of my letter he is

[2]See documents V and VI.
[3]Chapter XI, document V.

making allusion when he says that the notices of the demarcation survey which I include, in my official letter are the only maps of the territory in my possession [to which they relate], but they are not satisfactory. I have tormented my spirit, but have not been able to find a single phrase in all my letter which gives rise to such a slighting statement as announced. What limits are outlined in it? If the prefect himself of whose proposition I made literal use when treating of the pretensions of France, only speaks indeterminately, who fixed them and how can it be imputed that I have pointed them out?

These I find extraordinary as I have already mentioned that the *Comandante-General* has not taken more active measures because of an erroneous confidence, and I fear that this same confidence will injure the promptness of the dispositions which should be taken to stop the progress of Merry. And thus it has appeared to me proper to my duty to inform Your Excellency, so that instructed of everything, it may please you to take the steps which may be best.

God, etc., Sept. 15, 1804

[unsigned]

Most Excellent *Señor,* Don Pedro Ceballos.

Don Pedro Cevallos to *Señor* Marqués de Casa Calvo⁴

The King has been kind enough to approve the official letters sent by Your Excellency to Don Nemesio Salcedo, *Comandante-general* of the *Provincias Internas* for the purpose of stopping [detaining] the expedition of the American Captain Merry Weather directed to reconnoitre the territory which belongs to His Majesty, and with this motive [and in] replying to Your Excellency's official letter number 41 I am informing you that His Majesty has ordered me to instruct his Minister Plenipotentiary in the United States that he complain to that government against so manifest an offense against the sovereignty of the King.

May God keep Your Excellency many years.

January 17, 1805—

Pedro Cevallos [rubric]

Señor Marqués de Casa Calvo.

⁴Original in A.G.I., P. de C., leg. 176B.

XII.

[DRAFT] TO SALCEDO, SEPTEMBER 20, 1804¹

By authentic advice received from the Post of St. Louis, Capital of the establishments of Illinois in Upper Louisiana, under date of June 23

¹Written in Spanish. Draft in A.G.I., P. de C., leg. 2368,

last, news is had that Captain Merry Whether [sic] who had entered by way of the Missouri River to explore its course and place of its origin, was in good health as well as all of his party, finding himself when he wrote, more than 91 leagues from the Mississippi without having suffered any discomfort whatever in the Indian nations through which he has crossed.

By a prudent calculation at the beginning of May the above mentioned Captain found himself at the distance which is indicated by the notice from Saint Louis, and for the same reason I consider that at that time he might be credited with the navigation of more than 300 leagues on the said river, and consequently was quite advanced into the *Provincias Internas* under Your Excellency's command, to whom I give notice of it in fulfillment of my duty. This same places me in the position of advising Your Excellency that the party which is to examine the Colorado and Arkansas Rivers has put off its departure until next spring[2] a thing which makes it very urgent to reinforce the garrison of Nacogdoches without neglecting Sabinas and the other points which Your Excellency better than I might consider more exposed to the incursions of our ambitious and intriguing neighbors.

God, etc. September 20, 1804.
Señor Don Nemesio Salcedo.

---

[2]Dunbar-Hunter expedition. See Cox, *Early Exploration of Louisiana.*

XIII.

[DRAFT] TO CEVALLOS, NEW ORLEANS, SEPTEMBER 24, 1804[1]

No. 15.

Most Excellent Sir:

I have just received a letter from the subject known by number 13, making use of the precaution which I manifested to Your Excellency I would use in my correspondence by my official letter No. 11, of May 18 last, whose tenor is the following:

Washington, June 18—"Monroe is in Madrid," etc.

I should add that by authentic advice received from the Post of Saint Louis, capital of the establishments of Upper Louisiana, under date of June 23 last,[2] there is notice that Captain Lewis Merry Wheather who had entered by way of the Missouri River to explore its course and the place of its origin, was, when he wrote, at a distance of more than 91 leagues from the Mississippi without having suffered the least discomfort by the

---

[1]Written in Spanish. Draft in A.G.I., P. de C., leg. 2368.
[2]See document XII.

Indian nations through which he had passed, news of which I have communicated to the Commandant General of the *Provincias Internas*.

As I have not received up to now any orders from the Ministry other than those communicated in April, neither have I been able to make any progress concerning the boundaries; and because of the lack of funds by which I am bound, it has not been possible for me to reconnoitre the mouths of the Sabina, Nemintas, and Calcusine Rivers, an operation which I judged best before undertaking the demarcations, and proper in order to form the small establishment in Sabinas which no. 13 indicates in his letter; there remains likewise without effect the aid which he asks for in money. I am taking advantage of this opportunity to bring to Your Excellency's attention that on the part of the Americans there are up to date no delegates appointed, at least ostensibly, for the demarcation.

May God keep etc. New Orleans, September 24, 1804.
Most Excellent *Señor* Don Pedro Ceballos.

XIV.

CASA CALVO TO PRINCE OF PEACE, NEW ORLEANS, SEPTEMBER 30, 1804[1]

Most Excellent Sir:

Sir:

The enclosed copies are transcripts of the representation and document that I am sending on this date through the Minister of State. As Your Excellency will see I am reflecting upon the information recently communicated by Colonel Don Carlos de Hault de Lassus, former Lieutenant-Governor of the settlements of Illinois; and discussing the memorial presented by Regis Loisel,[2] I set forth the imminent danger to which the *provincias internas* are exposed, if the Americans retain the west bank of the Mississippi.

It is evident, *Señor General,* that these dangers must be feared, all the more so because of the easy and continuous communication by water from Hudson Bay to the Gulf of Mexico, without other obstacle than the sole portage of one-half league overland near the upper part of the Missouri, as demonstrated in the memorial. Consequently, I propose the remedy that has appeared most suitable to me and even adequate, and that is the employment on the frontier of New Mexico of the author of the memorial as

---

[1] Written in Spanish. Index and draft in A.G.I., P. de C., leg. 2368; duplicate in A.G.I., Sto Dom., leg. 2600, printed in Houck, *Spanish Régime in Missouri*, II, 355. I have retranslated this document.
[2] Document VII.

agent of the Indian nations,[2] with two subordinates to aid him in restraining the entrance of English and Americans.

I am informing Your Excellency of this for your superior consideration.

May God Keep your Excellency many years. New Orleans, September 30, 1804.

Most Excellent *Señor*
The Marqués de Casa Calvo   [rubric]
Most Excellent *Señor,* The Prince of Peace.[4]

Number 47 *Reservada.*

Your Excellency:

Colonel Carlos de Hault de Lassus, ex-Lieutenant-Governor of the settlements of Illinois in Upper Louisiana, under date of August 10,[5] secretly informs me of the results of his observations on the movements and conversations of the Americans in respect to the acquisition which they have made of that province.

He shows me clearly that the general idea of that nation is that their boundaries will pass through the very kingdom of New Mexico, carrying their lines to the Bravo River, and penetrating by several points and following various small streams, showing only too clearly that they are making vast calculations, in consideration of the profits that they will make from the lands and the working of the mines.

They are planning to send troops to the headwaters of the Missouri, for which object, and through others, officials, whom they are sending into Illinois, they are informing themselves in an efficacious manner and with continued eagerness from the Indians, hunters, and traders, in regard to the shortest paths by which to penetrate to Santa Fé and to other places of the New Kingdom. The traders Jeannot Metoyer and Bautista Lalande, who were to be joined among the nations by the trader called José Gervais, went as early as the month of July via the said Missouri River for that purpose, leaving St. Louis with merchandise and boats. All three are to work in concert, and have been equipped and supplied by Evan Morrison, a wealthy inhabitant of Kaskaskias, an American post on the east bank of the Mississippi. Gervais, who knows the road well, will guide them and show them the way into the New Kingdom.

---

[2]See document VII, note 1, letter of Delassus.
[4]Royal order given January 18, 1805. Original sent by brigantine "Los Dos Amigos," Captain Dominil de Norast. Duplicate sent by Frigate "Carmen," Captain Juan Sardina.
[5]This is a certified copy; draft in A.G.I., P. de C., leg. 2368; duplicate in A.G.I., Sto. Dom., leg. 2600; printed in Houck, *Spanish Régime in Missouri,* II, 356-358. I have retranslated this document.
[6]Document IX. See my editorial notes to that letter, which is very similar to the contents of this document.

This same Gervais is the one who last year conducted the Panis tribe to make peace with the Governor of Santa Fé or with the Commandant-General—a voyage which it appears he has repeated this spring, and upon his return Metoyer and Lalande are to meet him. With the same intention and in order to facilitate the undertaking Lorenzo Deroche and Santiago d'Eglisse have gone to the upper waters of the Missouri. They are recognized as *voyageurs* of the greatest knowledge and experience. The latter was employed by the Company of the Discoveries of the Missouri and since he has not returned this year it is inferred that he has penetrated into New Mexico.

The American Captain of Illinois, Mr. Stoddard, and [Mr.] Brush, in conference with the Osage Indians, have incited them to take the warpath and pillage the silver convoys which ply between different points, as they succeeded in doing some years ago.

The said Lieutenant-Governor advises that those posts abounded, at the time of this writing, in all sorts of the finest drygoods, and although there were more than three-fourths above the ordinary consumption, more were being brought in daily, with the idea of sending them to the Mexican frontiers. He is of the opinion that unless the most efficacious measures and the most exact precautions are taken in order to restrain the contraband, in a short time the silver will go from the New Kingdom of Mexico by the Missouri instead of the furs which are the only product of the commerce of that river.

On the same occasion, he remits to me the memorial whose translation accompanies this letter.[7] This document, while it at the same time enforces and confirms whatever has been said in regard to the navigation of the Missouri, its proximity to New Mexico, and the fatal consequences that must be feared from the ambition of our neighbors, proves the urgency and the absolute necessity of not yielding even one foot of the west bank of the Mississippi, although it may be necessary to have recourse to arms for that purpose. Any other means, even delay in preventing by real force those dangerous neighbors from entering our possessions will occasion their inevitable loss.

The water communication from Hudson Bay to the Gulf of Mexico, as soon as it is known and frequented, can increase the British and American commerce to the extreme of power, and they will meet their greatest support and encouragement at the passage of the inland rivers. Because of the treasures that they will tear from the very bosom of Spain, they will totally ruin our commerce. What is even more to be feared, I believe, is that they will alienate the affection of the Indians [from us], and may, perhaps, cause other consequences of the greatest consideration. At the

---

[7]Document VII.

bank, then, of the Mississippi must be established and raised solidly the dike that will restrain the rapidity of this current. If what I have shown happens, that dike ought to be procured at all cost. It will be easier now, however, by means of the most exact and continual vigilance of our governors and commandants to cut off the communication of the English who may penetrate by way of Hudson Bay, and of the Americans who may penetrate into the Missouri by other currents than that bay.

The author of the memorial, Regis Loisel, proposes a method which is one of the most adaptable, and I am even so bold as to pronounce it one of the most adequate. Loisel has been an inhabitant of Illinois for some time, and both by his written statement and by the verbal conferences which I have held with him in order to instruct myself thoroughly of the matter, he advises me that he understands thoroughly and that he knows practically about 500 leagues of the course of the Missouri. He is active, young,[8] and enterprising,—and I consider him suitable, and consequently, faithful in the discharge of his promises. With these qualities, and since he possesses a knowledge of the English and French languages, at the same time that he preserves the goodwill of the tribes by means of trade, he will be able to easily destroy the projects of the English and Americans, if he be employed on the frontier as agent of the Indian tribes, and if he also be given liberty to select one or two other men to help him, who shall receive a fixed salary.

I must beg Your Excellency to please keep in mind numbers 1—15 *reservadas,* with the exception of the 4th, 6th, and 7th, which are so closely connected with the present irrefragable testimony, which urges more and more the arguments and reasons in those settlements wherefore the Americans should not be permitted under any consideration to retain the possession of the west bank of the Mississippi; and why this river should constitute the line of division between Spain and the United States, from its source to its discharge into the Gulf of Mexico, even if we should not succeed in retaining possession of the island of New Orleans on the said west [*sic*] bank, which I have also proposed, and which I ever conceive as the most advisable thing.

---

[8]He was just thirty-one at the time of his death in October, 1804. Loisel left from St. Louis for New Orleans most likely in August. See Delassus to Casa Calvo, St. Louis, October 3, 1804, A.G.I., P. de C., leg. 73. He probably died of the "New Orleans fever." His will, made at the home of M. Perillat in New Orleans, is in Missouri Historical Society, Auguste Chouteau Collection. In his will, Loisel states that he had some men in the upper Missouri in the care of Tabeau; that he has had business with Clamorgan "for quite a long time"; that the firm of Clamorgan, Loisel and Company owes him about 5000 *livres.* Auguste Chouteau and Clamorgan were named his executors in St. Louis and Manuel de Lisa was to take care of his cases pending in New Orleans against Peyroux and La Fourcade. Part of the accounts of the executor Auguste Chouteau is in the Missouri Historical Society, Auguste Chouteau Collection. In this account Auguste Chouteau had two-thirds and Loisel one-third in the equipment of the voyages for [of the] Loisel-Heney enterprises. Clamorgan had a one-third interest in part of that company. Chouteau equipped two-thirds of Loisel's trip in 1803.

I entreat Your Excellency to please bring this to the superior notice of His Majesty, in order that he may opportunely give the orders that are deemed most advisable for the preservation of those vast dominions in the imminent risks to which I believe them exposed.

May God keep Your Excellency many years.
New Orleans, September 30, 1804.

Your Excellency,

The Marqués de Casa Calvo.

His Excellency, Don Pedro Cevallos.

[certified copy. El Marqués de Casa Calvo   [rubric]].

[Reply][9]

I have given an account of the contents of You Excellency's confidential letter number 47 to the King which he will take under consideration. At present His Majesty orders me to tell Your Excellency that the author of the memorial, Regis Loisel, be well employed in the capacity which Your Excellency may consider most useful and advantageous with the commission with which he has been charged; it being consequent to the important faith which the King has in the person of Your Excellency to concede to you the aid of a subject whose knowledge and activity for the benefit of the state will be as conducive as Your Excellency manifests in the cited official letter number 47. May God keep Your Excellency many years. Aránjuez, January 18, 1805.

Pedro Cevallos   [rubric]

Señor Marqués de Casa-Calvo.

[9]A.G.I., P. de C., leg. 176B.

XV.

CHOUTEAU TO GALLATIN, ST. LOUIS, NOVEMBER 7, 1804[1]

After my arrival at St. Louis[2] I occupied myself without cessation to obtain the best information concerning the commerce with the savages in order to transmit it to the government, which has been for a long time now the only resource that the inhabitants of this country have.

We dare to hope that they will fix for this reason the view of the government, always attentive to what might prove flourishing to the commerce of the United States.

I dare to hope that you will interest yourself for me with the Minister of War in order to obtain for me a private license for a post of the

[1]Written in French. Missouri Historical Society, Pierre Chouteau Letterbook, pp. 10-11.
[2]From his trip with the Osage and other Indians to Washington. Some documentation on this matter is contained in Nasatir, *Imperial Osage*.

Missouri in order to be able to place there the funds which I have always had in commerce. However if I thought that the request was contrary to the views of the government I would renounce it, not wishing to ever ask anything which might be opposed to it in any manner.

My brother will remit to you the present. I dare to hope that you will kindly accord him your good offices and your protection.

Copie de l'apperçu de las Consommation annuelle des marchandises pour les traittes sauvages de ce District.

Missouri	Savoir	Prix de Londre
Grand Osages		$35000
Petit Osages		8000
Kansas		8000
Hotos		8000
Missouris		4000
Panis		5000
Republique		4000
Loup		3000
Mahas		10000
Poncas		1500
Sioux Pour le moment & beaucoup plus considerable à l'avenir		15,000
Mandannes		2500
Ricaras		2000
		104000
Mississippi		
Sakias		40000
Renards		20000
Ayouas		12000
Sioux de la rivière des moines, etc, and la Rivière St. Pierre		4000
		216000

XVI.

Apercu de la population des diverses tribus du District de la Louisiane[1]

Arcansas	130 hombres
Loup ou Delawars	100
Chawanon	100

[1]Attached to letter of Pierre Chouteau to Secretary of War Dearborn, St. Louis, November 19, 1804, original in Library of Congress, Jefferson Papers; unsigned copy in Missouri Historical Society, Pierre Chouteau Letterbook, pp. 9-10. This *aperçu* is on page 12. See Colonel Chouteau's "Notes on the Various Indian Nations," *Glimpses of the Past*, VII, 119-140.

Piorias	50
Ayouas	250
Sakias	500
Renard	450
Sioux	12000
Grand Osages	1200
Petit Osages	300
Cances	350
Hotos	120
Missouris	80
Panis	500
République	300
Loups	400
Mahas	300
Poncas	250
Mandanne	400
Ricaras	500
Gros Ventre	700
Chayenne	400
Padodos	300
Laytanne qui bordent les Côtés d'espagne	15000

Envoyée à Mr. Le Président et à Mr. Le Sécretaire de la Guerre.

XVII

Casa Calvo to Prince of Peace, New Orleans, July 19, 1805[1]

Number 18.

Encloses a copy of a paragraph from the Gazette of that capital giving news of the expedition of Captain Lewis on the Missouri.

Most Excellent *Señor:*

By the Gazette of this city of the 17th, whose news proceeds from the government, I have seen the paragraph of which I include a copy for you for your information and that you may be instructed of the progress

---

[1]Written in Spanish. A.G.I., Sto. Dom., leg. 2600. See Thwaites, *Original Journals of the Lewis and Clark Expedition;* and "Descriptive Observations on certain parts of the country in Louisiana by Anthony Soulard, Esq. in a letter to J. A. Chevallie translated from the French manuscript by Dr. Mitchell, St. Louis, March, 1805," *Medical Repository,* second hexade, III, 305-313. Soulard states that he ascended the Missouri, whose sources are still unknown, about 500 leagues. Soulard describes the geography, tribes, trade, etc. of the Missouri.

of the American expedition commanded by Captain Lewis who on April 14 of this year, eleven months since his entrance on the Missouri had gone 1609 miles up river, counting even on that which remains of it to make the six hundred that seem to be the number to the head of the river, and flattering themselves that they will winter on the Pacific Ocean.

The statement does not depart from the news that we have, and for that reason and conforming much to the memorandum of the deceased Loisel[2] transmitted in dispatch number 47[3] of September 30 of last year, I believe it exact enough and I am persuaded of the prudence and propriety of the medium selected to assure ourselves the knowledge of the intentions of the Americans with the appointment of the subject who is to accompany them on the expedition ready for the exploration and examination of the Colorado and Arkansas rivers.

May God keep Your Excellency many years. New Orleans, July 19, 1805.

Most Excellent Sir
El Marqués de Casa—Calvo   [rubric]

Most Excellent *Señor* Príncipe de la Paz

[Enclosure]

Gazette of New Orleans, July 17, 1805 — Lexington, Kentucky, July 18 —.

The party of discovery under the command of the Captains Lewis and Clark left the mouth of the Missouri the 19th of May, 1804, and a special messenger who left them in their winter headquarters the 14th of April arrived a short time ago at St. Louis with dispatches. By the same occasion their correspondents in Kentucky have received letters from Captain Clark: A gentleman of the County of Jefferson has had the kindness to furnish the editor of the Kentucky Gazette with the following narration that he was able to obtain from one of those who returned with the special messenger, and from the letters which some of the party wrote. The party fortified itself in November last on the margin or bank of the Missouri at 1609 miles from its entrance into the Mississippi, according to the actual measurement in North latitude 47°21'. They gave to this place the name of Fuerte Mandana after the Indians who live in that vicinity and who have shown themselves to be very friendly to them. On their trip up the river they had the delightful view of a beautiful country for the distance of some 200 leagues to the Platte or Chato River which empties on the south of the Missouri; from there to the district where they have wintered they did not find it so fertile. The special messenger who brought the parcels of letters

---

[2]Document VII.
[3]Document XIV.

[*pliegas*] speaks of an aperture made by the river one mile wide between two high bluffs. The bed of the river occupies about one quarter of the mile, and the remainder of the bottom [a dale] or glide is entirely composed of coarse sand covered with cottonwood trees. This bottom is continually crumbling on one side or the other and piling up on the opposite. The banks in some places are covered with red cedar, which with the cottonwood trees and some few small black ash trees are the only ones that are found in the country. From the high places as far as the eye can see, and in that which they have explored there is not a tree or stem to be seen; from the river the earth is perfectly level with few exceptions—and the plains are covered with grass. They passed the mouths of a great number of streams the most of which have names which the French have given them. To one of them was given by the people of the expedition the name of Floyd to perpetuate the name of a young man of the party, who died with much grief on the 10th of August. They related that the Indians, with the exception of a few, have shown themselves to be friendly. The Sioux, which are the most numerous, are distributed in parties under different names: they wander from one part to another from the banks of the river to the plains following the game and the opportunities to plunder without having a fixed place of residence, and are in a continual state of war. They are the Indians who have most inconvenienced the party of discoverers, showing jealousy that the Indians farther up trade, receive arms, etc. However the further up the expedition has penetrated, the more friendly and better armed they have found the savages. They have a trade or commerce more regular with the Northwest Company from which they receive merchandise via Lake Winnepeg. The Mandanas cultivate maize of small grain, with which the party and the hunters have maintained themselves in abundance during the entire winter. They say that the buffalo are found in numerous herds, and that they are of great corpulence. They describe two species of deer, the one which resembles the common ones of this country is larger, with a tail of eighteen inches, and the hair of the body much longer. The other species has a black tail. The elk and mountain goats are very numerous. The geese are in abundance, and before the falls of the river there is an abundance of water hens. The fish are scarce, and are of the barbed species [*barbudo*]. The Indians from above, who visited the Fort, wore some skins of white bear; but those of the expedition have not seen any animal of that kind. The Indians have horses, of which they make use entirely for the hunt and for war.

From the information which they have received concerning the upper country, it is yet about six hundred miles to the great cataract or falls which are formed by the chain of mountains named Rocky, in which it is presumed the Missouri ends or begins. In its winter season the river is about a mile wide; and it is as turbid and muddy as at its mouth; it is the same rapidity with little change so far as they have reached, although with considerably less depth, so that the great [*bercha*] cannot follow any higher. From the information that they have been able to obtain of the course of the upper part of the river, they are more to the north of it. From the winter quarters to the Falls the navigation is almost to the south. The descriptions given by McKenzie of the headwaters of this river are true.

They have sent to the President of the United States a fairly exact diary together with a map of the country through which they have passed.

Six of the expedition have returned, so that it is now composed of twenty-eight men and two officers. All have enjoyed perfect health; none has been sick with the exception of the unfortunate youth who died in a few hours of colic, or stomach convulsions. There has existed among all the greatest harmony and those who have returned speak in the best terms of the humaneness, care, and extraordinary attention which Captains Lewis and Clark have had with all; that they left them very happy, and completely convinced that they will winter on the Pacific Ocean. They have spoken of six nations of Indians, through which they will have to pass before arriving at the falls, only one of which they suspect anything, which are called the Serpents, and are all up-river. Curiosities of different species of animals, birds, various boxes of minerals, a pair of extraordinary horns from the sheep of the Rocky Mountains, some feet of a new kind of *fresa* called *fresa de cíbolo* have been brought by the people of the expedition and have been deposited in the hands of the commanding officer of St. Louis [to be forwarded to the president].

Within a few days we expect more news about this interesting journey.
El Marqués de Casa — Calvo.
[rubric]

Esteemed Sir:

The Marqués of Casa-Calvo in his report of last July 19, number 18, enclosed to Your Excellency a copy of the paragraph from the Gazette of that capital of the 17th of this month, through which news is given of the expedition of Captain Lewis on the Missouri, he who at eleven months since his entrance on this river, has ascended the 1609 miles to 47° 21' north latitude, where his party has fortified itself, giving the name of Fort Mandana, which is that of the Indians of those environs who have shown themselves to be very friendly. Up to the River Plate or Chato that empties into the Missouri about 200 leagues after its entrance into the Mississippi is a beautiful country of delightful view, and from there to that of the Mandana there is the maize with which they maintain themselves, and with which the party of discovery has been supported in the winter: The courier who brought the letters speaks of an aperture a mile wide through which the river passes, which occupies the fourth part and the rest sand and some trees. In all those surroundings nothing is seen from the heights but plains of grass; they passed the mouths of a great number of streams, the most of which had names the French have given them: the Indians, with exception of a few, had appeared friendly; the Sioux which are the most numerous and wander around are those which have most inconvenienced them; farther up they are more peaceful and have some trade with the Northwest Company from which they receive merchandise via Lake Winnipeg. They continue speaking of the kinds of animals, almost reduced to buffalo and two species of deer, and mountain goats. They lack yet about 600 miles to the south to arrive at the Falls of the Rocky Mountains where they believe that it begins, for from Mandana the bottom diminishes much, and the large boat cannot go on! They have to pass toward the source six nations of Indians among which the last is that called Serpent which they mistrust; they believe they will make the second winter quarters on the Pacific Ocean; they have sent various curiosities of plants, birds, etc. and among them some deposits of minerals; the diary and map of it they have given and they have for corroboration the description given by McKenzie, which seems to be that of the deceased Loisel[4] sent to you in letter number 47 of September 30, 1804.[5]

[4]Document VII.
[5]Document XIV.

XVIII.
[Casa Calvo] to Cevallos, July 19, 1805[1]

Number 20, July 19, 1805
[Marginal notations]

Advises that the American expedition which entered the Missouri on May 19, 1804, was on April 14, 1609 miles from its mouth, it counting upon navigating during the remainder of the year the 600 miles which they estimate there are as far as the head of the said river and wintering on the Pacific Ocean. What confirms this proposition[?] of having appointed the subject, of which my preceding letter treats in order to witness the operations of the reconnaissance of the Colorado and Arkansas rivers.

Number 19, July 18, 1805

Informs with documents that the President of the United States renews his project of examining and reconnoitering the Colorado and Arkansas rivers as far as their sources; Manifests the means which he saw himself in the necessity of adapting, without compromising himself, with the

[1]Written in Spanish. Index of letters to Don Pedro Cevallos, A.G.I., Sto. Dom., Sección de Estado, leg. 14.

object of availing himself of the most useful and advantageous knowledge [documents] which must result from it, appointing Don Thomas Power to accompany the commissioner of the United States as an individual member of the Commission of limits; And he solicits royal approbation.[2] No. 20. His Most Excellent Sir

In the newspapers of this city dated the 17th., the notices from the government; I have seen the paragraph, a copy[3] of which I am enclosing to Your Excellency and which instructs you of the progress the American Expedition under the command of Captain Lewis, which on the 14th. of April of this year eleven months after its entrance into the Missouri had covered 1609 miles of the upper river. [They expect] in this year to make the 600 miles which appear as far as the source of the said river and to winter on the Pacific Ocean.

The account is no different from the notices which we have nevertheless and conforms well with the Memorial of the defunct Loisel remitted in *representación* number 47 of September 30 of last year. I believe it to be sufficiently exact. And I am persuaded of the certainty and propriety of the means chosen to assure to us the knowledge of the designs of the Americans by the appointment of the subject who may accompany them on the voyage ordered for the exploration and reconnaissance of the Colorado and Arkansas rivers.[4]

May God, etc. June 19, 1805.[5]

[To] *Señor* Don Pedro Cevallos.

[2]Index, letters, and enclosures are in A.G.I., P. de C., leg. 2368.
[3]Enclosure is here but is same as enclosure in Document XVII.
[4]Dunbar, Freeman and Hunter. See Cox, *Early Explorations of Louisiana.*
[5]There follows the excerpts from the *Gazeta de Orleans,* of July 17, 1805, given in document XVII.

XIX.

Cevallos to the Prince of Peace, San Yldefonso, September 18, 1805[1]

War.

San Yldefonso September 20th-informed of this opportune step return the official letter.[2]

Most Excellent *Señor*

My Dear Sir, I send to the hands of Your Excellency for whatever use you may wish, the enclosed official letter of the *Señor* Secretary of State, in which he manifests that having notified the Marqués de Casa Calvo, Commissioner of the limits of Louisiana of there having arrived to his notice that the government of the United States had

[1]Written in Spanish. A.G.I., Sto. Dom., leg. 2600.
[2]Marginal notation.

commissioned Captain Merry Weather to reconnoitre the course of the Missouri as far as its origin, it was notified to His Majesty's Minister in the United States to give the proper complaint to that government concerning the violation of the Spanish Territory; even though the government of the United States has not answered concerning this business, our government finds itself authorized to impede the progress of his commission if he should try to extend it within the dominion of the King.

May Our Lord keep the life of Your Excellency many years, as I wish. San Yldefonso, September 18, 1805

Most Excellent *Señor*

Pedro Cevallos [rubric]

Most Excellent *Señor*

Príncipe de la Paz.

To His Most Excellent *Señor,* Don Pedro Cevallos, Madrid, September 25, 1805

To the Minister of War:

The *generalísimo* has been informed of what was represented by the Marqués de Casa Calvo concerning the commission that the Government of United States gave to Captain Merry Weather to reconnoitre the course of the Missouri River to its origin. His Excellency appreciated the opportune step and recommends that the official letter be returned to the said minister, the official letter which the *Señor* Minister of State has remitted

Most Excellent *Señor:*

The *Señor Generalísimo* Príncipe de la Paz, received the official letter from Your Excellency the 18th of the current month, and the one which was enclosed of the *Señor* Secretary of State in which is manifested that as a result of the advice which the Marqués de Casa Calvo gave concerning the commission with which the Government of the United States charged Captain Merry Weather of exploring the course of the Missouri River to its origin, it was brought to the attention of His Majesty's Minister, resident in said states, to give the proper complaint to the Congress over the violation which would be made of the Spanish Territory in case of carrying forward the commission when our government finds itself authorized to stop it. And said superior chief has been pleased to resolve: that he remains informed of the opportune step, and that the cited official letter be returned to Your Excellency.

I am executing this, informing Your Excellency by disposition of the *Señor Generalísimo.*

May Our Lord keep the life of Your Excellency many years which he can and I beg.

Madrid, September 25, 1805

Most Excellent *Señor:* Don Pedro Cevallos.

XX.

CHOUTEAU TO WILKINSON, ST. LOUIS, APRIL 12, 1806[1]

St. Louis, April 12, 1806
Genl. J. Wilkinson

Governor &c. &c.

Sir, I would that I were able to give you with all possible precision a statement of expenses incurred by the Spanish government in regard to the Indian department, but these expenses varied so much according to circumstances that I can send you only a general estimate. I shall add to it a detail of the causes and circumstances which contributed most to the increase or decrease of these expenses, and finally I shall submit to you my ideas regarding the expenditures to be made this year for the Indian Department.

Under Spanish Government, the Indian department was entirely under the direction of the Lieutenant Governor of Upper Louisiana and the Commandants of the various posts under his jurisdiction, who might be looked upon as sub-agents, as they were authorized to give out provisions and small presents to the Indians from whom they received yearly visits, whether they happened to stop on their way to St. Louis or whether they came solely for the purpose of keeping up a good understanding with these subordinate Commandants, or to bring back stolen goods or to deliver over some culprit. The subdivision of powers was perfectly adapted to the place and the circumstances. The posts of New Madrid, Cape Girardeau, Ste. Geneviève are too far away from St. Louis to carry on prompt intercourse with this place and it was necessary that there should be in these different places, persons specially commissioned to oversee the conduct of the Indians and to provide for their support; otherwise these Indians might indulge in disturbances which would be disastrous to the inhabitants. The post of St. Charles, although not far away from St. Louis, being necessarily the passage way for the Nations of the Mississippi and the Illinois river who come to the Missouri to hunt, has also a sub-agent; and the anxiety which the inhabitants of St. Charles suffered on the departure or the return of these nations, such anxiety as made them spend several nights under arms, seems to demonstrate the wisdom of the Spanish government in the establishment of her sub-agents. It is impossible to determine the emoluments which were attached to these places, those who

---

[1]Missouri Historical Society, Pierre Chouteau Letterbook, pp. 87-93. This translation from the French was made by the late Mrs. Nettie H. Beauregard.

possessed them were at the same time both Civil and Military Chiefs, but an estimate may be made for provisions and presents at

New Madrid $1000.00
Cape Girardeau 400.00
Ste. Geneviève 400.00
St. Charles 400.00

The expenses incurred at St. Louis by the Spanish government may be divided into two classes, current or yearly expenses, and unusual and unexpected expenses. The first are those which I have described above, which vary according to circumstances. When Spain took possession of Louisiana, she felt the necessity of winning to herself the Indian nations of this district who through prejudice, hallowed by long habit, seemed to regret the French and to be less attached to their successors.

The method employed to attract their affection, and which succeeded, was to show them more generosity than did the old government and yet to reduce, each year the number of their presents to restrain them within just bounds. When in 1777 Spain was at war with England, she greatly increased her presents to the Indians to counterbalance the presents and the counsel which these same Indians were receiving at that time from the employees of Canada; but despite these presents, the nations of the Mississippi, hired and assisted by the English, attacked even St. Louis. Finally at the time of the war between the United States and the Indians living on the East bank of the Mississippi, the Spanish, in order to restrain the nations antagonistic to the whites in general, and anxious for war, were obliged to increase the number of their presents. I believe that one will make no mistake in stating that the maximum of yearly expenses incurred by the Spanish Government for presents, distributed among the Indians, during the time of its possession of Louisiana, was $30,000.—and the minimum of these same expenses was $8000.—which amount covering approximately forty years when Louisiana belonged to the Spanish, and calculating on ten years of heavy expenses, and thirty of ordinary expenses, the average would be 13500.—. The heavy and unexpected expenses, under the Spanish government, varied always according to events, and were not of much consequence. There were circumstances, however, which made them mount up considerably, such as the expedition, made to New Madrid, in recent years, for the execution of some Indian murderers.[2] The Lieutenant-Governors were authorized by their permits to make these expenditures, without a special authority required, this was always granted them, without difficulty; this sort of full power was necessary in many circumstances where the Lieutenant-Governors could not have obtained orders

---

[2]See documents in Houck, *Spanish Régime in Missouri*, II, 318-321, and Billon, *Annals of St. Louis, op. cit.*, pp. 318-332.

from the Governor at New Orleans as promptly as the occasion demanded. I do not think that in ordinary years these expenses ever exceeded 3000 g^{ds}. Recapitulation of expenses incurred by the Spanish Government, for every disbursement made during approximately 40 years during which time Spain was in possession of Louisiana.

Expenses for provisions and presents distributed in the various posts under the jurisdiction of the St. Louis post.................. $2,200.—

Current expenses in presents 8,000

     "   "   for provisions 3,500

Unusual   "   3,000

Not including any salaries of employees 16,700

I do not include in these expenses, the upkeep and the pay of a small party of militia which was constantly stationed at the Osages[3] by the government.

If the expenses incurred by the Spanish government are to serve as a basis for those to be incurred by the American government, it would first be necessary to compare the position of the Spanish and the Indians of Louisiana with the position held today by the United States, toward these same nations. The intercourse between the government and the Indian nations, has greatly increased since Louisiana has belonged to the United States. The voyage of Captain Lewis has attracted many nations to St. Louis, which had never come here before. The bond of affection and trade did not extend any further up the Mississippi than "Rivière des Moenes." Those nations of the Upper Mississippi and of the St. Pierre river, although living on land confined to Spanish boundaries, had no intercourse in trade or bond of affection with any but the English nations living at Prairie du Chien or directly with Canada; in fact the nations residing on the Arkansas river had no intercourse with St. Louis; therefore, the nations which received presents and provisions from the Lieutenant-Governor of Upper Louisiana, were the "Loups" [Wolves], the Shawnee, the Peorias, a small part of the "Machecoux," the "Cances," the Ottowas, Iowas, Sacs and Fox, Kickapoos.—In short the Spanish government owned the whole extent of territory from the Mississippi to the Sea in the West and could afford to neglect the nations living in the centre of this vast territory without fear that a powerful neighbor might turn these nations against it, who by their geographical position could have intercourse with none but the Spanish of New Mexico or of Louisiana. The position of the United States differs in this in every respect. The expeditions sent out by order of the government to Upper Missouri and the Mississippi, have and will attract to St. Louis Indian nations who until then had never come, such as the Ricaras,

[3]At Fort Carondelet of the Osages. Full documentation is given in Nasatir, *Imperial Osage.*

the Sioux from the river "Des Moines," Sioux from the Upper Missouri, Mandans, Mahas, Pawnees, Mahas, &c. If it be the intention of the government to attract to the Eastern ports of the United States or to New Orleans the trade of fine peltries, which hitherto have been taken to Canada it is necessary in order to attain this to cultivate the affection of the Sioux and of [illegible] those [?] living on the northern limits, and to win the affection of an Indian nation, one must make it presents. In fact the "Aytanes," a very numerous and powerful nation living in the immense prairies which are supposed to reach beyond the western limits, must become, owing to their position, the most important ally of the United States. The intercourse of affection, politics and commerce with the Indians, therefore, becoming stronger day by day, may be considered as necessary to the United States. It follows that the sum which was considered sufficient by the Spanish government for the ordinary year, to carry on this intercourse, would not be sufficient today; but considering the economical and wise administration which characterizes the United States government, one may hope for better results from the same amount of money used by the Spanish government.

In order to give a reasonable estimate of the expenses to be made this year for the Indian department, one would have to be thoroughly apprised of the political relations existing between the United States and the neighboring powers. One would also have to know the plans which the government may have for the prosperity of the trade. Having no idea regarding these points, I shall confine myself to a few private thoughts. The establishment of sub-agents at the posts of the Arkansas, New Madrid, Cape Girardeau, Ste. Geneviève and St. Charles, seems to me necessary; these sub-agents will be instructed to watch the conduct of the Indians who shall pass through their posts, to find them lodging, wood and provisions which shall be necessary without being authorized to make them presents and in a case where the government would have some claim to make against any Indian nation or anything to transmit to them, it shall be the duty of the sub-agent, to execute all the orders that may be received in this matter. There has been no interpreter appointed by the government for the Kansas, Missouris, Ottos, Panis, Mahas, "République," Mandans, Sioux of the St. Pierre river, the Northern Sioux, "Aytanes," "Sauteux," Arkansas. When any parties of these nations come to St. Louis, it is very difficult and at times even impossible to procure an interpreter to communicate with them, and besides this difficulty, if the government sends out any expeditions among any of these nations, it would have to employ interpreters for the voyage, who would then insist on very high wages; in fact, in choosing for this position, only trustworthy and intelligent men, would contribute more than any other way to keep the Indians in a peaceful attitude. The unforeseen and unusual expenditures cannot be estimated and depend entirely upon circumstances, but I think it would be advantageous and even necessary that the Superintendent of the Indian Department should be authorized to spend a certain stipulated sum which unforeseen circumstances might exact at the moment without having to depend on orders from his higher chiefs.

Therefore the annual expenditures or current ones estimated on the several Indian nations who come to St. Louis every year, and calculating on visits from some of the Chiefs from the Upper Missouri and the Mississippi, may necessitate presents amounting to $8,000, which is the most moderate price which was paid for these same presents under the Spanish government. In adding to this sum that spent in appointments and wages and for provisions to be given to the Indians in the St. Louis as well as the subordinate posts, and finally expenses that are unforeseen and impossible to calculate, one will get the exact total of expenses required by the Indian Department in Louisiana.

I have tried Sir, in this estimate, to answer accurately and in detail all the points mentioned in your last letter, but to make it perfect, I should have had more information than I have. All that I have to offer is my experience of over thirty years, acquired under the Spanish government, by continuous contact with the Indian nations of the Missouri and the Mississippi and an ardent desire to co-operate, with all my might in the plans of the government, in obeying punctually, the orders which it will be pleased to give me.

Enclosed is a list of the present employees in the Indian Department.

I have the honor to be

&c.&c.　[Pierre Chouteau]

Louisiana Territory　　　　　Indian Department

Names	Employ	Residence	Appointments
L. Laurimier	Sub-Agent	Cape Girardeau	$400.00 per year
Nᵉ. Mongrain	Interpreter	Grt. & Little Osages	365.00　do
H. Bolon	Ditto	Peorias, "Loups" "Shavans," Kickapoos	365.00　do.
Pᵉ. Dorion Sr.	"	Sioux, River Des Moens	1.50 per day
Lˢ Dorion, Son	"	Iowas	1.50 " "
Graveline	"	Ricaras in United States	1.50 " "
Fisher	"	Sacs & Fox; Wm. Ewing	1.50 " "

INDEX

NOTE

In this index, when a letter or other document is noted as "cited," it means, of course, that the source of it is to be found indicated on the given page. As a space saving device, citations have not been mentioned in the index for the several hundred documents included in these volumes: the source for all of them are indicated in footnotes on appropriate pages. Therefore if the index says: "letter to Carondelet cited, 134n", or "*mémoire* from Mesnager cited, 43n", it means that the editor has seen and translated [where necessary] that document, but has not necessarily included it in this publication. He is merely telling the source of it, in what publication or collection of documentary material it may be found; and the index is pointing the way to that information. An effort has been made to include in the index page references to nearly all such citations, certainly to all the important ones.

In subject matter other than names in the index, the plural is intended to include the singular; for example, *Geese*: if one *goose* is mentioned it will be entered under *Geese*.

INDEX

Abbadie, M. d': See Dabbadie.

Abnaki Indians (Abenaki, Abenaky, Abenaqui) : 357; 439; 696.

Acadians: colony to be planted, 65; Peyroux once interpreter for, 598n.

Acosta, M.: 441.

Account and risk: in Todd-Clamorgan agreement, 464.

Adaes, presidio: See Los Adaes, presidio of.

Adaes Indians (Adais, Adayes) : habitat, 120.

"Aerostatic chariot"; 683.

Aesetone Indians: Iberville lists, 8n.

El *Afortunado* barge: 476n.

Agents for traders: suggested regulation about, 313.

Agriculture: declining, but petitioners will promote it, in exchange for trade contract, 679; De Lassus tries to promote, 676; extensive area suitable for, in Louisiana, 684; Government point of view, 652ff; hindered by fears of Osages, 199; range in crops, 686; reduction in duties would promote, 394; source of prosperity, 454; the civilizing of the villages the goal: agriculture the means, 691, 695; vs. fur trade, 652ff.

Agua Fría: location, 121.

Aguardiente: for distribution to the Indians, 129, 168, 185, 250.

Aile de Corbeau: 180.

Air view (imagined) of Louisiana: as described by L. Vilemont, 680-687.

Ajonis Indians (Iowa) : habitat, according to Toscan, 72.

Alabama Indians: See Alibamon Indians.

Alange, ——: extract from letter from Miró, 157-160.

Albany Fort: 501.

Alcides (Alcide) : 699.

Alcudia, Duque de, Secretary of State: dispatch from Carondelet cited, 340; extract from letter from Carondelet, 230n; letter from Carondelet, with annexes, 385-410; letter from Viar and Jaudenes cited, 79n; marginal note, on Carondelet dispatch, 395n. See also Manuel de Godoy and Prince of Peace.

Aldea de la República (Maniguacci), village: 123.

Alibamon Indians (Alabama, Alibamones, Alibamu) : habitat, 120.

Allegheny Mountains: 2; 685.

Allies, Indian: See Indians friendly to French; to Spanish.

Allouez, Claude Jean, Father: a history of Missouri based on his information, 4n.

Álvarez, Eugenio: 184; 234n; 235; given license to trade on Missouri, 162; letter to López y Ángulo cited, 614n; letter to Morales cited, 614n; witnesses statement, 666.

American claims: to territory, following Louisiana purchase, 748.

American Philosophical Society: sponsors of proposed Michaux expedition; 164; synopsis of proceedings in the matter of Michaux expedition, 166-167.

American Revolution: effect of, on British traders, 76; on Spanish dominion, 71.

American settlements: description and distance up the Missouri, 486; several on east bank of Mississippi, 542.

American territory: in Mississippi region and on Lake Michigan listed in report on English commerce, 180; extent of, 684.

Americans: 157n; 343; 408; 409; 424n; 442; 508; 513; 542; 583; 588; a band of, observed fortified in a blockhouse, 365; are industrious and behave well, 543; character of, 440; forts needed to protect against encroachments of, 393; in Spanish territory needed an interpreter, 544; measures concerning usurpation by, 398; reason for their superior grain, 535; supersede English in Indian trade, 528; to become masters of traders, 407.

Amiens: See Congress of Amiens; Treaty, or Truce of Amiens.

Ammunition: See Munitions. See also Gunpowder.

André Cayouga and Company: See Cayouga Company.

Anglo-Spanish rivalry: 71-72; 75-76; 78; 79; 80; 81; 83; 85; 101-102; 109; 111; 131; 145-146; 204; 212; 302-303; 322-323; 336; 337; 338; 347; 354-355; 364; 364n; 385ff; 425; 433; Carondelet proposes measures to stop clandestine commerce of the English, 385-386; proposed measures covering, 207-208.

Anglo Spanish war: declared by Spain for reasons given, 431n; with war impending, Carondelet advises Trudeau, 478n.

Animals: 378; 379; 380; in Missouri region, 11; many different ones found in Rocky Mountain region, 498; "new" ones on Upper Missouri, 99, 316-317; on Nodaway River, 488. See also bears, beaver, bison, buffalo, cows, deer, dogs, elk, ermine, goats, horses, martens, otter, wild cats, unicorn.

Ansa à la Grasa (L'Anse à La Graisse, New Madrid) 146n.

El *Antelope,* ship from London: 508; 512; bringing merchandise ordered by Todd, 507; lengthy correspondence about merchandise brought, cited, 512n.

Apache Indians: 2; 147; 148; threatened by French-Pawnee alliance, 17; Comanches enemies of, 42; See also Lipans.

Apaches, Lake of: 4n.

Apalache: 157n.

Aranda, Conde de: letter from Carondelet cited, 79n.

Arcanzás (Arcansa) : See Arkansas.

Arikara Indians (Aricaras, Arricarás, Caricara, Kikara, Ree, Ricarra, Richaare, Riis, Rik, ka, ras) : 28; 33; 34; 59; 60; 74; 78; 82; 83; 88; 89; 90; 91; 97; 98; 100; 101; 109; 110; 121; 123; 124; 233; 258; 260; 262; 263; 265; 267; 270; 272; 273; 275; 277; 285; 286; 287; 289; 291; 292; 294; 295; 296; 297; 304; 305; 307; 310; 326; 338; 340; 341; 342; 360; 362; 365; 374; 379; 384; 388; 390; 411; 416; 418; 426; 428; 441; 453; 456; 490; 495; 496; 527; 596; 673n; 748; 749; estimate of annual value of merchandise for, 759; estimate of population, 760; Evans finds fort built by merchants of Montreal, 540; expedition sent out by American government will attract these Indians to St. Louis, 769; horses stolen from second village, 303; live on Upper Missouri, 11; location and number, 540; location and number of warriors, 126-127; number of men using arms, and amount of trade, 706n; numbers, 25, 53; numbers and divisions, 299-303; one killed by Poncas, 353; salary paid interpreter for, 771; seen by Loisel, 739; speak same language as Pawnees, 12; suffer from raids, 19; trouble with Poncas and Sioux reported, 99.

Argote, Villalobos Antonio: 642.

Arkansas: John Law colony, in eastern part, a good market for slaves, 20.

Arkansas Indians (Quapaw): 214, 321, 747; estimate of population, 759; habitat, 120; Iberville lists, 8n; location, description, number, 53-55; report Missouri attack on, 27, 27n.

Arkansas River (San Francisco de Arkansas, Arcansa, Arcanzás, Rivière des Arcs, Rivière des Argues) : 8; 12; 13; 17; 59; 121; 124; 126; 158; 320; 365; 379; 439; 486; 521; 538; 539; 684; 750; 763; 764; a fort projected on, to restrain Osages, 151; Americans send expeditions to explore source, 749; Fabry reaches, 30; Frenchmen there, reported attacked, 28; gold mines in region, 683; Indians have no intercourse with St. Louis, 769; Mallet party descends, 28; post at mouth urged, 14.

Arkansas River post and district: 158; 173; 325; 343; considered important, 64; establishment of sub-agent for Indian affairs seems necessary, 770; soldiers needed to defend, 24.

Armenta River: See Mermentao River.

Armesto, Manuel Andrés Lopez de: 240; 674; enclosure, in letter from Moro, with marginal note by De Lassus, 663-664; extract from letter from Clamorgan, 520n; letter from Manuel Moro, about Lisa *mémoires*, 660-663.

Armstrong, John, Lieutenant: 79; biography and explorations, 135n-136n; expense account, 141; extract from letter, Harmar to Knox, 137n; letters from superiors about his expedition to the Missouri, 135-140, 142; report to General Harmar, 140-141.

Arricarás Indians: See Arikara Indians.

Arrows: 332; 334; 380.

Articles of agreement, Loisel-Heney partnership, 636-638.

Articles of incorporation, Missouri Company, 217-228.

Artillery: 152; 355.

Arundel, William: extract from letter to John Evans, 99n.

Arundel, *Sieur,* merchant at Cahokia: 414; assortment of merchandise to be furnished to, by Clamorgan firm, 469.

Ascanis Indians: See Yscanis Indians.

Ash trees: 762.

Assiniboine Indians (Asseniboine, Nasseniboine, Osseniboines, Osniboine): 332; 335; 381; 382; 391, 400; 435; 437; 492; habitat and numbers, the wandering part and the settled part, 383.

Assiniboine River: 32; 94; 95; 103; 110; 161n; 331; 332-333; 334; 335; 383; 491; 492; 493; 500n; 620; 660; English building forts on, 337.

Atakapa, Atak-apa, Attakapa Indians: See Attacapa Indians.

Atlantic Ocean: 394, 491; 684; explorers to try to find water route from, to Pacific, 715.

Attacapa Indians (Atakapa, Atak-apa, Attakapa): 59; 685; habitat, 120.

Attacapa post: 746.

Attotactoe Indians: See Oto Indians.

Aubry, Charles Phelipe de, successor to Dabbadie as Director-General of Louisiana: as acting French governor, 64; extract from letter to Minister, 63; letters to Minister, New Orleans, cited, 64n.

Aulneau, Father: with La Vérendrye party, 32.

Autawa Indians: See Ottawa Indians.

Autman (Auteman), Frederic: acts as witness, 515.

Autocdata Indians: See Oto Indians.

Ayaguis Indians: 747.

Avoyelles Indians: exclusive trade with, proposed, 458n.

Awls: 271.

Ayetan (Ayetanes) Indians [Ietan]: habitat, according to Ríu, 70.

Les Aymons: on Iberville list, 8n.

Ayoa, Ayoua, Ayoués, Ayowas, Ayouwai, Ayowai Indians: See Iowa Indians.

Ayres, Stephen: extract from journal of trip in the Mississippi valley, 607n.

Aytanes Indians: See Ietan Indians.

Azanza, Mr.: letter from Carondelet cited, 355n.

Bache, B.: contributes to fund for proposed exploration, 167.

Bacon: 200.

Bahia: 157n.

La Baie Denoc: 180.

Bald Island: distance from mouth of Missouri, 488.

Balls: See Bullets.

Bankruptcy: staring Clamorgan in the face, 570n; threatens Missouri Com-

777

pany, because of Clamorgan's management, 567.

Banners: 251; 359. See also Flags.

Barrancas, Commandant of: See Folch.

Barrancas de Margot: See Écores à Margot.

Bartélemy, Juan: trade with Republican Pawnees granted, 135.

Basq, M.: French geographer, 713.

Basque Island (Ile aux Basques): 266; distance from mouth of Missouri, 490.

Basquez, Benito: See Vasquez, Benito.

Bauvais, Sainte Geme (Saintgeme Bobé): 33n; 62.

Bay of Juan de Fuca: 671.

Bay of St. Bernard (San Bernardo Bay): See Bay St. Louis.

Bay of St. Louis: See Bay St. Louis.

Bay of the West: See Pacific Ocean.

Bay St. Louis (Bay of St. Bernard, San Bernardo Bay, Bay of St. Louis): 439; 685.

Bear Creek: 260.

Bear grease for cooking: 159.

Bears: 125; 488; 538; 762.

Beaudouin, Juan: given license to trade on Missouri, 162.

Beauharnois, Count de, Governor at Quebec: 26; 32; 33; letter to Minister cited, 40n.

Beaver: 6; 36; 39; 70; 95; 125; 249; 261; 264; 266; 271; 283; 311; 322; 378; 379; 380; 382; 412; 488; 538; abundant in Upper Louisiana, 684; "beyond all belief," 381; in exchange for guns, 263; plentiful in Hay River, 498; price in powder for each pack, 301.

Beckwith, Major: asked to investigate stranger, 133n.

Begnis, Michel: letter to Villermont cited, 7n.

Belêtre (Bellêtre Belestre), Picoté de: 72; draft of letter to, cited, 72n; granted trade with Osages, 146n; letter to Miró cited, 146n.

Belisle, Jean Baptiste[?]: order to steal horses, 22n.

La Belle Rivière: See Ohio River.

Belliaur, William: accuses Butler of stealing his horse, 617.

Bellier, Jean Baptiste: acts as witness in depositions, 575, 576.

Bellin, Jacques Nicholas: Armstrong's map traced from "Carte de Louisiane", 142.

Bellivos, Charles: 403n.

Benito [Vasquez?]: 316.

Benoist (Benoît), Jean Baptiste: See St. Claire, Jean Baptiste Benoist (Benoit), Sieur de.

Benoît, M.: trade granted, for 1802, 592.

Benoît, François M., son-in-law of Sanguinet: 592; 646; 650; 664; 705; 741; 741n; acts as witness, 703; concession, by Salcedo, of exclusive trade, 688-689; granted, with three others, exclusive trade, 644; petition against exclusive trade, with Robidoux and others, 624-627; petition for exclusive trade, with Lisa and others, 677-680; share in note to Chouteau, 680n; signs power of attorney for Lisa, 667.

Berger, Pierre (Periche): 247; 267; 292.

Bergier, Marc, Father: successor to St. Cosme, 6; tells of French plans for Missouri fort, 8n.

Bernard, Father, of Pointe Coupée: 373.

Bertet, M. de: commandant at Illinois: 40; 40n; 41; plan to stop fraud and violence of traders outlined, 35-36; sent to the Illinois as commandant, 35.

Betegon, Josef: member of Spanish committee, 727.

Biddle, Mr.: 90.

Bienville, Jean Baptiste Lemoyne, Sieur de, governor of Louisiana colony: 8; 9; 24; asks to found post on Missouri, 13; directs Du Tisné activities, 18-19; extract from letter about murder of voyageurs, 25; extract from letter about Osage attack on hunters, 25; 27;

extract from letter about silver mines, 25; instructions to Fabry, 29; journal fragments cited, 16n; letters to Minister cited, 26n, 34n, 35n; recommendations quoted concerning trade with Spaniards, 16; relations with La Salle, 10n; requests award for Bourgmont, 13; sends party to New Mexico, 28; writes Boisbriant about sending Bourgmont to Upper Missouri, 20.

Bigbellies: See Gros Ventres Indians.

Big Horn River: 110.

Big Manitou River: location and distance from mouth of Missouri, 486.

Big Osage River: See Osage River.

Big Osages: See Osage Indians.

Big Rabbit, Omaha chief: 280; 281; 292; cheats in exchange of merchandise, 288.

Big Sioux River: 264.

Bilbao: birthplace of Gardoqui, who held official positions there, 130n.

Biloxi Indians: habitat, 120.

Billiard table: 589; François Vallois the owner of one, 644; Gerónimo Hebert, also, 645.

Billiards: 559n.

Billon, F. L.: 548n.

Birch-bark: to be used on expedition to record observations, 165-166.

Birch trees: 381.

Biscuits: 267.

Bison: herds make nomads of the Sioux and the Sauteux, 693.

Black Bird (Pájaro Negro), Omaha chief: 98; 357; 358; 359-360; 363; personality and power, 282ff; rascality, 290; slander against Truteau, 294.

Black Hills (Costa Negra): 111; 738.

Black Pawnee Indians: See Wichita Indians.

Black River: 684.

Blackfoot Indians (Pieds Noirs, Pieds Négros): 333; 383; 739.

Blackwell, R.: contributes to fund for proposed exploration, 167.

Blankets: 272; 287; 291; 361; as presents to Indians, 129; for trading with Mahas or Poncas, 248; English get two furs for one blanket, 364.

Bleakley, Josiah (Bleaklay, Blakely): 387; petition, with Todd, 403-405.

Bloom, Lansing B.: 113.

Blue-bead Nation: habitat, 384.

Blunderbusses, 374.

Boats: 175; 292; 294; bull boats, 110; Carondelet order cited, to confiscate English, 403n; flat-bottomed ones, armed and manned, to patrol expedition waters, 434; number, on Missouri, 150n. See also Galiot; Galleys.

Bobé, Saintgeme: See Bauvais, Sainte Geme.

Bodega y Cuadra, Juan Francisco de la, explorer: 713.

Boilvin, Nicolas: 376n.

Bois Blanc River: See James river.

Bois Brulé Indians: See Tetons of the Burned Wood.

Boisbriant, Pierre Duqué. *Sieur* de, commandant of Illinois: 18n; identified, 16; recounts French dilemma in Indian relations, 16-17.

Bolduc (Boleduc) of Ste. Geneviève: 324; 367; assignment and share of trade, 210.

Bolon, H.: annual salary as interpreter for several Indian nations, 771.

Bon Homme Island (Good Man's Island): 265; description and distance up the Missouri, 486.

Bonds: 220; 221; 222.

Bondsmen: for Missouri Company members, 226; 226n.

Bonparé, Louis (Bonpart): 194; given license to trade with Missouris, 162.

Bordas, Luis: 467n.

Bordley, J. B.: contributes to fund for proposed exploration, 167.

Bossu, N.: 18n; "New Voyages . . ." cited, 22n; publishes narrative of the Missouri, 5.

Botany Bay: 131.

Boudon, M., a Canadian: says there are many tin mines on the Missouri, 9.

Bougainville, De, M.: estimates annual trade of Osages and Missouris, 50.

Bouligny, Domingo: 232.

Boundaries: 2; 254; 385; 584-587; 731-732; Anglo-Spanish, 607n; Collot writes about, to Talleyrand, 668-671; facts and settlements to mark, 393; in trade, 83, 84; Louisiana-Texas, 725-727; of American territory, 743; 743n; of Louisiana: historical account by Casa Calvo cited, 743n; official letter from M. Salcedo to Cevallos, discussing historical background, 745-750; Spain vs. United States, 719n; treaty necessary, following acquisition of Louisiana by the United States, 724; violation of, 95. See also Jurisdictions.

Bourbon, Duke and Duchess de: entertain Indians who accompanied Étienne de Bourgmont to France, 21-22.

Bourbon, Prince, son of Condé: mysterious stranger claims to be, 132-133.

Bourgmont, Étienne Veniard de: 28; activities at Detroit and in exploring Missouri, 12-13; among Osages, 13; appointed commandant, 18; arrival in New Orleans, 20; diary cited, 12; Journal and documents about, cited, 22n; knowledge of the Upper Missouri, 23n; lives among Missouris, 12; post on Missouri established by, 14, 748; recommended for post, as peacemaker, 17; seeks friendship of the Padoucas, 20-21; takes Indians to France, 21-22, 22n.

Bouvet, Mathurin: witness to partnership agreement, 239.

Boyer River (Boyér): 126; distance from mouth of Missouri, 489.

Brabo River: See Rio Grande.

Branciforte, Marqués de (Branceforte): copy of letter from Carondelet, 439-440; letter to Prince of Peace cited, 439n; prefix to letter, 439n.

Brandon House, Hudson's Bay Company post: 103; James Sutherland heads, 461n.

Brandon House Journal: cited, 460n; 461n; extracts, 461-464.

Brandy: 38; 46; 48; 283; 516; 538; gift from Sioux to Mahas, 517; Ortiz and friends corrupt the Osages by selling out of turn, 717.

Brau, - - - - : grant to, 62.

Breda, Antonio, agent for Missouri Company, 92; 98; 351, 353; 363; misfortunes, 528.

Bribery: to Englishmen, noted in McDonnell letter to Evans, 503.

Bridles: Mandans have Mexican, 82, 161; several nations have Spanish, 333.

Brindamoor, - - - - : French outlaw, 20n.

Brouton, Narso, public scrivener: certifies statements, 666, 667.

Brown, John: 131n.

Bruff, Major, military commandant of Upper Louisiana: report of conversation with two Osages about pillaging a caravan, 744-745; 756.

Brulé Sioux: See Sioux Indians.

Bucareli River (Cook River): 713.

Buffalo: 99; 124; 362; 378; 381; 382; 762; instruction about escorts for buffalo hunts.

Buffalo Island: distance from mouth of Missouri, 490.

Buffalo skins: 277; 333. See also Hides; Robes.

Buildings: for agency and employees among the Mandans, 243; shed measurements, 244.

Buisson, Jean François: See St. Cosme.

Bullets (Balls): 262; 272; 280; 281; 283; 287; 492; 710.

Bungees, Bungi Indians: See Sauteux Indians.

Burro, Bernardo: commands Spanish dragoons from Santa Fé, 591n.

Bustamente, Carlos María de: 713; narrative cited, 713n.

Cabanné, M.: 112; granted one-year trade with Kansas and Otos, 592; letter to Casa Calvo, offering to mediate between tribes in exchange for exclusive trade with them; with Calvo decision, and marginal note by De Lassus, 614-616.

Caddo Indians (Cadaux, Cado): 214; habitat, 120; Fabry gets some horses from them, and following their route, reaches Natchitoches, 30-31.

La *Cadena de Rocas:* See Rocky Mountains.

Cadillac, Antoine de la Mothe, *Sieur* de: reports to Minister cited, 10; 10n; 11n; 12n.

Cado Indians: See Caddo Indians.

Cadodachos, Cadodaquis, Caudachos Indians: See Kadohadacho Indians.

Cahokia (Kaokia, Kaokias, Kahokia, Cas, Kao): 6; 8; 43; 51; 132; 142; 372; 373; 469; 601n.

Cahokia Indians: 43.

Cailhol, E. G.: 109n.

Calamec, Petit: 180.

Calcasieu River (Calcasiu, Calcasine, Caricut, Cascacious): 685; 726; mentioned, in determination of boundaries, after Louisiana purchase, 750; no funds available for exploring mouth, 754.

California: 7; 8; 77; 236; 337; 390; 391; 611; 620; French activities in, cited, 5n; occupied by Spain simultaneously with Louisiana, 3; the Californias, 399, 434.

California, Sea of (Vermillion Sea): 92; Charlevoix suggests two routes, 23n; French seek exclusively owned route, 2; Marquette hopes to reach, 3; need for maps, 7. See also Pacific Ocean; Western Sea.

Calumets: 52; 123; 287; 305; 306; 361; 370. See also Peace-pipe.

Calvo, Casa, Marqués de, successor to Gayoso de Lemos: 113; 690; 730; 765; 766; decree, granting trade to Clamorgan; decree granting trade to Sanguinet, 631; distributes trade for 1800 and 1801, 591-592; favors Loisel as Indian agent, 115n; letters from Cevallos, 752, 758; letters from De-Lassus, 613-614; 631; 638-639; 639; 641-645; 719-721; 742-745; letters from De Lassus cited, 114n; 115n; 594n; 614n; letter from N. Salcedo, 732-734; letter from N. Salcedo cited, 746n; letter from Sarpy and Cabanné, 614-616; letters to Cevallos, 727-728; 750-752; 755-758; 764-765; letters to Cevallos cited, 115n; 735n; letters to De Lassus, 617; 627-628; 629; 629-630; letter to De Lassus cited, 614n; letter to Lopez y Ángulo mentioned, 594n; letter to Price of Peace, 754-755; report to Prince of Peace about Lewis expedition, 760-761; letters to Prince of Peace cited, 735n; letter, jointly with M. Salcedo, to N. Salcedo, 731-732; letter and draft of letter to Somuerlos cited, 614n; petition of Clamorgan for restitution of trade, 608-611, with notation in reply, 611; petition of Clamorgan for trade, 635; petition of Sanguinet for exclusive trade, 630.

Caminanbiches Indians (Caninanbiches); 301; 304; 309.

Campillo, Miguel Gomez del: See Gomez del Campillo.

Canada: British in, 3; sphere of interest, 7; English carry on contraband trade from, 387; gathering place of boats for merchandise used in trade, 175; stranger's interest in, 133n; and every other page.

Canadian River: low water slows progress of explorers, 28, 29, 30; Mallet party descends, 28.

Canadians: a few deserters from boats on Upper Mississippi help to increase the population of St. Louis, 214; travel on Missouri and Mississippi in early eighteenth century, 8, 9. For other references about Canadians see Detroit; Companies, English; Michilimackinac; Hudson's Bay Company; Traders, Canadian; Traders, English.

Cancé, Cancis Indians: See Kansa Indians.

Caneenawee Indians (Caneenawees): habitat, 496.

Caninanbiches: See Caminanbiches Indians.

Caniones Indians: make peace with Spaniards, 749.

Cannes: See Kansa Indians.

Cannibalism: between two tribes reported by Du Tisné, 19.

Cannon: 339; 345; 360; 399; for patrol boats on Missouri, 389. See also Guns, Swivel guns, Munitions.

"Cannon ball": Sutherland says it will be deposited among the archives, 501.

Canoes: 31; 89; 150; 175n; 177; 178; cargo of, among English traders, 179; Canadians use birch bark, 491; English use bark, 392; number from English posts wintering in American and Spanish territory, 180; of ox skin, 264.

Cans River: See Kansas River.

Cape Girardeau: 106; 108; 203; 232; 535; commission to oversee Indians necessary at, 767; establishment of sub-agent, Indian affairs, deemed necessary, 770; estimate of amount spent for provisions and Indian presents, 768; location and description, 534.

Carbine (Carabines): stolen by Osages, 214. See also Rifles.

Carbonneaux (Char Bonneaux), poor old school teacher: on list, and *mémoires,* of individuals against exclusive trade, 645, 646, 651; signs power of attorney for Lisa, 667.

Cardin, [Louis, Jr?]: 94, 94n.

Caricara Indians: See Arikara Indians.

Caricut River: See Calcasieu River.

Carlos IV of Spain: See Charles IV, King of Spain.

Carmen, frigate: 755n.

Carondelet, Spanish settlement on Mississippi: 534; 537; location and description, 537.

Carondelet, François Luis Hector, Governor-General of Louisiana, succeeding Miró: 97; 100; 107; 109; 159; 253; 398; 399; 400; 401; 407n; 481; 524; 531; 534; 536n; 541; 546; 563; 573; 598n; 603; 608; 609; 610; 618; 621; 633; 661; 662; 748; approves Missouri Company and plans, 86; approval of regulations of Missouri Company, 433-434; concessions made by Court on recommendation of, 437-438; confiscation order cited, 403n; commission of James Mackay, 428-429; decree, 195; decree approving Missouri Company, 227-228; decree granting Todd petition, 410; decrees free trade, 84; decrees trade free to Spanish, 80; fear of American and British aggression, 393n; forwards Clamorgan report to Prince of Peace, 92n; instructions to Trudeau, 151-153; is aware of English usurpation of trade, 433; letters from Clamorgan, 421-424, 424-425, 429, 431-432, 452-460, 470, 475, 477-478; letter from B. Collell, 241-242; letter from Deblanc, 365; letter from De Lassus (extract), 425n; letter from Deluzières cited, 442n; letter from Dorchester cited, 392n; letter from Gardoqui cited, 402n; letters (extracts) from Gayoso de Lemos, 438n, 513n; note from Grandpré, 573; letter from C. Howard, 514-515; letters from Howard cited, 106n, 523n; letter from Langlois cited, 318n; letter from Morales cited, 370n; letter from Morales cited, 512n; letters from A. Todd cited, 522n; letters from Trudeau, 155, 156-157, 160, 167-169, 171-173, 174-175, 181, 184-185, 185-186, 197-203, 204-205, 205, 207-208, 208, 214-217, 229-230, 230-233, 317-319, 320-322, 322-324, 325-326, 328-329, 329-330, 343-345, 345-348, 348-351, 369-371, 373-375, 416n-417n, 423n, 430n, 440-442, 519-522; letters from Trudeau cited, 77n, 81n, 84n, 86n, 168n, 170n, 193n, 444n, 512n; letter to Alcudia (extract) 230n; letter to Alcudia, with annexes, 385-410; letter to Alcudia, 395-396; letters to Alcudia cited, 253n, 318n, 340; letters to Aranda cited, 79n, 253n; letters to

Azanza cited, 355n, 519n; letter to Branciforte, 439-440; letter, in substance, to Branciforte, with quotation and citation, 424n; letters to Clamorgan, 213, 236-237, 420n-421n, 442-443, 450, 452; letters to Clamorgan cited, 356n, 388n, 473n; letter to Dorchester cited, 392n; letter (draft) to B. Fernandez cited, with extract, 499n; letter to Gayoso de Lemos cited, 478n; letter (extract) to Godoy, 122n; letter to Howard cited, 531n; letters to Las Casas cited, 146n, 149n, 230n, 355n, 519n; letters to Morales, 426, 430-431, 457n (extract), 470-472; letter to Pérez, 196; letter to Portell cited, 230n; letters, with enclosures, to Prince of Peace, 503-506, 507-512; letters to Prince of Peace cited, 87n, 355n, 473n, 519n; letters to Trudeau, 163, 163-164, 167, 173-174, 196, 212, 212-213, 235-236, 315-316, 325, 341, 365, 371, 426, 427, 427-429, 476; letter extracts, to Trudeau, with citations, 175n, 194n; letters to Trudeau cited, 82n, 156n, 170n, 193n, 370n, 388n, 438n, 458n, 478n, 505n; marginal comment on supplementary regulations for the Missouri Company submitted by Clamorgan, 445-450, 453-459; marginal notes on letter from Trudeau, 341, 342; mémoire from Clamorgan cited, 193n; military report (extract) to Las Casas, 253-256; nullifies two articles of the instructions to Truteau, 87, 325, 325n; opposes erection of certain forts, 140n; orders swivel-guns for forts, 425n; petition from Clamorgan, 226-227; petition from D'Église, 234-235; petition from Meunier, 194-195; petition from Meunier and Rolland, 237-238; petition of St. Louis merchants, 181-184; petition of A. Todd, 407-410; proposals to suppress hostile incursions, 435-436; receives from Clamorgan premature congratulations on promotion, 429; recommends reimbursing Todd for goods confiscated, 436-437; report, favoring Todd, 405; report from Clamorgan and Reilhe, 335-340; report from Trudeau

on Missouri commerce, 175-180; St. Louis merchants complain to, 84; summary of proposals to stop English encroachments, 402; trade regulations proposed for Illinois trade, 186-190; value of presents distributed annually, 701n.

Carroll County, Missouri: Fort Orléans established, 20n.

Cascacious River: See Calcasieu River.

Cascaquias: See Kaskaskia.

Castañedo, Juan de, brother-in-law of Lisa: 642.

Castor Indians: number and habitat, 383.

Cat skins: 264.

Cataka Indians: Wandering nation, seen by Loisel, 739.

Cataract of St. Antoine: See Falls of St. Anthony.

Catapoé, Catapoi River: See Qu'Appelle River.

Caterpillar pest: 329.

Catholics: effects of limiting immigrants to, 559; Mackay argues against limiting immigrants to, 587n-588n; many possible immigrants from the United States, 542; marriages and baptisms must be performed by, 543; Stoddard pleads for retention of three clergymen, 742.

Cattle: 153; wild, 282, 287, 288.

Catupe River: See Qu'Appelle River.

Caudachos Indians: See Kadohadachos Indians.

Cauldrons, Copper: 707. See also Kettles, Cooking.

Cavalier, Robert: See La Salle, Robert Cavalier, *Sieur* de.

Cayechingá, Indian chief: medal for, solicited, 326.

Cayne, François: name on Lisa *mémoire*, 667.

Cayogua Indians (Cayougas): 301; 304; 309

Cayouga Company (André Cayouga and Company): 112.

Cayouva Indians: wandering nation, seen by Loisel, 739.

Cedar Bluff: distance from mouth of Missouri, 489.

Cedar Island: See Isle of Cedars.

Cedar River (Cedros): 122.

Cedar trees: 122; 205; 381; 762.

Census, Annual: 368; 372; 372n; résumé cited, 368n.

Ceret: See Cerré.

Cerré, Gabriel (Ceret): 71; 72; 194; assignment and share of trade, 210; commended by Gayoso de Lemos, 597; letter from, cited, 72n.

Cerré, T. S.: signs Lisa *mémoire* against exclusive trade, 651; signs power of attorney for Lisa, 667.

Cevallos, Pedro (Ceballos), Commandant General of Interior Provinces: 725; decree, 714; letter from Casa Calvo, 727-728; letter (draft, unsigned) from Casa Calvo, 750-752; letters from Casa Calvo, 754-755; 755-758, 764-765; letter (draft, unsigned), from——?: 753-754; letters from Casa Calvo cited, 735, 743n; letter to Casa Calvo, 752; letter from Fr. Francisco Gil and others, 723-724; letter, with marginal notation, to the Prince of Peace, 765-766, and reply, 766; letter from M. Salcedo, 745-750; letter (with enclosures: 731-735) from N. Salcedo, 729-731; letters from Yrujo, 712-714, 715-716, 723-724.

Chactos Indians: See Choctaw Indians.

Chafalaya River: arm of the Mississippi, 685.

Chaguennes, Chaguiennes Indians: See Cheyenne Indians.

Chaguinne River: See Cheyenne River.

Chaony Indians: 310.

Chaoïnes Indians: wandering nation, seen by Loisel, 739.

Chaplains: 15; 324; pay too low, 22n; Sr. Mariette commissioned, 22n. See also Clergymen, Missionaries, Priests.

Chapuis, Jean: 42.

Chariton River (Charatón): 122; 261; distance from the Rio Grande, 123; two rivers: location, navigability, and distance from mouth of Missouri, 487.

Charles IV, King of Spain; 100, 413; royal decree, declaring war on England, cited, 431n; royal order, in regard to cost of maintenance of militia, 619.

Charles Mix County, South Dakota: 88; 388n.

Charlevoix, Pierre F. X. de: 10n; 33n; his suggestions followed, 31; letters cited, 23n; suggests two routes to Vermillion Sea, 23n; used by French to gather facts needed in plans for search for western sea, 31.

Charron, Noel: hunter with Truteau, 265, 278, 280, 282.

Chassin, ——: 22; 23; extract of letter cited, 23n.

Chato River: See Platte River.

Chauvin, Jacques (Santiago Chovín): 72; 112; 218; 690; draws lots and gets share of Osage trade, 210; given license to trade with Otos, 591; granted exclusive trade with Panis Bon Chef and Panis Tapage, one year, 592; granted trade with Panis, one year, 592; with Panis, 629-630, 630n, 705; granted share of trade with Otos, 605; inconsistency on subject of exclusive trade, 643; on list and *mémoire* of individuals against exclusive trade, 644, 646, 651; petition, with Robidoux, against exclusive trade, 624-627; signs power of attorney for Lisa, 667.

Chavanon Indians (Chawanon): See Shawnee Indians.

Chayé [Dubé?]: 103; 105; 479; 503; possible identity, 104n.

Chepanchie Indians: Iberville lists, 8n.

Cherry-Branch River: 384.

Cheyenne Indians (Chaguennes, Chaguiennes, Chaguyennes): 88; 90; 101; 262; 294; 296; 297; 298; 301; 304; 305; 306; 309; 310; 332; 334; 377n; 379; 380; 384; 389; 418; 448; 456; 496; 673n; 706n; 711; estimate of population, 760; wandering nation, seen by Loisel, 739. See also Chouta and Ouisy Indians.

Cheyenne River (River Chayennes, Braso, Fork, Fourche, Rió Que Habla, Riviére Qui Parle, White): 56; 89; 111; 113; 301; 379, 380; 382; 384; 498; 737; 738.

Chiabey (Le Couteau): gorget requested for him, 327.

Chicago River: 154n.

Chicagou: wintering spot for English canoes, 180.

Chicagou Indians: 21.

Chicasaw Bluffs: See Écores à Margot.

Chickasaw Indians (Chicasaw): 45; 54.

Chicot Island: 265.

Chido Whaguegran (Le gendre du Coupiqué): gorget requested from him, 327.

Childbirth: 259.

Chiouitanon Indians (Chionitones, Chiouitounes): habitat and number, 385; Truteau instructed to inform himself about them, 245.

Chipiwian Indians: 385.

Choctaw Indians (Chactos, Tchaktas): 54; habitat, 120.

Chorette, Joseph; 303; drowning, 306-307.

Choumans: See Jumano Indians.

Chouta Indians [Cheyennes]: habitat, 379.

Chouteau, Antonio, mestizo: given license to trade on the Missouri, 162.

Chouteau, Auguste: 63; 71; 72; 114; 173; 184; 218; 316; 316n; 320; 321; 343; 344; 345; 420n; 421n; 426; 430; 441; 530; 539; 544; 557; 580; 640; 641; 663; 679; 688; 741; acts as agent for A. Todd and A. Reilhe, 575; appointed to press D. Clark's claims against Clamorgan, 570n; assignment and share of trade, 211; claims loss suffered from purchase of merchandise, 705; commended by Gayoso de Lemos, 597; delivers swivel-guns to Trudeau, for Clamorgan, 444n; effects of his

methods on Osages, 623-624; good influence on Osages, 538; granted exclusive trade with Osages, 458n, 526-527; granted licenses to trade with Osages, 591, 605, 628, 662; granted license to trade with Missouris, 162; granted one-half of trade with Kansas, 135; Journal cited, 63n; letter to Gallatin, enclosing estimate of Indian trade, 758-759; letter to Gayoso de Lemos cited, 560n; letter to Grant, 513-514; letters cited, 570n; litigation over Osage trade privilege, 680n; long-term contract for Indian trade recommended, 624; memorial to Trudeau concerning Clamorgan company indebtedness, 576-579; named one executor for R. Loisel, 757n; "Notes ... on Boundaries of Various Indian Nations" cited, 742n; offers capital for Loisel-Heney partnership, 636; petitioners object to his exclusive trade grant, 677; quoted on distance to Pacific Ocean, 99; trade assignment for 1800, 623; Trudeau owes him money, 328, 329; witnesses Loisel-Heney articles of agreement, 638.

Chouteau, Pierre (Pedro): 162; 184; 214; 215; 318; 320; 321; 326; 345; 346; 350; 367; 370; 372; 373; 375; 464; 469; account of Osage threats of vengeance, 144; assignment and share of trade, 210; given license to trade on Missouri, 162; letter to General Wilkinson about Indian affairs, 767-771; uses tactful methods with Osages, 623-624; winters peacefully with Kansas, 143.

Chovin: See Chauvin.

Christinaux Indians: 383.

Church: previous discussions on construction, 559n; Trudeau suggests selling trade shares to construct a needed church at St. Louis, 559.

Church, Mission: benediction of, 132.

Cius: See Sioux Indians.

Clamorgan, Jacques (Santiago, St. Yago, Morgan), Director of the Missouri Company: 88; 91; 92; 96n; 114; 194; 206n; 208; 209n; 212; 218; 225; 229;

ter to D. Clark, 569-570; memorial of A. Chouteau concerning indebtedness, 576-579; owes large sum to Loisel, 757n; petitions for permission to deposit documents in archives, 464n; represents Missouri Company, 541; successors to Missouri Company, 109; to be permitted to deal with the House of Todd, 427; Trudeau asked to inspect books, 573.

Clark, Daniel, merchant of New Orleans: 420; 464; 464n; 524; 576; 577; 579; 581; documents showing efforts to collect debt from Todd cited, 572n; letter cited, 587n; letter from Clamorgan, Loisel and Company, 569-570; Missouri Company in debt to, 567.

Clark, William, explorer: 3; 109; 367; 749n; 761; "Papers" cited, 115n; sent to explore route to Pacific, 115.

Clarkson, M.: contributor to fund for proposed exploration, 167.

Clergymen: plea for retention of three Catholics, established under Spanish government, 742. See also Chaplains; Missionaries; Priests.

Clermont, chief of Big Osages: 346.

Cloth: for distribution to Indians, 129, 185, 249, 272, 275, 287, 291, 361, 495, 538; blue, for trade with Mahas or Poncas, 248, 707; scarlet, for Black Bird, 283, 707.

Clothes: 310; 329; 707.

Coates, S.: contribution to fund for proposed exploration, 167.

Coiteux, M.: 319.

Coliere, M. M.: assignment and share of trade, 210.

Collars: 154; 232; 318.

Collell, Boneventura (Bentura, Ventura Collel, de Collel): 82; 135; 218; 233; 315; 440; 442; claims losses caused by Garreau, 256-257; letter to Carondelet asking for trade with Kansas, 241-242; trade with Otos granted, 135.

Collin, N.: role in the matter of financial support to Michaux expedition, 167.

Collot, Victor: 376n; 520n; *mémoire* to Talleyrand about administrative problems, 668-671; spends nine months in North America collecting information for the French Republic, 383n; "State of Indian Nations" [list], 383-385; suggestions as to his reception by Trudeau, 519.

Colorado River: See Red River, and Red River of the North. [Note: Since the word Colorado, in Spanish, means *red* or *ruddy*, both rivers referred to above were called both Red and Colorado. Neither one is the river now known as the Colorado.]

Colorado-Arkansas River project: 749; 750; 753; 761; 764; 765.

Comanche Indians (Cumanches, Padoucas, Padós [Laytanes]: 2; 12; 18; 42; 91; 148; 301; 329; 330; 379; 673n; alliance with, important to French, 20; Bourgmont parties seek alliance, 20-21; chief agrees not to war on French, 21; furs, 706n; go against Pananas, 147; letter of Fernando de la Concha to Pedro de Nava discusses Commanche-Apache strife, 146-148; party sent to spy on and stop M. Lewis expedition, 730; threaten peace, 17; to be used to reconnoitre, 734. See also Laytanes; Ietans.

Comandancia-General of the East: made up of four provinces, 147.

Combs, 271.

Commandants: duties and privileges, 544; need secretaries, 544.

Commerce: 13; 67; 174; 686; Clamorgan pleads for aid against English usurpation, 633; effects of exclusive trade on, 647-648; England takes advantage of fictitious boundary line, 669; Howard instructed to arrange destruction of English commerce on rivers, 514; of the Missouri; English ambitious to obtain, 154; of the Missouri: to be free, 151; on upper rivers to need protection from English, 425n; prohibition against Osages threatens loss of Missouri commerce to the English, 155; superiority of English over Spanish, 81; Trudeau report on English commerce with Indians, 175-180; water communication, Hudson's Bay to Gulf of Mexico can increase both English and American, 756; will be increased by change in duties levied, 392-393.

Commerce Syndic of: See Syndic of Commerce.

Commercial company: Clamorgan plea for, 207-208.

Commissioners: Clamorgan suggests Missouri Company article about commissioners, to adjust differences between traders, 192; *commisaire* appointed to oversee distribution of presents to Indians, 328; of Indian affairs urged by Vilemont, 693, 695, 698; Vilemont's eleven definite suggestions for, 700-702.

Commissions for Indians: See *Patentes*.

Commissions on merchandise: in Todd-Clamorgan agremeent, 465, 466, 467, 469.

Committee of Fortifications and Defense of the Indies; names of members of Committee, 727; opinions on limits of Louisiana and Texas.

Commons: land beyond that necessary for pasture to be divided, 153.

La *Compañia del Comercio Yglés:* 181

Companies, English: formed to penetrate Spanish territory can reach Platte River, 439; have penetrated to Arikaras and Mandans, 748; incite Sioux against Missouri Company, 505; their activities threaten Spanish plans, 620.

Company for the Exploration of the Country West of the Missouri: designation of the about-to-be-formed commercial company.

Company of the Indies: 24; 36; directors entertain Indian visitors in Paris, 22; extract from letter to Perrier and La Chaise, 22n-23n; is given fantastic ideas for opening up commerce, 16; orders Bourgmont's appointment as commandant on the Missouri, 18.

Company of the Missouri. [Note. Here follow seven names, found in the documents, used to designate the company later commonly known as the Missouri Company. For additional names see Spanish Company . . .]
Company of Commerce and Discoveries of the Missouri;
Company of Commerce of the Upper Missouri;
Company of Discoverers of the Missouri.
Company of Discoveries. This is the name under which the company was authorized and licensed. See page 193.
Company of Discoveries of the Missouri;
Company of Explorers of the Upper Missouri;
Company of Missouri: used by A. Chouteau in memorial to Trudeau, 579.

Company of the North, and of the Northwest: See Northwest Company.

Compasses: 137; 479: Gayoso de Lemos purchases a costly astronomical one, 586.

Concha, Fernando de la: letter to Pedro de Nava, 146-148.

Confiscation of boats and merchandise: 387, 387n; 433; 438n; belonging to A. Todd, 398; itemized accounts of goods confiscated, 403n.

Congress of Amiens: 668.

Constant, Gabriel: signs Lisa *mémoire* against exclusive trade, 650; signs power of attorney for Lisa, 667.

Convention du Commerce: See Loisel-Heney trade agreement.

Cook, James, Captain: 131; 131n; 699; 699n; 713; his "Voyage to the Pacific" cited, 713n.

Copper: 14.

Corbeaus, Corbeaux Indians: See Crow Indians.

Corks: profit allowed, in Todd-Clamorgan agreement, 468.

Corn: 177; 381; 440; 493; 494; 538; sought by J. McDonnell, 479.

Cornel, Mr.: letter to Saavedra cited, 614n.

Coropa, Ta: village of the Sioux, 295, 310.

Corps du Commerce, St. Louis; 85.

Cortes, Pedro de: member of Spanish committee, 727.

Costa Negra: See Black Hills.

Cottonwood Swamp: See Marais des Liards.

Cottonwood trees: 295; 377; 762.

Council of Louisiana *(Le Conseil de la Louisiane):* 20; extract of letters, 22n; minutes cited, 21n.

Council of State, Spain *(El Consejo de Estado):* 388n; 504; 506; 507; minutes, 432-439; minutes cited, 386n, 403n.

Cour Qui Brule, Kansas chief: letter to De Lassus, 607-608.

Coureurs-du-bois: 4; 7; 10; 12; 40; 43; 49; 187; 284; 313; abuses by, 34; captured by Indians, 5n; undesirable characters, 41.

Courrois Indians: defeated by Arkansas, 54, 55.

Courtois, Louis: amount of debt to Clamorgan company, 577.

Cowhides: 36; 264; 298.

Cows: 233; 278; 279; 310; 331; 379; 521.

Crawford, L.[?]: entrusted by Meriwether Lewis with *parole* and speech for Ayouas and Sioux, 741; 741n.

Crazy Bear, Arikara chief: 305; 306; 308.

Creek Indians ("Machecoux"): 131n; 157n; among the nations receiving presents and provisions from the Spanish, 769.

Creoles: 300; 536; 543; 594; 700.

Crow Creek agency, S.D.: 88.

Crow Indians (Corbeaus, Corbeaux, Cuerbos): 110; 295; habitat, 381, 494; wandering nation, 739.

Crow-Quill Indians: 384.

Crow River (Yellow Rock River): 384.

Crow Wing River (Aile de Corbeau): 180.

Cruzat, Francisco, Lieutenant-Governor, Spanish Illinois: grants trade to Belêtre, 146n; lists Indian nations in report to Gálvez, 70-71; letters to and from cited, 72n; puts forth little effort to overthrow British monopoly, 76; reports cited, 71n; second term in office, 130n; warned to be vigilant against Americans, 72.

Cruzat, Josef (José): granted trade with Otos for one year, 617, 617n, 629n.

Cuadra: See Bodega y Cuadra, J.F.

Cumberland, 146n; 328; 345.

Cypress trees: plentiful in Louisiana, 683; 695.

Dabbadie (Abbadie, D'Abbadie), ——, Director-General of Louisiana: Journal cited, 64n-65n; once offered Maxent exclusive trade privilege, 66; régime, 60-63; trade free after death of, 67.

Dakota River: often called James River, q.v.

Daoiz, Fernando: member Spanish committee, 727.

Darac, Ensign: ascends Missouri, 9-10; character, 10n.

Dartaguiette, Diron: extract from *mémoire* on Louisiana, 10n; extract on Osages cited, 26n; forbids commerce with Osages, 26; is told of many tin mines in Missouri country, 9; reported resolved to avenge murders by Osages, 25; retaliatory measures, 26; states what he has heard about course of Missouri River, 10; thinks exploration of the Missouri important, 10.

Dauphin Island (L'île Dauphin): 6.

Davion, Antoine, Father: 6-7.

De Bertet, M.: See Bertet, M. de.

De Bon, M.: correspondence concerning him cited, 133n; much mystery surrounds the travels in America of this French subject, 132-133.

De Bougainville: See Bougainville, De.

D'Église, Jacques (Jacinto, Jacobo, Hiacinthe, Santiago; Egliz, Yglesia, Léglise, L'Yglesse: 81; 83n; 84; 87; 88; 88n; 89; 93; 95; 101; 101n; 109; 112; 113; 160; 160n; 161; 163; 164n; 181; 233; 235; 242; 247; 249; 250; 262; 263; 267; 275; 285; 289; 291; 292; 293; 294; 298; 330; 331; 334; 341; 342; 344; 371; 417; 452; 520; 707n; 756; Carondelet's recommendation, 315; claims to have discovered Mandans, 256; guns, powder, bullets, and other merchandise stolen by Poncas, 289, 290; killed in New Mexico, 113; on list and *mémoire* of individuals against exclusive trade, 644-646; petition for exclusive trade denied, 83; petition to Carondelet for trade contract, 234-235; promissory notes to Clamorgan, 703, 704; reaches Mandans via Missouri, 82; reported to have left on trip up Missouri, 744, 744n; reports to Trudeau, 82; signs power of attorney for Lisa, 667.

De Ganne's *mémoire:* says Indians claim that the Western Sea can be reached by water. The citation, 11n, indicates a long *mémoire.*

De la Barre, M.: assassination, 45-46; 45n; 46n.

De la Chaise: See La Chaise.

De Lassus, Charles Dehault, Lieutenant-Governor of Louisiana: 204; 231; 236; 319; 591n; 598n; 641n; 652; 688n; 731; 754; 755; at Ste. Geneviève, 202; certified statement, 661-667; decree, 646; letters from Casa Calvo, 627-628; 629; 629-630; letter from Cour Qui Brule, 607-608; letters and draft of letter from Gayoso de Lemos, 597-599, 600; *mémoires* from Lisa, 665, 716-718; report from Loisel, 735-740; letter from Loisel cited, 115n; letter from Moro cited, 680n; letters and draft of letter from M. Salcedo, 672, 689-690, 705-706, 720; letter from M. Salcedo cited, 718n; letter (draft) from [Governor of Louisiana?] 725; letter from Trudeau cited, 386n; letters to Casa Calvo, 613-614; 622-624; 631; 638-639; 639; 640-641;

641-644; 742-745; extract, 736n; letters to Casa Calvo cited, 594n; 614 n; 629n; 630n; 641n; letter to Casa Calvo and M. Salcedo, 719-720; letter (extract) to Carondelet, 425n; letter to Carondelet cited, 172n: letter to Gayoso de Lemos; 605-606; letter to Gayoso cited, 600n; letter to Morales, 675-677; letters to M. Salcedo, 664-665; 674-675; 673; other letters cited, 112n, 634n, 647n; letter to M. Salcedo and Casa Calvo, 719-720; list of protestants against exclusive trade, 644-645; marginal notes, 616; 664; 675; 677; note to François Saucier, 596; order concerning land for Saucier family, 602; petition of Loisel for land, 611-612; petition of James Mackay for land, 603-604; receives petition from Clamorgan, 112; reply to Mackay petition, 604-605; summary of trade licenses at St. Louis, 590-592.

De Liette, (Deliette), *Sieur:* 22n; 23; 23n.

De Luzières, Delassus; Letter from Rousseau cited, 318n; letter to Carondelet cited, 442n.

De Mézières y Clugny, Athanase (Atanasio) Lieutenant-Governor and Commandant at Natchitoches: 20n; 743n; 746; 746n; correspondence sheds information important in Texas-Louisiana boundary settlement, 749.

De Volsay, François (Volsey): death and will, 368; letter to Governor cited, 72n; recommended for trade already reserved for others, 72. See also Volsay.

Dearborn, Henry, Secretary of War: draft of letter from Amos Stoddard, 740-742; estimate of population of Indian tribes sent by Pierre Chouteau, 759-760; 759n.

Deblanc, Luis, commandant at Natchitoches: letter to Carondelet, 365; letter to Carondelet mentioned, 354.

Dée, M.: with two others, granted exclusive trade with Missouris, 60.

Deer: 124; 125; 265; 277; 278; 279; 280; 378; 380; 488; 538; 762.

del Campillo, Miguel Gomez: See Gomez del Campillo, Miguel.

Del Pensamiento: the river called La Lutra empties at this spot, 122.

Delaware Indians (called Loups by the French) : estimate of population, 759.

Delinó, Ignacio, Commandant of Arkansas: 144n; wise action foils English attempt to induce Arkansas nation to join in a revolution, 45, 45n.

Delisle, Guillaume: 23n; 33n, map of Missouri cited, 6n.

Derbanne, ——: 9.

Derbigny, Pedro: 324; certifies accuracy of translation of Lisa *mémoire,* 674n.

Derouin, Francisco: goes on expedition to the Otos, for the Missouri Company, 109; Trudeau report on the information obtained from questioning, 516-517; examination cited, 109n.

Deroute: See La Deroute.

Deruisseau, M.: builds fort, according to agreement, 41; checks abuses, 41; exclusive grant one means of increasing fur trade and preventing frauds, 40; granted trade of entire Missouri River, by Bertet, 35; terms of agreement, 36-40.

Des Moines River (Des Moins, Demoine, de Moin, Rivière Des Moines, River of the Frayles, River of the Friars, River of Monigona, Mongoina River, Moingona River): 72; 73; 78; 80; 81; 198; 207; 214; 255; 256; 268; 311; 322; 323; 364; 378; 382; 420; 422; 511; 520; 554; 614; 669; 693; 710; 769; Carondelet recommends fort on, 402; description, 741; foreign traders penetrate Spanish territory by way of, 565, 566; Iowa Indians live on banks, 163; number of hunters, 627n; Perez and Cruzat write letters proposing fort at mouth, 76; Pratte asks trade on, 627n; Pratte granted trade, 592, 641, 641n; suggestion for fort at entrance, 145.

Des Pères River, 7.

Deserters, 366; 371; 389; 399; 503.

Desmarais, Jean Baptiste (Mr. De Murier) interpreter, Northwest Company: 103; 104; 479; 499; 499n.

Despins, M.: 46.

Detroit: See Fort Detroit; Strait of Detroit.

Les *Deux Cornes:* See Renombas.

Les *Deux Rivières:* See Two Rivers [Wis.].

The DEVIL!: granted exclusive trade contract, all Indian nations, 592.

Didier, Father: 132n; 215-216; 231; 350; 368; 373; letter to Carondelet [?] cited, 559n.

Diseases: See Dysentery, Measles, Smallpox, Venereal disease.

Dishes, Tin: 251.

Distances, Table of: See Table of Distances.

Divorce: 257-258.

Dog-field trading post: See Prairie du Chien.

Dog sledges: 492.

Dogs: 279.

Dorchester, Lord, Governor of Canada: 401; 409; 436; complaints received from, 392; letters cited, 133n; letter to Carondelet cited, 387n, and from Carondelet, 392n; letter to Duke of Portland cited, 387n; letters to Carondelet and Portland cited, 392n; role in apprehending mysterious traveler, 133n.

Dorion, Lewis: acts as witness, 240; salary by the day as interpreter for the Iowas, 771.

Dorion, Pierre, Sr.: salary by the day as interpreter for the Sioux on the Des Moines, 771.

Dorsey, J.: contributor to fund for proposed exploration, 167.

Los *Dos Amigos,* brigantine: 755n.

Douay, M.: companion of La Salle, 4n; narrative of expedition cited, 4n.

Drawing lots for trade: 431n; 453; 477n; 530; 531; 568; 568n.

Drunkenness: 538.

791

du Lac, François Marie Perrin: See Perrin du Lac, François Marie.

Du Tisné, Charles Claude: activities among Indians, 18-19; alliance with Pawnees, 17; in temporary command, Natchitoches, 18, 18n; letter to Bienville cited, 19n; plants royal flag among Panis, 19; reports cannibalism, 19; sent to stir up Missouri valley tribes against the Foxes, 25n; shot by a Fox Indian, 18n; twice in command at Fort de Chartres, 18n.

Dubois River: Meriwether Lewis to spend the winter on, 720.

Dubreuil, [J?]: 194; 218; assignment and share of trade, 210; member of Missouri Company, 225, 226.

Dubuisson, Charles Regnault: letter to Vaudreuil cited, 10n; receives aid from Missouris, 10.

Dubuque, S., interpreter: journal of council of Maha chiefs, called by the English, cited, 633, 633n.

Duchouquet, Henri: to conduct the voyage of *Le Missouri,* with merchandise for the Clamorgan company, 467.

Duchouquet, Jean Baptiste (Juan Bautista): to be in charge of Chouteau's boat, with merchandise for Clamorgan company, 467.

Duchoquet, Pierre (Pedro): given license to trade on Missouri, 162.

Dulonpré, M.: salary as interpreter, 50.

Dunbar, William: 586n; 749n.

Dunbar-Hunter expedition: 761; 764; Freeman added to explorers, 765n; organized to examine source and course of Arkansas and Colorado [Red] Rivers, postponed, 753; 753n.

Dunegant, François, Father (Dunegan): falsely accused by a fellow priest, 215-216; Gayoso de Lemos orders he be paid salary of commandant, San Carlos de Florisante, 536n-537n; made captain of militia, St. Ferdinand, 536n-537n; petition to Gayoso, for salary, cited, 536n.

Dunn, William, millwright: brought from the United States to build watermills, 688n.

Dunn, Major: 131n.

Dupre, ——: killed by Little Otos, 35.

Duquesne, Ange, *Sieur* de Menneville, Marquis de; Governor-General of New France: favors free trading, with exceptions, 49, 50; letter to Rouillé cited, 49n.

Duquet, François (Duquette, Doquelt?): signs Lisa *mémoire* against exclusive trade, 650; acts as witness in deposition, 576.

Durocher, Laurent (Lorenzo, Deroche): believed to be carrying instructions about an expedition, from Captain Stoddard, 744; Clamorgan seeks his deposition concerning Todd accounts, 573; deposition in regard to sale of Missouri Company share, 574-575; Mackay bespeaks a billiard table for him, 589; member of Missouri Company, 225, 226; purchases share in Missouri Company as agent, 574; signs Lisa *mémoire* against exclusive trade, 651; signs power of attorney for Lisa, 667.

Dysentery: 494.

Ear-rings, Silver: coveted and appropriated by a savage, 710.

East Indians: 416.

Écores à Margot (Los Écores, Ecors de Margot, Chicasaw Bluffs, San Fernando de Barrancas): 328; 343; 343n; 344; 345; 372; 373; 420n; 685; 697.

Elk: 762.

Emigration: from European countries urged upon Spain by Vilemont, 681n.

Employees: number, for licensed traders, 162; of traders may not be negroes, half-breeds or savages, 192; salaries of men in service on Missouri Company expeditions, 339, 340, 349.

Endrevil: See L'Andreville, Andrés.

Enemies, Indian, of French; of Spanish: See Indians hostile: to French; to Spanish.

English traders: See Traders, English.

Ermine: 498.

Ernest House: 501.

Escamany (le Poux Blanc): *patente* of first medal requested for, 327.

Escarpado River (Rugged River): 123; 124.

Evans, John T. (Even, Jean, Juan), companion of James Mackay: 97n; 106n; 108; 108n; 351n; 520; 562n; 583; 585; 660; acts as surveyor, 106; crossing of Mandan nation reported to Howard by Mackay, 515; experiences on journey to Mandans, 540; instructions from James Mackay, 410-414; Journal cited, 90; Journal extracts, 495-499; Journal extracts cited, 389n, 463n; leads expedition to penetrate the west to the ocean, 100-106; "liquor has deranged his head", 599n; letter from Jusseaume, 474-475; letters from John McDonnell, 478-480, 502-503; letter (extract) from McDonnell, 105; letter and extract from Mackay, 415-416, 101; letter from Mackay cited, 89n; letters from Sutherland, 104-105, 462, 499-500; letter from Turner, 99; letter from Turner about strange animals, 316-317; letters cited, 105n; letter to Sutherland, 462-463; overland journey to the Arikaras, 98-99, 99n, 101, 101n; seeks information about Welsh Indians, 98-99.

Ewing, William: 771.

Expeditions: cost, to dislodge English from Mandan posts, 435; Dunbar-Hunter plans, 753, 753n; men and equipment necessary for river exploration, 9, 15; of Missouri Company: capital outlay for three expeditions, 339-340; obstacles, cost, etc., 388, 441, 608-609; continuing Missouri Company: first expedition, conducted by Truteau, 86-91, 259-311, 527, 539-540; second expedition, conducted by Lecuyer, 91-92, 114, approximate time, 328, 351, pillaged by Poncas, 351, 360, 362; third expedition, conducted by Mackay, 93-94, 95, 96-98, 97n, 528, 540, date of

departure, 351, 351n; Journal: See entries under Journals.

Expense accounts: Lieutenant Armstrong's, 141; Spanish government in Louisiana, 768, 769, 771.

Explorers: See entries under names; e.g.:
Armstrong, John
Bienville, *Sieur* de
D'Église, Jacques
Evans, John
Iberville, *Sieur* d'
La Bruyère, Fabry de
La Salle, *Sieur* de
La Vérendrye, *Sieur* de
Le Sueur, Prem
Loisel, Régis
Mackay, James
Mackenzie, Sir Alexander
Perrin du Lac, François Marie
Truteau, J. B.
Vancouver, George
Vial, Pedro

Eyes of the Partridge: See Maniguacci.

Fabry: See La Bruyère, Fabry de.

Fagot la Garcinière, Andrés: 82; fails to use trade privilege with Kansas, 146n.

Falls of Saint Anthony (St. Antoine, San Antonio) 398; 682; 698; 741.

Falls of the Ohio: 135n.

Falls of the Rocky Mountains: 762; 763; 764.

Famine: 200.

Farming utensils: President Jefferson keeps peace among Indians by sending them, 695.

Fermiers: 37; 38; 39.

Fernández, Bernardo: draft of letter from Carondelet cited, 499n.

Feuilli, Luis: 42.

Figueroa: See Rochay y Figueroa, Gerónimo.

File, Mr.: signs Lisa *mémoire* against exclusive trade, 651.

Fines and penalties: 190; 191; 250; 313; 314; for violating trade regulations, 189.

Fire Prairie (Prairie of Fire, Prado del Fuego): 125; 261; location and distance from mouth of Missouri, 487.

Firearms: 334; 388; 390; Indians provided with English, 161; prohibition against providing to Indians, 325.

Fires: at New Orleans, 556, 556n; John Evans cautioned about, 411-412.

Firs, North American: 381.

First Prairie: location and distance from mouth of Missouri, 487.

Fish: scarce, and of the barbed variety, 762.

Fisher, Mr.: salary, by the day, as interpreter for the Sauks and the Foxes, 771.

Fitzgerald, Edward, Lieutenant: 131; 131n; plans to cross wilderness to Mexico, 78.

Flag Pond: location and distance from mouth of Missouri, 487.

Flagier, M., Abbé at Vincennes: 324; 350.

Flags: 19; 101; 102; 251; 262; 268; 285; 291; 304; 305; 309; 341; 359; 361; 362; 374; 402n; 420n; 496; 611; 634; given Osages, 144; order received by Trudeau, 430; with the Burgundy cross, 426, 430.

Flags, Royal: 447; 456; 496; extract from letter of Clamorgan about, 374n; plea from Clamorgan for supply, 499.

Flancour, ——: 34; letter to Salmon cited, 27n; 34n.

Flax: 124; can be grown in Louisiana, 686; inhabitants east of Mississippi producing abundance, 657.

La *Flecha,* galiot of war: 323; 616.

Flints: 272.

Floods: 535.

Florida: 607n; 682; 685.

Floridablanca, José de Monino y Redondo, Conde de: brief biography; 130n-131n; letter from Gardoqui cited, 78n.

Florissant, M.: 132n.

Les *flots à peser:* profit allowed, in Todd-Clamorgan agreement, 468.

Flour: 265; 369; 370; 423n; 588; Americans monopolize sales, 679; cost, 160; gift to Evans, 500; means to produce, in Louisiana, 683; scarcity, in Louisiana, 424n; superior grade possible, 543.

Flour mill: fire destroys Grégoire Sarpy's, 678.

Floyd River: named for a young man of Lewis' expedition, 762.

Folavoana Indians [Menominees]: number of English canoes wintering among, 180.

Folch, Vicente, Lieutenant-Governor of Barrancas: receives order from Carondelet to deliver swivel-guns to Chouteau, for Clamorgan, 425n; Trudeau writes Carondelet of their delivery, ultimately for the Missouri Company, 444n.

Food: 265; 267; 270; 279; 281; 298; scarcity retards construction of a fort by Truteau, 359. Note. The following edible items or ingredients of prepared food are mentioned in the documents, as either cultivable or wild, as gifts to others, consumed for sustenance, or, as in the case of dog's flesh, part of an Indian ceremony.

Apples: 371.

Bacon: 200.

Beans: grown by Mandans and other nations, 493, 494; wild ones a winter's sustenance, 290.

Biscuits: 267.

Buffalo flesh: received from Mahas in exchange for gunpowder, 710.

Chocolate: gift to Evans, 500.

Coffee, 407; 538; can be grown in Louisiana, 686.

Corn: 177; 381; 440; 479; 493; 494; 538.

Deer: 265; 267; 277; 278; 279; boiled hides ("bad feast"), 280. See also Venison.

Dog's flesh: included in ceremonial of war preparation: Perrin du Lac finds it "extremely disagreeable", 710.

Ducks: 124.

Geese, 125; 762.

Grapes: can be grown in Louisiana, 686.
Herbs: the only food of some hungry Indians arriving at Truteau camp, 281.
Maize: 160; 163; 200; 233; 265; 280; 359; 379; 380; 521; 762; 763.
Meat, Dried: 265; 292; 298; 411.
Muskmelon: Mackay sows seeds, 494.
Pancakes: 276.
Pears: gift to Mme. Carondelet, 204-205.
Pheasants: 124.
Pigs: 233.
Poultry: 233.
Pumpkins: 493; 494.
Rice, Wild: Truteau and his men feasted on bad wild rice, 270.
Rose-buttons: Truteau and party have nothing else for three days, 278.
Soup: hungry Indians watch Truteau party eating, and fight over soup bones thrown to them, 270.
Sugar: 61; 407; 538; can be grown in Louisiana, 686; gift to Evans, 500.
Sugar, Maple: Chouteau orders, 514.
Tea: 524.
Turkeys: 124, 280.
Venison: 37. See also Deer.
Watermelon: Mackay sows seeds, 494. See also Flour; Wheat.
Foreigners: defined, 189.
Foreman, Grant: 742.
Fork River: See Cheyenne River.
Fornerel, M., interpreter: 701.
Fort au Cèdres: built by Loisel, 114; Loisel detained there, by Sioux, 737.
Fort Barrancas de Margot: See Écores à Margot.
Fort Carondelet of the Osages: 320n; 326; 343; 584.
Fort Cavagnolle: built following abandonment of Fort Orléans, 28; location, 28, 42, 50, 52; possibly the one built by Deruisseau, 41; repair, 48.
Fort Charles: 462; 463; erected by Mackay, 98, 99; Evans escapes to, pursued by a band of Sioux, 101, 101n.
Fort de Chartres, near Kaskaskia: 42; 44n; 45n; 51; 52; 55; 601n; ceded to

the British, 64, 67; Du Tisné twice in command, 18n.
Fort Detroit (Pontchartrain du Detroit): 132; 133; 133n; 232; 349; 407; 425; besieged by Foxes, 10, 10n, 12.
Fort Erie: 133.
Fort Espérance: Joncquard makes trading journey from this post to the Mandans, 95; winter post of British traders, 94.
Fort La Reine: built by La Vérendrye, 32; La Vérendrye party returns to, from Mandans, 34.
Fort L'épinette: Joncquard spends a year here, 333.
Fort Mackay: built by Evans, 500n.
Fort Mandana (Fuerte Mandana): site of Lewis and Clark camp, 761, 763, 764.
Fort Maurepas, established by La Vérendrye on Lake Winnipeg, 32.
Fort Miami: 44n.
Fort Natchez: 684; 697.
Fort of Carlos III: location, 120.
Fort Orléans: abandonment, 22, 23n-24n, 28; erected by Bourgmont, 20; from here he visits the Osages, later the Kansas, 21; from here Father Mercier visits the Osages and Missouris, 22; map cited, 20n; re-established, 23n.
Fort Pitt: 135n.
Fort Randall: 88; location, 388.
Fort Recoude [Reconde?] de l'homme: Joncquard spends a winter here, 333.
Fort St. Charles: established by La Vérendrye on western shore of Lake of the Woods, 32.
Fort San Carlos: 70.
Fort Washington: headquarters of General Harmar, 137.
Fortifications: 80; 346; Clamorgan promises to build, on Platte and Kansas Rivers, 634; military protection necessary, 24; of Arikara village, 295-296; Pérez urges, 78-79.
Forts: 38; 65; 255; 386; 386n; 389; 390n; 393; 402; 420n; 422; 477;

among Mahas necessary, 609; among Mandans to be destroyed, 93; being erected by English, in Spanish territory, 430; cost of maintenance of a chain, 390; description of a fort, officer's quarters, and guard house to be built by Deruisseau, 36-37; directions and drawing for a fort among Mandans, 243-244, 243n; easy for French, with Indian aid, to hold post, 15; Evans takes over British fort among Mandans, 101, 102; Evans takes possession of English, 496; Howard to destroy English fort among Mandans, 514; imaginary ones constructed by Clamorgan, 567; Loisel promises to build one, if granted land, 612; Mackay appointed commandant on Upper Missouri, 428; many built by English, 389, 434; maintenance of those among Mandans necessary to block English penetration, 610-611; militia and maintenance needed for, 563; of English on Assiniboine menace Missouri Company establishment, 620; Omaha and Arikara forts established, 418; one constructed by English among Mandans, 385; one projected on the Arkansas, 151; Pérez' suggestion to Miró, for construction of, 73; personnel necessary to maintain post on Upper Missouri, 14-15; plea by Pérez for fort to restrain Osages, 150; proposal for grant to Missouri Company to maintain, 399-400; proposed by Chouteau, to subjugate Osages, 526; proposed fort can not prevent illegal trading, 157, 158; proposed, to stop influx of English traders, 145n; protective chain recommended, 59-60; reactions of Miró and Las Casas to Pérez' suggestion about construction, 146n; Spanish need train of, 337; to be built by the Americans, 543; to be built by the English on the Assiniboine, 337; to be built by Todd, 402n; under construction by Mackay, 360. See also Albany Fort, Nogales Fort, Osage Fort, Pine Fort, Rivière Tremblante, Souris Fort.

Fotman [Tremont], Juan: 92; examined by Trudeau, who certifies his statements about Missouri trip, 330-333.

Foucault, M., Commissaire Ordonnateur: writes to Minister, 62-63.

Fourche River: See Cheyenne River.

Fox Indians (Renards, Reynards): 5; 23; 150; 180; 420; 421n; 423; 430; 742; among nations receiving provisions and presents from Spanish, 769; at siege of Fort Detroit, 12; Dubuisson besieged, 10, 10n; English trade with, 81, 707n; estimate of annual value of merchandise for, 759; estimate of population, 760; expedition with Lahontan doubtful, 5; habitat, number of warriors, value of merchandise received, skins sold, 694; other nations preparing for war against, 25n, 26; receive annual presents, 120; salary paid interpreter, 771; threaten to kill Little Osages, 168.

Fox River (Rivière des Renards): 154n; 180; 693.

Franquelin, J. L.: map of Missouri cited, 5n.

Frebucher, ——: companion of Joncquard, 333.

Freedom of trade: 49; 50; 60; 61; 61n; 62; 63; 71; Carondelet decrees, 84, 151; Carondelet's instruction to Trudeau about, 152; copy of edict sent to Carondelet by Trudeau, 155; regulations set up, 84-85; St. Louis merchants complain, 84; will promote growth of Louisiana, 394.

Freeman, Mr., explorer: 749n; 765n.

Freemen [independent traders]: 94.

French: accomplishments, and acquisition of geographical knowledge during régime, 55-57; motives in exploration of Missouri region, 7; ousted from the "heart of America", eighteenth century, 2; plans for holding and expanding against the Spaniards, 14; progress of discovery along the Missouri, 3; policy with the Indians, 50; rapid advance in explorations beyond the Mississippi, seventeenth century, 2.

French and Indian war: 50; 55.

French emigrants: 542; plan designed to attract, 556n.

French explorations: by Satren, Chapuis, and others, 42, 42n; of Fabry de la Bruyère party, 28-31; of Mallet party, 28.

Fruit juice: as ink, 411.

Fuel: 295.

Fult [?]: signs power of attorney for Lisa, 667.

Fur trade: See Trade, Fur.

Furs: 89; 161; 176; 178; 264; 266; 292; 306; 322; 363; 394; 421; 423; 423n; 465; 466; 493; 513; 514; 538; 673n; annual yield of Missouri-Mississippi trading posts, 625-626; average number of packs from Osages, with value, 539; beaver and otter the richest furs in the Missouri country, 73; diverted by English traders to Montreal and Quebec, 407; English get the best, 204; gift to Carondelet, 371; Jusseaume letter to Evans, to straighten accounts, 474-475; large quantity assured, under Todd plan, 435; obtained by Todd, will enrich the treasury, 400; of the Missouri Company shall bear the mark C D M, 248; Osages offer the best, 13; peltries, 10, 158, 159; quantity Todd will undertake to supply, 409; special order for Clamorgan, 249; spoken of by Captain Cook, 131; value of peltries from posts on the Missouri, according to Lisa, 647-648, according to Government, 653. See also Beaver, Ermine, Lynx, Martens, Otter, Peckans; Trade, Fur.

Gaillard, M.: leads advance party to Padoucas, 21.

Galiot (Galiotte, Galliot), a small, swift galley: 370; 371; 374; patrol of Missouri by armed galiot recommended, 389.

Gallatin, Albert: letter from A. Chouteau, seeking post on Missouri and enclosing estimate of annual trade with Indians, 758-759.

Galleys (Galères): 399; 425.

Gallipolis, Ohio: on Perrin du Lac's travel route, in America, 707n.

Gallut, ——: identified, 15; comments on importance of controlling the Missouri region, 15-16.

Gálvez, Bernardo de, Governor-General of Louisiana: administration exceptional in conduct toward the savages, 691; instructions concerning Indian relations noted, 147; letters from Cruzat, Martigny, and De Leyba cited, 71n; letter to De Leyba cited, 71n; list of Indian nations submitted by Cruzat, 71; orders Cruzat to submit a list of licensed traders and an account of Indian nations, 70-71.

Garaua, Garaut, Gareau: See Garreau.

Gardoqui, Diego María de (Gardoque): biographical sketch, 130n; calendar of correspondence cited, 130n; letter from Montarco cited, 402n; letter from Morales about the death of Todd, 481-482; letter from Morales about duties, 483-484; letter from Morales about the expense of maintenance of militia, 480-481; letter from Morales about Todd affairs, 472-473; letters to Carondelet cited, 402n, 438n; letter (extract) to Floridablanca, 130; letter to Floridablanca cited, 78n; letter to Governor of Louisiana cited, 438n; letters to Intendant Rendón cited, 402n, 438n; pleads for discovery of river routes to the Pacific, 78.

Garments for women: part of merchandise D'Église carried, 298.

Garo, Garon, Garraut: See Garreau.

Garreau, Joseph (Garaua, Garaut, Gareau, Garon, Garo, Garraut): 95; 101n; 103; 105; 109; 233; 234; 235; 242; 248; 249; 250; 267; 274; 297; 298; 334; 503; 503n; owes the price of a horse, plus a slave girl, 479; sent to hunt on the Upper Missouri, 81.

Gasconade River: 51; 122; 260; 261; description, source, and distance up the Missouri, 486.

Gaultier, Pierre de Varennes: See La Vérendrye, Pierre Gaultier de Varennes, *Sieur* de.

Gayoso de Lemos, Manuel, Governor-General of Louisiana, successor to Carondelet: 343; 347; 347n; 349; 349n; 369; 371; 373; 604; 623; diary cited, 369n; index of *carta reservada* to Saavedra, 582-583; letters (extracts) from Carondelet, 427n, 438n; letters from Carondelet cited, 438n, 478n; letter from Clamorgan, 560-561; letter (extract from draft) from Clamorgan cited, 553n; letter (draft) cited, 553n; letter from De Lassus, 605-606; letter from De Lassus cited, 600n; letter from Mackay, 587-589; letter (extract from Mackay, 107; letter from Mackay, protesting regulation about Catholics, cited, 587n; letter from Morales cited, 537n; letter from Robidoux, requesting exclusive trade with Kansas, 548; letter from Robidoux, with postscript by Trudeau, 592-594; letters from Trudeau, 373-375; 525-529; 534-544; 581-582; letter from Trudeau, enclosing Mackay narrative and map, 545; letter from Trudeau, giving reply about attracting settlers, cited, 556n; letter (extract) from Trudeau, 442n; letters from Trudeau cited, 427n, 545n, 553n, 647n; letter from Vasquez, soliciting trade from Kansas, 546-547; letters from José Vidal cited, 587n; letter (extract) to Carondelet, with citation, 513n; letter and report to Carondelet cited, 369n; letters to De Lassus, 597-599, 600; letter (draft) to De Lassus, 600; letter to De Lassus mentioning his Indian god-child, 597, 597n; letter (draft) to Morales, 554; letter to Morales cited, 545n; letters (extracts) to Mackay, 108, 599n; letter to Saavedra, 583-586; letters to Santa Clara cited, 370n, 587n; letter to Trudeau, 556-557; letter to Trudeau about Clamorgan affairs, 571; letter to Trudeau about Missouri Company matters, 555; letter to Trudeau, giving statement on division of Indian trade, 529-532; letter (extract) to Trudeau, 524-525; letters to Trudeau cited, 427n, 537n, 547n, 553n, 556n, 647n; letter to Trudeau on church construction cited, 559n; letter to Vásquez cited, 547n; petition from Robidoux for cancellation of Clamorgan trade contract and his exclusion from Missouri Company, 548-553; summary of trading licenses ordered, 590-592; urges Trudeau to examine Robidoux's claims and take steps in his behalf, 553n.

Gazeta de Orléans: See New Orleans *Gazette.*

Genêt, Edmund, French minister to the United States: 84n; 366; 366n; Peyroux recommended to, 598n.

Gengembre, R. (Gingembre): 194; absent from merchants' meeting, 211.

Les *Gens des Feuilles* (Feuillets): Fotman and Joncquard report hearsay about them to Trudeau, 332, 333, 335; named by Loisel as a wandering nation, not seen by him, 739.

Les *Gens des filles:* Fotman and Joncquard report hearsay about them to Trudeau, 332, 335.

Geographical knowledge: digest of information on Missouri region in account by Miró, 73-74; names of men best informed on the geography of the Upper Missouri, 485n; résumé of knowledge picked up by Truteau, 73-74; summary of knowledge of the Missouri received by Rengel, 77-78; summary of geographical knowledge acquired during the French régime in Louisiana, 56-57.

Georgia: 157n; 345; 682.

Gervaes, Josef (José Gervais): 755; 756; to guide others to New Mexico, 743-744.

Gibault, Pierre, Father: 132; correspondence and accounts cited, 132n.

Giguière, M.: murdered by Little Osages, 44.

Gil, Francisco: communication setting forth opinions of the Committee of Fortifications and defense of the Indies, on boundaries, Texas and Louisiana, 725-727.

Gingembre: See Gengembre.

Glassware and window panes: profit allowed, in Todd-Clamorgan agreement, 468.

Glorieux: 417n.

Goats: 124; 762.

God-child: of Gayoso de Lemos, 597, 597n.

Godoy, Manuel de, Spanish minister: learns about Mackay explorations from Carondelet, 96; receives suggestion from Carondelet about expedition to restrain English trade, 112n; responsible for dismissal from office, and imprisonment of Floridablanca, 130n. See also Alcudia, Duque de; Prince of Peace.

Gold: 59; Spaniards give, as copper, 14.

Gomez del Campillo, Miguel: statement about a map, 389n.

Good Man's Island: See Bon Homme Island.

Goodman's Island: distance from mouth of Missouri, 490.

Gordon, Harry: 64; Journal cited, 65n.

Gorgets: 326; list of chiefs for whom Trudeau requests, 327.

Goth [Hosty], M.: given one-year license to trade with Poncas, 591.

Gourds: 493; 494.

[Governor of Louisiana?]: letter to De Lassus, concerning journey of Meriwether Lewis, 724.

Grand, M.: See Grant, Cuthbert.

Grand Manitou: point touched by Larche on his way to the Kansas, 46.

Grand Osages: See Osage Indians.

Grand River (Great River, Grande Rivière): 89; 125; 180; 207; 707; 708; description, source, navigability and distance from the Mouth of the Missouri, 487.

Grand Portage: 154n; 333; 490; 491.

Grand Traverse Bay: inlet on Lake Michigan, where English canoes winter, 180.

Grande Colome: 180

Grande Macoquité River: See Maquoketa River.

Grandpré, M. (Grand Pré): abstract of letter to Carondelet, 513; letter from Carondelet cited, 458n; letters to Carondelet cited, 458n, 513n; proposes exclusive trade contract, 458n.

Grands Eaux: See Osage Indians.

Grant, Mr., merchant at Michilimackinac: letter from Chouteau, 573-574.

Grant, Cuthbert, "a nor'wester interior leader": 474; letter to Evans, 460-461; letter to Evans cited, 103n; writes to John Evans, expressing dissatisfaction with Company handling of business and his desire to withdraw, 102.

Grant, Peter (Piter Grante): director of small trading company, Montreal, 332; his company mentioned, 334.

Grant, Robert (Roberto Legrante): 94; director of Great Company, Montreal, 332, 333.

Gratification [fee paid by *voyageurs*]: 46; 47; 48.

Gratiot, M.: 218; absent from merchants' meeting, 211; letter to Charles Buyon cited, 482n.

Graveline, Mr.: salary by the day as interpreter for the Arikaras, 771.

Gravier, Jacques, Father: Missionary, letter cited, 5n.

Great Britain: 582; 584; 585; 586.

Great Trading Company of Montreal: one of several companies said by Fotman and Joncquard to have established posts on the Assiniboine River, 332, 333, 334.

Great-foot Indians: habitat and number, 383.

Great Lakes: 4n; 383n; French frontier, in early seventeenth century, 2.

Great Nation: habitat, 383.

Great Nemaha River (Big Nemaha River): 125; 126; 263; description, navigability, and distance from the mouth of the Missouri, 488.

Great North River: Knox wants General Harmar to trace distances from southern branches of Missouri and streams that empty into this river, 136.

Great Osages: See Osage Indians.

Great River: See Grand River.

Great Sioux River: 384.

Gredomanse (Cheveux Blancs), Indian chief: large medal solicited for him, 326.

Grenadiers: two officers appear as witnesses, 516.

Grenville, William W.: letter from Hammond cited, 80n; letter from Hammond cited, with extract of observations on western trade, 154n.

Grimaldi, Marqués de, Minister of War and Marine at Madrid: urged by Vilemont to establish a Spanish post among the Missouris, to offset English activities with the Indians, 60; three *informes* from Vilemont cited, 60n.

Grist mills: 561n.

Gros Ventres Indians (Grovanders, Bigbellies, Ventrudos): 90; 92; 94; 95; 110; 297; 301; 303; 304; 307; 309; 331; 332; 333; 334; 376; 380; 381; 384; 448; 450; attitude toward women, 258; called Grovanders by Sutherland, 464; destruction of English fort among, 620; estimate of population, 760; seen by Loisel, 739.

Les *Gros Ventres de la Montagne des Roches:* 333; 335.

Les *Gros Ventres des Prairies:* 332; 335.

Groseilliers, Médart Chouart, *Sieur* de: believed to have visited the Missouri, 4n.

Guémez Pacheco de Padilla Horcasitas, Juan Vicente: See Revilla Gigedo, Conde de.

Gulf of Mexico: 2; 75; 121; 136; 383n; 424n; 439; 726; 738; 756; 757.

Guns: 89; 262; 263; 270; 272; 274; 281; 283; 292; 306; 310; 331; 332; 334; 352; 357; 358; 361; 381; 402n; 492; 706; 707; as presents, 129; in trade, with Indians, 19; not to be fired by John Evans, 411; spurned by Iowas, 185; stolen from D'Église by Poncas, 290; wanted by Osages, 29.

Gunpowder: 38; 61; 262; 270; 272; 280; 281; 283; 286; 287; 294; 306; 331; 339; 358; 440; 456; 706; 707; 710; as gift to Indians, 29, 129; Clamorgan suggests it be provided as protection for forts, 447; cost in exchange for furs, 301; Gayoso de Lemos needs, for Indian trade, 554n; order for, to provide for Indian nations, 430-431; price, in Todd-Clamorgan agreement, 468.

Guthrie's Geographical Grammar: McDonnell sends Evans a copy, for his amusement, 103, 479.

Habitation: description and distance up the Missouri, 486.

Haha [?] River: 122.

Hahitannes Indians: habitat, 91; wandering, bald-headed people beyond the Platte River, 379.

Hamilton, Alexander: contributor to fund for expedition to the Pacific, 167; letter to, cited, 150n; stand on Northwest Territory, 79, 79n; writings cited, 80n.

Hammers: 272.

Hammond, George: letter to Grenville cited, 80n; letter to Grenville cited, with extract of observations on western trade 154n.

Hardy, Arthur Shelbourne: 442n.

Harmar, Josiah, General: extract of letter to Knox, 138; extracts from two letters from Knox, 142; letters to Armstrong, 137, 139; letters from Knox, 135-136, 137; letter to Knox, enclosing Armstrong report, 142; letter from Governor St. Clair, 140; letter to Governor St. Clair, 138; Papers cited, 137n.

Harris, Lieutenant-Colonel: letter concerning De Bon cited, 133n.

Howard, Carlos: 370n; 458n; 516; 520; 521; 598n, 624; letter from Trudeau cited, 523n; letter to Carondelet, 514-515; letters to Carondelet cited, 351n, 523n; secret instructions from Carondelet cited, 355n.

Huachage Indians: 148.

Hubardau of Ste. Geneviève (Hubardeau): 367; assignment and share of trade, 211.

Hubert, ——: *mémoires* inform about Missouri and branches, 12, 12n; *mémoire* on Louisiana cited, 12, 12n; *mémoire* urges appointment on the Missouri, 14; proposes to reconnoitre the Missouri, 13, 13n.

Hudson's Bay (Hudson Bay): 114; 131; 178; 332; 381; 388; 390; 392; 399; 424n; 461; 475; 515; 607n; 609; 659; 687; 737; 738; all Indians below, favor French, 746; English may penetrate by way of, 757; water route to Gulf of Mexico will be advantageous to British and Americans, 756.

Hudson's Bay Company: 76; 94; 95n; 332; 334; 337; 386n; 434; 500; activities threaten Spanish hold on territory, 620; exempt from import duties, 436; Missouri Company must combat trade, 566; rivalry with Northwest Company, 95n, 104ff.

Hudson's Bay Company Archives: See Brandon House Journal.

Huitauyrata Indians: allies of Pawnees, 148; habitat and number of warriors, 148.

Hunkpapa Indians (Oncpapas): wandering nation, seen by Loisel, 739.

Hunter, Dr., botanist and mineralogist: 749n; arrives at Natchez prepared for explorations west of the Mississippi, 750; explorations cited, 743n.

Hunters: 125; 126; number in Mandans, Cheyennes, Manitouris, 706n; number in three tribes trading with the English, 707n.

Hunting: 41; 160; 161; forbidden to travelers, in Deruisseau contract, 39.

Hunting licenses: 82; 342.

Hutchins, Thomas: 150n; death mentioned, 131n.

Iberville, Pierre Lemoyne, *Sieur* de: 6; 7; *mémoire*, included in Journal, lists Indian nations on Missouri, 8; *mémoire* cited, 8n; plan for relocating Indian tribes, 8, 8n.

Ietan Indians: 48; 49; can be attracted to St. Louis and should become an important ally of the United States, 770.

Île Perrot: Deruisseau, Seigneur de *en partie de* l'isle, 35.

Illinois, Spanish (Ilinoa, Ylinoa, Ylinueuses): 27; 77; 82; 421; 449; 453: beginnings, 63-64; British encroachments upon, 62, 92, 95; Carondelet grants free trade, 84-85, 186-190; domain at first, Ste. Geneviève and St. Louis, 64; fear of British incursions gives reason for forts on Missouri, 65; fort construction at mouth of Missouri ordered, 65; invasion from Canada feared, 109; lacking in animals, 160; name by which Upper Louisiana becomes known, 77; St. Louis the capital of Spanish possessions in the district, 67; Spanish settlements in, 534; spends large sums for presents to Indians, 328. For names of administrators, see O'Reilly, Piernas, De Leyba, Cruzat, Pérez, Trudeau, De Lassus. For trade activities, see Missouri Company. For chief posts, see St. Louis and Ste. Geneviève. For explorers, see D'Église, Evans, Mackay, Truteau, etc.

Illinois country, 4; 5; 7n; 22n; 51; Du Tisné returns to, 19; name by which Upper Louisiana is better known, 670.

Illinois post: 22n-23n; 63; 325; "Literary News" from, 132-134; soldiers needed to defend, 24.

Illinois Indians: 15; 180; 529; conspiracy against French, 43-44; English trade with, 81; French formed first establishment among them, 747; Iberville lists, 8n.

Illinois River (Rivière des Yllinois) : 128; 154n; 594; 602; 603; 707; Armstrong sends map, to Harmar, 141; manuscript description and map cited, 142; Kaskaskia Indians move from, to Des Pères River, 7.

Immigration: Collot makes some observations, 670.

Import and/or export duties: 408; 409; 510; evasion of, by English and Americans, 508; exemption enough to counterbalance difficulties, 392; King grants reduction, 510; lowered, by Carondelet, for Todd trade, 393, 400, 435, 484; none on goods from Canada, 407; official reduction, 438; pertinent article in supplementary regulations, Missouri Company, 447; plea for permanent decrease, 394; reduction will benefit Louisiana, 401; Todd petitions for prewar duty, 435.

Indian affairs: administration, philosophy, and expense, under Spanish government, with recommendations, 767-771.

Indian chiefs: 299; 303; 305; 307; 308; 309; 332; 417n; 495; list of medals and gorgets requested for, 327. See also the following names of chiefs: Big Rabbit, Black Bird, Cayechingá, Chiabey, Chido Whaguegran, Clermont, Cour Qui Brule, Crazy Bear, Gredomanse, Kichetabaco, Naugy, Pauxblanche, Petit Arc, Pontiac, Prince of the Nations, Sac de Médecine, Stabaco, Toangerest.

Indian Department in Louisiana: Pierre Chouteau's list of present employees, 771.

Indian girls: 300.

Indian nations: 17; 27; 59; 71n; 72; 72n; above the Mandans, 332-333; according to Truteau, 378ff; as listed by V. Collot, 383-385; between the Mandans and the Rocky Mountains, 336; described by Truteau, 296-303; habitat of nations encountered by Fotman and Joncquard, 332, 333, 334, 335; hostility of some tribes, 14; Iberville lists nations on the Missouri, 8, 8n;

La Salle catalogues some native tribes of the interior, 4n; Laussat lists those who visit New Orleans, 701n; listed by Cruzat, 71; in trade with Spaniards, 66; location and description in Miró letter, 119-127; on Missouri and branches, 12; Perrin du Lac's list, 706n; residing in fixed villages along New Mexico mountain chain, 739; receive presents from Spanish government, 769; Ríu statement cited, 66n; size, dwellings, etc., to be obtained and noted by John Evans, 411; that may be induced to come to St. Louis, 769-770; Vilemount's report to Talleyrand, 694; wandering nations seen, and some not seen, by Loisel, 739.

Indian trade: See Trade, Indian.

Indian villages: of the Arkansas, 120; of the Kansas, 41; of the Mahas, 98, 489; of the Mandans, 102n, 498; of the Missouris, 487; of the Osages, 486, 487; of the Otos, 351, 352, 488; of the Panis, 19; of the Pawnee Hocá, 332; of the Poncas, 490; of the Sauks, 742; of the Sioux, 295, 310; on drawing of Missouri basin, 451; Petit Arc, 490, 710; Washcanda Nipishi, 489.

Indian warriors: numbers: 124; 125; 126; 127; 148; 172; 299; 358; 379; 386; 673n; of Osages, 624; of Poncas, 710; of Sauks, 742; Vilemont report to Talleyrand, 694.

Indian wars: 16; 19; 44; 50; 99; 125; 126; 144; 147; 148; 168n; 170n; 232; against Americans, 153, 153n; French and Indian, 50, 55; threats of, among Missouri nations, 303ff.

Indiana: a few straggling villages of Sauks in, 742.

Indians as slaves: 9; Carondelet prohibition against, 197; Padoucas, 16; Pawnees, 19; sold to Foxes, 17.

Indians friendly to French: 9; 21; 23; 27n; 29; 30; 45; 45n; 50; 51; 54; 55; 59; 60; 74; 78; 82; 83; 88; 89; 90; 296ff; Arkansas, 53; Kansas and Osages, 52; Kansas, Missouris, Osages, Otos and Pani-mahas, 17; Osages make overtures, 25.

Indians friendly to Spanish: 48; 79; 82; 83; 86; 87; 89; 90; 98; 101; 147; 148; 297; 382; 389.

Indians hostile to French: 17; 21; 23; 25n; 27; 27n; 43-44; 45; 54; 55; 269ff; 282ff; French learn not to trust Missouris and Osages too much, 22.

Indians hostile to Spanish: 60; 82; 98; 107; 147.

Indians of the north: 147.

Indies Company: See Company of the Indies.

Indigo: 61; can be grown in Louisiana, 686.

Ingersóll Jared: Contributor to fund for proposed exploration, 167.

Ink: 100; 411.

Insurance: 176; 177.

Interior Provinces (Provincias Internas): 73; 77; 119; 325; 390; 390n; 391; 393; 395; 399; 400; 409; 424n; 434; 435; 439; 440; 499; 728; 746; 749; 750; 752; 753; the only way to prevent ruin is to arrest Captain Merry Weather, 731.

Interpreters: needed for nations that come to St. Louis, 770; salary, 771.

Iowa Bluff: distance from the mouth of the Missouri, 489.

Iowa Indians (Ayoa, Ayoues, Ayoua, Ayowas, Ayowai, Ayowais, Nacion Ayoas): among nations receiving provisions and presents from Spanish, 769; Carondelet regrets stolen horses, 163; estimate of annual value of merchandise for, 759; estimate of population, 760; friends of Missouris, 52; habitat, number of warriors, value of merchandise received, and of skins sold, 694; know upper reaches of Missouri, 23n; letter concerning horse theft by, 197; location and number, 52; number of hunters, 707n; pillage Kansas, on the Missouri, 323; return stolen horses, 184-185; salary paid interpreter, 771; steal horses, 160; suffer from smallpox, 631; treachery, among Kansas, 185; two traders beaten by, 316; waylay and pillage French traders, 318.

Iowa River (Rivière des Ayouas): 12; 81; 180; 364n; location and distance from the mouth of the Missouri, 489.

Iron: 10n; 370; 538; 708; claimed discovered in Missouri region. See also Mines.

Iron and steel articles: profit allowed, in Todd-Clamorgan agreement, 468.

Iscanis, Isconis: See Yscanis Indians.

Isla à Cabaret: Indian traders to go through quarantine here, because of smallpox in the district, 631.

Island of La Ballena: 585.

Islands: 122; 125; 377. See also Bald Island; Basque Island; Bon Homme Island; Buffalo Island; Chicot Island; Dauphin Island; Goodman's Island; St. Joseph's Island; Isla à Cabaret; Isle of Cedars; Tessalon Island.

Isle aux Basques: See Basque Island.

Isle of Cedars (Cedar Island): 266; 267; 612.

Jacques River: See James River.

Jago, Andrés, sub-lieutenant of militia: his debt, 134.

James River (Jacques River, River Bois Blanc, River White Wood, now Dakota River): 265; 737; 738; navigability and distance from the mouth of the Missouri, 490.

Janin, l'Abbé: 350; plea for his retention, 742, 742n.

Janis, Antonio (J. Janis): on list, and mémoire sent De Lassus, of individuals against exclusive trade, 645, 646, 667; signs Lisa mémoire against exclusive trade [signed: J. Janis] 651; signs power of attorney for Lisa, 667.

Jaudenes, Josep de: letter, with Viar, to Alcudia cited, 79n.

Javelins: 334.

Jay-Gardoqui treaty: 130n.

Jay's treaty: 347; 347n; 393n; 396n; 407; 409; 436; 515n; 523n; Articles 3-4, 396-398; Carondelet certain England will carry out provisions, 424n; treaty cited, 79n; results, 433.

256; 261; 315; 316; 318; 321; 384; 426; 430; 431n; 477n; 559; 568n; 643; 644; 673n; 709; 710; among the nations receiving provisions and presents from the Spanish, 769; amount of merchandise assigned for, 209; Chouteau spends winter among them and reports to Pérez about Osages' wrath over trade denied, 143-144; Clamorgan gets trade for one year, 635, for two years, 672; Clamorgan petitions Casa Calvo for trade, 635, and seeks from Salcedo, exclusive trade, 634; description, 708; estimate of annual value of merchandise, 759; estimate of population, 760; friendly to French, 17; habitat and number 52, 125; known, when French made first settlement, 747; location of villages, 488; medals and gorgets requested for, 326-327; number, and trade relations, 539; number of men using arms, and amount of trade, 706n; Osages seize merchandise intended for Kansas, 149, 150; portions of trade, and share to traders, 210-211; Pratte and Vásquez petition for trade, 531n; receive presents annually, 120; Robidoux seeks trade, 548; Sarpy and Cabanné offer to mediate between Pawnees and Kansas, 614-616; trade assigned by Pérez, 134, 135; trade divided among St. Louis merchants, 597; trade for 1801 granted G. Sarpy and Cabanné, 592; trading license issued to M. Bernal, 591; trading license issued to Beral Sarpy, 605, and to G. Sarpy, 590, 622; trading license issued to Sarpy brothers, 568; trade shares, and value, 530, 531; traders pillaged by Iowas, 323.

Kansas River: 7; 36; 37; 38; 39; 112; 123; 125; 126; 261; 262 263; 316; 384; 488; 708; 711; Clamorgan petitions for exclusive trade on, 634; description, navigability, and distance from the mouth of the Missouri, 487; distance from the village of the Missouris, 12; noted on Le Maire map, cited, 13n; post to be transferred, 41.

Kao, Kaos: See Cahokia.

Kapouk Indians: habitat, number of warriors, value of merchandise received and of skins sold, 694.

Kaskaskia (Kaskaskias): 18; 46; 48; 139; 142; 165; 324; 350; 676; 743; an American post, on east bank of Mississippi, 755; Armstrong goes beyond, 140; Governor St. Clair there, 138; home of William Morrison, rich merchant, 113, 755.

Kaskaskia Indians (Kas, Cascaquias): English canoes winter among them, 180; move to mouth of Des Pères River, 7; receive presents annually, 180; visit Missouris and Osages, 5.

Kaskaskia River: 5.

Kaydesce, La Croix: signs power of attorney for Lisa, 667.

Kayguechinga (Le Petit Chef): large medal requested for him, 327.

Kayoha Indians: habitat, 384.

Kellogg, L. P.: 5n; 6n; 7n; narratives cited, 4n.

Kentucky: 131n; 157n; 343; 583; 652; 682; Lexington correspondents of William C'ark have received letters from him, 761.

Kerlérec, Louis Billouart de, Governor of Louisiana: favors free trading, 49, 50, 60; letter about trade abuses cited, 51n; letter to Minister cited, 50n; lists Indian nations in contact with French, 50-55; succeeds Vaudreuil, 49.

Kettles, Cooking: 272; 274; 281; 283; 310; 361; 501; profit allowed, in Todd-Clamorgan agreement, 468.

Kicapu, Kicapus: See Kickapoo Indians.

Kichai Indians (Kitsais, Quitsais): 31; move south and raid Spanish Texas, 20; Spanish treaty of peace with, 749.

Kichetabaco, Ponca chief: 290.

Kickapoo Indians (Kikapou, Kicapu, Quiapou): 27n; 180; 199; 529; among nations receiving provisions and presents from Spanish, 769; English trade with, 81; Lisa claims to have prevented warriors from going against Osages,

717; listed in Iberville *mémoire*, 8n; salary paid interpreter, 771; threaten to kill Little Osages, 168.

Kikara Indians: See Arikara Indians.

Kiowa Indians: 380; wandering people, allies of the Cheyennes, 379.

Kitsai Indians: See Kichai Indians.

Knife River: 110.

Knives: 270; 271; 272; 278; 281; 286; 305; 306; 707.

Knox, Henry, Secretary of War: letter from General Harmar, 142; letters (extracts) to Harmar, 142; secret, private letters to Harmar, 135-137, 137; letter to Armstrong, 137; letter to Governor St. Clair, 138.

Kuchechire (La Grande Piste): *patente* of first medal requested for him, 327.

Kueéhagachin (Le Batard): small medal requested for him, 327.

La Baie Denoc: an English canoe winters there, 180.

La Brosse, Joseph: witnesses statement, 241.

La Bruyère, Fabry de: 30; attempts to secure horses, 30; expedition to New Mexico, 28-31; Fabry gives up, 31.

La Chaise, M. de: gets an inquiry from the Company of the Indies, about Missouri post, 22n-23n; letter (extract) from the Company, 23n; reply (extract), 23n; letters cited, 23n, 24n.

La Deroute, Joseph: Truteau sends him to the Arikaras, 267.

La Fleur, M.: assignment and share of trade, 210; present at organization meeting of the Missouri Company, 218.

La France, Jean Baptiste: 105; 105n; 106; 502; 502n.

La Grave (Laggrave): 103; 105; 334; 503; 503n; reprehensible conduct, 479.

La Grillade, ——: reported killed by a Missouri Indian, 27, 27n, 34.

La Harpe, Bénard de: 17; 20; Journal cited, 19n; says Mentos and Panis at war, 19.

La Jeremaye, ——, nephew of La Vérendrye: accompanies uncle on exploring expedition, 32.

La Jonquière, M.: 47; letter to Minister cited, 45n.

La Lutra River: 122.

La Pérouse, J. F. G. de: 699; his "Voyage . . . autour de Monde" cited, 699n.

La Rocque, François Antoine (Laroque): 390n; activities a threat to Spain, 3; Journal cited, 94n.

La Salle, Nicolas de: urges exploration of the Missouri, 9, 10n.

La Salle, Robert Cavelier, *Sieur* de: 53; arrival at the Missouri, 4, 4n; assassination mentioned, 4, 5; documents and narratives about him cited, 4n, 5n; relations with Bienville, 10, 10n; writes of Frenchmen among the Missouris, 5.

La Souris River: See Souris River.

La Ventane Indians: 60.

La Vérendrye, Pierre Gaultier de Varennes, *Sieur* de: biographical sketch, 31; British subjects follow the trail he blazed, 76; efforts to reach the Western Sea, 31-34; extracts from Journal, 33; extent of explorations, 56; Journal and Letters cited, 34n, 93n; sons accompany him on explorations, 32, 33, 34.

Labadie: See Labbadie.

Labbadie, Pierre: acts as witness, 704.

Labbadie, Silvestre (Labadie): 71; 184; 218; assignment and share of trade, 211.

Lac du Bois: See Lake of the Woods.

Lac Sant Croix: See Lake St. Croix.

Lace: 68.

Laclède: See also Maxent, Laclède and Company.

Laclède, Jean de: attempts to salvage brother's estate, 63n; *mémoire* cited, 63n.

Laclède Liguest, Pierre (name *written* Laclède Liguest and *signed* Laclède Liquet): associate of Maxent, 60, 67, 68, 69; founder of St. Louis, 1; selects site for post, 63-64; trade of, 64.

Lacroix, Joseph Baptiste: on list and *mémoirs* of individuals against exclusive trade, 645, 646, 651.

Lafillard, Pedro (Lafilar): acts as witness, 646, 667.

Lagotenee, Vincent: signs Lisa *mémoire* against exclusive trade, 651.

Lahontan, Louis Armand de Lom d'Arce, Baron de: narratives fact or legend? 5, 5n; publishes narratives on Missouri River experiences, 5.

Lahoye: See Lajoye.

Lajoye, L., fils (Lahoye, Lovejoy, La Joye): 72; 218; absent from merchants' meeting, 211; signs Lisa *mémoire* against exclusive trade, 651; signs power of attorney for Lisa, 667.

Lake Erie: 133; 683; Armstrong explores communicating waters, 136n.

Lake Inférieur: 694.

Lake Lapluie: See Rainy Lake.

Lake Michigan: 141; 180; 514; 683.

Lake Oanipik: See Lake Winnipeg.

Lake of the Woods (Lac du Bois): 397; 491; 584; 585; one end of a boundary line, 669.

Lake Onepik: See Lake Winnipeg.

Lake Ontario: 683.

Lake Ouanipik, Ouinipique: See Lake Winnipeg.

Lake Placotee: 383.

Lake Saint Croix (Lac Sant Croix): 180.

Lake Superior: 177; 178; 333; 389; 399; 490; 566; 632; 683; English have a chain of forts from this lake to the Rocky Mountains, 434; La Vérendrye activities on or near, 31, 32.

Lake Winnipeg (Oanipik, Onepik, Ouanipik, Ouinipique): 385; 492; 584; 585; 611; 632; 659; 738; 762; English company established there threatens Spanish dominion, 620; size, latitude and longitude, 491.

Lalande, Bautista (Baptiste Le Lande): Morrison puts claims against him in Pike's hands, 113n; one of several traders interested in a short route to Santa Fé, 113, 743, 755, 756.

Lama [animal]: 165.

Lamate [?], Francisco: his information about Americans in a blockhouse, 365.

Lami, Baptiste: 321.

Laministre [Manistee River, Michigan?]: wintering spot for English canoes, 180.

Lamothe, Nicholas: documents from him, forwarded to Carondelet, speak of American penetration of New Spain, and what he can do about it, 513.

Lancaster: on Perrin du Lac's travel route, 707n.

Lance, Cheyenne chief: 309-310.

Land: Clamorgan asks land grant, 560n-561n; Gayoso de Lemos makes offer to attract new settlers, 556n; Gayoso proposes to use Evans and Mackay on land claims business, 108n; Loisel petition for, 611-612; Mackay petition, 603-604; plans for exchange of Indian land, 723-724; requested by F. Saucier, to support a large family, 601; Trudeau promises land to Evans in recognition of services, 108.

Land grants: to R. Loisel, 612-613; to James Mackay, 604-605; to Saucier family, 602.

Land office: 347.

L'Andreville, André (Landréville, Lendresill, Endrevil): among petitioners for authority to form an exploring society, 194; assignment and share of trade, 210; given license to trade on the Missouri, 162; on list and *mémoires* of individuals against exclusive trade, 645, 646, 650, 650n; present at organization meeting of Missouri Company, 218; signs power of attorney for Lisa, 667.

Langlois, M.: commands the galiot *La Flecha*, 323; letter to Carondelet cited, 318n.

Languages, Indian: Big Osages speak the same language as the Iowas and the Otos, 52; the elder branch of the Arkansas, the Little Osages and the

Kansas speak the same language with differences in accent, 51.

Lanusse, Pablo: 688.

Lanut, A.: his gift to Evans, 479.

Larche, Sr.: Macarty receives from him the news of difficulties among the Little Osages, the Iowas, and Missouris, 46.

Larivière, François conducting a boat carrying a large load of maple sugar for Chouteau, 514.

Las Casas, Luis de, Captain-General, Havana: 146n; 157n; 159; extract from military report from Carondelet, 253-256; letter cited, 79n; letters from Carondelet cited, 230n; 355n; letters to and from Carondelet cited, 146n; letter to Governor of Louisiana cited, 370n; letter to Minister of War cited, 146n; draft of letter to Cayetano Payeto cited, 146n.

Latitude: 164; 165; 440; 441; marking territory of proposed commissioners, 701; of first winter party of Lewis and Clark, 761; within which explorers seek water route to the Pacific, 713.

Latitude and longitude: 412; 493; 584; of northern lakes, 491; of tribes or rivers in Collot list, 383-385; to be noted by John Evans, 411.

Laudrain [?], C.: his undated *mémoire*, giving some information as to extent of French establishments, mentioned, and cited, 58, 58n.

Laurain, M.: gives Bienville account of travels, 8.

Lauson, Mr.: a bad man, who insults the Sioux, 267, 274.

Laussat, M., prefect: delivers Louisiana to American commissioners, 723; gathers information about presents to the Indians, 701n; letter to Minister of Marine, Paris, cited, 701n.

Lavalinière, Abbé de: papers accuse Ste. Geneviève priest, 373.

Lavallée, John (Lavalé, Lavalée, Lavellée): among petitioners for authority to form an exploring company, 194; among those present at organization meeting, 218; assignment and share of trade, 211.

Law, John: documents about him cited, 20n; his colony in eastern Arkansas a good market for slaves, 20.

Laytan Indians : ask the Osages to make peace, 321; considered the best warriors on the Missouri, 127; estimate of population, 760; have horses to spare to other Indians on the Missouri, 125; Interior Provinces suffer from their incursions, 325; location and characteristics, 127; wandering Apaches, 127. See also Comanche Indians.

Le Bartz, Sr.: *mémoire* cited, 14n.

Le Conte, M. (Pedro Lecont): 72; 467n; among those present at organization meeting, exploring company, 218; assignment and share of trade, 211.

Le Dru, Jean Antoine (Ledru), *ad interim* curate at St. Louis: discontent in his parish, 203; letter to *Monsigneur* cited, 132n; officiates at benediction of church, 132.

La Maire, ——: doubts Lathontan narrative, 5n; gave space in his *mémoires* to the Missouri, 13; map, cited, shows the Missouri, Kansas, and Osage rivers, 13n; says few Spaniards live on the Missouri, 10-11, 11n.

Le Norman, ——: his murder reported, 26.

Le Page du Pratz, Antoine S.: 17n; 21n; claims about Bourgmont activities, 13; his "History of Louisiana" cited, 56; writes about mines, 13.

Le Raye, Charles: activities, with party, on the Missouri, 110-111; Journal cited, 111n.

Le Sueur, Pierre: corrects map based on travels of La Salle, 142; map based on his *mémoires*, and other source material cited, 6n; searches for mines and finds tin and lead, 6.

Lead: 9; 233; 278; 370; 707; received by Sioux Indians in exchange for skins, 706. See also Mines.

Lead-Mine River: 384.

Leavenworth, Kansas: Portneuf post near present site, 47n.

Lecuyer, —— (Léquiyé: 98; 114; 328n; 351; 353; 354; 360; 362; 388n; activities as leader of third expedition for Missouri Company, 91-92; bad conduct, 441.

Lecuyer, Na.: 295.

Lee, Patrick (Patrice, Patricio): on list and *mémoires* of individuals against exclusive trade, 644, 646, 650; petitions, with Robidoux, against exclusive trade, 624-627; signs power of attorney for Lisa, 667.

Legac, Charles, ex-director, Company of the Indies: supplies information, 16.

Legal procedures: discussed in Gayoso de Lemos letter to De Lassus, 598.

Legantois, M.: 36.

Leggings: 298.

Legrante, Roberto: See Grant, Robert.

Lemos, Gayoso de: See Gayoso de Lemos, Manuel.

Lemoyne, Jean Baptiste: See Bienville, Jean Baptiste Lemoyne, *Sieur* de.

Lemoyne, Pierre: See Iberville, Pierre Lemoyne, *Sieur* de.

Leroy, Jean: signs Lisa *mémoire* against exclusive trade, 651.

Lewis, Meriwether (Merry Weather, Merryweather, Captain Merry, Captain Merry Whether, Captain Lewis Merry Wheather, Captain Wheather): 3; 109; 722; 728ff; 733; 734; 749n; C. Calvo finds it difficult to impede his progress, 750-751; De Lassus ordered not to hinder him, 725; his apprehension would be useful, 735; Journal cited, 110n; letter, Calvo to Prince of Peace, gives digest of *Gazette* account, 763-764; letter from De Lassus to Salcedo and Calvo gives information about proposed trip, 719-721; letter (extract) from Jefferson, enclosing "a map of a mr. Evans", 98n-99n; "literary journey" authorized by Jefferson, 721; official

report and newspaper account of expedition, 760-763; proposal to arrest, 732; rumor about his objective, 745; sent to explore route to Pacific, 115; shows passports from British and French *chargés d'affaires*, 720n; Spanish minister authorized to lodge a complaint against him, 766; Stoddard writes of the beginning of journey, 740-741.

Lewis and Clark expedition: 79n; 749n; 765; complaints about expedition to go to King of Spain, 752; diary and map sent to the President, 763, 764; has created Indian friends and brought them to St. Louis, 769; Jefferson's pet project, 115; map cited, 107n; Journals cited, 83n, 90, 111, 164, 377n; progress of expedition as reported from an official to Cevallos, 752-753; purpose, according to Spanish officials, 719n.

Leyba, Fernando de, Lieutenant-Governor of Spanish Illinois, successor to Cruzat: alleged that he gave licenses to those who could afford to pay, 71; letters to and from Gálvez cited, 71n.

Licenses: See Hunting licenses; Trading licenses.

Lile Dauphin: See Dauphin Island.

Limestone: 607n.

Limoges, Joseph J., Father: makes known desire to plant the cross among the Missouris, 6.

Linden trees: 695.

Lions, Mountain: 125.

Lipane Indians; Spanish instructed not to take part in inter-nation war, 147; thrown out of their territory by Comanches, 148.

Lipiyanes Indians (Lipillanes): thrown out of their territory by Comanches, 148.

Liquors, Intoxicating: 40; 62; 63; 312; 314; given Indians by English, 81n; sale prohibited, 38; sales tax suggested, for benevolent purposes, 559n; trade regulation, 190. See also *Aguardiente;* Brandy.

811

Lisa, Manuel de: 664; 687n; 688n; 705; 741; 741n; bickering over payment of share of note, 680n; concession of Osage trade, by Salcedo, 687-689; given share of Osage trade, 592; insulting *mémoire* to De Lassus, 716-718; jailed for presenting insulting *mémoire*, but released, 718n; letter, De Lassus to M. de Salcedo, about Lisa and two powers-of-attorney, 664-665; letter to Moro cited, 741n; marginal notation of Salcedo, approving grant, 677; *mémoires* to De Lassus, 645-646; 665; *mémoire* to Intendant-General, against exclusive trade, 667-668; *mémoires* to M. de Salcedo, 646-651, 677-680; notation on copy of *mémoire* to Salcedo, 646n; opposes Clamorgan, 553n; petition mentioned, 660; petitions to De Lassus cited, 718n; power-of-attorney document, 666-667; relinquishes share of trade but buys Sarpy's, 592; signs *mémoire* against exclusive trade, 650, 650n; submits a list, and *mémoire* with names of inhabitants against exclusive trade, 644-645, 646; to take care of legal matters for Loisel estate, 757n; with friends, granted Osage trade, 689.

"Literary News": translation of French document, 132-134.

Little Manitou River: description and distance from the mouth of the Missouri, 486.

Little Missouri River (Tranquil Water): 275; 277; 378; 384; course and source, 124.

Little Nemaha River: 263; distance from the mouth of the Missouri, 488.

Little Platte River: description, navigability, and distance from the mouth of the Missouri, 488.

Little Salt River: location and distance from the mouth of the Missouri, 486.

Little Sioux River: 264; 378.

Livingston, Robert R.: negotiations with Talleyrand, 115

Llaneros Indians: thrown out of their territory by the Comanches, 148.

Lobos Indians: See Loup and Panimaha Indians.

Loisel, Régis (Loiselle): 371; 421, 421n; 641n; 690; 742n; 761; 764; acts as witness, 703, 704; amount of debt to Clamorgan company, 578; buys share in Missouri Company for A. Todd, 574; commended as explorer by De Lassus, 736n; death mentioned, 763n; just a young man when he died, 757n; letter cited, 611n; letter to De Lassus cited, 115n; memorial cited, 115n; narrative of his expedition cited, 354n; New Orleans fever probably killed him, 757n; partnership with Heney, 114, 114n; party to partnership agreement, 636; petition to De Lassus for land, 612; qualifications as a frontier agent, 757; report to De Lassus on explorations, 735-740; requests depositions, 575; trips contemplated by notes to Lisa and Meunier, 736n; will, copy of will, and provisions cited, 114n, 736n, 757n.

Loisel: See also Clamorgan, Loisel and Company.

Loisel-Heney trade agreement: A. Chouteau had a large part in equipping enterprises, 757n; agreement cited, 114n; articles of agreement, 636-638; articles cited, 636n.

Loison, M.: servant of Garreau, 95, 334.

Lom d'Arce, Louis Armand de: See Lahontan, Louis Armand de Lom d'Arce, Baron de.

London: 176; 177; 178.

López, André: See Armesto, Andrés López de.

López y Ángulo, ——, Intendant at New Orleans: letter from Álveres cited, 614n; letter from Casa Calvo mentioned.

Lorimier, Louis (Laurimier, Luis), Commandant at Cape Girardeau: 172n; 231; 232; 526; 534; difficulties with Portell, 203; his oratory could move Indians, 698; letter from Trudeau cited, 198n;

position in Indian Department, residence, and salary, 771.

Los Adaes, presidio: 14; 726; 743n; Spaniards occupy, 12n.

Louis XIV, King of France: orders five posts established on the Missouri, 11.

Louis XV, King of France: *mémoire* cited, allows freedom of trade and urges the giving of presents, to keep Indians friendly, 61n.

Louis XVI, King of France: 204.

Louisiana: See also New Orleans.

Louisiana, American: boundaries, 726, 730; discussion of boundaries, 745-750.

Louisiana, French: 16, 40n; 43; 50; 56n; 57n; 70; 253n; as described in Vilemont letter to Talleyrand, 680-687; Bourgmont information useful, 13; Cadillac reports hearsay about it, 10, 10n-11n; Lahontan narrative doubted, 5n; Le Page du Pratz writes a history, after sixteen years' residence, 56, 56n; "Plan" for Louisiana written in 1763 indicates existing geographical knowledge, 59-60, 60n; possibility of mines, 14; problems arising, after delivery to the United States, as seen by Yrujo, 723-724; strategic location, 3; transfer of Upper Louisiana to the United States, 719n, 725, 725n; Vaudreuil writes a *mémoire* on the jurisdictions of Louisiana and Canada, 41, 41n; work on the close of French rule cited, 55n.

Louisiana, Spanish: 70; 73-74; 77; 78; 113; 119-127; 236-237; 253n; 385; 400; 409; Carondelet report, 253-256; Carondelet's fears of conquest, 424n; expense account, forty years, 769; income and cost of administration, 686. See also: Illinois, Spanish.

Louisiana purchase: United States takes over, 723; boundaries, 747; text of treaty cited, 747n.

Loup Indians: 112; 173; 180; 199; 203; 231; 232; 357; 364; 431n; 453; 454; 526; 529; 673n; amount of merchandise assigned for, 209; estimate of annual value of merchandise for their trade,

760; estimate of population, 760; located on Clamorgan map, 451; number of men using arms, and amount of trade, 706n; portion of trade, and share to trader, 210; receive provisions and presents from the Spanish government, 769; salary paid interpreter, 771. See also: Pani Loup and Panimaha Indians.

Loup River: home of Panimahas, 71n.

Lovejoy, *fils*: See Lajoye, *fils*.

Luttig, John C.: Journal cited, 82n.

Luzière, M. de, Commandant of Ste. Geneviève: 535.

Lyman County, South Dakota: Fort au Cèdres near, 114.

Lynx: 371.

M. Y. A.: Lisa says *mémoire* previously presented to, 678.

McConnell, Mr.: contributor to fund for proposed exploration, 167.

McCracken, Hugh: 93.

McDonnell, John: 460; 461; diaries cited, 94n, 333n, 480n; Journal refers to traders from Fort Esperance among the Mandans, 94; letters to John Evans, 103; 478-480, 502-503; letter (extract) to Evans, 105; letter (extract) to Evans cited, 104n; sends present to Evans, 103.

McGillivray, Mr.: Miró fears he may deprive the Creeks of part of their land, 157n.

McKay, Mr.: 462; 479; 480. See also Mackay.

McKee, Alexander: letter concerning De Bon cited, 133n.

McKina: See Michilimackinac.

McTavish, Simon: 154n.

Macarty, Major, Commandant at Illinois: 48n; 60; 62; letters (extracts) to Rouillé, 48; 49; letter to Rouillé cited, 46; letters to Vaudreuil cited, 47n; role as Commandant, 46-49.

"Machecoux": See Creek Indians.

Mackay, James (Diego McKay): 89; 99; 101; 101n; 104; 341; 342; 346n; 365; 416n; 418; 421n; 422; 423; 424;

441; 442; 460; 496; 520n; 562n; 582; 585, 586; activities as leader, third expedition of Missouri Company, 93-94, 95, 96-97; appointment as Captain of militia and Commandant of San André del Misuri, 545n; blamed for Missouri Company losses, 519; character, 97, 97n; commended by Gayoso de Lemos, 599; commission as commandant of forts desired, 418; commission as Commandant: document, 428-429; commission sent to Trudeau, 427, 427n; cost of expedition, 97; description of Missouri, in Journal, cited, 110, 110n; directed to sell land for Clamorgan, 704; divergent opinions about date of departure on expedition cited, 351n; experiences among the Omahas, on third expedition, 540; experiences on third expedition, 97-98, 97n, 529; given license to trade with the Omahas, 591, 605; instructions to John Evans, 410-414; instructions cited, 100n; Journal, Oct. 1795 to Jan. 1796, 356-364; Journal and letters sent to Carondelet, 100n; Journal sent by Carondelet to Prince of Peace, 354, 354n; Journal extracts, 89n; 94-95, 102-103, 490-495; Journal extracts cited, 90n, 103n, 389n; Journal cited, 90n, 96n, 100n, 103n, 389n, 417n; letters (extracts) from Gayoso de Lemos, 108, 599n; letter (extract) from Trudeau to Gayoso about Mackay's map and ambitions, 545n; letter (extract) to ---[?] 92; letter to Clamorgan and Reilhe, 351-354; letters to Clamorgan cited, 92n, 97n, 98n; letter to De Lassus [?] about theft of horse, 617; letter to De Lassus cited, 614n; letter to Evans, 415-416; letter (facsimile) to Evans, 533; letter to Evans cited, 89n; letters to Gayoso de Lemos, 561-563, 587-589; letter to Gayoso, protesting limitation on immigrants, cited, 587n; letter to son, giving biographical data, 96n; map of voyages cited, 243n, 545n; nomination as Missouri Company agent approved, 371; petition to De Lassus for land, 603-604; receives recognition for services, 108;

remuneration, 93; sends John Evans on expedition, 495; summarizes his activities, in petition for position, 107; Table of Distances along the Missouri, up to the White River, 485-490; to stop violation of boundaries, 95; to survey land to be deeded to Saucier family, 602; well-informed on geography of the Upper Missouri, 485n. See also Mckay.

Mackay, John Zeno: son of James, 96n.

Mackay (Mckay?), [Neil or Donald?]: 102, 102n; 460n.

Mackay, Mr. [S ?]: 479.

Mackenzie, Sir Alexander (McKenzie, Makensi): 585; 712; Lewis and Clark find his description of the head waters of the Missouri accurate, 763, 764; second trip proves no water route to the ocean exists, 713-714; "Voyages from Montreal . . . to the Frozen and Pacific Oceans" cited, 712.

Mackenzie, Charles: activities threaten Spain in North America, 3.

Mackenzie River (McKenzie): 585.

Mackinac: See Michilimackinac.

Magazines, European: gift to Evans, 103, 479.

Maha River: 12; 128.

Maha Indians: See Omaha Indians.

Mahi Indians: among the most distant nations of the Missouri, according to Piernas, 59.

Maison Todd: See House of Todd.

Maissonneuve, Jean de la: 590n.

MaKay: See Mackay.

Makensis: See Mackenzie.

Makinak: See Michilimackinac.

Maldonado, Lorenzo Ferrer: 713, 713n.

Malespina, Alejandro, explorer: 713.

Mallet, Paul: 28.

Mallet, Pierre: group reaches Santa Fé and Taos, 28.

Mallet brothers: blame Fabry de La Bruyère for difficulties, 30-31; expedition to New Mexico, 28, 28n; members of party guide Fabry, 28, 29.

Mammoth: 165.

Manchiamany (Le petit Maigre) : gorget requested for, 327.

Mandan Indians: 34; 76; 81; 83; 87; 87n; 89; 89n; 90; 91; 92; 93; 94; 95; 96; 97; 100; 101; 104; 109; 110; 111; 164; 181; 229; 233; 234; 235; 245; 246; 247; 248; 249; 250; 251; 252; 258; 260; 263; 277; 285; 286; 287; 292; 294; 295; 297; 299; 301; 303; 304; 307; 309; 315; 326; 330; 331; 332; 333; 334; 335; 338; 340; 341; 342; 344; 346; 351; 352; 354; 357; 364; 371; 376; 379; 380; 384; 385; 389; 390; 399; 411; 413; 418; 426; 428; 434; 437; 448; 456; 461n; 462; 477; 492; 493; 496; 497; 500; 514; 520; 584; 596; 610; 660; 669; 673n; 682; 699n; 706n; 748; 749; 762; always at war with the Sioux, 161; are in communication with Spaniards, 161, 164; attitude toward women, 258; blank *patentes* requested for, 327; can be attracted to St. Louis, 770; D'Église reaches, via Missouri, 82; destination of Truteau, 243; distance from St. Louis, 539; English dare to erect factories among, 554; English fort certain, 515; English menace Company establishment there, 620; English to be dislodged from nearby posts, 435; estimate of annual value of merchandise for, 759; estimate of population, 760; Evans crosses successfully, 106; fort maintained by the Company among, 609; friendly to La Vérendrye, 32-33; later expedition to, cited, 96n; Mackay takes possession of fort, 563; seen by Loisel, 739; trade directly with English, 161, 161n; Truteau to build a fort there, 86.

Mandeville, Sr.: *mémoire* cited, 10n.

Maniguacci (Eyes of the Partridge) : 123.

Manitou (Maniton), spirit: 699; a dried serpent represents, 50n. See also Watchi-Manitou.

Manitouris Indians (Manitaris, Minitaree, Munitarees, Munitaries) : 492; 496; 673n; 706n.

Manners and customs of Indians: the female of the species, 259; ceremony on reception of *patente*, 305; childbirth, 259; clothing and ornament, 380; divorce, 257-258; food eaten in preparation for war expedition, 710; Mackay instructs Evans to note, 411; marriage, 257-258; medals: see references under Medals for Indians; noted by Evans, 499; polygamy, 257; presents: see references under Presents to Indians; religion, 543; 696; treatment of, and attitude toward women, 39, 258, 259, 300, 300n, 414; Truteau's observations about huts, clothing, etc., 380.

Mantanes, Manton Indians: See Mandan Indians.

Maple sugar: See Sugar, Maple.

Maps: gathered by Collot now in French archives, 383n, 719n; suggested to Michaux by Thomas Jefferson, 165. The following single maps are mentioned or cited: one, of English chain of forts menacing Spanish territory, 385, 395; cited as missing from folder, 389n, 395n; one of Fort Orléans, cited, 20n; one, of Jesuit missions, cited, 7n; one, of Louisiana and West Florida, cited, 253n; one, traced from original, of Missouri basin, 451; one, based on information derived from *coureurs-de-bois* and Indians, cited, 10n; one, of Missouri, cited, 88n; another, cited, 107n; one of Missouri valley, cited, 4n; one, a conjectural map, based on Mackay's instructions to John Evans, shown, 415; one, a topographical map of the Upper Mississippi, cited, 406n; a topographical map showing a chain of English forts, cited as missing from folder, 389n, 395n; a topographical relief map mentioned as having been deposited by Vilemont in Madrid, 682, and cited 682n. In addition, the following maps, associated with some personal name, are mentioned or cited in the text: Armstrong's of the Missouri, 142n; Bellin, based principally on travels of La Salle, 142; Bourgmont, cited, 22n; D'Anville, cited, 56, 56n;

Dartaguiette, already cited, 10n; De Bon, 133; Delisle's cited, 6n; English traveler's, 131; Evans map, presented to President Jefferson, 719; Franquelin, 5n; Jolliet's lost map of the Mississippi, cited, 4n; Le Maire's cited, 13n; Le Page du Pratz, of Louisiana, 56, 56n; Lewis and Clark, cited 107n, 377n, 485n, 520n, 612n, 719n; Mackay's, 243, 520, 545, 545n, 563, 604, discussion of them cited, 520n; Marquette's cited, 4n; Perrin du Lac's, believed to be the work of Mackay, 545n, of Upper Missouri cited, 111n, 376n-377n; Pitot's, 700n; Soulard's, 257n; Vermale's indicates course of Osage River, 13.

Maquoketa River (Grande Macoquité): 81; 180.

Marais des Liards (Marais de Liars, des Liars, Cottonwood Swamp): has American families, 442; near the village of San Fernando, 537.

Maramec, Marameck, Maramek River: See Meramec River.

Marchesseau, Nicholas: 387; petition, with Andrew Todd, 403-405.

Marest, Gabriel, Father: letter cited, 6n; letters about mission, on site of St. Louis, cited, 7n; sends Iberville geographical information, 6.

Marié, Alexis: signs Lisa *mémoire* against exclusive trade, 651; signs power of attorney for Lisa, 667.

Marié, Joseph: assignment and share of trade, 210; given license to trade on Missouri, 162; on list and *mémoire* of individuals against exclusive trade, 645, 646.

Marié, Jean Baptiste: signs power of attorney for Lisa, 667.

Mariette, François: commission as chaplain issued, 22n.

Marin, M.: peacemaker, among Mississippi Indians, 50.

Marmillon, Francisco: 72.

Maroteau, Juan Luis: captain of frigate *Mississippi*, 472.

Marquette, Jacques, Père: 6; discovery of Missouri, 3; religious motive in exploring, 4n.

Marain, ——: granted exclusive contract for trade on the Missouri, and Ouabache, 24.

Marriage: 257-258.

Martens: 36; 38; 203; abundant in Upper Louisiana, 684.

Martigny, J. B.: letter to Galvez [?] cited, 71n.

Martigon: wintering spot, in American territory, for English canoes, 180.

Martínez, Esteban José, explorer: 713; 713n; report about American territory cited, 743n.

Martinique: 746; 747.

Marujuy, Pierre: letter to the Governor [Carondelet], 241.

Mascouten Indians (Mascou, Mascuten, Mascutin, Maskoutin): 66; 180; 529; English trade with, 81; habitat, number of warriors, value of merchandise received and of skins sold, 694; Iberville lists, 8n; threaten to kill Little Osages, 168.

Maskegon Indians (Maskego): habitat, 385.

Maskoutin Indians: See Mascouten Indians.

Maurelle, Antonio Francisco, explorer: 713; 713n.

Maurepas, Comte de: letter (extract) from Perrier, 24; letter cited, 24n.

Maxent, Gilbert Antoine: 62; 63; 63n; 72; list of merchandise, 68; plea for trading license, 66-69.

Maxent, Laclède and Company: 62; assets of company listed, 69; Company dissolved, 63n; grant canceled, 63; granted exclusive Missouri commerce, 55; Maxent, Laclède and De, 60.

Maxwell, James (Diego), Father: 442; 442n; plea for his retention, 742, 742n.

Meadows: 123; 124.

Meares, John: a work of his cited, 713.

Measles: 44.

Medals for Indians: 98; 101; 144; 168; 251; 257n; 262; 284; 285; 287; 291; 304; 305; 309; 326; 329; 359; 374; 402n; 418; 420n; 426; 496; 611; 634; list requested by Trudeau, 327; received by Trudeau, for distribution, 430.

Medehiaquoin Indians: Iberville lists, 8n.

Membré, Zenobius, Father: narrative cited, 4n.

Mémentan River: See Mermentao River.

Menard, ——: 82; 89; 90; 91; 93; 93n; 161; 232; 304; 331; 332; 381; 390.

Mento Indians: Du Tisné gives them slaves to sell, 19; Osages planning war, 29, 30; suffer from raids, 19-20.

Meramec trading post: American families settled in, 442.

Meramec River (Maramec, Marameck, Maramek): 122; 170; 170n; silver mines in region, 683.

Merchandise brand: of Loisel-Heney goods, 636.

Merchandise for Indian trade: 144; 144n-145n; 178; 179; 278; 402n; assignment of amounts, 209; big chiefs preempt the best, 283-284, 288; Black Bird evades payment for, 290; expense of shipment, 510; Chouteau's estimate of annual consumption, 759; instruction to confiscate, 246; lengthy correspondence about cargo of *El Antelope* cited, 512n; of foreigners, may be confiscated, 192-193; pillaged, from Truteau, by Sioux, 271, 272; Poncas cheat in exchanging pelts for, 293; profit allowed, in Todd-Clamorgan agreement, 468; profits, to English traders, 176; Register of, submitted by Maxent, 68; stolen by Osages, 150; stolen from D'Église, 289; value of entire trade of Missouri, 210, value, three expeditions of Missouri Company, 339, 340; what D'Église carried, 298.

Mercier, Claudio: 72; Clamorgan seeks extension of time for payment of debt, 170, 171.

Mercier, Jean Baptiste, Father: work among Indians, 22, 22n.

Mermentao River (Mémentan, Mermenta, Armenta, Nementao, Nemintas): 685; no funds available for exploring mouth, 754; Spaniards fix on a line, involving this river, in boundary discussion, 726, 750.

Merry, Captain: See Lewis, Meriwether.

Merry, Mr., British Chargé d'Affaires at Washington: letter to Hawkesbury, about boundaries, cited, 719n.

Merry, Mr., nephew of André Todd: to continue management of uncle's interests, 523.

Mesnager, Le Bailly: *mémoire* advocating exploration of sources of Missouri and Mississippi cited, 43n.

Messigamea Indians: See Michigamea Indians.

Messouri: See Missouri River.

Metchagamis, Metchigamea Indians: See Michigamea Indians.

Meteyer, Jeanot (Jeannot): embarked on journey to discover shortest route to New Mexico, 743, 744, 755, 756.

Meunier, Jean Baptiste (Juan Munier, Bautista Monier, Munié): 88; 208; 215; 235; 262; 280; 287; 290; 292; 293; claims about discovery of Ponca Indians, 194-195, 195-196; decree of Carondelet, requiring Pérez to report, 195; does not know how to write, 239; false claims about discovery of Poncas, causing contract to be withdrawn, 207, 212-213; given license to trade on the Missouri, 162; letter from Carondelet granting petition, 196; letter from Carondelet, granting trade contract, 240; name on list and *mémoires* of individuals against exclusive trade, 645, 646, 651; obtains exclusive trade with Poncas, 81-82; partnership agreement, 238-239; partnership with Rolland, 194n; petition to Carondelet, for trade with Poncas, 194-195; petition, with Rolland, to Carondelet, for restoration of license, 237-238; report of Pérez, recommending, 195-196; statements of friends certifying his discovery of Poncas, 240-241; Trudeau writes Carondelet about voided license, 256.

Mexico: 76; 145; 424n; 582; 585; Spaniards hoping for aid from Viceroy, 750; the goal of English and American traders, 146; the Missouri the route to, 652.

Mézières: see De Mézières.

Miami Indians: English conspire with, 43; 48.

Miami River: 154n.

Michaux, André (Micheau, Micheaux): 79; 366; 598n; correspondence cited, 366n; ideas about establishing France in former American possessions, 164n; Jefferson's instructions, for western expedition, 164-166; statement about date of departure of Mackay expedition, 97n, 351n.

Michaux expedition: contributors to fund for, with amounts, 166-167.

Michigamea Indians (Messigamea, Metchagamis, Metchigamea): Iberville lists, 8n; one chief goes with Bourgmont to France, 21-22.

Michilimackinac trading post (Mackinac, McKina, Michilimackinack, Michilimakinak, Michilimaquina): 42; 51; 76; 81; 131n; 162; 177; 178; 179; 180; 185; 323; 339; 344; 349; 387; 388; 390; 391; 392; 394; 398; 399; 400; 404; 407; 408; 433; 434; 435; 437; 476; 513; 514; 541; 580; 687; 693; 697; English traders here exempt from import duties, 436; merchants get fees for permits, 134; turned over to Americans, 515.

Military defense: preparations for, 584-587, 587n.

Militia: See Soldiers.

Miller, Hunter: Treaties cited, 747n.

Mills: See Flour mills, Grist mills, Saw mills, Water-power mills.

Milwaukee (Miloaki): wintering site for canoes for Folavoana trade, 180.

Mine River: 122; 125; description, navigability, and distance from the mouth of the Missouri, 486.

Minerals: 23; 38; 59; samples collected by Vilemont, 682.

Mines: 6; 8; 9; 11; 24; 36; 48; 128; 449; 459; 462; 486; believed Spanish are traversed by the Missouri, 10, 14; Mine of St. Barbe, 15; objective of river exploration, 7; said to have been found by *voyageurs*, 13; Trudeau recommends working the mines in Illinois, 537; variety near Kansas River fork, 12; also the following specific references to mines of: coal, 121; copper, 9; 671; gold, 14; 449; 459; on Arkansas River, 683; iron, 537, 671; lead, 6, 9, 11, 24, 421n, 486, 537, 671, 683; silver, 9, 14, 449, 459, claimed found among the Arikaras, 25, 28, on Meramec River, 683; tin, 6, 9, 671.

Miniconjou Indians (Minikaojoup): wandering nation, seen by Loisel, 739.

Minister, Versailles, France: letters from Bienville cited, 26n, 35n; report from Cadillac cited, 10n-11n; letter from Salmon cited 26n; letter (extract) from Vaudreuil, 43, with citation, 43n; letter (extract) to Beauharnois, 33; letter (extract) to Bienville, 26-27; letter to Bienville cited, 35n; letter (extract) to Dabbadie, 62, with citation, 62n; letter to Perrier cited, 23, 23n; letter to Salmon cited, 26n; letter to Vaudreuil cited, 50n.

Minnesota River: See St. Peter's River.

Miró, Esteban Rodriguez, Governor-General of Louisiana: construction of forts suggested, 386n; describes Missouri valley, 72-74; full contents of *informe* to Alange noted, 157n; *informe* (extract) to Alange relative to political state of Louisiana, 157-159; letter from Cruzat cited, 72n; letters from inhabitants of Ste. Geneviève cited, 134n; letter from Oro cited, 72n; letters from Pérez, 128-130, 134-135, 143-144, 145-146, 149-150; letters from Pérez cited, 134n, 146n; letters from Pérez and

Vallière cited, 73n; letter (draft) to Belêtre cited, 146n; letter to Cruzat cited, 72n; letter (extract) to Pérez, with citation, 130n; letters to Pérez cited, 146n, 149n, 144n-145n; letter to Rengel, 119-127; letter to Rengel cited, 74n; Pérez says Osages respect Miró, 144; report to King, on New Orleans fire, cited, 129n; suggests measures to preserve and strengthen Louisiana, 157n; warns against English and American traders, 72.

Missionaries: 22n-23n; 25n; Indians ask for, 22. See also Clergymen, Chaplains, Priests.

Missions: along or near the Missouri, 6-7; Jesuit missions needed by France, to keep Spaniards off the Missouri, 14.

Missisourie: that's the way Cuthbert Grant spells it, 460.

Mississippi, frigate: 472.

Mississippi Indians: 73n.

Mississippi River: 2; 53; 131n; 158; 254; 383; 383n; 385; 391; 395; 400; 413; 424n; 436; boundary treaty will restrict navigation, 747; commercial competition expected on upper river, 425; English and Americans to be denied permits to cross, 152; English from Michilimackinac trade on, 162; lands beyond, unknown in 1700, 7; latitude of mouth, 120, 684; line of demarcation, in boundary settlement, will cut, 747; list of posts to which English traders come, 180; routes to, via five rivers, 154n; source, 15, 58, 669, 684; sources of information on discovery cited, 4n; Spain must not yield one foot of west bank, 756, 757; tributaries, 56.

Mississippi River valley: documentary material cited, 129n; *mémoire* listing Indian nations cited, 8n; officials seek military defense and patrol of Spanish possessions, 109; source material for history of, cited, 83n; sources of information cited, 4n.

Missouri: meaning of word, 6.

Le *Missouri,* boat: 467.

Missouri Company: 83; 89; 96; 97; 100; 102; 105; 109n; 211; 212; 217; 302; 304; 315; 321; 335; 357; 380; 387; 391; 402; 403; 413; 419; 420; 421; 428; 433; 472; 473; 476; 480; 503; 557; 579; activities among tribes on the Missouri, 109; Articles of Incorporation, 219-224; Articles cited, 86n; authorized and licensed, 193-194; Carondelet approves the incorporation, 86; Carondelet urges the formation and approves the creation, 398, 748; Clamorgan and Loisel acquire all shares, 558; Clamorgan petitions for reformation of Company, 553; concessions to, on recommendation of Carondelet, 437, 438; construction of forts, 426; difficulties, 505, 541; expeditions: first, 87-91, 87n, [Journal] 259-294, 294-311, 328, 527, 539-540; second, 91-92, 328, 328n, 374; third, 93-94, 95, 96-98, 102-103, 351n, 356-364, 519, 528, 540; expenses and losses, 565; fate of expeditions, 441-442, 527-528; financial and other difficulties, 619ff; formation, 84-87; granted exclusive trade privileges, 398; guns belonging to Company held by Poncas, without payment, 89; heavy expenses, 422-423; membership cited, 86n; list, 225, 226, 541; obstacles met in expeditions, 381, 399, 434, 539-540; price for a share, paid by Durocher, 574; profit motive, 108; regulations and supplementary regulations, 186-190, 190-193, 445-450, 453-459; report of expeditions, 335-340; shares bought by A. Todd, through agent, 573-574; St. Louis merchants seek to form company with exclusive trade privileges, 85; Todd's death a blow, 482; Trudeau to collect accounts due, 554-555. For earlier names used to designate the Company, see the entry under Company of the Missouri.

Missouri Indians (Misuris): 5; 10; 11; 12; 18; 26; 27n; 34; 44; 45; 46; 48; 50; 51; 55; 65; 66; 70; 71; 72; 112; 445; 453; 454; 565; called "people of the canoes", 6; complaints against traders, 34; contacts with, cited, 43n; estimate of annual value of merchandise, 759; estimate of number, 34, 760; friendly to French, 17; habitat and number, 52, 125; Iberville lists, 8, 8n; known when French made first settlement, 747; mission to them not safe, after abandonment of Fort Orléans, 22; nations noted by Piernas, 59; Osages steal merchandise intended for, 149; receive presents annually, 120; their trade allowed to Ste. Geneviève commandant, 135; used, to fall upon Foxes, 23, 25n, 26n; Vasquez granted trade for one year, 592; young princess goes to France, and is baptized at Notre Dame, 21-22.

Missouri River (Messouri, Misuri, Missoury): 17; 18; 20; 47; 48; 78; 125; 126; 158; 254; 383; 383n; 384; 385; 391; 400; 401; 413; 424n; beginnings of exploration, 7; Beinville writes of branches, 16; called Rivière Blanche, 10; course, 10, 58, 120-121, 497, 498; discovery, 3; estimate of length, 57n; Evans to discover sources and passage to Pacific, 410; explored by Bourgmont, 12-13; importance, 9, 14; knowledge of, increasingly important, 77ff; legendary narratives, mentioned and cited, 4-5, 5n; maps, cited or mentioned, 10n, 88n, 107n, 111n, 142, 142n, 243n, 257n, 376n-377n, 485n, 520, 520n, 545, 545n, 563, 604, 612n, 700n, 719, 719n, 763, 764; maps shown, 415, 451; names, 3, 4n, 10, 49; navigability, 4n, 57n, 150n, 332; "of unquestioned preference" as route to the Pacific, 165; possible route to Vermillion Sea, 3; source, 6, 113, 120-121, 332, 410, 498, 620, 670-671, 684, 747; silver mines reported, 25; Spain believes confluence with Mississippi should belong to her, 726; Table of Distances, 485-490; tributaries, 56, 121-124, 261, 263, 265, 737-739; Truteau's "Description of the Upper Missouri" (extract), 376-382; "Description" cited, 90, 90n, 91, 91n, 93n, 110n, 111, 111n, 115n. See also Little Missouri River.

Missouri River, Lower: 434.

Missouri River, Upper: 23n; 178; 180; 430; English penetrate as far as Mahas, 134; silver mines reported, 25; trading activities, 110-114; Truteau's "Description of the Upper Missouri" (extract) 376-382.

Missouri River region: 1; 5; geographical information, 6, 73-74; information in early mémoires, 12; knowledge of, at close of French régime, 56-57; many posts essential to development, 59-60; more French settlements a prerequisite to exploration, 5n; report to Rengel on geography cited, 74n; Spanish penetration, 9; visit of Father St. Cosme, 5.

Missourias: location of village, description, and distance from the mouth of the Missouri, 487.

Misuris: See Missouri Indians.

Mitchell, N.: letter cited, 79n.

Mitchell, Thomas or Medad: 84n; 376n; autobiography and letter to Alexander Hamilton cited, 79n; letter of Las Casas about him cited, 79n; letter to Hamilton cited, 150n-151n.

Moami River: 141.

Mobile: 18; 682.

Moccasins: 298.

Moingona River: See Des Moines River.

Moncach-Apé ——: searching for Western Sea, 33n.

Moncharvaux, Captain de: served on the Missouri, in 1757, 50.

Monchauvaix, Jean Baptiste: cadet soldier on the Missouri, 50.

Mongona River: See Des Moines River.

Mongrain, half-breed: Osage relatives avenge his murder by Loups, 173.

Mongrain, Baptiste: given license to trade on the Missouri, 162.

Mongrain, N.: position in Indian Department, residence, and annual salary, 771.

Mongrain, MM., and Co.: 524.

Monin, David: killed by Sioux, 94.

Monino y Redondo, José de: See Floridablanca, Conde de.

La Montagne des Roches: See Rocky Mountain.

La Montaña de Peñas: See Mountain of Cliffs.

La Montaña que Canta: 121.

Montañas Blancas: See Rocky Mountains.

Montañas Relucientes: See Rocky Mountains.

Montarco, Conde de: 506; letter to Carondelet, 402-403; letters to Carondelet, Gardoqui, and the *Ministerio de Hacienda* cited, 402n; letter to Prince of Peace cited, 437n; returns documents and "topographical plan" sent him by the Prince of Peace, 402n; summary [believed prepared by Montarco for the Council of State] of methods proposed by Carondelet to suppress contraband trade, 398-402.

Montardy, Pedro (Motardi): 235 [Montard]; 284; 352; given license to trade on the Missouri, 162.

Montbrun's Cave: description, and distance up the Missouri, 486.

Montigny, Father Dumont de: 6-7; 59.

Montreal: 32; 133n; 177; 178; 180; 331; 333; 341; 388; 390; 396; 399; 407; 409; 434; 490; 682.

Monument: erected by Perrin du Lac, 711.

Morales, Juan Ventura, Intendant of Louisiana: 504; 505; 674n; decree mentioned, 471n; letter from Álverez cited, 614; letter from Carondelet, 426; letter from Carondelet, enclosing Clamorgan *mémoires,* 470-472; letter (extract) from Carondelet concerning pay of militia, 457n; letter from Carondelet cited, 430n; letter from De Lassus, 675-677; letter (draft) from Gayoso de Lemos [?] cited, 554; letter to Carondelet, opposing financial support of militia, 473-474; letter to Carondelet cited, 472n; letter (extract) to De Lassus, with citation, 677n; letters to Gardoqui, 472-473, 480-481, 481-482, 483-484; letter to Gardoqui

cited, 470n; letter to M. Salcedo, 671; letter to C. Soler, 722; letter (draft) to Trudeau cited, 467n; letters to Varela y Ulloa cited, 512n; *mémoire* from Lisa, 667-668; opposition to maintenance of militia from royal treasury, 621.

Moreau River: description and distance from mouth of Missouri, 486.

Morgan, Mr., independent trader: killed by Sioux, 94.

Morgan: See Clamorgan.

Morières, *Sieur* de: 26; 26n.

Moro, Manuel Gonzalez, first sergeant, St. Louis: 333; 335; acts as witness, 330; letter to Armesto, 660-663, enclosing petition to Governor-General, 663-664; letter to De Lassus cited, 680n; letter from Lisa cited, 741n.

Morris, Robert: contributor to fund for proposed expedition, 167.

Morrison, William (Morrisson), wealthy merchant of Kaskaskia: 755; advances merchandise for explorers, 743; equips traders, 113, 113n.

Mortars: 345.

Motard, Joseph (Montan, Mostard; José): assignment and share of trade, 210.; Clamorgan seeks his deposition concerning Todd accounts, 573; deposition declaring sum paid for share and interest in Missouri Company, 576; deposition in regard to sale of Missouri Company share, 575; member of Missouri Company, 225, 226; on list and *mémoires* of individuals against exclusive trade, 645, 646, 650, 650n; one of those interested in founding exploring company, 194, 218; purchases share in Missouri Company as agent, 574; signs power of attorney for Lisa, 667.

Motilones Indians: See Pelé Indians.

Motte, M. de la: 15.

Mt. Vernon: 707n.

Mountain of Rock (Montaña de Penas): See Rocky Mountain.

Mountains: 78; 113; 124; 165; of New Mexico project into Upper Louisiana,

14; Spanish mines located there, 14. See also Rocky Mountains.

Mountains of the Black Rock (Roca Negra): See Rocky Mountains.

Mourelle, Antonio Francisco (Maurelle): 713, 713n.

Mouse River: See Souris River.

Muddy River: description and distance from mouth of the Missouri, 486.

Mules: 29; 492; Du Tisné receives a mule in trade, 19.

Munié, Munier: See Meunier.

Munitaries: See Manitouris Indians.

Munitions: 144n-145n; 171; 172; 172n; 264; 305; 332; 334. See also Guns; Gunpowder.

Murray, Major: letter to Dorchester, concerning De Bon, cited, 133n.

Muskets: 358.

Mysterious stranger: See Stranger, Mysterious.

Nachitoches Indians: See Natchitoches Indians.

Nación Ayoas: See Iowa Indians.

Nasseniboine Indians: See Assiniboine Indians.

Nasseniboine River: See Assiniboine River.

Natchez: 11; 586; 685.

Natchez Indians: French get aid from Arkansas, in war with them, 54.

Natchitoches (Nachitoches): 12n; 19; 62; 63; 120; 172n; 325; 354; 439; 584; 726; 743n; 746; founded by St. Denis, 17; French claim to have established, 15; soldiers needed to defend, 24.

Natchitoches Indians: 346; 365; exclusive trade with, sought, 458n; habitat, 120.

Natchitoches River (San Francisco de Natchitoches): 749.

Naugy, Morrest, Ponca chief: 290.

Nava, Pedro de, Commandant-General, Western Interior Provinces: letter from

Fernando de la Concha, 146-148; letter to Alcudia cited, 355n.

Navajo Indians: punished for barbarity, 734, 734n.

Navarro, Martin: report on New Orleans fire cited, 129n.

Navigation: Article 3, Jay's treaty, allows freedom to both Americans and Spanish, 396; decrease in duties will increase Spanish, 394.

Negroes: 345; 366; 656; 696.

Nelson River, formerly York: 385; 738.

Nemaha rivers: See Great Nemaha, Little Nemaha River.

Nementao River: See Mermentao River.

Neve, Felipe de, Commandant-General, Interior Provinces, and Governor of the Californias: requests account of Missouri valley, 73; wants information about Indian nations, 119, 119n.

New Bourbon: 214; 534; 536; location and description, 535.

New France: dependence of Illinois upon, 51n; documentary history and description cited, 10n; documentary material cited, 4n.

New Kingdom of Mexico: See New Mexico.

New Madrid: 172; 172n; 256; 317; 319; 324; 343; 345; 349; 367; 441; 674; estimate of amount spent for provisions and Indian presents at, 768; Indian commissioner necessary, 767; necessity of sub-agent of Indian affairs, 770; Peyroux made Commandant, 674. See also Ansa à la Grasa.

New Mexico (New Kingdom of Mexico): 2; 7; 8; 8n; 14; 42n; 70; 73; 76; 120; 124; 171n; 325; 379; 385; 395; 583; 620; 652; 684; 698; 726; 730; 737; 738; 739; 756; 769; Americans seek a boundary passing through, 755; belief Missouri flows to, 10; expedition to, proposed, 355; French traders reach, 27-28, 42; mineral wealth, 37; river routes to, 113, 114; route sought by Canadians, 16; Spanish claim no silver found, 9; Spanish fear British encroachment, 78; 79; 80; 113.

New Orleans: 20; 21; 24; 29; 40; 63; 64; 129; 133n; 144; 344; 408; location, 120.

New Orleans *Gazette:* published account of Meriwether Lewis expedition, 761-763.

New Orleans Island: in boundary settlement, Spain hopes to retain possession, 757.

New Spain: Little Osages border on, 120; mixed motives lead Spaniards to protect, 2-3.

Niagara Falls: 133n.

Niobrara River (Rivière Qui Court, Río Que Corre, River-that-runs): 3; 71; 73; 74; 124; 126; 265; 378; 384; 710; 738; home of Ponca tribe, 81-82; source and course, 123.

Nipigon trading post: La Vérendrye appointed commandant, 31.

Nishnabotna River (Nichenanbatoné): 123; 263; description, navigability, and distance from the mouth of the Missouri, 488.

Nixon, Mr.: contributor to fund for proposed exploration, 167.

Nodaway River: navigability and distance from mouth of Missouri, 488.

Nogales Fort (Walnut Hill): 697.

Nolan, Philip: 732; his horse-trading ventures, 732n.

Nonbonbechie (Le Mangeur de Canards): *patente* of first medal requested for, 327.

Nootka Sound: 165; 337; 385; 386; 388; 390; 395; 399; 424n; 434; 585; 683; Spanish intention to dislodge English, 443.

Nootka Sound controversy: 3; 77; 79; 133n.

North Company: See Northwest Company.

North Platte River, 590n; 591n.

North Sea: 424n.

Northwest coast: 77; explorers on the Missouri to continue to, 715.

Northwest Company (Company of the North): 3; 76; 95; 102; 114; 161n; 331; 389; 399; 434; 460; 764; activities a threat to Spain, 3, 620; Indians near head waters of Missouri have trade with, 762; location of post, 103; rivalry with Hudson's Bay Company, 95n, 104; trade with Mandans, 94; volume of commerce of two English companies, now united in one, 178.

Northwest passage: attempts to find, 713.

Northwest Territory: its importance in diplomatic relations, 79; treasurer, is Armstrong, 136n.

Notary public: St. Louis needs one, 544.

Noy, Charles: signs power of attorney for Lisa, 667.

Oak trees; plentiful in Louisiana, 683.

Oarsmen: 389; 399; to each canoe, 177, 178.

Ochanya Indians (Ochania): habitat, 120.

Ockendanne Indians: wandering nation, seen by Loisel, 739.

Oconona Indians [Sioux]: 379.

Octoctata Indians: See Oto Indians.

Octohues Indians: 747.

Oeil de Fer: distance of this "large hill upon the southern bank" from the mouth of the Missouri, 489.

Officers and troops, Louisiana: list cited, 42n; salaries, 50.

Ogapá Indians [Arkansas]: habitat, 120.

Ohio: 542; 543.

Ohio River (La Belle Rivière): 8; 139; 140; 141; 158; 232; 233; 321; 367; 383n; 385; 391; 394; 400; 401; 408; 435; 436; 440; 534; 652; 683.

Oil cloth: used for letter pouch and tent, 140.

Oklahoma: Du Tisné reaches a Panis village, 19; Panis-Noirs raided, 19.

Omadi, Nebraska: 98; 352n.

Omaha, Nebraska: Oto village near the site of, 48.

Omaha Indians (Otomies, Mahas): 71;
72; 88; 89; 97; 98; 99; 109; 111; 112;
180; 198; 206; 213; 248; 249; 250;
260; 262; 263; 264; 265; 284; 286;
289; 290; 291; 292; 293; 302; 322;
326; 351; 352; 362; 363; 370; 374;
378; 384; 388; 388n; 389; 390; 399;
416n; 418; 424; 425; 426; 430; 431;
434; 441; 442; 448; 456; 478; 494;
495; 497; 498; 517; 520; 528; 540;
541; 559; 565; 567; 600; 611; 614;
635; 643; 644; 673n; 710; amount of
merchandise assigned for, 209; can be
attracted to St. Louis, 770; Englishmen
trade with, 145; estimate of annual
value of merchandise for, 759; estimate of population, 760; experience
of Company expeditions in relation to,
608ff; habitat, number of warriors,
value of merchandise received and of
skins sold, 694; Iberville lists, 8n; located on Clamorgan map, 451; location and number, 52, 539; location of
village, and distance from mouth of
the Missouri, 489; medals requested for,
327; Missouri Company given exclusive trade, 539; number of men using
arms, and amount of trade, 706n; portions of trade for, and shares to traders,
210, 211; prevent passage of Missouri
Company traders, 634; Robidoux seeks
exclusive trade, 599n; Sanguinet petitions for exclusive trade, 631; shares
of trade to, with value, 530; Spaniards
trade with, 79; subsidized by the English, this nation shows hostility to Company traders, 633; to be punished for
bad behavior, 541; trade granted to
Clamorgan, 591, 622, 628; trade
granted to Mackay, 591, 605; trade
granted to Pratte, 135; trade granted
to St. Cyr and Sanguinet, 591; traders
to be quarantined because of smallpox, 631.

Omaha River: 710; distance from mouth
of the Missouri, 489.

Oncpapa Indians: See Hunkpapa Indians.

Onepik Lake: See Lake Winnipeg.

Opelousas post and district: 63; 746.

Opelousa Indians (Opelouses, Opeluzás):
de Rassac recommends a post among,
59; habitat, 120.

Opuchigie (La Bombarde): *patente* of
first medal requested for, 327.

Ordinance of 1787: 366n.

Ordway, Sergeant: Journal cited, 110n.

Oregon River: 165.

O'Reilly, Alexandro, Conde de (O'-
Reylly) Lieutenant-General, Louisiana:
70; 70n; orders presents to go to many
tribes, 120.

Oro, Antonio de: 72; letters cited, 72n;
Peyroux succeeds, as Commandant,
Ste. Geneviève, 598n.

Ortiz José: See Hortiz, Joseph.

Osage fort: letter, Moro to De Lassus,
summarizing difficulties, cited, 680n;
Lisa and friends offer to maintain, 679,
688.

Osage Indians (Great Os, Ozages, Grands
Eaux): 4n; 6; 11; 22; 29; 42; 43; 45;
47; 48; 50; 55; 60; 65; 66; 67; 70;
71; 80; 110; 122; 125; 132; 134; 143;
158; 257n; 318; 319; 321; 344; 350;
365; 384; 421n; 426; 430; 458n; 558;
584; 640; 673n; 705; amount of merchandise assigned for, 209; attacked by
Loups, 173; ban on trade partially
lifted, 156-157; boat fired on by Sauks,
741, 741n; Bourgmont lives among
and writes about them, 13; characteris-
tic behavior, 26; commissions and gorget requested for, 326-327; commit
murders, 25-27; concession of trade,
to commandants, as extra pay, 544;
continue vengeful because traders denied them, 149-150; correspondence relating to, cited, 134n; document conceding trade to Lisa and others, 687-
689; effects of interdiction of trade
with, 183, 184; estimate of annual value
of merchandise for, 759; estimates of
number, 34, 124, 760; exclusive trade
requested by Lisa and others, 678, 680;
finally and fully subdued through activity of A. Chouteau, 145n; French
had a post among, 748; French traders
exchange arms for furs and slaves, 19;

friendly to French, 17; habitat, 486; habitat, number of warriors, value of merchandise received and of skins sold, 694; history of trade cited, 680n; intercept traders on the Missouri, 159; location and number, 51; number of men in both villages, 539; number of men using arms and amount of trade, 706n; number of warriors, 172; one Osage goes to Paris, 21-22; order received from Governor-general banning trade with all Osages, 133, 144n-145n; party threatens vengeance for prohibition of trade, 144; perfidy mentioned, 143; pillage a caravan carrying silver, 744-745, 756; plans for war against, 171-173; portion of trade to, with total value, 530; portions of trade for, and shares for traders, 210; reaction to prohibition of trade with them, 154; receive annual presents, 120; remarks expressing pride in fort, 320; restrained in piracies by A. Chouteau, 538; rob and pillage, 345-346; salary paid interpreter, 771; savages complain of forays by, 168n; Shawnees and Loups declare war on, 526; suspicions of Fabry de la Bruyère, 30; their *manitou*, 50n; trade for five years granted Lisa and others, 592; trading license issued to A. Chouteau, 590-591, 605, 623, 628, 662; treachery, 19, 20; Trudeau urged to restrain them, 151; Trudeau letter reporting difficulties, and plans for war against them, 197-203; two in irons for murders, 520-521; Vaudreuil's relations with, approved, 50n; villages united by Du Tisné, 18.

Osage Indians, Little: 47; 51; 60; 66; 71; 72; 171; 201; 257n; 321; 426; 430; 558; 747; accused by Great Osages of their own deeds, 156; amount of merchandise assigned, and estimate of annual value, 759; ban on trade with, 133, 134, 134n; habitat and number, 57, 120, 124-125, 486, 487, 694, 760; kill and rob, 173; kill Frenchmen, 44, 48; letter, Trudeau to Carondelet, about theft of horses, 167-169; portions of trade for, and shares of traders, 210; receive pres-

ents annually, 120; salary paid interpreter, 771; shares of trade, with total value, 530; Shawnees and Loups declare war on, 526; trade for five years requested by Lisa and others, 678, 680; trade contract granted A. Chouteau, 590-591, 605; trade contract granted Lisa and others, 592; value of merchandise received and of skins sold, 694.

Osage River (River of the Grand, or Great Osages): 7; 18; 51; 70; 122; 260; 707; description, navigability and distance up the Missouri, 486; distance up the Missouri mentioned in Hubert *mémoire*, 12; navigability, 214; noted on Vermale and Le Maire maps, 13, 13n.

Osibedocá (Le foulier Monillé): gorget requested for, 327.

Osmoboines River: See Assiniboine River.

Osniboine, Asseniboine Indians: See Assiniboine Indians.

Otamoroas Indians: Iberville lists, 8n.

Otave Indians: See Ottawa Indians.

Othochita, Othocatatas: See Oto Indians.

Oto Indians (Athochtata, Attotactoes, Autocdatás, Hotas, Hotos, Octoctata, Octotata, Othochita, Othos, Otoctatas, Otoctotas, Otoe, Otoktata, Otos, Ototatoes, Ottos, Toctata): 6; 8; 16; 23; 27n; 59; 66; 67; 70; 71; 72; 73; 74; 96; 109; 112; 211; 215; 249; 262; 263; 264; 289; 322; 323; 326; 338; 349; 351; 352; 353; 356; 357; 370; 374; 384; 389; 390; 399; 418; 422; 425; 426; 428; 430; 434; 445; 451; 453; 454; 477; 478; 520; 559; 565; 567; 600; 611; 629n; 709; amount of merchandise assigned for, and shares to traders, 210; distance of old village from the Missouri, 489; experience of Missouri Company expedition in relation to, 608ff; friends of Missouris, 52; habitat, number, amount and value of merchandise, 52, 125-126, 494, 539, 694, 706n, 759, 760; kill two Frenchmen, 35; location of first fort, and distance

825

from mouth of Missouri, 489; medals and gorget requested for, 327; Missouri Company deprived of trade, 635; Missouri Company expedition to, as revealed by Derouin, 516-517; Missouri Company given trade, 531; Missouri Company traders among Mahas forced to withdraw to, 633; needs supplied by Missouri Company, 596; receive presents annually, 120; shares of trade for, with value, 530; to have no merchandise for a year, 541; trade granted Chauvin and Ortiz, 591, 605; trade granted Clamorgan, 591, 622, 628; trade granted Collell, 135; trade granted Cruzat, 617, 617n; trade granted to G. Sarpy and Cabanné, 592; trade sought by Clamorgan, 634; trade sought by Robidoux, 593; trade with English, 80, 145; traders to be quarantined because of smallpox, 631.

Oto village (Octoctata) : 351; 352.

Otoctatas, Otoctotas, Otoe, Otoktatoes: See Oto Indians.

Otomies: See Omaha Indians.

Otos, Ototata Indians: See Oto Indians.

Otouy, a village of the Arkansas: location, 120.

Ottawa Indians (Autawa, Otave, Otovoa, Outacuagas) : among nations receiving provisions and presents from Spanish, 769; English canoes carrying goods to them have winter locations on Lake Michigan, 180; habitat, number of warriors, and value of trade, 694.

Otter: 73; 125; 261; 264; 266; 283; 301; 322; 378; 379; 380; 412; 538; in exchange for guns, 262; plentiful on Hay River, 498.

Otter River: description and distance up the Missouri, 486.

Ottos: See Oto Indians.

Ouabache River: See Wabash River.

Ouachita River: 120; 684; 750.

Ouanipik lake: See Lake Winnipeg.

Ouify [Ouisay] village: 304.

Ouisy Indians [Cheyenne] : habitat, 379.

"Oumissouries": 3.

Ounipique Lake: See Lake Winnipeg.

Oupas [?] River: England establishes posts on, 669.

Outacuagas: See Ottawa Indians.

Outagamis: See Fox Indians.

Outcasts: Carondelet warns against, especially American or English, 151.

Outlas, M.: given trade contract, conditionally, 24.

Outlaws, French: Brindamoor, 20n.

Ox skins: desired by Clamorgan, 249.

Oxen, Wild: 310; 311; herds make nomads of the Sioux and the Sauteux, 693.

Paca [animal] : 165.

Pacana Indians: habitat, 120.

Pacific Ocean (Bay of the West, Pacific Sea) : 99; 121; 165; 166; 316; 336; 337; 364; 412; 413; 417n; 422; 424; 445; 461; 462; 491; 493; 515; 562; 563; 582; 585; 593; 618; 620; 682; 702; 713; 761; 763; 764; 765; Charlevoix estimates distance from Sioux to the ocean, 23n; discovery the object of expedition of M. Lewis, 720; Evans instructed to penetrate to, 410, 495; Michaux, also, 164; rumored that Lewis plan for discovery is just a pretext, 745. See also California, Sea of; South Sea; Western Sea.

Padodos Indians: estimate of population, 760.

Padós Indians [Comanches] : formerly numerous, reduced by wars to four small, wandering groups, 127; habitat, 301; number of warriors, 127.

Pados River: 126.

Padou Indians: habitat, 384.

Padouca Indians, later called Comanche: 18; 70; 72; 228; 490; Bourgmont parties seek alliance, important to France, 20-21; chief agrees to peaceful relations, 21; estimate of number, 58; relations with French, 16-23; sell slaves to Foxes, 17. See also Commanche Indians.

Pájaro Negro: See Black Bird.

Panana Indians: See Pawnee Indians.

Panas Indians: Iberville lists, 8n.

Pani Blanc: See Pawnee Indians.

Pani-Picqué Indians: 45; continually warred on by Big Osages, 44; savages on the road to Santa Fé, 60. See also Panis-Piqués.

Paniguacey (Eyes of the Partridge): See Pawnee Indians, Republican.

Panimacha Indians: 71n.

Panimaha Indians (Pani-Maha, Panimahás, Panis-Maha, Panismaha): 6; 8; 16; 45n; 66; 70; 71n; 72; 263; 296; 299; 384; called black, 747; friendly to French, 17; habitat and number, 52, 126; habitat, number of warriors, value of trade, 694; kill a Frenchman, 35; lose slaves in raids, 19; Salcedo thinks their friendship worth winning, 749; trade granted to B. Vasquez, 135. See also Loup Indians.

Panis Indians: See Pawnee Indians.

Panis Blancs Indians: See Pawnee Indians.

Panis Bon Chef Indians [Pawnee]: 112; amount of merchandise assigned for, 209; annual division of trade, and value, 530, 531; portion of trade for, and share to trader, 210, 211; trade contract granted Chauvin, 592.

Panis Loups: annual share of trade, with value, 530, 431; Clamorgan petitions for trade, and gets it, 635.

Panis-Noirs Indians (Panimai): 59; aided by Laytanes, at war with Osages, 44; Osages say they are allies of Foxes, 45; raided, for horses, 19; raided in Oklahoma, move to Kansas, 20.

Panis-Ouasas Indians (Paniouassas): Du Tisné tries to visit, via Missouri, 18; French purchase horses from, 16.

Panis Picotés Indians: habitat, according to Toscan, 72.

Panis Piqués Indians: Vilemont said they were savages on the road to Santa Fé, 60.

Panis Republican, Panis République: See Pawnee Indians, Republican.

Panis Ricaras Indians: 306; number and divisions, 299-303; their character, as observed by Truteau, 296-299.

Panis Tapage (Pani-Topage) [Pawnee]: amount of merchandise assigned for, 209; portion of trade, and share to trader, 210, 211; share of trade, with value, 530, 531; traders licensed by Ríu, 66.

Panisses: See Pawnee Indians.

Panton, Guillermo: 393; 400; 509; privileges accorded his company, 436.

Papin, Jean: among those interested in formation of Company of Discoveries, and present at organization, 194, 218; assignment and share of trade, 210.

Parlamentarios: 372; 373.

Parques River: Truteau camped there, one July day, 261.

Partnerships: Articles of Agreement, Loisel and Heney, 636-638; Meunier and Rolland, contract, 238-239; cited, 82n.

Paruananinuco Indians: 146-147.

Passports: 160; 189; 323; 324; 370; 509; 529; 530; 541; 611; 614; 704; De Lassus pleads for revenue, 606; fee, 368, 526; M. Lewis presents two, 720, 720n; number, with charges, six years, 532; to be denied to English and Americans, 151; Trudeau deprived of revenue from fees, 527, 544.

Pataka Indians: 60.

Patentes [commissions, letters patent]: 185; 257n; 305; 309; 325-327; 359; 420n; 426; 430; 611.

Patuca Indians: See Padouca Indians.

Pauxblanche, chief of Sauks: 741.

Pawnee confederacy: 71n.

Pawnee Hocá Indians (Pawnee Ocá): 332; 334; 389; habitat, 331.

Pawnee House: See Ponca House.

Pawnee Indians (Panis, Panisses): 6; 8; 33; 42; 48; 66; 71; 72; 73; 112; 125; 180; 198; 228; 264; 306; 321;

329; 330; 357; 364; 384; 425; 431n; 439; 453; 454; 500n; 502; 643; 644; 669; 673n; 690; 709; 710; 743; 747; 756; can be attracted to St. Louis, 770; cataloged by La Salle, 4n; Comanches go against, 147; De Lassus shares trade, 591; deprived of trade, as punishment, 541; Du Tisné secures alliance, 19; Englishmen trade with, 145; habitat and number, 126, 148, 539, 694, 706n, 760; led by Villasur, 16; located on Clamorgan map, 451; Pratt and Clamorgan seek trade, 477-478, 471n, Pratte and Vasquez, 431n, 477n, 531n; Robidoux interested in trade, but Trudeau does not favor him, 593, 596-597; Sarpy and Cabanné offer to mediate, 614-616; trade granted by DeLassus, 591; trade granted Chauvin, 629-630, 705; trade gratned P. de Volsay, 135; trade sought by Clamorgan, and granted, 477-478, 477n, 634, 591; trade sought by Moro, 663-664; value of merchandise, 694, 759; Vasquez granted portion of trade, 547n, 591, 605, 628; villages, location and estimated number, 12, 58.

Pawnee Indians, Republican (Paniguacey, Republican): 71; 112; 123; 261; 673n; 709; amount and value of trade, 209, 706n, 759; attitude toward women, 258; habitat, 126, 384, 488; number, 126, 706n, 760; portion of trade and share for traders, 210-211; share of trade, with value, 530, 531; trade granted Bartélemy, 135; trade granted Bernal, 591; trade granted G. Sarpy, 622; village name and location, 123, 488.

Pawrangy (Les Beaux Cheveux): *patente* of first medal requested for him, 327.

Payeto, Cayetano: draft of letter from Las Casas [?] cited, 146n.

Paysá: 79; 151n; 164n; 230n; 602; Americans plan military post here, 595, 602.

Peace: 349; 372; 373; 408.

Peace of Amiens: See Treaty of Amiens.

Peace of Basle: 431n.

Peace of 1783: 348.

Peace-pipe: 196; 270; 412. See also Calumets.

Peale, ——: role in matter of financial Support to Michaux expedition, 167.

Peckans [pécans]: 36; 38; 371.

Pedrejosas Mountains: See Rocky Mountains.

Pekitanoüi River: name given the Missouri by early French explorers, 3, 6.

Pelé Indians (Pele) Motilones: 246; 325.

Pembina [North Dakota]: trail from, to Missouri, 94.

Pénicaut, André: narrative cited, 6n.

Pensacola (Pasachola): 157n; 474n; 509; 682; Bourgmont helps capture, 13.

Peoria Indians (Piorias): 43; 529; among nations receiving provisions and presents from Spanish, 769; English canoes winter among, 180; estimate of population, 760; salary paid interpreter, 771.

Peppermint: a bottle given to John Evans, 479.

Peran Indians: number of hunters, 707n.

Pérez, Manuel, Lieutenant-Governor of Spanish Illinois: 76; 78; 145n; 146n; 240; 386n; 687; letter from Carondelet, granting Meunier petition, 196; letter (extract) from Miró, 130; report to Carondelet, about Meunier, 195-196; letters to Miró, 128-130, 134-135, 143-146, 149-150, 153-155; letters to Miró cited, 78n, 80n, 134n; reports on English smuggling, 79, 80; reports to Miró, 72; succeeded by Z. Trudeau, 80; suggests forts at entrance of Des Moines and San Pedro Rivers, 146.

Pero, Duchêne: See Perrot, Duchêne.

Pérouse, J. F. G. de la: his "Voyage . . . autour de Monde" cited, 699n.

Perrault: See Perrot.

Perier, Governor: 22n; 24; 24n.

Perrin du Lac, François Marie: extracts from his "Voyages dans les Deux Amériques", 673n, 706-712; narrative cited, 111n; travel purpose and route, 706n, 707n; visits Upper Missouri, 111.

Perrot, Duchêne (Perrault): "Narrative" cited, 392n; petitions against trade abuses of English, 322, 322n.

Perrot, L'isle: See Île Perrot.

Petit, Solomon (Salomon): 88; 287; 290; 292; 293; 294.

Petit Arc, Omaha chief: 490, 710.

Petit Arc village: distance from mouth of Missouri, 490; distance from second river of the Sioux, 710.

Petit Calamec, on Lake Michigan: winter quarters for English traders to Otovoa, 180.

Petit fost [village or settlement?]: 180.

Petit Jean: killed by Little Otos, 35.

Petites Cotés village: 132.

Petits Eaux, Petits Os: See Osage Indians, Little.

Petizó Indians: 66.

Petujean: killed by Osages, 26.

Peyroux de la Coudrenière, Henri (Enrique): 317; 323; 719; 721n; 757n; biographical sketch, 598n; covets de Volsay post, 370; discontent with administration, 202; letter from Thomas Jefferson about Lewis undertaking, 721; letter to *Monsieur* cited, 79n.

Philadelphia: 99; 166; 171n; 349; 370; 720; 730.

Piankashaw Indians (Piankesaw): 46.

Piché, ——: on list and *mémoires* of individuals against exclusive trade, 645, 646, 651; signs power of attorney for Lisa, 667.

Pichon, L. A., French Chargé d'Affaires at Georgetown: issues passport to Meriwether Lewis, 720n.

Pickaxes: 272; 278.

Pieds Ganes [Piegan?]: wandering nation, 739.

Pieds Negros, les Pieds Noirs: See Blackfoot Indians.

Piepez, Juan Bautista: signs Lisa *mémoire* against exclusive trade, 650.

Piernas, Pedro, first Spanish Commandant of Upper Louisiana: 65; 72; attitude on exclusive trade, 626; reports on Indian nations, 59; reports on Missouri area, 70; reports to Unzaga cited, 59n, 70n.

Pike, Zebulon Montgomery: 113n; 749n.

Pinckney's Treaty (Treaty of Friendship, Boundaries and Navigation, Treaty of San Lorenzo el Real) 420n; 437; 438n; 473; 499n; 586n; date, 676; effects of terms, on Spanish territory, 439-440.

Pine Fort: 94.

Pine trees: 381.

Pirogues: 87; 90; 97; 149; 242; 260; 262; 264; 294; 351; 352; 357; 358; 378; 381; 741; with twelve rowers, 15.

Pistols: 332; 334; 497.

Pitacaricó Indians (Higados Duros): habitat, 127.

Pitapahotos (Pitapahata): 301; 304; 309; 379; habitat, 384.

Pitot, Citizen, a New Orleans merchant: makes a map, according to instructions to geographers of Louisiana, 700n.

Pittsburgh: on Perrin du Lac's travel route, 707n.

Plants: samples collected by Vilemont, 682.

Platte River (Rió Chato, Rivière Platte): 7; 12; 28; 52; 73; 77; 92; 97; 108; 112; 114; 123; 125; 126; 263; 275; 301; 351; 352; 353; 354; 355; 356; 357; 364; 376; 377; 379; 381; 384; 425; 439; 454; 488; 539; 709; 761; 763; Clamorgan petitions for exclusive trade, and gets it, 634, 672; indispensable passage for the Missouri Company, 478; longitude of mouth suggested as a trade boundary, 445; navigability and distance from mouth of Missouri, 489; source, 114; source and course, 737; Spaniards reach it, 71.

Plu, Indian unit of value: 708.

Plum River: distance from mouth of Missouri, 490.

La Pointe Basse de la Rivière au Se: See Salt River Bottom.

Pointe Coupée (Punta Cortada): 122; 373; insurrection of negroes here mentioned, 345.

Poisons: 283.

Polygamy among Indians: 257.

Pomme de requête: fancy name for prickly vegetation found on prairies, 277.

Ponca House (Pawnee House): 88n; Truteau's first wintering camp, 90.

Ponca Indian post: distance from mouth of Missouri, 490.

Ponca (Ponka) Indians: 82n; 88; 89; 92; 98; 99; 109; 112; 123; 193; 196; 206; 215; 235; 237; 238; 240; 241; 246; 247; 248; 249; 250; 259; 260; 262; 263; 266; 279; 280; 283; 287; 288; 289; 290; 292; 294; 302; 322; 326; 338; 349; 351; 353; 360; 362; 363; 370; 374; 378; 382; 384; 388; 388n; 389; 390; 399; 411; 416; 418; 426; 428; 430; 434; 437; 441; 494; 540; 559; 611n; 635; 643; 644; 669; 673n; 749; chief, 359; estimate of annual value of merchandise for, 759; experience of Company expeditions, in relation to, 608ff; habitat, number of warriors, population, amount and value of trade, 126, 694, 706n, 710, 760; location and characteristics, 126; location and distance of village from mouth of Missouri, 490; medals requested for, 327; Meunier petitions for exculsive trade, 194-195; Missouri Company given trade, 531; "nothing but Mahas who have left the tribe", 206, 212-213; prevent passage of Missouri Company traders, 634; their rascality, 293; rob Missouri Company expeditions, 527; rob Spanish of *pirogue* of merchandise, 372; Sanguinet petitions for trade, 630; Sanguinet to arrange for part year of Clamorgan's trade, 631; to be deprived of merchandise for a year, 541; to be quarantined because of smallpox, 631; trade contract given Sanguinet, 591; trade given Clamorgan, 622, 628; trade given Meunier, 81-82; trade given Yosti, 600n, 605; trade sought by Robidoux, 593, 596, 600.

Pondret, *voyageur:* incites Missouri villages against Foxes, 26n.

Pontiac, Ottawa chief: leads uprising, 75.

Population: 157n; 172; 197; 245; 344; change in import duties will increase, 394; increase desirable, 151, 171n, 542, 543, 686, 687; of eight villages on the Missouri, 161; of Spanish settlements, 535, 536, 537.

Porcupine: fringes of, for ox skins, 249.

Portage La Prairie: 32.

Portage of the Sioux (Le Portage des Sioux, San Ysidro de Los Sioux): 121; founding, 594n, 601n; letters, Trudeau to Saucier about establishment and command, 594-595, 602-603; quarantined against visitors because of smallpox in the district, 631; Saucier, founder, appointed Commandant, 601, 601n, 602.

Portages: 178; 413; 601n; 671; number and nature, for English traders, 177, 392, 491.

Portell, Thomas: 172; 204; 232; 328; 367; difficulties with Lorimier, 203; letters from and to Carondelet cited, 230n, 370n.

Portland, Duke of: letters from Lord Dorchester cited, 387n, 392n.

Portneuf, *Sieur* de: activities at Missouri post, 44, 46-48.

Potawatomi Indians (Pou, Poux, Pu, Pus, Pouteatamia, Pouwatoumis): Enlish canoes wintering among, 180; envoy brings assurance of friendship, 322; habitat, number of warriors, amount and value of merchandise exchanged, 694; savagery, 199; threaten Little Osages, 168.

Powder horn: See Horn, Powder.

Powder River: 110.

Powell, Ewing S.: contributor to fund for proposed exploration, 167.

Power, Thomas: appointed a member of the commission on boundaries, 765.

Power of attorney: given D. Clark, in Todd-Clamorgan affairs, 430, 569, 570; given John Hay, by A. Todd, 571-572; given M. Lisa to act in regard to exclusive trade, 661, 664, 665, 666, 667-

668; not legalized by De Lassus, 664-665.

Prairie du Chien trading post (Dog-field): 76; 81; 109n; 111; 180; 503; English gather Maha chiefs there, 633; principal rendezevous of Canadian merchants, 706.

Prairie of fire: See Fire Prairie.

Prairie St. Michael: description and distance from mouth of Missouri, 488.

Prairies: 124; 125; 264; 266; 276; 295; 377; 379; waiting to be plowed, 684.

Prat of Ste. Geneviève: See Pratte, Juan B.

Pratte, Bernardo: 597; 641; barters for trade, offering to erect a fort, 614n, 627n; granted trade on Des Moines River, 592, 592n; mémoire cited, 641n; petition for Panis trade, 431n, 477n, 531n.

Pratte, Juan Bautista (Prat), of Ste. Geneviève: 215; 367; assignment and share of trade, 210; given trade with Omahas, 134.

Pratz, Le Page du: See Le Page du Pratz, Antoine S.

Preneloupe, ——: 590n.

Presents to the Indians: 10; 15; 19; 20; 21; 22; 29; 37; 38; 40; 41; 43; 45; 65; 70; 73; 78; 90; 98; 99; 100; 101; 106; 108; 120; 130n; 132; 133; 140; 144n-145n; 157; 174; 185; 196; 197; 198; 249; 262; 271; 286; 308; 309; 328; 338; 359; 361; 362; 363; 412; 417n; 418; 423; 453; 454; 494; 495; 497; 516; 607-608; 633; 697; 701; 708; Anglo-Spanish competition in, 566, 768; Chouteau explains their usefulness, and estimates necessary expense, 768-769, 771; "foreigners" bribe savage nations, 736; from English at Michilimackinac, 81n; Laussat gathers information about amount and value, 701n; Pérez pleads for more merchandise to distribute, 129-130; range of yearly expenditure for purpose, by Spanish government, 768.

Presents to white men: fascinating gifts from McDonnell to Evans, 103, 479;

Sutherland to Evans, and Evans to Sutherland, 500, 501, 502.

Price control: 191; 312-313.

Price cutting: by English traders, 392, 398, 401, 407, 433, 436, 541.

Priests: 25n; 350; two paid by Congress. See also Chaplains; Clergymen; Missionaries.

Prieur, priest of St. Charles: on list and mémoires of individuals against exclusive trade, 645, 646.

Prieur, [Noel Antoine, Jean François, Antoine]: signs Lisa mémoire against exclusive trade, 651, 651n; signs power of attorney for Lisa, 667.

Prince of Peace (El Príncipe de la Paz): letter from Branciforte cited, 439n; letter from C. Calvo cited, 735n; letters from Carondelet, 354-356, 503-506, 507-512; letters from Carondelet cited, 355n 386n, 473n, 507n; letter from Cevallos, 765-766; letter from Montarco cited, 437n; letter to Cevallos, 766; letter to Montarco cited, 402n; report of Clamorgan and Reilhe forwarded by Carondelet, 335n. See also Godoy, Manuel de, and Alcudia, Duque de.

Prince of the Nations, Omaha chief: 418; special gift medal for, 420n.

Prisoners: 185; 197.

Pritchard, William, Philadelphia bookseller: 98n; 99.

Prizes and rewards: offered by Carondelet for discovery of the South Sea, 388, 388n, 398, 434, 452.

Profits in trade: allowable in Todd-Clamorgan agreement, 468; English have rich trade with "uncommon profits", 178, 179; Illinois trade regulation prohibits private profit, 191; Spanish trade, and profits, on lower Missouri dwindling, 83.

Promissory notes: D'Église to Clamorgan, 703-704, 744n; cited, 703n, 704n.

Property rights and title: suggested by Clamorgan, for Missouri Company, 448, 456-457.

Proulx, Basil (Basilio, Basille): 403n; on list and *mémoires* of individuals against exclusive trade, 645, 646, 651; signs power of attorney for Lisa, 667.

Proulx, Gabriel (Cabil): signs Lisa *mémoire* against exclusive trade, 651, 651n.

Provencher, Mr.: his boat carries the mail, 674.

Provincias Internas: See Interior Provinces.

Puankaska Indians: habitat, number of warriors, and value of trade, 694.

Puant Indians (Puantes, Puanti, Puants): English trade with, 81, 180; pounds of powder required for, 431.

Pujol, Juan Bautista, *fils* (Batiste): signs Lisa *mémoire* against exclusive trade, 650; signs power of attorney for Lisa, 667.

Punges: McDonnell sends Evans ½ doz, 479.

Puñita Cortada: See Pointe Coupée.

Pursley, James: reaches Santa Fé via Missouri, 113n.

Pus Indians: See Potawatomi Indians.

Quadra: See Bodega y Cuadra, Juan Francisco de la.

Quapaw Indians: See Arkansas Indians.

Qu'Appelle River (Catapoye, Catapoi, Catepoé, Catupe): 103; English dare to establish a post on, 669; furthermost western wintering spot of Canadain traders on this river, 96, 492; Joncquard spent some time there, 333, 334; river post the point of departure for Mackay, on journey to Mandans, 94.

Quarantine procedures: 631.

Quarries, Red stone: 52; 123; 378.

Quartel: construction and cost, 205, 205n.

Los *Quatro Hermanos,* barge: 467n.

Quebec: 232; 396; 682; a young Englishman left there with a compass, headed for Mexico, overland, 131; M. De Bon has great curiosity to see it, 133n.

Quebec, Bishop of: letter from St. Cosme cited, 5n.

Quebec, Mr.: 294; 295.

Quenel, Pierre (Quennell, Pedro): 235; 352; certified statement about Meunier, 241; given license to trade on Missouri, 162.

Quenneville, Mr. (Quenville): 262; 267.

Qui Court River: See Niobrara River.

Qui Parle River: See Cheyenne River.

Quiapou Indians: See Kickapoo Indians.

Quitsai Indians: See Kichai Indians.

Quivira: chain of mountains that starts east of Santa Fé goes to this province, 121; its lure is known to the French, 4n.

Radisson, Pierre Esprit: believed to have visted the Missouri, 4n.

Rainy Lake (Lake Lapluie): one of the lakes through which English traders pass, 491; post established by La Vérendrye, 32.

Rapid Indians (Rapides, Rápidos): Grandpré proposes exclusive trade contract for, 458n; habitat, 120.

Rapid River: distance from mouth of Missouri, 490; three miles below Ponca village, 710.

Rassac, Redon de: "Plan" for Louisiana, 59-60.

Rate of exchange: *piastres* vs. shillings, 467.

Records of observations: possible methods of keeping secret, 165-166.

Red-Bead Indians: habitat, 384.

Red People: 496.

Red River (Río Rojo, Vermillion, Colorado): 13; 14; 17; 56; 120; 365; 439; 684; 685; 726; 746; 761; 764; expedition to discover the source being sent by Americans, 749-750; expedition postponed, 753.

Red River [of the North] (Riviére Rouge, Colorado River): 94; 180; 382; 383; 500; 584; 585; 669; 738.

Redondo [Moñino y Redondo]: See Floridablanca, Conde de.

Reilhe, Antonio (Reylhe, Antoine): 87; 91-92, 218; 252; 311; 335-339; among those interested in organization of merchants for trade and discovery, 194; assignment and share of trade, 211; Clamorgan seeks his deposition concerning Todd accounts, 573; declines to take action against Clamorgan, 553n, 582, 582n; deposition as to sale and price of share in Missouri Company, 575-576; member of Missouri Company, 225; name on list and *mémoire* of individuals against exclusive trade, 644, 646, 650; petition, with Robidoux, against exclusive trade, 624-627; purchases share in Missouri Company, as agent, 574; signs power of attorney for Lisa, 667.

Relf, Richard: witness, 467; 468; 469.

Religion: 543; 696.

Rémonville, *Sieur* de: compares Missouri and Mississippi rivers, 8n.

Renard Indians, Renards: See Fox Indians.

Renaudot, ——: letter from Tonti cited, 4n.

Rendón, Francisco, Intendant of Louisiana: 391; 393; 394; 400; 401; decree granting petition for trade, 410; letter from Gardoqui cited, 402n; petition from A. Todd for trade contract, 407-410; petition from Todd, for reimbursement for goods confiscated cited, 404n; statement (in Minutes of the Council of State) that Carondelet and the Intendant had granted Todd a reduction in import duties, 435.

Rengel, Antonio, Commandant of the Interior Provinces: 77; 77n; letter from Miró, 119-127; letter from Miró cited, 74n.

Renombas (Les Deux Cornes): a captain's medal requested for, 326.

Republican Nation, Republican Pawnees: See Pawnee Indians, Republican.

Requeña, Francisco: member of Spanish committee, 727.

Revilla Gigedo, Juan Vicente Guemez Pacheco de Padilla Horcasitas, Conde de, Viceroy of Mexico: Concha writes of his warning not to provide escorts for buffalo hunts, 147.

Revolution of 1768; 204, 204n.

Reynal, Antonio (Antoine), surgeon: 588; name on list and *mémoire* of individuals against exclusive trade, 645, 646, 651; signs power of attorney for Lisa, 667.

Ribbon, Blue: as payment for favors Indian women bestow, 258.

Ricaras: See Arikara Indians.

Ricaras Pawnees: See Panis Ricaras Indians.

Ricarra, Richaare Indians: See Arikara Indians.

Rifles: gift from Sioux to Mahas, 517; theft of, 320; See also Carbines.

Riis, Rik, ka, ras Indians: See Arikara Indians.

Río Bravo del Norte: See Río Grande River.

Río Chato: See Platte River.

Río de Adaes: important in connection with boundary determination, 746.

Río del Norte: See Río Grande.

Río Grande (Río Bravo, Río del Norte, Brabo River): 78; 121; 123; 743; aspired to, by Americans, as boundary, 755; French activities extended to, 17; its mouth determines one end of a boundary claimed, 731.

Río Que Corre: See Niobrara River.

Río Que Habla: See Cheyenne River.

Río Rojo: See Red River.

Ripperdá, Baron de, Colonel: 743n; 749.

Ríu, Francisco, Captain: makes report on the known geography of the Missouri, 70; report cited, 70n; role as commandant beyond the Missouri, 65-66; unpublished manuscript cited, 65n.

River Bois Blanc: See James River.

River Chayennes: See Cheyenne River.

River de Cancés, or Cans: See Kansas River.

River de Lupas (Papas): See River de Papas.

River de Nimahá (River of the Great Nimahá, Nemahas): See Great Nemaha River.

River de Papas (Lupas) [Lobos, Wolves]: the Panimahas live up this river, and hunt from here to the Platte, 126.

River Gasconade: See Gasconade River.

River Jacques: See James River.

River La Bombe: 498.

River Niangá: 122.

River Nichenanbatoné: See Nishnabotna River.

River of Monigona: See Des Moines River.

River of Rocas Pagizas: See Yellowstone River.

River of the Bunch of Cherries: 379.

River of the *Chits:* 685.

River of the Frayles, of Friars: See Des Moines River.

River of the Grand, or Great, Osages: See Osage River.

River of the Great Nimahá (Nemahas): See Great Nemaha River.

River of the Little Nemaha: See Little Nemaha River.

River of the medicine bluff: See Rivière de la Côte de Médecine.

River of the Mine: See Mine River.

River of the old Englishman: See Rivière du vieux Anglais.

River of the Poncas: distance from the mouth of the Missouri, 490.

River of the Sioux (Sius): 123; source of first river, navigability, and distance from mouth of the Missouri, 489; same, for second river, 490.

River of the Split Rock: description and distance from the Mouth of the Missouri, 486.

River of the red stone: 378.

River of the Yellow Stone: See Yellowstone River.

River St. John: description, and distance up the Missouri, 486.

River San Francisco: 535.

River-that-runs (Rivière Qui Court, Río, Que Corre): See Niobrara River.

River White Wood (Bois Blanc): See James River.

Rivers: above mouth of Missouri, navigable rivers come from northwest, 686; great length, 699; in Louisiana, 683, 684; named and described in Truteau's narrative, 260ff, 378ff; seen by Loisel in voyage up the Missouri, 737-739.

Rivers of the boeufs: 684.

Rivière à la Barque: distance up the Missouri: 12.

Rivière à la Mine de Plomb: distance up the Missouri, 12.

Rivière au Portchicore: distance up the Missouri, according to Hubert, 12.

Rivière Bêtes Puantes [Skunk]: one of the rivers on which English canoes wintered, 180.

Rivière Blanche: English canoes winter here, among the Ottawas, 180. According to early accounts, the Missouri also was so described, 10.

Rivière de la Côte de Médecine (River of the medicine bluff): Loisel wishes land nearby, and promises to build a fort, 612.

Rivière de Roche Jaune: See Yellowstone River.

Rivière des Arcs [des Argues?]: See Arkansas River.

Rivière des Ayouas: See Iowa River.

Rivière des Grands Osages: See Osage River.

Rivière Des Moines (Des Moins): See Des Moines River.

Rivière des Panis: 12.

Rivière des Renards, Reynards: See Fox River.

Rivière des Sauteux: English canoes winter here, 180.

Rivière des Yllinois y los Pés: English canoes winter here, 180.

Rivière du Foin: See Hay River.

Rivière du vieux Anglais (River of the old Englishman, Vieux River?) : 490; 612.

Rivière Pekitanoüi : See Pekitanoüi.

Rivière Père Marquette (Mar Ket) : English canoes winter here, 180.

Rivière Platte: See Platte River.

Rivière Pomme de Terre: English canoes winter here, 180; English traders from here enter Spanish territory, 81.

Rivière Qu'Appelle: See Qu'Appelle River.

Rivière Qui Court (Río Que Corre) : See Niobrara River.

Rivière Qui Parle (Río Que Habla) : See Cheyenne River.

Rivière Saint Pierre (Sant Pierre) : See St. Peter's River.

Rivière Tremblante: 102n.

Rivière Tremblante Fort: the favorite residence of Cuthbert Grant, 102.

Rivoire, M.: writes against exclusive trade, 62, 62n.

Robbery: 158; 159; 173; 200; 202; 271; 272; 284; 288; 318; 391; punishment for, 173-174.

Robes: 463; 479; among D'Église's merchandise, 298; Sutherland wishes to trade buffalo robes, supposing them "not to be connected with the Fur Trade", 103, 462.

Robidoux, Joseph H. (Robidou), Lieutenant of militia: 82; 112; 113; 113n; 218; 235; 242; 528; 582n; 596; 600; 718n; assignment and share of trade, 210; attempt to get power of attorney fails, 647n; certifies that power of attorney document was presented to De Lassus, 667; letters to Gayoso de Lemos, 548-553, 592-594; letter to Gayoso cited, 647n; membership in Missouri Company, 225, 226; name on list and *mémoires* of individuals against exclusive trade, 644, 646, 650; note to Clamorgan, 718; petition to Gayoso de Lemos for cancellation of Clamorgan contract, 548-553; petition, with others, to C. Calvo, against exclusive trade,

624-627; refusal to appear against Clamorgan, 553n, 581-582; shows envy and jealousy of Clamorgan, 627n, 647n; signs Lisa power of attorney, 667; underhanded attacks on Clamorgan, 431-432.

Rocas Pagizas river: See Yellowstone River.

Rochay y Figueroa, Gerónimo de la: member Spanish committee, 727.

Le *Rocher:* post of Kansas to be transferred to, 41.

Roches Jaunes river: See Yellowstone River.

Rocky Mountain (La Montagne des Roches, La Montaña de Roca) : 332; 333; 335; 342.

Rock Mountains (La Cadena de Rocas, Montañas Relucientes, Shining Mountains, Montañas Blancas, White Mountains, Pedrejosas Mountains, Rocky Chain, Stony Mountains) : 55; 78; 87; 92; 97; 107; 121; 245; 295; 337; 338; 340; 344; 389; 399; 412; 416; 422; 434; 462; 491; 493; 494; 497; 498; 515; 585; Mackay's estimate of distance to ocean, 100.

Rolland (Roland) : 215; 315; claims loss caused by revoked license, 256; contract for partnership with Meunier cited, 194n; letters to Carondelet cited, 82n, 194n; partnership agreement, 238-239; petition to Carondelet, 237-238.

Rope factory: Clamorgan asks land for, 561n.

Ross, John: contributor to fund for proposed exploration, 167.

Rouillé, M.: letter from Duquesne cited, 49n; letter from La Jonquière cited, 45n; letter from Macarty discussed and cited, 49, 49n.

Rouin, Estevan de: given license to trade on the Missouri, 162.

Rouin, Quenache de: Trudeau reports he and his party were pillaged and beaten by Iowas, 316.

Rousseau, M.: 328; letter to De Luzières cited, 318n.

Roy, Antoine (Antonio): among those interested in organizing Company of Discoveries, 194; among those present at organization meeting, 218; assignment and share of trade, 210; given license to trade on the Missouri, 162.

Russian settlements: to the north of California, they say, 236, 413.

Russian threats to Spanish dominion; 3; 77; 388; 399.

Saavedra, Francisco de, first Secretary of State: index of and official letters sent by Gayoso de Lemos, 582-586; letter from Cornel cited, 614n; letter from Gayoso de Lemos cited, 108n.

Sabine River (San Francisco de Sabinas): 685; 750; no funds available for exploring mouth, 754; true boundary between Texas and Louisiana, 746.

Le *Sac de Médecine:* Oto chief, away visiting, 262.

Sac, Sacue Indians: See Sauk Indians.

Saddlecloths: 380.

Saddles: possession of Mexican saddles and bridles by the Mandans proves that they communicate with the Spaniards, 82, 161.

Sagan, Mathieu (Sagean): stories of the Missouri mentioned and cited, 5, 5n.

Sahaskawan River: See Saskatchewan River.

Sailors: See Oarsmen.

St. Andrews (San André du Missouri): 416n; 562n; 599; 603; 604; 614n; Mackay becomes Commandant, 108, 586; Mackay builds a road to St. Louis, 588; Mackay wants good, honest farmers, regardless of religion, 588n.

Saint-Ange de Bellerive, Louis: 25n; assumes control, St. Louis, 64; correspondence cited, 65n; lists Indian nations, 70; report cited, 70n; visits Padoucas, 21.

St. Anthony, Falls of: 741.

St. Barbe: mines in chain of mountains passed by French, 15-16.

St. Charles trading post: 132n; 163; 173; 185; 197; 260; 324; 350; 597n; 601; 742; Durocher lives there, 574; establishment of sub-agent for Indian affairs deemed necessary, 770; estimate of amount spent for provisions and presents to Indians, 768; horses stolen from, 160; in danger from savages, 201; Indian agents important, on route of Indian hunters, 767; location, 534; location and description, 485; Mr. Pratte a resident, 597.

Saint Cire: See St. Cyr.

St. Clair, Arthur, Major General, first Governor, Northwest Territory: 135; 201n; 348; 349; 349n; defeat by Indians, 80; letter to Harmar, 140; letter from Henry Knox, 138; letter to Knox, 139-140.

St. Claire, Jean Baptiste Benoît, *Sieur* de, Commandant at Illinois: 34; 42; 45; 47; learns of Indian treachery, 27; letter to Captain Raymond quoted, 44; letter to Salmon cited, 27n; report quoted, 43.

St. Clin, M. de: induces Illinois Indians not to listen to Big Osages, 45.

St. Cosme, Jean François Buisson de: 7n; letter cited, 5n; visits Missouri region, 5.

St. Cyr, Mme. Helena, wife of Jacinto: signs for her husband, member of Missouri Company, 226.

St. Cyr, Jacinto (St. Cire, St. Sire): among petitioners to Carondelet for freedom of trade, 184; among those interested in forming Company of Discoveries, 194; among those present at organization meeting, 218; assignment and share of trade, 211; given license to trade with Omahas, 591; membership in Missouri Company, 225, 226.

St. Denis, Louis Juchereau: founds Natchitoches, 17; seeks commerce with Spaniards, 18.

St. Ferdinand de Florissant (San Fernando de Florisanta): daylight slaughter here, 199; gossip about a priest, 215-216; location, 534; location and description, 536-537; population small and not increasing, 350; turns attention to agriculture, 214.

St. Francis River (San Francisco River) : 60n; 158; 535; 684.

St. James River: 490.

St. Joseph trading post (San Joseph) : 111; 180; 514; turned over to Americans, 515.

St. Joseph's Island: 515n.

St. Lawrence River: 683.

St. Lawrence River basin: French occupy, early seventeenth century, 2.

St. Louis (San Luis de Yllinois) : 70; 71; 73; 81; 95; 131n; 141; 158; 172; 330; 387; 388; 389; 414; 554; 711; becomes important post, 65; Carondelet report on, 254-256; distance from Santa Fé, 79n; establishment of mission, 6-7; former existence of Indian village on site established, 7n; founding, 63-64; garrison needs to be increased, 543; latitude, 684; letters and other accounts cited, 7n; location, 120, 534, 536; merchants complain about restrictions on trade, 181-184; merchants write sugestions to the Editor, 312-315; strategically located for trade, 1; Trudeau, commandant, 152.

St. Louis church: all inhabitants of St. Louis to be required to contribute money or labor, to build a church, 152.

St. Louis River (St. Lewis) : 384.

Saint-Michel, Archange: 10; 11n.

St. Peter's River (St. Pierre, San Pedro, Rivière Sant Pierre) : 63; 73; 81; 214; 254; 256; 301; 311; 359; 363; 364; 378; 382; 402; 402n; 430; 431; 554; 614n; 669; 681; 769; Carondelet proposes construction of a fort on it, with fifty armed men, 386; concerning desirability of forts on, 76, 78-79, 145, 386, 420, 443; expectation of competion in commerce on, 425; foreign traders penetrate Spanish territory by way of, 565, 566. Howard to arrange expedition to, 514; rendezvous for Canadian merchants, 706.

St. Pierre, M. de, Father: 373; 442; to be recalled, 324.

St. Pierre River: See St. Peter's River.

St. Sire: See St. Cyr.

Ste. Geneviève: 111; 131n; 133; 172; 199; 202; 214; 232; 319; 321; 324; 334; 367; 421; 467n; 526; 534; 536; a flood likely at, 521; Armstrong visits, 141; commandant given trade with Missouri, 135; establishment of sub-agent for Indian affairs deemed necessary, 770; estimate of amount spent for provisions and Indian presents, 768; important Illinois post, 64; inhabitants have horses stolen, 167; lead mines nearby, 683; letter from inhabitants to Miró, 134n; location, 120; location and description, 535; person commissioned to oversee Indians necessary at, 767; Peyroux appointed commandant, 598n.

Salcedo, Juan Manuel de, Colonel, Governor-General of Louisiana: 611n; Clamorgan petitions for trade on Kansas and Platte rivers, 632-634; concedes trade privileges to Lisa and others, 592, 689-690; letters from De Lassus, 673, 674-675, 705-706, 719-721; letters from De Lassus cited, 634n, 635n, 647n; letter from Morales on exclusive vs. free trade, 671; letter to Cevallos discussing boundary question, 745-750; letters to De Lassus, 640, 672; letter to De Lassus cited, 112n; letter, jointly with C. Calvo, to N. Salcedo, suggesting arrest of Meriwether Lewis, 731-732; many trades, above mouth of Kansas River, granted to Clamorgan, 112; mémoire of Lisa and others, petitioning for exclusive trade, 677-680.

Salcedo, Nemesio, Commandant of the Interior Provinces: 750; 752; dispatch on Texas-Louisiana boundary mentioned, 726; letter (draft), unsigned, to him about progress of Lewis expedition, 752-753; letter to C. Calvo, concerning Lewis expedition, 732-734; letter to Cevallos, with three enclosures, 729-731, 731-735; letter to Cevallos, suggesting Indians spy on Lewis expedition, 734-735; letter to M. Salcedo and

C. Calvo cited, 746n; letter to J. de Yturrigaray, 728-729.

Salcy Indians: wandering nation, 739.

Salle, Nicolas de la: writes about Missouri explorations, 9, 10; letters cited, 9n, 10n.

Salmon, ——, ordonnateur: 26; letter from Flancour cited, 34n; letter from St. Claire cited, 27n; letters to Governor of New Mexico and to Minister cited, 29n; writes to Governor of New Mexico about Fabry expedition, 29.

Salt: deposits, 537; factory of Clamorgan, 170, 170n, 372; mines, 459; springs, 122, 449.

Salt River Bottom (La Pointe Basse de la Rivière au Se): land in area granted to Saucier family, 602.

San André du Missouri (del Misuri): See St. Andrews.

San Bernardo Bay: See Bay of St. Louis.

San Carlos de Florisanta: Father Dunegant to be paid salary of Commandant, 537n.

San Carlos de las Pequeñas Cuestas: 143.

San Carlos del Missouri (Misuri, Misury): See St. Charles trading post.

San Fernando de Barrancas: See Écores à Margot.

San Fernando de Florisanta: See St. Ferdinand de Florissant.

San Francisco de Arkansas River: See Arkansas River.

San Francisco de Natchitoches River: See Natchitoches River.

San Francisco de Sabinas River: See Sabine River.

San Francisco River: See St. Francis River.

San Ildefonso: See Treaty of San Ildefonso.

San Joseph: See St. Joseph.

San Louis de Ylinueses: See St. Louis.

San Pedro River: See St. Peter's River.

San Vrain (St. Vrain), Santiago de, Captain of militia: ordered to cruise at entrance of Des Moines River, 613.

San Ysidro de los Sioux: See Portage of the Sioux.

Sanguinet, Charles: 72; 194; 218; 640; 674; 688n; 705; accorded trade contract with Big and Little Osages, 592; assignment and share of trade, 210; change of heart about exclusive trade indicated, 639; decree granting Maha trade to, 631; does not use contract, second year, 592; granted trade of Mahas and Poncas, 112; inconsistency on subject of exclusive trade, 643, 673; membership in Missouri Company, 225, 226; name on list and mémoire of individuals against exclusive trade, 644, 646; petition, with Robidoux, against exclusive trade, 624-627; petition to C. Calvo for exclusive trade with Poncas and Mahas, 630; petition, with Lisa and two others, for trade with Osages, 677-680; protests action of partners on contract drawn up in his absence, 680n; Salcedo rescinds his grant, 634n; Salcedo yields to his solicitations for Osage trade, 687-689; signs mémoire against exclusive trade, 650; signs power of attorney for Lisa, 667; to pay a share in note to Chouteau, 680n; to share with Lisa and others trade with Osages, 689-690.

Sans Peur, M.: killed by Panimahas, 35.

Santa Clara, Conde de: 582; 583; letters from Gayoso de Lemos cited, 370n, 587n.

Santa Fé, trading center, Spanish and Indian: 3; 17; 114; 329; 329n; 330; 354; 355; 385; 682; 698; 748, 748n; distance from St. Louis, 79n; French traders reach, 28, 42; Spanish expeditions from, early eighteenth century, 748, 748n; traders from Illinois penetrate to, 113; trail to St. Louis, 113n. See also New Mexico.

Santa Fé River: 489.

Santa Genoveva: See Ste. Geneviève.

Saone Indians (Saoñes): wandering nation, seen by Loisel, 739.

Saques, Saquias: See Sauk Indians.

Sardina, Juan, Captain: 755n.

Sargent, Major: 138.

Sarpy, Bernal (Beral): assignment and share of trade, 211; trade contracts granted, 591, 605.

Sarpy, Bernardo: 218.

Sarpy, De l'Or: 218.

Sarpy, Gregoire (Gregorio): among those interested in organizing St. Louis merchants, 194; brother petitions in his name, 677; difficulties over construction of a mill, 688n; gives his power of attorney to Lisa to act against exclusive trade, 664; has share in note to Chouteau, 680n; his bad luck, 678; inconsistency in regard to exclusive trade, 643; letter to C. Calvo, 614-616; mix-up over Osage trade, 705; name on list and *mémoire* of individuals against exclusive trade, 645, 646, 650; promised license to trade with Kansas, 556; sells share of trade to Lisa, 592; signs power of attorney for Lisa, 667; trade concessions, 556, 592, 622, 638, 688, 689.

Sarpy, Juan Bautista, older brother of Gregoire: cared for in his old age by Gregoire, 678; petitioner, for Gregoire, for exclusive trade, 677, which is granted, 688.

Sarpy, Lille: holds power of attorney for brother and signs for him, 680, 680n; petition cited, 680n.

Sarpy family: Gayoso de Lemos wishes to help, 556; unnamed members mentioned, 72; 112; 129; 568; 597.

Sarsi Indians (Les Sarcis): 335; habitat, 332.

Saskatchewan River (Sahaskawan): latitude and longitude, 383.

Satren, Pierre: traded with the Comanches via the Arkansas River, 42.

Saucier, François, Jr. (Francisco Saussier, Socier), Commandant of Le Portage des Sioux: correspondence cited,

594n; letters from Trudeau, 594-595, 602-603; *mémoire* to De Lassus, requesting land grant, 601; note from De Lassus, 596; proposed by De Lassus, as Commandant of Le Portage des Sioux, 594n; to take measures to prevent spread of smallpox, 631.

Saucier, François, Sr. [J. B.?]: 601n.

Sauk Indians (Sac, Sacques, Sacue, Sakias, Saques, Saquias): 150; 264; 420; 421n; 423; 430; among nations receiving provisions and presents from the Spanish, 769; attack boat carrying Osages, 741, 741n; English canoes winter among, 180; English trade with, 81, 707n; estimate of annual value of merchandise, 759; estimate of numbers, 694, 742, 760; habitat, 383; habitat, number of warriors, value of trade, 694; in threat to Little Osages, 168; kill Osages, 318; receive presents annually, 120; salary paid interpreter, 771.

Saukee Prairie: location and distance from mouth of the Missouri, 487.

Saussier, Francisco: See Saucier, François.

Sauteux Indians (Saulteux, Bungi, Bungees): 66; 385; 391; 400; 435; 437; 669; habitat, 383, 491, 694; habitat, number of warriors, and value of trade, 694; number, 383; one of the most populated nations, 693.

Savannah of St. Michael: 708-709.

Savoie, M.: 294, 295.

Saw mills; 370; 543; 561n.

Scalping: 143; 295; Little Osages guilty of, 44; Big Osages also, 29.

Scarlet, I. [J?]: 416.

Scieus: See Sioux Indians.

Sea of California: See California, Sea of.

Sea of the West: 92; 245; 338.

Seitz, Chistoval [Christoval?]: signs Lisa *mémoire* against exclusive trade, 651.

Sereyra, Sergeant: 204.

Sea-otters: 414.

La *Serena,* frigate of war: 583.

Serpent Indians, Serpientes: See Snake Indians.

Sesemany (Le Gauché): gorget requested for, 327.

Shareholders in the Missouri Company: rights and obligations suggested by Clamorgan in supplementary articles submitted, 445, 446, 455.

Shawnee Indians (Shavan, Chavanon, Chavanones, Chawanon): 199; 203; 232; 526; 529; among those receiving provisions and presents from the Spanish, 769; English trade with, 81, 180; estimate of population, 759; salary paid interpreter, 771.

Shells: 380.

Shepherds River: 486.

Shining Mountains (Montañas Relucientes): See Rocky Mountains.

Shirts: distributed as presents, to Indians, 129; mysterious stranger left debts but gave away suits and shirts, 133.

Shivitauns: habitat, 494.

Shoes: 267; 277; 380.

Shore-that-sings: 124.

Shoshoni Indians (Shoshones, Chionitones): Truteau to inform himself concerning them, 87, 245.

Shot bag: gift to John Evans, 479.

Silver: 15; Osages pillage a caravan carrying white metal, 744-745, 756; unwrought, 283.

Silverware: among presents English traders bestow upon Indians, 185.

Simcoe papers: cited, 154n, 230n.

Sinaloa: Cevallos warned that Americans covet, 719n.

Sioux Indians (Cius, Sios, Siu, Sius, Brulé Sioux, Dakotas): 44; 50; 66; 73; 73n; 78; 82; 88; 89; 98; 99; 110; 114; 120; 126; 127; 233; 260; 262; 267; 268; 269; 278; 279; 280; 281; 285; 287; 289; 290; 294; 298; 301; 302; 305; 310; 311; 332; 334; 340; 361; 362; 378; 379; 382; 384; 388n; 391; 400; 417; 418; 435; 437; 449; 458; 476; 491; 505; 517; 564; 669;

706; 709; 710; 711; 739; 741; 764; always at war with Mandans, 161; attack Arikaras, 441, 527; can be attracted to St. Louis, 770; cause most inconvenience to Lewis and Clark, 762; Charlevoix suggestion for mission, 23n; English trade with, 707n; estimate of annual value of merchandise for, 759; estimate of population, 760; feared and dreaded, 296; force presents from Truteau party, 527; habitat, number of warriors, and value of trade, 694; in Canadian sphere of interest, 7; kill three persons, 295; La Vérendrye attempts to placate them, 32; number listed by Iberville, 8n; obstruct Truteau's progress, 539; on the war path, 109; one of the most populated nations, 693; salary paid interpreter, 771; their wandering life makes exploration difficult, 748; three factions at war with, 148. See also Oconona Indians, Teton Indians.

Sioux of the Grand Detour, or Great Bend of the Missouri: 562; John Evans meets them, above the Omahas, 494; not favorable to whites, 495; spend spring and fall on borders of White River, 494.

Sioux of the Plains: 494.

Sioux, Yankton: See Sioux Indians.

Sioux River (Sius): 121; 378; first river, 709; second river, 710. See also Big Sioux River, Little Sioux River.

Siriton Indians: wandering nation, seen by Loisel, 739.

Skidi Indians: See Panimaha Indians.

Skins: of bears (white), 762; of deer, 179, 538; of hares and kids, 380; of oxen, 249; of roebucks, 703; of squirrels, 706n, 709; of wolves, 709. See also Robes.

Skunk River: 81; 214; 364n. See also Bête Puant.

Slaughter houses: 561n.

Slave girl: 104; 480; Garreau "owes" one, 479; Sutherland wishes to purchase one, 500.

Slave Lake: 585.

Slave trade: 10; 16; 17; 20.

Slaves: 17; 19; 41; 282; fugitive, 366; number, 687.

Sletter (Slettar), Mr.: 463; 501n; 502.

Smallpox: 44; 710; affects Arikaras, 299; most terrible of all scourges, 494; quarantine procedures, 631; several tribes suffer, 631; weakens Kansas, 52.

Smugglers: English traders so called, 145.

Smuggling: 392; 394; 433; Todd plan will prevent English, 436. See also Trade, Illegal.

Snake Bluff; location and distance from mouth of the Missouri, 487.

Snake Indians (Serpents, Serpientes): 34; 87; 245; 381; habitat and number, 385; one nation Lewis and Clark distrust, 763, 764; wandering nation, 739.

Snakes: 487.

Soap: 538.

Socier: See Saucier.

Soil: 123; 124; 165; 494; 543.

Soldiers (Armed men, Army men, Militia, Militiamen): additional, needed for French post on the Missouri, 14; annual cost, for forts, 390; Carondelet writes of permission granted, to arm and maintain, at cost of King, 542; Clamorgan solicits pay for, 457-458, 470-471, 475, 503-504, 563, 565, 566, 609-610, 618-622, 633; essential for safety at posts, at Arkansas, Natchitoches, and Illinois, 24; *fermiers* may appeal for, 38; pay, 15, 448, 480-481; quibbling over interpretation of order on maintenance of, 473, 473n, 474, 504-505, 506; royal order in regard to maintenance, 619; who is to pay depends on His Majesty's decision, 471n.

Soldier's River: description and distance from mouth of the Missouri, 489.

Soler, Miguel Cayetano: letter from Morales, containing news of arrival of Captain Lewis, 722.

Somuerlos, Marquis de: letter and draft of letter from C. Calvo cited, 614n;

letter to Governor of Louisiana cited, 370n.

Songs of death: 294.

Sonora: Cevallos warns that Americans covet, 719n.

Soulard, Antoine (Antonio), Captain of militia, St. Louis: 324; 335; 370n; recommended as adjutant, 597-598; letter to Gayoso de Lemos cited, 370n; petition to the King cited, 370n; statement on registration, and on survey and location of land for Saucier, 602; to assist Saucier in establishing a post, 595; to put Mackay in possession of land requested, 604-605. Descriptive observations cited, 760n.

Souliers Indians [Zapatos]: among nations with fixed villages, 739.

Souris River (La Souris, Mouse): 94; 103; 161n; 331.

Souris River fort (La Souri): 94; 95; 104; McDonnell once leader of, 480n.

South Fork: 416.

South Platte River: 590n-591n.

South Sea [Pacific Ocean]: 33; 115; 356; 364; 386; 389; 390; 393; 395; 399-400; 417n; 424n; 434; 442; 671; 699; 712; 731; explorers to examine possibility of communication by water, 715; from Illinois, communication should be opened with, 670; Mackay attempts to reach, 96; prize offered for reaching, 254; route to, of interest to French, 4n. See also California, Sea of; Pacific Ocean; Western Sea.

Spanish Illinois: See Illinois, Spanish.

Spanish Company, Spanish Company of Discoverers to the West of the Mississippi, Spanish Company of Discoveries of the Missouri, Spanish Company of Discoveries to the West of the Missouri: See Missouri Company.

Spanish régime: 58ff; termination, in Illinois country, 96.

Spanish settlements in Illinois: names, location, population, 534-537.

"Spectateur, le Fidel": letter to the Editor, on behalf of St. Louis merchants, 312-315.

Tayenne Indians: 83; 234; 235; reached by D'Église, via Missouri River, 82.

Tayon, Carlos, Captain of militia, Commandant at St. Charles: 201; 514; 613; 614n; signs Lisa *mémoire* against exclusive trade, 651; signs power of attorney for Lisa, 667; to take quarantine measures against smallpox, 631.

Tchaktas Indians: See Choctaw Indians.

Teguayo province: somewhere near the Rocky Mountains, 121.

Tennessee River: 138.

Tessalon Island: 515.

Teton (Titon) River: 384.

Teton Indians [Sioux]: 382; ferocity and treachery, 269ff.

Tetons of the Burned Wood (Bois Brulé): wandering nation, seen by Loisel, 739.

Texas: 4; 120; 682; 730; 733; 749; boundary, 726; Gallut writes of Spanish activities, 15; raided for horses, by several tribes, 20.

Thecis River: 685.

Thompson, David: 390n; leads Canadian traders to Mandans, 95.

Thornton, Edward, British Chargé d'Affaires: Meriwether Lewis shows passport from, 720n.

Timouian, Ara: 376n.

Titon River: See Teton River.

Toangarest, Indian chief: 281.

Tobacco: 90; 200; 251; 262; 270; 272; 292; 303; 304; 306; 311; 361; 379; 381; 475; 495; 538.

Tocaninanbiche Indians (Tokaninambich): 380; habitat, 384; wandering people, allies of the Cheyennes, 379.

Toctata Indians: See Oto Indians.

Todd, Andrew (Andrés, Andris), originally British subject residing in Canada; later Spanish subject: 3; 108; 374; 375; 403; 420; 421; 422; 423; 425; 430; 433; 435; 436; 437; 443; 449; 458; 458n; 472; 473; 507; 508; 509; 510; 511; 522n; 523; 528; 541; 563; 565; account of his relations with

Spaniards cited, 433n; advances made, in Company transactions, 554, 554n; amount of investment at New Orleans, 524; appeal for reimbursement for goods confiscated, with statement of losses, 403-405, 403n-404n; becomes associated with firm of Clamorgan and Loisel, 419; articles of agreement with Clamorgan, 464-469; buys Missouri Company shares through Loisel, 574; Carondelet *reservada* urging favor for, cited 395n; changes citizenship after Jay's treaty, 523n; character, 524-525, 541-542; Clamorgan letter requests legalizing of statement about accounts, 573; concession granted, for fur trade with reduced duties on merchandise, 438; concerning confiscation of goods, 387, 398, 438n; death causes the Company new difficulties, and interrupts customary discoveries, 505, 564; death from yellow fever, 481-482; duped by Clamorgan, 552; good results from contract with, 423n; his exclusive trade on Mississippi now handled by Clamorgan, 557; his firm to be given an interest in Missouri Company, 427; his property demanded by Clamorgan, 573; jealousy of, suggested, 429; letter (extract) from Carondelet about him, 478n; letters to Carondelet cited, 387n, 522; letter to Clamorgan, about Missouri Company business, reported missing, 580; nephew of Isaac Todd, 522; no objection to his carrying on trade with Sauk and Fox Indians, says Carondelet, 421n; petition and letters cited, 404n; petition for permission to carry on fur trade for Spain, 407-410, granted, 410; petition to Carondelet cited, 392n; proposals in regard to upper Mississippi trade discussed by Carondelet in letter to Alcudia, 391-394; proposals summarized by Montarco, 400-402; proposes changes in his exclusive trade contract, 402n; remark to Motard about buying share quoted, 575.

Todd, Isaac, uncle of Andrew: 154n; 522; 524; John Hay a substitute agent

843

for, 572; letters to Clamorgan company missing, 581; letter to Trudeau, sent by him to Carondelet, 523-524.

Todd, McGill and Company: 80n; petition of company, through J. R. Jones, cited, 404n; petition to Carondelet cited, 387n; statement of value of goods confiscated, 403n-404n.

Toguibacós Indians: See Padós Indians.

Tokaninambich Indians: See Tocaninanbiche Indians.

Tokiouako Indians (Tokiwako): habitat, 384; wandering people, allies of the Cheyennes, 379.

Tollibois [Jollibois?] : 416.

Tomahawks: 199; 200.

Tongenge Indians: Iberville lists, 8n.

Tonkawa Indians (Tankahueis): move south and raid Texas, 20; Salcedo sends Cevallos a copy of Spanish treaty of peace with them, 749.

Tonti, Henri de (Tonty): letter to Renaudot cited, 4n; narrative of La Salle expedition cited, 4n; reference to Missouri map, 4n.

Topography: as observed by Evans, 497; as observed by Mackay, 491-492; of Upper Missouri region, 761-762; to be observed and noted by John Evans, 411. See also Geographical knowledge.

Toquibacos Indians: See Padós Indians.

Touacara Indians: post among them proposed, 17.

Trade abuses: 34; 35; 41; 51; 51n; 60; 84; 95; 131; 134; 242; 322; 323; regulations to control, 85; suggested regulations to prevent, 313.

Trade Contracts, Exclusive: 24; 46; 47; 49; 55; 62; 63; 63n; 194-195; 228; 229; 315; 321; 420; complaints against, 60-63; contract for trade on Kansas and Platte Rivers sought by Clamorgan, and granted, 634; contract for trade on all of Missouri River and branches granted Deruisseau, 35; contract for trade with Kansas and Pawnees sought by Cabanné, 615, granted, 616; con-

tract for trade with Osages given A. Chouteau, 526-527; contracts given Meunier, 81-82, 196, 240; contracts granted members of "Company of Discoveries", 193; contracts granted to "Company of Explorers", 83, 434, 445, 453, 527; D'Église petition denied, 83; extent and conditions of A. Todd's contract, 458n; Lisa complains that Ortiz and others infringe on his trade, 717; Lisa incites others to protest against, 644-645, 646, 650-651; list of contracts, five-year period, 590-592; list of exclusive contracts granted by Spanish officials, 112; *mémoire* of Lisa and others presenting disadvantages, 646-651; Moro straddles the issue and petitions for contract with Pawnees, 660-664; plea from Clamorgan for trade with Otos and Pawnees, 477-478; reasons for, 61; Robidoux and others inveigh against, 624-627; Robidoux seeks contract for trade with Kansas, 548, with Otos, Omahas, and Poncas, 593; Robidoux wants Clamorgan's canceled, 553; several others were proposed, 458n; trade of some consequence should be made exclusive and conceded to opulent persons, says Casa Calvo, 628.

Trade, Fur: 10; 36; 63; 64; 103; 175; 180; 223; 229-230; 230n; 298; 423; 435; 490; 625-626; all trade of Osages and Missouris in furs, the best of the region, 13; British, 175n; decline of, and some reasons for it, 676, 676n; difference between French and English prices cause trouble, 48; effects of exclusive trade privileges on, 647-649; estimate of annual trade of Osages and Missouris, in number of peltries, 50; Government says agriculture would develop the country faster, 651-660; inroads on, by English, 387, 392, 433; Journal of Luttig fur trading expedition cited, 82n; La Vérendrye helps develop, securing monopoly in north, 31, 32; value of annual trade in Illinois, 529; value and quality of annual yield in furs on the Missouri, 673n.

Mississippi, and desire to reach Mexico, 80, 146; effects of Jay's treaty on, 407; encroach on Spanish territory, 94-95, 111-112; exemption from duties, 401; food and wages, 177; forts proposed to stop influx of, 145n; list of places in American and Spanish territory where they winter, with merchandise for the Indians, 81, 180; Mackay prohibition against all British subjects, 461-462; make good use of Mississippi, 540-541; methods superior, and threaten Spanish trade, 86n, 207-208; more daring than those of Illinois and Louisiana, 302; reported to have caused the destruction of Missouri Company agent, Heney, 632; routes they follow, 94, 492; sole possessors of commerce on Upper Missouri, 407; strategy, trickery, boldness and daring, 497, 500-501, 554; their annual haul in furs, 682; Trudeau advised to work hostilely against, 478n; Trudeau report on English commerce, 175-177; ways of stopping, 323; will use every method to gain Illinois trade, 150.

Traders, French: records exist of Frenchmen among Osages, Missouris, Arikaras, and Mandans in late seventeenth and early eighteenth centuries, 5; 5n; 8; 16; 23; 24; 34; 42; 49; 50; 51; 66; 747; 748.

Traders, Spanish: 65; 66; 70; 82; 109; 111; 156; go into Iowa country to prevent influx of English traders, 145n; new period of activity undertaken from St. Louis, 81. For activities see Missouri Company.

Trading companies: 332: See also Great Company of Montreal, Hudson's Bay Company, Missouri Company, Northwest Company.

Trading Company of the Upper Missouri: See Missouri Company.

Trading expedition, French: in Colorado, falls in with a party of Spanish dragoons, 591n:

Trading licenses: 41; 51; 51n; 65; 66; 66n; 71; 71n; 72; better regulations

desirable, 40n; fee, 152, 156; list to be sent to government, 153; Maxent's plea for, 66-69; prerequisites, 84; revocation of Meunier's 212-213, 237, 238; summary for five years, by De Lassus, 590-592; Trudeau list for one year, 162; to be granted to selected men, 34, 35. See also Trade Contracts, Exclusive.

Trading posts: distribution of, on the Missouri, 209-211; French policy to establish French influence through establishment of posts, 32; Iberville proposes, on Arkansas, Ohio, and Missouri rivers, 8; military protection necessary, 24; reasons for establishing a post on the Missouri, 11; small posts established on the Missouri, 40n. See also Forts.

Traiteur, Un ancien: speculation as to identity of the person who accompanied Perrin du Lac, 91; 111; 376n; 707n.

Tranquil Water: See Little Missouri River.

Treaties: 697n; with Comanches and Jumanos, 42. See also Jay's treaty, Pinckney's treaty, and the following.

Treaty of Amiens: 668n; Collot makes a suggestion for it, 670.

Treaty of 1803: by which the United States purchased Louisiana from France, 747, 747n.

Treaty of Friendship, Boundaries and Navigation: See Pinckney's treaty.

Treaty of Greenville: 347n.

Treaty of peace of 1763: 75; 254; 746.

Treaty of peace of 1783: 669.

Treaty of peace with Indians, 1771: 749.

Treaty of San Ildefonso, 1800: by which Spain ceded Louisiana to France, 668n.

Treaty of San Lorenzo el Real: See Pinckney's treaty.

Trees: many full-grown trees on Upper Missouri, and many varieties on the Yellowstone, 381. See also Ash, Birch, Cedar, Cottonwood, Cyprus, Firs, Linden, Oak, Pine, Poplar, Willow Trees.

Trinkets: 707; 709; 710; received by Sioux in exchange for furs, 706.

Trogs, Pier (Piertrog): signs Lisa power of attorney, and *mémoire*, 667, 651.

Trudeau, Zenon, Lieutenant-Governor of Spanish Illinois, successor to Pérez, and Commandant at St. Louis: 90; 93n; 95; 97; 99; 100; 108; 156n; 162; 171n; 194n; 197n; 205n; 207n; 208n; 209n; 212n; 225; 234; 242; 252; 260; 361; 386n; 387; 401; 410; 414; 420n; 421n; 424; 426; 437; 493; 514; 515; 546; 593; 601; 604; 605; 608; 609; 621; 642; 651; 658; 687; acts as notary in partnership agreement, 238-240; asked to preside over meeting of merchants, 186; asks for *patentes* and medals for Indians, 257n; authorized by Carondelet to organize an expedition against the Osages, 172; carries out orders to confiscate contraband goods of A. Todd, 398, 433; decree authorizing attachment and seizure of Clamorgan company assets, 579-580; decree on free trade published, 81; decrees issued in settlement of accounts of Todd estate, 573, 574, 576, 581; deposition of L. Durocher, 574-575; deposition of J. Motard, about Todd conduct, 575; deposition of A. Reilhe, concerning transfer of his interest in Missouri Company, 575-576; examination of Derouin about expedition, with facsimile of part of document, 516-518; fire destroys his property, 324; gives instructions about traders, 80; grants Vasquez shares of trade with Pawnees, 547n; has one share of Kansas trade, 211; initiates and promotes idea of trading company, 549, 550; instructions about traders, 80; instructions from Carondelet on his duties as Commandant at St. Louis, 151-153; instructions to Truteau approved, 87; is in continual fear of American and British aggression, 393n; issues permit to St. Louis merchants, to assemble, 218; legal notification in connection with settlement of Todd estate, 580; letters from Carondelet, 341, 365, 371, 426, 427, 476; letter from Carondelet about English competition in trade, 212; letter from Carondelet about horse theft, 197; letter from Carondelet about Meunier and the Ponca trade, 212-213; letter from Carondelet about Missouri Company, 325; letter from Carondelet concerning trade contracts, 315-316; letter from Carondelet, with enclosure to be delivered to Clamorgan, 427-429; letter (extract) from Carondelet about impending war, 478n; letters from Carondelet cited, 82n, 86n, 170n, 425n, 431n; letter from Carondelet, about A. Todd, cited, 478n; letter from Carondelet, forwarding Clamorgan's *mémoire*, cited, 478n; letters from Clamorgan, 169-171, 563-566; letter from Clamorgan about distribution of trading posts, 209; letter from Clamorgan about Meunier and Ponca trade, 206-207; petition from Clamorgan regarding convocation of merchants, 217-218; letters from Gayoso de Lemos, 524-525, 553-554, 556-557; letters from Gayoso about Clamorgan affairs, 571; letter from Gayoso about Missouri Company matters, 555; letter from Gayoso in behalf of Sarpy, 556-557; letter from Gayoso in reply to letter about Kansas trade, 568-569; letters from Gayoso cited, 537n, 553n, 647n; letter from Gayoso suggesting methods of attracting French emigrants from Canada, cited, 556n; letter (draft) probably from Morales, cited, 467n; letters to Carondelet, 173-174, 204-205, 208, 214-217, 229-230, 230-233, 317-319, 320-322, 322-324, 328-329, 329-330, 343-345, 345-348, 348-351, 366-369, 369-371, 373-375, 440-442, 443-444; letter to Carondelet about construction of *quartel*, 205; letter to Carondelet about difficulties with Osages, 156-157, 197-203; letters to Carondelet about Mandans, 160-161, 181; letters to Carondelet about medals, 185-196, 325-326, 430; letters to Carondelet about Missouri Company affairs, 341-343; letters to Carondelet about stolen horses, 160, 173-174, 184-185; letter to Carondelet telling about examination of Fotman and Joncquard,

330-335; letter to Carondelet conveying list of Missouri traders licensed, 162; letter to Carondelet enclosing Articles of Incorporation, Missouri Company, 228-229; letter to Carondelet enclosing letter from Clamorgan about competition of English traders, 207-208; letter to Carondelet enclosing letter from I. Todd, 522-523; letter to Carondelet enclosing memorials from traders, 256-257; letter to Carondelet, submitting report on Missouri commerce, 174-175; letter to Carondelet transmitting edict for free trade, 155; letter (draft) to Carondelet, 171-173; letter (extract) to Carondelet, about expeditions contemplated, 87n; letter (extract) to Carondelet establishing date of Truteau's return to St. Louis, 91n; letters (extracts) to Carondelet, 91n, 92n, 93, 416n-417n, 423n; letters to Carondelet enclosing maps drawn by Soulard cited, 257n; letters to Carondelet cited, 77n, 81n, 82n, 84n, 86n, 168n, 170n, 193n, 194n, 427n, 431n, 444n, 458n. 505n, 512n; letters to Clamorgan cited, 82n, 386n; letter to De Lasus cited, 386n; letters to Gayoso de Lemos, 372, 525-529, 557-560, 596-597; letter to Gayoso de Lemos about Kansas trade, 568; letter to Gayoso about Spanish settlements, trade, expeditions, 534-544; letter to Gayoso enclosing Robidoux memorial, 596-597; letter to Gayoso enclosing Mackay narrative and map, 545; letter to Gayoso[?] giving statement of distribution of Indian trade, 529-532; letters (extracts) to Gayoso, 427n, 442n, 581-582, 582, 581n; letters to Gayoso cited, 87n, 370n, 545n, 546n, 547n, 553n, 559n, 561n, 587n, 597n, 647n; letter to Howard cited, 523n; letter to Lorimier cited, 198n; letter to Morales cited, 512n; letter to Saucier about establishing a post, 594-595; letter to Vallé, 316; letter (addressee unknown) on English trade cited, 86n; makes gift to Carondelet, 371; makes long report on English trade, 81; memorial from A. Chouteau in regard to debts of Clamorgan firm to Clark firm, 576-579;

memorial from Clamorgan about conduct of John Hay, fugitive, 571-573; memorial from Clamorgan and R. Loisel, asserting ownership of shares in Missouri Company purchased from Durocher and others, 573-574; memorial from Clamorgan concerning Todd-Clamorgan correspondence, part missing, 580-581; memorial from Clamorgan seeking further deposition from Motard, 576; memorial from Clamorgan seeking notarized statement that Reilhe and friends were only agents for A. Todd, 573-574; order by Carondelet to confiscate English boats cited, 403n; ordered by Carondelet to strengthen defenses of St. Louis, 146n; proclamation about free trade, 155-156, cited, 84n; proposes appointment of surveyor, 257n; report concerning the Spanish Illinois cited, 89n; report on aid to Truteau cited, 92n; report on English commerce with the Indians, 175-180; Robidoux pleads with Gayoso for a recreated Missouri Company under direction of Trudeau, 553; son born to 560, 560n; statement to Carondelet about meeting of merchants, submitting additional trade regulations, 190-193; submits trade regulations, 85; succeeds Pérez as Lieutenant-Governor, Spanish Illinois, 80; urged by Gayoso to examine Robidoux's claims against Clamorgan, 553n; writes postscript on letter, Robidoux to Gayoso, 594.

Truteau, Jean Baptiste (Juan Bautista): 93; 96; 101; 101n; 109; 115n; 229n; 233n; 236n; 252; 331; 341n; 349n; 351; 364; 388n; 416; 417; 707n; activities for Missouri Company, 87-91; Clamorgan's instructions to, 243-253, approved by Trudeau, and, months later, by Carondelet, 87, cited 87n; "Description of the Upper Missouri" (extract), 376-382; "Description" mentioned, 90, 111, cited, 90n, 93n, 110n, 111n; directors of Missouri Company select Truteau to head expedition and give him instructions, 86-87; experiences on expedition, as told by Trudeau in letters, 527-528,

539-540; Journal, first part, 259-294, second part, 294-311; Journal cited, 82n, 86n, 87n, 89n, 90n, 93n, 331n; Journal sent to Carondelet by Trudeau, 328, 342, 342n, 389n; plat enclosed in instructions cited, 389n; "Remarks on the Manners of the Indians" (extract), 257-259; seeks information from Cheyennes about a river flowing toward the setting sun, 91; time of return to St. Louis, 91, 91n; to give assistance to John Evans, 411.

Truxillo, Francisco Xavier de, secretary: 732; memorandum to N. Salcedo, 735.

Tulima Indians [Arkansas]: habitat, 120.

Tupes Indians, popular name for Yamparika Indians, q.v.

Turlington's Balsam: gift to John Evans, 479.

Turner, Benjamin: 317n.

Turner, G., of Kaskaskia: 99; letter to John Evans, 316-317.

Turner, Judge (Tourner): 366.

Turtle Mountain: 492.

Two Rivers: distance from the mouth of the Missouri, 489.

Two Rivers [Wis.] (Les Deux Rivières): 180.

Uguitate, Mr.: signs power of attorney for Lisa, 667.

Ulibarri, Juan de: 17.

Ulloa, Antonio de, Governor of Louisiana: 58; 64; instructions to Ríu cited, 153n; letters from St. Ange and Ríu cited, 66n; Trudeau urged to observe his instructions, 153.

[Unicorn]: said to be found in Rocky Mountains, 412.

United States: 136; 140; 164; 232; 393; 394; 396; 416; 436; 437; 439; 515; 534; 543; 582; 585; ambitious views in connection with newly-acquired Louisiana, 730, 733; delay urged in Spanish negotiations, 157n; has an interest in the treaty of Amiens, Collot suggests, 670; suspected by Carondelet of political machinations, 424n.

Unzaga y Amezaga, Luis de, Governor of Louisiana: report from Piernas cited, 59n; reports cited, 70n.

Vadon, Abbé de, priest of Cahokia: makes accusation against another priest, 373.

Vallé, Baptiste [Jean Baptiste?]: 214; 232; 367; an Upper Missouri trader, 111.

Vallé, François (François Valois, Vallois, Valoi, Francisco): 316; 319; 535; acts as witness, 575, 576, 646; name on list and *mémoires* against exclusive trade, 644, 646, 651; replaces Peyroux as Commandant, Ste. Geneviève, 598n; signs power of attorney for Lisa, 667.

Vallé, Mme. (Villar), sister-in-law of Baptiste Vallé: has a share in an old mill, 214-215.

Vallière, Josef (Valière) Captain, Commandant at Arkansas post: 73; letter to Miró cited, 73n; proposes construction of a fort, 158.

Valverde, Cosio Antonio: learns of French-Pawnee alliance, 17.

Vancouver, George, Captain: 713; his "Voyage of Discovery . . ." cited, 713n.

Vandenbemden, Louis: 370n; asked to draw up a plan for a church, 559n.

Varela y Ulloa, Pedro: letters from Morales cited, 512n.

Varennes, Pierre Gaultier de, See La Vérendrye, Pierre Gaultier de Varennes, *Sieur* de.

Vasallo, Josef: member of Spanish committee, 727.

Vaseur, Basille (Bacilio): certified statement that Meunier discovered the Poncas, 241; given license to trade on the Missouri, 162.

Vásquez, Benito (Basquez): among those interested in organization of St. Louis merchants, 194; bondsman for St. Cyr, 226; letter to Gayoso de Lemos, soliciting trade with Kansas, 546-547; membership in Missouri Company, 225, 226; petitions for trade with Kansas, 431n, 531n; recommended by Gayoso de Le-

849

Vomits [Emetics?] : gift to John Evans, 479.

Vossay: See Volsay.

Voyageurs: 16; 18n; 23; 25; 26; 26n; 27; 28; 30; 32; 34; 41; 46; 47; 47n; 49; 51; 55; 269; 756; Bienville letter about murders committed by Indians, possibly Osages, 25; eleven reported killed, 24; licensing to be limited, 18; some independent ones reported to have found mines, 13; their trickery, 48; unable to discover Missouri source, 9.

Wabash Indians (Ouabache): 43; 45; 141.

Wabash River (Ouabache): 53; 154n; Armstrong explores, 136n; English conspire with Indians, 43; Lahontan visit doubted, 5; post to be reduced to ten men, 23n.

Wachanto: 708.

Waepiton Indians: wandering nation, seen by Loisel, 739.

Wage regulations: 312.

Wages of hired men: for wintering, 177.

Walnut Hill: See Nogales Fort.

Wanutaries Indians: 107; 563.

War dances: 22.

War of Spanish succession: 31; effect on Iberville scheme, 8n.

War plans: 197-202; 198n; 614n; against Osages, 171-173; Carondelet instructions, in case of war, 152.

War scares: fears of invasion of Spanish territory, 582, 583, 583n, 587n, 614n; fear of war between the United States and France, 587n; Trudeau in continual fear of American and British aggression, 393n.

Warin, aide-de-camp of Collot: 670n.

Wars mentioned: American Revolution, 71, 76; Anglo-Spanish war, 431n, 669, 669n; French and Indian war, 50, 55; Revolution of 1768, 204, 204n; War of Spanish succession, 8n, 31.

Washcanda Nipishi: location and distance from mouth of the Missouri, 489.

Washington, George: 79; contribution to fund for proposed expedition to Pacific, 167; Diaries cited, 80n.

Washita River: 521. See also Ouachita.

Watchi-Manitou (Welcé): 696. See also Manitou.

Water: healthful quality of, 124.

Waterfalls: 498. See also Falls.

Water-power mill: a bone of contention among petitioners, 688n; Lisa and friends offer to construct one, and do so, they say, 679, 716, 717.

Watson: 463.

Wattasoon Indians: 492; habitat, 496.

Wayne, Anthony, General: 347n; 372.

Weeping River: 709.

Weeping water River: 123; distance from mouth of Missouri, 480.

Welcé: See Watchi-Manitou.

Welsh Indians: 98; 98n; 99; 99n.

Western Sea: 15; 33; 33n; 49; 422; 424; 609; an enthusiastic Englishman reports about a river leading to, 131; Evans' instructions for expedition to, 100; Fabry and party fail to discover it, 29-31; Father Charlevoix gathers data needed for exploration, 31; Michaux route toward, 164-166; Spanish explorations pave the way for American, 115; Truteau seeks information about river route to, 91; Winnipeg-to-the-Pacific, 32. See also California, Sea of; Pacific Ocean; South Sea.

Whacetonchiga (Le Petit verd de gris): *patente* of first medal requested for, 327.

Whachanguia (Le Geur qui brule): small medal requested for him, 327.

Whahongaché (Le gendre de la Butte): gorget requested for him, 327.

Wheat: 54; 124; 163; 233; 311; 521; 538; bad harvest, 160; can be grown in Louisiana, 686; good harvest, 442.

Wheather, Captain: See Lewis, Meriwether.

Wherry, Mackey (Makay): name on list of individuals against exclusive trade, 645, 646, 651; signs Lisa power of attorney, 667.

White, William: contributor to fund for proposed exploration, 167.

White Bear Lake: 684.

White men, or Spirits: 300; 304; 305; 306; 310; 382; 496; compared by Truteau with the barbarians, not to their disadvantage, 297-298; Mackay finds the Mandans more or less corrupted by communication with the whites, 493, 498; the Panis Ricaras respect and defer to the white men, 296.

White metal: See Silver.

White Mountains (Montañas Blancas): See Rocky Mountains.

White Pawnees: See Pawnee Indians.

White River (Rivière Blanche, Río Blanco): distance from the mouth of the Missouri, 490; Evans ascends the Missouri to, 99; Perrin du Lac ascends to, 111, 706.

White Wood River (Bois Blanc): See James River.

Wichita Indians: kill four deserters from Missouri post, 49; move to Kansas, 20; procure horses from Spaniards, 11.

Wilkinson, James, General: 131n; 157n; 230; 433; letter from Pierre Chouteau, 767-771; proclamation about cession of Louisiana mentioned, 723.

William, Edward: 98n.

Willow trees: 295.

Wine: 38; 707.

Winnipeg, Canada: La Vérendrye seeks route, Winnipeg to the Pacific, 32.

Wisconsin River: 154n; 180; 693.

Wistar, ———: role in matter of financial support to Michaux expedition, 167.

Wold Indians: See Loup Indians. See also Panimaha Indians.

Wolf River: 384; distance from mouth of the Missouri, 488.

Wolf skins: 264; 380; 709.

Women, Indian, Treatment of, and attitude toward: dissolute behavior frowned on, 39; jealousy unknown, except among the Sioux and the Cheyennes, 258, 300, 300n; Mackay's injunction to Evans, 414.

Women and children, Indian: 268; 271; 274; 275; 279; 281; 411; taken prisoner, 185.

Wood: 61; suitable to the construction of ships, available in profusion, 686; to be cut only with a knife, John Evans is instructed, 411.

Wood River: description and distance up the Missouri, 486.

Yamparika Indians (Yambaricas), popular name for Tupes Indians: are furnished help against the Pawnees, 146-147; habitat, 439.

Yankton Sioux: See Sioux Indians.

Yasou Indians (Yasou): See Yazoo Indians.

Yatasi Indians (Yatasés, Yatasse): Fabry follows route of, to Natchitoches, 31; habitat, 120.

Yazoo Indians (Yasou, Yasu): 55; defeated by Arkansas, 54.

Yatasse Indians: See Yatasi Indians.

Yberville: See Iberville.

Yellow Bluff; distance from the mouth of the Missouri, 489.

Yellow fever epidemic: 482; 482n.

Yellow Mountains: 383; 384; 385.

Yellow Rock River: See Crow River.

Yellowstone River (River of the Yellow Stone, Rivière de Roche Jaune, Roches Jaunes, River of Rocas Pagizas): 91; 109; 110; 115; 381; 416; 498; description obtained from the Indians, 101.

Yllinois Indians: See Illinois Indians.

Ynctan Indians: wandering nation, seen by Loisel, 739.

Ynctoannan Indians: wandering nation, seen by Loisel, 739.

York River: See Nelson River.

Yorston, Mr.: 463; 501n; 502; 502n.

Yosti, Emilian (Yostie, Yostiz; Emiliano, Emileon) : among those present at organization meeting, Missouri Company, 218; assignment and share of trade, 211; name on list of individuals against exclusive trade, 645, 646, 650; recommended for trade contract, 600; signs power of attorney for Lisa, 667; trade privileges granted, 600n, 605.

Yostiz, C.: 194.

Yrujo, Carlos Martinez, Marqués: 720; letters to Cevallos about Jefferson project, 712-714, 715-716; letter to Cevallos concerning conditions arising from acquisition of Louisiana by the United States, 723-724.

Ysanty, village of the Sioux: 295.

Yscanis Indians (Ascanis, Iscanis, Isconis, Yscanes) : move south and raid Texas, 20; Spanish treaty of peace with, 749.

Yturrigaray, Joseph de: draft of letter to N. Salcedo, 729.

Yutas Scihuahuanas Indians: allies of Spanish, 148.

Zamora, Bishop of: 350.

Zapatos Indians: fixed nation on the Missouri, 739.